A Hero for High Times

IAN MARCHANT

A YOUNGER READER'S GUIDE TO THE PUNKS, RAVERS, AND DOG-ON-A-ROPE OF THE BRITISH ISLES,

A HERO FOR HIGH TIMES

BEATS, HIPPIES, FREAKS, NEW-AGE TRAVELLERS BREW CREW CRUSTIES 1956-1994

JONATHAN CAPE

Jonathan Cape, an imprint of Vintage Publishing,
20 Vauxhall Bridge Road,
London SW1V 2SA

Jonathan Cape is part of the Penguin Random House group of companies whose
addresses can be found at global.penguinrandomhouse.com.

Penguin
Random House
UK

First published by Jonathan Cape in 2018

www.vintage-books.co.uk

A CIP catalogue record for this book is available from the British Library

ISBN 9780224097086

Typeset in India by Integra Software Services Pvt Ltd, Pondicherry

Printed and bound in Great Britain by Clays Ltd, St Ives PLC

Penguin Random House is committed to a sustainable future for
our business, our readers and our planet. This book is made
from Forest Stewardship Council® certified paper.

MIX
Paper from
responsible sources
FSC® C018179

Violet and Grace,

this book is for you.

It is called
A Hero for High Times

(Being an account of the Life and Times and Opinions of
Mr Robert Rowberry)

Or,
A Younger Reader's Guide
to the Beats, Hippies, Freaks, Punks, Ravers,
New Age Travellers
and
Dog-on-a-Rope Brew Crew Crusties of the British Isles,
1956–1994,

together with an Epilogue, entitled

'How to Get Your Head Together in the Country'

and an Appendix and an Afterword

It is by me,

Ian Marchant,

and I am your grandfather.

This book, my darling granddaughters, is mostly about a small group of people who called themselves Freaks. They have called themselves many other things over the years. The Beats, the Hippies, the Punks, the Ravers, the New Age Travellers. Freaks will do for them all.

The Freaks thought the world was broken, and that they might have found a new way of mending it. They wanted freedom, and happiness, and a world in which people could be themselves, which meant that there would be no war, no famine and no disease.

The Freaks thought that in order to make this happen, everyone and everything needed to change. And to change everyone and everything, the Freaks were going to teach the world to play.

The Freaks wanted everybody to look at everything in a new way.

A new way which allows people to live their lives how they choose, no matter what anybody else thinks or says. A way where we can dance and sing and play all day. A way where Love is the most powerful force in the universe, and where people see that the world is a wonderful, magical place. A way where we all realise that we are in the here and now, just this once, just in this pregnant moment of the eternal creative life of the cosmos, and that we are the eyes and hands and souls of Creation.

It didn't work, my darling girls, of course it didn't. But between about 1956, when your grandmother Rowan was born, and about 1994, when your mummy was fourteen, the Freaks *tried* to make it work.

Lots of my friends were Freaks. You can read about one of them called Bob Rowberry in this book. I was a Freak, too – still am – and I'm sorry it didn't work. Sometimes it even looks like we made things worse.

Just like every other human in history, you have been born into a world that is broken. I don't know if the world can be mended. On the evidence of what I've seen, I almost want to say it can't be. But I still believe with all my heart that the world is worth trying to mend. The thing is to try. It is always hard, so trying may be your only reward.

I hope you will try one day, and that your way, whatever it might turn out to be, will be better than ours.

Presteigne, Radnorshire, July 2017

You know, there really exist certain people to whom it is assigned, at their birth, to have all sorts of extraordinary things happen to them.

Mikhail Lermontov

The Past is Only a Pleasant Void

Deep in a wood in a valley in the Marches of Wales, alongside a long-ago abandoned railway line, there lives a seventy-five-year-old man called Bob Rowberry. His home is a superannuated school bus, now painted battleship grey, whose engine has died and whose wheels have fallen off.

This is the story of how he ended up in this broken-down bus, on this abandoned line, in this lost and forgotten part of the world.

I've come up here today – pulled up a farm track off the A44 onto the old permanent way, driven along the rutted trackbed between overhanging trees, and parked up alongside the corrugated-iron shed where Bob keeps his tools and parks his quad bike – to see if he can mend my writing stool.

I write sitting on a 1960s draughtsman's stool. I am a big lad. Yesterday part of the base snapped, and it has felt unsafe all morning. Bob will be able to mend it, I know. He's a travelling metalworker; from the roughest blacksmithing to the most delicate jewellery, Bob can make and mend pretty much anything. He's a highly skilled man. Besides, I want to talk to him. I have had an idea.

He says he's always pleased to see me, and I trust him. I know I'm always pleased to see him. He looks at the stool, and props it up on his bench.

'You big fat fucker,' he says. 'Come and have a coffee and I'll fix that in a minute.'

A third of the bus is filled with Bob's bed, a ginger cat dozing on the Afghan throws that cover it. The rest is part kitchen, part metalworking shop. A box full of lettuce seedlings sits on top of the dashboard. Next to the bed, a wood-burner smoulders, even on this muggy late-summer day, with a kettle keeping warm on top. The bus smells of hot metal, coffee and woodsmoke. And Bob. Smelling like Bob is a good thing, to judge from his startling success with the ladies. Perhaps it helps that he is officially a gypsy; Powys County Council designated him as such a few years back, so that he can continue to live in this wood, which he rents from a homeopathic vet for 5p a year. He's a looker, even at seventy-five; he looks a bit like David Essex might have, if David had dressed in

Hereford Hospice Shop chic and actually lived a great deal of his life outdoors hitting hot metal.

Bob wasn't always a gypsy. Society has had a few names for Bob over the years. He was a Beat in the fifties, a Face in the sixties, a Freak in the seventies, and a New Age Traveller in the eighties. Bob calls himself a Raver. I call him my friend, for thirty years now.

We take our coffee outside. The wood is loud with birdsong.

'Do you know why there are so many birds in my wood?' Bob asks me.

'Isn't it because we're in a wood in the middle of nowhere?'

'No, it's because I've killed all the grey squirrels, so the birds lay more eggs.'

I've seen Bob do this. I've sat outside his van at the Abergavenny Food Festival, and watched him kill a squirrel from thirty yards with a ball bearing fired from a catapult.

The wood might belong to the homeopathic vet in law, but it's Bob's patch. Here and there, in clearings in the wood, he grows his own veg, and his own requisites. There's no spring, but Bob catches the water he needs in rain butts. His meat he often shoots himself; lots of rabbits and pigeons, and even, on one occasion, a squirrel. The meat was too greasy and tough to repeat the experiment. He husbands the trees, thinning them for fuel, and making sure the strongest trees grow stronger still.

Under an awning on the side of the bus, there is a welder's bench where Bob makes psychedelic spinning tops from old pennies and fabulous mobiles out of feathers and scrap metal, which he sells at festivals in the summer and at high-end garden centres and Surrey art galleries in the winter. Students make their way out here; young craftsmen and women who stay for a day or a week or so, learning how to work with metal, sleeping in what was once Bob's Other Van, but is now his spare bedroom.

On top of a high pole mounted to the bus roof, three solar panels charge an array of 12-volt car batteries. The panels need to be high because although today sunlight is dappling the floor of the wood, in winter sunlight can be hard to come by under the trees.

There is a fire space between the workbench and the shed, where logs burn on cold evenings when Bob and his guests want to sit outside and chat and smoke. It's too warm to have the fire going this afternoon, but we sit, Bob and I, in one of the four old wheelchairs that are gathered round the fire space, drinking Bob's thick coffee, sweetened with honey and evaporated milk.

'What were you supposed to be writing before you broke your stool?' Bob says.

'Do you remember,' I ask, 'Theory & Practice, General Builders?'

Bob laughs.

'Yeah.'

The idea was a good one, I always thought. It came to us one afternoon in 1989. Bob was outside our house fitting a radio to my car, whilst I sat indoors, revising for an electronic engineering exam at the Polytechnic of Wales.

'Come out and I'll show you what I'm doing, you stupid wanker,' Bob shouted up at the room where I was trying to do hard sums. 'That'll teach you more about how to do electronics than some fucking equations.'

I came down to make him tea.

'You know I'm not good at doing stuff,' I said. 'You do Practice, and I'll do Theory.'

Thus was born the idea of 'Theory and Practice, General Builders'. We'd go round to people's houses to do mending and shit, and while Bob handled the practical side of the job, I could discuss theoretical aspects of the project with the homeowners.

We never got much work.

'What about Theory & Practice?' says Bob.

'I'm still at it,' I say. 'Theorising while you practise.'

'What are you theorising about?'

'Hippies. Hippie culture. The Freaks. You, I guess.'

'Me?'

'Yeah, man, you.'

You, Bob. And what you seem to represent.

If I have ever added one nugget of fact to the sum of human knowledge, it is to help prove that Bob really did once own the cat after which Procol Harum were named. This legendary cat-ownership claim was one of the initial stories Bob told me when I first met him. In 2007 a music journalist, Marcus Gray, following up on my report of Bob's story in my book *The Longest Crawl*, confirmed it to be true. There really was a cat called Procol Harum, owned by Bob, after which the band was named. In the Appendix at the back of the book, you'll find links to the full story on the Procol Harum fan website.

Bob has told me a lot of stories over the years. Sleeping rough in Soho in the fifties, living the Beat dream – reciting *Howl* on buses, bopping at Ken Colyer's club on Great Newport Street. Eric Clapton's facility with the banjo. Throwing quoits over Long John Baldry's erect cock. Bukakke nights with Diana Dors.

He told me once, 'I was the first person to sell R.D. Laing acid,' and I believed him.

After thirty years, you might think he'd be coming to the end of his stories, but I see no sign of it. The best place to buy a gun in Kandahar. The best way to test it. Why Afghan coats smelled of piss, and whose piss it was. His fashion spread in *Vogue*. The thing with Howard Marks and the IRA. The time he was freed from jail in Mexico by a popular uprising of the peasantry who had come to know him as 'El Maestro'. The run-in with Saddam Hussain, for fuck's sake. I tend to believe them all. Why not? If a chap tells you that Procol Harum were named after his cat, and if top-level investigative journalism proves it to be the case, why not just go with the lot?

'What about me?' says Bob.

'You know I've got this job at a university?'

'They put you in charge of young people?'

'It is odd, I know. But ... it's got me thinking.'

And so it has.

When I started work at Birmingham City University in 2006, there was something nagging at me from Day One. Something was missing, but I couldn't work out what. It took me the best part of my first term to put my finger on it. It was the virtual disappearance of student politics. There were no flyers, no posters, no overheated student union meetings; nothing. Even the poor old SWP seemed to have gone. Twenty-five years ago, you couldn't have got near a university campus without encountering a cost accountant's daughter from Kettering desperate to sell you a copy of *Socialist Worker*. All gone. I was shocked to see copies of *Nuts* and *Zoo* in the student union shop; when I was a student, the sisters campaigned to get rid of this kind of stuff.

Who let it back in?

Feminist politics, and student politics in general, seemed alive and well when I graduated in 1992. I myself had thrown an egg at Norris McWhirter, and occupied the Senate Room at Lancaster University; to what end, I'm afraid, I can no longer remember. On graduation, I lived amongst the Freaks, writing songs and trying to write a book, in cat-infested rented houses, in a caravan, in a London squat and, latterly, for four years, in the extraordinary bubble from reality that is an Arvon Foundation house.

By the time I emerged back into the real world in 2006, after a long absence, radical student politics seemed to have disappeared. Any politics that was left seemed to focus around the Islamic Society. The students I was meeting liked to get drunk on beer and jägerbombs at weekends; but, by and large, they were clean, hard-working and well behaved; one might almost say wholesome.

What had gone wrong?

Then one lunchtime, I mentioned the *OZ* trial to a colleague, a specialist in Norwegian literature, aged, I would guess, in his late thirties.

'What's the *Oz* trial?' he asked.

Something, I thought, from a lost world. Ozymandius, the Schoolkid's Edition.

In seminars and in tutorials, I've teased students with references to this lost cultural world, but the Aldermaston marches, *Spare Rib*, Operation Julie, the *International Times*, the *I Ching*, *Catch 22*, *Illuminatus*, *Zen and the Art of Motorcycle Maintenance*, the NUSS, the Angry Brigade, R.D. Laing, the Divine Light Mission, the Incredible String Band, the *Little Red Schoolbook*, the Socialist Party of Great Britain, the Revolutionary Communist Party, the Revolutionary Communist Party of Great Britain (Marxist-Leninist), the Pink Fairies, Throbbing Gristle, *Sniffin' Glue*, Crass, John Seymour, John Michell, Greenham Common, the Peace Convoy, Beanfield, Swampy – all seemed to have been forgotten. I started to think of this lost world as Freak Culture. I thought about how it was the culture in which I'd been raised, and about how it is fading away now, and about how I wish Younger Readers could know something of the cultural world of their parents and grandparents before it has gone, and while some of the perpetrators are still with us.

This is a quote from the Preface of Theodore Roszak's *The Making of a Counter Culture*, first published in Britain in 1970:

> It strikes me as obvious beyond dispute that the interests of our college-age and adolescent young in the psychology of alienation, oriental mysticism, psychedelic drugs, and communitarian experiments comprise a cultural constellation that radically diverges from values and assumptions that have been in the mainstream of our society at least since the Scientific Revolution of the seventeenth century.

He admits that he is 'quite aware that this constellation has much maturing to do before its priorities fall into place and before any well-developed social cohesion grows up around it.'

A few paragraphs later he writes,

> I am at a loss to know where, besides among these dissenting young
> people and their heirs of the next few generations, the radical dis-
> content and innovation can be found that might transform this
> disorientated civilisation of ours into something a human being can
> identify as home.

He was wrong. The adolescent young might be interested in playing
Alien Nation on their devices, but that's about it. No college-age young
person has thrown the *I Ching* these last twenty years. It is fair to say
that Minnie, my Millennial daughter, has shown a good deal of interest
in psychedelic drugs, but her interest in communitarian experimentation
does not extend to sharing her Pringles.

But, for me, for my generation in particular, he was dead right. The
people that Roszak writes about – Herbert Marcuse, R.D. Laing, Alan
Watts – they built our intellectual life, though we knew it not at the
time. For us, growing up in the seventies, it seemed obvious that only
the idea of radical discontent and innovation could possibly bring about
'something a human being could identity as home'. These were the big
hip cultural ideas of our youth. We were spoon-fed it. John and Yoko in
bed for peace. 'Something in the Air' at school discos. The *NME*. We
grew up in the seventies, when the lights didn't work, when the State
shook, and when, O Glorious Day!, anarchy was declared in the UK. We
were the heirs of those Freaks Roszak was writing about, the next generation, the clear inheritors of this world-changing cultural constellation.

But Roszak was wrong. So we were wrong too.

I was born in 1958 on 14 March. Elvis Presley joined the US Army ten
days later. This event traditionally marked the end of the Golden Age of
Rock 'n' Roll. The fact that I was born in that Golden Age has always
seemed to me important in terms of how I have lived my life. 1958 also
saw the publication of Michael Young's satire *The Rise of the Meritocracy*,
the tragic misinterpretation of which has had untold consequences for
my Younger Readers, to whom this book is addressed, as you'll notice
from the subtitle.

By the mid-seventies, my hair was long, my flares were wide, and my
politics were radical. This was the case for lots of young people. The
seventies were a highly charged and politicised time to be young. No
one could ignore politics, not when politics turned off your lights at ten
every night; not when your dad was on strike for long periods of time;

not when bombs were going off in towns like Guildford, the town my parents were from, the town where I'd been born.

When punk came along, it voiced these realities. Punk rock swept aside the flabby prog rock with which we'd been suffocated, but its anger wasn't just musical. Punk castigated the 'rock dinosaurs' for being not radical enough. For 'selling out'. For not being real enough. 'Anarchy in the UK'. 'White Riot'. Punk was a child of the failures of 1968, an attempt to try again. I'm still grateful to the young teachers at my school who were *soixante-huitards*, out to change the world by radicalising their pupils; who gave us tools for trying to understand why everything was shit.

The punks still form part of the soundtrack of our times, but the radical anger has gone. The nasty spate of riots that swept the country in 2011 looked like shopping with violence, rather than a radical uprising of any kind. Somebody will always play a bit of Clash, a bit of Pistols and The Specials' 'Ghost Town' on the soundtrack to the News. The music still gets played, but the Freak Culture from which the punks sprang, and which they revitalised for a time, has gone. The Ramones are a popular T-shirt.

There seemed no real way to account for this disappeared culture to my students. How, for example, do you explain Maoist student movements to students who have never heard of Mao? A student in a creative writing class, asked to write something from the point of view of a New Age Traveller, didn't know where to start. Not only did she not know what a traveller was in this sense, she had no idea what was meant by 'new age'. Sometimes, it seems like all that has survived is some of the dullest of the music, transmuted into Dad Rock, the stuff of nothing but an endless circuit of washed-out summer festivals.

To a Freak like me, coming to adulthood as I did in the intellectual world that Roszak describes, the idea that shopping should be taken seriously or that the Kardashians or the *X Factor* or *Geordie* fucking *Shore* would be interesting to anybody is incomprehensible. Why young, talented, creative and intelligent people in their early twenties would be the least bit keen on getting jobs and mortgages is still quite beyond me. These world views, mine and those of my students, are incommensurate, I thought. Perhaps there is some kind of paradigm shift going on; or perhaps, more likely, the paradigm shift in the way we live demanded by the advocates of the Freak Culture had never reached the point of crisis. It was, after all, the call for a revolutionary paradigm shift in modes of living that was at the heart of the Freak Culture ...

'Yeah .... hello? That's a whole shitload of theory,' says Bob. 'What the fuck are you on about?'

'Ah. Yes. Well. It's all about the philosopher Thomas Kuhn. He talked about the way ideas change over time. He called the moment when ideas change a "paradigm shift". He said that when two ideas don't match they are "incommensurate"; and when two ideas are incommensurate, one of them will win out, and one will die away. The moment when the new idea grows as powerful as the old is called the crisis point.'

'I'll skin up,' says Bob.

'Will it help you follow my argument, do you think?'

'No. But it might make it seem funnier.'

I ignore him, and plough on.

'See, the Freaks' method of bringing about this paradigm shift was Kuhnian as well. Kuhn suggested that old paradigms finally die out as the stakeholders of the old paradigm die. This, in effect, was what the Freaks predicted: the death of the corrupt old world as the old and corrupt died away. This is the dawning of the Age of Aquarius. Never Trust Anyone Over Thirty. And although there were antagonisms between various subsets of the Freak Culture (as between "hippies" and "punks", or "ravers" and "crusties", for example), it seems to me that there was a shared continuity of thought – an aim, a goal – which was to overcome alienation ...'

'I just thought we were trying to have fun,' says Bob.

'You were in practice, yes. But in theory, you weren't. In theory, you were trying to overcome alienation.'

'I don't even know what alienation is.'

'That's probably because you've overcome it.'

'How can I overcome something if I don't know what it is?'

'Right. Alienation is an idea based on the early writings of Marx. Alienation is the bit of the system that takes our intelligent engagement with the world and saps all our pleasure in what we do, in order that we fulfil our economic function as consumers. For example: *Growing* a coffee bean tree on common land, cropping the coffee beans with your smiling friends, roasting and grinding the beans, singing folk songs together about the spirit of the bean, heating water from a communal well over a renewable energy source, pouring it over the ground beans and drinking it from a hand-thrown earthenware mug together with your neighbours is a non-alienated cup of coffee. I've never had one, but it sounds quite nice, I think.

'*Going* into the caff, and saying, "Morning, Frank, can I have a coffee and a crispy bacon sandwich please?" is a slightly alienated cup of coffee, because everyone understands that Frank bought that big catering-sized tin of Maxwell House from which he is spooning the granules to make your coffee from a Cash and Carry, and now he is selling it to you for more than he paid. Frank paid price X and is now selling it to you at price Y, where $Y = X + $ Frank's costs + a small profit so Frank can get his fags and have a bet and save up a bit to take his wife on their annual holiday to Eastbourne, but where $X = $ a large profit to Maxwell House, a smaller one to the Cash and Carry, and a tiny one to the people who grew the coffee beans. But Frank asks nothing else of you than your money; it's a fairly simple deal.

'*Visiting* Starbucks or Costa or Caffè Nero, queuing for the services of a barista, standing, waiting, reading wall signs assuring you of the passionate commitment of the barista to his or her craft, reading little notices on displays of cakes, supposed to look like they've been hand-written in chalk saying "Choose your favourite" (what else would you choose?), reading a notice on the back wall in the same faux-chalk script offering you a choice you didn't know you wanted between a range of coffee drinks whose names you can't pronounce, differing in ways which are unknown to you, in various sizes described in a language not your own, and then being forced to watch the barista as they exercise their craft . . . . . . to come to believe that it *is* a craft . . . . . . that is a fully *alienated* transaction.

'Admittedly, the coffee served with passionate commitment by a trained barista in a special cup is better than poor old Frank's, though I'm not sure it's worth all the palaver.

'We never used to mind it in Frank's caff, and you could get a crispy bacon sandwich on white bread, rather than a quinoa and mung bean spelt flour wrap. Frank only wants 90p for your coffee, and perhaps a chat about football or what you fancy in the 2.30 at Lingfield, because the only things he's passionately committed to are Brighton and Hove Albion and the gee-gees.

'The franchised coffee shop coffee costs £2.90 *and* it demands your interest in their passionate commitment to coffee. If you work as a barista, the company demands your passionate commitment to their profits; your intellect, your time, your life. At no point do you own anything that you have made – none of that passionate commitment, nor your education, your brain, your soul, etc., none of it belongs to you. It all belongs to your employer.

'As a consumer, while your coffee is being hand-crafted, you can look at leaflets containing assurances about the company's passionate

commitment to their ethical and moral policies re. fair trade/environ-
ment/equal opportunities, etc. – even though they have neither ethics
nor morals, so far as I can see – and you are made to look at large black-
and-white photographs on the wall of smiling people in Venice drinking
the stuff and smiling people in Vietnam growing it, and the train is leaving
in three minutes and all you want is a CUP OF FUCKING COFFEE.
That's Alienation.'

'I see. Bad one,' says Bob.

'Essentially, alienated capitalism doesn't just exploit our labour, it
exploits our souls. It degrades all our transactions. It renders our lives
meaningless. Joyless. Empty. Inauthentic. Untrue. No Fun.'

'I'd agree with that. Do you remember my hooks?'

'I've got a bunch of them in my house.'

One of Bob's products is this lovely little hook, made from the wire
on the fence that still runs the length of the abandoned railway line.
Perhaps an inch long, with a twist in the shaft and a curlicue on the end,
they are the very thing to put up in your weekend cottage kitchen to
hang your Le Creuset pots on. Back in the nineties, Bob sold some to a
woman who, unbeknownst to him, was a writer for *Country Living*. She
publicised Bob's hooks, printed a picture of them, and told her readers
where they could get them. Orders flooded in, and Bob started to make
real money. So much so that some people still call him 'Bob the Hook'.
He was making so much money that he rented a small workshop in the
village closest to his wood, and even took on an assistant.

'Problem was,' says Bob, 'I suddenly realised that I was working in
a factory. I mean, it was my factory and that, but it didn't make any
difference. It was still a factory. No fun at all. So I thought, fuck it, and
jacked it in. Now I only make a few hooks when I need a bit of extra
money.'

'So, they are de-alienated hooks. Leaving you free to mend my stool.'

'Is that what you were supposed to be writing about before your fat
arse broke your stool? Alienation?'

Yes. Alienation and its enemies. I want to write about the Freaks and
their lost culture. A history of the British underground. A history book
to explain to my students, my daughters, my stepdaughters, my granddaughters, my Younger Readers, what the Freaks were up to in their
war on alienation, their failed, imperfect, valiant revolt against the long
slow death of the human soul.

I've come up with two dates for my history, to bookend the project.
1956 and 1994.

1956, because it was the year of Suez, which saw the collapse of Britain's view of itself as having importance in the world.

1956, because it was the year of the Soviet invasion of Hungary, which fatally wounded traditional Communist support, and forced radical ideal-ists to look towards Mao, Trotsky, Gramsci, Tolstoy, Kropotkin, Bakunin.

1956, because the UK was right in the middle of a Christian revival that swept through what the historian David Kynaston calls 'Family Britain', and was, to the young Freaks, a dull, hide-bound, suffocating prison.

1956, because it was the year Elvis released 'Heartbreak Hotel' on the RCA Victor label. This might seem trivial, but to the earliest Freaks, hearing 'Heartbreak Hotel' on Radio Luxembourg seems to have changed how they saw themselves and opened new possibilities of ways to live. As John Peel, the great DJ of Freakdom put it: 'Before Elvis there was nothing. After Elvis, there was something.'

I chose 1994 to end my history because it was the year of the Criminal Justice Act, which ended traveller life and the big outdoor raves.

Bob nods.

'Yeah. After that it became really hard to find a park-up.'

By 1994, it was clear which ideas were ready to be taken up by a dominant culture. Some of the ideas had become something approaching mainstream, especially ideas around food and concerns about the medi-calisation of health. Vegetarian restaurants existed in Everytown, and brown rice and wholemeal bread had become de rigueur in middle-class homes. By 1994, everyone was rubbing arnica on their bruises, and everyone was keen to reuse and recycle. Everyone had gay friends. Men appropriated the most creative and enjoyable household tasks, and although we still left our wives to clean the loo and to assemble the IKEA furniture, at least we were doing *something* about the place, and had begun to fully comprehend the implications generated by the rediscovery of the clitoris.

'Communism' had failed in 1989; and there seemed no alternative but unrestricted capitalism. History had ended. The alienation that had been the Freaks' concern didn't seem to worry a population stunned by Neo-Liberalism. Compulsory drug education at school had warned chil-dren off harmless substances like marijuana, LSD and ecstasy, and weaned them on to the lethal but legal pleasures of alcohol. The internet had come into existence a few years before, and one of its first victims was the old underground press. 1994 was also the great year of Brit Pop; ironic, cool, cynical, well-dressed and clean cut, Pulp, Blur and Oasis were simply a great deal better than Chumbawumba, or the Levellers. Pop music, so vital as a means of sharing ideas within the Freak culture, was moving away from cultural criticism or political involvement. Now pop music seems to have lost interest in everything, except expressing and expressing and fucking well expressing a 24/7/365 emotional weather report in voices cracking with self-pity.

1994 was the year that Blair was elected to the leadership of the Labour Party. Sadly, big-tent politics turned out to be too small a tepee to include the dog-on-a-rope crusties, eco-warriors, drug liberationists and anarchist techno-geeks who were by then all that remained of the Freak culture. Roszak's wrongness was now self-evident and I still fail to see anything that looks like home.

If a paradigm shift implies a change in consciousness, then 1994 is as good a moment as any to draw a line, and admit that, so far from uptight, war-mongering, plutocratic, phallocentric, racist, environment-despoiling late-period capitalism dying out, it had, once again, adapted itself enough so that it had pretty much beaten down the alternatives. Very few people, in the end, could cope with the enormous responsibilities of turning on, tuning in and dropping out.

Freak culture has gone.

It is lost.

Alienation, so far from being overcome, has never been in better health.

'I haven't gone,' says Bob. 'I'm still here.'

'Yeah, I know. But I was talking to Chas the other day ...'

'How is Chas?'

I feel a lump gather in my throat. Old Chas Ambler, my sixty-nine-year-old piano player and musical partner of twenty years, is dying of oesophageal cancer in a friend's house in Glasson Dock, just outside Lancaster. I've been driving the 400-odd miles round trip most weekends to spend time at his bedside, to offer limited comfort, and to garner what I can from his fading memory – because Chas, only five years younger than Bob, is a Freak if ever there was one. It hurts to talk about him, and I don't want to cry.

'He's not good. Lot of pain when he eats. Finds it all but impossible to eat, actually.'

I take a breath. The hippies all are going, fading away.

'Anyway, he was telling me about how once, in about 1974, he was on tour as a drummer with a left-wing theatre company, and how he had nothing to read, so he went into a radical bookshop in Cardiff, and bought and then read Guy Debord's *The Society of the Spectacle* in the van between shows.'

'Yeah?'

'Don't you see? There used to be radical bookshops in pretty much every fair-sized city. People could buy Situationist tracts in them. There were left-wing theatre companies touring all over the shop. Drummers read books. What the fuck happened? And why did you go to Mexico?'

'I wanted to do that thing that Gurdjieff did in *Meetings with Remarkable Men*.'

'What thing?'

'That thing where he just set up in a place and mended things for people. I wanted to do that.'

'I haven't read *Meetings with Remarkable Men*,' I said.

'Loads of it's bollocks,' said Bob. 'He reckons he crossed the Gobi Desert on a raft of sheep.'

'But you read a book, and thought the mending was worth a try?'

'We all read.'

'I know. You had cult books. No such thing any more. You read *On the Road* and went on the road. I read all sorts of stuff and threw caution to the wind as a consequence. These days, if my students read anything, they read fucking *Twilight* and wish they could be vampires.'

Bob rolls his eyes at me.

'Kids today, eh?' he says.

'That's not what I'm saying. It's not that they aren't taught to think about the past any more. It's just this story has very few people left to tell it. It's never really been rolled up and put into one book for them to read.'

'So this is what you were writing? When you broke your stool?'

'Sort of. But it's too big. Too baggy. Too theoretical. It needs practice. It needs you.'

'Why me?'

'Because you were there. Really there, from the word go.'

'I was, yeah.'

'You were a Soho beat in the fifties. I want you to tell me all your stories. The time you met the Beatles in the 2i's. Busking with Clapton. CND. Profumo. R.D. Laing. Why you went to Afghanistan. I want you to tell me it all. Running backstage at the Isle of Wight Festival. The one about Sly and the Family Stone, the ambassador's son and the air crash. Mexico. California. The Peace Convoy. You're like Zelig in the Woody Allen film. Or Forrest Gump. You were everywhere.'

'But who'd read a book about an ordinary bloke?'

'You're not an ordinary bloke. You've lived an amazing life, and stayed true to yourself. Besides ... have you ever read *Stuart: A Life Backwards*?'

'No.'

'I'll lend it you. It's about this homeless guy in Cambridge, written by one of his friends. It's fabulous. Game-changing. And Stuart's life was tragic. Yours has been ... heroic.'

Now Bob is laughing, but I know I'm right.

Bob gets me to hold my stool steady in his vice as he welds the wonky leg back together, and then, while it cools, he makes another pot of coffee.

'You're happy to talk, then? About the past?' I ask him.

'Of course,' says Bob. 'The past is only a pleasant void. No harm talking about it.'

'The future?'

Bob sips his coffee, and rolls a fag.

'The future is a less pleasant void, waiting to be filled,' says Bob.

And he gestures round at his clearing, at his home, at the place where his wheels have fallen off.

'But the present,' he says, 'is lovely.'

I had a Reputation as a Foul Mouthed Fucker

On dark winter days in the woods, the light hardly makes it down to the ground, like it can't be arsed; or, as the Freaks might say, like it can't get its blanket out of its muesli.

The mountains which rise to the west shut the last of the sun out from the valley where Bob's wood grows by 4 p.m. In winter, the problem of living in the woods is the wet rather than the cold, because although you can crank a wood-burner in a living vehicle up to a temperature approaching that of the surface of the sun, rain makes mud, and this winter is as wet as anybody in the Radnor Hills can remember. The ground is like a sponge. Every step is wet. There is a place just in front of the doors to Bob's bus where water collects and mud accumulates, Glastonbury deep. Bob has no running water in the woods other than the rain; he collects it in butts which are placed to collect the run-off from the sheds and the roof of the bus. Water is a good thing, and like all good things, you can have too much.

This winter, the wet has been too much. Bob's bones are hurting. He is seventy-five. His brother just died.

Any wood can seem a cheerless place at this time of year. Bob can't get up into the trees to manage the timber; his gardens are unproductive mud wallows, and even the squirrels won't come and get shot.

The reluctance of light to get through the gloom has consequences. There's not enough of it to get the solar panels fully powered up, so energy has to be conserved. Even though it is daytime, a small gas hurricane lamp purrs and putters. Bob puts a few logs on the wood-burner, whilst I fill the stove-top moka with water for coffee.

The logs are to dry things out as much as to warm up the van; the coffee to give us an excuse not to talk, to avoid the subject. Because, after all, where *do* you start to talk to somebody about their life?

I mean, this might do as an opening question.

'When were you born, Bob?'

'Sixteenth of August 1942. In Yeovil, on the RAF base. My father was a ...'

I suddenly realise the full implications of my question.

It's all very well for Bob to tell me the date of his birth, on this wet winter's afternoon in the gloaming of his bus, by the heat of the wood-burner and the light of the hurricane lamp, in the kick of strong coffee and the buzz of a little hashish that I had brought over, but if I'm to write Bob's Life *and* Times, then I need to do a bit of work first.

I know that Younger Readers don't always want dates, but this is important. Who else was born in 1942? What else? What ideas? And what ideas had brought the ideas of 1942 to being? What had happened long before Bob was born, so that when Bob *was* born, at such and such a place and such and such a time, he was the heir to certain ideas that had already been tried, which enabled him to travel in the wake of certain people who had already tried to live as authentically as they could.

This then, is where to start telling the story of someone's life – long before their birth.

'Let me stop you there, Bob!'

'Why?'

'Because you weren't the first hippie.'

'What the fuck difference does that make? When did I ever claim to be the first hippie?'

'You didn't. Because you weren't.'

'I never said I was.'

'I know. Because you weren't.'

'Who was, then?'

'Not you.'

Scholars might argue who the first hippie really was. Maybe it was Krishna or the Buddha or Jesus. Maybe it was one of the Levellers, or the Diggers, or the Anabaptists. I don't know for sure.

So I think I'll pick my own candidate, and say that he was the first, and leave others to argue.

My candidate's name was Henry David Thoreau. He was an American writer and troublemaker who was born in 1817 and who died from tuberculosis in 1862. He came from the small but important town of Concord, Massachusetts, which was also where the well-to-do poet, critic and philosopher Ralph Waldo Emerson lived. Emerson befriended Thoreau on his graduation from Harvard, and encouraged him to write.

From July 1845 until September 1847, Thoreau lived in a one-roomed shack that he'd built for himself close by the shore of Walden Pond, in a tract of woodland owned by Emerson, and only about a mile and a half from his family home.

He wanted to live simply, without compromise. He wanted to be free, and he thought that freedom could only be won by learning how to live as lightly as was possible. He wrote that

> I went to the woods because I wished to live deliberately, to front only the essential facts of life, and see if I could not learn what it had to teach, and not, when I came to die, discover that I had not lived.
>
> I did not wish to live what was not life, living is so dear; nor did I wish to practise resignation, unless it was quite necessary. I wanted to live deep and suck out all the marrow of life, to live so sturdily and Spartan-like as to put to rout all that was not life, to cut a broad swath and shave close, to drive life into a corner, and reduce it to its lowest terms.

Thoreau cannot have read what Marx wrote about alienation, because although they were working at roughly the same time, Marx's theory of alienation would lie undiscovered for another seventy years. But Thoreau had realised that jobs are shit. It is better to grow your rows of beans, to hew your wood and fetch your water, than it is to work for the benefit of someone else. It is always better to listen to the sound of birds in the woods, to watch the ice grow on your pond, to sit in front of your hut and write your book, than it is to accumulate so-called wealth.

There is a sense in which *Walden*, the book he wrote as a consequence of his life in the woods, is a book of natural history. Thoreau earned himself the time to sit and watch and listen to 'nature'; but his idea of nature was a liberal one. *Walden* is pro-science, not anti. Thoreau practises as a scientist. He is not merely a bucolic poet. He observed the behaviour of birds, he watched and recorded the nature of ice, and he accurately measured the depth of the pond. He includes in 'nature' (and with some admiration) 'the iron steed', as he calls the new railroad which cut through a corner of his wood. For Thoreau, the problem isn't the modern world; not innovation, not technology. The problem is the way things are valued. He said, 'Love your life, poor as it is.'

Thoreau didn't look as we might expect a Freak to look (though he was 'ugly as sin' and 'dressed like a tramp'), and so far as we can tell he didn't take recreational drugs. But Thoreau loved the little house that he had built for himself – 'a tight-shingled and plastered house, ten feet wide by fifteen long ... with a garret and a closet. A large window on each side ... one door at the end and a brick fireplace opposite.' Having built it, he set out to change the world by trying to change us. What is perhaps his most famous line – 'Most men lead lives of quiet desperation' – if not a condemnation of alienation?

Bob has never done that, lived in quiet desperation. Most of us have, at one time or another, but Bob hasn't.

'Can I tell you about what happened after I was born yet?' Bob asks me.

'No. Not quite. I'm still setting your scene.'

'I had jaundice, and I had a pointy head, and I was covered in fur. I was so fucking ugly that the doctor offered to flush me away.'

'That's not kind.'

'And I was nearly dead, so they sent me up to a specialist hospital in London, and I was only five days old and the fucking hospital was bombed.'

'Soon. A bit more about Thoreau, then some stuff about the Nature Boys, then you.'

Bob lumps another log into his wood-burner, rather than me, which I sense at this moment he might like to.

'You been behind the door, Bob?'

'You know I have. Have you?'

'Yes. For a day. Non-payment of fines. Same as Thoreau.'

On one occasion when Thoreau strolled into Concord (as he did a couple of times a week; he wasn't a hermit), he was arrested for non-payment of his poll tax, which he had refused to pay because the proceeds were being used to fund slavery, as he saw the case. Although he was only held for one night, jail shaped his consequent writing. His later book *Civil Disobedience* is an account of his political ideas. Thoreau felt that he was seeking a 'form of government beyond democracy', where individual conscience would be respected as 'a higher and different power'.

He said,

> Cast your whole vote, not a strip of paper merely, but your whole in-fluence. A minority is powerless while it conforms to the majority ... but it is irresistible when it clogs by its whole weight .... Let your life be a constant friction to stop the machine.

Thoreau's writing has an underlying commitment to a democratically oriented recognition of the claims of others. And the claims of others, their rights by necessity, include claims on water, food, energy, resources, etc.

And therefore, it is good, it is best, it is democratic, to take only your share; to live as simply as you can. To fell your own wood, to build your own shack, to cultivate your own bean-rows.

Walden was published in 1854; John Updike (in his introduction written for the 150th anniversary of its publication in 2004) said that it 'risks being as revered and unread as the Bible'. This is probably true. But *Walden* is one of the most beautifully written books of the nineteenth century. American schoolkids have to read him like we had to read, say, *Lord of the Flies*, and so they do not always enjoy it as much as a non-American audience who have not been force fed the thing all through school. It's a bit opaque at times. In fact, I've never met anyone who has read it all the way through, other than me. I've met lots and lots and lots of hippies, and no one has ever claimed Thoreau as their great-grandfather.

But he is.

If the day and the night are such that you greet them with joy, and life emits a fragrance like flowers and sweet-scented herbs, is more elastic, more starry, more immortal – that is your success. All nature is your congratulation, and you have cause momentarily to bless yourself. The greatest gains and values are farthest from being appreciated. We easily come to doubt if they exist. We soon forget them. They are the highest reality. Perhaps the facts most astounding and most real are never communicated by man to man. The true harvest of my daily life is somewhat as intangible and indescribable as the tints of morning or evening. It is a little star-dust caught, a segment of the rainbow which I have clutched.

This seems to me an all but note-perfect summation of what the hippies came to believe. All that I've come to believe, in a way.

'In that case,' says Bob, 'I'll continue. Five days old, and I'd already been bombed ...'

'Not yet,' I say. 'Not quite yet. I need to talk more about your shadow time.'

'My what?'

'Your shadow time. The time before you were born, that you sort of grew up in, even though you weren't there to see it. The writer Colm Tóibín says we all inhabit shadow times. For me and my generation it's the war ... for you, it's ninety years' worth of Freaks. Ninety years between *Walden* and you.'

Ninety years; that's no time. Back when I was a Younger Reader; back in 1980, say, when I was twenty-two and a new father, many of the sixty-year-old guys I knew had fought in the war. My grandmother was a Victorian woman, born in 1888. My stepfather's father fought at Jutland, in the First World War. My mother watched her grandmother piss into a bucket while smoking a clay pipe. My shadow time, like Bob's, is set in times very different from ours, but not that long past. My parents were conservative country folk, born and raised in abject poverty. Their ideas are not mine, but they are part of who I am.

Maybe someone complicated, like Bob or you or me, needs hundreds, thousands of mothers and fathers. Who else other than Thoreau shall we take from the nineteenth century? Who might be the grandmothers and -fathers of the counter culture?

There was Marx, writing *The German Ideology*. There was Darwin, of course there was, because Darwin changed everything for everybody. There was George Bernard Shaw, dressed in natural materials, eating vegetarian food. There were the Aesthetes and the Apostles shading into Bloomsbury, queer boys and clever-clever women acting in concert. There was the birth of Bohemianism, and perhaps, at least arguably, the appearance of something that we might recognise as modern friendship amongst the group of beautiful young people around Rupert Brooke in the years just before the First War, the Kaiser's War. There was mass industrialisation, the invention of the music industry, the growth of the clerkly class, the introduction of free compulsory education, the invention of the bicycle . . . all of this might go some way to account for Bob, and his moment.

And then there's religion.

A big problem that people faced in the late nineteenth century, at least in part as a consequence of Darwin's postulation of the theory of natural selection, was that God was Dead. The writer who found this out was a German called Friedrich Nietzsche. This staggering event, the Death of God, the long withdrawing roar of faith down Dover Beach, is a necessary condition for Bob, because it means that when he was born, in the middle of the greatest armed conflict in human history, he was born into a world where all certainty had been dissolved.

God left behind a void, which Humankind takes great pleasure in filling, so before we jump forward to that fateful moment in Yeovil on 16 August 1942, let's have one last nineteenth-century character. Let's have Madame Helena Blavatsky, mother of Theosophy. Madame claimed that she was in contact with the spiritual masters of the world, who lived high in the Himalayas, and who would be needed if God was dead.

Helena Blavatsky arrived in the USA in 1874 after extensive travels in Tibet, and with her came the cultish (and made-up by her) philosophy of Theosophy. Theosophy served up much spiritual apparatus that would be highly valuable to the New Age: *The Tibetan Book of the Dead*, for example, and the *I Ching* – Madame Blavatsky was the first important populariser of Eastern philosophies in the West. India, and in particular the mountainous north of India which borders Tibet, Nepal, Bhutan, Kashmir, Baluchistan and Afghanistan, will eventually become Shangri-La for the hippies. This is the roof of the world, and it is up here that we were keeping a whole new set of about-to-be-reborn gods, as Madame Blavatsky was one of the first to recognise.

We'll be back for them later.

Post-Christian ideas were particularly important in Germany, in the wake of Nietzsche's growing (and increasingly misunderstood) reputation. By the 1890s the widely available Theosophical publications that summarised in plain language the ideas of Egyptian religion, of Gnosticism, alchemy, Hermeticism and the various Hellenistic mystery cults were bestsellers in Germany, *The Da Vinci Code* of the day.

Ancient Chinese philosophy was also widely read in Germany, and subsequently by the Freaks. Up until the 1980s no self-respecting Freak would be caught without their copy of Richard Wilhelm's translation of the *I Ching*. I have spent many a cheerful night smoking spliff and casting coins with friends; people did this behind closed doors as much as they danced in clubs or put a ring around Greenham in public.

There were numerous attempts to translate Chinese texts into German, particularly the *Tao Te Ching*, the founding book of Taoism. Legend has it that this book was written under duress by Lao Tzu, 'Old Man', the 'founder' of 'Taoism'. The Old Man (who probably didn't exist in the sense that you or I or Bob exist, but who clearly did exist in a way we never can) was trying to leave China, around about 600 BCE, because he was sick of the place. He travelled over the mountains towards Tibet, but before he was granted an exit visa, the border guards made him write down all his wisdom. This he did, reluctantly, and, having finished the *Tao Te Ching*, he crossed over the mountains and was never heard of again. His simple philosophies will flow through this story, as we learn to go with it, man, the flow, the Tao, whatever it is, whatever stream it takes us along. This stream will bubble up from under our feet again and again, and it is by far the most important of the Freaks' philosophies, leaving peace and love nowhere. If life is to be lived to the full, then it is necessary to live in the present, and to follow the path that opens up in front of you.

Gustav 'Gusto' Gräser was one of the first translators of the *Tao Te Ching* into German. Born in 1879, he was a simple-life vagabond, a disciple of Nietzsche, who refused military service in 1901. He did five months in prison, and when he went home to his parents, they were horrified because of how he looked. He looked like a draft dodger should. He wore a poncho and home-made sandals and put his long hair up in a headband, and wore his beard untrimmed; in short, if you had encountered Gusto Gräser running a gong workshop at any music festival between about 1967 and today, you wouldn't think twice. But this was more than a century ago. A contemporary described Gusto:

> Long, chestnut hair falls over his shoulders, and a chestnut beard frames a fine, regular face of clear complexion, red-cheeked, with a lightly curved nose and a pair of magnificent clear brown eyes under unusually finely shaped brows and a smooth forehead. The upper body of this form is wrapped in a kind of chiton made of yellowy-brown coarse sacking fabric with the bare, lean, strong arms and slim veiny hands exposed. His legs are clad in tight trousers from the same material and his feet wrapped in sandals fastened up the shins with straps. A meshed wanderer's sack hangs over his shoulders.

For a time he was living in a cave outside the Swiss/Italian village of Ascona, a small fishing village on the Swiss side of Lake Maggiore. Between 1900 and 1920 Ascona became a focus for many of Europe's 'spiritual rebels' (including Carl Jung, Isadora Duncan, D.H. Lawrence and Franz Kafka) and many others disillusioned by life in industrialised German-speaking countries. Visitors became involved in activities including modern dance, Dada, paganism, feminism, psychoanalysis, nature cures, vegetarianism and, I'm very much afraid, naturism.

Ascona was full of 'seekers after truth', with an emphasis on a bloodless, vegetarian diet. And fruit. And nut butter. Gusto Gräser refused all cooked foods – an Englishman who wanted fried potatoes was asked to leave the village. The mountain on which the colony was founded was named Monte Verità, or the Mountain of Truth. Although it attracted 'certain idlers', Monte Verità quickly gained a reputation as a health centre, and as a centre of what became known as 'lebensreform'. Life reform.

Lebensreform was one of the many German social trends of the late nineteenth and early twentieth centuries. Up until the time of German unification in 1870, German culture and language had been regarded as *the* most vital culture and the most profound language for upwards of a

century, but with unification came Prussianisation, and thus militarisa-
tion. It is easy to remember the terrible consequences of some of those
German social trends. But there were others, some of which found their
way to California, and into contemporary ideas of 'the good life'.

Lebensreform thinkers such as Johannes Guttzeit and Richard Ungewitter
advocated vegetarianism, nudism, 'natural medicine', freedom from
alcohol and clothing reform. (If you think about how buttoned up the
Victorians were, you can see why 'clothing reform' mattered.) *Lebensreform*
was a huge project, as it would have to be (still has to be): at various
moments *lebensreform* adherents advocated settlement movements,
garden towns, soil reform, sexual reform, economic reform, liberation
for women and children, communitarianism, religious reform and a world
view emphasising the feminine, maternal and natural traits of existence.

Most 'life-reformers' adopted only one or two modes of reform, but
the *'naturmenschen'* were the full-on version, who attempted to radically
change all aspects of their life in relation to current customs. The most
fully committed of the *'naturmenschen'* roamed through German-speaking
countries proclaiming a message of natural life, preferring to fast or go to
prison rather than adopt normal customs and rules. Johannes Guttzeit,
for example, founded the 'League for Full Humanity' and believed Christ
was an early kind of *naturmenschen*. In his 1914 book *Die Nacktheit
(Nakedness)*, Guttzeit advocated abstention from meat, tobacco and alcohol,
and placed special emphasis on nudity in gymnastics and sport, especially
in co-education, though whether or not I would have enjoyed PE more
at school if we'd had to do it naked, I doubt. But for Guttzeit nudity was
aristocratic, and clothing plebeian, leading to decadence and that other
powerful late nineteenth-/early twentieth-century phantasm, degeneration.

The Lebensreformers had a youth wing, who were known as the
Wandervogel: which translates as migrant birds, or free spirits. The
Wandervogel were founded in 1895 by Hermann Hoffmann, a twenty-one-
year-old student, and started with nature walks, which soon led to rebel-
lion against the complacent materialistic and sexually hypocritical views
of their parents' generation. Anti-bourgeois and pagan in temper, they
were middle-class German children aged mainly fourteen to eighteen,
organised into autonomous cells around charismatic leaders. By 1911, the
Wandervogel had about 15,000 members, and by 1914 about 50,000. They
pooled their money, spoke 'hobo slang, peasant patois and medieval
vulgate', and wore torn clothing, woollen capes, Tyrolean hats and bright
scarves. They went in for long hikes, with singing, guitars, mixed bathing
in lakes and camping in the countryside and in ruined castles. The

Wandervogel formed the basis of the Youth Hostel movement, first in German-speaking countries, but ultimately across Europe. They said that they were 'seeking communion with nature' and the 'ancient peasant folk spirit'.

It is terrible to contemplate what happened to them, first in the coming Kaiser's War, and then in the Nazification of Germany in the 1920s and '30s.

Sad to know that there might have been a radically different future. On Christmas Eve 1912, in the city of Darmstadt, a chemist called Anton Köllisch who was working for the German pharmaceutical giant Merck filed a patent for a new anti-coagulant drug called MDMA. Imagine if the *Wandervogel*, when they got herded into the trenches, had 'E' to go with their Nietzsche and their bright scarves and their guitars. Militarism might have been backed against a wall and laughed out of existence. As it was, Köllisch was killed on the Western Front in 1916, and his discovery was sidelined, and not even tested on humans for certain until the 1970s.

Gusto Gräser was the most well-known of the early *naturmenschen*, and not just because of his work on the *Tao Te Ching*. In 1906, the writer Hermann Hesse visited Ascona, and met Gräser in his cave. Hesse found the experience immensely powerful. Although critics have disputed the extent to which Hesse was influenced by Gräser, a long-standing friendship seems to have developed between the two men. During his stay, Hesse was impressed enough that he tried out some of Gräser's ideas. Hesse lived naked and alone at Ascona, slept on a stone floor wrapped in a blanket, fasted for a week, and spent a day buried up to his armpits. Each to their own.

Herman Hesse was to become the most widely read and translated German writer of the twentieth century, and writers are important in this story. Bob was, is, a great reader, and so were many of the Freaks. You could argue (I am arguing) that early Freakdom was a literary culture. The counter-culture was, after all, cultured, and the reading list of books that they held in high esteem is long. Not always great, in critical terms, maybe, but long. And one of the first writers who was widely read was Herman Hesse.

His novels are like morality plays. They start in a metaphorical Garden of Eden and end with a metaphorical Apocalypse. The first, published in 1904, is called *Peter Camenzind*, and it established Hesse's great theme, and to some extent that of the counter-culture – that of the individual in search of their authentic self. The last novel is called *Magister Ludi*, or *The Glass Bead Game*, and was published in 1943 ...

'1943. When I was a baby,' said Bob. 'This is supposed to be my life story ...'

'And when Albert Hofmann ingested LSD through his fingertips and went for a ride on his white bicycle. Life and times, Bob. Life and times. I'm getting there ...'

Although Hesse won the Nobel Prize for Literature in 1946, by the early 1960s, he was almost forgotten, and little read, until he was promoted by Timothy Leary (of whom more later) and Colin Wilson, a British writer who was in vogue in the wake of his 1956 book extolling the virtues of existentialism, *The Outsider*. Hesse's revival was in full swing by the late sixties when all self-respecting Freaks had read *Steppenwolf, Siddhartha, Narcissus and Goldmund* and *Journey to the East*.

Steppenwolf is probably the best known. There's the band, of course (*Born to be Wild*), and a Steppenwolf Theatre Company, but the book is also remembered for the idea of the 'Magic Theatre', which became a popular metaphor for psychedelic drug use. The novels are, I suppose, a bit heavy going, but they are heavy going in a good way when you are a Younger Reader; achievable, and worth achieving, even now. Hesse is one of the key figures in Freak Orientalism, the idea that everything is more far out the further east you go. And through his books, the ghost of Gusto Gräser with his long hair tied up in a headband, travelling around Germany and Switzerland with his wife and baby in a horse-drawn caravan, is transmitted to the High Sixties. And the spirit of Ascona was reborn in the 1960s, too. The Esalen Institute in Big Sur on the West Coast of California was founded in 1962 with the aim of becoming a 'Monte Verità on the Pacific'.

One unlooked for consequence of Prussian militarism was the exodus of a number of Lebensreformers to California in the period just prior to, and during, the First World War. One of the first to arrive was Arnold Ehret, who had run a sanatorium in Ascona, treating illnesses with fasting and a fruit diet. Ehret came to California in 1914, and wrote and lectured in the LA area on fasting and the 'mucusless diet'. He wrote that 'life is a tragedy of nutrition', and that 'the direct rays of the sun on the naked body supply the electricity, energy and vitality to the human storage battery renewing it in vigour, strength and virility'. He claimed that 'We start the resurrection of man by reconstructing the paradise, planting fruit trees, vineyards and gardens as our new residence. We bring not only a scientific system of healing based on natural laws, but a regeneration, a complete resurrection of the flesh by water, air, "spirit", and by the divine foods of God, i.e. fruits.'

Hermann Sexauer was born in Germany 1883, but came to the USA in 1907, 'in search of freedom', and worked his way to California. He studied forestry and worked as a tree warden in Santa Barbara, but he was refused citizenship as he would not swear to bear arms, having been influenced by Tolstoy's idea that militarism and freedom did not belong together. In 1934 he opened the 'Sexauer Natural Food Shop', in Santa Barbara. He was against the things that all the *naturmenschen* were against: tobacco, alcohol, sugar, coffee, white flour, medicine, doctors, vaccination, God, war and vivisection, and in favour of vegetables, Esperanto and, inevitably, nudism. Sexauer believed that abolition of meat eating would end wars, and who is to say he was wrong, since no one seems to have tried it. He was responsible for the wide distribution of many types of fruit trees in the Santa Barbara area, especially avocado, sapote, carob and cherimoya, all sold in his health food shop.

He is quoted as saying, 'Coffee is poison. But it kills you so gradually it is impossible to detect it,' with which there is no arguing. He is credited with being the founding guru of the 'straight edge' movement, that odd post-punk bubble of the late 1980s and early 1990s which eschewed meat, drink and drugs, and which I never fancied.

Perhaps of more importance for our story, this story of the attempt to live as truthfully as possible by one old hippie in a van in a wood on the borders of England and Wales in the early twenty-first century, is John Richter. Born in North Dakota of German descent, Richter was fascinated by the ideas of *lebensreform* and the *naturmenschen*. With his wife Vera, he opened the 'Eutropheon' live foods café on Laurel Canyon Boulevard in LA, which lasted from 1917 until 1942. After living for fifteen years on a largely cooked vegetarian diet, Richter adopted the 'live foods' (i.e. raw) philosophy. He believed that 'live food' could allow people to live to 140. He was, inevitably, opposed to coffee, sugar, salt, tobacco, meat, dairy and cooked food, and promoted massage, heliotherapy, iris diagnosis, sun gazing, bare feet and, as you have probably guessed, nudism. In short, you could bump into his descendants up in the Healing Field at the Glastonbury Festival today, and get them to rebalance your chakras. Richter might seem like yet another example of wholefood nuttiness, but for the fact that he had followers.

One of the most important of his followers (perhaps allies would be better) was another immigrant from Germany called Bill Pester. There is a picture of him sitting outside his self-built hut playing the slide guitar, taken in 1917, looking very like the Beach Boys drummer Dennis Wilson would fifty years later; naked but for shorts, hair well over his shoulders, beard down to his chest, he looks the archetypical California hippie. No one would look at him twice in Santa Barbara today. But this photo was taken at the same time that US troops were arriving in Europe to fight in the First World War. It took something beyond courage to live like that and to look like that at that moment in history.

He lived not far from Palm Springs. He did the naked thing, the raw foods bit and the wandering about. He said, 'All man's troubles, sickness, anxieties and discontent comes from a departure from nature.' In the 1920s he started an organic farm, and in the 1920 census he was counted as an 'Indian', much as Bob is now counted a gypsy. People like these are as hard to compute as ever.

Pester and Richter were charismatic men. The lifestyle they were promoting seemed a lot more attractive than fighting in the trenches or working on Cannery Row to a handful of young idealistic men like 'Gypsy Boots', 'Gypsy Jean', Fred Bushnoff, Maximilian Sikinger (another German immigrant), Emile Zimmerman, Buddy Rose and Bob Wallace, who started to hang out at the Eutropheon. Gordon Kennedy, the expert on these proto-hippies, says in his excellent book *Children of the Sun*, the Eutropheon was the torch where they lit their lamp'. Richter inspired them to eat 'live' foods, to try their hands at organic farming and to promote *lebensreform*. They called themselves the Nature Boys.

California's Nature Boys all worked at one time or another at the Eutropheon, shopped at Sexauer's shop and adopted the lifestyle and philosophy of the *naturmenschen*. Richter encouraged the Nature Boys to wear their hair long, and to live 'native style' up in the mountains. These ideas made sense during the 1930s economic depression, just as they make sense now. If times are bad, new ways have to be found.

And so, there came one day into the Eutropheon a boy, a very strange enchanted boy, who had been born in 1908 in Brooklyn, and christened George Alexander Aberle. He had been adopted by a family called McGrew, and came to maturity in Kansas City, where he worked as a dance band leader. By the early 1940s he had wandered across to California, and changed his name to eden ahbez (he didn't believe in capitalising names other than that of God). Before he came into the Eutropheon, he had previously been living in a cave in Tahquitz Canyon near Palm Springs, where he had met and become influenced by Bill Pester, whom ahbez described as his 'mentor'. He started to play the piano in the Eutropheon, and to hang out with the Nature Boys. The Boys would visit Pester in Tahquitz Canyon, and there ahbez wrote the song that would immortalise the Boys and their mentor. 'Nature Boy', with its heart-expanding chorus, is therefore the first song of the Freaks.

One day in 1947 ahbez left a manuscript with the doorman at the Lincoln Theater in LA where Nat King Cole was performing. The tattered and rolled-up sheet music made its way to Cole's manager, Mort Ruby, who saw potential in the tune. Cole took to it immediately. 'Nature Boy' was Nat King Cole's first hit record; it spent eight weeks at number one in 1948, and meant that ahbez never had money worries again. But, as the cliché has it, success didn't change him. ahbez lived with his wife and child for a time under the Hollywood sign, and when he had to travel to New York, he slept in a sleeping bag in Central Park. ahbez told *Life* magazine, 'I am the wind, the sea, the evening star. I am everyone, anyone, no one.' He died in 1995, aged eighty-five, from injuries received in a car accident, which seems heart-breaking to me.

The Nature Boys, even after they became the subject of one of the greatest of American pop songs, stayed true to themselves. In *On the Road*, Jack Kerouac noted that while passing through Los Angeles in the summer of 1947 he saw 'an occasional Nature Boy saint in beard and sandals'. eden ahbez once told his friend Gypsy Boots, as they were hanging with Bill Pester in Tahquitz Canyon sometime in the 1940s, that, 'Someday there will be a million beards.' And you can't argue with that.

There is a playlist in the Appendix, as well as a reading list, and 'Nature Boy' is the first song on it. When you hear it, think of the Boys, tanned and naked in the California sun, and the pioneering Freaks up in the canyon with Pester, eating raw food and making music.

Bob has made us both another coffee. The rain has started again, black rain it looks like, in this dark wood, like this thick coffee. He's impatient to tell me his story, with all its adventure and guns and drugs and fucking and appearing on stage with Led Zep, and I want to hear him talk. But I just need a moment to think about 1942, the year when Bob first happened.

Lots of people were born in that year who would effectively become the counter-culture; in the USA, for example, Jerry Garcia, Jimi Hendrix and Brian Wilson; and in the UK, Paul McCartney, Brian Jones, John Cale, Graham Nash, Ian Dury, Nobby Stiles, Derek Jarman, Peter Greenaway, Terry Jones . . .

'Nobby Stiles?'

'Yeah. And Oxfam. And the first Famous Five book . . .'

There must have been a series of events which meant that these people from this time would do things that had never been done before, and that these people born in this moment would try to find new ways and means of expression, – and I would beg your indulgence for a little while longer to imagine what some of those 1942 things might have been.

It must be hugely significant, for example, that the British babies – the McCartneys, the Brian Joneses, the Derek Jarmans, the Bob Rowberrys – would find themselves growing up in a world where the government thought it would be a good idea to do away with want, with disease and with ignorance, because the founding document of the Welfare State, the Beveridge Report, was also born in 1942. And here's a thing: the future British counter-culturistas would have found themselves growing up in a world where soap was in short supply; 1942 was the year when soap rationing was introduced, and so the hippies were dirty from the moment of their birth.

Perhaps there was optimism in the air, a vibration (an idea with which the Freaks became obsessed) – faint, noticeable only to a newborn, sensitive to the world as no one ever is again. The Soviet Union had swapped sides. The USA had entered the war. And in North Africa, there was the first real British military victory at El Alamein. Fortunes were turning for the better.

And perhaps you could argue that 1942 marked the end of high modernism, and that in order for a counter-culture to thrive, it is necessary that 'High Culture' be in some difficulties.

Let me elucidate, Younger Readers.

Modernism in the Arts had been born after the First World War. Kevin Jackson, in his book *Constellation of Genius*, claims that Modernism's 'Year Zero' was 1922. By 1942, I would say, it was on its last legs. Virginia Woolf, the advocate of the highest of 'High Culture', had drowned herself the year before, a few miles up the Sussex River Ouse from where I went to school and had been forced to read her class-hate-filled prose, while I stared longingly at Jackie Sinclair, and carved 'Free Wayne Kramer' on my desk. James Joyce, whom Woolf called 'a callow board school boy', had also died in 1941. In 1942, T.S. Eliot published 'Little Gidding', the last of *The Four Quartets*. Although he would continue to write plays, and occasional verse, 'Little Gidding' was the last of his serious poems. If no Eliot, we might argue, then no modernism; certainly no High Modernism in capitals. So perhaps this was the last year of the highest of high culture. After all, in America, in New York, girls were screaming at Frank Sinatra.

On 30 December 1942, Sinatra was third-billed on the programme behind Benny Goodman and his Orchestra at New York City's Paramount Theater. Goodman had never heard of him. When Goodman announced

Frank the audience roared and shrieked for five minutes. Goodman's response was, 'What the hell was that?' Once Sinatra started to sing, the audience continued to shriek during every song. Something had changed.

1942 was the year when American forces first landed on British soil, in Belfast as it happens. In terms of the transmission of popular culture, few invasions have ever proved more important; the story of Van Morrison in Belfast or the Beatles in Liverpool listening to R&B records imported from the States must be well known even to the youngest Younger Readers.

So perhaps, we might argue, by 1942 the very notion of 'high' and 'low' culture was in trouble. After all, Theodor Adorno and Max Horkheimer in their seminal *Dialectic of Enlightenment*, published only two years later—

Bob draws the line at Adorno and Horkheimer, as well he might.

'What the fuck?' he says. 'I only want to be born.'

I sigh.

'Oh, go on then ... You're born. Tell me your earliest memory.'

'I have three really early memories. The first is: I was in one of those garden air-raid shelters covered with turf – a Morrison or an Anderson, can't remember which – knocking my head against the wall in time to the bang bang bang of bombs.'

'Fuck. Where was this?'

'Kingsbury. Wembley, that way. That's where we lived. That's why they sent me to hospital there, I guess. My second memory, a bit of an odd one I suppose, was an out-of-body experience, running through the streets of Eastbourne, one hand in Mum's, and the other one in my Aunty Pat's, being dragged along, feet off the ground, ARP blokes shouting get off the fucking streets, an air raid going on, near a searchlight and anti-aircraft battery, all that boom boom boom ... but I was aware of the scene from above and behind, like I was an observer.

'And my third memory was at the street party at the end of the war; middle of the street ...'

'Still in London?'

'In Kingsbury, yeah, with trestle tables going out of sight, loaded with food and stuff, a great atmosphere, and then this bloke in an RAF uniform comes up with a trombone, and I'd never seen a trombone before. He says put your hand in there, and I do so tentatively, then he gives it a big UHHHH, and I fucking freaked. I was inconsolable, had to be taken home, just a few steps away. I missed the whole party.'

'You made up for it later.'

'I did.'

'Tell me again about Yeovil and the fur-covered pointy-head thing.'

'When I was born ...'

'At an RAF Station in Yeovil. On the sixteenth of August 1942.'

'Yes. I had jaundice, and I had a pointy head, and I was covered in fur. I was so fucking ugly that the doctor offered to flush me away.'

'That's not kind.'

'And I was nearly dead. I had to be put on a life support machine, but there were no spare ones at the Yeovil air base where my father was working, so they sent me up to a specialist hospital in London, and I was only five days old and the fucking hospital was bombed.'

'Did your mum split up with your dad at the moment of your birth?'

'Don't know. My mum would refuse to answer any questions about him, but the one thing she did tell me was that he schlepped off with an heir to the Pickfords fortune. In later life she told me, "You're just like your father; he was a bastard too."'

'And that's it. That's what you know?'

'I know more now. He came from the Rhondda, that way.'

One of Bob's girlfriends found the family tree on the internet, with a photograph of Bob's father. He married after the war, and had other children.

'The family must know of my existence, but they don't want to know me, so fuck 'em. Being the eldest son of the father might raise a few complications, maybe.'

Bob was taken to Wembley, because there was a child-care unit in the hospital there, but mainly because Bob and his mother were to live with Nan and Gran, the couple who adopted her at birth and named her Gwendoline Gertrude Craven.

Bob still isn't sure if Nan and Gran were lesbians, but he strongly suspects this might have been the case. The only grandparents he knew, therefore, were cuddly round smiling Nan, and Gran with an aquiline nose and an aristocratic demeanour.

They had a piano, and seem to have encouraged Gwen in mildly bohemian ways; she wrote poems, played guitar, and was a belly dancer in later life; an enthusiastic amateur, but a proper dancer. She was good looking, in what Bob describes as a 'Pre-Raphaelite sort of way', with dark wavy hair.

Because Bob never asked, or Gwen wouldn't say, he doesn't know how his mother got to Yeovil, or how she met David Rowberry. In fact, he didn't know until he was fifteen and leaving school that Rowberry was the name on his birth certificate. Until that moment, he thought he was called Robert McGregor, instead of David Robert Rowberry, which is what he is called really. And he thought his father was called Jack McGregor.

'When did Mr McGregor appear in your mum's life?' I asked Bob.

'In the war. So, but, perhaps even prior ... because I don't know why Mr Rowberry fucked off. He might have had very good reason; because my mum might have been fucking Mr McGregor, who wasn't the Scotsman that you might expect, but was in fact a German. I didn't know that till much later. I went through school telling everyone I'm a direct descendant of Rob Roy. Little boys build them selves up, like; and then I discovered I wasn't descended from Rob Roy, but a fucking German.'

Bob's stepfather's real name was Herman Kouri; Jack McGregor was picked off a list of the dead. Bob doesn't know when or why he fled from Germany, but at the beginning of the war he was sent to an internment camp on the Isle of Man, where he was recruited into an early parachute commando regiment. Many of the internees joined the British forces, because they often had good reason to hate the Nazis. Many of them found their way to the Commandos because they had the motivation that comes from hate of this kind.

'A big handsome bloke in commando uniform; the airborne commando badge must have carried a bit of weight with the girls,' says Bob.

'He never talked about what he did in the war, but he was really casual about his weapons. He kept all his weapons in the garden shed – real guns and real sacks of ammunition. I played with them, for fuck's sake; a little kid in shorts with a real fucking army real rifle to play with, a little .22.'

'So how did you end up Aldershot way?'

'I suppose McGregor just knew that area. Just where he was when he was discharged, I guess. I was five when we moved from Kingsbury. Sandhurst and Camberley one way, Aldershot was about six miles away. I was in Mytchett ... near Frimley, near Ash.'

'I lived in Ash when I was a kid,' I tell Bob.

'Did you? Fuck me.'

'I told you years ago. My mum and your mum both worked at different times as cleaners at RAE Farnborough.'

'Well, I'm fucked,' says Bob.

'What did McGregor do?'

'He fancied himself as a chef, but most of the work he did was driving manure lorries for D.C. Bushell of Sandhurst. Sometimes I went out on the shit lorries with him. Once I saw him deal with some bloke in a transport café with a knife; fuck me, he dealt with him. He was a hard man. Handy. Like in the films.

'But he wanted to be a chef. Sometimes he would take all the family's weekly food coupons to buy stuff for just one dish which would take two days to prepare, and then was just a meal for him.' (Younger Readers might forgive me for reminding them that wartime food rationing didn't end until 1954, six weeks before Bob's twelfth birthday.)

'He wasn't a nice man. He was a bastard, he tortured me.

'Try it one day. Stand against the wall. With just your nose touching the wall, no other part of your body, and your hands held up above your head like that, and if any other part of your body touches the wall you get hit. It's all right for a few minutes, but fucking try it. Half an hour and you're weeping and your knees are buckling. It's fucking agony. You don't have to try it really, you could just take my word for it.'

'Yeah, all right, I will ... but he was Sandy's dad, though?'

Sandy was Bob's kid brother, the cause of a great deal of trouble later on in our story, and a recurring character; Bob just got back from his funeral in Margate a few days ago.

'Yep. He was Sandy's dad .... wee Sandy McGregor. Alexander was his proper name. I hadn't seen him for ten years before the funeral. Didn't see him then, either, of course. I didn't want him to know where I lived. He was two years younger than me.'

'Tell me about your stutter. How you caught it.'

'Aldershot Lido. Most wonderful swimming pool. Huge, fucking enormous, wonderful place. At that time, either my mother or father was working there. They were both swimmers, with swimmers' badges on their trunks. I spent a lot of my childhood at swimming pools. One time, one hot July day, we were sitting on the grass, and this geezer came over who knew McGregor. He was notable partly because one of his bollocks was hanging out of his trunks, but also because he had this terrible stutter. And my mum reckoned that before that geezer turned up, I had never stuttered, and from that moment on, I did. It's a strange one. Was it a defence mechanism? Though why I'd absorb such a thing ... but apparently I did.'

Bob's stutter was bad, cataclysmically so. You can still hear it scarring his speech now.

Bob, as is his way, made the best of it. He enjoyed his weekly speech therapy.

'Sadly, it coincided with art classes, which was one of the only classes that I liked, but it did have the advantage of Miss Peachy, who was a

vast old dragon of a woman. She used to make me lie on my back on
the ground. Then she'd say, "Breathe like I am. You'll have to put your
hand on my chest to feel how I'm breathing." So I could feel her tits,
and periodically her hand would *so accidentally* brush against my then
erect willy in my baggy short trousers … so I used to love it.

'The speech therapy did me no good, except for this strange erotic
experience with Miss Peachy. It was only after puberty and moving up
to London and interjecting profanities that I learned to control the stutter.
"Blinking" in polite company, "bloody" if I wasn't and I was going to be
stuck on a word, then, later, "fucking". Some people knew me as Blinking
Bob, because I had a reputation as a foul-mouthed fucker.'

'Entirely undeserved.'

The stutter might make it sound as though Robert McGregor was a
nervous child. He wasn't. He was a lunatic nutcase of a child, exactly
the sort of child that Younger Readers were not allowed to play with.
The family were double dirt poor. Bob went to school in dead man's
shoes, and was always the scruffiest kid at school. Already, your parents
are looking at him nervously, and so they should.

'Almost all the children of my age in the village weren't allowed to
play with me.'

'Why not?'

'Cos I'd bring bombs home! Actual fucking bombs. I used to put live
.303 rounds on a fire. We had a big sack of .303 rounds we'd found, we'd
put a handful of 'em on a fire, and stand back. Either end, the casing end
or the bullet end, would have fucking destroyed you, because they would
have been rotating, they'd be going end over end, and they'd made a
hole you could put your hand in …. Either end of 'em would at that
range.

'And I'd bring adders home. Vipers. Real adders. They were common
in that area. Lift up any sheet of tin, and you'd find an adder, and I'd
take 'em home. Mother wasn't delighted.

'I'd put vinegar and bicarbonate of soda in a lemonade bottle, give it
a shake and throw it. They'd explode. I used to have scars on my body
from one that exploded before I'd let go of it. Of course people didn't
want their kids to play with me!'

Bob pauses.

'I tell you who I did play with at primary school, though. John
Renbourn. Lived in quite a posh house. I played round there quite a bit.'

'John Renbourn?'

'Yeah.'

'The Pentangle guitarist?'

'Yeah. He was playing in Brecon a few years back, and I went up afterwards and re-introduced myself. I thought we might have played together when we were in secondary school, but he said no, he went to the Grammar, and that it was when we were in primary that we played together.'

John Renbourn, therefore, becomes the first name-drop in this story, the first of many.

I remember from my far distant childhood (we moved from Ash when I was six) that our house in Ash Vale backed onto a sewage farm, and then the heath, the Ash Ranges, a battleground fought over since time immemorial by soldiers in training. Bob's house backed onto the Ranges, too, and that's where he used to play.

'It was so great. It was lovely: endless heath for all intents and purposes. It was sandy, with bracken, and heather and Scots pines, but not only that, but there were real tanks there you could play in, and if you went over to the mortar ranges, real bombs that hadn't gone off that you could pick up and throw at your mate, whole trench warfare trench systems, with loads of lost and discarded stuff you could pick up. The war had just finished. You'd see really badly wounded men around Aldershot. With open wounds, some of them. It had only just stopped. The heath was fucking heaven.'

Bob had a favourite game.

'Have you ever seen a military rifle range?' he asks me.

'On TV.'

'There's a bank of earth about a small house high, in front of which the targets go. Then in front of that there's a trench where the guys who are operating the targets are hidden. Then, heading back towards the firing places, there were more mounds of earth, five foot high, which run about a hundred yards across the range every fifty yards or so. When they're firing from the three, four or five hundred yards mark, there's several of these long mounds between the firers and the targets – and my trick was luring my brother or a mate down to share this experience with me. We'd crawl down through the bracken to the end, and make our way along, covered by a mound of earth, and crawl between the targets and the shooter and then make our way to the apex of the mound. You'd get as far up as you could, but still be covered by it. And when you get loads of blokes firing rifles, Bren guns, Vickers machine guns, all at the same time, well, to me it was awesome, hundreds of bullets whistling over, a hand away from your fucking head ... Whssh! Whessssh!

'And an extension of this game was to get about a quarter of a mile behind the target area. I'd found out where all the bullets landed from the shooters who were so fucking inept that not only they didn't hit the target, but they didn't hit the bank as big as a fucking house behind the target. I worked out where all these bullets would land, because you found loads of bullets, and it was quite a thrill to just hang around that area and hear the bullets. ShsssstP! ShsssstP!'

'Weren't you scared?'

'No. Thrilled, yes.'

Bob gets out his tin, and rolls a fag.

'It's strange behaviour, I can see that now. But that's what I used to do.'

'You talked to me before about Kipling? Was that part of it? Bullets on the redoubt? Boys' Own Adventure?'

'I loved Kipling. That's why I always wanted to go to Afghanistan – to meet the wily Pathan. I loved all that as a kid. I still do. I recently bought a volume of his verse, and I still think it's great. The man had soul, no doubt about it. And guts.'

'How did you find out you were a great shot? Two things from the whole story of your life are constant, it seems to me: reading and shooting.'

'I always had guns. Guns used to come to me, and I've always been a shot. When I was a kid in shorts I found three revolvers on separate occasions. How many other people do you know who in their childhood found three revolvers?'

'I don't know anybody who even found one.'

'Just after the war, round about Aldershot there were all these retired colonials coming back with their revolvers from the first war, and their fucking assegais from the Siege of Mafeking. And they died or they got fed up with 'em or had to sell the house and they chucked 'em over the hedge. I found what I now know to be a Napoleonic short sword with a brass handle and a double-edged blade. They'd just chucked the whole lot over a hedge.

'And I always had airguns, German original make. The first one was longer than I was, go right through both sides of a galvanised iron dustbin. So I taught myself to shoot. I sat in my bedroom window and shot all the heads off the neighbour's flowers. One after the other. He never said a word.'

'You wouldn't.'

'But I'd destroyed his garden! And lupins, in particular. Because they have a fat hollow stem, you had to hit 'em in the same place to fell them. You had to be a nifty shot to be able to fuck someone's lupins from thirty yards.'

Bob has always been a maker, a mender and a bit of a petrolhead. There are some remarkable vehicles around his van, like the chassis and engine of an antediluvian dumper truck, which he still uses to drag felled trees around his wood. It started with the bikes.

'When I was eleven I got my hands on an enormous, heavy Panther 600 cc motorcycle, with old hand-change gears on the tank, and it was broken when I got it, and on me own initiative and with no tools I was able to mend it.

'Me and Sandy and our pal Hughie MacDonald we'd ride it three-up down the main road. And every day bits would fall off. It had no silencing, tyres stuffed with grass, and we'd ride it down the main road, as long as we had petrol. The tank was fucked up, so I got a National Dried Milk tin, and somehow got the fuel pipe to stay in the tin. You couldn't have too much petrol in there, so you'd have one of you perched on the frame, standing on the footpegs, no chain guards, going down the main fucking road with someone leaning over you pouring petrol into an open milk tin from a bottle, with flames pouring out of the engine. But we never went up in flames.'

'Have you ever wondered how you're alive?' I ask.

'Yeah, I have. Behind our house, there was a railway line. I watched 'em doing the conversion from steam to electric during the time I was there. They'd laid a cable on the ground, looped on the fence as an emergency signal cable. I just wanted to cut the cable; I don't know why. I didn't want to nick the copper; I just wanted to cut it. I had this cheap folding penknife that had lost its plastic covering, so it was just metal. I cut through this cable, about half an inch thick, and apparently stopped all the trains from Waterloo to Alton. The next day this geezer knocks on the door. Says we been told you cut the cable. I'd been grassed up. Terribly pleasant guy, he was, under the circumstances. I'm just curious, he said. Can I see the knife you did it with? So I showed him, and he said, it can't be that knife, because there's hundreds of fucking volts running through it. You should be dead, he said.

'I used to pick up two-inch mortar bombs, remember, high-explosive bombs. They had a killing range of about a hundred feet. And I'd chuck 'em a few feet.'

'Would they still go off?'

'In theory, yes. They did for other kids. The dead kids.'

We laugh, and Bob stirs on the bed where he is sitting, and leans across for his tobacco tin. The skin on his hands is like leather. He has earned those hands, I think. I've always been jealous of his hands. My hands are rather beautiful, unworked like those of a dowager duchess, though with very slightly thickened keyboard-dabbing pads and a shrunk away to almost nothing pen callous on my right middle finger. A theory boy's hands. I've earned them, too.

'Then there was the lad who pissed on the live rail. He didn't live to tell the tale. We used to stand on the wall of the bridge at the end of the village, and piss on the trains, like boys do. He didn't wait for a train, and formed a perfect circuit. It was said he died of the broken bones from being thrown across the road.'

'You were a smart kid.'

'I passed the written part of the 11-plus. Couldn't pass the verbal. Who wants to be a grammar grub?'

'School not your thing?'

'School ... it was complete discipline, the master person above you says something, you do it, and there's no questioning it. That's what I was raised in, but by the time I left school I was starting to question it.

'And the thing that really brought it home was when the headmaster made an announcement at assembly that he would no longer be giving corporal punishment, but that instead we'd be having after-school detention. As the most caned boy in the school, this was clearly relevant to me.

'"Any questions," he said.

'I lived four miles away, and needed to get a bus home, and I knew what the roads were like; almost all that distance was main roads, and no pavements. In detention, you're kept in for an hour after school. In winter by half past four it's already dark before you got out the school gate, and you've got no money for the bus, because you get the free school bus normally. To walk at night on a main road with no pavements for over an hour, seemed really fucking dangerous ....

'So I wanted to ask what they were going to do about it but at the time I had the terrible stutter, and couldn't articulate a sentence, so the head said come to my study.

'I asked him what about the kids who come by school bus, it'll be dark. I could see from his face that he hadn't considered this. You could read it in his face, the struggle to regain the moral and intellectual ascendancy.

'I mean, he should have had the upper hand in this and he had hugely failed, because he said to me by way of response to my perfectly valid fucking query, "Would you rather be hung or go to prison?"'

'And I said, "Well, go to prison."

'"Well, there you are, then," he said.

'And at that moment, I left school, because I could see they had nothing to teach me if that's the best they could do. I abandoned school at that moment.'

'How old were you?'

'Just before my fifteenth birthday.'

'Summer 1957?'

'Yeah.'

So here we are, plumb dab in the 1950s. Right at the moment where, on the cover of this book, I promised it would start.

Bob is a product of his moment in space/time, as are we all. There is fucking and dancing ahead, and guns and adventure, high politics and low-down dirty rock 'n' roll.

Everything is in place. The welfare state has arrived, rationing has ended, acid and E have been invented and things are looking up. The Bomb has been dropped on Hiroshima and Nagasaki, and it's like the end of the world is coming, and, who knows? It might be fun. The Nature Boys have had a worldwide number-one hit, sung by the first black showbiz millionaire. Bob has left school, unqualified, well read, a great shot, and a danger to his friends and society. Society is just about as dull as it's ever been, but there are stirrings just off the Charing Cross Road, as we shall discover.

At night, under the bedclothes, boys and girls are tuning their transistor radios to Luxembourg, and what they hear goes AWOPBOPALOOBOPALOPBAMBOOM.

The gods up in the Himalayas are stretching and coming to.

And Bob has got a job in a tractor factory.

Elvis was a God to Me

'And that was the moment,' says Bob, 'that I found out my real name.'

'How come?'

'When I started work, they told me they needed to see my birth certificate. So I said to my mum, "Where's my birth certificate?" And she says it's in the sideboard. I look through the sideboard, and found a bunch of them, for all the kids. "Who's David Robert Rowberry?" I ask.

'"Oh, that's you," says my mum. "Always meant to tell you."'

'Fuck.'

The rain is hammering on the roof of the van. Bob says, 'Would you like something to eat?' and I agree.

Bob puts some bacon to sizzle in a frying pan on top of the wood-burner. I've brought over some soda bread made by my wife, and Bob cuts four slices on his workbench, and butters them.

Now the van smells of hot metal, Bob, smouldering wood, bacon, toast, tobacco and coffee, which Bob is brewing up again. We eat, Bob sitting on his bed, and me on an old school lab stool by Bob's workbench.

We are talking about what the world was like when Bob was growing up, both from Bob's 'I was there' angle, and my book-larnin' perspective.

'The late 1930s was a period of material growth,' I say, 'as the big economies recovered from the Crash of 1929. It was interrupted by the war, but by the mid fifties, this underlying economic strength was starting to make itself felt again. Think of Eisenhower's America: cars and washing machines and TV sets, and all that. That was starting to pick up over here, too. There was full employment, even for layabouts like you. But it was a dull time, a morally restrictive time. In 1951, the British Conservative Party was the largest voluntary organisation in Europe. The mid fifties saw a series of Christian revivals. C of E attendance was rising; the fifties saw the highest church attendance rates of the twentieth century. The Revd Billy Graham's revivalist mission saw him preach to thousands of people at Wembley Stadium. And then there were the Watch Committees. Every borough seemed to have one. Busybodies who assumed power over what people saw or heard or read. They banned films or plays that they deemed to be obscene. You know the old seaside postcards ... Boy – "Do you like Kipling?" Girl – "I've never Kippled, you naughty thing", that sort of thing?'

'Course I do.'

'The most famous ones were by an artist called Donald McGill. Orwell wrote an essay about him. McGill had been producing them since right after the First War. But in the 1950s he was jailed for obscenity.'

'No ...'

'Straight up. There seems to have been a moral backlash after the sexual licence of the war. Sexual intercourse stopped on 9 May 1945, and didn't get going again till 1963, according to Philip Larkin, anyway.'

The historian David Kynaston argues that British society was frozen for ten years after the war; and that there was an 'instinctive retreat to familiar ways, rituals and relationships, all in the context of very slowly lifting austerity'.

In *Family Britain* Kynaston cites the example of how, in 1951, the *Evening Argus* in Brighton ran a competition looking for the 'typical British family'. They gave some idea of what they were looking for:

> They must enjoy the simple pleasures (she likes best a quiet evening at home with her husband relaxing and making a mess with his pipe and the family watching television, or walking in the country with their dog Rover).
>
> A husband who doesn't drink, except for a sherry at Christmas, and who doesn't grumble.
>
> A wife who, although told by her employer that she was a career girl who would never enjoy married life, makes a success of it, and who loves making such dainties as lemon meringue pie and fruit flan for a most appreciative husband.
>
> A husband who doesn't mind doing the washing-up on his Sundays off ....

Then as now, pop music is a useful map of the emotional landscape of the times. On 14 November 1952, the first UK singles sales charts were published by the *New Musical Express*. The top five consisted of records (still 78 rpm shellac discs) by American crooner Al Martino, British singer Jo Stafford, the immortal Nat King Cole, Bing Crosby (with just about his last hit record) and Guy Mitchell, who was a sort of country-lite singer. This was the moment of my parents' adolescence and late teens. Nat King Cole was my mum's favourite singer; Guy Mitchell my father's. My mum always had much better taste. Nat King Cole followed 'Nature Boy' with a series of beautifully sung and arranged ballads, whilst Guy Mitchell made corny novelty records. In his cups, my father would sing Mitchell's 'She Wears Red Feathers (and a Hooly Hooly Skirt)' to the unending shame of his children. My mum and dad had the misfortune to be too old for Elvis, and were therefore eternally caught between rock and a dull place.

In 1952 ballroom dancing was the second-largest entertainment industry; second only to cinema. There were annual admissions of around 200 million at dance halls. In the early fifties, dancing consisted mainly of old-fashioned styles; people were still fox-trotting and quick-stepping, just as they are on *Strictly Come Dancing* in our own conservative times. Dancing was done to the tunes of respectable band leaders like Victor Silvester and Joe Loss. My mum's favourite bandleader was Ted Heath, whom she followed around Surrey and south London – and although his band was regarded as exciting, a bit edgy even, to contemporary ears it is hard to understand the fuss.

It is this time which Conservative politicians look back at with the greatest nostalgia. Hard-working families enjoying themselves in whole-some ways, National Service for the boys, motherhood for the girls, Everest conquered, Stanley Matthews winning the Cup with Blackpool, Gordon Richards winning the Derby – and crowds of people sleeping on the pavement not because they were homeless, but because they were waiting for the Queen to pass on the way to her Coronation.

'It was fucking dull,' says Bob.

'Andy Yurt told me a funny story about you,' I said.

'Oh yes?'

'Him and Vicki were camped up near you at a festival, a few years back, and there was some bloke also parked up there in a van, with a couple of wind-up gramophones, DJ-ing old British dance-band tunes: Ambrose and his Orchestra, Geraldo, that kind of thing. And you emerged from your van with a chainsaw going, and threatened to cut the bloke's head off if he didn't stop playing the stuff. And then ten minutes later you came out and apologised, saying that it was the music you'd spent your whole life trying to escape.'

Bob laughs. 'I don't remember that,' he says.

'Andy Yurt was adamant.'

'It was shit, all that crap,' says Bob.

'So there you are, fourteen years old, nearly fifteen, leaving school ...'

'I was called in for a careers interview just as I was leaving, but I had no fucking idea of what I was going to do. Next to the building where the interview was held, a steel-frame building was going up, and at the top there was an arc welder. There were all these cascading blue flashes, and I thought it looked beautiful, so I said, I'll be a welder. So I became a welder. And rather bizarrely, I still am. Odd, when you think of all I've been through, cos for years I didn't do any of that stuff.'

'Didn't you?'

'No. When you're a tearaway and a scallywag living on the streets of London, you can't get the oxyacetylene.'

'When I first met you, you were making jewellery. And now you make wind sculptures and jewellery and hooks and beautiful things. So I guess I thought you must have always been at that kind of thing. I just think of you as someone who makes things.'

'Not for years. I had a head-bone which was good at those kinds of things. I'd mended the bike and that. But I didn't make anything for twenty years, I guess.'

'Were you too young for National Service?'

'Just. Year before, two years before. Just missed it; and I was very fucking glad.'

'You were the first generation to miss it?'

'Yeah, and we were the generation that became hippies. How much that's related, I dunno.'

'That's really interesting. Imagine all those crusty old colonels saying about the hippies, "Little shits, National Service is just what they need." No wonder they hated you. But you could have joined the Army, even though you'd missed National Service. Given your love of guns and that.'

'Not fucking likely. Because I lived near Aldershot, I watched it, and it was really fucking awful. A line of geezers and the RSM with his nose right up against theirs spluttering and calling them all the cunts under the sun, and being thoroughly obnoxious, and I knew I'd never put up with that. But I joined the Territorials when I first left school and was working.'

'You were in the TA?'

'I joined as a boy soldier. I was fifteen. I had no interest in uniforms or square bashing, but I did want to get me hands on the current weaponry. And you got a bit of extra cash, and a heavily subsidised bar with half-price beer. No, I was there for the shooting. I won the Southern Area Rifle and Light Machine Gun Cup.'

'But you liked action, and adventure and guns. You must have been tempted by the Army ...'

'Really, not at all. I'll tell you another reason. When I was in the TA, we went on an exercise up in Norfolk and we were given an officer who was new to us, who wasn't one of our own officers. A group of about a dozen of us and this officer came up to this wood, and there was a hut in the middle of a clearing. And we were told that this hut was full of geezers with machine guns and we were to take it, and this officer said to us, right, all stand in the clearing with rifles at the hip, and at the word of command fire one round. Well, that's Napoleonic war, squares and all that bullshit, and I knew that if we did that, we'd all be dead within five seconds. So I had this cold realisation that if the exercise was for real, I'd have to shoot this cunt, the officer, cos at least then you'd have a chance of surviving it. Whereas if you did what he said, you'd have no chance.'

'So tell me about your job.'

'It was with All Wheel Drive Ltd, Camberley, Surrey. I was an indentured apprentice engineer, on three quid a week. At the time I started, their main business was converting lorries to four-wheel drive, mostly for civilian use. But then the company got a contract from a US company in Michigan to produce these massive four-wheel-drive earth-moving things, like you see on the motorway. At the time, I was in the Research and Development and testing department, cos when you were an apprentice they moved you around. The rumour went around the works that the Army was interested in these things, and if the Army took 'em, it would save the company, cos the company was in trouble.

'The Army tested 'em, and loved 'em, but they wouldn't buy 'em because they couldn't drive in convoy. All army vehicles have to be able to drive in convoy, at about 12 miles an hour. These things had those big fucking tyres like balloons, and if they got on a hard surface, they'd start bouncing. And it would become really pronounced. They would bounce so much that all four wheels would be off the ground. You could get out of it by braking, or weaving about, but you can't do that in convoy.

'But I knew that if you drove 'em in reverse, this wouldn't happen. And it would be an easy matter to detach the seat, or slightly alter the cab, just for driving in convoy. No retooling. A really simple job.

'So I mentioned this to the chargehand, and he didn't seem to take any heed.

'But then a few days later I saw a notice saying he'd been bunged a grand. A grand was a fuck of a lot of money in those days. You could buy a house with it. And this chargehand had been promoted from a blue-collar to a white-collar job. And my mate told me it was because he'd saved the company, with my idea.

'I was upset, and went to the works manager, and broke down in tears. But he said, "What can we do? We can't take the money off him."'

'That was it. That was working. The bosses would rip you off every way they could. I went on a wild-man spree, deliberately turning forklifts over every day, and all shit like that. So I left the company.'

'How long were you there?'

'About a year.'

'And that's the only job you ever had?'

'Yeah. The only job job, if you know what I mean.'

'When's this? 1958?'

'About then, yeah. And by this time, I had discovered jazz and middle-class girls.'

'Bob.'

'What?'

'I need to do some theory. I need to explain Suez, Hungary and Elvis. I need to go back a couple of years. I need to do a bit of times before we do more life. I'm not ready for the jazz and middle-class girls bit.'

'Go on then.'

I explain again why my story begins properly in 1956, when Bob's had already been going for fourteen years.

'I'm arguing there are three vital events which mark the end of one thing and the beginning of another, and that these three events mark the beginning of the Freaks in Britain. These are: the Russian invasion of Hungary, the Suez crisis and the release of Elvis Presley's "Heartbreak Hotel" on RCA-Victor records.'

Bob nods sagely, and pops one together while I go on.

The political crises of Suez and Hungary were twins, born and dead in the same few weeks. Suez was a post-colonial disaster, which demonstrated that Great Britain had lost its grip, its power, whilst Hungary was about the taking and holding of colonies, about the Soviet Union tightening its grip and increasing its power. As the crises played out over the autumn of 1956, their implications for the old political order became clear. Suez showed the world – and the British people in particular – that Hitler's war had marked the end of Britain's global reach as a military power; that Empire was ebbing away like the tide. And Hungary showed the radical left that it could have no trust in the Soviet Union, and that if Jerusalem was to be built, then new plans would have to be drawn up.

I think it must be puzzling for Younger Readers that some people in Britain once thought of themselves as communists or even belonged to the Communist Party. In the 1945 post-war election, two Communist MPs were elected to Westminster.

Now, the modern Stakhanovites lighting the path to a more prosperous future are smiling clean-cut privately educated entrepreneurs called James. Everyone is encouraged to aspire to be an entrepreneur just like James. Primary schoolchildren are taught in 'Enterprise Week' to design, manufacture and market their own products (usually 'smoothies', in my experience), which their parents toddle up to the school to buy. There are television programmes, including children's television programmes, devoted to buying and selling, to adding value, to getting on. These programmes generate enthusiasm for the Jameses of the world.

James started selling smoothies with just a stall on Borough Market and thirty grand from his parents. (Smoothies are like milkshakes, but with added alienation – Mango and Lemon Grass! Banana and Nettle!) James uses only fresh organic ingredients sourced locally by means of Fair Trade. From these immodest beginnings James has built up the business, so that now the company has a turnover of five million and employs seventeen people on an industrial estate in Kettering. He is thinking of running in the Conservative interest in the marginal seat of Corby. He is married to Tamsin, and they have a lovely home in North London, an old hunting lodge outside Melton Mowbray which Tamsin has made so lovely that it featured in *Elle Interiors*, and three lovely boys who attend Uppingham School on the proceeds of the smoothies. Thus begins the cycle over again.

The TV shows demonstrate to Young Readers that entrepreneurship is the way forward. There are dragons in your path, and if only they can be overcome, then the promised lands await: money, power, trophy wives. But with a few honourable exceptions, most entrepreneurs are very like James; and though it may be shocking to some Younger Readers, James and his people mostly come from one particular social class.

Meanwhile you, Younger Reader, if you are lucky, get to work in the industrial unit in Kettering making and packing the smoothies. If you are very lucky, and you live in Stoke Newington, you might get to work on designing the website to advertise the smoothies. You might run the social media side of things, letting people know that those smoothies are so great, so clearly, manifestly better than a milkshake, that everyone should post pictures of the smoothies on Instagram, captioned 'Nom! Smoothies!', and thus work unpaid for the marketing department of James and Tamsin and the kids.

It was not always so. After the disgusting horrors of the First World War, the Depression of the 1930s, and the depredations of the war against Nazism, by 1945 millions of people in Britain thought that it was time to change, to end class deference, and to share the spoils of their work more equally. Attlee's radical Labour government won the election by a landslide. But for hundreds of thousands of other people, including many 'intellectuals', the Labour Party did not go nearly far enough. Since the time of the Russian Revolution in 1917, many of these people had drawn hope from the Soviet Union that there could be a better way of doing things. For many people in the West, Moscow was the moral centre of the universe, the place where, despite a few unfortunate local difficulties and necessary sacrifices, capitalism had been thrown over to be replaced by a society devoted to equality; equality both political and economic.

It is evident that capitalism is a cruelly flawed and exploitative way of running the world, so it is unsurprising that people have tried to think of better ways of organising things. Sadly, the only other way of organising things that has ever been really tried was State Capitalism, as characterised by the Soviet Union; and it was a cruel and unjust system, crueller and more unjust than Western Capitalist democracy. Make no mistake, I would rather live here than there.

State Capitalism, whether it was in the Soviet bloc or Mao's China, sacrificed its citizens by the million in the name of class solidarity. In order to continue to admire the Soviet Union throughout the 1930s, it was important not to look too closely. During the war, twenty million Soviet citizens were killed. 'The Great Patriotic War' they called it, and this sacrifice enabled Western intellectuals to see Stalin as Uncle Joe, smiling benignly under the shelter of that moustache. But by the early 1950s, it was obvious that the Soviet regime had nothing about it to aspire to, and it became harder for the British Left to look away. The British Communist Party was a Russian satellite, funded by Moscow, and taking Moscow's line, but still appealing to leftist intellectuals hoping to overturn capitalism. Apart from a few tiny splinter parties, like the Independent Labour Party to which Orwell belonged, there really was no alternative to the official party. Communist meant the Communist Party; and if you weren't a Communist, what were you?

The Hungarian Uprising of 1956 marked the moment when the European Left could no longer look away.

After the 'liberation' of Hungary from Nazi occupation in 1945 by the Red Army, a Stalinist regime was put in place by the Russians. Between 1945 and until after Stalin's death in 1953, 300,000 Hungarians were purged:

exiled, imprisoned or killed. But with Stalin's death, it seemed as though the new regime in Moscow led by Nikita Khrushchev might have some slight reformist agenda; might even, in comparison to Stalin at least, be just the teensy-ist bit liberal. As a token of this new attitude, Moscow appointed a reformist leader, Imre Nagy, to lead Hungary; still a reliable Moscow-trained Communist, but with less desire to kill and oppress his own people than his predecessors. His softer approach to power gained him much popular support. Life improved for Hungarians; goods appeared in shops, and political prisoners were released. But Nagy became too popular for the Kremlin's liking and in April 1955 the old-style Stalinists were put back in power by Moscow, although Nagy remained a hero.

With the old regime back in charge, arrests continued, and the AVO, the Hungarian secret police, was busier than ever. Discontent simmered and people longed for the return of Imre Nagy.

In February 1956, Khrushchev made a 'secret speech' to the Soviet Politburo attacking Stalin and his policies. The widespread leaking of this speech led to further hopes of reform in the satellite states, first in Poland and then in Hungary. On 23 October 1956, students in Budapest staged a peaceful demonstration. The night before, student leaders had drawn up a list of sixteen demands. Among them were the demands for a new government led by Imre Nagy and for the removal of Soviet troops from Hungarian soil.

By the evening of the 23rd, the demonstrators had reached 200,000 in number. 'Russians go home!' they shouted. Red stars were torn down from buildings. A 30-foot bronze statue of Stalin in the city's Hero Square, erected five years previously as a gift to the dictator from the Hungarian people, was pulled down, leaving only his boots on the plinth.

The police opened fire and killed several demonstrators. The Stalinist government condemned the protest and sent in the troops, but, to its dismay, found that many of the soldiers sided with the demonstrators. At 2 a.m., the Soviet tanks began arriving. Martial law was imposed. What had begun as a peaceful demonstration had turned very quickly into a full-scale revolution. The citizens of Budapest took control of the radio; the state broadcasters were happy to cede control and confessed to having been instruments of the state: 'We lied by night, we lied by day, we lied on all wavelengths. We, who are before the microphones, are now new men.' On 24 October, the Kremlin responded by putting Imre Nagy back in charge, believing that 'limited concessions' were necessary to satisfy the Hungarian people. Nagy promised his people reform in return for an end to the violence.

Nagy and his new government were sworn in on 28 October, and on the same day Khrushchev withdrew his troops over the border. The Uprising sensed it was winning. Long-banned political parties reformed; one-page broadsheet newspapers were plastered up on shopfronts, trees and lamp-posts. Hundreds of Hungary's secret police were lynched, in revenge for their years of torture and oppression. Nagy, catching the wave of optimism, promised open elections and a coalition government. On 1 November, he went even further, promising Hungary's withdrawal from the Warsaw Pact.

Nagy had gone too far. The Soviet Union was regretting the concessions, which they decided had been too generous. Nagy hoped for and expected support from the West but Britain and France were distracted by the emerging crisis over the Suez Canal, and the USA by presidential elections. The help never materialised. Chinese Communist leader Chairman Mao heckled Khrushchev for being weak, and encouraged him to get nasty. So Khrushchev, taking advantage of the West's preoccupations, ordered the tanks back in. They crossed the border into Hungary on 3 November and entered Budapest the following day.

Nagy appeared on Radio Budapest at 5.15 a.m. on the morning of 4 November as the tanks started to enter the capital:

> This is Imre Nagy speaking. Today at daybreak Soviet forces started an attack against our capital, obviously with the intention to overthrow the legal Hungarian democratic government. Our troops are still fighting; the Government is still in its place. I notify the people of our country and the entire world of this fact.

And that was it. Nagy's voice disappeared and was never heard in public again. A couple of hours later, at 8.10 a.m., Radio Budapest broadcast its last appeal – 'Help Hungary … help, help, help' – before being taken off the air. The Soviets quickly and ruthlessly crushed all opposition. Thirty thousand Hungarians had been killed, and a further 200,000 fled across the border into Austria. Nagy was tried in secret, and was hanged in 1958.

The official British Communist Party, funded by Moscow, had no doubts as to the rights and wrongs of the Soviet invasion. The Party newspaper, the *Daily Worker*, ran the headline, 'Anti-Fascist Government in Action' (Nagy and the revolutionaries being the Fascists in this case), with the sub-heading 'Soviet troops called in to stop White Terror'. As a consequence, the British Communist Party started to lose a great deal of its membership, including some of the leadership, and most especially the intellectuals, unable to turn a blind eye to what Stalinism meant any longer. By the fall of the Iron Curtain in 1989, the British Communist Party, still clinging with a dog-like devotion to the skirts of Mother Russia, was a laughable rump, with only a few hundred members left. One of these was the Marxist historian Eric Hobsbawm, who called the Soviet invasion 'a tragic necessity'. The depth of his insight is shown by the fact that, also in 1956 and writing as 'Francis Newton', the jazz critic on the *New Statesman*, he described Elvis as 'a peculiarly unappealing Texan lad, with a line in suggestive belly-dancing'.

'Elvis was from Tennessee, wasn't he?' asks Bob.

'He was, yes. Hobsbawm was a twat. But I'm not ready for Elvis yet. Suez first.'

Bob sighs. 'Really?'

'Yes really,' I say. 'It's amazing. Because in the same week that utopian dreams were being turned to nightmares in Hungary, the world discovered that the British Empire was fading into obscurity.'

The British Empire ended a long time ago – long before Suez. The schoolroom maps with one-third of the world coloured red are a thing of legend; I remember them from my old-fashioned primary school, but these days they are to be found only on eBay or in antique shops. But once it was real, the greatest Empire in extent the world has ever seen. Once, the Empire reflected Britain's status as the richest and most powerful industrialised and militarised nation on Earth. Being a British subject conferred bragging rights. The British walked with a swagger; dukes and dustmen alike could imagine that they were somehow blessed. Suez was the end of that.

One of the principal reasons that Egypt had been fought over so cruelly from the 1870s, through the First World War and then through the Second, was the Suez Canal; by the early 1950s, two-thirds of European oil came through the canal. Egypt had effectively been a British possession from 1875 until 1936. Even after that date, up to 40,000 British soldiers were stationed in the 120-mile strip adjacent to the Suez Canal. In 1951, the Egyptian government tried to call a halt, and demanded the immediate withdrawal of all British troops from their territory.

The Suez crisis was to a great extent a face-off between two men, Egyptian leader General Gamal Nasser and British Prime Minister Anthony Eden. General Nasser was determined to force the British from the Canal Zone, and by October 1954 he had struck a deal with Eden, then Foreign Secretary. The British would withdraw from the Canal

Zone within eighteen months, unless any of the Arab League countries were attacked by 'an outside power'. In 1955, Nasser declared that he was buying armaments from Soviet-controlled Czechoslovakia, and in 1956, Britain and America, fearful of what they saw as Nasser's closeness to the Communist bloc, withdrew 200 million dollars' worth of funding from the Aswan High Dam project. Nasser was outraged. He appeared in Alexandria on 26 July 1956 to make a fiery speech, which was broadcast on state radio. He talked about de Lesseps, the engineer of the canal; an interesting history lesson to his immediate listeners, perhaps, but in actuality, the code word for his army to occupy the Canal Zone.

Eden had become Prime Minister in 1955. He was popular, charming, experienced, patrician and good-looking. He had conducted the negotiations for British withdrawal with Nasser (Eden spoke Arabic, and read Arabic and Persian poetry by way of relaxation), but he was unprepared for the General's nationalisation of the Suez Canal.

Because actually, Eden, despite his outward qualifications for the job of Prime Minister, was weak, isolated within his Cabinet and physically sick. By 1956, it appeared as though he had lost the support of the Tory Party he purported to lead. Nasser's nationalisation of the Suez Canal gave Eden what he saw as a chance to reassert his authority; so much so, that he came to see Nasser as his personal enemy.

This sense of personal outrage seems to have been shared at first by much of the British electorate, who didn't see why Nasser should get away with taking control of the canal. The press likened Nasser to Mussolini and Hitler; Eden had resigned from Neville Chamberlain's government in 1938 because of its policy of appeasement towards Hitler, and now it seemed to him as though non-appeasement was once again the sensible course of action. Military action was inevitable, and Eden invited the Americans to the party. President Eisenhower, on the brink of an election, declined to attend.

For six weeks, the planning dragged on, whilst the Americans tried to persuade Eden that military action would cause more problems than it would solve. And as Eden fiddled, the support for intervention dropped. Military planners chopped and changed their ideas. His health failing, and his popularity within the Conservative Party withering away, Eden needed something to happen, and deliverance seemed to come in the middle of October when he was approached by the French Government, who had been in secret negotiations with the new Israeli state. France wanted to teach the Arab world a lesson because of growing problems in their Algerian colony; Israel wanted Gaza and the Sinai Desert. The plan, the conspiracy really, was that Israel would invade Egypt, and that Britain and France would launch a joint operation to secure the Canal Zone. The Israelis would therefore agree to act as the 'outside power' that would grant Britain the right to keep its troops in Suez. On 24 October, Britain, France and Israel signed 'The Protocol of Sèvres' in secret, agreeing to what was known as 'Operation Musketeer'; a week later, Israeli forces invaded the Gaza Strip and the Sinai Desert, heading towards the Canal Zone.

On 2 November Britain and France vetoed a UN Security Council motion calling for an immediate ceasefire, claiming the right to act as a 'police force' in the international interest. On 4 November, the same day that the USA managed to get a resolution calling for the establishment of a peace-keeping force, 30,000 anti-war protesters gathered in Trafalgar Square, where they listened to the 'architect of the NHS', Aneurin Bevan, condemn military action. This was the largest anti-war demonstration that London had witnessed up to that point. And a few of these protesters were art students, with coffee on their breath, wearing duffel coats and with hair down to their collars.

On 5 November, as the Soviets secured Budapest, British and French paratroopers dropped into the Canal Zone. Militarily, Operation Musketeer was a success. Alexandria was bombed, the key points in the Canal Zone captured. The old European powers looked as though they had regained the canal. Diplomatically, however, it was a disaster. The British economy was in crisis, and US support was vital to prop up the value of the pound. And the Americans, worried by the growing crisis in Hungary and on the verge of an election, were very angry. If Eden had hoped that Eisenhower would come round once the boots were in the sand, he was very wrong.

On 7 November the UN again called for an immediate ceasefire, and for a peace-keeping force to be sent to Egypt. Neither Britain nor France would be allowed to have troops in the peace-keeping force. The Chancellor of the Exchequer, Harold Macmillan, told Eden that without an American approved loan from the International Monetary Fund, the pound would collapse in value. Eden conceded, and took himself and his wife off on holiday, to stay with James Bond author Ian Fleming at his villa in Jamaica. Britain (and therefore France) had no alternative but to withdraw its troops, if Britain were to receive the vital American backing for the pound. Suddenly Britain, as millions of people saw it, was great no more; just a client state of the Americans, and no longer powerful enough to assert itself against the will of the United Nations.

In January 1957, Anthony Eden resigned as Prime Minister due to ill health, brought to the point of crisis by the strain of Suez. He was succeeded by Harold Macmillan, who began the process of negotiating independence for most of the old colonial territories of the British Empire.

Although in fact the sun had been setting over the British Empire for years, most people hadn't really noticed. The Suez crisis showed the world that Britain was no longer a true world power. The writer Peter Vansittart 'sensed a change, in the streets, at bars, in homes and in the media after Suez; a lowering of expectations, a feeling that the good times had gone'. Actually, in many ways, the good times were about to roll.

Pumped up with American money, the British economy found new legs, and sales of cars, televisions and washing machines were booming. The first Moka coffee bar had opened in Soho in 1953 (with the Italian actress Gina Lollobrigida performing the ceremony), and by 1956 were starting to be the places to hang out for those long-haired art students, newly liberated from the threat of National Service. The Angry Young Men were attracting notice; also in 1956, John Osborne's *Look Back in Anger* opened at the Royal Court. Rock 'n' roll had arrived in Britain. These social and cultural stirrings were to become important to the radical Left, who would see them as useful in a new cause. Because if Suez showed the world that Britain was finished as a world power, the Soviet invasion of Hungary showed the Left that the USSR was finished as a moral force.

'For the Freaky new-born New Left, this was the start of the attempted re-appropriation of power and morality from empires to the individual. And now we can talk about rock 'n' roll,' I say.

'Thank fuck,' says Bob. 'I'd loved rock 'n' roll from the start. Elvis was a god to me. I used to hang about in Camberley after work. There were Americans stationed there, and they drove these fuck-off cool cars. And there was a really hot jukebox in one of the coffee bars. Not just Elvis, but wilder, harder stuff too. I loved Gene Vincent and Carl Perkins, because they looked like they might carry flick knives.'

Elvis, I wish to argue, is another of those things that must be hard for Younger Readers to understand. Of course, they have heard of Elvis. Everyone has heard of Elvis. They have seen plenty of impersonators of Elvis, and they might even be able to impersonate him themselves. He is fat and laughable, a ludicrous figure in a glittering jumpsuit, who died from burgers and squirrels and prescription drugs while having a shit. His true greatness died on 21 March 1958 when he was conscripted into the US Army. This moment is taken to mark the end of the Golden Age of Rock 'n' Roll, and so I'm chuffed to have been born a week before. I don't remember it, of course I don't, but I was there, like a babe in arms who survived the sinking of the *Titanic*. Perhaps the moment of my birth qualifies me (I am qualified in innumerable other ways) as a full-on card-carrying Dad Rocker. And proper Dad Rockers will point out to you that Elvis became great again after the '68 Las Vegas Comeback Show, and so I will too. Your record collection, if it is to be any good at all, *must* include the Sun Sessions album, the RCA *Greatest Hits* album, and the live album recorded at the '68 comeback show. But there is really no need for anything else. Elvis didn't make albums in the modern sense (nobody did until the Beatles), and he didn't write his own stuff, even the stuff he got songwriting credits for. The whole point of Elvis is that he was first, the first real modern pop star, seated for ever at the top table, the originator, the source, the wellspring.

Bob Stanley in his superb history of pop music *Yeah Yeah Yeah* says that 'no one has had the pop culture impact of Elvis Presley', and I'm sure that's true. The Beatles were extraordinary; no one had seen a group playing their own instruments and writing their own songs before. But Elvis was the first real pop star, in the sense that we now understand it. Imagine if you had never seen a pop star, ever. Imagine that all you had seen was sexless songbirds dressed like your mum and safe crooners that your dad could warble along with. Then imagine this beautiful sexy creature, gyrating his hips, wearing eyeliner, dressed like a black boy, in heaven's name (and remember, in Britain in 1956, outside of the major cities you had probably not seen a black boy), and singing like nothing and no one else. And imagine the extra thrill of liking something that your parents simply couldn't stand, that turned their stomachs, dried their mouths, that filled them with righteous horror.

He was discovered by small-time producer and independent record label boss Sam Phillips, in Memphis, Tennessee. Phillips loved black R&B, and had been looking for a way to cross it over into the pop charts. Elvis was a shy and silent mummy's boy, whom no one at his school really noticed. All that he had ever been interested in was singing and looking great; he bought his clothes from Lansky's on Beale Street, and was pretty much their first white customer. He wore pink jackets, frilly shirts, grew his hair long and then greased it back. In 1953, aged seventeen, he came into Phillips' Sun Studio and recorded a demo of two songs; and then he spent the next year nagging Phillips to make a proper record with him. In 1954, Phillips decided that if nothing else, the boy had persistence, and put him in the studio with guitarist Scotty Moore and bass player

Bill Black. At first, nothing gelled. Moore and Black were experienced Memphis musicians, Elvis an untried kid who had never played a gig. Phillips stuck with them, wasting tape, until Elvis started playing Arthur 'Big Boy' Crudup's R&B hit from 1946, 'That's All Right', and Scotty and Bill followed on. Phillips worked them hard; the version you hear today is take 18. This is key to the understanding of rock 'n' roll; from its start, it was the first musical medium that used the recording studio as an instrument. Phillips piled on the echo, weirded it up. There are other records which can claim to be 'the first rock 'n' roll record'. Bill Haley would certainly have the first world-wide rock 'n' roll hits. But 'That's All Right' is the first rock 'n' roll record made with studio trickery by the first rock 'n' roll star. It is beautiful still.

Phillips cut the acetate, or demo, of the song, and took it straight to his friend and namesake, Memphis DJ Dewey Phillips, who played it that night on his R&B show, and it lit up his phone lines. It was a hit before it had been released. When Phillips actually put it out a week later, it sold thousands, first in Memphis, then all over the south-west. Elvis had never appeared live in front of an audience, so he and Scotty and Bill started making appearances, at first playing only 'That's All Right' and its flip-side, 'Blue Moon of Kentucky'. He got very good, very quickly, but fought to overcome his nerves; nerves to which Elvis attributed the leg-shaking that was to drive girls bonkers in the first few years of his glory, and which saw him filmed only from above the waist for his first appearances on the legendary *Ed Sullivan Show*.

Roy Orbison, then nineteen, was in the audience when Elvis performed in Lubbock, Texas, in the spring of 1955. The headliner was Hank Snow, the star act of the vile Colonel Tom Parker, who had just signed an exclusive management deal with Presley. Orbison said of the first time he saw Elvis, 'His energy was incredible, his instinct was just amazing. I just didn't know what to make of it. There was just no reference point in the culture to compare it.'

By 1955, it was clear that Presley was going to be huge, and after four singles for Sun, and under pressure from Tom Parker, Phillips sold his contract with Elvis to RCA-Victor for the then unprecedented sum of $35,000.

Peter Guralnick, in his wonderful biography of Elvis, *Last Train to Memphis*, emphasises the strangeness of 'Heartbreak Hotel'. Written by Mae Axton and Tommy Durden (and Elvis, if you believe the songwriting credits, which you shouldn't, Elvis only being credited as a co-writer by Axton out of the goodness of her heart), it was an odd choice for Presley's first release on a major label. Drowning in echo, gloomy to the point of being suicidal, producer Steve Sholes wasn't at all sure that 'Heartbreak Hotel' would do as a song to launch Elvis on a national and then world-wide stage. RCA were similarly unsure, but they'd paid a lot for Presley's contract, and gave the boy his head. Guralnick writes that there was no other musician working at that time who had the insight and taste of Presley. Released in March 1956, by June Presley was awarded Billboard's 'Triple Crown' award for topping the charts in sales, DJ and jukebox plays (all of which fed into chart placings at the time). And in Europe, under their bedclothes, listening to Radio Luxembourg late at night, the young men and women who were to grow up to become the first generation of hippies were having their minds blown. Rock 'n' roll had arrived, served up by the strangest and most beautiful boy anyone had ever seen.

And now I feel it necessary to explain what rock 'n' roll is to Younger Readers, because chances are they don't know, never having been taught. Younger Readers have no taxonomy with which to decipher rock 'n' roll. So I'm going to use an example from biology, which is much less puzzling. Rock 'n' roll, if it means anything to Younger Readers, probably means a genus (a 'genre', if you will) which includes the species Elvis, Little Richard, Chuck Berry, etc.

But actually rock 'n' roll is a family, which includes genera (genres) such as, rock, indie, metal, etc., etc. When Younger Readers say they like 'rock' or 'indie' or 'punk', all these things are sub-divisions of the family rock 'n' roll, which is itself a member of the order post-Stephen Foster American pop music, class, non-art music, etc., etc. (Stephen Foster incidentally, who lived from 1826 until 1864, was the inventor of modern pop music. His compositions include 'Oh! Susanna', 'Camptown Races' and 'Beautiful Dreamer').

To push the biological analogy as far as I can, Elvis was a mutant, who found a niche amongst teenagers (a term first used in 1946), and who then fathered many imitators. Oddly, as will become evident, by 1959 rock 'n' roll seemed to have faded away, to be replaced by folk and traditional jazz in the hearts of hip British teenagers. It would be up to the Beatles to bring rock 'n' roll back to prominence. But the Beatles didn't start by playing rock 'n' roll. They started by playing an odd genre, part blues, part folk, and all home-made, which, although originating in 1920s America, was reinvented not far from where Bob was growing up, in 1949. It was called skiffle, and without it, the Beatles, and thus the revival of rock 'n' roll, would have been unthinkable. And skiffle's founder in the UK was a man called Ken Colyer.

Bob has been dozing, as he always does when I tell him about my putative taxonomy of rock. But at the mention of Ken Colyer, he perks up.

'Ken Colyer invented skiffle?'

'According to Bob Stanley in *Yeah Yeah Yeah*, er, yeah.'

'Fuck me.'

'I know.'

'Ken Colyer changed my life.'

'Ken Colyer changed everything. He's the most influential British musician that no one has heard of.'

'Is he?'

'It's time, Bob. It's time for jazz and middle-class girls. I think you'd better tell me about Ken Colyer.'

Or was that Merleau-Ponty?

'Trad jazz is hard to understand these days, I think,' I say.

'How do you mean?'

'If Younger Readers have ever even encountered it,' I say, 'it's in a dull old pub on a Sunday lunchtime with their grandparents, watching a bunch of ancient old fucknuts in stripy waistcoats tootling away at "When the Saints".'

Bob nods.

'And for me it was the first music I ever hated,' I add, clearly still bitter.

'Was it?'

'Yep. I can remember being four or five and fed up with "Stranger on the Shore" by Acker Bilk. It was on the radio and TV all the time.'

'Acker Bilk was like a god to me ...'

'Like Elvis?'

'Yeah. Except I met Acker Bilk. Bummed a fag off him, and kept the dog-end Sellotaped to my wall.'

'Yet it seems so naff now. So crusty ... gone really. You never even hear it on Radio Two. But for you ... it was like the Pistols to me when I was eighteen. The hottest, trendiest thing there was.'

Bob leans back on his bed.

'It was.'

'But why? Never mind Younger Readers, I don't get it myself.'

'Middle-class girls liked it.'

'I see.'

'The girls who were around, that I went to school with and all that – I mean, you were lucky to get a feel of a tit. Certainly nothing else. I mean, other fellas might have, but they didn't have an appalling stutter, and they weren't from a known white-trash household.'

'But middle-class girls ...'

'Middle-class girls would let you feel their tits and more. And I met middle-class girls through jazz.'

'Go on.'

'When I left school and was working in the company I had the apprenticeship with, I got matey with the bloke in the draft office there, Taffy

Evans, and he said, "Do you want to come to the jazz club on Friday night?" It was in the village hall which I passed every day, and I had seen this sign for "High Curly Stompers Jazz Club" outside. I was into Elvis Presley, and I was prejudiced, the normal prejudices of country boys to things they know fuck-all about. But I thought fuck it, all right, and I went to the High Curly Stompers Jazz Club. And it was great.'

'Why?'

'I loved the music and I loved the wildness of the girls. And some of these girls, only a year or two older than me, had cars, when your parents didn't. And it soon turned out that they all lived in big houses, where the parents seemed to go away and not mind if the daughters had parties there. I mean, wonderful mansion places ...'

'You look up to heaven, it's as though a light just hit you.'

When Bob smiles, I can see the memory in his face.

'So when like a few months later, this group I was part of by then, said, "Do you want to go to Ken Colyer's club for the weekend?" I said yes please, because by then I knew who Ken Colyer was and the sort of music he played, and the thought of an all-night jazz club in London was heaven. Seven of us piled into a Vespa bubble car and went from Camberley to Soho, and I just loved it. We started going most weekends, and it was one of the reasons I moved to London, in fact, because I really fancied that all-night jazz club London sort of life, twenty-four hours a day.'

'Ken Colyer's club in Great Newport Street has a blue plaque outside it now. As it happens, I used to run a bookshop on Great Newport Street. Last time I was in Town, I went past on a psycho-geographical *dérive*.'

'You what?'

'I went and had a look.'

'Quite right. Great place.'

'He was a great man ... the most important British musician you've never heard of.'

'You said. I didn't take much notice, really. I liked the beat. And the girls.'

'History is wasted on some people.'

'Fucking go on then.'

Pete Frame in his history of early British rock 'n' roll, *The Restless Generation*, says, 'If you're one of those people who like to put exact dates on seminal events, then it has to be October 1949. It was in a corrugated iron hut, round the side of the White Hart public house in Bath Road, Cranford, that Ken Colyer and his mates introduced a handful of curious punters to a primitive musical diversion, a style they had devised for themselves, based on whatever appropriate instruments were at hand, and whatever songs they felt like singing.' Ken's brother Bill came up with a name for this style – skiffle.

Brother Bill was an important figure in Ken's musical development. Not only did he play occasional washboard with his younger brother, and act as his manager, but it was he who left a large and interesting collection of jazz records behind when he went to fight with the Army in the Second War. Good stuff: Sidney Bechet, Lead Belly, Duke Ellington. When Ken joined the Merchant Navy after the war, he bought himself a trumpet, and practised whilst crossing the Atlantic. He arrived in New York in 1948, and heard Eddie Condon, Pee Wee Russell and Oscar Peterson, and came back home to form the Crane River Jazz Band. That first gig in 1949 might have been in a corrugated-iron hut, but their last gig, in 1951, was at the Royal Festival Hall in front of HRH Princess Elizabeth: not averse to a trad stomp herself, if legend be true, though otherwise counter-cultural in no other sense, so far as I have been able to ascertain.

But Ken was a purist, and the Crane River Jazz Band were slipping out of his control. He was a seeker after 'authenticity', an idea that has both informed and blighted the Freaks ever since. But whatever atrocities have been subsequently committed in its name, it was after all what eden ahbez and the Nature Boys were chasing down: the right way, the truest way, to do things, the truest thing to be.

Ken rejoined the Merchant Navy in 1952, and got himself back across the pond. This time, he was heading for New Orleans, the heart of jazz authenticity in Ken's mind. When his ship docked in Mobile, Alabama, in November 1952, he jumped ship, and got a twenty-nine-day visa and a ticket for the Big Easy. He listened to, played with and recorded with as many New Orleans jazz legends as he could find; but on Christmas Day 1952, his twenty-nine days were up. Only he had miscalculated; it wasn't until after the holiday that he went to renew his visa. He was arrested and incarcerated in New Orleans Parish Prison until 5 February 1953, when he was released on bail prior to deportation.

During his time in the Parish, he'd written letters to his brother Bill, which were published in the *Melody Maker*. Even before he landed back in Southampton, he was a hero for many British jazzers. He was met at the dockside by Bill – and Chris Barber, the trombonist and bandleader, who had come to make him an offer. A new band, the Ken Colyer Jazzmen, with Ken on trumpet, Barber on trombone, Monty Sunshine on clarinet, and a hot three-piece rhythm section: bass, drums, and, on banjo, Lonnie Donegan. During intervals, Ken and Lonnie would play guitars, and Barber would play bass, and they would perform some of the old American blues songs they all loved. And Bill remembered the corrugated-iron hut in Cranford, so skiffle was reborn. The intervals were in danger of becoming more popular than the main sets, and the band changed their name to Ken Colyer's Jazz and Skiffle Band. Ken was once again haunted by authenticity: he left the band because it was becoming too much like show business. After he left, it changed its name to the Chris Barber Jazz and Skiffle Band – which, Ken sensed, was what Barber had been aiming for all along. He left the band in search of authenticity at the very moment that the band, and the skiffle interludes in particular, were about to become big time. The intervals had become showcases for Lonnie Donegan.

Tony 'Lonnie' Donegan was a fine blues guitarist, as well as a banjo player, but one with an eye on the main chance, rather than some notion of being true to your roots. By the late 1950s, he was having novelty hits like 'My Old Man's a Dustman' and 'Does Your Chewing Gum Lose Its Flavour', which is a bit like Johnny Rotten going on from the Sex Pistols to make 'Agadoo'. Or butter adverts. But, make no mistake, Donegan's 1955 hit 'Rock Island Line' was the most influential British record of the 1950s. As Bob Stanley says in *Yeah Yeah Yeah*, 'It's one of the unlikelier facts of history that a song about illegally importing pig iron is British pop's fountainhead.'

The version that Donegan played was arranged by legendary bluesman Lead Belly, after he had heard it whilst accompanying folk song collector Alan Lomax to the Arkansas State Prison in 1934. It would be a mistake, however, to think of it as a link to the rhythm and blues roots of rock 'n' roll. Lead Belly may have been hard as nails, but his was not the same hard-edged Chicago blues that inspired the Rolling Stones. Lead Belly and his songs were popular with a white folk audience, rather than a black R&B one. Just the job for Britain in 1955.

Lonnie Donegan taught British teenagers something astounding: that here was a music they could play themselves. A couple of guitars, a few chords, a washboard for percussion and an upturned tea chest with a bit of string stuck to a broom handle for a bass, it was, as the punks later pointed out again, cheap and easy. It is estimated that by 1958 there were some 40,000 skiffle bands in Great Britain, which is a lot of bands. Skiffle bands were where the rock greats of the sixties learned their trade. Some of them were very good, and some of them were not. One of the least regarded skiffle bands, glued to the bottom of the bill at church fetes and school dances in Liverpool, were called the Quarrymen. They got better. It was Lonnie Donegan and skiffle that started British teenagers playing music – not Elvis, not Bill Haley, but Lonnie Donegan. And it was Ken Colyer who had given skiffle to Donegan, and walked away in search of something else.

'Like the club,' says Bob.

'Like the club. It had been called Club 51, but Ken persuaded the management to put his name on the club, and let him front the house band – with the young Acker Bilk on clarinet. They got a recording contract, and the club gained in popularity ...'

'I fucking know. I went there every weekend. It was packed. Fucking rammed.'

'What was it like?'

'Just one room, with a pile of coats in one corner, and the band playing in the other. And a sweaty room full of people dancing.'

'A pile of coats?'

'There wasn't a cloakroom, so people just piled their coats up. Nobody's coat ever got nicked. It was a thing that happened at jazz clubs. I used to shag my girlfriend in just such a pile of coats.'

'Did you, by gum?'

'I did.'

'In Ken's?'

'In all the jazz clubs. Once in a pile of coats at the Eel Pie Island Hotel.'

'This was before you moved up to London?'

'No, just after. But we went to Eel Pie Island with the people from Camberley too.'

'But Ken's was still the main place?'

'For a year or so, yeah.'

'Then fashion changes, I guess. Hip young things go to the UFO, or the Roxy, or the Factory, or the Ministry of Sound, and then the old places die off.'

'They do.'

By the late 1950s the club was closed, and Ken was ill, very ill, with stomach cancer. Although he recovered, and continued to lead the Ken Colyer Jazzmen until the early '70s, the great days were gone, and there was nothing in Ken that could make him wear a striped waistcoat and a bowler hat and play his equivalent of 'Stranger on the Shore' like Acker Bilk, or appear on endless sixties and seventies light entertainment shows like Kenny Ball and his Jazzmen. He continued to play sporadically throughout the '70s and '80s, guesting with other bands, but he could go months without a gig – and he died, in some poverty, in France in 1988. Ken Colyer was the real deal, the authentic father of much that came after him. No Ken, no Beatles, you could argue.

There's something secret at the heart of fashion – real fashion, not the stuff you see on the catwalk or in the press. These people aren't always self-consciously hip; John Peel wasn't, nor, I think, was Tony Wilson, founder of Factory. Only a tiny handful of people get to start something, and Ken Colyer was one of those. The authenticity that he spent his career chasing can be heard in his recordings, one of which is in the playlist. It's not authentic New Orleans jazz, but an approximation of it. What it is is authentic British trad, none more authentic. I still don't get it, but Ken takes me as close as I'll ever be. When I listen to the Ken Colyer Jazzmen playing 'The Sheik of Araby' I can just hear it echoing up Great Newport Street, and, over in the corner of a poorly lit room, see an unwashed young Bob trying to get off with middle-class girls over by the coat pile.

Bob still looks a scamp, there is no doubt. I look at him stirring his fire. I find it all but impossible to imagine him other than as he is, here and now. But it still takes a leap to believe that trad jazz was the light that lit the path that ended up with him in this old bus, in this wood.

'But what made you, a boy from Mytchett, who has done a bit of engineering and been good at that, what made you chuck it all in and go and live rough in London? I mean, how many times had you been to Ken Colyer's club before you decided?'

'Just a few weekends, but I really liked it and I was living for the weekends to go up to Ken Colyer's; and then I learned about Eel Pie Island and we went up there one weekend too. And I just decided this is what I want, I want this full time. And I'd met people of my own age who were living rough on the streets, so I threw my lot in with them, and didn't regret it. It was fun, a lot more fun than working for £3 a week. It just appealed to me, that's what I wanted. These were the people I wanted to be mixing with, the music I wanted to be listening to, and that whole bohemian beatnik thing was very appealing to me, life beyond the normal confines of society. I read a book recently, where some space-ship had a wonderful name, *Operating Beyond The Normal Bounds of Convention*.'

'By Iain M. Banks, presumably … which one was it?'

'That's him. Can't recall which book. But the name of that spaceship struck me. That was what I wanted when I was seventeen.'

'And still now.'

'Yeah. It seemed like a door that was opening to me, so I took it. I still try to do that, though fewer doors are open these days.'

Bob shifts to get comfortable after doing the fire.

'So there just came a day? Did you tell your mum and McGregor?'

'Yes. My mum made me a packet of sandwiches, but I threw 'em away in a bush after about a hundred yards.'

'I bet you regretted that later.'

'Of course. And I knew I would when I did it. But it felt like a declaration of independence. I'd saved up thirteen quid, and I had a sleeping bag in a duffel bag, and off I went.'

'Not in a bubble car, presumably?'

'No. Hitching. And somewhere between Staines and London Airport, on the A30 it would have been, this car stops, picks me up. The geezer said, "Can you drive?" and I said I've not driven a car before, and he says, "Maybe we should practise your gear changes. I'll do the clutch if you change gear." and he puts his hand on mine, that was as far as anything went before he dropped me off. Oddly enough, several years later on the same route, hitchhiking – and I'd learned quite a lot in the intervening years – this same geezer, and he starts on the same fucking rap. So I was a bit harder nosed by then, and I said, "We've been here before – you're going to take me to exactly where I'm going, otherwise you're in trouble ..." And he did, he took me exactly where I was going. I thought sad git; he spends all his free time driving up and down the road hoping to find hitchhikers he can bugger.'

'It's no life, is it .....? So that's your first night? You haven't even made it to Soho yet.'

'Soho is more me than Chelsea, but the first night in London, when I'd left home, I thought Chelsea, I'd never been there before, but I thought that's where the bohemian crowd were supposed to hang out. I walked down the King's Road and I saw a coffee bar called The Sa Tortuga and lots people in it with striped T-shirts, the French sailors' type, so I thought this must be an arty crowd, but they were all snotty types really. I went in there and just finished my coffee, and these people completely ignored me. I was scruffy, poor looking, and was just about to go when some geezer said, "Do you want to go to my place round the corner?" and I thought, "He's a queer." But I thought, "Fuck, it's a door that's open, a path that's revealed, take it and see what happens." So I went round the corner and he's there, and he gives me a drink, puts some music on, says, "Shall we dance?" We do a holding-on sort of dance which I'd never even done with a woman before, let alone a geezer, so I wasn't happy with the situation. I say I'm going to get a drink of water so I go into the kitchen and there's a window open and I nip out of it. Not taking the several pound notes that were on the kitchen counter. I thought, "He hasn't done anything to me." And I had thirteen pounds of my own in my pocket, so I was all right, and just slipped out the window and legged it to Soho.'

'So that first night, what was it like after you'd escaped?'

'Where I spent that first night I honestly haven't a clue. On the Embankment maybe? But the next day, I already knew where *the* coffee bars were in Soho, and I teamed up with the right crowd then.'

'But can you remember waking up? What was the first thing you did? Did you go to the coffee bars? Who were your pals?'

'I'd have met some people when I was coming up at weekends. I quickly sussed out the hard-core group living the life – they were more attractive to me, so I threw in my lot with 'em. And because of the nature of that situation, they were open ...'

'That situation being, essentially, voluntary homelessness on the streets of London?'

'Yeah. But you had to pay the toll, which was being upfront; no money, no food, nowhere to live, just a sleeping bag; not even a change of clothes; that was an easy club to join, once I was there and doing it. And as that grew, and I met more and more people, I was readily accepted into it, and once you're accepted into that Soho scene, then you can get into the clubs you want to get into without having to pay.

'You've spent fucking hours hustling, being nice, but just hustling till they let you in. I quickly found you no longer had to pay to get into these clubs, because for some reason, the Soho jazz clubs wanted us in, the kids who were living rough on the streets.'

'Why?'

'Because they knew that the main clientele, the ones who paid, they wanted to be part of the authentic jazz scene and all that. And that was us, so we just walked in.'

'So they wanted you because you were the cool kids. The real kids, the authentic beatniks. So if you were in the club, that made it ... the scene, I guess.'

'Oh yeah. And it lasted ages. A few years later, I could still get into loads of clubs, exclusive ones.'

'Who were the first people you met?'

'Frankie, who was a girl. Trunkie, Buck, Bluey. They called themselves the Viccy Boys, because they wore Victorian clothes. Not Teds – they were more authentic; they had shoulder-length hair, and they beat the shit out of people who took the piss. I thought they looked pretty fucking cool; they were fun. Not at all pretentious; they could fight, they were tough, you know?'

'So how did you live?'

'You got to know the backs of restaurants where you could arrive just when they're throwing out the remains of a perfectly good meal, a whole lamb chop still warm, and that sort of stuff, and various little blags you'd know, like Schmidt's delicatessen on Charlotte Street, this big German-Jewish delicatessen. The old lady obviously had a soft spot for whatever she thought we were, artists probably, and for a shilling you could buy all the salami ends, a fucking great bag, you'd get to the last inch or so of a salami, which they had a lot of, she just put them in a bag, probably about a kilo of salami for a shilling. Things like that. And whoever your current girlfriend was, generally some little art student girl, who fancied the life but really wanted to live at home because she wanted the toilet and the bathroom, that sort of thing, you'd send them down the tube station with the rap, "Oh, I've lost my tube fare money, can you give me a shilling so I can get home?" sort of thing, and you'd come out of there with enough for a meal or a couple of pints.

'It was a self-regulating thing, you know, looking like I did. I already went to London with shoulder-length hair, but now I had long hair, sewn-on jeans, and not having been in a bath for quite a while. When you're living on the streets of London you get pretty bloody grimy, so there's not a lot of places that will let you in. And the ones that did, well, they obviously had bohemian pretensions, simple as that. If that's what you fancied, then it worked, because you couldn't go into a normal caff, they'd chuck you out, wouldn't let you sit down. The only reason you'd go into a normal caff, which I regularly did, was if you saw someone leaving a half-finished meal, like burger places, just go in and grab it and out the door ....'

'So that whole world was beyond the realms of convention. But how was it cool? Who were the older boys and girls? Did you all spontaneously arrive at the same point, or was there a face who went, "Yeah, this is cool, this is modern ...."?'

'The slightly older people were traveller types, who when they were in London would be at the places I've mentioned, but winters they'd spend on Ibiza, when apparently no one else did, or the southern Spanish coast. But, no, we were the "faces". We lived from day to day. We slept in bomb sites or half-destroyed houses that would keep the rain off you. I was slightly concerned about where my next meal was coming from, and I was often quite hungry, but not starving. I was pretty fucking hungry sometimes, to be honest, but we weren't thinking, "What am I going to do, how am I going to be respectable?" I didn't want to be respectable, because I was in awe of existentialism ...'

'What? Wait! Existentialism?' I feel anxiety tightening my chest.

'Yeah, of course. That's the whole fucking point.'

'S'pose I'd better do some theory, then.'

Bob sighs and leans back. I feel my mouth drying. I start talking.

'If people think anything about hippies, or whatever, the Freaks, what-ever, it's Peace and Love. But that's bollocks, isn't it?'

'Yeah. Or, Peace and Love was only fashionable for a short time.'

'But really, this whole story is about what happens if you decide to live as an "existentialist", isn't it?'

'Yeah.'

'So, we need to pin down what an existentialist was. Or is.'

'Go on then.'

'Right. I will.'

'Yes?'

'It's difficult.'

'You're the theory guy.'

'I know. I may not have paid as much attention at university to this bit as I should.'

'Try.'

'Right. Well, if I remember rightly, and, as I say, this is difficult stuff ...'

'Go on ...'

'Well, existentialism derives from the nineteenth-century Danish philosopher Søren Kierkegaard, who wanted to distinguish man from God by arguing that man had agency separate from that of God. Man was free. So, then, at the beginning of the twentieth century you have a bloke called Edmund Husserl, and he, er ....'

'Yes?'

'Well, I never quite worked out where he fitted in. He invented this idea called phenomenology, which holds that the job of philosophy is simply to describe the world ... I think ...'

'You're doing very well ...'

'Er, and then you had Martin Heidegger, who was a bit Nazi, and he said that if you really wanted to describe the world, you needed to distinguish between things and man, and that the main difference between them was that things can't choose what happens to them, but that humans can, except that because man exists in time, the only thing you can say for sure is that men die. And to live authentically, you have to face up to that. It's fucking hot in here, isn't it?'

'You certainly appear to be sweating,' says Bob.

'And then you had Jean-Paul Sartre ...'

'I've read *Nausea*.'

'And he said that we are totally free. And to live authentically, you need to choose. That you are only not free *not* to choose; that we face free choices at every moment our whole life, limited only by our facticity.'

'And what the fuck is that?'

'Oh, like I can't choose to be Aretha Franklin, even though I would have liked to have been Aretha Franklin, because I'm not a black woman, but a fat white bloke from Newhaven. But, facticity aside, having freely chosen what to do or how to live – he called it realising yourself – you then live with the consequences of that choice. And if you can't live with your choice, then you are living in bad faith.'

'So, we are free?'

'Yes. And to be truly free, to be truly authentic, you had to reject bourgeois rationality. Or was that Merleau-Ponty?'

'So,' says Bob, 'what's the point in worrying? What's the point in being respectable? We pays our money and we takes our choice, and then we live with it?'

'Let's settle for that,' I say, mighty relieved.

'Well, that's what I've always done.'

'And the point is, again, to be authentic. To live authentically.'

'That was why I wanted to live on the streets of London. Cos I was a fucking existentialist. I was a beatnik, man!'

Beatniks, or beats, appear on the cover of this book, which shows us that we are, at last, starting to get somewhere. If we settle for Bob's definition of existentialism (as I think we must, because he self-avowedly is one, and it's a bugger to define), and then if we marry that essentially French idea to an American sensibility, we come up with the Beats.

In particular, the Beats were a generation of American writers, whose best known and most widely read members were Jack Kerouac (*On the Road*), Allen Ginsberg (*Howl*) and William Burroughs (*The Naked Lunch*). Kerouac said that there were 'two kinds of beat hipsters – COOL: bearded, sitting without moving in cafés, with their un-friendly girls dressed in black, who say nothing; and HOT: crazy, talkative, mad shining eyes, running from bar to bar only to be ignored by the cool subterraneans.'

Bob was (and is) clearly one of the latter; and, to judge from his first night in Chelsea, the former were very much in evidence in 'fashionable' London, and still are in popular consciousness. The Simpsons' next-door neighbour Ned Flanders was the son of beat hipsters, who had goatee beards and played the bongos.

This is an important point; the Cool are always more numerous than the Hot. In my book *Parallel Lines*, I equate Cool with the idea of the Classic, and Hot with the idea of the Romantic. Classic is safe, safer than Romance. If life is a process of choice making, the Cool always have fewer choices to make, and the choices they do make are to some extent made for them, because they are concerned first and foremost with whether or not the choices they do make are cool or not. The Cool don't get in trouble. I have an old friend who is Cool, and his record collection is great. Everything in it is Cool; there's not a hair out of place. There's nothing in it you wouldn't want to hear. But the thing is, you've already heard everything in it before. There are no risky choices; nothing bought just to hear what it's like, nothing intriguing, nothing funny, nothing naff. Everything has been run through a Cool check, and everything has passed. It's Cool; but dull.

In Kerouac's book *On the Road*, his hero is the Romantically Hot figure of Dean Moriarty, based on Kerouac's friend Neal Cassady. But this book you are reading is a book about Bob and the British Freaks, and enough has been written about Neal Cassady to be going on with for now, or maybe even for ever; there are novels, biographies and poems and films and songs. More to the point, *On the Road* is still being read by Young Readers. Whatever magic it had is clearly still there, though I must admit I can't be doing with it myself. It was published in 1957, but it concerns a series of journeys Kerouac took with Cassady in the years from 1947 to 1950. Kerouac said that on the day after it was published, he 'woke up famous'.

'When I first met you,' I say to Bob, 'you told me that you read *On the Road*, and the day after you finished it decided that was what you were going to do yourself: go on the road.'

'Pretty much, yeah. I remember buying it on the Charing Cross Road, so that must have been when I was still working.'

'Ever heard of Lucien Carr?'

'Nope.'

'He was Ginsberg's room-mate at Columbia. Ginsberg was in love with him, and *Howl* was originally dedicated to 'LC' before Carr demanded that his name be removed. He was beautiful and brilliant, and attracted both men and women, though, so far as anyone can tell, he was entirely straight. He befriended a fellow Columbia student, Edie Parker, who introduced him to her sailor boyfriend, Jack Kerouac. Lucien Carr had a stalker, his ex-scoutmaster David Kammerer, who had been at school with William Burroughs, and through Kammerer, Carr introduced Burroughs to both Ginsberg and Kerouac. Carr was a campus star, one of those students who blaze brightly, of whom great things are expected, but who never seem to realise their potential.

'Lucien Carr it was who formulated what we might think of as the Beats' aesthetic, which he called "The New Vision" – "1) Naked self-expression is the seed of creativity. 2) The artist's consciousness is expanded by derangement of the senses. 3) Art eludes conventional morality."' Kerouac and Carr planned to cross to France together, hoping to be the first American visitors to Paris after the liberation by the Allies from Nazi occupation. On 13 August 1944 (three days before Bob's second birthday), they even managed to smuggle themselves onto a ship heading for France, but got kicked off at the last minute, and went for a drink instead. After Kerouac left the bar, he bumped into David Kammerer, Burroughs' friend and Carr's ex-scoutmaster stalker, who asked Jack where he could find Lucien. Kerouac directed him to the bar, where Kammerer persuaded Carr to come with him to Riverside Park, where Carr killed him by stabbing him in the chest with his Boy Scout's penknife. Kammerer had come on to Carr one time too many. (The author Caleb Carr, Lucien's son, said that 'the fact that my father later killed Kammerer with his Boy Scout's knife is not something that any psychologist or detective I know would ever dare to call a coincidence'.) Carr dumped the body in the Hudson River, and then went round to see first Burroughs and then Kerouac, before turning himself in to the New York District Attorney. He did two years for second-degree murder. A few years back, there was a film made about it called *Kill Your Darlings*, with that bloke out of Harry Potter as Ginsberg. Carr is portrayed as a young man in denial of his (homo) sexuality, who killed Kammerer rather than face up to his gayness, but this is pretty much based on Ginsberg's account – he thought that all men were really gay – rather than on any actual evidence. In fact, Kammerer had haunted Carr for years; he had become his father figure at the age of twelve, and because he was the scoutmaster, he persuaded Carr's mother to grant him unusual access to Carr and then followed him about the country for ten years.

Rather than Carr being confused by his sexuality, it is much more likely that under relentless sexual pressure, he finally turned on his abuser.

Carr had been 'the glue that held the Beats together', according to Ginsberg, and now, with this murder, he became the subject of some of their earliest fiction and poetry.

When he got out of jail, Carr went to work for the United Press, but stayed close to the others, Kerouac in particular. When Kerouac got back to New York in 1951, after several years of travelling with Neal Cassady, he went to share Carr's apartment. Jack was experimenting with 'spontaneous prose' in which the writer simply writes or types as fast as possibly with 'no discipline other than rhythms of rhetorical exhalation and expostulated statement'.

And here's a thing I bet you didn't know: Jack had once been the speed-typing champion of the greater Boston area; so typing hell for leather suited him. The only thing slowing him down was the fact that he had to keep stopping to insert new bits of paper into his typewriter. Lucien Carr, employed at the United Press, had access to Teletype paper and brought home a 130-foot-long roll for Jack to write *On the Road* on. So Carr had provided the Beats' aesthetic, their inciting incident and even the means by which Kerouac composed *On the Road*. It's a shame he only gets remembered as a closet queen who killed his lover, when he wasn't. There were the big three: Kerouac, Ginsberg, Burroughs. Maybe there would have been a fourth, but for the murder.

'Burroughs I never got on with, despite the guns,' says Bob.

'Me neither. But Ginsberg?'

'Oh yeah, I loved Ginsberg. Oh yeah, of course ... If we were on a bus, me and my girlfriend would go up and down reading out *Howl* to the passengers.'

'Did you? You did that?'

'Literally that. *Howl*. "I saw the best minds of my generation" – I'm seventeen at the time – "I saw the best minds of my generation destroyed by madness, starving hysterical naked, dragging themselves through the negro streets at dawn looking for an angry fix, angel-headed hipsters burning for heavenly connection to the starry dynamo in the machinery of night" ... and some people would give us money. We weren't looking for money, though we'd always take it as we had none. It was odd, actually, we'd do it for the reactions, because some people really didn't like it, they'd get almost violent. And some people would say, "No, don't stop, more, more" sort of thing. It did bring those extreme reactions out. Reading poetry and listening to jazz all went together.'

I can't help but be impressed that Bob can still quote *Howl* off the top of his head.

'Yeah, we read loads of beat poets; not just Ginsberg, but Corso, Ferlinghetti, all that. We'd sit all day on the Circle Line when it was cold, reading poetry, and reciting it too. If the mood took me, I'd just stand up and recite to whoever was there.'

Allen Ginsberg is still the best known of the Beat poets, and *Howl* his best known work. Ginsberg described it as a 'jazz mass'; the long lines of the poem are each supposed to be a breath long, and Ginsberg saw himself as following in the tradition of saxophonist Charlie Parker, whose breath control was legendary. Ginsberg launched *Howl* at a reading on 7 October 1955, at the Six Gallery in San Francisco. There were only about a hundred people there, one of them Kerouac, who shouted 'Go, go', at the end of every line. It is not one of the poems which has 'influenced' many subsequent poets, far from it; but that night, beyond all question, was the most important and influential poetry reading of the twentieth century. Ginsberg had invented performance poetry.

One of the people who were there that night was the owner of San Francisco's City Lights Bookstore, Lawrence Ferlinghetti, who at the time of writing is still with us, aged ninety-seven. He agreed to publish *Howl* along with others of Ginsberg's poems, which he duly did in 1957. An undercover cop bought a copy, and Ferlinghetti was prosecuted for obscenity, largely on the basis of the line

who let themselves be fucked in the ass by saintly motorcyclists, and screamed with joy

Ferlinghetti was acquitted after testimony by literary experts. The trial is therefore the US equivalent of the *Lady Chatterley* trial in the UK.

A note on where the word 'Beat' comes from. Burroughs, older than the rest of the group, urged them to read Oswald Spengler's *Decline of the West*, which was not a nice thing to do, as anyone who has had a go will testify. The group equated themselves with the 'Fellaheen', who Spengler described as 'people living on the ruins of a civilisation'. But it's not a catchy term (not much in Spengler is; I retired hurt after thirty pages).

Herbert Huncke, Huncke the Junkie, a friend of Burroughs, introduced the term Beat to the group; it was a junkie term, meaning beat down, ragged, whipped, outside the game. But Kerouac also saw it as meaning 'beatified', that is to say, sainted. And Herb Caen, columnist for the *San Francisco Chronicle*, added the '-niks', by way of insult.

As to what a Beat was, I don't think you can top Beat poet Diane di Prima's definition. In a letter to her daughter, di Prima wrote: 'Honey, you see, we all thought experience itself was good. Any experience. That it could only be good to experience as much as possible.'

'That's good,' says Bob. 'I'm a Beat.'

'No you're not. You *were* a Beat, I admit, but you've been lots of other things since. But I met one of the very last of the breed, an unreconstructed beatnik: beard, sandals, bongos, concrete poetry, the lot. A bloke called Bob Cobbing – ever meet him?'

'Don't think so.'

'Me and Chas appeared on the same bill as him a couple of times. He was a sound poet; it was quite funny to hear, but he took it utterly seriously. He was in his eighties, and unchanged since 1954, when he ran Better Books on the Charing Cross Road. It wasn't a club, but a bookshop that held "happenings". He was authentic, authentically Beat, but, oddly, his view of authenticity never changed. The gigs we did with him were in – what? – 2000, 2001? And he wore sandals with socks, and a smock, and had a goatee. Like an ancient Ted at a Butlins rock 'n' roll weekender with a DA held together with product in the face of overwhelming male pattern baldness. Or a sixty-year-old punk.'

'Like you.'

'Fuck off. I'm fifty-nine. And my punk credentials are long gone.'

'Well, we were authentic. The real beatniks. As opposed to ravers.'

'What were ravers?'

'A raver was like a weekend beatnik; lived with Mum and Dad, had a job, grew their hair a bit, had a stripy T-shirt and a duffel coat, and came up from the suburbs to pose about in Soho. They weren't living in bomb sites and spending as much time as possible in dark cellars listening to music, all fucking week, like us. They were a bit of a target, to be honest, because they had money. I feel a bit ashamed, actually … You'd pick up girls, as much for getting a meal out of them as a fuck. The sex was nice, but a meal inside you was more important.'

'Tell me about the girls ….'

'Well, I'll tell you about the first girl I ever fucked. Her name was Jo Bramley, and I met her in Ken Colyer's. I was thinking about her face just the other day. She was a bonny-looking lass, a round face with blonde hair. Long straight hair, and what you'd call a Rubenesque figure. Nice, warm, soft.'

Bob is smiling at the memory.

'We were both virgins, and we'd been going out for a few weeks, but the opportunity hadn't quite – well, she wasn't quite ready for it. And we'd gone on to Eel Pie Island, and it was in the last of the days when you actually had to be rowed across, before they built the bridge. An old lady in a rowing boat would ferry all the punters to Eel Pie Island. She'd get about five punters in her boat, and row 'em there, all night, for about a penny or tuppence each. Anyway, we go to Eel Pie. There'd be the main Edwardian gin palace sprung dance floor and all that, so the plebs would be on the main dance floor. But there was a group of boys, the boys who were a bit cool, above the herd, an unspoken, tacit thing, sounds a bit snobby but there it is. Loads of times I've danced up there with Mick Jagger and Keef. Anyway, so in the morning after that, we're all back at a friend's place in Richmond, and someone's trying to revive some spaghetti from the day before, and Jo and I find ourselves in the bedroom there, and we had a fuck.'

'That's the most romantic thing I've ever heard ....'

'And from then on, in the jazz clubs at the time, everyone would just chuck their coats on a heap, literally, there'd be a heap of fucking coats this high – there were no cloakrooms or anything. And Jo and I would just burrow into them, and just do it, like, in the club, while it was going. And we did it in Oxford Street, at the Tottenham Court Road end of Oxford Street, against a Keep Left sign, just for the hell of it.

'But I think the second time we did it was in St James's Park. They have a little island of shrubbery sort of thing, amongst the lawn bit, and within the middle of one of these, we're just getting it together, one of the first times I've ever used a rubber johnny, and we're just getting to it when suddenly I hear this noise behind us, and I look and there's a geezer there. He says in a very posh voice, "Do you mind if I watch?"

'Of course, being a twat I don't say, "Give us a fiver and you can." Instead, I just sort of jumped to my feet with trousers round my ankles, pulled out this fucking commando knife I had and chased after him while pulling up my trousers, dagger in hand, across the park .... He must have had a good chuckle over that.'

'Well, up to a point ...'

'She was great, Jo. She was very good at going down the tube station, saying I've lost my tube fare home, and getting money. I felt like a pimp.'

'Because you didn't have any money to eat otherwise?'

'No.'

'So when you got a bit of money, where did you go? Coffee bars and that?'

'Coffee bars, caffs, pubs, clubs ...'

'Because this was the era of the coffee bar, really, wasn't it?'

'It was.'

'Which was your favourite?'

'Well, there were caffs and coffee bars. One for eating and one for hanging out. The Star was the cheapest restaurant in London, one and six for spaghetti, one and nine for spag bol and chips. A lot of it too. If you got a bit of money, there was Jimmy the Greek's, four and six for wonderful stewed lamb, with professionally surly Greek waiters. They'd drop your plate from just above the table, *bang*, and grin while they were doing it. They were playing a part. The coffee bars were something else again.'

'I suppose the 2i's was the most famous?'

'Yeah, but it was a bit over, really, a bit touristy.'

The 2i's was a coffee bar in the basement at 59 Old Compton Street, in Soho, which existed between 1956 and 1970. (It's a Vietnamese restaurant now.) It was owned by Paul Lincoln, an Australian wrestler. It became famous as the place where skiffle broke loose from the Colyers and Barbers, and so wasn't exactly the go-to place for the Beats, who were through with skiffle by 1958. So were Liverpool's Quarrymen, who had changed their name and were rediscovering their rock 'n' roll roots.

'Though I did meet the Beatles there,' says Bob.

'Of course you did. Where else?'

'Yeah, years later. 1963 maybe? I was with Long John Baldry. They'd just toured with him, and I was walking past with him, and he said come in and meet the lads. So I did. Paul and George, it was.'

'What did you think?'

'Not much. I was a hip jazzer. What would you think if you met One Direction?'

'Not much. How did you meet Long John Baldry?'

'At the Gyre and Gimble. The "G's" it was known as. It was off the Strand, down John Adam Street. It was the first coffee bar I was taken to by people who already knew London. Very early on, I met Long John Baldry. Baldry was already a star on the fringe folk scene, he wasn't big anywhere else. Baldry was rated on the Soho folkie circuit; and that's where Eric Clapton was playing banjo and later learning guitar with him. It was a good place, was the G's, open till four in the morning, and they didn't mind us sitting there all night with a coffee. The only problem was a couple of Guardsmen from the nearest barracks had found out about it, would occasionally come down the steps and punch everybody in the fucking face. But I had this mate called Paddy, runty-looking geezer about seventeen.

He was like a hurricane, laid into 'em both. They were twice his size; he just waded in – gave 'em both a thrashing. They never come down again.'

'So how did you come across Donovan?'

'Because he regularly used to sit at the door at the Duke of York pub on Rathbone Street. That pub was rammed with beatnik types, dirty, long hair. The owner of the pub was the Major, he somehow didn't mind all these beatniks. He had this big dog called the Colonel, and the dog was famous because in the film of *The Hound of the Baskervilles* he was the hound, dressed up. Anyway, Donovan used to be very often sitting outside the pub, playing guitar, singing. Wizz Jones too.'

'So at the moment of the appearance of *On the Road*, this world you were part of was beginning to rise sharply in the fashion stakes ...?'

'Yeah, and the Parisian, and I suppose the American, Juliette Gréco existentialism, beatnik-y, bohemian ... Yeah, all that started being fashionable.'

'Because, those of you who were the Soho contingent were the authentic thing, weren't you?'

'Yeah, we were or aiming to be. We certainly had our foot on the bottom rungs of that ladder, yeah – just because we were living there, and around all the time, we got to meet all the people, the musicians, we'd be a known face around the scene, just from being around and not being an obnoxious, boring sort of person.'

'And that's a story that happened again and again,' I say. 'A group of people suddenly found themselves at the front of things. The hip kids out of which pop culture grew, you were one of those kids.'

Bob scratches his nose.

'Yeah. We were the seeds from which the English side of the hippie thing grew.'

'Where else would the hippest kids in London go?'

'The really cool place, but you needed to buy something to go in there, so I didn't go in very often, was the House of Sam Widges. Now that was cool, the best jukebox in London I suspect, they only had classical music and the best of cool jazz on the jukebox, no rock 'n' roll whatsoever. And they used to have modern art action painting in the basement, some of which would involve shotguns and cans of paint, and naked girls being dragged across canvas.'

The House of Sam Widges (and its downstairs happening area, known as 'The Pad') was founded by the poet Neil Oram, who was later to write the longest play ever performed, *The Warp*, which lasts for twenty-two hours. It was directed by Ken Campbell, one-time Professor of Ventriloquism at RADA, and one of the people I would most like to have met.

'It's interesting to me that Sam Widges would be playing modern jazz. In a narrative history of jazz at that time, you're either trad or modern,' I say.

'I'm not saying I liked all modern jazz then, and I don't like all modern jazz now, but some of the stuff was great. On the jukeboxes Max Roach and Clifford Brown were big. "Parisian Thoroughfare", I remember. Lots of Charlie Parker and Miles Davis. I don't think Mingus had even started then, or Ornette Coleman. That came a bit later, and that was more modern.'

'So, be-bop?'

'Yeah.'

'I think we might call it a day there, Bob,' I say.

'Why there?'

'Because I need to do theory.'

Bob walks me to my car. Not because it's a long way, but because he wants to keep talking, and I have to stop him. I am overloading. There is too much to tell you. I drive the six miles home, buzzing with coffee and the feeling that it is all but impossible to map a man's life in anything other than 1:1 scale. I should take seventy-five years to write this bastard. And I'll be dead by then.

A week later, and I've popped up to see Bob again. The Chinese restaurant in Presteigne contributes its old oilcans to Bob's cause, and I pick them up and take them over. Without these oilcans, Bob's work would suffer; he uses them to make the vanes on his mobile sculptures, and big cans like this can be hard to find. Besides, I have acquired a little skunk weed, by virtue of sitting by a dying friend's bedside, and it's good to share a smoke with Bob on an early spring afternoon.

'How's Chas?' Bob asks.

I shrug. 'Somewhere close to the end. A few more weeks, I reckon.'

'Really?'

'Yeah. He's asleep pretty much twenty-two hours a day now. But people keep visiting, and bringing him weed, which he doesn't smoke but gives away.'

'Let's have some then,' says Bob, and I oblige.

'Where else?' I say. 'Where else was *the* place to be?'

'Well, there was the Partisan, which was a pretty lefty, green-y type of place. Most of the people there were members of the Young Communists. But they had good folk music. Baldry played there often and they had lots of people there who were well-known folk musicians.

But the main thing about it was that they let little herberts like me in. You could buy a bowl of yogurt with brown sugar on for a tanner.'

'I've been writing about the Partisan,' I tell Bob. 'Do you know the story? Why it mattered?'

'Not really, no,' says Bob. 'Let's do it.'

Of all of the coffee bars of Soho, it's arguable that the Partisan was the most interesting. And the most left wing. Young Leftists, disillusioned by the Communist invasion of Hungary, and as disgusted with the Labour Party, wanted to make a new movement. Four Oxford scholars, Raphael Samuel, Gabriel Pearson, Charles Taylor and Stuart Hall (no, not the kiddie-fiddler, but a Jamaican scholar who would go on to be one of this country's most respected sociologists, and the father of Cultural Studies), set up a magazine in 1957 called *The University Left Review*, and subsequently a series of 'Left Clubs' based at British universities. In 1959, the *ULR* merged with by then ex-communist E.P. Thomson's *New Reasoner* to become *The New Left Review*, which continues to the present day.

They were young men; Hall was the oldest at twenty-six. Twenty-two-year-old Raphael Samuel, encouraged by the success of the Left Clubs, became convinced that the New Left needed a permanent home, and so he campaigned to raise money to buy a building at 7 Carlisle Street, in Soho. (*Private Eye* has its offices at number 6.)

Raphael managed to raise seven grand from investors and fellow travellers as diverse as the actor Michael Redgrave, theatre critic Kenneth Tynan, writer Doris Lessing, literary critic William Empson, and screenwriter Wolf Mankowitz (who wrote *Expresso Bongo*, set in the coffee shops of Soho, first a novel, and then a film starring, unlikely as it might seem, Cliff Richard). The offices of the *NLR* were on the top floor, the next floor down had a left-wing library, and on the ground floor was the Partisan itself, with its attendant basement.

Stuart Hall recalled that Raphael Samuel was 'completely scatty', and that the bills were never paid. None of the rest of the group wanted Samuel to open a coffee house, but he went ahead anyway.

His idea was to draw on the traditions of the seventeenth-century coffee house, or Mitteleuropean cafés, all in their day centres of dissent. So it was to some extent a historical recreation (it boasted earthenware cups and plates, for example), but it also saw itself in opposition to the 400 plus coffee bars which existed in Soho by 1957. The Partisan actively encouraged punters 'to stay for much longer periods than the espresso bars', because, above all, they wanted people to talk – primarily, of course, about left-wing ideas.

the Partisan
7,   CARLISLE ST   SOHO SQ   WI
(Tottenham Court Rd Tube)

A coffee house for the Left
An anti-espresso bar
Open seven days a week
10 a.m. to midnight

Bill of fare includes

Farmhouse Soup . . . . Old fashioned pea soup
. . . Borscht . . . Irish peasant stew . . . Baked
Yorkshire ham with sauce Cumberland . . . Liver
dumplings . . . Boiled Surrey fowl with parsley
sauce and Patna rice . . . Boiled Breconshire
Mutton with caper sauce . . . Frankfurters or
Vorscht with potato salad . . . Apple dumplings
with hot lemon sauce . . . Whitechapel cheese-
cake and pastries . . . Vienna coffee . . . . cafe
filtre . . . Russian tea

the Partisan coffee house 7 Carlisle St W1

They bought a monstrous Gaggia coffee machine, and came up with a
fairly adventurous menu – liver dumplings, anyone? – a menu which is
remembered by habitués as 'dreadful in the extreme'. The coffee wasn't
great, either; Stuart Hall, a coffee aficionado, admitted that he nipped
out for his coffee to a place over the road, where the coffee was less
right-on, but much better.

The New Left took the emerging youth culture seriously, in a way
that the Old Left was unable to do. The cultural critic and historian
Richard Hoggart, author of *The Uses of Literacy*, published about this
time, felt that the coffee bars offered 'spiritual dry rot amid the odour
of boiled milk'.

The Partisan was soon seething with visitors, as its policy of letting
people stay as long as they liked meant that no one was turned away.
Quentin Crisp (of whom more in the next chapter) sat at the front, challenging all-comers to a game of chess; that Crisp was happy to sit there
says something about how welcoming the place was. It later emerged
that Special Branch had an informant who sat for much of the day playing
chess in the Partisan; presumably he got to play with Crisp, which is an
enduring image.

Jeff Nuttall in his book *Bomb Culture* said that it had 'a puritan atmosphere you could cut with a knife'. The noticeboard was covered in peti-
tions calling for nuclear disarmament, for action on Algeria (at that time
fighting for liberation from France), on housing, on Labour Party reform.
Speakers read like a *Who's Who* of the London Left: E.P. Thomson, Stuart

Hall, Eric Hobsbawm, Doris Lessing, John Berger, Michael Foot, Raymond Williams, Christopher Logue, Kenneth Tynan. It hosted the fortnightly meetings of the London Schools Left Club, comprised of earnest sixth-formers. The Aldermaston Marches were organised from the premises. It had screenings of films, and rolling exhibitions of radical artists, mostly those who belonged to what became known as 'the kitchen sink school'.

The basement became a centre for the emerging folk scene. As Bob said, Baldry played there often, and Rod Stewart hung out there; as he put it, 'to meet the birds' (though he did go on the Aldermaston Marches of 1961 and 1962). And the smell of dope permeated upstairs from the basement, a smell which I have never associated with puritanical atmospheres myself.

So, it became trendy. Condé Nast approached the management about doing a piece for *Vogue*, though they were turned down. In 1959, the BBC's *Panorama* made a programme about the Partisan. One of the interviewees was Stuart Hall, who summed up what a lot of Younger Readers felt then and now about politics. He said that 'politics have become separate from real life, which is dangerous in the extreme'.

It lost money hand over fist; of course it did. Bad management combined with the policy which stated that 'nobody can be turned away except clearly undesirable elements' spelled business ruination, and despite an attempted restructuring where the management said 'the objectionable Soho ne'er-do-wells are being moved out' (as good a description of Bob at that time as is to be had), the Partisan closed in 1962.

'The politics side of it never interested you, did it?' I say.

'Not really,' says Bob. 'See, growing up when I did, what I thought of politics was that I didn't like Hitler, and I didn't like Stalin neither. And I've made a living from selling beautiful but useless things to rich people: jewellery and that, things to adorn their bodies and their homes. So I knew that communists just wear black suits and that, and I was never going to make a living off them. Besides, I'd seen what they were like, just going around killing and controlling people with machine guns.'

'But, that's the whole point. The New Left, the people behind the Partisan, they'd seen what Soviet Communism was like in Hungary. They didn't want to stop being socialists. But they didn't want what they'd seen in Hungary. They were looking for a new way. A way that meant socialists could adorn their bodies and homes with beautiful things.'

'See, that's all right in theory, but in practice, a lot of those people were cunts.'

'Always with you it's the practice, isn't it? I'm sure lots of them were cunts, but you've got to see it from my point of view.'

Bob sighs, and reaches for my tin of Chas Death Offering Weed. I am not to be stopped by his sighing.

'See, from my point of view, by the time I hit fourteen/fifteen, you guys were my heroes. You had opened paths that me and my friends could follow. You were like our Elvis. We believed in it all: love and peace, freedom, free love, free drugs, radical politics. We just bought the whole package. You smoked dope, you listened to the Stones, and you did a clenched-fist salute while going "'Ho Ho Ho Chi Minh'". That's what we aspired to do. That was all fairly mainstream when I was a teenager.'

'Yeah, but none of it ever worked in practice, did it?'

'No, Bob. But I am here to represent theory, and let me tell you, from a theoretical point of view, we've got it all sewn up.'

'If you say so.' Bob yawns, and puts the coffee maker on the stove.

'I'll tell you another thing I liked about the Partisan,' he says. 'The first time I ever got into a bit of posh totty was from the Partisan. She was called Susie Greenwood and she was the daughter of the then Shadow Housing Minister, Sir Anthony Greenwood. I met her because she was a friend of Baldry's and was on that Partisan scene, lefty, all that. And we had a bit of a fancy for each other, so she said, "Come back to my place", and we went up to Downshire Hill, a nice street in Hampstead. And it was a very nice Georgian house there, opposite the Freemason's Arms. I saw her write a note when we were down in the kitchen, before we went upstairs. Anyway, we went upstairs and had a pleasant night, woke up in the morning and there was a knock on the door. I say, "Oh fuck, shall I get under the bed?" She says, "No, it's all right." And a maid comes in with two breakfasts on a tray. You can imagine what I thought.'

'That was the subject of the note, presumably? Ordering breakfast?'

Bob smiles at the memory. 'Yeah.'

'You were sort of sucked into CND about this time?'

'Yeah. When I was up in Liverpool, I went for some chips, and they wrapped my chips in a Sunday paper, and fuck me, there was a picture of me on the front page, walking across Trafalgar Square with my bedroll, and the CND march about to set off in the background. I wasn't political; I was just there, and they must have thought I looked rough or something.'

'What was the paper? I'd love to find that picture.'

'Can't remember. I know it stopped publication soon after. Was it the *Sunday Pictorial*? It might have been *Reynolds News*, or it might have been the *Sunday Dispatch*. It was a fairly popular Sunday newspaper, not the

News of the World.' (Author's note: Despite a day in the Newspaper Library in Colindale, I have been unable to track this picture down.)

'But you went on the march?'

'Yeah, the second CND march. But I was part of a crew of scallywags who had no moral dilemma about going there to profit from it. Though we didn't want anyone dropping fucking atom bombs on us, or on anyone else. We were against people having atom bombs, seemed like a bad idea; but our principal minute-to-minute operation was looting and plundering. By some wonderful chance we were made baggage marshals. We did most of the march on the back of fucking lorries with everyone else's baggage. I'm sorry, but that is the truth, we were street kids and if we could do a bit of thieving and looting without much chance of getting caught then we were going to do it. And one of the places where the march stopped happened to be near a big road-house, a pub. So me and a couple of the others – the Soho contingent, we were called – were in this pub, and we were all skint, and the pub was absolutely rammed. So I fought to get to the bar, just to see, and there was a huge magnum of champagne behind the bar, and I just had to have it. So I leapt over the bar, and grabbed the bottle. One of the contingent was awake enough to toss him the bottle, hopped back over the bar, pushed through the crowd and out. And while we was putting in a bit of distance to sit down and drink this, there was a table full of salamis and nice French breads, which were there for people to buy and make their lunches out of. I picked up one of these salamis that was at one end of the table, looking the geezer whose stall it was in the eye, and went down the table going bang, bang, bang till I got to the end of the table, then I just walked off with his sausage. So that sorted lunch out for one of the days of the Aldermaston March.'

'Chas was ten, and living in Ealing. He watched the march go by the end of his road. It stayed with him. Part of what turned him into a Young Communist.'

'Daft old cunt.'

'Nevertheless, it stayed with him. Stayed with me, even though I was only a babe in arms; it entered the mythology of my generation. I grew up in the shadow of the Bomb.'

Younger Readers still live in the shadow of the Bomb, though they know it not. The organisation which has tried throughout my lifetime to keep the Bomb in political view is CND, the Campaign for Nuclear Disarmament. CND have tried to give some moral leadership on the subject, but they wane and ebb in the popular consciousness. At times, they appear only to have given Younger Readers a T-shirt design.

1957 was the year that the UK tested its first hydrogen bomb. The eminent writer J.B. Priestley wrote an article for the *New Statesman* entitled 'Britain and the Nuclear Bomb', in which he urged the government, having developed the H-Bomb, to show moral leadership to the world, and to give it up. Kingsley Martin, the editor of the *New Statesman*, was swamped by letters in support of Priestley, so he set up a private meeting at the flat of Canon John Collins of St Paul's Cathedral to establish CND.

The aim of CND, according to Priestley, was to persuade the government and people of the UK to get rid of the bomb, 'whatever other nuclear powers may decide', a policy which is called 'unilateralism', and a policy that still divides the Labour Party, though not proper radical political parties, who all support it. (The Green Party, for example, have always been in favour of unilateralism.)

On 17 February 1958, in Central Hall, Westminster, CND held its first public meeting. Five thousand people attended. Speakers included Canon Collins, Priestley, the philosopher Bertrand Russell and the historian A.J.P. Taylor, who listed the consequences of a hydrogen bomb attack, and then asked, 'Is there anyone here who would want to do this to another human being? Then why are we making the damned things?' When the meeting broke up, 1,000 people marched on Downing Street chanting, 'Ban the Bomb'.

The first Aldermaston March, which took place over the Easter Weekend (4–7 April 1958), was actually organised by the tiny 'Direct Action Committee', although it was supported by CND, who took over the organisation of the march for the following and subsequent years. The first march, from London to Aldermaston, attracted no more than 300 demonstrators, and none of the leadership attended; but it picked up when the march was swapped to run from Aldermaston to London, and was organised by CND. The 1959 event, at which Bob behaved so poorly, attracted an estimated 60,000 marchers.

In its first incarnation CND attracted many of the great and good: actors like Peggy Ashcroft, Edith Evans and Flora Robson; composers like Benjamin Britten and Michael Tippett; writers; politicians; sculptors Barbara Hepworth and Henry Moore, and the cricket commentator John Arlott. The great and the good are not generally known for radicalism. CND was widely supported, but very badly organised; run by Canon Collins, J.B. Priestley, Michael Foot and Kingsley Martin from Collins's flat, in the early days it had no useful democratic structure. In 1960, Bertie Russell stepped down from the presidency of CND to set up the Committee of 100, which was more committed to direct action. This split the movement, to a great extent, and it was not until the 1980s that CND found its mojo again.

The CND symbol was designed by graphic artist Gerald Holtom. It incorporates the semaphore letters for N and D, but Holtom himself claimed that he was inspired by a Goya painting of a peasant before a firing squad. It is now universally known as the peace symbol; though not everyone seems to remember this.

I tell Bob the shocking moment when I realised how debased the symbol had become.

'I was at the Secret Garden Party festival last year, doing a bit of walk-about theatre. I was playing the part of an ancient vicar. And I walked past this kid, who was wearing a T-shirt covered in CND symbols. So I do my vicar schtick on him. "Ah," I said. "CND. Marvellous. Ban the Bomb. I went on the marches when I was a young curate." And this kid says, "What?" And I drop out of character and say, "Your T-shirt. The CND symbol. Ban the Bomb." And he said, "Oh is that what it means? I just thought it was a cool symbol." I was stunned. I wanted to explain to him that, since he didn't know what it symbolised, it therefore wasn't any kind of symbol; just some shapes on a T-shirt. But I let him go.'

'Fuck, really?' says Bob.

'Really. That's why I'm writing this book. So people know what the CND symbol stands for.

We had Nothing in Common Except that we were Criminals

I've come up to see Bob for a chat and a coffee and a smoke. Even though it's the middle of March, there is a skim of snow on the Whimble, the tit-shaped mountain that overlooks Bob's wood. It's cold, and we sit in the van with the door closed and the wood-burner up high.

We talk about cool; the more I think about it, the more I'm sure that cool is part of the problem; part of the reason that the counter-cultural project of the fifties, sixties, seventies, eighties and early nineties failed; simply because cool moves on.

Bob has been building a guest hut with a local lass working as his labourer, and he takes me up the track on his quad bike to visit it. Not that it's far from the van: 100 metres, maybe. But it's been sleeting hard, and the track through the wood is claggy with thick mud; Bob doesn't want to slip, and I don't want half of Radnorshire on my boots, so I sit on the back of the quad bike, and crap myself with fear for the duration of the thirty-second ten-mile-an-hour journey through the wood.

The hut is great. Last time I was up, all he had of it was six upright pine poles resting on breeze blocks sunk into the ground; but now it's finished, with a home-made stable door, an insulated corrugated-steel roof, insulated wooden walls, a wooden floor, a wood-burner that Bob has made, and which he now fires up, and a work bench where he has clearly been doing some brazing. There are two LED lights on swinging iron brackets made by Bob, powered by a solar panel up on a pole outside the hut. I reckon it's about the size of Thoreau's hut next to Walden Pond. It cost 450 quid for materials, plus whatever Bob pays his labour: over-generous for the market, I suspect, but given Bob's rating of the lass ('the best worker I've ever had'), fair dues.

'It doesn't have a bed, though.'

'Ah, well, it's a forester's hut. I don't have planning permission for a house. But you see those bits of wood in the corner?'

'Yes.'

'Those assemble into a bed in about five minutes. I've already had a guest to stay.'

There is no doubt that you could live here, if you didn't mind shitting outside and collecting your water from rain butts. Four hundred
and fifty quid; once again, as so often when I'm with Bob, I see a window
into the future, rather than a nostalgic black-and-white film of the past,
framed in a dusty casement. The forester's hut is heated sustainably, lit
with LEDs, and if you pop a dongle on your device thing, you're
connected to the world. Young people don't have to be homeless; some
basic skills training, a radical overhaul of land-ownership and planning
regs, and low-impact micro-homes like this could pop up all over the
countryside.

It wouldn't suit everybody, clearly.

'If I'd been your age in 1958, instead of just being born in 1958, I reckon
I'd have been hot, but in my own way. Duffel-coated hot ....'

'Ah, you see,' says Bob, 'we'd have known you for a weekender at
once. The real street kids wore donkey jackets ...'

'Well, I'd have been a weekender, that's why. Hot, but at university.
Hot for Cambridge, or wherever I'd gone.'

Bob's life has been a life of action, and mine of inaction. Which is
better? Who can say? Bob is very well read, and I've had a few scrapes,
but reading books made Bob want to do things and go places, whilst
reading books made me want to read more books. And yet I have
authenticity, I think, and a high degree of freedom, freedom being the
most important currency with which writers are paid. But I would have
been a raver, a weekend Beat, just as, when my turn came, I was a
weekend punk. That I managed so much is only because I had some
lucky breaks: a shattered family, a fearsome seventies comprehensive,
long years singing for failing bands in quarter-full dives, an equal number
of years working for William Hill on the wrong side of the bandit screen
for below-subsistence wages. I've been 'vulnerably housed' (in a shed for
a winter and a Mom and Pop caravan for two years), and had an interest
in drugs that has sometimes veered towards over-interest. I've had three
wives (died, divorced, survived), countless breakdowns, grinding poverty,
and I have loved and been loved in return. But I was always faking street
life, even when I pretty much lived there. My purpose has not been to
take the path that opened before me, and take the consequences, no.
That's Bob's way. Once, my purpose was to be Daryl Hall out of Hall
& Oates, but for many years now, my purpose has been to become a
Bookman, a Man of Letters, a Broadcaster, a Stephen Fry-esque guest
on telly things, a National Treasure. I'd like a Grammy, a Bafta (or an
Oscar, thinking about it), FRSL, the Samuel Johnson, CH (or OM, can

never decide which is classier), the Nobel, quiet funeral, big memorial service in the Abbey. Bob doesn't think like that.

'The trouble with me,' he says, 'is I've got a criminal mind.'

'Ideal for when you went up to Liverpool. When did you do that?'

'1959? 1960?'

'And why?'

'Well, we'd heard there was a jazz and poetry scene up there, and we just wanted to check it out. So we hitched up.'

'You and Jo Bramley?'

'No. Me and a bloke called Ken.'

'Who was Ken?'

'A bloke, Ken Shelton, came from Hounslow, Southall sort of area, suburban boy who'd decided, much the same as me, that this was a much more interesting life than living out the other side of London Airport. And a tall, good-looking bloke, so he was a good buddy to knock around with. We were both after the same thing, a meal and a shag, basic sort of stuff ... And if you could get a shag with a bed, that would make you really happy. A shag with a bed and a meal, that would be all too much.'

'How often did you get a shag and a meal and a bed?'

'Very rarely; I mean the shag and the bed more frequently, but it was generally with girls who lived in the suburbs with their parents, and you certainly weren't going to be introduced over breakfast. You had to slip off before the parents got up in the morning, which as you probably only got there at two o'clock and then you had to get up at four or five in time to fuck off wasn't ideal, but, you know, three hours in a bed was better than no hours in a bed.'

'And much of that shagging. No rest for the wicked. So you hitched up to Liverpool?'

'Yeah.'

'What was it like when you got there?'

'Shit really, but amazing too. We'd get attacked by gangs of nine-year-olds with half-bricks. That was their weapon of choice. The whole place was covered in half-bricks. If London was still a bit of a bomb site, Liverpool was fucking all but derelict. And, although we knew how to survive on the streets of London, it didn't always translate to Liverpool.'

'Was there a jazz and poetry scene?'

'Yeah, but we were too scummy to get in many places. We often stayed in bombed-out basements with a group of other derelicts. We'd light campfires in the middle of the room, with floorboards and banisters, right in the middle of the room. No wonder people don't trust teenagers.

Fucking bandits at heart; I was, anyway. Once, I managed to nick a bone off a dog . . . .'

'I'm sorry?'

'Yeah, this dog had a big marrow bone, and I thought, "I'm having that." So I took it back to where my mates were, and we boiled it up in a tin can with a few veg we'd got after the market packed up. While we were eating it, one of the lads, Sean his name was, said, "I wonder what the poor people are doing?" And we pissed ourselves, because we thought we were rich.

'One time, I had an out-of-body experience in Liverpool. We'd met a girl with a flat, and we were staying there with some beatnik types. Up by where they were just finishing the Roman Catholic Cathedral; it was only a tiny flat, but she was quite happy to have four or five people dossing on her floor. I was lying on a bed – exhausted, malnourished – and it was like I floated up to the corner of the room, up where the walls meet the ceiling. I was actually looking down on my body. And I could see this guy called Rhodesian Mike reaching around in my bag. I mean, there was nothing in there to nick, but he was trying . . .'

'What did you do? Did you swoop down on him?'

'No, I just rolled over. The experience was over. I just looked at him, and he backed off.'

'So you were starving, really? What did you do?'

'Came back to London. After about six months. Jo Bramley had left me for Clapton when I got back.'

'This is Eric Clapton?'

'Yeah.'

'Is this when the busking with Long John Baldry and Eric Clapton thing happened?'

Bob smiles. He likes this story. It was one of the first stories he ever told me, when we met thirty years or so ago.

'No, the Clapton / Baldry thing happened a couple of years before that, when Clapton was a banjo player, and then Baldry started to show him guitar chords, and at that time me and Jo Bramley would go down and do the hat down by the arches at Villiers Street, while Baldry played guitar and Clapton played banjo, by the Embankment just outside Charing Cross Station. This was when he was just going from banjo to guitar.'

'So you would take the hat round while they were busking?'

'Yeah. And then one of the first shared places I lived in – there were about six rooms there – various people lived there and Baldry was one of them. We just hit it off. I've told you the thing about the hoopla with the Kilner jar rings, playing hoopla on his dick ....'

'Baldry was gay, wasn't he?'

'Oh yeah, no doubt about that. Fuck yes. In fact, he's the only bloke I've ever given a wank to, and that was at, don't know whose place it was, but it was in the morning after an all-night music thing, and there was some girl at this place who I don't know from Eve but I really fancied, and I thought, "I know how to get her interested." So I got hold of Baldry's cock and started giving him a wank ....'

'Did it work?'

Bob shakes his head ruefully. 'Nah.'

'Worth a try, though.'

'Definitely.'

Baldry was about eighteen months older and six inches taller than Bob. Like Bob, he came from the Kingsbury area of North London; and like Bob, pretty much his first memory was of bombing raids. Unlike Bob, his adolescent years were spent obsessing over blues records, an interest sparked by a very early TV appearance by the blues duo Sonny Terry and Brownie McGhee. By the age of twelve, he'd started a Blues Appreciation Society at school; another member was Stones drummer Charlie Watts. Baldry was busted for busking in Soho, aged sixteen, and although he didn't actually go on the streets, he was already an established figure on the coffee-bar scene by the time Bob rocked up. 'The kid who plays the blues,' they called him. Clapton later described him as 'a musicologist', and claimed Baldry as one of his earliest inspirations, not just as a guitar teacher, but because it was the first time he'd seen a white man playing the blues.

Long John Baldry was also funny, and he was the MC at Eel Pie Island, with a Noël Coward voice and a droll line in patter; his dress was described as 'flamboyant', and his gayness was very much in evidence, though he didn't come out publicly until the late seventies. He was the singer for Alexis Korner and Cyril Davies' Blues Incorporated (Charlie Watts was the drummer), the first amplified British blues band, and the band from which the Stones grew. After they split up, Baldry founded Steampacket, featuring Rod Stewart and Julie Driscoll on joint lead vocals (Baldry discovered Rod the Mod playing his harmonica on the station after a night at Eel Pie Island); and when they split up in 1966, Baldry set up Bluesology with Reg 'Elton John' Dwight on keyboards and vocals. The Elton John song 'Someone Saved My Life Tonight' is dedicated to Baldry, who talked Elton out of getting married to a lady, and helped him come to terms with his sexuality.

Long John Baldry runs through the story of British blues like trams through Blackpool; and if you think the British blues scene didn't amount to much, then I suggest you check out your Dad Rock history, because it gave rise to the Rolling Stones, the Animals, Them, the Yardbirds, and countless thousands of other sixties bands. So popular was the blues in the UK, it helped to repopularise and reinvigorate the blues in the States.

His spoken-word patter song 'Conditional Discharge' gives you a flavour of Baldry. He does a very good Kenneth Williams voice, and tells the story of his arrest for busking with great good humour. But on the whole, I'm not sure if the recordings do justice to the man. I can remember disliking his 1967 number one, 'Let the Heartaches Begin', a syrupy ballad where his cod-Mississippi Delta blues voice is replaced by a tremulous vibrato. His real moment was at the Gyre and Gimble, at Eel Pie Island, at the Partisan, and is gone. But his influence, and the scene he helped to create, can still be heard in the music of the Rolling Stones and Rod Stewart and their countless imitators.

'So did Baldry introduce you to the gay scene?'

'Not really. Baldry was a queer; but living on the streets of London you learned that lots of 'em were lovely people. There were a heck of a lot of queers about in Soho at night, but they were friendly. We used to go to the Nucleus Club. Fuck me, that was an eye-opener. It was a basement coffee bar, but the walls were covered with penny coins, big old proper penny coins. And they had good music on the jukebox. But what really shook me was two geezers on the little dance floor bit, dancing together, and one of them going down on the other in the middle of the dance floor.'

'Would make you think, that.'

'I'd just come up from the country, and had heard of queers and all that, but to see these blatant queers, one going down on the other literally in the middle of the fucking floor ... For a boy just up from Camberley ... bloody hell, people weren't batting an eyelid. So I came to embrace the gay scene as a good part of life.'

'You told me once that you met Quentin Crisp ...'

'That was in the first year of being in London, and living rough on the streets. He was part of that life. Purely because he would appear in Soho Square most days, and very often we were in Soho Square because it's the nice little bit in Soho, with nice seats and a nice garden; I always loved the building in the middle of it, the tool shed, the Elizabethan tool shed ...'

I furrow my brow with historian's anxiety.

'I'm not sure it's Elizabethan as such ...'

'It looks Elizabethan.'

'Yes. Anyway. Ignore me. Quentin Crisp.'

'Quentin Crisp had his lunch there every day, or every day when the weather was OK, and he was always happy to sit with us and share his sarnies.'

'So he was just a bloke who was about the place?'

'Well, he was obviously a strange bloke, because he had his dyed hair and his chiffon scarf, sort of electric pink round his neck, and was obviously very camp, but that was fine because one of the things you quickly learned if you're living rough on the streets of London is you've got to drop any prejudice you might have had. And you got more educated – black people, queers and that, you knew they existed but you'd never actually seen any, never had any dealings with them, and you quickly learn it's all part of the scene, part of the world. So we were quite happy to sit with Quentin Crisp. We'd have sat with anyone who'd share their sandwiches with us, we'd have sat with the devil.'

I'm not sure what I can say about Quentin Crisp that hasn't been said much better by Quentin Crisp. Here he is on Soho:

All I know of London is what I now call the reservation – that is to say, Soho. It's called the reservation in the sense that we are now able to live there protected, no longer shot at as though we were big game. We can do as we please. Most of the Soho life that I know is spent living in small cafés, which still exist in Soho. They used to exist in Chelsea, but Chelsea is now smart or pseudo-smart: King's Road, which once was full of small shops full of aniseed balls and dead wasps, is now full of clothes for women and clothes for men, and up and down the street walk debutantes hoping to be mistaken for art students. In Soho the people are still what you would call real; their attitudes are not derived, or not derived to the same extent, and these people can be met in cafés, perfectly ordinary cafés open to the street, cafés where the old layabouts from the happy time still go.

This is taken from a transcript of a programme made for the Third Programme in 1964, a programme which eventually led to the publication of his autobiography, *The Naked Civil Servant*, in 1968, and then the subsequent TV film of the same title in 1976, with John Hurt in the title role.

Sting (sorry) wrote a song about him, 'An Englishman in New York'. Crisp wrote two more volumes of funny, sad, brave, witty, bitchy, brilliant memoirs. He described himself as an 'effeminate homosexual'. He wore his long hair dyed scarlet, wore flamboyant clothes, painted his nails, and was the object of derision and violence for much of his early life. Born in 1908 (so in his early fifties when he was sharing his sandwiches with the Soho contingent), he died in 1999, and worked for thirty years as a life model for art students, until the success of the book and film, which liberated him to write and to perform a brilliant and funny one-man show.

He said, 'I have always lived my life in the profession of being', which still seems worth a try.

'But that gay thing ... that was always there?'

'Of course it was, yeah. Prejudice is just something you know fuck all about. But when you start meeting people who are gay, and some of them are mates ... At least one of our crew was a rent boy.'

'Er ... And you yourself?'

'I did get shagged up the arse once by some geezer. Do you want to hear about that?'

'I do, yes.'

'I bedded down on a bench on the Victoria Embankment, down near Charing Cross tube station. Just down the road from Hungerford Bridge, little embankment gardens there, used to be a lot of old-style homeless people sleeping there, tramps basically. It was winter, I just had the clothes I had on, just lying on this bench trying to sleep, and this guy comes up and says, "I live just over the river, do you want to come and stay at my place?" So I thought, "He's a queer," but for the opportunity of some food and a fucking warm bed I'd take my chances, so I said, "Let's go." It can't have been that late, because we got a tube and they didn't run late. Anyway, we got down to his place and I get into his bed, because that's obviously what's going to happen, and I let him fuck me up the arse and I really, really didn't like it, and I thought, "I'm never going to do that again," and in the morning he gave me fourteen shillings, making me a whore.'

'Fourteen bob. Fucking hell. Lot of money in those days. You'd think he'd round it up to fifteen, wouldn't you?'

I think I need to remind Younger Readers that in this period, in the late fifties, homosexuality was illegal. That's right. You may need to retreat to your safe space at this time. Crayons are provided. In the sixties, later on in this story, people said that the personal is the political, and everyone nodded. Now, of course, politics has gone, and the personal is all that's left. It is hard for Younger Readers, with their high emotional intelligence and their low knowledge of history, to comprehend. But it's true. Homosexuality was illegal until 1967.

So, for the Younger Reader, who may be gay, and will certainly have gay friends, and for whom homophobia is about the worst, wickedest phobia there is, you must know that nobody back then had any gay friends, not really, because being gay, or queer, was illegal. Therefore, on the whole, by and large, gay people were invisible. That's why Crisp was so brave in living out. There was one gay couple who I had any awareness of, and that was Julian and Sandy, played by Kenneth Williams and Hugh Paddick on the mid-sixties radio show *Round the Horne*. So I knew that such people existed, and that they were camp, rude and funny; and that they spoke a language of their own, called Polari. It never occurred to me, listening aged ten, that the reason why they needed to have their own language was because they needed to hide what they were up to. All I knew was that it was brilliantly funny.

Williams would say, 'Ooh, Mr Horne, how lovely to vada your old eek again,' and a whole generation of schoolboys learned how to do a poofy voice.

Nowadays, coming out (for middle-class people at least) is not far removed from a kind of Bar Mitzvah, a rite of passage: a bit cringey, but not much more than that. The parents are relieved that it's over with, friends smile and say, 'We Know!' There might even be a party. Pretty much everybody knows what to do. But the practice of homosexuality was illegal until 1967; and gay liberation wasn't really born until the 1969 Stonewall Riots in New York. No one 'came out' before 1967, apart from a tiny minority of courageous men and women. To have someone come out *to* you is now regarded as a great honour, and a sign of trust and friendship. We know that now. But I didn't, when, in 1973, my close friend H 'came out' to me. We were working at the time, stacking shelves at our local supermarket. We were in the warehouse at the back of the shop. He told me he was in love with the butchery assistant, whose name was John, twenty-seven, and married. We were fifteen. I was stunned, though perhaps I shouldn't have been, in retrospect, since H and I loved camping it up, and even had a camp comedy act which we performed at school shows. Only I was impersonating Julian and Sandy, whilst H was living the dream, getting wanked off by men up Newhaven Fort.

I can't really remember what I said. I was dumbstruck, I know that. I'm like Prince in this regard, as in no other; women and girls rule my

world. The whole existence of fifteen-year-old boys was founded on the
desire to get inside girls' bras, or so I had imagined. H made me promise
not to tell anybody, so I told pretty much the first person I met. And
pretty much everybody at school. Stayed with me, it has. I apologised
to H a year or so back, and he was as gracious as I had been dunder-
headed. Times have changed, and not always for the worse.

'An Acte for the punishment of the vice of Buggerie' was promoted
in Parliament by Thomas Cromwell in 1553. Up until that time, homosexuality had been tried in the ecclesiastical courts, but the courts lost
their power under the Henrician Reformation, and so morality was
brought under the control of the state, where it largely still resides.
Buggery was a hanging offence till 1861.

Fellatio between men, however, was not a crime until 1885, when
under the Criminal Law Amendment Act, gross indecency became an
offence. Since the punishments under the buggery laws were so harsh,
and so difficult to prove, gross indecency, easier to prove and with less
dire consequences, resulted in a lot more prosecutions. It was this that
did for Oscar Wilde in 1895 and Alan Turing in 1952. Wilde was sentenced
to two years hard labour, Turing to a cruel course of synthetic oestrogen,
which killed his libido and made him grow tits. He killed himself two
years later, by eating an apple laced with cyanide. Well-known gadget
salesman Steve Jobs thought this so hilarious that he used an apple with
a bite out of it as the logo for his products: doubly annoying since his
machines are not computers in the sense that Turing envisioned.

And so a culture of furtive secrecy grew up. If you weren't lucky
enough to be in Soho, what did you do? Allan Horsfall of the North
West Committee for Homosexual Law Reform, remembered: 'The story
goes ... of someone who went to work in a strange town and didn't
know where the gay community was. So he went into a pub and said,
"I've only been here two days – the first pub I went in was full of nancy
boys. I can't quite remember the name of it," and two or three people
turned round and said, "Oh, you mean the Rose and Crown." So he
drank up and went down the Rose and Crown, and that was the way
people found their way around in those days.'

In the mid-1950s, there was something of a witch-hunt against gay
people, with consequent opportunities for blackmail. Leo Abse, who
would eventually guide the Sexual Law Reform Act through Parliament,
recalled that, as a lawyer in Cardiff, his fees from criminals suddenly all
started coming from the account of one man. He investigated and found
he was 'a poor vicar. The bastards were bleeding him. I sent for one of

the criminals and told him if I had another cheque from this man, I'd get him sent down for ten years. I sent for the vicar and told him to come to me if they approached him again.'

The Lord Chancellor, Lord Kilmuir, led the opposition to law reform in the Lords, which was ironic, since he started the process when, before his ennoblement, he was Home Secretary, as plain old Rt. Hon. Sir David Maxwell Fyfe. He thought that by handing the issue over to a committee of the great and the good he could shelve it. He set up the Wolfenden Committee to examine the law around homosexuality and prostitution in 1954, just before he got kicked upstairs into the Lords. John Wolfenden was an educator, who had been headmaster of Uppingham. Perhaps Maxwell-Fyfe assumed Wolfenden would find against, in which case, he chose a curious chairman, because Wolfenden had a gay son, Jeremy. When Wolfenden accepted the job, he wrote to Jeremy saying it would be better if he wasn't seen around him too often in lipstick and make-up.

Wolfenden, not wanting to embarrass the ladies, especially the lady stenographers who had to type the thing up, called Homosexuality and Prostitution after the biscuit manufacturers, Huntley and Palmers: Huntleys for gay people, and Palmers for sex workers. The committee published its report in 1957, recommending that 'homosexual behaviour between consenting adults in private should no longer be an offence'. Geoffrey Fisher, the Archbishop of Canterbury, agreed; so did the British Medical Association, the Howard League for Penal Reform and the National Association of Probation Officers, who would have been aware that at the time of the report, over a thousand men were still serving time in British jails for homosexual offences. The Tory government threw up its hands in horror, and it was another ten years until decriminalisation took place in England and Wales, whilst homosexuality remained a criminal offence in Scotland until 1980.

It took a Private Members' bill under the socially liberal Labour Government of Harold Wilson to get it through Parliament. It was a real struggle, despite strong support from the Home Secretary, Roy Jenkins, who fought for the issue in Cabinet, and made sure that there was enough Parliamentary time to pass the bill.

At 5.50 a.m. on 5 July 1967, the Sexual Offences Bill, which decriminalised homosexuality, limped through its final stages in the House of Commons. Leo Abse needed a quorum of 100 MPs to get the final reading through; in the end, he got 101. Pity was one of the key themes of the reformers, pity for men with no chance of a wife and family, who should be treated with Christian compassion; the Act hardly stands as a great liberalising document. Same-sex relations were only legal between adults over twenty-one. It was also legal only in private. Gay rights activist and great human being Peter Tatchell says that this was interpreted as being 'behind locked doors and windows and with no other person present on the premises'. No one was going to be throwing coming-out parties.

Peter Tatchell also wrote that 'the tone of the parliamentary debate alternated between vicious homophobia on one side and patronising, apologetic tolerance on the other', which may well be the case. But that patronising tolerance was a start. Life did get a lot easier for gay men. People did start coming out, however slowly; H's courage in coming out to me in 1973, just six years after legalisation, has only really become evident to me over the years. Things did start to change; better patronising tolerance than homophobic hostility. Leo Abse was a great man, who played a major part in liberalising divorce and abortion laws in this country, as well as piloting the Sexual Offences Bill through the House, and he deserves to be remembered for his role, even if he had to utilise pity to force it through.

And yet, however much of a watershed the Act was, it took a very long time until full equal rights were granted to gay men (there had never been legislation about the behaviour of gay women, because no one could really believe that lesbianism existed). As late as 1989, 2,000 men were convicted of gross indecency.

'Anyway, buggering me was a move the geezer probably regretted afterwards, as at the time I had appalling scabies. I didn't know what scabies were, but I certainly had them. Someone said I had really bad scabies and I said, "What do I do about that?" And I learned you could go to the Holborn Cleansing Centre, which was a municipal place that was just for dealing with such things, and it mainly consisted of a row of good old solid Victorian baths, filled with what seemed like boiling water, you would get in and be given what looked like an old-fashioned floor-type scrubbing brush, and this geezer who's running it told us to scrub ourselves, and it's really boiling water, you could only just bear it. And there's me and Ken Shelton, we've both gone because we're both travelling round, sleeping in the same bomb sites, and so we both get out of this bath and we're both pink and naked and scabs bleeding all over, and this geezer has us stand on a rubber sheet, and he has a big distemper brush and a big bucket of this white paste, I forget now what it was called, something like Scabiestopol, and he starts painting us all over, from the chin down. And it's like being dipped in a bowl of fucking acid. Anyway, then he starts getting to the genital area, and he starts basically wanking us with this slippery creamy stuff, but when he starts ramming two fingers up one's arsehole one thinks this isn't good … And we just flee the place, covered in this stuff …. Nowadays you'd have the geezer hung …. no, we just got the fuck out and ran, putting our clothes on as we went …. Those were the days, eh? …'

'So did you and your pals start to go indoors at round about the same time? After you got back from Liverpool?'

'Yeah, people would start disappearing, and then you'd meet people on the scene who, most of them, were living in accommodation, flats, houses, rooms. You'd meet someone who was looking for another person to share a big flat somewhere – West Hampstead ours was – and you'd raise the necessary three quid or whatever it was. Those were the days when you could find a place for literally a few pounds.'

'Because it was still a bit of a bomb site, London, wasn't it? So people let out unregulated places, shit holes.'

'Yeah, but if you went indoors, you could start looking a bit sharper.'

'Of course. Why else would you want to live indoors, other than to look sharp? But it's starting to matter?'

'Yeah, at Ken Colyer's club everyone was trying to look as beatnik-y as possible. *We* were just looking like that because we had no option, those were our clothes, but the suburban kids who'd come in, they'd wear big jumpers and sandals, but it's not what they wore at any other time, they'd go to the office in suits. But on the modern jazz side of things it was definitely a bit more chic, still not trying to look straight but a bit cool and a bit smart, a bit different, a bit sharp.'

'And you liked that?'

'Yeah, very much so. And the mod scene was already under way, and I had my foot in the door of that, because some of the criminal lads, the thieves, were mod types. Some of the earliest mods were criminals, basically.'

'Criminals who started worrying about what they were wearing …'

'Who got into fashion, yeah, and were trying to outdo the others with what they were wearing. Someone would go to a theatrical costumiers and find a Scottish piper's jacket with a nice little rounded cutaway thing and turn up at the Lyceum wearing that, then they'd all go down to Sam Arkus the tailor and see if he can make them a jacket like that. Sam Arkus [whose shop still exists in Soho's Berwick Street], the majority of his clients were theatrical types, I think he was a tailor to the theatre, almost Savile Row but more approachable. He had a wider more catholic taste, and was prepared to make what people wanted.'

'So when did your own criminal career get going?' I ask. 'Did you arrive in London and start burgling?'

'No I'd been burgling since I was a kid. Not for gain but more for adventure. Near to Mytchett Lake, only a couple of miles from where I lived, there was a big old house, I suspect a late Georgian sort of manor house, in parkland and pasture. Anyway, I crept round that house, found a basement window open, went in there and there's a notice inside the place: "In this building Rudolf Hess was held as a prisoner." That was Mytchett Place. I broke into there.'

'He couldn't break out, but you broke in?'

'Yeah. And I'd actually got up in court for breaking into another house near the Basingstoke Canal, this time a big old Victorian house, but again it was empty. There were a couple of little wooden shields with a metal steel painted device, some college coat of arms, of no value at all. But the little kid in me liked it because it was shield shaped, it was the only thing in the place, so I just took them. And then someone reported us because we had them – "Where did you get that from?" – the Old Bill turned up and I'm in court over it.'

'That was your first time in court? How old were you?'

'I don't know, I had short trousers on but I had short trousers on until I was fourteen, so … maybe ten, eleven, twelve? But the worst thing, the one that had the greatest effect on the most people, was I burned down fucking hundreds of acres of Army land, just for the hell of it, and to hear the bombs and bullets go off, because there were lots of bombs and bullets scattered over the place. I think that was the worst crime of my childhood ….'

'But you didn't go to London to be a crim, did you?'

'Oh no, it was just circumstances that drove me to it, because you've got no money, you're hungry, and there's a little opportunity …'

'And you had some skills at getting in and out of places?'

'Well, yeah, I was an agile youth – climbing and jumping and that was second nature to me. It was just like I said, if you're hungry and you see the opportunity to get the value of a meal or two, then you take it. But I did start burgling when I became more settled in London and started living in shared flats and low-budget accommodation.'

'So from living on the street, now you've got a room in a flat. And Long John Baldry lived in this flat, too?'

'Yeah, and Roger the Prof, and a bloke called Angus Dudgeon, whose mum owned it.'

'Gus Dudgeon?'

'Yeah, why?'

'Elton John's producer? The bloke who produced "Space Oddity", Gus Dudgeon?'

'Really? Good on him. I knew he worked in a studio.'

'This is why you need me to write your story. You still don't know how cool you are.'

'Yeah, I do.'

'But you had to pay Gus Dudgeon's mum some rent, and pay bills and shit.'

'Yeah, I needed an income, so I did get more into crime as a means of revenue, rather than just to satisfy the immediate hunger. That is true. Because all around you there's criminals, most people on the Soho scene are some sort of criminal, so because you're a thief you're certainly not excluded from the company, because half the people round the table would be as well. And you get into a bit of competition, boys, particularly shoplifter types, would vie for audaciousness – who could do the most audacious crime, not even to steal, just to do it. But fortunately one learns other skills and moves on.'

'It's quite a jump to make . . .'

'But I made it before I left home, long before. I made that jump before I left fucking junior school. Because it was just part of the adventure, we were always trespassing, either on the Army land, which had "No Admittance" signs, or scrumping. Although we knew it was stealing, it was a sport, as well as a way to get apples and pears and that . . . . So trespassing and entering other people's property was just a way of life, really. So I didn't go to London and be corrupted by it, because I was already almost totally without morals.'

'But also without fear : . . . One of the reasons I didn't steal as a child was cowardice. You never had that, did you?'

'Oh, I had cowardice in all sorts of areas, but certainly not with regard to shoplifting from Woolworths or wherever, as a kid.'

'And sometimes you got caught, mostly you didn't?'

'Mostly I didn't. Very rarely. Never got caught for shoplifting.'

'But somewhere in there, you ended up getting caught and you got sent away?'

'That's true. Three months in a detention centre. A short sharp shock, as the magistrate described it. And I well deserved it – I was a nasty little thief. Well, not nasty . . .'

'A little cunt . . .'

'Yeah. I was a bit. You'd go to parties sometimes more to steal than to party.'

'So what was the one where they said, "You're going down"?'

'I'll tell you. I was living in a flat in Hampstead with a girl called Beatrice, a right bitch, who was Georgie Fame's girlfriend. We didn't really like each other but we lived together because of circumstances; we both needed a flat and there was a two-bed, kitchenette, bedsitting-y sort of place there, just 50 yards down the road from Gus Dudgeon's mum's place, so we got it. She was shagging Ronan O'Rahilly at the same time. You've heard of him?'

'Yes. You knew Ronan O'Rahilly?'

'Of course. I shared a flat with his fucking girlfriend. He and Clive shared Beatrice.' (Clive Powell, aka legendary singer and R&B Hammond organ genius, Georgie Fame.) 'They took it in turns to come round. A bit awkward, cos Ronan was Clive's manager. Irish aristocracy sort of thing, really cool guy. One of the schemes he used to talk about was projecting films onto clouds using lasers.'

The idea of projecting films onto clouds using lasers is only slightly more implausible than the actual scheme that O'Rahilly came up with, pulled off, and spent his life promoting: Radio Caroline, the first and greatest of the 'pirate' radio stations.

Astute readers will have noticed that when the young Freaks were hiding under their bedclothes listening to 'Heartbreak Hotel', they were listening to it on Radio Luxembourg, and not on the BBC. From 1948 until 1967, BBC Radio had only three stations: the Home Service, the Light Programme and the Third Programme. Commercial radio was illegal. Before the Second World War, there were a few stations on the Continent broadcasting English-language programmes via huge transmitters to the UK, but by the early fifties only the first and most powerful, Radio Luxembourg, was still transmitting. (It transmitted until 1992. I can remember tuning into all-night Radio Luxembourg 208 when I worked at a twenty-four-hour garage on Newhaven docks, and, in 1977, hearing for the first time of the death of Elvis Presley; which seems appropriate, as though it gives closure to Elvis's story.) The BBC's Light Programme was still playing dance-band tunes and soapy white ballad singers right up until its death, with only a few concessions to contemporary pop music; an honourable exception was *Saturday Club*, presented by Brian Matthew, who sadly died during the writing of this book.

The BBC had published a report in 1960, saying that it saw no need for an all-day music station. O'Rahilly was just one of the people who disagreed, because in 1964 the Local Radio Association was set up to lobby for the establishment of commercial radio in the UK. But Ronan

O'Rahilly was the quickest, the cleverest, the best connected and, quite frankly, the most piratical of all those who thought there was a place for all-day music radio, paid for by advertising.

First, he pirated the idea. A ship would be moored in international waters, just over five miles from the British coast, fitted with powerful transmitters, and play music and adverts all day. A similar idea had been in operation as Radio Nord off the coast of Sweden since the 1950s, and as Radio Veronica off the coast of the Netherlands since 1960. Australian music publisher Allan Crawford had been drawing up plans for a British equivalent for several years. His plans included detailed technical specifications. And by 1963, he had a ship: the *Mi Amigo*, bought from Radio Nord. O'Rahilly was keen to promote the acts he was managing, acts like Georgie Fame and Alexis Korner, and thought access to a radio station would be a great way to go about that. At a meeting with O'Rahilly in early 1963, Crawford handed over his plans, including the technical specs, because O'Rahilly had a thing that Crawford didn't: a port. Greenore, in County Louth, a third of the way up Carlingford Lough, faces Northern Ireland's Mountains of Mourne from the Irish side of the border, and until 1953, had been a port for ferries from Holyhead. It just happened to be owned by O'Rahilly's father. O'Rahilly arranged with Crawford that the *Mi Amigo* should be fitted out at Greenore. And then he started raising money to buy and fit out a ship of his own. Within a few weeks, O'Rahilly raised £250,000 from friends of friends; Crawford had struggled for a year to raise the finance. By the time Crawford got the *Mi Amigo* to Greenore in March 1964, the former Danish ferry *Fredericia* was already undergoing fitting out as a radio ship.

O'Rahilly tried to persuade Crawford to 'merge' with Radio Caroline, which, under pressure from the financial backers, Crawford pretty much had no choice but to agree to. O'Rahilly's fitters, seeing how well sorted the *Mi Amigo* was, pirated it for equipment. The *Fredericia* was ready first; the *Mi Amigo* joined it in the North Sea five miles off Harwich, where it started broadcasting as Radio Atlanta for a few months until it became Radio Caroline South, while the *Fredericia* headed for a mooring off the Isle of Man, and became Radio Caroline North. And Crawford was out of the picture.

Because Ronan O'Rahilly, the king of pirates, had pretty much nicked his ship, too.

On 29 March 1964, Caroline started broadcasting. It was a stunning success. Estimates vary as to the size of the listenership. The highest estimate is that up to fifteen million people a week listened to the two

Caroline stations. This success prompted imitators: Radio London, Radio England, Radio Jackie, Radio 390, Britain Radio. More accurate figures came from a 1966 National Opinion Polls survey. Both Luxembourg and Caroline attracted almost nine million listeners a week; Radio London was not far behind. Even the more obscure stations, like Radio 390 and Radio England were attracting listenerships of over two million a week.

They played pop music all day. The shape of British pop radio was determined on the pirate ships. Caroline DJs included Johnny Walker, Tony Blackburn, Simon Dee, Tony Prince, Dave Lee Travis and Emperor Rosko. Radio London ('Wonderful Radio London') had Ed Stewart, Kenny Everett and John Peel. Radio London was my mum's station of choice; we only listened to the Light Programme on Sundays when my father was home, with its schedule of shows that still fills me with horror: *Two-Way Family Favourites, Sing Something Simple*. Radio London in particular had a special relationship with the Beatles, and played a nightly series of interviews during the Fabs' last tour of the USA in 1966. London was the first radio station in the world to play *Sgt Pepper* in its entirety, on 12 May 1967, a few weeks before the official release.

Governments don't like pirates, and so the Wilson government acted to end pirate radio's brief reign. In 1967, at midnight on 14 August, the Marine Broadcasting Offences Act came into force, which made illegal the supply of music, advertising, fuel, supplies and water to any of the pirate ships or the offshore wartime forts that some of the stations also used. All of the stations went off air, except Caroline. Six weeks later, BBC Radio took on the shape we recognise today. The Home Service became Radio Four, the Third Programme Radio Three, and the Light Programme Radio Two. And they launched an entirely new service, Radio One. At 7 a.m. on Saturday 30 September 1967, ex-Caroline DJ Tony Blackburn launched the new service by playing 'Flowers in the Rain' by The Move. So pop radio in the UK was changed for ever by the guy who wanted to project films onto clouds using lasers.

And the station he founded has never quite gone away. After the *Mi Amigo* finally sank in 1980, O'Rahilly found a new ship, the *Ross Revenge*, which restarted broadcasting in 1983. And, ahem, if you'll forgive me, it was this version that described my then band, The National Game, as 'the best unsigned band in Britain'. As I've joked with my fellow members over the years, better to be the *best unsigned* band than an indifferent signed one. They never so much as smile. But, as you might imagine, ever since, I've regarded the Caroline DJs as discerning types. The *Ross Revenge* is still with us as a radio ship, maintained by volunteers and moored at Tilbury; Caroline have occasional use of it, under a restricted licence; and the BBC have used it too. And Caroline is still an internet radio station, and still innovating, technically, if not musically; I've just turned it on, and they're paying ELP's 'Fanfare for the Common Man', the extended version; a shame, but there it is. Google them; or you can find the link to Radio Caroline in the Appendix at the back of the book.

'Whatever,' says Bob. 'Anyway, there I was in this flat with Beatrice, and I needed some dosh, so I just emptied the gas meter on the landing, and the next-door neighbour's as well. Just finishing doing that when the next-door neighbour opens his door. So I went back into my flat. Then there's a banging on the door, and I looked round the corner, because I could see down the stairs, and it's the police. Some of them were already there with the neighbour, he's obviously phoned the police and he's letting them in. So I leg it. The only way out was the front door, so I keep going up the building, a five-storey Victorian place on West End Lane, next to the railway line. I get to the top floor, can't hear any boots coming up above my level, they've obviously gone into the flat where I've been living. I keep very quiet on the top-floor landing. Then the one door on the top landing opens, an old boy comes out, he's obviously seen something from the window because he shouts, "He's here, he's here!" I think, "Oh, fuck." There's boom boom boom up the stairs. And there's a window there, which I can only just reach because of the geometry of the place. I manage to open it. And my only option is to jump blindly through it. I think the buildings are still there, if you're ever driving down West End Lane in West Hampstead, where the railway bridge is, not the tube but the main suburban line; have a look at the building, I just jumped out of the top floor of that building because I didn't want to be caught by the police.'

'You jumped?'

'Blindly, not being able to see what's out there first .... Anyway, what was out there happened to be, fortunately, a one-storey tin shed that the greengrocer on the ground floor used as a storage place. And it had a corrugated asbestos roof, which both of my feet and my entire legs went through. So I had roof up to my bollocks, and a copper looking out of the window, and obviously not going to jump out after me. So I pull myself out of the roof, jump off and over the wall, and you're over it to the railway line, but it's a multi-railway line, it's not just one track, it's a whole load of tracks and a railway yard. Anyway, so I ran across the tracks, through the railway yard a bit and then I just lifted a tarp that was covering fuck knows what, and got under the tarp and just lay down there for an hour, because I knew they would be buzzing around the streets trying to find me, but if I just cooled it for an hour then they would have gone off on something else. So that's what I did. Then I met up with my mate that I was doing a bit of burglary with and we decided – because we couldn't stay in London – to do a burglary tour of the south coast.'

'The hotel in Bournemouth, was that the same tour? Where you're hanging on the balcony? You told me about that years ago.'

'Oh, I forgot about that, yeah ... We'd climbed up the decorative brickwork at the back of this hotel in Bournemouth, quite a posh hotel. And our plan was to get up to the balcony, break in through the French windows, get into the rooms, and plunder and loot. Anyway, this is all going well, we've just got to the French windows on the balcony, we're just about to force them open, and the door into the room from the hotel hall opens, the light goes on, and it's a couple, who immediately head for the fucking French window which we're the other side of. We haven't time to get down, we've just got time to get over the balcony wall which was substantial concrete pillars, of a sort of baroque shape, with quite a wide stone concrete top to them, more than a foot wide. But there's also a lip, on the floor level of the balcony, on the outside of the balustrade, which has just enough room for us both to lay down on it, edge on. And this couple come out on to the balcony, and they're standing inches away from us, just the other side of these concrete bollards. And they're obviously both married to other people, and they're having a holiday fling, and they're both coming out with such bollocks, such corny lines, you cannot believe .... and me and my mate, it's all we can do not to laugh, we're holding our hands across our mouths and snorting away as silently as we possibly can, listening to these absolutely ridiculous lines both of them are coming out with – we think, "Who's your scriptwriter? Sack 'em." But we didn't nick anything, we just decided to give up after that.'

'You gave up the burglary tour?'

'No, we kept on for a few more days. Got stopped and searched in Exeter, and they found us with two large suitcases full of swag. They locked us in a cell, and went through the stuff, and found a load of letters from Susie Greenwood, who had been writing to me while I was away. And this copper comes in and says, "Why have you got lots of letters from Miss Susan Greenwood?" – daughter, you remember of Arthur Greenwood, the Labour Housing spokesman – and I said, "Cos she's my girlfriend, like". The cop says, "I see." And a couple of hours later we were released without charge. It's not what you know ...'

Anxious to stop Bob from talking in dead metaphors, I chip in.

'Who was your mate, who were you with?'

'A bloke called Paul, a professional East End sort of criminal-class thief, part of the London underworld ...'

'Because you met that world of organised crime a bit, didn't you? there's that story about seeing Taffy stabbing one of the Krays ...'

Bob seems uncomfortable. 'Are you sure he's dead?' he says.

'I am. I know very roughly how and when. But he's dead, for sure.'

'Because if Taffy is alive, he might be displeased if you use his name.'

'He isn't alive. Anyway, there are lots of Taffys.'

'Not like Taffy, there aren't.'

'He's got to make a first appearance somewhere. Here is where he appears.'

Bob sighs, and lights his fag.

'Where you did you first see him? The Flamingo, wasn't it?'

'Yes, except it was the All-Nighter. It was the same premises, but after midnight it was taken over by different management, Rik Gunnell and his brother. The Flamingo was a teenybopper, disco sort of place, whereas the All-Nighter was much cooler. I had a job in the All-Nighter, which was down the lower part of Wardour Street, the Leicester Square end of Wardour Street over by Shaftesbury Avenue. I was collecting bottles and glasses. You wouldn't have been seen dead in there before midnight, but after midnight it was a very cool place to go. Mainly black American servicemen, that was at least half the clientele, they'd come for the music. Georgie Fame was the resident band, and Alan Price – I think he'd started playing with Georgie Fame – and Cyril Davies ... good R&B music. This was when I was sharing the flat with Georgie Fame's horrible girlfriend. And that was where I first saw Taffy. My job was, any empty bottles, just pick them up and lose them outside. So I was just going out to do that, and this strange-looking geezer, looking very wild and extremely urgent, came down the steps I was going up. And I was very surprised to see that the management on the door parted for him like the waves before Moses. I didn't know who the fuck he was or why he was looking so urgent, but he did, and the people on the door – and they're quite heavy, serious people on the door – obviously recognised his urgency and made no effort to stop him. Then they let him go, and he'd just stabbed Joey King up the arse. Joey King was a really horrible villain, he would do you over, slash your face, he was the Krays' heavy, to give you an idea of how horrible he was. That takes some bottle, to shove a knife up the arse of the Krays' heavy. And years later I met Taffy, and we travelled together for a few years after that. Because if you wanted adventure, he was the fella to travel with, Christ, non-stop ...'

'So that's your first memory of Taffy. In that sort of world. You're talking about the East London gangs and that. Were you starting to edge into those Richardson-y, Kray-y circles? ... Was that about?'

'Oh, it was certainly about, and I was certainly aware of all these people, but because I was big, they were just the sort of people I would stay very, very, very well clear of. Because I was just the sort of person that they would use as a demonstration. I'm serious. Like, I wouldn't go to their club, because I knew they'd deliberately pick a fight with someone like me, zero clout but big, they'd just duff you up to show they were hard and tough and mean and nasty, and here was an example of it. Well, I didn't want to be that example, so I stayed well away from all the places where they were. I was aware of the guy that Taffy stabbed before I even came to London, because 35 miles out of London you'd have heard of Joey King ... mean Maltese bastard from North London. It was never the sort of life I wanted any part of; they were just nasty, fucking people, not what I was looking for. I was looking for nice people; a bit of crime, because it's an adventure and you need to get some income from somewhere, but not being nasty to people with a knife.'

Taffy will be back in a few years' time. The next time he appears, it will be 1969, and an immeasurable amount of water will have passed under innumerable bridges. Bob, emaciated and ill after getting back from Afghanistan, will be running a bike workshop in Knightsbridge, and Taffy will be driving a converted bus which played a part in saving the world from all-out thermonuclear heck.

Throughout our lives, we have moments where we have big choices, and on which whole lives can turn. The next part of Bob's story strikes me as one such: an idyll, a dream of Merrie England – and although Bob disagrees, claiming his ragamuffin nature and positive lust for adventure would never have allowed it to last, I can picture a whole other Bob emerging at this part of the story, in a way which afterwards becomes unimaginable. Bob, after this, is forever himself. But see what you think.

'I'd come back from the tour of the south coast, and was in Kingston upon Thames, because when we were on the burglary tour, my mate's girlfriend turned up with a mate of hers, who I wouldn't have gone out of my way to pull but, as she was there, nature took its course. She seemed to be very keen for some more, and gave me her address and phone number. So I went back to London, thinking the hunt would have died down, and thought I'd check out this girl. I went out to Kingston to see her, and that all went fine. Afterwards, like, I was walking along the Thames, when I came across this exquisite Edwardian boathouse. It's that part of the Thames with the aits, little islands, and lots of boats moored out along what they call the trots, mid-river moorings on a chain with buoys. I thought, 'This looks like a lovely situation here.' I found Mike Turk who owned the place.'

'Turk's Boatyard?'

'The same company has one up by the bridge at Kingston as well.'

'I think it's the one in *Three Men in a Boat*.'

'But I'm on the upstream one, not the one by the bridge. I found Mike Turk, a very affable fellow, asked him, "Have you got a job?" And he said, "Yes, I could do with a boy about the place." So I said, "Have you got anywhere I can sleep?" He found a sail loft for me. I spent a very pleasant summer, hiring out boats, mucking about in boats. I learned to sail. The bloke who taught me to sail was a bloke called Something Holt: can't remember his first name. I knew he had some sort of boat business, but I later found that his family firm, Holt's, were designing and making world-class dinghies, like the Mirror. So it was like having Stirling Moss teach you to drive. And lots of nice girls about too, tasty birds. And we were allowed into all these really posh clubs, like the Leander Club, and the Remington, Leadenham, clubs like that ... It was a fucking great time.'

'So this might have been a whole other life? Working at a boatyard. You might have had an apprenticeship or something.'

'Yeah, it might. It might well. I liked the life. But I don't think I'd have stuck it. Anyway, I didn't have the choice, did I? Your sins will find you out.

'See, I decided I didn't want to see this girl I'd originally turned up to Kingston to shag, as there was a girl hanging round the boatyard, much more the sort of girl I actually fancied, so I sort of dumped that first girl. She rather took the hump to it. Her dad was a copper. There is some truth in "hell has no fury like a woman scorned", she definitely proved that. So I was bringing a boat in, to tie up on the landing stage, and a couple of geezers were waiting there. I thought they wanted to hire a boat. And as I was stepping off the boat they asked, "Are you Robert Rowberry?" And foolishly I said I was; next second they had the handcuffs on my wrist. And I was hauled off, first to the police station, then the magistrates' court.'

'In Kingston?'

'No, in Marylebone, in fact. Because I had done the crime in West Hampstead, and Marylebone was the nearest.'

'And the crime was?'

'Stealing money out of a gas meter and evading arrest. So I spent a couple of weeks in Feltham jail, a proper prison for young offenders, just outside London, before I was sentenced. I was held on remand there.'

'And then when I was sentenced I got three months' detention, in a detention centre, which was extremely rigorous. I mean, by eight o'clock in the morning you would have changed your clothes about four times and done something like an hour of extremely strenuous PT, like bunny hops, squatting then propelling yourself forward, and when you have to do several lengths of a basketball court like that – there were lads my own age falling down and weeping because it hurt so much, but you had to keep on doing it.'

'How old were you?'

'I was nineteen when I went in, and I had my twentieth birthday there.'

'What was it called?'

'Blantyre House, Goudhurst.'

'In Kent?'

'Yeah. And I realised then that me and the criminal classes don't have a lot in common – in fact, we had nothing in common except that we were criminals. I know that sounds like an odd thing to say. But at a place where you were only permitted, I think, a total of one hour in a day where you were allowed to speak, the main topic of conversation – the only topic of conversation – was, "What you're going to do to the niggers when you get out?" And obviously I had no part in this conversation, because all I wanted to do to the niggers when I got out was listen to their music and dance with them. So I thought, "I don't want to go there again; I don't like these people." And of course they were the sort of people who didn't like my type either.'

'And they cut your hair, and all of that.'

'And all of that. And no music and no girls, OK, that wasn't good, but it was the people I was in there with that was by far the worst thing about it. The people you're locked up with. There were a couple that were OK, but mostly not. So I got out of there, in about 1962. I went straight back to West Hampstead, to Gus Dudgeon's flat where Baldry was still living.

'And by coincidence there was another geezer there the same age, and he had also been released the same day, not from a detention centre but from borstal. So we were both absolutely skint, and we both wanted to kick back. So I said, "I know a gaff we can go and burgle at Marble

Arch." It involved going up the stairs, and dodging the hall porter to make sure he didn't see us go by. I only knew this because this mate of mine, that I did the tour with, his girlfriend used to live in a similar place, and sometimes he'd have to climb in, go out of a window on the top floor, which was at least five storeys up, go along the window sills, which weren't right next to each other. You had to step from one to the other (certain death if you fall) and get to the bathroom window, which was never locked: you could just open it and get into the bathroom. I mean, I shit myself – I just couldn't do it now, my legs are turning to water just thinking about it, but I did it then – got into the bathroom and let my mate in through the front door. Billy Crabbe, he was called. And there was fuck all in there – except a tiny little tranny radio, an electric razor, junk like that, nothing of any great value.

'But we nicked it anyway, and went out the front door. And then we heard the lift coming up. And because there's only two flats up there, it's fifty-fifty it's the bloke who's flat we've just burgled. And it's one of those old lifts that's not enclosed, but trellis work, like, an iron trellis, so as we go down the stairs, and the bloke's coming up, he gets a good look at us from the lift. The hall porter is back at his place, and he sees us run out the front, and he shouts, 'Stop,' but we're out the front door and out onto the street; Wigmore Street, I think it was. And there's a bus going by, so we hop on it, and we're away.

'Twenty minutes later, we're walking down Shaftesbury Avenue, and this police car comes cruising slowly past, with this same geezer in it, and he taps this copper on the shoulder, and points at us. And me and Billy both say to one another, "Don't run." So we keep walking, and this geezer looks at us again, and shakes his head, and the car drives on. So that was the last time I did any burgling, because I really didn't want to go back inside. But now I've got no sources of income, and nowhere to go.'

So, what to do? Why not play a small part in one of the most sordid episodes in recent British history, Bob?

Imagine, Younger Readers, that you are driving somewhere with your mum, and she's listening to Radio Two. On comes 'Nothing Has Been Proved' by Dusty Springfield and the Pet Shop Boys. It comes from the soundtrack of the 1989 film *Scandal*, which was about the Profumo Affair. If you listen to the lyrics, you'll hear references to Christine, Mandy, Stephen. Christine is Christine Keeler, Mandy, Mandy Rice-Davies, and Stephen, Stephen Ward. Younger Readers will have seen naked celebrities sitting facing the back of a chair, so that, although you know they are naked, you can't see their bits – a swizz, in my view. If you Google it, you'll see that chairs of this shape and design are now marketed as 'Keeler chairs', though they are based on a chair by Danish designer Arne Jacobsen. Christine was the first to pose this way. Photographer Lewis Morley's image of Christine Keeler wearing that chair has been endlessly reproduced; it's on the poster for the film, of course it is. What else would you choose?

While Stephen Ward was being tried, Catholic commentator Malcolm Muggeridge, married to a member of the aristocracy, wrote a piece about the end of the upper classes in relation to 'Profumo'. Britain was scandalised, not so much by the sex (they enjoyed reading about the sex, which, according to Philip Larkin, was just kicking off at this point), as by the hypocrisy and duplicity of the ruling class.

The affair turned *Private Eye* from a schoolboy rag mag into a serious and, for the ruling classes, increasingly scary organ (*Eyes passim*). Profumo put a rocket under the satire boom and the new wave of British comedy, which launched the careers of Peter Cook and Dudley Moore, Alan Bennett, and Monty Python. It caused the British PM Harold Macmillan to resign, and paved the way for the Labour victory of 1964, Swinging London being unthinkable without Harold Wilson as PM.

'Profumo' was another nail in the coffin of deference, showed the public that police and lawyers and politicians are corruptible, and was a great opening to the Sexy Sixties, part of a triumvirate of events that signified a change in atmosphere: the *Lady Chatterley* trial in 1960, the arrival of the Pill in 1961 and Profumo. After this sex was just going to get sexier.

We'll take a quick trot through the main events, before we can ask Bob about his part in the thing. It's yet another great story that I can't do justice to here, and so here's yet another set of reading recommendations if you'd like to find out more about the case – *An English Affair* by Richard Davenport-Hines is very good, as is *Honeytrap* by Anthony Summers and Stephen Dorril.

John 'Jack' Profumo was the Secretary of State for War (now known as Defence, but still the same nasty business). He was married to Valerie Hobson, the British film actress, best remembered now for her role as the straitlaced Edith D'Ascoyne in *Kind Hearts and Coronets*.

Valerie's glamour did not stop him from playing away from home, and on 8 July 1961, at Cliveden, Lord Astor's house, high above a reach of the Thames, he met the model and dance-club hostess, Christine Keeler. She was there as the guest of her landlord Stephen Ward, along with a Scottish prostitute called Ronna Ricardo. Ward was a portrait painter, but he derived most of his income from osteopathy.

During the war, Ward was posted to India, where he treated Gandhi for headaches and a stiff neck. On his return from India, other clients of Ward included Winston Churchill, Ava Gardner, Lord Astor, Anthony Blunt (the so-called Fourth Man in the Burgess/Maclean/Philby spy scandals); and also the head of MI5, Roger Hollis. Ward was the osteopath of choice for much of 'society', which was why he was invited to spend the weekend up at the big house; at the time, he was renting a cottage in the grounds of Cliveden. He was charming, well-connected, and, it's worth pointing out, quite comfortably off. At his trial, the court heard that his annual income from drawing and osteopathy was somewhere in the region of £5,500, a lot of money in those days. He didn't need to earn pocket money from pimping hard-working girls. He just liked them about the place.

At their first meeting, Keeler was swimming naked, and Profumo provided her with a towel as she got out of the pool. This is the sort of thing that stays with a chap, and Profumo (impressive in Keeler's eyes not because he was a Government minister, but because he was married to a film star) promised to be in touch. Also in the party that weekend was Yevgeny Ivanov, another friend of Ward's, and a naval attaché at the Soviet Embassy. Ward was keeping an eye on him for MI5, because Ivanov had been outed as a KGB agent by Oleg Penkovsky, the Soviet spy who saved the world (as a former head of MI5 pointed out to me over dinner one night).

After that weekend, Ivanov drove Keeler back to Stephen Ward's flat, where she later claimed to have had sex with him, though no one is sure if she was telling the truth. Ronna Ricardo thought Keeler was lying; 'Christine never went to bed with Ivanov. He was really innocent; he'd never seen anything like it.'

Profumo kept his promise to be in touch with Keeler, and they started an affair that lasted a few months; probably until August 1961, when Profumo was interviewed informally by the Cabinet Secretary, who warned him off Stephen Ward's circle of friends. From October 1961 until December 1962, Keeler ran a couple of boyfriends, Lucky Gordon and Johnny Edgecombe, both highly possessive men. In December 1962, Keeler was sharing a flat with her friend and fellow would-be model Mandy Rice-Davies, when Edgecombe appeared and in a jealous rage fired several shots into her front door. This upset Christine, and she started to talk about her affair with Profumo to whoever would listen.

By this time, rumours of the affair had already started to appear in the press; so much so that in January 1963, the Soviets recalled Ivanov to Moscow. Edgecombe was tried for attempted murder, but was found guilty on a lesser charge of possessing a firearm with intent to endanger life, and was sentenced to seven years. A few days after the trial finished, *Private Eye* started publishing accounts of the affair, and Christine sold her story to the *Sunday Pictorial*, though they didn't print it straight away. Profumo was interrogated by the Conservative Chief Whip Martin Redmayne, and was offered the chance to make a denial in the Commons of any wrongdoing in the company of Miss Keeler. This he did, on 22 March. He said, 'I understand that in the debate on the Consolidated Fund Bill last night, under the protection of parliamentary privilege, the Hon. Gentlemen the Member for Dudley [George Wigg] spoke of rumours connecting a Minister with a Miss Keeler and a recent trial at the Central Criminal Court.' (This was not Edgecombe kicking off, but Lucky Gordon, Keeler's other principal beau. Keeler, whom Gordon had attempted to assault, was the chief prosecution witness, but had skipped off to Spain for a few weeks, missing his trial, and upping the temperature still further.) 'It was alleged that people in high places might have been responsible for concealing information concerning the disappearance of a witness and the perversion of justice. I understand that my name has been connected with the rumours about the disappearance of Miss Keeler. I would like to take this opportunity of making a personal statement about these matters. I last saw Miss Keeler in December 1961, and I have not seen her since. I have no idea where she is now. Any suggestion that I was in any way connected with or responsible for her absence from the trial at the Old Bailey is wholly and completely untrue. My wife and I first met Miss Keeler at a house party in July 1961, at Cliveden. Among a number of people there was Dr Stephen Ward whom we already knew slightly, and a Mr Ivanov, who was an attaché at the Russian Embassy … Between July and December, 1961, I met Miss Keeler on about half a dozen occasions at Dr Ward's flat, when I called to see him and his friends. Miss Keeler and I were on friendly terms. There was no impropriety whatsoever in my acquaintanceship with Miss Keeler.'

At first, Christine Keeler and Stephen Ward backed Profumo's position, but due to aggressive police behaviour and increasing press harassment, Ward wrote a letter both to the Home Secretary and to Labour leader Harold Wilson, who was making great political capital out of the affair. Ward wrote:

I have placed before the Home Secretary certain facts of the relationship between Miss Keeler and Mr Profumo since it is obvious now that my efforts to conceal these facts in the interests of Mr Profumo and the Government have made it appear that I myself have something to hide – which I have not. The result has been that I have been persecuted in a variety of ways, causing damage not only to myself but to my friends and patients – a state of affairs which I propose to tolerate no longer.

And Christine was willing to sell her story to anyone who would buy it.

On 5 June, Profumo resigned after a series of accusations by Keeler and Ward, and was forced to admit to the truth of the affair. The Establishment was angry at the fall of one of their own, and somebody had to pay. Stephen Ward was their fall guy. Two days after Profumo's resignation, Ward was arrested and charged with living off the immoral earnings of Keeler, Mandy Rice-Davies, and 'two other prostitutes', Vickie Barrett and Ronna Ricardo.

Enter Bob.

'Back when I was living on the streets of London among the people who are living rough on the streets, in the few coffee bars where they have the music and where long-haired beatnik-y types would be allowed in, there were a couple of blokes about called Eric – Eric Clapton was one and the other one, he was always just known as Long-haired Eric. Anyway, he was an artist at St Martin's, where he mainly drew Nazis; and a girl joined him, and I think she was only thirteen at the time, called Gwen. Donovan was also matey with her. Some time later, after the detention centre, I met up with Gwen. I had just come out of nick, so I'd just turned twenty, and I bumped into Gwen, and this is at the time when all that Profumo thing was happening. And Gwen said, "What are you doing?" And I said I'd just done this thing, climbing up the brickwork five storeys up and we nearly got caught.

'I didn't want to go straight back inside. And Gwen said, "My sister is Ronna Ricardo."

'I knew I'd heard the name before, in the news – she was one of the mates who was a witness in the Christine Keeler / Mandy Rice-Davis thing. Now Gwen, who was living with her sister in a flat in Queensway, says, "She wants a biggish bloke around, because she's getting a lot of hassle from reporters and weirdos, so she just wants a bloke in the house that she feels OK with and is quite big and handy." And I had a little .22 pistol at the time as well, which is relevant. So that's what I did. Ronnie was a dominatrix, mostly, but I didn't really see any of that; I was just about, to lend an air of thuggery and menace if anybody stepped out of line.

There were lots of journos and weirdos about, so Ronnie was just pleased to have me there. Anyway, we're in London, in Ronnie's flat, and there's a knock on the door. I looked down, but someone else had already got halfway down the stairs, and I see top brass uniforms at the door – not ordinary coppers. So this top brass uniformed cop and a geezer in civvies came up the stairs. And because I'd got this little pistol, I thought, "I don't want these coppers seeing me and asking me any questions or who I am or anything." So I hid behind the sofa. I was thinking they'd probably go into the kitchen and have a cup of tea or something, but no, they came into the room where the sofa was. And basically told Ronnie that unless she said what they told her to say, which was, in fact, perjury, they would fucking take her children away. That shocked me, too.'

Margaret 'Ronna' Ricardo was a Scottish prostitute; one of the few actual prostitutes who were involved in the case. She was interviewed a total of nine times by the police.

Ronna was not a great fan of the police. During one interrogation, she lifted her skirt and pulled down her pants to reveal, written in large letters on her stomach, the words ALL COPPERS ARE BASTARDS.

The top-brass policeman Bob hid from behind the sofa was almost certainly Chief Inspector Samuel Herbert, who was alleged to be a client of Ronna's. As she later recounted, she was threatened by having her child removed from her (and also Gwen, who was under-age, and living as Ronna's ward). How many times she was threatened, I don't know; but certainly Bob was witness to one such occasion.

On 5 April, Ronna testified at Marylebone Magistrates' Court that Ward had told her that it would be 'worth her while' to come to Cliveden, and that she had subsequently slept with a US airman, 'Silky' Hawkins in Ward's flat for £25, and that she had given Ward some of the money.

At this point, Ronna, her baby, Gwen and Bob were taken to a 'safe house' in the country by *Express* journalist Tom Mangold; Bob can't remember where the safe house was. After being interviewed extensively by Mangold, Ronna changed her story. She had cried on Mangold's shoulder and told him, 'I've fitted up Stephen.'

So she went back to the police, on 20 July, two days before Ward's trial was due to start, and made a new statement:

I have come here this evening to make a statement about the Ward case. I want to say that most of the evidence I gave at Marylebone Court was untrue. I want to say I never met a man in Stephen Ward's flat except my friend 'Silky' Hawkins. He is the only man I have ever had intercourse with in Ward's flat. It is true that I never paid Ward any money received from men with whom I have had intercourse. I have only been in Ward's flat once and that was with 'Silky'. Ward was there and Michelle. The statements which I have made to the police were untrue. I made them because I did not want my young sister to go to a remand home or my baby taken away from me. Mr Herbert told me they would take my sister away and take my baby if I didn't make the statements.

Two days later, Stephen Ward's trial at the Old Bailey began. In the witness box, Ronna stuck to her new story, the true story, despite a blistering cross-examination by the prosecution counsel, Mervyn Griffith-Jones. She told the court:

> The statements which I have made to the police were untrue. I made them because I did not want my young sister to go to a re-mand home or my baby taken away from me. Mr Herbert told me they would take my sister away and take my baby if I didn't make the statements.

Stephen Ward was found guilty in absentia of living off the immoral earnings of Christine Keeler and Mandy Rice-Davies, but was acquitted of taking money from Ronna and Vickie Barrett. In absentia, because on the last night of the trial Ward attempted to kill himself with an overdose of sleeping tablets, and he died five days later. In *Honeytrap*, Anthony Summers and Steven Dorril claim that Ward was murdered by the security services.

Ward left suicide notes addressed to Tom Mangold, Ronna Ricardo, Vickie Barrett (who had testified against him), James Burge (his defence lawyer) and Lord Denning, who had already been commissioned to run an inquiry on Ward's links to MI5. I have been unable to track down what Ward said to Ronna in his note, but we can perhaps guess from what he wrote to Vickie Barret: 'I don't know what it was or who it was that made you do what you did. But if you have any decency left, you should tell the truth like Ronna Ricardo. You owe this not to me, but to everyone who may be treated like you or like me in the future.'

Whatever else can be said about the labyrinthine mess of 'Profumo', it was a great time for liars. Everyone lied – the police, the politicians, the judges, the lawyers, the press, Keeler, Mandy Rice-Davies, everyone. Only Ronna Ricardo, the prostitute, told the truth.

The Profumo Affair and its ramifications continue to fascinate writers, dramatists and composers. New books are published every couple of years. *Stephen Ward – The Musical* by Andrew Lloyd Webber premièred in 2013 – and a few years back, in 2015, in my local church, two minutes' walk away, during the Presteigne Music Festival, an opera called *That Man Stephen Ward*, by Thomas Hyde and David Norris, was performed.

Still prefer Dusty and the Pet Shop Boys, m'self.

'And immediately after that episode, I went up to Nottingham,' says Bob.

'But why? Why Nottingham?'

'The reason I went to Nottingham was a newspaper I read in the nick, saying there was an extraordinary amount of females in Nottingham, something like 5 to 1. It seemed like a good reason to check it out.'

'It's an urban myth, still running. Nottingham University was always supposed to have five times more female than male students. That's why blokes want to go there. I've always assumed, therefore, that there are more men than women in Nottingham, because girls don't want to go there, because of the lack of blokes, whilst men are drawn in their thousands by the mythical glut of girls.'

Bob pulls a little moue.

'Also my mum had moved up there, and I'd never been to the place. The only other town I knew was Liverpool, and it had memories of totally penniless existence and running from the law, so I didn't fancy an action replay on that one. All the contacts I had in Liverpool were the dodgy gutter-snipes, so I thought, "Well, I'll go and have a look at Mother." Mother had moved to a real black-and-white northern-town cobbled street, Crown Street, just by Stenton market, a tiny little Victorian terrace. I liked it, the house; but I did get my own place, a rented room, like. And then I met this girl, we fancied each other, nature took its course, and a mate of hers told me she was very well off … married, but an heiress.'

'I think it's so interesting that you were in Nottingham at the time when everyone in Britain knew what Nottingham looked like.'

'How come?'

'*Saturday Night, Sunday Morning*. The film is set in Nottingham, that's why everyone knows what it looks like. It reinforced that national image of the North … smoky chimneys, black and white – you were in that black-and-white world, at the moment when parts of Britain are on the cusp of going colour. And, in terms of the story – Nottingham is about D.H. Lawrence. He's from Nottingham, and he fell in love with a married woman, a very rich German baroness, whom he met when her husband was teaching. He was teaching the millions of girls at Nottingham University College. So you kind of lived that Lawrence dream, in Nottingham …'

'I was totally unaware of the parallel.'

'But that's what's interesting; we're all unaware of what history is up to. It's not till years later, often, that we go, "Oh yeah, that's what was happening." But with you, it's the Lawrentian dream, but it's also 1963 – between the *Lady Chatterley* trial and the Beatles' first LP – sexual intercourse has started, and there you are, between Nottingham and Liverpool.'

'It started years before that for me.'

'It's a poem. By Philip Larkin.'

'Has anyone ever told you you look like Philip Larkin?'

'Yes Bob, they have. And sometimes I feel like him. My childhood was a forgotten boredom, too.'

I move on.

'But, Bob, you must have missed London, and the rapscallion life?'

'Yeah, I did. But I wasn't gone all that long – nine months, maybe? And when I went back, I went back with the secret ingredient.'

'What's that, my friend?'

Bob smiles.

'Money.'

We Stuck our Fingers into it like it was a Sherbet Fucking Dip

I haven't been up to see Bob for a while. A lot has been going on. Chas
has died, and for most of the summer, I've been shuttling between
Presteigne and Lancaster, to do my best to be part of his care team. Chas
died of oesophageal cancer at the beginning of September, which gave
rise to more shuttling, as I'd been doing what I could to represent his
interests.

He died a hippie death, out of his nut on morphine, surrounded by
chatty stoners theorising about stuff, in a hippie house in the port village
of Glasson Dock, a few miles south of Lancaster on the Lune Estuary.
We held a hippie funeral, with a mini-festival by way of a wake, in a
hippie-owned new-planted wood high on the Tatham Fells above
Bentham. We buried him in the same place in a cardboard coffin painted
by his great friend Panit Dave. I ran the service. A hippie service, with
words from the Bhagavad Gita and the Upanishads, a prayer from the
Quaker William Penn, and a rewritten extract from The Book of Common
Prayer …' 'ashes to ashes, dust to dust', all that. Chas, like so many in
the hippie culture of which he was such a proud member, was something
of a spiritual magpie.

Back at last in the Marches of Wales, the weather has turned. It is
Fireworks Night, when any good Sussex man longs to be in Lewes. Low
mist has lain over Radnorshire like a mildewing duvet for about a week.
My spirits have been depressed by the mockery of grief and mourning
and the commodification of the unknown and the unknowable that is
Hallowe'en, followed immediately by the grandstanding of impersonal
nationalistic grief that is Remembrance. I feel under pressure to wear a
poppy, and, although I usually do wear one, this year it feels as though
we're all under heavy manners, as though not wearing a poppy says that
you don't care. A visit to Bob might lift my mood.

The old railway line is buried under leaves, which patter on the windscreen as they come down. It has been wet for a week, and raining all
day, and the mud is gaining a hold on the potholed trackbed. There is
smoke rising from the old bus's chimney, and the afternoon light is
already starting to dim. Bob is drowsy, but happy to see me.

'The other day,' he says as I arrive, 'I was in town, and my whole fucking body hurt. I didn't have much work on. The weather's shit. So I thought I'd take an opium holiday.'

He puts the coffee percolator on, while I skin up.

'What sort?' I ask. Bob is a cautious opiate user; cautious because he understands so well its dangers. If a little bit of gear comes his way from time to time, well and good. If not, that's OK too. You've got to be careful with it, very much so, and Bob is, though it's not easy stuff to be careful with. Opiates are a bit like Pringles – once you start, you can't stop. Except with opiates, when you do stop, you feel like shit, but when the Pringles run out you feel remorseful and ashamed, and glad they've gone. Also, the direct link between death and Pringles has yet to be established, whilst the link between death and opiates is like that between power and corruption.

'Poppy-head tea,' says Bob. 'A remedy for bone-ache. It tastes fucking horrible, but it's just the job at this time of the year. Stops me feeling the fucking arthritis.'

'Does it make you throw up, like smack does?'

Bob smiles. 'No. But it does make you sweat. To an outsider it might look like you're not having a very nice time. But, let me assure you, you are.'

'When heroin arrived on the hip scene, it was legal, wasn't it?'

Younger Readers take note. In 1963 – as Bob caught the train north to Nottingham, towards the black-and-white cobwebbed casements of Saturday night, away from the Technicolor sunny morning of London as it really got swinging – homosexuality was illegal, but heroin was legal.

'It was legal, and a lot of Canadian junkies were coming over and dying ...'

"I found a dead Canadian junkie on a train once,' I say.

Bob ignores this impressive gambit, and ploughs on.

'... because it was the first time they'd ever had pure heroin ... I suppose they could come into England without a visa, and they could speak the language ...'

'It's good heroin that kills people.'

'It is. The junkies are so used to shit, that a bit of quality kills 'em.'

'Wasn't there a doctor who used to sit on Sloane Square tube station, writings scrips for cash?'

'The one down on the King's Road is the one you mean.'

'Like in the Stones song? "You Can't Always Get What You Want"?' ...

'That was the scene, yeah. Not him, no. I used someone who went by the nickname Dr Bliss; I'd been to him because I'd had a gallstone. A mate said, "Go round to my doctor, say you're from me." He was just literally two doors down from me, I didn't know his name until I got there – "Oh, you're the famous doctor!"'

'Because that was how legal heroin worked. You got it on prescription?'

'Yes, pure boot smack .... Jacks were the parlance for them, as in Jack-and-Jill, pill.'

'Oh, they came in pill form? And in Cockernee rhyming slang.'

'Tiny little pills, only a little bigger than a saccharine pill, one-sixth of a grain for each one. Pure, pure heroin, and really good. Half of one of them jacks – and on the very few occasions when I would take one, I couldn't take a whole one – I felt really happy. Really happy.'

'You've been lucky with your heroin use, haven't you?'

'No, not lucky. I've been very firm. It wasn't luck. Certainly in London in the mid-sixties, we could get it as many times as we liked; and in Afghanistan you could go into a chemist and fucking just buy it, pharmaceutical smack, and coke, and mandrax. You probably remember mandrax?'

'I had some to help me sleep ...'

'Mandies, just to go to sleep? You twat, what a waste! No, heroin – I'd seen from very early on how deep it bites. And I wanted to try it, obviously, but I didn't want to become an out-and-out junkie, because I didn't want to have that tie. And you could see that the people who were junkies, they couldn't move without the prime thing being to secure their supply of smack. It was very, very limiting, and I was very much for zapping about all over the place, and didn't want to have that as part of my life – except the occasional opium holiday, such as I have been enjoying these last few days – and when I get back from my holidays, there have been quite a number of times when I felt achy and sniffly, but two or three days later it's a forgotten thing.'

'Cold turkey isn't as bad as people make out. I'm not saying it's great, but it's no worse than having the flu.'

'Well, it depends on people, I think. Some twat recently burned a house full of children, and I heard him referred to on the radio as a "marijuana addict". That's bollocks. He was just a psychopathic cunt who happened to smoke. From my own experiences, you could smoke hash every day for a fucking year, as often as you like, and if you've got something to do, like you've got to go through customs, say, and you don't have a smoke for a few days then it's no problem at all. You know, it's nice to have a little smoke, but if you don't, it ain't a problem, it ain't addictive. It might be addictive in someone's head, but that's different. With heroin it's a physical thing.'

'Like the fags.'

'It hurts and aches and your joints feel horrible.'

'That's how it is for me when I give up fags, though. Nicotine is the most addictive thing there is. You can be firm with smack, we can both live without spliff, but you and I are slaves to tobacco.'

'I would vote to ban tobacco, not that I've ever voted for any polit-ical thing, ever – never been in a position to, in fact. But any government in this country that said, "Right, we are going to ban the importation and sale of tobacco," I would vote for them – that would be a govern-ment with fucking balls. Because I know it would make smoking fags more fun.'

'You wouldn't contemplate giving up, of course?'

Bob snorts. 'I could grow tobacco; and people would smuggle it in, so I could buy it off them. It might cost a bit more, but fine, I'm happy to smoke less. It's the fact that it's so freely available.'

'Which is a really interesting difference with heroin that's sort of lost. Heroin taken in the right conditions isn't going to kill you, whereas even a couple of fags a day is killing.'

'I was absolutely delighted to come across a report on research into the effect of heroin on the human body, which said, "Small amounts of heroin taken occasionally delay the effects of ageing." Now I bet they wouldn't like that to get on the fucking mainstream news. It's the only time I've ever come across that information but it seemed to be from a reputable source ...'

'Oh, I can believe it. Look at John Cooper Clarke.'

'Because that's exactly what I do – occasional use of small amounts of heroin. I still do. Mind you, I've turned it down in the past week. Recently there's been some extremely good quality (in terms of its strength and its undilutedness) coming out of Hereford. It's obviously come in with the SAS, who happen to be conveniently parked in Afghanistan. But the last lot made me very ill in my stomach, gave me shitting snot sort of thing, and my mate who had got it, and who I got it off, had the same thing. You should be very suspicious of anything you put in your mouth that comes out of Afghanistan through any chan-nels ... The Afghans are a vengeful race. Much as I love and respect them, it doesn't blind me to the fact that they are vicious and very vengeful. So getting a bit of leprous dog shit and grinding it up, or who knows what, they've got a huge array of diseased things and manufactured chemical poisons about the place, so ....'

'I love your expression that it bites deep. A big load of deaths went through Newhaven a while ago, and it was good smack, reputedly.'

'The first time I took it, and I agree with what the geezer says at the beginning of *Trainspotting*, I was on my own, and I felt, "This feels like it has filled in the missing parts of me." Which was quite big. I feel now that there is a whole of me. Deluded, or whatever, maybe, but the fact that it gives you that feeling, that's why people take it – and because it's hugely physically addictive, of course. But the trouble is, though, from what I see, the more you take it the less of that you're going to get.'

'In 1950 there were something like four hundred junkies in the UK ...'

'All getting nice pure boot smack!'

'About twenty per cent of them were doctors.'

'In the biz, like ...'

'And therefore they're going to be using clean needles, not chasing brown off a bit of tinfoil ... well-injected stuff that they know how to use. They're not dying. If you don't get your gear off crims, and if you're using it under medical supervision, you're probably going to be fine. It makes sense. William Burroughs thought the UK had the best heroin regime on Earth. And if anyone should have known, it was William Burroughs. And it was rare. It was. But then Thatcher made it illegal, and now I could get you some gear tonight, in Presteigne.'

Bob says, 'And as the British stopped doing it so well, the Chinese just happened to have Gerrard Street handy. Because when smack was legal, start of the war sort of thing, I think there was one Chinese restaurant on Gerrard Street, at the end, towards Wardour Street where it looked down Gerrard Street, a couple of doors up from the Flamingo where I was working. And in fact the only other thing down Gerrard Street – it was a very bland street, no shopfronts or anything – was the original Ronnie Scott's place, and this gay twist club called the Peppermint Lounge or the Peppermint Twist or something. But then it became Chinatown, just like that, at exactly the same time as China smack started getting on the streets. So you could walk down the street, as I did with a friend who was there on that business, see various Chinese youths leaning against lamp-posts, and you'd give them a tenner and the little packet comes out from under the watch strap. I suspect the Chinese government was not unaware of all this – it would have been under Chairman Mao at the time.'

'When did dope appear in your life?'

'Well, at the end of the fifties when I was first in London, it was very rare. You knew there was such a thing, but you didn't get your hands on it. One of the types I first met at Ken Colyer's all-nighter, he used to turn up with big jars of powerful speed pills. He got them from the place he worked, which was at an egg production unit, and he claimed that these pills were ground up and put in the hens' food. At the time there was a slogan: "Go to work on an egg." Speed-freak chickens laying three eggs a day, under controlled light, plus speed, so you were getting three days out of every twenty-four hours. Chickens only last a few months. They were good pills, though. The first actual smoke I can remember was up in Liverpool. So it's really when we get back to London from Nottingham with money. And the only dealer I knew at first was Duncan Laurie, who was a picture restorer, working for the top firm in London. A very Dickensian-type outfit, who worked for the National Gallery. But then he got into dealing hash. You could get good Afghan hash for seven quid an ounce in London. I once asked Duncan, "Why do you put so much Sellotape round the hash?" – no one bought anything less than an ounce – and he said, "Do you know anyone else who can sell fucking Sellotape for seven quid an ounce?"'

Some Younger Readers will be rubbing their hands, thinking, at last, the drugs bit of sex and drugs and rock 'n' roll! Here we go! Sixties, wheeeee! Others will be horrified, as they have grown up in a world that regards the use of illegal drugs as up there with transphobia as a Bad Thing. But, forgive us. Bob and I come from a different generation from Younger Readers, and although we come from different generations from one another, too, we both participated in a different culture from most Younger Readers, a culture where drugs were socialised.

When I were a lad, the only bottle you'd take round to someone's house would be a bottle of milk for tea, in case your hosts were too fucked to get down the shops. Then, we'd sit around, chatting, listening to music, drinking tea, and taking drugs. That was the culture. We didn't go to the pub, not really.

But for now, we are in late 1963, and, having done some heavy-duty drugs, I'd like to ruminate on sex and rock 'n' roll at that moment in time, before we pop up to Nottingham to fetch Bob down.

Sex. Bob's had sex with girls, by this stage, not to mention the unfortunate arse-fucking and Baldry-wanking episodes. But it was different from how it was in the seventies and eighties before AIDS, and how it is now, where AIDS is in the world, but contained for those rich countries which can afford the medication. Bob will deny this, but he once told me that he didn't perform oral sex on a woman until the seventies. You rubbed 'em up, got 'em wet, and fucked 'em. This is England, girl; lie back and think of your Union Jack Mini. This is ten years before *The Joy of Sex*. In 1963, as Larkin said, sexual intercourse had only really just got going, and there was much to learn for everybody.

And then there's sex – gender, if you prefer. 1963 is a big date in the history of educated middle-class Western women, because Betty Friedan published *The Feminine Mystique*, regarded as the opening text of Feminism. For most of the sixties, although what we now know as 'Women's Liberation' was slowly starting to build up steam, it's not until the early seventies that it begins to make any sort of impact. Even in the very beating heart of sixties counter-cultural London, chicks made tea, and the hippies went home to their old ladies. The introduction of the Pill, although liberating in many ways, also meant that a lot of women were exploited for sex in the 1960s, because they had lost one of their main reasons for saying no. This will take time to change, and, like many things during this period, Bob managed to be around at an overlooked but fascinating moment of paradigm shifting, and to sleep with one of its instigators. But not until the early 1970s. Know this, Younger Readers, much of what you think about the sixties actually happened in the seventies.

And as for rock 'n' roll – 1963 is the date of its resurrection. Five years it had lain dead in the tomb, since March 1958, when Elvis joined the US Army. Bob last listened to rock 'n' roll on a jukebox in Mytchett in 1957. I hope it is clear how important music is and was to Bob, but he hasn't been listening to rock 'n' roll, these last few years, has he? He's been listening to jazz, trad jazz at that, Dad. He's been listening to poetry, and sat outside the Marquess of Granby listening to Donovan put some of it to the lilting strains of a plastic-stringed acoustic guitar. He's hung out with Baldry, so he's heard a lot of blues; and at the rhythm end of blues, he's danced with Jagger / Richards to Alexis Korner and Clive Davis. But rock 'n' roll? Nothing since Gene Vincent and Carl Perkins.

He even went to Liverpool in search of jazz and poetry, and found it too. He just never managed to catch the support band.

The story of the Beatles is the Greatest Story Ever Told, have no doubt. According to Mark Lewisohn's definitive and on-going biography of the Fabs, by 1963, no rock 'n' roll band in Britain, probably Europe, and maybe even the States, had spent so much time live on stage in front of an audience. Elvis, by contrast, had played no gigs at all at the time of his first Sun release in 1954. The Beatles, it was pretty obvious, were The Greatest Rock 'n' Roll band in the world, not least because they had so little competition. They were playing some of the same songs as Ken Colyer, such as 'The Sheik of Araby', but authenticity was not their thing. What they touched turned to rock 'n' roll. And they cleaved a lonely path, even in Liverpool, the only town in the UK where rock 'n' roll had clung on.

'Why Liverpool?' is a fair question, and one that matters to this story, I think. One reason seems to be the link with the USA forged by sea-going music lovers, which meant that older brothers were filling their kid brothers' heads with the latest releases: another link with Colyer, who had first heard New Orleans jazz through his older brother. The second reason was that Liverpool had great record shops (how else did the Beatles get to hear the Marvelettes, 'Please Mr Postman', for example? No one was playing it on the radio). Greatest of the shops was NEMS, owned and operated by Brian Epstein, the least counter-cultural of all the important founders of the British counter-culture, and soon to be the Beatles' manager. Thirdly, Liverpool had dozens of great venues where bands could play, though the Beatles found it hard to get gigs until they came back from Hamburg. They were too idiosyncratic. Lennon snarled, Pete Best glowered (he was the drummer before Ringo), George wasn't a good enough guitarist to look up from his fingering, Stu Sutcliffe (the bass player) was so shy that he could only play with his back to the crowd (that's one of the reasons he decided in the end to leave the band and stay in Hamburg). Even Macca looks hard in the Hamburg photos. They kept their DA haircuts whilst all about them turned Beat. They wore leather jackets, not duffel coats. Nor did they dress up as uber-Teds, like Rory Storm and the Hurricanes, whose soon-to-be-recruited drummer, Ringo Starr, was the only one of the Fab Four who knew how to do popular entertainment. If Younger Readers know nothing of the Beatles' story, Philip Norman's *Shout* is still a good place to start.

In 1963, rock 'n' roll returned from the dead. It's the first year of Beatlemania. Those oiks who had stuck to their outdated guns came back from Hamburg ready to rule the world. They were the hippest kids ever, but Epstein put them in suits, so it took time for people to latch onto their utter, perfect hipness. The counter-culture in this country would have been very different without them. It certainly wouldn't have garnered the mainstream attention it did. In particular, it would have been very different without Paul McCartney's interest in, and bankrolling of, counter-cultural activities.

1963, then, is the start of the High Sixties. Larkin's timing was spot on. It *was* an *annus mirabilis*. And Bob's stuck between Alan Sillitoe and D.H. Lawrence, and is in danger of missing it.

The light is dim in the van, and gets dimmer as we talk. Bob lights a candle.

'Do you struggle for power at this time of the year? I mean, there's no light under the mist.'

'The big problem is the leaves on the solar panels. My first job every morning is to get up and sweep the leaves off the panels. But no, it's all right so long as I'm careful. The sounds and the radio are on one circuit, and the lights are on another, so if one goes down, there's still one going.'

There are solar panels all over the site: one on the shed, one out by the new cabin, and the array above the van. There's an LED movement-activated light over the shelter where Bob does his washing-up. Still, it is dark in the wood; the rain has gone, but drops are falling with the leaves on the roof of the van. Bob puts a log on the stove, and we talk about Nottingham.

'I think I went up to Nottingham pretty well straight after Profumo and that. Late summer, 1963. You don't remember things when you're just scrounging your next meal, they just blur into each other. But I know I was twenty-one up in Nottingham.'

'So, you might have been a boat builder. If the firm who designed them were teaching you to sail Wayfarers, you might have raced yachts, met a nice girl, settled down in Kingston ... but instead that bitch dobbed you in, you went to prison and you ended up in Nottingham. As a washing-machine salesman. Just as London's really kicking off. Lacks glamour.'

'Yeah. And I was just humping the things around, a washing-machine salesman's roadie, basically. My mother's bloke had a stall selling 'em on Nottingham market.'

'And no burgling?'

'No, because I knew that I was on pretty thin ice with the law, and I didn't want to go back with a bunch of fucking racist bastards. No, man, I'd done with burgling.'

'Any sort of café scene? Were there drugs, were there bands ...?'

'Yeah, there was pot. There wasn't really any bands, but there was a very good pub scene there, probably the only time in my life I've really been into a pub scene.'

'The Trip to Jerusalem?'

'Not one of my favourites, a bit of a touristy one that was, but the Bell, Six Bells or Blue Bell or something, that was one, and Yates's Wine Lodge I rather liked, because it was so bizarre and Victorian.

'But the Black Boy was a favourite one, where I met Kate Stacey. I was in there on my own, it was pretty full but I wasn't with anyone, and I was just at the bar having a drink, and this woman came in wearing a sort of Mary Quant oilskin coat. And I just knew that underneath that coat she was naked. And no one was talking to her, she was right across the other side of the bar, so I ambled over to her and revealed my suspicions. And by way of reply she just slides her hand down the inside of my trousers, and cops hold of … Well, as it happened, that day I didn't have any underpants on. So I thought, "If I play my cards right I can have my way with her!"'

'I can see why you might have thought that.'

'… And from that day to this, I've never worn underpants … except once or twice when I've been horseriding and you need them to keep your balls out of the way …'

'In the hope that one day …'

'That one day Kate Stacey would show up and wank me off, yeah. She was fucking gorgeous. And married and all that sort of thing, but that didn't stop her inviting me back to her place, and me asking her back to my place, quite a number of times.'

'But she wasn't the heiress girl?'

'No, that was Vicki. She was a few weeks later.'

'What was she an heiress to?'

'A cotton mill.'

'An old Nottingham business?'

'Yeah, but she didn't own a cotton mill, she just had the money from it.'

'See, it's a classic Nottingham story. *The Heiress and the Beatnik*, by Lawrence Sillitoe. You've rocked up, Colin Wilson's *Outsider*, done a spell behind the door, but, poetry, bongo drums, goatee, and you run away with the boss's wife, who is bored by respectability and longs to escape the bonds of family and experience her wildness.'

'Yeah. She was married, too. The fucking cheek of it – I even assumed her husband's name for a while.'

'What was her husband's name?'

'Gary Andrew Hills. I had a driving licence in that name.'

'What happened to Gary Andrew?'

'I don't fucking know ….. I do know that I did visit Nottingham with his missis during the year after we'd gone away, and I saw that Gary had a pretty fucking juicy new girlfriend. So I took her outside and shagged her, just because I could. Which wasn't very nice of me, but ….'

'You weren't close to Gary?'

'No.'

'So how did you meet Vicki?'

'At a party.'

'What was a party like in Nottingham?'

'I tell you what, they were better than the parties in London. Because the parties in London, even the roughest, hippiest – well, there weren't hippies then, but – they were all trying to be cool. Nottingham, you could still get girls in the middle of the floor, "Go on, get your kit off, get your tits out," and they would. The parties were more fun.'

'Music?'

'Record players, not live music. But the people I was hanging out with, they had pretty sophisticated musical tastes.'

'Jazz still?'

'Still jazz, yeah. Mainly jazz, in fact.'

'So it's at a party, and you meet Vicki. Do your eyes meet across a—'

'No, just a room, and there's a handsome-looking girl there, so you ....'

'You take an interest.'

'We got it together, because there was mutual attraction – and can I stress the fact that when we first got together I didn't know there was dosh, she was just a woman that I fancied. But certainly when a mate of hers marked my card and told me she was an heiress, it didn't dampen my ardour – but I do want to labour the point that my ardour was there already.

'Well, Vicki was married to Gary Hills who'd been a corporal or a sergeant in the Army, and whether she was happy with him I don't know, but she probably wasn't since when I came along, we were shagging at every possible opportunity. I'd been invited round to her house to have dinner with them as a couple, and I was feeling her up under the table ... pretty full on and bold and upfront. So I said, "Why don't we go to London and get a place?" And she was up for that, so we went to London. We rented a place on Worsley Road just by Hampstead Heath. And that was the place where the landlord who lived upstairs was a mate of the screaming therapy geezer ... what's his name ...'

'R.D. Laing. Whoa, hang on. That's it? You just moved with Vicki down to Hampstead?'

'That's it. We had money. I mean, it wasn't fucking millions, it was a few tens of thousands, you know – in them days it was a lot more than it is now. It was enough to buy a big house in Belsize Park and a Jag and have plenty of dosh for change. And Swinging London and all that, and the beautiful people, well, there I was, which was great for Vicki because I was already a known figure on that London scene, so no problem at all slipping back into it, especially when suddenly someone who's never had any money now has any amount. Suddenly a whole lot of new friends, oddly enough, as people like you when you've got loads of dope, booze, good food, and a place and all that, smart clothes even.'

'So you've arrived back in London ... when, late spring 1964? You've got a beautiful rich bird, you're in Hampstead, you've got loads of money, you've got a Jag, and London is about to start swinging. I'm glad you weren't away any longer. Tell me the story about the bloke upstairs who smelled you smoking spliff ...'

'So, we rented 5a Worsley Road, a nice basement flat just 150 yards from the Heath, from a Mr Platt who owned the house, and lived upstairs. A very posh gentleman.

'One night, we were sitting out on this little courtyard behind the flat smoking some very tidy hash. Several of my mates, like Duncan Laurie, were smugglers who were running it back from Afghanistan, so I always had access to really good Afghani hash.

'So Mr Platt came down and said, "Can't help but smell the hash you're smoking here" – and he's very posh, remember. You've got to get the voice. Well, I wasn't going to deny it – I never rubbish people's senses when they're right.

'So then he said, "Because I hope you don't mind me asking, but I wondered if you could get hold of any LSD?" – and at this time I certainly could – "because my friend Laing wants some for his work." So I provided him with some acid. For his mate Laing. All that primal scream therapy stuff, wasn't it? Psychiatrist bloke who liked dosing his patients up with acid? Mr Platt told me later that I was the first person to help him get it.'

Now, as we go on, Bob will make claims to at least three firsts, all of them remarkable in the history of the counter-culture. (He will also have Procol Harum named after his cat, of course, but that could only happen once, so doesn't count as a first.) The acid for R.D. Laing thing is one; the others are that he was the first person to import Afghan coats into Europe, and that he was the first person to light a Pink Floyd gig with an oilwheel projector.

Imagine for a moment, if you would, that you are a film designer, presented with a script set in a British university in the early 1970s. Your lead character is a rebellious undergraduate. The opening scene is in his cold student bedsit; you imagine him, hugging his Afghan coat around him, listening to *A Salty Dog* on a Dansette, under a poster of *The Piper at the Gates of Dawn*, with the Floyd lit by oilwheels, while reading a copy of *Knots* by Ronnie Laing. I reckon you've done a lot of work, right there, establishing when the film is set. It's Early Seventies 101. Take Bob out of it, and what do you have?

'Any chance of another coffee, Bob?'

'Sure.' Bob gets to his opium-soothed arthritic legs, and starts knocking together a cup of his eye-opening brew, taken with evaporated milk. I need to occupy him.

Except for the odd redoubt of unalienated space in areas like Papua New Guinea, Antarctica or the Amazon basin, by the 1960s pretty much everywhere on Earth had been explored, mapped, colonised, bought and sold. Two kinds of absolute exploration remained, those of Outer and Inner Space. These two kinds of exploration were in many ways inimical. Exploring Outer Space could only be achieved by governments putting up the vast amounts of money necessary to get humankind to the Moon. You could watch it on TV, but other than that, you were merely a spectator. The Apollo programme wasn't exactly a participatory sport. They didn't even use volunteers in the NASA gift shop.

Exploring Inner Space, by contrast, was cheap and available to all. Before the Death of God, people in Europe and the USA had ways and means of exploring these vast spaces using prayer. Secular exploration was, and remains, a new adventure, still in its infancy. Nietzsche, Freud and Jung had begun the first primitive maps of the territory, but by the late 1950s new pathfinders were putting on their psychic solar topees and striking out across this undiscovered country of the secular mind. Wilhelm Reich, a one-time student of Freud, was exiled to the USA by the Nazis, and persecuted to the point of extinction by his new hosts. Reich died in a US prison where he was serving time for obscenity, because his ideas about the orgasm, which were going to come in handy for times of sexual revolution, were not to the taste of the Food and Drug Administration. Not content with locking Reich up, they also burned his books.

Medical psychiatry was starting to learn from psychoanalysis to some extent, and psychologists like Donald Winnicott and John Bowlby were reaching towards contemporary understandings of, for example, depression. But the best known of the new pathfinders was Dr Timothy Leary.

Tim was a rascal. There are innumerable books about him, but I reckon Jay Stevens' *Storming Heaven: LSD and the American Dream* is still the most readable. His famous formula 'Turn on, tune in, drop out' is less useful today than his ideas about how to use LSD; *not*, I would wish to argue, as a party drug, but as something wonderful which nonetheless needs to be treated with a degree of caution, under the right circumstances and in the right way. Leary was singing in the chorus on the Beatles live broadcast of 'All You Need is Love', from 1967. I struggle to find a better example of how times have changed. A contemporary pop video to accompany a massive worldwide number-one hit might have semi-naked children wriggling about in time to the music, but what it certainly wouldn't have would be a celebrity psychologist barred from practising because of his advocacy of universal LSD use as a religious sacrament, a man described by dear old President Nixon as 'the most dangerous man in the US'. 'Come Together', one of the late Beatles last great moments, was supposedly written as a campaign song for Tim's attempted run for the governorship of California. Tim, as I say, was a rascal, a man whose life never once stopped being interesting, although it was, for much of the time, insane. Read a book about him, and be on your guard against his charm.

Owsley Stanley, aka 'Bear', was the first private individual to manufacture LSD, at first for the benefit of the Grateful Dead, for whom he was the sound guy. Those who tried it claimed that it was the best acid ever, a theory confirmed by the fact that his LSD was used by Ken Kesey's Merry Pranksters (for more on whom Younger Readers should look at *The Electric Kool-Aid Acid Test* by Tom Wolfe), and on the Beatles' filming of *The Magical Mystery Tour*. Previously, LSD had been available for medical use from Sandoz Laboratories in Switzerland, where chemist Albert Hofmann had first synthesised it in 1938. It was not until 1943, however, that Hofmann discovered its psychedelic properties, most famously on 'Bicycle Day', 19 April 1943, when Hofmann took a small dose and rode his white bicycle home from work. The day is commemorated by psychedelic advocates as a day of celebration, and you can easily find Tomorrow's song from 1968 about the occasion, 'My White Bicycle'. An early British metal band, Nazareth, covered it in 1975, and it reached number fourteen in the charts. I well remember their appearance performing it on *Top of the Pops*. Again, if *TOTP* still existed, you can easily imagine songs by Rihanna going 'Money on my mind, money money on my mind' with her tits out, and no one turning a hair; but a song celebrating the discovery of LSD? I think not. LSD was made illegal in the UK in September 1966, a month before it was banned in the USA, so it was no longer available from Sandoz; but Owsley Stanley had opened the doors, and had proved it could be manufactured just as safely without the benefit of legality.

If Old Tim Leary had a UK equivalent, it is at least arguable that this was R.D. 'Ronnie' Laing, once described by a fan as 'The Elvis of the Psyche'. He was a Glaswegian psychiatrist, based in London, who died in 1989 aged sixty-one from a heart attack brought about by exercise on the tennis court, a sport which he'd taken up to stop him drinking, which just goes to show. His 1960 book *The Divided Self* sold in hundreds of thousands, and became a set text for the British counterculture. In the book, Laing took Sartre's ideas about existentialism and applied them to psychiatry. He wrote, 'I'm not an object to be changed, I'm a person to be accepted.'

For Laing it was about the liberation of the individual, rather than the liberation of a class, as in earlier Marxist thought; he shares this with Herbert Marcuse. He developed the idea of the double bind: parents tell children to do one thing, and then do another, which means that children grow up in permanent conflict. According to Laing, society is mad, not individuals; schizophrenia is a valid response to this societal madness, if only the logic of the patient can be understood. In short, going mad is a rational response to an intolerable situation. So Ronnie listened to people. His 1967 book *The Politics of Experience and the Bird of Paradise* contains several accounts of what schizophrenia is actually like from the point of view of a schizophrenic patient.

Laing wrote that 'Experience may be judged to be invalidly mad or validly mystical'; and to see how close madness walked this line, Laing gave his patients acid. And took it himself, to trip alongside them, though usually in smaller doses. He gave it to Sean Connery, who apparently had a bad trip. Laing acquired a licence to use LSD in treating patients, and despite my best efforts I am unable to confirm Mr Platt's assertion that Bob was the first person to get it for him. I suspect that after it was made illegal, Bob was the first person to sell him extra-legal acid; still a fair claim. Ronnie was regarded as a guru by the Freaks. It was pretty much impossible to find any radical event at which he wasn't present. And his books continued to sell. Perhaps the most readable and intriguing is *Knots*, from 1970, which is like a series of Zen koans, where he poses situations in the form of poems to illustrate the 'double bind', which Ronnie called 'incompatible knots'.

He had his critics at the time, and their voices have grown louder over the years. I spoke to two friends of mine and Bob's, Christine and Tony Lawson, partly because I seriously needed Tony's views on a subject

I find impenetrable, and partly to hear Christine's views on Laing. She told me, 'When I trained as a psychotherapist, it was on R.D. Laing's model, as a phenomenonological psychotherapist. His books were very much based on existential philosophy, especially Sartre's *Being and Nothingness*. The whole sixties thing was freedom, and where was it going to take you. That freedom was supposed to be a model for "being". But a lot of people ended up in a nothingness. I think a lot of us then had to look and try to find our way.'

But perhaps that's a critique of the whole counter-cultural project. Laing still has his followers. The organisation he founded, the Philadelphia Association, still operates as a therapeutic community, where the line between agent and patient is blurred, and where people live together, trying to find a way out of ... I hesitate to say madness. Their way out of a series of disturbing and unpleasant symptoms. And his definition of alienation is a corker: 'Alienation as our present destiny is achieved only by outrageous violence perpetrated by human beings on human beings.'

'So you provided Ronnie Laing with acid. Which begs the question, why was it so easy for you to acquire acid?'

'Not just any acid, either. Owsley acid.'

I skin up while Bob tells the story.

'I come back to London knowing I'm well fixed, I can rent a nice flat in Hampstead, can get myself fancy motor cars and that. And of course all my old mates think, "Well, he's well fixed" – so you're welcome, aren't you? And the music places were the same sort of places as before, so the same crew were around. And I met up with Duncan Laurie and his brother Bob. I'd previously shared a flat in West Hampstead with Bob and John Baldry and Gus Dudgeon and them. I became known as Big Bob and he was Little Bob, but I didn't like Big Bob, it's a bit John Wayne-y, the sort of name that can get you into trouble if there are gangster types around. So I was doing a lot of shopping, smoking a lot of dope ...'

'A lot of shopping? I can't imagine you shopping. I can't imagine you not smoking a lot of dope.'

'Quite a bit of shopping, for a while; because when for all of your life you've been absolutely skint, never had any sort of money, certainly not spare money, to suddenly find yourself in the position of being able to walk down the Burlington Arcade, see a pair of slippers that would probably cost several weeks' wages for a normal punter, and then, oh, when you're down the Burlington Arcade, measure me up for a couple of those nice blue Oxford shirts, please … I mean, yeah, one could happily spend a couple of years doing that.'

'What were you wearing?'

'OK; me casual stuff was not greatly different from what I'm wearing now.' (I find this highly unlikely, as Bob these days tends to wear pre-loved Radnorshire clothes – such as a hill farmer might reluctantly part with after three decades of hard wear to the Hospice Shop in Llandrindod – albeit with a great deal of elan.) 'Good quality jumpers, jeans, boots not dissimilar to these. I've always liked elastic-sided, easy-on easy-off boots. But that was casual. For going out, things like Young Jaeger suits, hand-made shirts from down Burlington Arcade, Savile Row 1930s-style suit. Pretty flash. And good cufflinks. Loudly quiet, sort of thing.'

'Northern flash thing, sort of Mod-y?'

'Yes, but not mod clothes styles, not really following anyone; classic English looks, really, but also with a touch of the French *blouson noir* as well, the black leather jacket, worn with Levi's and a black polo neck. There was quite a strong Parisian influence – apart from the American influence on music, the other part of the cool was the Paris cool.'

'And the dope? That's coming from Duncan Laurie?'

'Mostly from a bloke called Tom Harney. He's the guy who's bringing the spliff in. There were probably others, but he was one of our imme-diate crew. Driving Volkswagen cars out of Afghanistan and bringing back a few kilos. He had a lovely girlfriend called Patsy Hughes, blonde hair, a beauty … Later, we put together my first trip to Afghanistan, and formed a company to get the money out of the country …'

Always, Bob wants to get back to Afghanistan. A little longer, I restrain him.

'So, you, the Laurie brothers and Tom Harney started a shop?'

'Yes, because we was mates. So we started up in the Cleveland Street area, north of Oxford Street/Regent Street/Tottenham Court Road. We started up what was London's first hippie shop. Well, I say it was a shop, but we didn't have much of anything to sell. Joss sticks. Posters. A French girl called Lorraine turned up and taught me how to make candles using a bottle. So that was what Karma Sigma had, which wasn't a lot until we started to get the Afghan coats. It was called Karma Sigma, because we had some connection with this organisation, this philosophy called Sigma. I never knew what it was. It was some cosmic-y, esoteric … I never paid it any great heed. The people who were in it were all-right people, who were around our scene, so we thought it was a good name, tagged Karma on to it and thought, "That'll do!"'

You see, Bob. Lived experience is all right as far as it goes, but book larnin' is a great thing. Because I do know what 'Sigma' was. I long to jump up with joy as Bob tells me this, and I shall continue to hang onto that longing until after his acid story. But I cannot help smiling.

'Did you know Alexander Trocchi?' I ask.

'Scots Alex? Of course, yes, because we were the first hippie shop in London, so although we didn't have anything to sell, people used to hang out, and that was at the time when Trocchi was about. When we first opened the Karma Sigma place, we sold posters and candles as our main things, but we sold a few books. Scots Alex was very much about, as we had good hash and some sort of literary pretensions. And that's how this acid turned up, because Trocchi was one of the references that the LSD bloke gave us.'

'Tell me about the LSD bloke.'

'So one day this posh bloke wanders into the shop. Mentions he knows Scots Alex. And says, "I've just got back from San Francisco, where I was given this envelope full of LSD by a chap called Owsley, who asked me if I could turn England on, to which I foolishly agreed. Because I can't go and stand on fucking Piccadilly Circus giving it away, can I? So what to do? So Alex told me about this place, and I wondered if you might like it?" To which we said yes. It was a big brown envelope, stuffed with all these crystals. It wasn't the first acid we'd had. The first came from a chemist out by London Airport, where someone had discovered that if you could get hold of a chemist's letterhead, and make an order, they would supply you with Swiss Sandoz LSD, so we'd had some of that.'

Bob smiles.

'What happened with that envelope of crystals?' I ask.

'We stuck our fingers into it like it was a sherbet fucking dip, that's what happened. And you know, several days later, after coming down off the fucking ceiling, we realised we'd probably taken about a thousand trips at a time here. So after that we rationed it out a bit. We worked out you could dissolve it, and then use blotting paper to soak it up, and cut up the blotting paper. Then sold little squares of the paper.'

'What you are telling me here, therefore, is that you and your mates invented the blotter?'

Is this another first, I wonder?

Bob shrugs. 'I'd never seen 'em before. We did some on sugar cubes too, which had been more common. That envelope had many many many thousands of trips. I didn't need money, I already had access to enough to buy a house in Belsize Park, a Jag and so on, so I let the guys who weren't so well fixed do what they wanted with it. I took as much free acid as I wanted, obviously, but I wasn't so interested in the commercial distribution of it.'

'Except for the stuff you sold to Mr Platt to give to R.D. Laing?'

'I might even have just given it to him. It was free, after all. And it was sent by Owsley to turn England on. Which it did.

'The LSD guy, he hands us this envelope packed full with these crystals. And we emptied this envelope out into more permanent storage, and then we tore the envelope up into about six and shared it around our little gang, as we realised it was probably saturated with the stuff and it would be a handy trip. I just put it in a pocket. And a couple of years later I was looking for something I'd put into the same pocket and found this bit of paper. I thought, "What the fuck's this, there's no phone number on it," and then I remembered and thought, "Oh, it's the acid, but it will have all faded away by now." So I tore it in half and gave half to Vicki, necked the other half, and a few minutes later set off to drive to Marlborough. We only lived about six or seven miles from Marlborough but between us was Savernake Forest. We were just getting to the edge of the forest on one side and fields on the other, and I noticed how the landscape was beginning to seriously undulate, turn into liquid, so I asked Vicki, "Do you feel a big trip coming on?" And she said yes. So I said, "I don't think I can handle shopping in Marlborough at the moment, let's just pull into the forest here." It's a mature old forest, primarily beech. Anyway, we pulled in, a nice summer's day, and we just lay on the ground and you could feel the souls of the trees, the sentience of the trees, and dead branches would turn into iguanas and walk off, stuff like that. A trip and a half, that was.'

'I asked some friends who are "in the business" when you first told me that story. Apparently one of those crystals now sells for £10,000.'

Bob is silent.

'It's not often I shock you.'

Bob is still silent, so I release the whoop of joy that I'd been holding in since Bob told me that Scots Alex was part of the establishment at Karma Sigma. I always knew that I was going to have to face Situationism, and couldn't work out how to do it.

And up pops Alexander Trocchi.

Alexander Trocchi was a Scottish writer of Italian ancestry and, as he was always happy to admit, a junkie (and, it should be added, something of a war hero, having served in the Navy on the Murmansk convoys, not a fun gig.) He spent most of the fifties in Paris, the USA and Canada, joined the Situationist International in 1960, and turned up in London in 1962, having published a couple of novels along the way. In July 1964, he left the Situationists and produced the first of his Sigma Portfolios. Trocchi described the Sigma Project as 'a possible international association of men who are concerned individually and in concert to articulate an effective strategy and tactics for cultural revolution,' and for the next twenty years, until his death in 1984, Trocchi saw all of his work as part of Sigma. Bob, though he knew it not, was a cog in the retail arm of a theoretical art project.

Trocchi advocated as part of Sigma 'the spontaneous university', which he described at some length, right down to the site.

> The original building will stand deep within its own grounds, preferably on a river bank. It should be large enough for a pilot group (astronauts of inner space) to situate itself, orgasm and genius, and their tools and dream machines and amazing apparatus and appurtenances [sic]; with outhouses for 'workshops' large as could accommodate light industry; the entire site to allow for spontaneous architecture and eventual town planning.

Trocchi did manage a gathering of the great and the good of 1964 Freakdom to discuss his ideas. He held a weekend in Oxfordshire where guests included R.D. Laing and some of his allies; the last Beat standing Bob Cobbing, and Jeff Nuttall, whose book on the period, *Bomb Culture*, still divides the old Freaks, mostly between those who met Jeff (who say it's a load of shit) and those who didn't (who say it's good in parts). According to Nuttall, the weekend went very badly, with too much booze, infighting and terrorising of the kind people at the Quaker Retreat which had been foolish enough to let them in.

Trocchi managed to keep enough Freaks on board to inspire an exhibition in the basement of Better Books on the Charing Cross Road, which had been managed by Bob Cobbing since 1952. The exhibition was called sTigma, and by all accounts, it was not good. Nuttall wrote of one of the pieces that it consisted of 'a dentist's chair which had been turned into a figure, with sponge-rubber breasts and a shaven head. On the seat of the chair was a cunt made of a bedpan lined with hair and cods' roe. Detergent bubbles spluttered from between the slabs of roe, which remained spluttering and stinking for four weeks.'

In 1964 and '65, as Trocchi dreamed of an ideal university, actual new universities were bobbing up all over the place: Lancaster, York, Sussex, Essex, Warwick, UEA, which would become some of the most fertile breeding grounds and fiercest battlefields for the counter-culture. These were the so-called plate-glass universities, where students of the ideas of the Frankfurt School held positions of influence from their inception (for more on the Frankfurt School, see Bob's comments re. Adorno and Horkheimer in Chapter One), and where new students and early career lecturers would certainly have been coming across an 'idea of a University', not from Cardinal Newman, but from Trocchi and the Situationists (via their most successful and influential tract, *On the Poverty of Student Life* by Tunisian writer Mustapha Khayati). And from Ronnie Laing, who had read and been impressed by Trocchi's *Sigma: A Tactical Blueprint*, and in particular the idea of the spontaneous university. Laing introduced Sigma to American psychotherapist Joe Berke, who became Trocchi's greatest supporter in the USA. As a result of Berke's reading of Sigma, he and Allen Krebs set up the Free University of New York in 1965, and subsequently the Anti-University of London, in Rivington Street, Shoreditch, in 1968, which clung to existence for a couple of years. The Anti-University sounds great; lecturer Steve Abrams spoke of his time teaching there: 'Laing gave a course, Cornelius Cardew did courses on modern music. Yoko Ono did a course. I taught advanced techniques for turning on, and all my students had prescriptions for tincture. I'd give them lessons on joint-rolling, and so on.'

An earlier consequence of Trocchi's vision was 'The Dialectics of Liberation', held at London's Roundhouse in 1967, which was a hip academic conference, if you can imagine such a thing. Speakers included Ronnie Laing, Herbert Marcuse, Allen Ginsberg, Tim Leary and Black Power leader Stokely Carmichael. Entertainment was provided by the Social Deviants, by all accounts the best really shit band ever. The Social Deviants 'singer', Mick Farren, gives a brilliant account of the occasion in his excellent autobiography *Give the Anarchist a Cigarette*:

> Stokely Carmichael delivered what appeared to be a set speech, which was received with something close to a standing ovation. He then turned the tables by announcing he'd been reading a speech by Adolf Hitler and castigated the crowd as a bunch of white-mother-fucker closet Nazis.

Sue Miles went with Ginsberg, who felt that Carmichael's intervention turned the event scary. However, to give Younger Readers some feel of the attitude to blackness, in the hippest place at that moment on Earth, back at Ronnie's flat after the event, Laing said to Carmichael, 'The thing is, Stokely, I like black people, but I could never stand their smell.' Carmichael got up and left; as you would. Incidentally, no women speakers were billed to appear at The Dialectics of Liberation.

I wish I'd been there, though, because I'd have loved to have seen the Social Deviants in their pomp. Russell Hunter, the Social Deviants' drummer, playing his first gig for the band, summed up The Dialectics of Liberation thus: 'We were just up on a load of planks and steel girders, thrashing through this appalling set. There was an awful lot of talking, spouting, stuff like that.'

This talking was finding its way to the new university campuses, and reached fever pitch in 1968, as students revolted all over the world. It was still going strong in 1976 when I started as a student, and in 1989 when I started as a student again. It is gone now. The kind of ideas that Trocchi was espousing were those that made university an exciting place to be between about 1965 and 1994. They were also the same ideas that the System wised up to, the ideas that caused the reaction that caused the university ('uni', it's called now) to become the sort of place that Younger Readers go, where marketing has replaced madness. You can see it from the System's point of view, of course. They need technocrats, not fucking Freaks.

Trocchi's definition of how he saw the world, as described in the *Sigma Portfolio*, shows why he and people like him have been silenced in the university, one way or another:

> Automation, and a general socialisation of vital goods will gradually and ineluctably dispense with most of the necessity of 'work'; eventually, as near as dammit, the complete liberty of the individual in relation to production will be attained. Thus freed from all economic responsibility, man will have at his disposal a new plus-value, incalculable in money terms, a plus-value not computable according to the accountancy of salaried work ... play value. What is becoming is homo ludens in a life liberally constructed. There is no solution within the conventional economic framework.

Now we need to go back a few steps. Alexander Trocchi was a member of the Situationist International. The SI. The most – and I use this next word advisedly – influential art movement of the counter-culture. Lots of people have written about Situationism, almost none of them Situationists. But to understand the counter-culture, they need to be taken on board.

There are three texts; Guy Debord's *Society of the Spectacle*, Raoul Vaneigem's *The Revolution of Everyday Life* and *The Situationist Anthology*, a volume which collects together all the SI's journals and publications, including *On the Poverty of Student Life*. The assumption of my book is that Younger Readers know nothing, so I have no choice but to take the Situationists on and to become yet another non-Situationist writing about the Situationists. If you want to know more, try Mackenzie Wark's *The Beach Beneath the Street* (you need the hardback edition with the fold-out dust-wrapper) or, if you can get hold of it, Stewart Home's *Assault on Culture*. Vaneigem's book has just been retranslated, and is highly readable. Or you could live it; try, for example, to be as economically inactive as you can for a year, and tell people it's part of Project Sigma.

The Situationist International was established in 1957 at Cosio di Arroscia, a mountain village in northern Italy, at a meeting between French art theorist Guy Debord and his partner Michèle Bernstein, who represented an organisation called Lettrist International, and Danish artist Asger Jorn, the inventor of three-sided football, together with several of his followers, who had a scheme he called the International Movement for an Imaginist Bauhaus. Also there was the English artist Ralph Rumney, who purported to represent an organisation called the London Psycho-geographical Association, which didn't actually exist. The three organisations resolved to combine to form the Situationist International. Belgian writer Raoul Vaneigem joined in 1959, Trocchi in 1960. There were never more than twenty members. Between 1957 and 1969, the SI produced twelve issues of their journal, which were later collected in the *Situationist International Anthology*.

Stewart Home, in *Assault on Culture*, writes about a public meeting at London's ICA in 1960, where the SI spokesman Maurice Wyckaert said, 'Situationism doesn't exist. There is no doctrine of this name.' But also: 'The Situationists, whose judges you perhaps imagine yourselves to be, will one day judge you. We are waiting for you at the turning.' The audience were either stunned or bored; there was one question to the SI from a man in the audience: 'Can you explain what Situationism is all about?' Guy Debord stood up and said (in French), 'We're not here to answer cuntish questions,' and stalked out. (What 'cuntish' might be in French, we can only guess.)

As you might imagine, therefore, trying to say what Situationism was/ is all about is somewhat difficult, even cuntish.

So here's my Chestertonian explanation of Situationism; which is to say, having read loads of stuff about Situationism over the years, I'm going for my own definition off the top of my head, because that makes as much sense as anything. Please bear in mind, though, my explanation is as full as that of the American who explained the rules of cricket to a puzzled countryman thus: 'There are two teams of eleven players. The teams take it in turn to bat and bowl, the object being to score runs between the wickets. The winner is the team who scores the most runs.' I.e., all right up to a point.

Here goes: according to the Situationists, we live in a hypercapitalist world which keeps us alienated by means of 'the Spectacle'. The Spectacle is your phone, and all that entails. It's films. Adverts. The print media. Posters. TV. Pop music. News. Politics. Money. Keep it spectacular, and truth doesn't matter any more, and the ruling class can retain power. It's the task of artists to create situations which confront the Spectacle and show it to be what it merely is, i.e., a spectacle. Art is only valid if it wakes up the individual to their plight, and helps to destabilise the Spectacle. The revolutionary liberation of the individual leads to the revolutionary liberation of society.

One kind of 'situation', according to Debord, at least, was/is the psycho-geographical *dérive*. And what, I hear you ask, is a 'psycho-geographical *dérive*'? This is one, written shortly after I started work on this book:

It is Lady Day, 25 March, a day of coincidences. It is the Feast Day of the Annunciation of the Holy Virgin Mary, the day she gets with child. Only nine shopping months till Christmas.

I am writing this in an inexpensive hotel hard by Earls Court tube station.

I have come down from Radnorshire for an event at the London Review Bookshop, from which I am lately returned. This event was in honour of the publication of a new translation of Raoul Vaneigem's *Revolution of Everyday Life*.

This is what happened.

I looked at the book again on the slow train up from Hereford to London.

The last time I read it, thirty years ago, I lived alone in an abandoned artist's studio in a hidden valley in the South Downs. For company, I had a mono cassette player, and one C30 cassette tape, with the first Jesus and Mary Chain album, and just enough room for 'Portuguese Love' by Teena Marie, at the end, taped off the radio. I was mad at the time, mad with grief and drugs, but I did a lot of reading. I read *Walden* for the first time in that place.

I read about religion, too; mostly comparative and historical, Alan Watts on Zen, Don Cupitt on Christianity, that kind of thing. My main religious activity was to throw the *I Ching*, but when I looked up into the dark skies above the studio, I knew that Nietzsche was wrong in at least one respect: God, far from being dead, was alive in me, and I in Her. I smoked a lot of Nepalese Temple Balls. I was out of my fucking nut, frankly, but in a good way.

I read Vaneigem for the first time in that place and in that state, and found a call to action that I have, in part, tried to follow. His insistence that we all live lives full of transparency was clearly attractive to a man who lived in an artist's studio with a glass wall.

'I should have wished a book such as this accessible to minds quite unschooled in the jargon of ideas'; so Vaneigem says of his book, just as I wish for mine.

The train arrived at Paddington, and I headed for my hotel in Earls Court.

Vaneigem's call for a ludic existence still make sense to me. I had a blim of hash, and in the en-suite bathroom I turned on the shower and I smoked my blim in a little pipe I take away with me, hoping that the steam from the shower would disguise any smoke from the detectors.

This action seemed playful, but it was also a bit foolish, as I realised when I stepped out onto the pavement.

I managed to get back to Earls Court tube from the hotel, just barely. I reckoned I should head for Russell Square and that therefore I needed to get onto the Piccadilly Line. You have to do this by lift at Earls Court. I was confused and a bit anxious, and the lifts weren't helping, because it was soon clear that I was in great danger of trying to talk to somebody. I found I wanted very much to say 'Hello' to the other people in the lift, as I would in Radnorshire (not, I must admit, that I know of any lifts in Radnorshire, though I guess there might be one in Llandrindod Wells), but I overcame this desire, got down to platform level, and found a seat on a train.

During the journey I realised that I had kind of forgotten where the London Review Bookshop is, and so I got off at High Holborn, rather than Russell Square, because I reckoned that I knew my way better to Bury Place, where the bookshop is, from there than from Russell Square. I mean, I've been there lots, but where have I been?

I always seem to forget my *A to Z* when I come up. As I came out of High Holborn, I was immediately disorientated. A pair of Chinese tourists, a father and son maybe, asked me the way to the British Museum.

All I could do was to point them in the direction I was going, which, sadly for them, was the wrong direction by 180 degrees. But they seemed happy, which is the main thing.

I found out that I was going in the wrong direction by means of a remarkable coincidence. See, what I was up to was sort of kind of what you might call a psycho-geographical *dérive*. I had gone out of my way to disorientate myself before heading into an urban landscape, one which I thought I knew. In Guy Debord's original *dérive*, he had ingested a lump of hash and wandered around Paris. I hadn't had what you would call a lump, Officer, but I had had a bit. I was drifting, stoned. Although I didn't exactly want to get lost, I wasn't exactly ready to be found, either. I felt pleasantly vague. I was in no real hurry. The event was due to start at seven, and now it was about 4.15.

What happened at this juncture proved to my satisfaction the greater usefulness of friendship than satnavs. Because, crossing the road with maybe a hundred other people, sure that I was heading the right way, sure, at this time, that I had told the Chinese guys the right way, a voice from behind called 'Ian'; and I turned to see a cheery long-haired geezer coming towards me.

'John Rogers,' he said, introducing himself with his hand outstretched. But I knew his name; I knew him from Facebook, but mostly I knew him because two years before I'd interviewed him outside the Westfield Shopping Centre in Stratford for a Radio Three programme that I had presented about psycho-geography. John had used algorithms to help people get lost, and so therefore rediscover their town.

I had been found by a bloke who is in the finishing stages of writing a book about getting lost in London. I told John where I was going and why, and he put me right, turned me around, walked me through Bloomsbury, a territory where I am *not* at home, to the LRB shop. Isn't that a thing you couldn't put in fiction? Lost in a big city because of hash smoking and on my way to a Situationist-esque do, I am rescued by a psycho-geographer, a man I first met while recording a programme about Debord, psycho-geography, etc., etc.

No, I hear you say. There's a bookshop do about Raoul Vaneigem round the corner. Clearly, all of London's remaining psycho-geographical types will be in that part of town. But you're wrong – John Rogers is going to a similar talk at Housmans Bookshop on Friday, but he didn't even know tonight's talk was on.

We perch on stools in the London Review Bookshop caff supping lattes and chatting about matters Situationist. This is as far as Theory gets you. I'm even wearing two polo-necked sweaters, one under the other, to fend off the cold.

We talk about the Socialist Party, the good old dear old Socialist Party of Great Britain, who are not the Trotskyist fucks who used to be called Militant and who changed their name in 1990-ish, but the proper Socialist Party, formed in 1904 and dedicated to the overthrow of alienation. We chat about the old Revolutionary Communist Party of Great Britain (Marxist-Leninist), and their most famous member Cornelius Cardew, and whether or not his very late-period songs ('On the founding of the Revolutionary Communist Party' is one) are better than the stuff with AMM or the Scratch Orchestra and such like matters. McCartney went to see AMM once, in 1965, and ended up jamming with them, biffing about on a radiator.

John tells me about his new book, called *This Other London*, which is being published soon. I tell him about this book, this very book that you are reading; and I then tell him about my idea that there is a real resistance, however quietist it might have become, and that we are part of it. That Younger Readers can be part of it as well, and keep something alive – a memory, perhaps, of when the world seemed full of possibilities; faith, perhaps, that the world is still full of possibilities, even if it is hard sometimes to see them. Then I tell John about the spliff in the shower, and why it was so great that he had rescued me – and he laughs and heads home.

The event is a bloke called Donald Nicholson-Smith in conversation with a bloke called T.J. Clark about Raoul Vaneigem's *Revolution of Everyday Life*, which Nicholson-Smith has translated – for the third time. Both Nicholson-Smith and Clark were at one time members of the SI.

I'm far from being the only middle-aged man with a shaven head and wearing big specs and a black polo-necked sweater at this do. Although I share a family resemblance with most of the men here, I know nobody, except Stewart Home. I also met Stewart through the psycho-geography show, and he comes in late, and sits at the front, wearing a tracksuit and a Yankees baseball cap; and I knew that I should have worn my hi-vis dog-walking jacket, because then I wouldn't look a lot like all the other pointy heids.

It starts badly from my point of view, because Nicholson-Smith opens by calling both Debord's *Society of the Spectacle* and Vaneigem's *Revolution of Everyday Life* '*sui generis*', and in my present state I can't quite remember what *sui generis* means.

Vaneigem's title for his book was *Totality for Kids: A Younger Readers' Guide to the Facts of Everyday Life*. As you can tell, I have stolen the subtitle.

In Situationist terms, I've done a bit of *détournement*. I ask a question when the time comes: why didn't Nicholson-Smith take the opportunity to change the title in his latest translation, so that people would think it was a whole new book, and buy it again. He laughed, and said he felt he was stuck with *The Revolution of Everyday Life* after all these years.

The thing is over by half-eight-ish, and I wander off to find something to eat; I settle on an Indian place on Endell Street that doesn't look as though they would find it odd for a bloke to be eating on his own ... a chicken dhansak, rice, a naan bread; three times what you'd pay in Birmingham, but still good. Afterwards, I walk onto Long Acre, and go for a coffee in Starbucks. These streets were part of Bob's beat, and not everything has changed; three very glamorous boys sit in the window in leather and diamanté, and I suspect them of looking for trade; could be wrong.

The staff are as alienated as alienated can be, alienation being much on my mind. They are clock watching. 'Half an hour till we close, twenty-five minutes.' As anybody comes in, the staff tell them of the imminent closure. The late-night punters are looking for somewhere that stays open; the chief barista tells a young man with a big bag that the branch over by the Trocadero is open till one.

I think of Bob. He was a Beat on these very streets, on darker nights than this; he sat in cafés, eking out a coffee, listening to Baldry and Wizz Jones. I leave, and head towards Leicester Square. I want to walk down Great Newport Street, where I used to run a secondhand bookshop, and where Bob had come night after night to hear Ken Colyer play. There is a plaque up on the wall, commemorating the site of Colyer's club; tonight the building is covered in plastic sheeting and scaffolding which announce that it is being made over into 'The Colyer Apartments'. This had been Bob's Mecca; this was where he'd run away from home to; in a corner of this club, under a pile of duffel coats he and Jo had shagged their brains out; here they had shouted *Howl* at one another; one door down from the bookshop I ended up managing for eighteen months in the early noughties, and where I launched my second novel, *The Battle for Dole Acre*. For one day only the bookshop windows were full of my book, and no other. Bob appears as a character in the book, thinly disguised as 'Ash'. Tonight, I stood outside my old shop (it's a Patisserie Valerie now), looking at the soon-to-be Colyer Apartments, and thinking about how Bob's life had bumped up against mine.

Then, on the tube back to Earls Court, there is a Poem on the Underground: 'Gherkin Music' by Jo Shapcott, who just happens to live in the village over the hill from where Bob has his wood. 'Under the pavement – Radnorshire.'

That's a *dérive*. Try getting lost in the city yourself, and seeing what happens.

In their time, we will be back to visit the SI's greatest moments: the 1968 student unrest in Paris; punk rock in London, *circa* 1976, and the burning of a million quid by the KLF on a Scottish island in 1994. In the meantime, Younger Readers, *Ne Travaillez Jamais*, as Debord once wrote on a wall.

Bob was not above setting up Situations himself, although he knew nothing of this till I told him.

'I'll tell you a little sociological experiment I did when we had Karma Sigma. It had a basement to it, which we just used as a sort of "happening" space. I had a couple of *epées*, you know, swords. I took the little button off the end of it and sharpened it into a point, got hold of an old army kitbag, scrunched up loads of newspapers and stuffed this kitbag. Hung it up in the basement so it was body height off the ground, punchbag height, with this sword just sticking in there. The reason I did that was to clock people's responses, because the little area I was making the candles in, you could see in the basement. And it happened with every fucker who went down there, and the only ones who went down there were definitely the middle-class intellectual, upper-echelon head types. You'd see them think, "What's this, then?" And they realise they can touch it, and interact with it, and it's all very sweet. It already had lots and lots of holes in it because I'd put lots in. So anyone could think, "Another few holes wouldn't make any difference." And I'm not saying everyone fucking went bananas on it, but a lot of them did. It was the same pattern, they'd touch the sword and I'd deliberately left it loose and easy to pull out of the bag. So they'd eventually pull it out, do a few waves in the air with it, then look at the bag and go mental, frenzied at it ... Hippies, peace and love, yeah!'

'You never really bought into that stuff, did you?'

'No, it was bollocks. I'm not saying a peaceful life ain't a fucking good life, but I know that in the world a lot of people would hurt a lot of people if they could get away with it, as any conflict will show you. Yugoslavia, Rwanda – folks would just be walking down the streets lobbing hand grenades through windows just because someone might be there – not someone who's going to come out and do them any harm, but just for fun. I'm sure you'd be able to get a good number of people, if you put a firearm or some weaponry in their hands, and said, "Those people over there, you can shoot them," a lot of people would do it. Some wouldn't, but a lot would.

'I'd be one of the people who wouldn't, except that one of the people who would would probably have a go at me, and then I'd become one of the ones who would ... You can't say, can you? It'd be like living in America.

'A lot of the thing is, as soon as you put on uniform, you are offered absolution, that's the deal. If you kill people we tell you to, you won't get into trouble, and not get told off, put in prison or anything. A lot of people would fucking love to do that, if you gave them an automatic weapon and said, "You can walk down the street shooting anyone you like, mate, and nothing will happen, it's all right, you can blow out some of the windows as well if you like." They'd love to do that – I mean, come on! I'd love to walk down the main street with a fucking automatic weapon shooting out windows; I think that would be fucking wonderful fun! And to fire one of those automatic weapons, the modern equivalent of a Gatling gun, shooting out astronomical numbers of bullets per second – I'd love to fire one of them. You could get a group of trees and they'd all dissolve into splinters. I know it's awful, and terrible, but I know I'd love to do it.'

As much as I love Bob, he has just made a very good case for gun control.

'That wasn't the beatnik agenda, was it? Peace and love?' I say.

'No, not at all.'

'In fact, the beatnik agenda was often quite violent, because it's about truthfulness somehow, isn't it, being anti-hypocritical; whereas "Hey, let's all like, yeah, peace and love" sounds hypocritical, because we know that life's not like that.'

'Not always, no.'

A note here about structure. This chapter is about Bob's times in sixties London, as experienced by Bob over four or five years or so. If I was to write it in strictly chronological sequence, I would have to break it up with the first two trips to Afghanistan, whereas I've decided to make High Sixties Swinging London counter-culture this bit, and the first two trips to Afghanistan the next chapter. This is because the trips to Afghanistan constitute *the* great adventures of Bob's life, the Boys' Own Adventure he'd always longed for. I decided that this would let the adventures of what Bob calls Afghan One and Two breathe a little, and I have promised myself I would save my ruminations about the hippie trail and hippie orientalism generally for Afghan Three, which was a different beast again. But Afghan One changed the fortunes of poor struggling Karma Sigma (not to mention sixth-formers' outer wear) for the next several years.

'So when did Karma Sigma become Forbidden Fruit?'

'Once we got the Afghan coats in, that established it as a place people would go to for clothes, then we moved to the Portobello Road and Vicki and I a got proper house, and the Laurie brothers set up production using outworkers and that, and just started manufacturing clothes.'

'When you got the coats, you moved the shop?'

'To Portobello Road, yeah. Just by the Westway flyover. Just that first block of shops between Oxford and Cambridge Gardens, in fact. We were next door to the Black Panther headquarters – I've got a photograph somewhere of me outside that building doing a stall, wearing Afghan boots. And the Black Panther headquarters, I think it's a tutu shop now or something, but there were a lot of Black Power types hanging out there. I went into our shop one day and Little Bob, Bob Laurie, was there and he said, "Oh, man, I'm glad you've come; there are a couple of black guys there and they're just loading themselves up with suede coats, and they've got a gun, and they're just going to fucking rob us." So I thought I suppose I'd better handle this, so I go over and say, "What's happening, fellas?" And the geezer pulls out a revolver and points it at me. I know a bit about guns, and I look at the gun and I can see straight-away that no bullets are going to come out of the end of it because the end of the barrel is blanked off, and it's got just three small holes in the blanked-off bit at the end of the barrel. That didn't take me long to ascertain, so I say, "Put that away and fuck off." And you can see them think: "What, this is a guy who can have a gun pointed at him and just be totally contemptuous of it." (They didn't know I knew anything about guns.) So they did: they dropped all the stuff they were going to nick and fucked off. Not long after this, we were doing some alterations to the basement, making a cutting-room extension so you could lay out cloth and cut it, and one of the guys who was working with us has his hand up under the roofing material, double layer, asbestos probably with hardboard, and he says, "Fuck me, look what I've found," and he pulls out this same fucking gun that the geezers had pointed at me. I said, "Give it to me, that's up my street," and I break it open and found it was loaded with these funny-looking, what I took to be blank cartridges, because sure enough there was no bullet on the end, brass like a shotgun cartridge but with paper on the end – just a very loud blank. Anyway, I take it into the building, with both the Lawrie brothers, and just fire it at the ground. And, "Ah, fucking hell, it's a tear-gas gun" ... so I thought, "Glad I didn't learn that the hard way – but anyway, worth having."'

'And you bought a house? Where was that?'

'Belsize Square, between Belsize village and Swiss Cottage. Big five-storey Victorian house. With it painted up it looked very smart. I thought it would be a good investment; I knew there were always lots of people looking for cheap bedsits, so you were never without funds – all you had to do was to go round once a week and collect the money. We bought this big house and I said, because of where I am with securities in life, "Look, we'll put this in both our names, so we're both the legal owners." I'd been on the streets a couple of years, so I thought if we buy a great big house we can rent out most of it and keep a nice flat for ourselves, seemed a sensible thing to do.'

'You've arrived back from Nottingham of all places, into Swinging London, at the moment when London is starting to be the hippest city on Earth. With lots of money. What was that like?'

'It was fucking great. We were just enjoying ourselves ... I'd say, let's jump in the motor and go down to Brighton for fish and chips ... or let's put an advert in *Exchange & Mart*: Wanted, rent or buy, secluded house within a hundred miles of London, and then go out and look at them, dozens and dozens of responses we got to that. All of which were less than a thousand pounds, can you believe? We looked at a lot of nice houses, all of which had something wrong with them, like one of them was in Norfolk ...'

Bob makes a face, as though Norfolk is the worst thing ever. I like Norfolk myself, but there's no accounting for taste.

'Sorry, you're from that part of the world, aren't you?'

'No, from Brighton. Just outside. Newhaven.'

'There weren't any secluded houses offered in Brighton, sadly, I'd have probably gone for that. In the end we rented one in Wiltshire, because that was the nicest house, nicest location, and it was a renter rather than a buyer ... And then I started making the trips to Afghanistan and that ...'

I can feel him straining at the leash; the closer we get to the Afghan trips, the more he wants to go there again. I keep trying to slow him down. Perhaps we need a musical interlude, to account for some of what is to come. Because by the time Bob was back in London, the music he had been listening to was about to change for ever. To help us through this change, to get from pop, folk and trad jazz safely across to 'rock', we need Dylan.

The first recognisable rock band, one that we could comfortably go and see and think, 'Oh a rock band; they look like a rock band, they act like a rock band, and they sound very much like a rock band,' was the Paul Butterfield Blues Band backing Bob Dylan at the Newport Folk Festival in 1965; and subsequently at the Manchester Free Trade Hall in 1966, this time with a group called The Hawks, who would soon change their name to The Band.

Watch them on YouTube: electric guitars lick, riff and solo; a rhythm section rocks out; someone is leaning hard into a Hammond organ, someone else is playing a rock-'n'-roll figure on piano, and Dylan sneers into the mic. Seeing footage of these events today, it is hard to imagine the fuss they caused. After all, that's what we expect when we go to see a rock band. It is when the camera turns on the audience that we see what extraordinary events these were. The band, we recognise. The audience, however, are your grandparents, and they are clearly stunned, and have no idea what to do. No one moves.

The idea of 'genre', so central to Younger Readers' ideas of popular music, has barely been born. Excluding soapy ballads, young people in the early sixties only encountered three 'genres': pop music, folk music and jazz, particularly trad jazz. What Mr Bob Rowberry would have called pop music also included the Beatles, please remember. Like trad jazz, folk music clung to ideas of authenticity, and to the idea that 'pop' was a sin, because it was inauthentic, false, alienated. In Britain in particular, folk authenticity was the order of the day, and it was culturally policed by artists such as Ewan MacColl. Dylan appeared in this world in 1962, and by 1965 had acquired the status of a prophet. His direct line of descent from Woody Guthrie, his anti-war anti-boss songs banged out on an acoustic guitar and breathed in through his harmonica meant that Dylan became the first folk superstar. His appearances at the Newport Jazz Festivals from 1962 until 1964 were spoken of in reverential terms.

Problem is, Dylan didn't want to be a prophet. He wanted to be a musician. He'd been listening to what an American guitar band called the Byrds had been doing with his songs. The Byrds had been listening to the Beatles (and, it should not be forgotten, the twelve-string guitars of the second-best Merseybeat band, the Searchers). Roger McGuinn from the Byrds thought he could take the sound of the Searchers and the Beatles, and put it to Dylan's songs. Dylan liked it, and decided to do it himself. (The Beatles, meanwhile, liked the Byrds too, and started to write better lyrics.)

Therefore, when Dylan stood on stage at Newport in 1965, with what to his worshippers looked like a pop band, like a stupid filthy rock 'n' roll band playing stupid inauthentic amplified musical instruments, his fans turned from reverential to outraged. And when, a year later, he brought his new band to Manchester to perform in front of your mystified grandparents, an audience member shouted, 'Judas!' And Dylan said, 'I don't believe you, you're a liar,' and pumped up the volume to 'Like a Rolling Stone'.

Oddly, two of the most lied about gigs in the history of rock 'n' roll happened in the Manchester Free Trade Hall: Dylan in 1966, and, ten years later, in 1976, the Sex Pistols at the Lesser Free Trade Hall. Millions of people claim to have been at these gigs, even though there were only a couple of thousand at the Dylan 'Judas' gig, and no more than forty for the Pistols, and maybe only one person who was even possibly at both: Tony Wilson, local TV presenter and one day owner of Factory Records and the Hacienda (though he did like to big himself up, so it's also possible that he was simply the only person with the nerve to lie about both gigs).

But I have a pal who was for sure at the Dylan gig: radio producer Peter Everett. I'm breaking a self-imposed rule, which is only to talk to people who actually know Bob, but I have made an exception, so that I can be sure of my ground. I could find any number of people who a) know Bob and b) claim to have been at the Judas gig, but I have decided that in this case, it's best to stay safe. After all, *I* know both Bob and Peter Everett. In fact, knowing someone who really was at the MFTH gig leads me to suspect that maybe I *was* there myself, aged eight, and I've just forgotten some of the details.

When I tell Peter these feelings, he says, 'You were there in spirit,' which was kind.

Six or seven years younger than Bob, by the time the 1966 gig happened, Peter was a student, with a corduroy jacket and a hankering after a pipe; just at the moment when that idea of what it meant to be a student was about to disappear for ever. This makes Pete sound square, which is not the case at all.

'We were catching up with Carnaby Street. We still hadn't worked out how to look. This was before *Sgt Pepper*, remember, and Manchester was not London. There was a rock audience, but they didn't look like rock audiences till years later.'

Peter has been working on a taxonomy of pop for many years, and traces his interest back through Donegan to the rootsy blues stuff, rather than through the heavily policed Ewan MacColl idea of authenticity.

'I went to folk clubs in the early sixties, including a few where guitars were banned because they weren't authentic British folk instruments. Concertinas, dozens of fucking penny whistles, and a coin being rattled in a beer glass, and that was about it. Twats.'

I asked him if the MFTH gig was the first time he'd seen an amplified band.

'No, not at all. I'd seen Them, the Kinks, the Animals. And we were listening to the Stones and the Beatles and The Who. And Dylan; after all, by the time he got to MFTH, he'd already had two electric albums out, one and a half anyway.'

'The electric thing didn't annoy you?'

'I thought it was great.'

'So you didn't agree with the bloke who shouted Judas?'

'Not remotely. He was a gobshite who spoke for no one but himself.'

'Where were you sitting?'

'Left front stalls. And the shout came from the centre front stalls, really loud. What you can't hear on the recordings is everyone turning around and glaring at him.'

'You don't think the audience were on his side?'

'No. And I don't think he was objecting to the electric thing. Like I said, Dylan had made some electric albums, done "Subterranean Homesick Blues". No, in my view he was objecting to Dylan abandoning protest songs for the more cerebral stuff.'

'Really?'

'Yes. All that trad jazz, all that folk stuff, all those sloppy joe and Aran sweaters, all that was through. That was the previous generation, the fifties.'

As is often the case with seminal moments, no one involved seems to be aware that the moment they were in was the least bit seminal. From Peter's account, very few audience members were outraged by the electric thing. But in the history of Dad Rock, it has become a symbol of something important; the moment when 'rock music' shakes free from 'pop', when trad jazz hastened its journey from being the hippest thing in London to being six old geezers in the pub on Sunday lunchtime; and when folk music, as such, bid goodbye both to Dylan and to Aran sweaters, and started to undergo its own revolution, one in which no one would object to electric instruments, so long as they were played with an English accent.

So now, Younger Readers, let's plunge into the world of rock music.

'So who were you hanging out with?'

'My main mate at the time was Guy Stevens, who you can probably find on your computer.' (Note to Younger Readers: Bob has just insulted me, as Guy Stevens was something of a hero to my generation, and I don't need a bloody computer.)

Guy Stevens is still waiting for his biographer, which is a shame, because if anyone deserves a biography, it's poor old Guy. Drink was his poison, unusually for his time, and drink it was that did for him. The music business has largely forgotten him, which is a tragedy, in my view. His three interventions in popular music history are all worthy of note. First, as a record collector, DJ and A&R man. Guy was the DJ at Ronan O'Rahilly's Scene club. He bought records by the truckload, particularly on labels that were pretty much unknown in the UK at that time, such as Chess, Stax and, in particular, Sue. He provided The Who with a compilation tape of American R&B tunes that ended up constituting their early set. Not much of a businessman, but hugely persuasive, he managed to be the licensee for American label Sue in the UK, and was taken under the umbrella of Chris Blackwell's newly formed Island Records, the first and, I guess, most important of the UK's independent record labels. Stevens released four compilations of Sue sides, which helped give impetus to the burgeoning Northern Soul scene. Northern Soul DJs were always trying to out-do one another in their quest for records, but thanks to Guy, they could all rely on being able to find the latest Sue sides. While he was working at Island in A&R, he signed and produced Free and Spooky Tooth.

Second, as an inventor of, and collaborator with, ridiculously named bands. Procol Harum were not under his aegis for long, but long enough for Stevens to name them (after Bob's cat) and to introduce songwriter Gary Brooker to lyricist Keith Reid; 'Whiter Shade of Pale' is still the stand-out track, of course, but Guy failed to persuade Chris Blackwell to release it on Island. It's the signature Procol tune, one which has sold an estimated ninety million copies, but a handful of others stand the test of time: 'Conquistador', in particular, still gets occasional radio play. After Procol Harum, Stevens helped psychedelic poster designers and not-quite exactly musicians, Hapshash and the Coloured Coat, to make a couple of albums; but above all, he poured his energies into the last and greatest of his ridiculously named bands, Mott the Hoople, named after a novel Guy read while he was in prison for drugs offences in 1966.

It's hard to underestimate how much boys like me loved Mott. When I came to true pop consciousness, about 1972, I soon realised there wasn't much to tickle my fancy in the mainstream. Bowie and Roxy Music were in the singles charts (good), but the album listings were dominated by cock rockers like Led Zep, Deep Purple and Uriah Heep (bad). Mott was one of the first bands that I was crazy about; not just because of the Bowie penned and produced 'All the Young Dudes', but because of the album of the same name, which I pretty much wore out through playing. I was going to see Brighton play football most weekends, and the group of lads I was going with were all similarly enamoured of Mott. I think time has shown them to be a lads' band (like the Faces), but when 'All the Way from Memphis' comes on the radio, I still crank it up loud. I never got to see them, to my eternal regret, but their shows were legendarily rowdy. Up until Bowie's intervention, in fact, this had been their main problem, as well as their great glory: fabulous live shows, supported by albums (four before *All the Young Dudes*, three produced by Guy) which nobody bought. The band decided to jack it in before being persuaded by Bowie to let him give them a song. Guy was pleased that Bowie took Mott on; but he was out of the picture by then, the drink having very much taken hold.

Another Mott nut was Mick Jones, co-founder of the Clash, and he it was who drafted in Guy Stevens for his third moment in pop's history: his 'production' of The Clash's masterpiece, *London Calling*. Guy was not easy to find by the time of the album's recording. Joe Strummer told the *NME*'s Charles Shaar Murray about hunting him down:

> I well remember searching through all the pubs in Oxford Street looking for him. I found a row of blokes sitting slumped over the bar staring in their beer. I looked down this row and I spotted him because of his woolly hat. I went up to him and tapped him on the shoulder, he looked round and it was like son-finding-father in one of those corny films. He looked up at me and said, 'Have a drink.'

By most accounts, Guy didn't so much as touch a slider, and spent much of the time pissed. But for Jones, for whom Mott were his teenage passion, Guy's mere presence spurred the band on to their greatest moment. You can see why. As Guy told Charles Shaar Murray:

> That electricity, that manic intensity. It's a kind of madness, not a 'mad' madness . . . but like Dean Moriarty and Sal Paradise. Chasing, chasing. I've always felt that way about making records. Making a record is an event. Big letters: AN EVENT. It's not just 'another session': I hate people with that attitude. It's electricity. It's got to be.

It may be hard for a company like CBS to accept a concept like this, but I could quite well die while making a record. It's that important. That's why – if it came to it – I could produce anybody.

I can't very well afford to take out a small ad in the classifieds, so you couldn't print my phone number so that people can get hold of me, could you? It's 699-4999. Ask for Guy. Record production a speciality.

'Anyway,' says Bob, bored by my fan-boy enthusiasm, 'he was the fellow who discovered Procol Harum. The Paramounts, as they were called.'

'When did you meet Guy Stevens?'

'Guy was living nearby to Belsize Square; where I first met him I don't remember, but he lived at the Primrose Hill end of Regent's Park, off Regent's Park Road, one of the central social streets. We became bosom buddies. The hash might have had something to do with it, he was at my place a lot and we'd go out clubbing several times a week. And my brother had turned up, and was basically poncing off me. I was looking for ways to get him standing on his own two feet, and Guy had just found Procol Harum and they were looking for a van and a roadie. So I bought a van and gave it to my brother and said, "You've got a job." I told you the whole thing about my cat and the name?'

'Uncountable times.'

'So Guy's found the name on my cat's pedigree, that's the name, well, that was how I was able to give my brother the job of being their first roadie and all that.'

At the back of this book, you'll find the URLs which will enable readers to follow the exciting detective story that led music journalist Marcus Gray to Bob's metaphorical door. Gray proved beyond all doubt, and to the satisfaction of Procol Harum fans the world over, that the band were named after Bob's cat (Vicki's cat really). I hope and trust that other journalists in the future, researching diverse subjects such as where R.D. Laing got his acid from, or who first thought of using oilwheel projectors to light Pink Floyd, will beat a path to Bob's door.

'I didn't know your brother *was* the first roadie for Procol Harum.'

'Oh yeah.'

'So was Sandy reasonably respectable at this point? He hadn't gone to prison?'

'He hadn't done any time at this point, though you'd never call him respectable. The job he had before this was photography on the beach at Margate, and I think he was fairly successful; he had easy charm and nice looks. But it was a summer job, so then he came up to London, and blagged off me basically, and I wanted to get him doing something on his own two feet. Then he met up with the Led Zeppelin boys, and understandably decided they'd got to be more fun than the Procol Harum boys, who were basically not, so it seemed to me, the brightest fucking stars in the firmament ... they just lucked in, I suppose. So Sandy gets the job with Zeppelin and went on all their American tours when they're first becoming really big. And in the middle of that he jacked the job in. I asked him why, as you would, and he said, "It's because I'm not up there on the stage getting all the adulation." I said, "Fuck me, surely you're getting all the pussy you can deal with and more," which is bound to be the case. If you're roadie for Led Zeppelin you're – well, if you can't shag one of the band members one of the roadies will do, sort of thing ... So I thought that was a pretty sad excuse to give up a fucking good job like that, well paid as well as a lot of fun, you know, doing all the main American tours. And he was well liked. To give up such a job because he wasn't on the stage, getting all the cheering and knickers being thrown at you, I thought it was sad.'

'Yeah, it is a bit.'

'Anyway, so Guy Stevens and myself went out almost every nightclub-bing. Vicki didn't want to go, she didn't like the club scene, so I'd leave her at home and go to the groovy clubs of the time, like the Scotch of St James, or a place called Blazes where you could see Jimi Hendrix on the stage, a little tiny stage they had, not much bigger than this table, and he played because he wanted to play. And the beautiful people were there.

'Anyway, so there we were, me and Guy, we were doing a lot of clubbing, like the famous re-meeting with Clapton – we were very affable, me and Eric, because the last time we'd seen each other we'd been in rags, and now we're well dressed, with posh-looking birds on our arms. I'd been to prison, come out of prison, gone up to Nottingham, met a girl who was very rich, came back down to London, bought a house in Hampstead and I'd just arrived at Scotch of St James in London, parked my XK20 Jaguar there in the car park, was heading towards the door of this club that I had free access to, and there was Eric, coming out of the club with a girl I now know to be one of the Ormsby-Gore girls, and we're both surprised to see each other, because we haven't seen each other for a few years, but we're both looking very well and prosperous and the groovy clubbers of the moment, and it all went well until I say – because I didn't know he was Eric Clapton, though I'd heard of Eric

Clapton and liked his music, but I didn't know that was Eric – "Are you still playing banjo, then?" And he just walked off in a huff, didn't reply, thought I was taking the piss or something. And it was only when the manager of the club came over to me, before I'd even got to the door, and said, "I didn't know you knew Eric Clapton" ...'

'Presumably his bird wasn't Jo Bramley?'

'No.'

'Scotch of St James, I've heard of.'

'A bloke I'd met up in Nottingham had got the job of being the manager of Scotch of St James. Often Hendrix would just be jamming in there; and Keith Moon, a lot of the sixties big names, Spencer Davis, Stevie Winwood, that sort of crew. There would be a stage, no bands booked, ever, but guitars, a bass, drum kit, amps just there, and if anyone had the balls to get up and play, it would be top-of-the-bill musicians. And it was free, no one getting paid. It was a great time, you were seeing top bands, it doesn't matter who you were (well, it did at Scotch of St James, you had to be in with the in-crowd, because there would be a queue of people from the suburbs, all done up to the nines, who just couldn't get in). But there were loads of other clubs like Blazes, the Cromwellian and others, the Four and Twenties, for very little money, like ten bob or something, you'd be in – it wasn't "only cool people can get in here, mate" it was anyone who wanted to go, and it was always rammed. And the spade clubs, whose names I don't remember but they all had good music, blue-beat type music ...'

'Playing records?'

'At the spade clubs, yeah, but bands at most of the others. Hendrix seemed to spend a lot of time wandering around places, picking up a guitar and just playing. He was often down at Blazes, which was just off the Gloucester Road. I saw Bob Dylan there. I was with Keith Reid, who wrote Procol Harum's songs, and he was a huge fan of Dylan's – and he was in the same little room as him, there was a back room to Blazes behind the main stage. I didn't talk to him, didn't want to, that was how you kept in fine with people, not bother the big names with pointless chat if you had nothing relevant to say. But Keith couldn't manage to say, "I'm a big fan of your work, mate, I'm a songwriter too," and I bet he regrets that.'

'But you don't know that Dylan isn't also going, "Skip the light fandango", wish I'd written that ...'

'I bet he isn't.'

'What about UFO?'

'That was down at Covent Garden, where John Peel would sometimes be DJing, Pink Floyd had their early gigs there, the Soft Machine, those sorts of bands.'

'Was it a slightly different sort of band that would be playing at Scotch of St James? The Who weren't playing at UFO?'

'There was definitely the acid hippie world and the straighter, just pot-smoking or no dope at all sort of world. But one of the best places was the Shamrock Club, an Irish club. Hang on ... no. UFO was at the Shamrock Club, on Tottenham Court Road, it was Middle Earth at Covent Garden. Wednesday was not a good night for the Paddies so they'd rent it out to the hippies, Joe Boyd had something to do with it. One of my girlfriends was a girl who worked for Island, so she knew a lot of American people like Joe Boyd. My impression of him wasn't so favourable; I thought he was a bit snotty. I recently read a book called *White Bicycle*, and that really confirmed that, because reading his book you'd think that the whole scene of the period we're talking about hung on the Ormsby-Gores, the whole upper-echelon aristocratic types, who were certainly around but they were trying to get in on the scene. Which they were able to, because of all they had, but it wasn't a scene that was focused on them, it was a scene that those types were trying to connect up with. And Joe Boyd was from New England, where they were far more into that class stuff ...'

'So posh boys know posh boys, and they give a posh-boy account of things. After all, History is the study of books people have written about things that happened, not the study of what happened. And books are usually written by posh people.'

'Yes. But like him or not, Joe Boyd did get things together,' Bob admits.

He did, though, in fairness. Boyd was the sound guy for Dylan at the Newport Folk Festival in 1965, and in 1966 he set up the UFO club (which, as Bob remembers correctly, was held in an Irish club on the Tottenham Court Road). But it is as a producer that he is best known. He produced Fairport Convention as they invented folk rock, the first Pink Floyd single, pretty much all the Incredible String Band albums, everything by Nick Drake and the legendary Vashti Bunyan. On his return to the States in 1970, Boyd produced 'Duellin' Banjos', Maria Muldaur's 'Midnight at the Oasis', and the first two Kate & Anna McGarrigle albums. I can't help thinking some people are entitled to be a bit snotty.

'Mick Farren wrote a book, and lots of that was about Joe Boyd and UFO.'

'I knew Mick. He was the doorman at the UFO. Good bloke. Always let me in for free. His band were fucking terrible.'

'I can imagine UFO, because I've read so much about it. And seen pictures of the Floyd on stage, with psychedelic stuff projected on to them.'

(Here it comes, future investigative journalist ...)

'Duncan and I did their first light show. A church hall, All Saints Church, Notting Hill, which I'd later squat the vicarage of, years later. The church hall at All Saints hosted some of Pink Floyd's first gigs. We'd seen some American West Coast stuff, San Francisco, the Grateful Dead, on film, and we'd seen their light shows, the oily, bubbly things, and figured out how to do that. Got a cheap second-hand Aldis projector, one of us loading, one putting the things in, and we did the messiest fucking job we'd ever seen. Sheets of glass, photographic slide glass, oil and ink, slap another sheet of glass on top, no sealing whatsoever, and when it's practically slid out the bottom, slap the next one in. Because the heat from the projector bulb really gets it moving, livens it up, in time to the music, you manipulate it with your fingers while the other one's preparing the next slide. So we made a few of them – and of course, we made acid rock 'n' roll history there, though we didn't know it at the time. It was fucking messy, we knew that.'

'So who else was about at that time?'

'John "Hoppy" Hopkins I knew well, he was part of our crew ...'

'Ah, sorry, Bob. Got to stop you there. I promised Perry Venus that this would be the first book that he'd read about the sixties which had no mention of 'Hoppy' in it.'

'Oh right. Well, Charlie Radcliffe I used to know well, he was connected with that printing stuff, *Friends*, I think, that sort of thing.' (Charles Radcliffe was that rarest of beasts, an English member of the SI.) 'Because in that area where we set up Karma Sigma, there was also a lot of publication stuff. It was the time of the birth of the underground press. And all those people were very much in the same pool as we were in, Sue Miles and so on ...'

'Barry Miles was Sue Miles's husband. He was the founder of *International Times*, wasn't he?'

'Was his name Barry? I only knew him as Miles.'

I almost regret my pledge to Perry Venus not to have too much about Hoppy Hopkins in my book, because though I take his point – Hopkins does appear in a lot of sixties memoirs, most especially in the books by Barry Miles, in particular *London Calling* and *In the Seventies*, both of which are highly recommended as further reading – Hoppy did get about a bit. At his 1966 trial for cannabis possession, the judge described him as a 'pest to society', which makes him hard to resist. But, to keep it brief, in October 1966, Hoppy Hopkins, on his release from prison, got together with his friend Barry Miles (always known as 'Miles') to found the *International Times*. Miles ran the Indica Gallery and Bookshop, part funded by Macca, which Miles described as an 'experimental powerhouse', and where on 9 November 1967 John Lennon would meet Yoko Ono for the first time. The Indica Bookshop, 102 Southampton Row, became the editorial offices of *IT*.

Issue Two lists the original editorial staff. The list includes editor Tom McGrath, who had an unfortunate obsession with Nazi sympathiser Ezra Pound, and his assistant editor David Mairowitz, with Hoppy on 'Headlines', and Jack H. Moore as 'Man-at-Large'. Miles sat on the editorial board, along with Jim Haynes, McGrath, Moore and Hoppy. Moore and Haynes had set up Edinburgh's Traverse Theatre, and ran the Scottish equivalent of Indica, the Paperback Bookstore. They had been the first to join Hoppy and Miles in their new venture; and in fact, their plans for an underground newspaper were more fully formed than those of Hoppy and Miles, so it is disputable as to who joined who. And in charge of advertising, Barry's wife, Sue. This was still no place for women. Mairowitz in particular liked to print pictures of Dolly Hippie Birds, in as pornographic poses as he felt he could get away with. In 1966, in the hippest magazine in Swinging London ... chicks did the classified ads, typed, posed for pictures, made the tea and swept up.

IT was successful, in its own terms; the largest print run was 44,000. But it never made any money. Presteigne resident and long-term Bob ally Mark Williams used to hack down to Southampton Row from Birmingham once a fortnight to pick up copies to sell, barefoot. Would he always pay for his copies? Miles never knew if the people who distributed the paper actually handed over the money they got from selling it. Mark Williams must have been one of the honest ones, as he was taken on as *IT*'s first music editor. He told me how *IT* in its heroic phase lasted until 1973, when the paper was closed for running gay contact ads. Mark subsequently founded hippie biker's monthly, *Bike*. And had a relationship with Sue Miles. At the same time as Bob. When we get back from Afghanistan in a few chapters' time, things might get messy.

On 15 October 1966, *IT* was launched at a happening in the Roundhouse in Chalk Farm. When I used to go there in punk days, I knew woefully little about Britain's railway system, so I thought the Roundhouse had once housed an engine turntable, but now, older and wiser in matters locomotive, I know that it had held the winding gear that helped trains up the slope out of Euston. These considerations aside, in October 1966, the Roundhouse was an abandoned industrial building, falling into what seemed like terminal decay. It was cold, filthy and dangerous. What better place, then, for what has been described as Britain's first rave? It was advertised as a 'Pop/Op/Costume/Masque/Fantasy-Loon/Blowout/Drag Ball. All-night rave to launch *International Times*, with the Soft Machine, Pink Floyd, steel bands, strips, trips, happenings, movies. Bring your own poison and flowers & gas-filled balloons & submarines & rocket ships & candy & striped boxes & ladders & paint & flutes & feet & ladders & locomotives & madness & autumn & blow lamps.'

And who better to describe the event than the writers of *IT*? Nothing tops this account, or gives a better flavour of *IT*:

2,500 Ball at *IT*-Launch: Two and a half thousand people dancing about in that strange, giant round barn. Darkness, only flashing lights. People in masks, girls half-naked. Other people standing about wondering what the hell was going on. Pot smoke. Now and then the sound of a bottle breaking. Somebody looks as if he might get violent. There was a lot of tension about. The Pink Floyd, psychedelic pop group, did weird things to the feel of the evening with their scary feedback sounds, slide projections playing on their skin (drops of paint run riot on the slides to produce outer space/prehistoric textures on the skin), spotlights flashing on them in time with a drum beat. The Soft Machine, another group with new ideas, drove a motor bike into the place, in and around the pillars that held up that gallery we had been warned wasn't all that safe. A large car (some said it was Oldsmobile, others a Cadillac) in the middle of it all, painted bright pop art striped and explosions by Binder, Edwards and Vaughan, a London team of artists who someone said put stripes over everything (and who were responsible for the light show that night). Contrary to earlier stories, this car was not previously exhibited at the Robert Fraser Gallery [Author's note: that would have been a Cobra which BEV also painted and which was owned by Tara Brown, immortalised in the Beatles song 'A Day in the Life'.]. Simon and Marijke Koger, the Amsterdam couple who are opening Karma, designed an interesting cubicle with coloured screens and nets, and within the box one of them, in suitable dress, read palms and told fortunes.

In another part of the Roundhouse, Bob Cobbing and the London Film Coop gave an all-night film show featuring films like *Scorpio Rising*, *Towers Open Fire*, under the most difficult of conditions. The audience stood in front of the projectors, on top of the cables, on top of Bob Cobbing. Yet the films went on. It may, though, have been just the right setting for those particular films. Burroughs' inner-space disappearance in *Towers Open Fire* somehow had more impact because of the vibrations from the 'party'. 'Famous' people turned up: Antonioni and Monica Vitti, Paul McCartney disguised as an Arab, Kenneth Rexroth. Of course several things went wrong. There was that narrow entrance for an unpleasant start. That communal toilet that ended up in flood. A giant jelly made in a bath for the party was run over by a bicycle ... After the party, the crowds caused a traffic jam in the streets outside. It should be said here that throughout the event the police were cooperative ... Perhaps it was just relief that something has at last happened in the Roundhouse. It was a good party, and just to prove something really *is* going on in London, another, bigger, better one is currently being planned.

Daevid Allen of the Soft Machine described the event as 'one of the most revolutionary events in the history of English alternative music and thinking. The *IT* event was important because it marked the first recognition of a rapidly spreading sociocultural revolution that had its parallel in the States. *IT* was its London newspaper. The new year came ... bringing an inexpressible feeling of change in the air.'

And the *Sunday Times* said: 'At the launching of the new magazine *IT* the other night a pop group called the Pink Floyd played throbbing music while a series of bizarre coloured shapes flashed on a huge screen behind them. Someone had made a mountain of jelly which people ate at midnight and another person had parked his motorbike in the middle of the room. All apparently very psychedelic.'

'I was at that,' says Bob. 'But who was playing, fucked if I can remember. But there were films projected on the wall there, Kenneth Anger films, and that.' They say that if you remember the sixties, you weren't really there. Bob really was there, and the occasional gap in his memory can be excused, I think.

IT had dozens of imitators. *Black Dwarf. Gandalf's Garden. Frendz. Ink.* Later on, *Zig Zag* and the punk fanzines like *Sniffin' Glue* followed in *IT*'s uncertain footsteps. The three most important magazines to follow on from *IT*, however, were *OZ*, *Spare Rib* and *Time Out*, the sole survivor of the alternative press, which is still indispensable to London life, even in our app-driven age. We'll curl up with *OZ* and *Spare Rib* after Bob gets back from Afghanistan.

International Times has never quite gone away. It has been published on and off ever since, currently as a webzine; you can find the links in the Appendix. Also available online is the entire *IT* archive; all the issues, ever. For readers of my other books (which I highly recommend buying and dipping into), Chris Brook, who came with me and Perry Venus on the leg of the journey from Glasgow to Islay in *The Longest Crawl*, was the last ever editor of the last ever print edition of *IT*, in 1986. He it was that began the process of getting the archive online, and he and Perry discussed it on our trip. For me and Perry and Chris and many of our generation, *International Times* mattered, even if it was hard to get in Newhaven, or Amesbury, or Bradford; even if the real thing was through, and the occasional copies we might see were second or third iterations. *IT* represented something we wanted when we were fifteen, sixteen, seventeen. It certainly had resonance for me in 1972, when the Soft Machine were the first band I ever saw live.

The best legacy of the underground press, from the point of view of seventies music geeks like me, is that the writers moved from the underground to the blessed *New Musical Express*, whose story, like that of *OZ* and *Spare Rib* is on hold until the seventies. And to complete this little orgy of foreshadowing, Chris Brook was also involved with the team that perpetrated the last 'happening' of the counter-culture: the burning of a million quid on Jura by the KLF on 23 August 1994 – which is where our story will eventually end.

Maybe Bob has dropped enough names for now. I shall allow him two more.

'Simon and Marijke, they were Dutch painters, they had quite a lot of involvement with us early on, when we were setting up our hippie shops. They did the designs and stuff.'

My head spins. According to the quote from *IT*, Simon and Marijke were actually 'setting up' Karma; but then, they were bullshitters of the first water.

'OK. Were they known as The Fool, by any chance?'

'Yeah, that's right. How have you heard of The Fool?'

Once again, I assert the superiority of reading about things rather than merely doing them. Anyone who has read a Beatles biography will be sucking air through their teeth at the mention of The Fool. If Younger

Readers only read one sixties book from the books I have recommended, let it be Philip Norman's *Shout*. Then you too will suck air through your teeth at the mere mention of The Fool. There were four of them. Three of them were Dutch – Marijke Koger, Simon Posthuma and Yosha Leeger. The fourth member was Englishman Barry Finch, who was Leeger's fiancé.

Soon after arriving in London, Marijke met musician-cum-magician Graham Bond, who 'turned her on' to tarot. She named the group The Fool after the first and last card of the Major Arcana, and you can detect the influence of the classic Rider Waite pack in much of their subsequent work. This will puzzle Younger Readers, unless they have a tarot app on their devices, which I doubt. Wait until Bob gets back from Afghanistan, and we will set up a school for wannabe wizards. We will learn what our rising sign is. We will throw the *I Ching* together.

The Fool's look became *the* look of high-end psychedelic London. Their posters and clothes for Cream, the Hollies, The Move, Procol Harum, their album covers for The Incredible String Band, brought them to the attention of Brian Epstein, who was leasing the Saville Theatre, where he used them to design a cover for one of his theatre programmes. Which in turn brought them to the attention of the lads. The Beatles loved The Fool. They painted Lennon's piano, and a mural at George's house. They dressed the Beatles for 'All You Need Is Love' and 'I Am the Walrus'. The Beatles loved them so much that they gave them forty grand (a very great deal of money in those days) to become the lead designers for their shop, the Apple Boutique, which opened in December 1967. The Fool were responsible for both the interior and the exterior design (though they were made to take down their original mural covering the building by Westminster Council, who felt it would upset bus drivers). They had experience of shop design, because they'd already designed Karma Sigma, but not actually of the realities of what to sell. The clothes they sold in the Boutique were beautiful, but hugely expensive, and ideal for shoplifting. The shop closed after seven months, having lost somewhere in the region of £100k. The Beatles decreed that on the last day everything should be given away; they naturally took care to go round themselves and pick up stuff the night before. There was naturally something of a scrum on that last day.

This, then, is the cause of the teeth sucking: that The Fool ripped off the Beatles, or, at least, were so out of their nuts on acid that they didn't really notice what was what. But the Beatles didn't give a fuck about the shop, regarding it as a bit of interesting fun. They seemed to like The Fool, like their designs, and not to care too much that it didn't work out. A pub quiz question for your dad: what was both the first solo album released by a member of the Beatles and the first album on Apple Records? Answer, *Wonderwall Music* by George Harrison. It's the soundtrack to the 1968 movie *Wonderwall*, with clothes and interiors designed by The Fool. There were clearly no hard feelings. They might have been bullshitting stoners, but everyone seemed to like them, and they did make lovely things, except, Younger Readers, for their two albums, which were dreadful beyond belief.

'Did I tell you about the funny-ish but sad story of Guy Stevens' record collection?' says Bob.

'I don't think you did.'

'He had gone to the States and toured and bought a whole lot of 45s, really early Elvis stuff, stuff on Chess, Checkers, Sue, other names I can't remember, Stax I think, an amount which would cover about a double-bed area all stacked close together. And he used to compile LPs out of them, some of which were issued as *The Sue Story*. One of them had a picture of Elton and Guy Stevens on the front, if I remember.'

'Elton?'

'Yes.'

'Elton John?'

'Yes.'

'You knew Elton John?'

Bob sighs. 'Of course I did. Him and Rod Stewart were Baldry's backing singers, weren't they? I thought you wanted me to stop name-dropping?'

'Just for a few minutes. What happened with Guy's records?'

'He was getting further and further out, going off on strange solo jaunts, like he was discovered unconscious in the bath at the Holiday Inn, wearing ladies' clothes, all that sort of stuff. Anyway, he gets back from one of these jaunts and he sees a kid in the street near where he lives, selling secondhand 45s for ninepence each. Guy bends down to look at them and very quickly realises they are his fucking records, and it turned out this kid had broken into his fucking gaff and stolen all his records, some of which would be worth many hundreds of pounds now, and flogged them all.'

'Really sad.'

'I don't think he ever recovered from that, actually.'

'But this was still in the sixties? Before he invented Mott the Hoople? Or produced *London Calling* for The Clash?'

'Yeah. He was pretty fucking mad by the end, you know.'

Guy Stevens died in 1981 of an accidental overdose of the prescription drugs that he was using to come off alcohol.

'One of the guys I knocked about with was bisexual, and he was Lord Montagu's bumboy. And as a result of that me and a bloke called Mike Delaney, who was a really good-looking London Irish geezer, film-maker, cameraman, and assistant photographer for a famous French photographer whose name I don't remember, anyway, through this connection, I get invited to these gay parties. It was all cool, they know me and Mike aren't gay, but that we're just lovely-looking boys, well dressed and with some semblance of manners. And of course Edward Montagu was at all of these parties. I mean, I was at parties in the fucking Albany. At one of 'em, Diana Dors was shagging a boxer in the middle of the floor while other people watched and had a wank. I didn't stay long at that one.'

'Actually, you just say "Albany", not "the Albany". Stephen Fry lives there now.'

'Doesn't surprise me. It's a whole world of its own, it really is.'

'So you went to Albany? To gay parties in Albany? With Edward Montagu?'

Younger Readers may be aware of Lord Montagu of Beaulieu as the man who set up the National Motor Museum. They may be less aware that he was Britain's best known 'out' bi-sexual, whose imprisonment for gross indecency in 1954 was one of the drivers for the establishment of the Wolfenden Committee.

'Yeah. Ed Montagu introduced me to a High Court Judge and asked, "Can you get him any hash?" And as it happened I had a couple of ounces back at home which wasn't too far away, so I jumped in the XK, tore back home, came back with a bit of hash which I sold to the judge, not being unaware of the irony of the situation.'

'You never went to the Beaulieu Jazz Festival?'

'No, that was years before. It turned into the Reading Jazz and Blues Festival in the early sixties. But I went to Beaulieu, just to Montagu's place, as a guest, and went out in his very nice speedboat. When we were out in it, he says, "Pull over by that boat over there." I had already worked on the Thames for a few months so I had a sort of eye and sort of idea for what was absolutely the dog's bollocks, none better than the kit on this boat. And this boat exceeded all my previous – I hadn't seen anything like it. It was Alec Rose's boat, just before he went off to sail round the world in it. Alec Rose was on it, I chatted to him.'

Sir Alec Rose was the second man to circumnavigate the globe single-handed, in his boat *Lively Lady*, which had so impressed Bob. He set off on his trip in July 1967, so this must date to shortly before that time, just before Bob's second trip to Afghanistan.

Back in the van, Bob says, 'Did I ever mention Dennis Rolfe? That's a whole scene I probably never told you about, before Afghanistan. This mate of mine Dennis was a book cover photographer for Penguin. He was shagging Hezza, the girl who was in charge of that department. And I was the model, if a book cover needed a person, a male – you can even see me naked on the cover of a book called *First and Last Men* by Olaf Stapledon. There is a blacky-orangey cover with a naked silhouette of a bloke – that bloke is me. That wasn't the most fun job ...'

'Did the most fun job have guns in?'

'Yes. The most fun job we had was a book of *The Eagle Has Landed* or something, about what it would be like if the Nazis had won the war. And Dennis hired the appropriate model convertible Mercedes, with all the appropriate flags on it, so we've got this 1930-something Mercedes with fucking Nazi pennants on the wings and all that. He hires three SS officer uniforms – playing it for laughs, he had one of them himself. There's myself and my brother Sandy as the passengers in this car, complete with Schmeisser sub-machine guns. Now they obviously didn't fucking work, but they were real de-activated Schmeisser machine guns, and they certainly looked the business. So he wants to take "us on a village green outside a ye olde English pub" sort of photograph. So we drive out of London in this Mercedes fucking Nazi staff car wearing Nazi fucking uniforms, and we go into deepest Wiltshire, driving around the place looking for the right place to be this village. And of course me and my brother were shouting "*Schweinhund*" and pointing the guns at everyone – and we did the job, this all takes about half a day. And how many calls do you think we got – fucking none. That you could drive around the countryside brandishing machine guns at people, menacing them as much as we could, tells you something about the English not wanting to make a fuss.'

'I know the edition of the Olaf Stapledon book you mean. I used to be a book dealer, so I can picture it. I've read it too, a sort of futurology thing. It's very odd, but I liked it.'

'Well, if you ever come across another copy ...'

Bob yawns and stretches. For a man on an opium holiday, he's done very well. Maybe I should leave him be. As I drive back down the old track-bed, the rain has stopped, but the trees drip water and drop leaves. One of my headlights has stopped working on dip, I notice.

This weather, this damp, gets in your bones.

It is time, perhaps, to find the high dry places of the East.

Those were the First Afghan Coats in London

I am alone, except for Peggy the dog, in a wooden cabin up on stilts on the west bank of the rising River Severn, a few miles north of Tewkesbury, where I have come to finish my first draft. Storm Imogen is tearing up the Bristol Channel, funnelled through the broad flat valley of the Severn by the Cotswolds on the east bank, and on the west by the high ground of the Forest of Dean and the Malvern Hills. It has been raining for days; both here and, more importantly, in the mountains of mid Wales, which drain into the Severn. The water is rising fast. This morning I chatted to a boat owner who told me that on Saturday morning the river was only a couple of feet above its summer average; by Sunday morning it had risen six feet, and it is rising still. All I can see from the cabin's picture window is the fast-moving river turned from bottle green to cappuccino by flood. Whole tree trunks sweep down the centre of the channel, and a picnic table, one of those A-frame ones with bench seating, glides down the river as though it were a potential prize on *The Generation Game*.

Now night has come, and it is hard to see how high the river has risen. I stand out on the decking in the teeth of the gale, and shine my torch over the waters. It has risen a lot. I realise I am now on an island.

I am alone on an island, with an idiot dog, in a place I don't know, in a cabin that creaks under the strictures of winter storms, and with dark water rising all around me.

It's a fair analogy for life, really.

I lived for a couple of years at the turn of the millennium in an old Mum and Dad caravan, parked up next to a quilt of allotments in the centre of Lancaster, just me, a bed, a wood-burner, my writing stool, an ancient desktop computer, and an ex-battery hen called Ginger, who had the run of the place and who liked to come and sit on the bed in the mornings while I was writing. I loved living in my caravan.

After that, I moved to London to live in a squat. London was a bit hectic for a mid-Wales hippie like m'self. At night, as goods trains from the adjacent railway shook the old house, and as the crack den next door said a noisy good-night to its punters, I lay trying to sleep. I did what the sleep experts suggest, and imagined myself in My Happy Place. Which was my old caravan, wood-burner red hot, rain only a few millimetres from my head. It had gone from being where I lived, to being My Happy Place, about which Younger Readers will know.

Over the years, My Happy Place has evolved. Now it's like something from the cabin porn websites; still with the stove, and the ancient desktop computer, and Peggy the dog instead of Ginger the hen, but now with minimalist retro styling, electric blankets and a reliable source of mains water. Something very like this actual cabin.

In short, I am actually living in My Happy Place. It is even better than you might imagine.

There is no internet in the cabin, and I find I don't miss it. All I have for company apart from Peggy is the radio. And listening to the news, it sounds like the whole world is at war. Refugees seek safety in a beleaguered Europe, bombs in Turkey, millions of refugees escaping the horror of Syria, Kurds attacking Daesh, Turks attacking Kurds, Russian bombing, UK France US bombing, Libya burning, Africa convulsed by war and drought and famine, Iraq and Iran closed, and Afghanistan and Pakistan wild with hatred, like hornets stirred up by the big sticks of Russia and the USA. Bad bad times. Bob's journeys to Afghanistan, to some extent blazing what became known as the Hippie Trail, are now impossible.

It was never an easy trip, the Hippie Trail, but it has been closed for a long time. While it's odd to meet a hippie of Bob's generation who didn't at least try to get overland to India, none of my contemporaries even had a go. The Russian invasion of Afghanistan and the Iranian Revolution, both in 1979, and the Iran/Iraq War of 1980 to 1988 pretty much closed the overland route. And it gets worse year by year. Now the traffic is the other way, except the intrepid travellers to the West make the whole journey in mortal danger, rather than in a spirit of adventure.

For Bob, there were three trips to Afghanistan. This next part concerns the first two trips. Afghanistan is Bob's great caper, the central adventure of his life, the one he had dreamed of since he read Kipling and Rider Haggard as a boy. He gets to meet 'the wily Pathan', and to feel like a player in the Great Game. So far as possible, I'll use his words to tell this story. His adventure, not mine. I would always have stayed at home, even when the Hippie Trail was possible, smoking spliff, looking after the womenfolk, knocking about in recording studios, and reading books. Though tonight, home feels a bit edgy; the cabin rocks and the water rises as Imogen shrieks up the river. It is time to pull the chair closer to the stove, poke up the fire and to listen to stories.

*

My first trip East was when I went with Vicki in a really old Volkswagen Beetle I'd bought. We'd gone down to spend some time on the Italian Riviera, then down to Naples just to have a look at it, then across the country, got on the ferry to Greece, and then drove across Greece. Autumn 1966.

And then we continued on the road, and got to Istanbul, and it was the coldest place I'd ever been in my fucking life, much to my surprise. There wasn't much snow in Istanbul, but it was like an English winter, damp cold. It was so cold that Vicki just blacked out in the street with hypothermia. She had clothes on and everything but it was just so cold. Quite embarrassing when your woman just collapses in the street, people think too much hashish, or pissed. But it was the cold.

So, winter 1966, November I guess, cos we were trying unsuccessfully to escape the weather, was my first time in Istanbul. I liked it. I like Turkey, it's an interesting country. It's beautiful, it's very varied, you can have Boy's Own adventures there at the drop of a hat, even when you don't particularly want one. On that first trip to Istanbul there was the Topkapi lion cage incident, have I not told you about that? I'm walking with my girl in Istanbul. It's all hills, but we're on this hill overlooking the Golden Horn, the bit of water goes through the middle of the town. And on the other side of the road there's a big, ancient wall, a bit of a bank then this big wall, which we don't know what it is. There's a gate in this wall, just a small pedestrian gate, and next to it a little sentry box. An army uniformed mush comes out of this sentry box with an Al Capone type tommy gun which he points at us. I don't speak a word of Turkish at this time, and he's equally handicapped by his lack of English. But when someone points a .45 calibre sub-machine gun at you, you tend to concentrate on finding out what they want. When we get up to the sentry box there's a plain-clothes man in there who's got a shooter in his hand, an automatic pistol, and he's also gesturing. There are now two guns pointing at us and they look quite serious. The plain-clothes guy's got a key and he unlocks this wooden door in this big wall, and they push us through the door. I'm not making a big fuss or struggling, because it's only going to make it worse, you don't speak a word of their language and they don't speak a word of yours, and they've got guns pointed at you and obviously they're earnest about whatever it is.

And as we're going through the wooded grounds of this place, we can see 70 yards away there's huge massive buildings, ancient buildings, mosque-y type shapes. This bloke's blowing a referee's whistle. And you realise that behind almost every bush there's a soldier with an Al Capone gun, those machine guns with round magazines, a very common gun over there, for the city armies. Anyway, we get to this office-type building where there are a few more plain-clothes people. They talk to each other, then some guy says in English, 'Would you like some tea?' or something like that. 'Yeah' – anything rather than being shot sounds good. Some geezer makes a phone call, chats away in Turkish for a bit, then hands me the phone. And a voice on the other end of the phone says, 'There is murder. It is you.'

Click. Hang up.

Now that is not a very good message to get ... Are you supposed to be the murderer or the victim-to-be? None of it is reassuring. Vicki asks, 'What was that?' And I say, 'Not loads to tell you ...' because there didn't seem much point. So the tea comes, nobody speaks English, and the geezer who speaks a word or two has fucked off. Anyway, we have the tea, and then the plain-clothes guy who brought us in off the street, and another plain-clothes guy who seems to be his mate, grab hold of us and take us out, walk us round from this office-y building to another door, into quite a big room.

It's an odd room, actually, because it's got a chest-high division down the middle of it. And the side of the division that's not occupied by us is occupied by three lions. It's a fucking lion cage we're in. I don't mind a bit of surreal, but this is pushing the boundaries. There's a uniformed guy with a machine gun, and the two guys in plain clothes who've both got automatic pistols, and they push us over towards the barrier, then they start to sexually grab me and the girl. It becomes clear that they're going to fucking rape us and feed us to the lions to save a few quid on the fucking lions' feed. Well, I ain't going to just lay back and enjoy it – this is all a micro-second thought – so I shove the geezer off me, and go for the geezer who's grabbing hold of my girl, expecting to get a shot in the back from one of the other guys behind me, but fuck it, I'd rather be shot in the back than raped and then shot in the back. And just at that moment when I'm grabbing hold of the geezer who's on the girl, the door we've come in opens, and some civilian-dressed geezer comes in who's obviously in authority above the clowns who are trying to fuck about with us – he comes in and gives them a bollocking, and he doesn't seem very happy with us either, he was pretty unpleasant with us. But he's presumably just saved our lives so I wouldn't hold that against him. He was obviously the captain of the watch and he'd just heard what was going on, probably from the bloke who spoke a bit of English, and came to put a stop on it. Anyway, he took us out through a gate on the other side of the grounds from the side we'd entered it in, and boom, I realised where we were, and I said to Vicki, 'Oh, fuck me, this is the Topkapi Palace we've just come out of.' So we were nearly fed to the fucking lions in the Topkapi Palace.

And the next day, or a day or two after that, I was in the British Embassy checking for mail, and I mentioned it to the assistant whoever it was, and asked, 'Do you ever lose any tourists around here?' and gave him a quick précis of what I've just told you, and he said, 'Well, if you do insist on coming to countries like this, it's your own fault,' sort of thing. I wasn't expecting anything more, but he asked, 'Have you any other questions?' So I said, 'Yes, is the tap water drinkable here?' He did not fucking know. He didn't know whether the tap water in the town he'd presumably been living in for years was drinkable. That is poor, isn't it?

When we got back from that trip, I wanted more. I knew Tom Harney from the early beatnik days, hanging round the Duke of York and places like that, he was a face on the scene. And he got into driving out to Afghanistan and bringing back a few kilos of hash, selling it for seven quid an ounce. He had paid three and a half quid a pound for it, so the profit margin was pretty good. But the risks involved! You've got to cross more than half a dozen borders, some of them with severe rules against drug smuggling; you're looking at life in the nick if you get caught. So for a few hundred quid, and the effort in driving 6,000 miles each way, the majority of it over dirt roads after the first 1,500 miles, and some of them bad dirt roads, it didn't seem worth it. But Tom had come back wearing this sheepskin coat with embroidery on it, and I thought, 'We could sell these', because the hippie thing was just beginning to blossom, and we had a shop. And so I thought. 'Let's go out to Afghanistan and buy a load of these coats.' And Duncan Laurie thought it was a great idea. So Vicki steered some finance towards this project.

There was this exchange control act, you were only allowed to take fifty quid out of the country. And when you're setting out to Afghanistan it's not feasible to say, 'I've only got fifty quid, mate' – so we had to form a company, and get special permission from the Bank of England to take money out of the country. I knew both Duncan and Tom were going to do hash as well, but I didn't want anything to do with that because I had a criminal record and they didn't, which was fair enough because obviously I would have got pulled out of any line at the airports and looked at quite closely.

Anyway, we put together a trip, the three of us, and formed a company to get the money out of the country, called David Rowberry and

Company. You couldn't just send money out to a bank in Afghanistan, you had to take it with you. Travellers' cheques, that sort of thing. It wasn't a vast amount, but it was money you could have bought several houses in this area with – about three grand. I bought a good-condition Volkswagen van, and Tom had a long-wheelbase Safari Land Rover.

I'd met an old mate called Ian Rock, who was sometime manager of the Gyre and Gimble, who had just come back from India, and he told me about this way you could legally go and buy a gun and ammunition in England, and take it out of the country. They provide you with this wonderful piece of paper. It was not very big, but by Christ, everything you could possibly do to a bit of paper to make it look impressive had been done to that bit of paper – embossings, perforations, water markings, lions and unicorns and crowns all over it. I suspect it was only produced for British agents, so they can carry a gun with some impressive piece of paper to back it up, because it's got the name and number of the gun on it. Supplied by the Board of Trade, this piece of paper was, and all you had to do was go into a gun shop, say, 'Could I look at your pistols?' and make your selection. I chose – because I knew they'd be cheap as chips and I knew they was good – a British Army .45, which this gun dealer had a great many of. I bought one of the last stock of British Army pistols designed to be fired from a horse; £5 for the gun, £5 for the ammo, a big box of ammo. All I had to do was supply the gunsmith with a destination address. I just made one up. I mean, I was going to Afghanistan, what have they got, a street directory of Afghanistan? No. So you can make up any name you want to invent, but more specifically they needed a point and date of departure from the UK. So I asked, 'How does this get to their end?', thinking it would be fucking posted or something. And the gun dealer said, 'Well, I can appoint a special messenger.' And then I realised that he meant he could appoint me as his special messenger, which he did. So on the appointed day I arrive at the gun shop, pick up the gun, just in its holster, and the ammunition, take it down to Dover and introduce myself at customs as the special envoy for Future Supply Company, Cleveland Street, and I'm delivering this gun to you to be collected by Mr David Rowberry and delivered to Afghanistan. And just for my own amusement, knowing I could keep a straight face because I had prepared for it, I stepped back, and stepped forward again, and said, 'I am David Rowberry, and I've come to pick up a gun to deliver to Afghanistan,' and they're like, 'What? You're a fucking hippie.' But I had this bit of paper, and so there I was, I had this shooter.

We stopped in Munich, cos we had a contact there, and we bought a Volkswagen estate car, a Variant, the S version, so quite swift compared to the Land Rover and the van. We bought that, not because we needed another motor, but because Tom had arranged to do a deal with a bloke called Abi Bulla in Quetta, who was sort of the flash-boy head of the local mafia.

So leaving Munich, we've got this little convoy: Tom and Patsy in the Land Rover, Duncan Laurie driving the VW Variant, and myself in my VW van. We'd come through Germany, Austria, Yugoslavia and Bulgaria. Got to Istanbul, and by chance we met a bloke there named Vic, who had been a Newmarket jockey, whom I used to know from my days living rough on the streets of London. Anyway, he was heading in the same direction, and he had a driving licence, so it seemed a good idea to have another driver along, so he became part of the trip.

Somewhere in Turkey we picked up a Belgian junkie who just wanted a ride and was willing to pay a bit, but we got fed up with him because he was always shooting up opium, boiling up opium into a liquid and injecting it. We got fed up with him on dirt roads, trying to cook up opium in a spoon; we wouldn't stop for him to cook up. So I said, 'Give me your opium.' I took it all and put it all in the windscreen washer bottle of this motor, pulled off the pipe that supplies the nozzle, put his needle on, said, 'when you want some, push this fucking button.' He wasn't a very happy bunny.

We went down to the south coast of Turkey and played around there for a while before heading on. Almost the entire coast, several hundred miles, and nobody there. Locals, and maybe one other lot of foreigners there, camping on a beach, but no tourists. Beautiful beaches. Scorpions on the beach, though, fucking millions of them.

We've just driven along the Mediterranean coast of Turkey, gone past Adana and Gaziantep, which is just above the Syrian border, and it's got very hostile, everyone we meet, in this caff particularly, the entire clientele were standing around us while we were eating, and they started to nudge us and knee us and elbow us and it was a very bad vibe. And we got out of there, got into our vehicles, and they all piled out and got into a vehicle of theirs, and started to chase us up the road. And it was only when I fired a couple of shots – not particularly at them, but just to let them know that I was armed – that they gave up chasing us. And everywhere we stopped for the next few days, we were having to stand guard, gun in hand, by the motors, because the kids was trying to puncture our tyres, and it was really quite heavy. It was only when we got to Tehran that we found out that we had been just a few miles north of the Syrian border when the Six-Day War was on. (Author's note; i.e., sometime between 5 June and 10 June 1967.)

Anyway, crossing into Iran was a worry, because of my .45 revolver. Going into Iran, they were obviously going to find it, and when they did they said, 'Oh no, you can't take that into Iran,' and I said, 'It's all right, I've got this paper,', and of course they can't read a fucking word of it, but it's just the embossments, and the lions, the unicorns and all this, and it was my name and the same name on the passport, so they say, 'OK, you can take it into the country, but we've got to put a seal on it so it can be taken off when you get to the other side of the country.' So they wound a bit of wire round the trigger in the pull position, put a lead customs seal on it. And this is the sort of strange person I am. The fact that before I was out of the customs compound I had pulled off that fucking lead seal, loaded up the gun and fired it out the window. While still in the fucking customs compound. Now I think I must've been mental.

A couple of days after that we'd gone through Tehran and then headed up the Caspian coast and down into Mashhad, and from there into Herat in Afghanistan. That road between Mashhad and Herat is a mountainous road, it's at night, we're in convoy. I'm driving the back vehicle in the Volkswagen van, Land Rover's in front and the VW Variant's in the middle. And the Variant has got Vic the jockey driving it and the Belgian junkie who was still with us. I'm driving half a mile behind them, because there's a huge amount of dust. And suddenly I see the lights of the Variant go in strange directions, their headlights and their tail lights and then the headlights again, they're revolving in more than one plane, so I knew this ain't good. The dust is getting really big-time. So we stop. And what there is is a mountain dirt road. And they'd put heaps of fucking stones to repair the road, and it's all the same colour stuff, with no signs what-soever. Nothing. And there was a row of these heaps of small stones. Vic's hit the first of these, then bounced off and hit the second, bounced and battered all along these fucking stones. By the time we get there the Variant is unbelievably fucked up, every side, front, back, rear, top, everything is fucked. One of the wheels is broken right off, so it's obvi-ously not going to be driving anywhere. And they'd picked up a fucking Iranian soldier earlier on in the day, and he could pick up a car while you changed a wheel, because you get a lot of punctures out there and he'd done that twice – he'd picked up the fucking car and held it while they changed the wheel. Which indicates that he's a strong bloke, and a bit of an idiot too, because we had a jack.

Now those three people who were in the motor, they're a little battered, a bit of blood, but nothing remotely serious, a bit shocked and knocked about, but fine, all still alive. So I thought what I'd better do was belt down the road and catch up with Tom and Patsy in the Land Rover to let them know what the situation is. Which I do, they've gone quite a way, but I find them at the first caff for hundreds of miles and they're having a meal, so I say I'm going to get back now.

So I get back and this Iranian soldier has got Duncan up against the wall and is stripping him of everything he's got. Because he's saying, 'You were all smoking hash' which is really big time against the law there, and he's a soldier, he's in uniform. So he said, 'Give me everything you've got or I'll grass you up.' And this is all going on as I arrive there, and just because I arrive he ain't backing off, he's still going for it, presumably going to turn on me. And I've got the .45 in the back of my jeans, so I was, 'Right, although you're a foot shorter than me I've seen you lift up a car, you're obviously very strong, and a pretty bold fellow by the look of it.' But I had a .45 fucking revolver, which does make a lot of difference psychologically. I wouldn't have pulled it on him, unless there was no other option, but it does give you a lot of confidence. He doesn't even know I've got it, but I know I've got it. You can go into a face-out with someone with far more enthusiasm and confidence than if you hadn't got a .45. Anyway, so I come into him like 'I'm crazier than you are', and he just gives it up then, because he can see I'm serious and I'm going to get cross with him. But then I just want to get rid of the fucker.

In fact, I had more sense than to try to get him to give up everything he had just stripped off Duncan – I got him to give some stuff back but I let him keep a lot, a watch and a bit of cash, so he's not totally fucked off. There's very few vehicles on the road, but about the third car that came along, they took him off. Then we had to get the Variant from there to the nearest customs, which was about 150 miles away, up on one of the Caspian Sea ports, and we had to tow it. Because we had to get it written off Duncan's passport, otherwise they might think he'd sold it, car smuggling and that, which would cost hugely more than the £3,000 I had for coats. The import duty on a vehicle was six times the new price. If you turn up at your port of exit from the country without the car that is written in your passport, well, you're fucked. You've either got to give them huge amounts of money, or Go to Jail Now. The only way you can get the car written off your passport is to get the car to the customs place so they've got the car. So that's what we had to do – we had to tow it. Dirt mountain roads, on three wheels ... with no wind-screen as well, and this is dust country.

I was steering it. One of life's interesting situations. I had a scarf round my face and all that. But we got back to this customs place, got the car taken off Duncan's passport, and headed back for Herat.

This was before the Hippie Trail had really got going. It was in full steam the time I was out there the same time as Taffy, the third trip. It was before the common people had got on to it, if you see what I mean. When we went the first time, it was semi-professional adventurer types.

We passed through the town of Mashhad and I bought a load of turquoise there, because that's where it comes from, they've got a load of it just nearby there. The trip across Iran – and the fact we'd lost a vehicle and a lot of time – was not a great deal of pleasure, because it was an unfriendly country, where every time you stop you get secret policemen blatantly watching you. They're not trying to hide; they're just there, following you around, everywhere you go. So you're just glad to be out. They leave the cars of foreigners who have crashed and died, they leave them like warnings beside the road, and one of these motors the brother of a mate of ours was in, and we stopped to pay a bit of homage by the vehicle and some locals came along and started mocking and laughing. I was very nearly tempted to get out the fucking shooter and let them have it, but I restrained that impulse.

Just before the border, we come across a bunch of tents with all these nomads, and I think, 'That looks interesting,' and of ethnological interest. So I go over and say, 'How are you?' And they say, 'Have you got a gun?' And I say, yes, and show it to them, and after that we're welcome, and they make us tea. In my experience, in that part of the world, if someone asks you if you've got a gun, it's always best to say yes, yes I have. Then everyone's happy, because we know where we stand.

Anyway, crossing the border into Afghanistan, near Herat, which is pretty much the first place you come to, there's an immediate sense of relief – we've got to Afghanistan, and it just lightens up hugely. We do the customs thing, no hassle at all. Within the customs compound there was this tiny little teahouse, you literally couldn't stand up in it, no furniture at all, everyone sitting on the floor, and the main centre of entertainment was this big hubble-bubble pipe, full of hash. Our little crew goes in, which makes it pretty crowded with all the local types in there. But they see us as a source of entertainment and a bit of revenue, so we're welcome. Patsy, Tom's girlfriend, who's young, blonde, beau-tiful, dressed respectfully, scarf on her head, but obviously blonde and foreign and exotic; they're astonished when she stands up when it's her turn on the pipe. Now this Patsy could smoke like you cannot believe. The Afghans thought she would keel over and they could have their wicked way with her. I had one toke on this pipe and that was enough for me, I thought if I have another one I won't be able to crawl let alone fucking walk, but Patsy, she fucking smoked them all under the table, because they got into the macho thing of, 'Well, if she can have another one, I can have another one.' That was a pretty good entrance into the country.

Coming from the west there's no road going north, unless you've got a camel, or a really good four-wheel drive, and are prepared to build the road as you go along. There is a road that goes across the middle, but it's easier to do on horseback than to drive. You can drive across it, people have done, but it's seriously problematical – it ain't really a road, it's a track that's sometimes working, sometimes not. So there was only the road that the Russians built from Herat to Kandahar. The Russians also built the bit from Kandahar to Kabul. And there's the road that goes over the Hindu Kush mountains from Kabul to the north of the country, and the road that goes down to Pakistan through the Khyber Pass. Those are basically the only roads in the country that you'd call usable. So you've got to go to Kandahar unless you're prepared to spend weeks and weeks driving across the country and having to be dragged out by teams of horses.

Between Herat and Kandahar, there was a place that Tom and Patsy knew about because they'd been there before, what they called the Russian Hotel, literally in the middle of nowhere. Between Herat and Kandahar there's absolutely nothing on the road except for this hotel. And it's enormous, with a swimming pool, kitchens to cater for thousands, it was obviously ready for when the Russian Army came, they'd already got a huge field kitchen. This was many years before the invasion, but it was already set up. You couldn't sleep in the hotel, and although the kitchen was four times the size of your house, when we asked for food they got a bit shifty, so we said we'd have eggs and tea. The geezer leaps over the wall, out of the building altogether, and I was interested to see where he was going. About twenty feet below us was this tiny little home-made shack, where the geezer had a little dung fire and was cracking some eggs into a frying pan and cooking our food.

One of the few regrets I've had in my life was that I bought a box of matches from this geezer. And I regret that I did not keep the box of matches he gave me and the change, from a tuppenny piece or something.

The box, the matches themselves, the block-printed label, was from the Pashtun Match Company, and I kick myself afterwards because I thought, 'They've got to be worth a fortune to matchbox collectors.' The matches were handmade, each one hand dipped. And the change he gave me – for my fuck-all – was a huge heap of coins, none of them I'd ever seen. And thus it was revealed that there was such a thing as pulis, a whole division of the currency I was completely unaware of. Coins, and some of them were nearly fucking hand-minted, probably what Genghis Khan would have had. I looked at them and wondered, 'What the fuck's a puli?' A puli is a hundredth of an Afghani, and in them days you were getting 340 Afghanis to a quid. So a puli is a hundredth of a 340th of a quid. (Author's note: although an Afghani is still officially divided into 100 puli, there are currently no puli coins in circulation.)

So we get to Kabul, and Tom has taken the Land Rover out there to sell, not to drive around. And he's got to keep square with the geezer down in Quetta that he's promised this Volkswagen Variant to, that we'd written off in Iran. So we put a Land Rover for Sale advert in the caff where the Ministry of the Interior had put up a noticeboard for English-reading Afghans and travellers. Next day a couple of local geezers, looking nothing special come in. 'You've got a Land Rover for sale? Can we go out in it?; Tom goes out with them, puts it through its paces, they're satisfied with it, and say, 'We'll be back tomorrow to finish the deal, with some money.' And these two geezers fuck off, and the hotel manager comes over and says, 'Do you know who that is? That's the Crown Prince of the country, the King's oldest son.' True to his word, next day he comes back with this big bag of money he's taken out of his dad's bank. Not his dad's bank account. His dad's bank.

The Afghan money was real shit quality. He'd gone down and taken all the returned reject notes, and there wasn't a note among them that wasn't Sellotaped together, pinned together, all in several bits (and there were a *lot* of notes). But even if we would have preferred nice clean notes, money is money, and we were planning to spend it there anyway. He brought his sitar along with him as well, so he spent a couple of hours sitting with us, smoking, drinking and playing his fucking sitar with us: the Crown Prince of the country and a bunch of hippies. There was Patsy, and a couple of other tasty young women, which probably influenced his keenness, but he just turned up with his mate/minder sort of thing, and sat with us.

So Tom's capital is now liquid – he was going to be doing his own scene with Pakistani geezers. And I had dosh to buy the coats with – Tom bought some coats, but I think he owed this Pakistani geezer Abi Bulla some money, down in Quetta.

On the road out we were just sleeping in the vehicles, because it was the only way you could keep them secure. But once we got to Kabul, we looked around the town, and there was a place called the Nur Hotel which was a beautiful, old, all-wooden place with really lovely gardens, right in the middle of town, and there was just an arch entrance, like a coaching inn entrance, with a big fucking gate and all that. I don't think there was any sign up or anything for it, but it was a really exquisite place, aesthetically spot on, and cheap as chips.

It was exclusively Westerners in the Nur Hotel. The only people who weren't Westerners were the staff, a manager and a gardener. When we got there, there were a few Freaks there, not more than a dozen; but it wasn't rammed or anything, it was exquisite.

So, settled in, you have a wander round the town, spend a day or so getting to know the layout of the town – which was very small, really. There were only half a dozen clothes dealers in Kabul, and most of their stock we didn't consider up to scratch, we just wanted the best, sort of thing. So you do a deal, and you'd haggle, you'd buy the best of what they'd got and say we want some more like this, not like that, like this. We'd make it clear that we wanted the good quality stuff. And other stuff you see in the bazaar that you reckon you can turn a profit over, which wasn't hard to do in Afghanistan then. Almost anything that was made locally, you couldn't go wrong, it was absurd.

The variety of normally thrown-away objects that people would make their homes from, like hammered-flat tin cans, just pierced, then wired together, hundreds of them, someone obviously had a source in the embassy dustbins to get tin cans; flatten them out and make your house from them, literally ... And you're talking about a place where the winters are much worse than here, people don't realise that, they're serious winters, they're Arctic ... big, big snow, every year, quite a lot of months of every year as well. Summers are very hot but the winters are really cold.

It's because the winters are so cold that the coats are so good, and three grand bought a fuck of a lot of good coats. We shipped a lot by rail through Russia, destined for England. But I had the van stacked and they had to be baled up to leave the country, because it wasn't just a couple of touristy souvenir coats, it was a lot of coats. They had to be baled up, with sacking sewn round, bundles of a cubic metre, and you had to have it marked where the destination address was, it had to be

stencilled on the sack to get it out of the country. I planned to take them
to Sweden initially, and then take what remained to London. I had a
mate in Sweden go round and line it up. So there was just enough room
below the roof to sleep, cos the Volkswagen van was stacked to within
eighteen inches of the roof with coats, fucking hundreds of them. So I
drove back with them to Stockholm. They smelt very badly of piss,
because they use piss to tan the hides. And they smelt of me, by the end,
I guess.

Everybody else was doing their own trip. Vic, he was making his own
trip anyway, it was just coincidental he was handy – well, I say handy,
he cost us the fucking motor, but he was just heading the same way.
Duncan had done some deal with this American girl who'd turned up
out there who had a brand-new Volvo 122S, and Duncan had arranged
to meet her in London after he'd driven the Volvo back to England with
a load of hash in it. Which succeeded, and the American girl was around
for a little bit and then she wasn't and Duncan had the car, so I never
bothered to query the ins and outs of the deal. Tom and Patsy, I honestly
don't remember whether I left them in Kabul or whether they had gone
on somewhere else.

I drove ten days between Kabul and Stockholm. 7,000 miles and most
of that on very bad roads. And a lot of customs as well. That's fucking
going, mate, I tell you.

I did have a passenger on the eastern side of Iran, which was very
fortunate. I can't remember who it was, but I didn't leave Kabul with
him, so I maybe picked him up in Herat or wherever. But crossing that
Iran desert again, the track rod end came off; it connects the wheel to
the steering wheel. One of these just broke, so it meant that the wheel
on one side wasn't connected to the steering wheel, which is not ideal
for driving along the public road. So I tied it together with rope the best
I could, which was partially successful, in that it kept you within a 45
degree angle of the direction you were going. You want a bit better than
that really, so I had this mush drive and I was hanging out the door to
keep it balanced. And the AA aren't coming, but robbers might. And no
one's going to come along and help – you could maybe find someone
who would give you a lift into town so you could arrange something
else, but when you got back out to your vehicle it wouldn't be there, or
not much of it would be there, it would be stripped or completely gone.
So you've got to do what you can to keep going. What else would you
do, just sit beside the road and bleat? Anyway, it worked, dunno how
far it was, about 150 miles or something, a long way, got to this little

town and there was a geezer there who had a hand-painted sign with VW on it, amongst the other stuff, a tiny little one-man garage. He saw the problem, rummaged round his kit and finds a track rod end off a Jeep, which he can weld on to the rods there and it will be roughly in the right direction. I said fine, go ahead. About half an hour later we were back on the road, and that bodge repair lasted. I sold the vehicle later on in England with it still on there.

Most of the coats and stuff was going by train through Russia to England. The reason I wanted to get the lot I had with me to another market was so we didn't have two shipments turning up at the same time. Sweden, Scandinavia, seemed like a good market for the sheepskin coats, especially as the hippie thing was just coming in there. I had an English mate called David Lindahl, married to a Swedish girl, who lived halfway up Sweden. They knew where Stockholm was at, and what the shops were, so I had them just check out the potential market. And he had a nice place to stay, and all that. So I got them to Stockholm, where people bought the coats.

When it got really funny was catching the ferry from Denmark to Sweden, going across the Skagerrak. Some customs fellow had given me this thing I'd never seen before, the red and green card thing, 'nothing to declare, something to declare', that one. I'd never come across this before and I was looking for the third way, but it turned out the third way was saying nothing. Well, there I am, I've got over half a ton of sheepskin coats sewn up in bales with 'Transit to Sweden' written on them, so it ain't hard to see, because there's no partition between the back and the front, so they ain't hidden in any way, they're very obviously there. I drove off the boat without doing this card, and the customs guy is all, 'Where's your card? Have you anything to declare?' And he's looking over my shoulder seeing these fucking sacks, you can see his eyes widening. I'd got this big .45 revolver and I showed it to him, and he says, 'You can't bring that in.' 'Oh, really?' 'You must surrender it here and we'll give it back to you when you leave the country.' 'It'll be here when I leave the country?' 'Oh yes, just produce this paper and we'll give you your gun back.' They settle that, give me a bit of paper, wave me through. Without my gun, but full of Afghan coats.

On the way out of Sweden, I had a huge amount of krone and I thought for the laugh I'd get the gun back. I was going to have to surrender it at the port anyway – probably Harwich – but I went for the hoot. I was a bit late getting to the boat, and Vicki had come out to meet me so we could do the last bit of the journey together. And Vicki and the car were on the boat, and the customs guy is, 'Oh fuck! We've taken the gun into our office in town, and the boat's here and just about to go. We can do it!' And they get into this customs car, police-type car, and they go off, squealing tyres, blaring siren ... Less than ten minutes later it's come back, lights flashing, squealing into the fucking customs, the boat is already moving, and the drawbridge is going up, and the guy gets out of the motor which he's squealed to a halt, I'm already running for the boat, he's up to it, he's with it and he fucking throws me the gun – a big gun – which I catch and stick into my waistband and just manage to jump on to the drawbridge of the boat, which is moving out. I only just make it and clamber on, in full view of hundreds of people, open-mouthed at this ... and no fucker from the boat came up and said, 'Excuse me, I couldn't help notice that you're carrying a fucking great shooter.' I get up to the exchange place, where you exchange money, and I have a great toilet-roll-sized bunch of krone: 'Can I change this into sterling, please?' Fuck me, how things have changed.

The whole roof of the van was covered in made-to-measure Afghan tin trunks, to go up on this roof rack. Just galvanised metal, basic square trunks with padlocks. The whole roof of the van was covered in them. We'd just come from fucking Afghanistan, with a gun, and they did not fucking search the van in Harwich. They did not even open the boxes on the roof, can you imagine that? I was pretty amazed. Maybe they hadn't begun to suss the drugs connection. I handed in the gun, and that was it. It didn't have many bullets in it when I gave it back.

We made a lot of profit, far more than the three grand Vicki put in. From the three grand came everything, 300 quid for the motor, the purchases and all the living expenses – yeah, we made loads of profit. We'd have made more than that from the sheepskin coats in Sweden, and then there were the coats that went to London, and other incidental stuff. That was what changed Karma Sigma into Forbidden Fruit. Because those were the first Afghan coats in London. I never did any books, or offered any tax returns, or anything – nothing. I wasn't remotely interested in business. I liked the thing of buying stuff and selling stuff, but people are trying to take some of it off you and make life as complicated as fucking possible, whichever way you go. I try getting on with my life and ignoring them.

And when I get back, I realised I wanted to live in the country. That's why I put an advert in *Exchange & Mart*: 'Wanted, rent or buy, secluded property within 100 miles of London.' Got a fucking sack of replies to that. Very few of them were for more than £1,000 to buy. And at that time I could have bought all of them. But I just wasn't interested in buying. The reason we bought the five-storey house in London was because it was in a handy area, but I just wanted to be in the country. I wanted to go out on a motorbike, on a dirt bike, carrying a shotgun, and in Wiltshire there was space enough to do that, if you didn't mind trespassing on Army land, which I had always enjoyed.

But it was obvious that Vicki and I was over. I said so, and I said I was going back to Afghanistan. And Vicki said OK, but I'm going to come for the first part of the trip.'

A trip that was a very different kettle of fish.

Me, Vicki, and this girl called Carol whom I was shagging at the time, a lovely, sexpot woman, all went off in this really ancient decrepit Volkswagen van I'd got, because I wanted to do a trip without anyone else's finance. The last trip was financed 100 per cent by Vicki. I really liked everything about the trip, it ticked all my boxes, but I wanted to do it again under my own steam. So we went out in this really ancient VW bus, me, Vicki and Carol.

And my brother Sandy had taken himself along as well. I'm planning to go east and then out to Afghanistan but without him, or Vicki and Carol. Carol's got some art school place in Istanbul. And after Istanbul, Vicki was going back home. I'd figured that taking this van further east ain't going to be good because it's pretty fucked, and I hadn't got any money, and I knew that public transport was really cheap. So why did I have Vicki and Sandy with me while I was still heading east?

I can't remember. But I did. And we were heading east along the southern Mediterranean coast of Turkey again. I'm heading for the Iraqi border, because I'm going to Baghdad. And I could see on some maps there was a bridge into Iraq, and on other maps there wasn't. So I think maybe I was planning to take Vicki down to Baghdad and then she flies back, I don't really remember, but I know I was going to Baghdad and then into Iran, so I must have been taking Sandy and Vicki along. Carol by now had split.

We were on the Mediterranean road heading for Alanya, and then onto Adana. Mountains come all the way down to the coast, and it's a dirt road, so dusty as fuck. There's a lorry with Alanya plates on it, it's going 35 miles an hour, putting up huge amounts of dust, and I just wanted to pass. There are plenty of places, but each time I tried to pass it would pull over, and bearing in mind that there is a sheer drop to the beach a hundred yards below, you don't want to fall down, and the other side it's a cliff, mountains. So trying to overtake him inside and outside, same result, he'd just try to push me off or into the wall, being a complete cunt. My first bad judgement was I should have just stopped and made a cup of tea and had a spliff beside the road. But I didn't, because I was with my brother, and we were both getting pretty pissed off with this geezer, and to exacerbate it, it was getting dark, and he had a big fuck-off spotlight, an ordinary car headlight but on the back of the motor, the back of the chassis, which he switches on. So not only have we got this dust at 35 miles an hour, we've got this blinding fucking light. Now, anyone with a brain in their head would have stopped and had a cup of tea. But I didn't have a brain in my head.

We get to the edge of Alanya, and I've made my little plan. I give a pair of pliers to Vicki while we're still driving and I say, 'Right, me and Sandy'll go around this geezer before he gets out of his cab, and just give him a load of verbal.' I told Vicki, 'Go round the back of his vehicle, because everyone will be concentrating at the front where we are, and with these pliers not only cut the wires but cut sections of wire out so he can't just join them together. Give us a sign when you've done that and we'll fuck off.' I don't know if Vicki actually did cut the wires, but the bloke hasn't got out of his cab, and he sees we're a couple of big blokes, and he knows he deserves it and don't want to face the consequences. But he understands the situation, I understand the situation, so it's cool. He's not going to get out of his cab unless we try to drag him out, which I'm not going to do. And I know enough Turkish abusive language by this time to be calling him the son of a cocksucking donkey or whatever, and he's giving it back.

But what I hadn't taken into account was that the telegraph-pole setting-up crew, which was working at this teahouse where we had stopped, might become overly interested in what's going on.

This is really brought to my attention quite sharply, when my brother suddenly pitches forward; he does this because a geezer's come up behind him with a large fucking rock and bashed him on the back of the head with it. Which really gives my anger a bit of focus, so I go for this geezer. And this is very fortunate, because the chair that would have hit me on the head, which I hitherto hadn't noticed, hits me on the back. So, distracted by this, I withdraw the chair from the hands of the fellow who was previously holding it, and I'm about to hit him with it, when I see that no, a better use for this chair is to use it to stop this fucking shovel which is coming quickly towards my head, edge on. And after that moment I don't remember precisely what happened, because it was very busy. There were a lot of geezers, most of them armed with these long-handled pointy shovels that they use in some places, shovels that are pointed at the bottom and a long handle rather than a cross-piece handle. Those that haven't got pointy shovels have got something in their hands they're trying to hit us with. I lost count of the exact number of blows, but there were plenty of blows going all round. I had things in my hand I was hitting them with, they had things in their hands they were hitting me with, me and my brother. Fortunately, I'd left the motor of the Volkswagen running because I thought we might want to make a quick getaway. I see that Vicki is in the van, so I shout to Sandy, 'Come on, get in!' I get in on the driver's side and put it into gear, and Sandy comes in also on the driver's side, but not in any way so he can drive, and it's not like I can just slip over because he's got his limbs going all ways to try to fight off these five million Turks trying to kill us. And anyway, it's in first gear, my foot's got Sandy's foot on top of it and the throttle pedal underneath it, so the pedal is on the metal fully, the engine is screaming, but we've got to go off, and I look forward and I'm rather alarmed to see that a bunch of these road crew guys have picked up a telegraph pole and are running battering-ram style straight at the front of the fucking van. So I think I've only got one option here, and I take my foot off the clutch. The engine is still screaming flat out and I know if I don't stop it from screaming, and I can't get my brother off my foot, and I'm also having a bit of trouble with people trying to get through the other window, so I take my foot of the clutch, the motor is going full scream, the van leaps forward, and this alarms the guys who've come with the battering ram towards the front. So they let go of the battering ram, but it's still hovering in the air, like in cartoons. I duck down and it comes through the windscreen, through the partition behind me, and stays there with probably a third of it in and the other two-thirds out the front. And because it's on my back, I can't see, and Sandy's still on top of me as well, so I'm trying to drive screaming flat out in first gear, twenty foot of battering ram out the front, and Sandy is trying to get up so I can see where the fuck we're going. Where we're going is we're just about to hit a building, with policemen sitting outside. It's obviously the fucking police station and we stop inches away, we crash through the garden, through the fence, and we're in the partially destroyed garden of the police station, the battering ram almost touching the fucking wall. We get out, we're all covered in blood, and the cops start laying into us with rubber truncheons. It wasn't the best of days.

All that stuff is the reason I like going to those sort of places, because that kind of stuff was generally on the menu. Does that sound odd to you? But I'm the person who would go to a military firing range and get between the shooters and the fucking targets.

So we move on, and sure enough there is the bridge, so I thought great – I had a visa for Iraq. I guess the others were going to turn back – why the fuck were they there? But there was a blockade across the bridge – I said I wanted to cross it and they said no, if you try we will shoot you, and if we don't shoot you the Iraqis on the other side will certainly shoot you if you try to cross that bridge. It's getting dark, time to bed down for the night, so we bedded down near this bridge, and a soldier walks by and slips a note through the partly open window. It's in Turkish, so I look at it and decipher it, and it says, 'They are going to kill you.' The note is clear. So I think I'll move on.

It's after we've been beaten up, threatened with murder and, incidentally, robbed at a petrol station, that I turned to Vicki and said, 'Look, this isn't going well, this trip, we're all stitched up and bloodied and damaged and the motor isn't going too well and I've got to get across the border some place else,' and we're driving along and I said, 'I ain't sure whether to keep going east or go back to Istanbul.' I said, 'I need a sign. And as I said 'I need a sign', there is a thwack on the windscreen. Everything is covered in dust, it's a really dusty road. And on the windscreen there is a perfect imprint of a bat. So I didn't know what that meant in Turkish, but I knew it would mean something, because it's very much a language where 'bat' will mean something. So I got out the Turkish–English dictionary, and looked up the word 'bat'. And it did mean something in Turkish. It meant 'west'. I kid you not, it meant west. And I'd just fucking asked that question, and bang, smack on the windscreen. And when you consider how many times you've seen bats bump into things ... they fucking don't, do they? Well, that fucker did. And we weren't far away from a road that turned west, and as soon as I turned that steering wheel west, the whole atmosphere just lightened up. So although I don't give a fuck about all that cosmic stuff, I certainly recognise there is more to this planet than we know about.

I drive back to Istanbul, where I bump into a geezer in a Mini Cooper S, whom I've met on the first trip, I met him somewhere along the line, the Mini Cooper S loaded up with hash. Anyway, I said, 'Look, I want Vicki to take this van to London, back to England, but it's a bit shitty. Do you mind driving in convoy with her?' And that was the arrangement, so I got on a bus.

So now I'm on a Turkish bus on my own, heading for Baghdad. Crossing Turkey on the northern route, the only route the buses would go, then going south along the Iranian–Turkish border, to get to where Turkey ends and Iraq begins. So I get to that border crossing, and yeah, I've got a visa, and the Border Guard says, 'No, geezer, your visa ran out yesterday' – unbeknownst to me.

Next day there's a bus comes along that's going back to the nearest town, which will have an embassy or whatever they call it to issue a new Iraqi visa. And it's fucking Ramadan, which is a pain in the arse if you smoke. Because they count smoking as 'things in the mouth', sort of thing – you can't even give your mate a blow job. So I go to – can't remember the name of the town now, but it will be on the map – get a visa and get a lift back to the border in the back of a big pick-up. With a bunch of local guys, and they've got bags of lemons. All these guys are mates, they all know each other. And one of them chucks me a lemon and says, 'Eat it.' I say, 'No thanks' – trying to keep it polite, but I don't want to eat a lemon. And the guy comes on a bit fucking heavy, insisting, 'Eat the lemon.' And I really don't like eating lemons, and I think, 'I ain't going to eat a lemon just because you want me to.' But they're all getting a bit 'Eat the fucking lemon', sort of thing, so I think, 'Hmm, looks like I've got to eat the lemon', because what's the point of getting into a fight with half a dozen geezers who are probably armed, and might just kill you and throw you out of the truck, end of story, nobody knows you're on the fucking truck, so I was just like. 'Oh, OK, I'll eat the fucking lemon' – not happily, but I opened the lemon up, and WHAT! It's a sweet lemon. I've never had a sweet lemon before. And they're all cracking up; they know they're sweet lemons, *mosambi* they call 'em in India. Really nice to eat, actually, and they were just having a laugh because they knew they were sweet lemons, and they knew that most people in the world don't want to eat a lemon, particularly if a gang of menacing blokes is telling them to. So we had a laugh, and we were great mates for the rest of the trip.

I spent quite a few months in Baghdad. What was odd, I went to the British embassy the first day I was there, to see if there was any mail for me, and to see if there was any local information I could get my hands on. I got my mail, then said to the bloke who I was chatting to – head of security there – did he know any decent cheap hotels in the town? He said, 'I don't know, but you can stay at my place,' and I thought, 'You must think I'm somebody else, but yes, I'll stay at your place, head of security at the British embassy, see what happens ...' And I stayed there for a while, but they soon realised they had made a mistake, and things got a bit chilly. But not before – it must have been the Queen's birthday, because I went to a British embassy party. They're fucking weird, those people, they're on a different planet. You cannot believe them, but then again, it's very rare that I meet ultra straight people. I was thinking, 'These are the people who get into governments and run things.'

So I'm out of there, in a cheap hotel, being followed by the police all the time. I phoned up a carpet dealer I was dealing with to see if they had any of the carpets I was going to be buying, if they'd come in from the village yet, and arranged to meet. And I'm going out of the hotel, and my 'spy', the guy who's following me about, it was so uncool, he said, 'Are you going to blah blah blah [whatever the name of the place I'd arranged to meet this carpet dealer was]?' So I said, 'Yes, I think we should share the taxi and pay half each' – and he did, he went along with it. I thought if he's going to be there with me anyway, I might as well put him in an embarrassing situation. Anyway, he pays half the taxi fare, because he gets that I'm on to him, and his bosses will be pleased, because his expenses are low, aren't they?

One day, I was walking across the Al Jumhuriya Bridge, one of the main bridges over the Tigris (or the Euphrates, I don't know which to be quite honest, because they both run either side of Baghdad), and a field gun goes off. Because I lived in Aldershot, I know what a field gun sounds like, because I used to hear a lot of them. And I hit the deck. In the middle of a large busy bridge. I'm looking round expecting everyone else to dive for cover, but they're all laughing their tits off at me lying in the gutter. One geezer actually fell off the side of a bus – they hang off the side of the buses – he was laughing so much. It was signifying that the sun had gone down and they could eat. Ramadan, remember? I thought it was some coup kicking off, if you hear a field gun going off in the middle of a fucking town. When you think, not very long ago, the last king, they disembowelled him and dragged him through the town behind a jeep, his family with him.

All the carpet buying's going good, I'm getting these embroidered type of carpets, rather than woven, chain-stitch embroidery, peculiar to one village – so that's all going OK. And I'm in the bazaar, walking through, and I kept noticing these stalls, and they were all the same in that they were extremely austere – no furniture, no goods on display, very little of anything in there at all other than a small charcoal brazier, a box containing silver tools and metals, and a picture on the wall of some geezer with a green turban. And it gave me a psychic shock sort of thing, because all the other stalls are a riot of colour, all gaudy, smelly, how the bazaar is, but these were completely the opposite. About the fourth one of these stalls, the guy who was working had a blowpipe – a jewellery technique where you blow down a tapering copper pipe onto charcoal and you heat up the work. A technique I'd seen before, in Afghanistan, but I wanted to talk to this geezer about 'who the fuck are you lot, then?' because I knew they were obviously linked, but I didn't know what it was – probably something to do with the green turbanned geezer. And it was one of those things where neither of us had a word of the other's language, but I asked him, 'Who are you geezers?' And he told me they were followers of the school of John the Baptist, the Mandaeans. And he then went on to say that he and the others I'd noticed around the place, they all had to be silver-workers and they had to work and live near running water. Doesn't sound too bad, live and work near running water. And I did my first bit of silver-work there, in fact, at that stall. He said, 'Do you want to have a go?' which was a simple piece of work, joining rings, so I did. I had never any intention of doing it again, but it turned out I did. I still do. But that was where I started, with these followers of John the Baptist.

Anyway, soon after that, I'm sending off a shipment of carpets from the airport, and it's a nice day, it's midwinter in Baghdad but as far as English people are concerned it's a beautiful day. It's not very far, and I hadn't had much exercise walking round the town, so I thought I might as well walk from the airport to the town. But between the town and the airport there's an army barracks beside the road. Between the buildings and the road someone was learning to drive an old Churchill tank, an old English tank. And when a tank is being driven just a few yards away from you by someone who obviously doesn't know how to drive it too well, you tend to look at it, keep it in your range of vision, which is what I did. But I had no camera with me, I didn't even slow down, I just wanted to get past the thing without it running me over.

So I get to the first caff on the edge of town, go in there, order up chicken and rice, which I'm just finishing when a mush comes in with a pistol in his hand and demands my passport. Which I take out of my pocket and hand to him, and he immediately puts it in his pocket without opening it. And I think, 'That is not a good sign.' He grabs hold of me, and the restaurateur jumps in front of him and says, 'Don't take him yet, he hasn't paid.' So he takes me out, he has an old Merc outside, he puts me in the back, there's another guy inside, a local guy, with a pistol in his hand which he keeps on me. And we drive to a series of police stations, get various mild rough handlings, nobody speaks any English so I don't know what the fuck's going on, not much I can do about it. I'm in their hands, sort of thing. And the last of the police stations we go into, we go into a compound, and there's a banner over the gate that says in Arabic and English (well, I don't know what the Arabic said, but I know what the English bit said), 'We hang all spies and traitors.' So by this time I get the idea they're bringing me in for being a spy, aren't they? It's a hard thing to talk your way out of, if they say, 'We think you're a spy.' Anyway, we eventually get to the people who can speak English – and behind the desk it's fucking Saddam Hussein, isn't it?

Didn't work it out at the time – he was just another Arab, a lot more suave, the others were just thugs. It wasn't until fairly recently, about five years ago I think, I was looking through a magazine article about the life of Saddam Hussein, and there he was, in his younger days, when he was just the head torturer at wherever, and it was the fucking geezer who was on the other side of the desk. He was a lot suaver – I sussed him for being gay. I don't know if he had any reputation for that, but I would have said he was gay, just the body language. Or maybe my gaydar ain't so hot.

He wanted me to interpret a letter from some English guy who'd been pulled in for being a spy in Kirkuk – a place up in the north of Iraq, in the Kurdish area. And he was in prison, writing a letter, ostensibly to his wife, saying pretty ordinary, mundane things, particularly the sentence, 'Don't forget to pay the gas bill.' These Iraqis, Saddam Hussein and his mate, were saying, 'What does this really mean?' How the fuck do I know? I think they gave up on me, I think they sussed that I wasn't really a spy, just there buying carpets and having a bit of an ethnological nose about the place, not the ancient culture, but the culture of today.

The only thing I saw that was good about the place was the guys I was dealing with, with the carpets, who were polite and fine enough, but apart from the aforementioned silver-worker followers of John the Baptist, they all seemed pretty shit really. When I was on the public bus going down to Kuwait, about a dozen times we were pulled over by jeeps and geezers with the 50-calibre twin-barrelled fucking machine guns, who just pulled up beside you – they're not firing them, but you know, it wouldn't take much for them to be firing them.

In Baghdad, both sides of the road, there were millions of broken bottles. Kuwait is like Saudi – alcohol no. Baghdad, although Muslim, has quite a thriving alcohol market – all fucking vile. I had a few samples, fuck me, the worst booze anywhere. The only bottle of booze I've ever poured down the sink – Iraqi arak was foul beyond belief. The road towards Kuwait has a solid embankment, both sides of the road, and because rich Iraq Kuwaitis are fucking rich, there's car wheels with punctured tyres. They don't bother to put the punctured tyre in the boot, they just leave it there, put on the spare and just leave the punctured tyre beside the road, and buy another one. Then you get into Kuwait and it's weird …

I know it's a strange reason to go anywhere, but I'd heard on the grapevine that you got twenty quid in Kuwait for a shot of your blood. Well, twenty quid out there, in them days, could get you a fucking long way. When you consider that on the return from that trip I got from Quetta to London on twenty pence, you can appreciate twenty quid is quite a lot of money. And to have a look at Kuwait, which is just down the road, cost hardly anything. So I got to Kuwait, asked a taxi driver where's a cheap hotel, and he showed me, and I went in there and said, 'The cheapest bed you've got please,' and the guy says, 'It's right on the top, on the roof,' and I said, 'Fine, sounds good.' I get up on to the roof, and it's got the walls eighteen inches high, with just a home-made shelter on the proper roof. Made of palm leaves, and it's full of beds, dozens and dozens, it's quite a big area. And every person in there, apart from me, is a really purply-black Sudanese geezer. But they were fine, though it was a bit strange. Anyway, I didn't want to hang about there long, because it was a strange place.

And I sold my blood. They were a bit excited to get my blood, as I have a rare blood group. I was excited to get the equivalent of twenty quid. I went into a little local supermarket, purely to see what sort of stuff they sold in a Kuwaiti supermarket. I'm looking around, not particularly looking to buy anything, even though I now had twenty quid. There were a couple of customers in there, and one of them sees this pentagram I had round my neck at the time, a five-point star. One of them, obviously a pretty dumb fucker, mistakes it for a six-point star, a Star of David, which it wasn't. But he immediately pulls out a long shiv, shouts, 'Yehud' – Jew – and starts going for me with this blade. So I realised it wasn't the time to start arguing the toss about how many points this star has got, and fucking legged it out of there.

When I was coming back out of Kuwait to Iran, I wanted to avoid Baghdad because of all the Saddam Hussein fucking shit. I could see you could get a water crossing rather than going up to Baghdad and going round by land. Anyway, there was just a lovely little slipper stern launch, like the ones that go round with the Boat Race, like a 1930s one, which was acting like a bus going into Iran, which was just the English Channel width away. So I paid my fare to go across to Iran on that. My fellow passengers ... some of them were speaking Farsi, which I had a bit of, though I've still got virtually no Arabic at all, but from the tone and the few words I could understand, one half of the boat was suggesting killing me and dumping me over the side, but luckily the other half was succeeding in arguing against my death. You feel a bit of a twat sitting there while they're arguing about whether to kill you. They'd dump you in the Persian Gulf and that would be end of story – they're not going to get off the boat and say, 'We've just murdered an Englishman and dumped him in the sea.' Anyway, that never happened, but it was touch and go, I reckon.

I landed in the Marsh Arab territory, the Iranian side, where they had the smartest fucking customised trucks I've ever seen – not a speck of paint on them, just delicately fretted wood, beautiful, no windows, no glass, no doors, just a sort of roof, and all the woodwork surround was exquisitely fretted, beautifully done, and all the paint just wind-blasted off.

I'd made the mistake of buying something in a chemist in Baghdad, which had the longest word I'd ever seen in my life and 'Opium', on the label of this jar. So I thought, 'Oh, that's got to be for upset tummy. I'll have two of them.' And I necked them. And I didn't shit for about two weeks.

From that bit of the Persian coast, going across Iran, I got a lift virtually the whole way in this petrol tanker, all through the oil fields, all these big burn-off gas flares going, and we stopped at every caff on the road, because it was about 150 miles between each one. And I noticed that the driver didn't seem to be having much in the way of meals, but he'd nip into a back room. And after he'd done this a couple of times I thought, 'There's something going on,' because I knew he wasn't eating anything, he came out of the back room and the truck went away again. So before the third stop, he said, a bit bashfully, 'Do you know opium?' So the next caff we both go straight in the back room and they've got these quite big opium pipes, like a coconut shell but smaller, and a nicely made stick, and a little hole, just one tiny little hole, no cup or anything, a tiny hole on one side. And the boy comes along, and he smears a great wodge of opium next to this hole, and then he'll stand there with a brazier with little bits of charcoal in, and a big pair of tweezers which will hold a bit of charcoal very near to the opium, while you toke away and you get a big hit. And you can if you like chase the dragon with morphine, which was particularly what the driver was into, so we chased the dragon all across Iran, both of us.

This time, I was going to Quetta in Pakistan before heading up into Afghanistan. I don't remember crossing the border. I must have come into Pakistan via Zahedan; I have no recollection of getting from Zahedan to Quetta, which is probably due to the fucking opium. Quetta's just below the Afghan border. It's opposite Kandahar – loads of miles in between, but Kandahar is north of Quetta. And so I'm in Quetta, waiting to have a shit basically. Also not helped by smoking opium. I got to know Quetta, which was fortunate because on the same trip on the way back I had to spend quite a while in Quetta.

I had a shit, anyway, and I then crossed over to Kandahar on a bus. So I'm in Afghanistan, travelling through Kandahar, there was absolutely zero about, got to Kabul and winter was setting in. I went straight to the Nur Hotel, and that for some reason wasn't happening, I don't know what, it had become something else. I found another hotel, completely lacking in all the olde-worlde type charms of the Nur Hotel, but along the river. Called the Shah Fuladi Hotel, along the banks of the Kabul River. Forget about verdant rivers and all that, it wasn't like that – there wasn't much water in it, and far more turds than water, because it was the local public loo. People would go down there, they'd have a shit, scoop up a bit of water and wash their arse – any time you could see half a dozen people down there having a shit. That's what I call a room with a view.

I was skint, I had no money, I had no capital. I was just making myself busy round the town, getting bits of dosh. I had a good eye for little items in the stalls, loads and loads of tat stalls, junk stalls, all the junk was really tasty stuff, it was all local stuff, not manufactured, some of it made hundreds of years ago, and I had a pretty good eye and could buy items for like ten pence, that I could sell later on, soon after that, for fifty pence, to some American chick or someone who was looking for stuff. And connecting people up to small amounts of dope. I wasn't interested at that time in connecting people to bigger amounts of dope, it was just that I needed day-to-day money. You could live well on 50p a day there, hotel, taxis, restaurants – that's all covered in the 50p. And there'd be a few pence left over to buy some little bit of whatever in the town.

And then the weather improved, it got springier. And people I knew started turning up from Europe.

Like a bloke called Dave Lindahl particularly. He's ostensibly an old mate. He was my contact in Sweden when I went back from the first trip, he was married to a Swedish girl and living in Sweden, and had lined up some sales. So he'd done me some good, but I don't think it outweighs the not-so-good that happens next, though we made it up. I moved from the hotel and was staying in a house, a spare room in a house where he was staying, with a whole bunch of people. It was quite a big house, compared to all the one-storey houses in the local area. And in a sort of compound. And one of the geezers there is a German mercenary who had just come up from Angola. He had driven his jeep, with machine guns dismounted sort of thing, from Angola to Afghanistan. And we see him take the engine out one day, we can't believe him, he's got one foot on either wing, he's got the bonnet right off, it's an American-type jeep, he's loosened the engine and I think, 'He's fucking lifted the engine out of there.' He was sweet as a nut, a really affable geezer, but he was a mercenary.

The first time I punched an Afghan was by that house, I was on the roof. There was a door into an orchard that wasn't part of the house, but there was a door from one to the other, their compound into this orchard, presumably at one time it would have been part of the same property but they must have rented the house without the orchard. So I go into the orchard where the ladder, presumably used for picking the apple trees, is leaning against the side of our house, and I go up on the roof there just to have a little quiet sunbathe. It must have been early spring, so not terrifically hot. Anyway, the ladder moves that I'd come up on. I look down there and there's an Afghan bloke, a young fellow, who's taken the ladder away. It's not a big deal; it would be hard to climb up the wall but not a problem to jump down from it. So I say, 'What are you doing?' And to show his displeasure about me having used his ladder to go up on the roof, he picks up this fucking enormous rock, and there's a dog that lives in the house, a little dog. He heaves it hard at this little dog's ribs, did for the dog. Cunt. So I just leapt off the roof, jumped straight off it, and before I got to the ground I hit him, punched him as hard as I could in the face. So he's got all the weight, and the momentum, and all that, and he goes down really quick. So I left him down and went back through the door – if he's armed, it's going to take him a few seconds to recover from that, and I don't particularly want to be in his sight when he recovers, if he's got a blade or a shooter. It's the only time I hit an Afghan.

See, a dog is an unclean animal, and a dog that's hanging around with unbelievers is doubly unclean. One day in Kabul, I see this American girl sitting on the banks of the river, the wharf, along both sides of it, where you could sit or display a carpet. And she's in a more populated part of the bazaar where the river's not used so much as a shitter. And she's got this dog, a city dog, a wild dog basically, and she's hugging it and kissing it, and I know she hasn't been in town long and I go up to her and say, 'You really shouldn't be doing that; the animals aren't like they are back home, they've got a lot of diseases.' And she was really rude to me: 'Fuck off and mind your own business', sort of thing. She was dead two days later. The next day she got seriously ill, she went to the American Embassy, they put her on the next plane to the States, she died on it. Something had eaten her liver.

So you had to be careful what you ate. All along the streets in the middle of town there's handcarts with fresh vegetables on them, salads and fruit, they all look nice and moist and crisp and fresh. Behind the geezer, or next to him, there's the ditch-cum-sewer, but it's open, like all the sewers in Afghanistan. And all these geezers have got an old tin can by them. They dip it in, and they sprinkle it over the vegetables, the salads, the lettuce particularly. But I survived.

And my fortunes were doing this and doing that, like gathering together the bags, such as that bag you're sitting on. I got a couple of them, and when they're in good condition they've got a very neat sort of fastening with loops that interlock with each other, you can thread one through the last one through the last one, like the fronts of old tents. They are incredibly robust and it's good to have a bag you can buy for a couple of quid and sell for thirty or forty quid when you've emptied it. So I had a couple of bags stuffed with a variety of things I'd got for a good price and which I knew were good quality and that I could sell, like a couple of proper nomads' dresses and all sorts of other stuff. And somehow I'd done something to get this really old VW van. But it needed a small amount of work on it that had to be done in a garage, it needed parts and that, but I had to get out of the country before it could be done, because of my visa running out.

So this David Lindahl, he'd bought loads of antiques and tasty stuff, and he wanted me to take them back to London, and said he'd pay all the fuel and I'd get a bung on top. And he'd pay for the repairs on the van. So it's all good, suits me, that gets me and my stuff back. Of course I told him what would happen if he attempted to put any drugs in it, I would give him up straight away if I'd seen what happened, and when I eventually got my hands on him I would fucking do him.

So I said, 'Right, the best thing is if I fuck off over the border to Quetta before my visa runs out. You drive the van down, meet me, and I'll take over from there, and you go back to Kabul.' And he said OK. So I left Kabul with a tenner, and got down to Quetta.

Where I was for far longer than I was expecting to be.

Because of the outward trip I was a little bit known. In Quetta I saw this building – apparently it's not still there – this building that gobsmacked me, in the garden of what used to be the residence of a British diplomat, who was obviously mad as a March fucking hare, or his wife was. There's this beautiful Georgian house, and in the garden ... you know the nursery rhyme 'There Was an Old Woman who Lived in a Shoe'? Well, imagine that boot twenty foot tall with a fucking old woman and a load of kids living in it. I kid you not, a painted red boot, black soles, eyelets all picked out and everything. Fucking lunatics had had it built, 'build me that and find a woman and a load of kids to live in it', and that's exactly what was going on.

It's a very small town; I had a few geezers, contacts, connections. It's going all right, but a few days rolled into a few weeks, and there are no phones to speak of. Where is David with the van and the stuff?

And then, fuck me, they had a financial crisis. The government announced one morning that all bank notes above a middling amount are no longer valid. And this is a country that don't trust the banks, and any money they've got, they keep in a roll of cash. And of course if you keep money in a roll of cash you always go for the highest denomination bills you can get your hands on, to make the roll appear smaller. So obviously there were hundreds of people on the streets, who had rolls of cash which the day before would have been a fortune, and were suddenly worth nothing at all. They protested and shouted and stamped, and the Army were there in great numbers. So it was quite exciting.

At the same time, I learned how to sell apricots in all the local dialects. One of my mates in the town, he owned a cheap hotel, and it was an old traditional style: perimeter wall with all the rooms inside the wall and a lovely garden in the middle. All the traditional buildings, they try to make it like the description of Heaven in the Koran. Most of the space in the walls is open space. Anyway, this particular open space had half a dozen apricot trees. And this mush was complaining that nomad types kept sneaking in, because there's no security on the place, there's a big open entrance where you could drive a cart through if you wanted to, people just slip in there, grab as many apricots as they could. And he was getting pissed off with this, and I said, 'Well, I tell you what, how about I gather up the apricots that are ready, and I use your cart and I'll set up a pitch on the street just outside your place and sell apricots?' I mean, it was apricot season, so obviously there are many, many, many apricot sellers on the street. I sort of listened to them, and I studied people's clothes a bit. Because there are quite a lot of tribes in that area, there are the Pathans and the Baluchi, and the Sindhs, and then there's the Burusho, loads of different tribes. So I'd learn just a few sentences in all these languages and I developed a multi-lingual way to say, 'Apricots, they are cold, they are sweet, they are tender, I haven't got many left ...' It was good, even though there were a million other apricot sellers.

The other real pain in the arse thing, they had closed the border to tourists. To travellers. They closed the borders at the same time as this dosh thing, so there weren't any hippies coming through. I was the only Freak in town. I was the only foreign person in town, let alone hippies; I didn't see any other foreigners, other than my mate Boris who I met there. What I did see was the inside of the government opium shop, saw that a couple of times – 'Come in and buy your government opium' – but rather more amazing than that, they have these quite blatant teahouses. They're teahouses but their main business is hash. They're not there to sell hippies hash to take away; they're there to sell the punters who come in 5, 10p's worth of excellent hash. Five quarter-inch cubes, two bob. You'd put it in a water pipe which belongs to the house, they would come by with a bowl and charcoal and some tweezers and you'd put the charcoal into a hole in your pipe ... a bit too much for me, to be honest, I couldn't smoke that much. Anyway, I was in one of these places, and this Malung turned up, who are quasi-holy beggars. You don't want to fuck with a Malung because it won't do you any favours with the other people around. Not that I ever had any desire to fuck with a Malung, but some people think that because they're poor beggars they can be rude and horrible to them, which doesn't do you any favours. And they all dress in rags, complete rags. Anyway, this geezer comes in and he sits next to me, and fuck me, he buys a big handful, a couple of ounces of hash. They get out the biggest pipe – they obviously know him, the people there – he fills this up, a heap of really good hash, and the boy's there with the charcoal, puts several lumps of red charcoal on, he's puffing away at the water pipe, and gets it going. Once it's going, he takes the stem with the business bit out of the fucking water pipe, sucks it like a fucking orange and when he stops sucking a cloud of sparks three foot high leaps into the fucking air. And he does this repeatedly. A couple of ounces of hash in a minute and a half. And he sits down and he gesticulates 'Here, what do you think of this?' And he starts unravelling one of the rags that's around his waist, puts his hand in, and he's caught a scorpion in it, like a fucking crayfish, and I think, 'Fuck off ...'

One day, this other geezer turns up at the apricot stall. I'm fairly near the edge of town, and he's coming in from out of town. If you'd seen him in a film, you'd think, 'He's a bit over the top, this geezer.' He is not a Malung, but something else, obviously a wild man, because Malungs have these special bowls and stuff, but no, he's another type. Same fucking rags and all that, but he's got these big wide leather things round his wrists, with stud-y things on them. He's got, not a stick, it's a fucking club – you know the clubs that are skinny at one end, then wide, they've got nails in them – he's got one of these. And he got a raggy old turban on, and his face is big scars all the way down, a triple row of fucking scars right down his face. His eye's OK, but he was lucky.

And it's a pretty safe bet that what made those scars was the eagle on his shoulder. He's got a fucking full-sized eagle on his shoulder. And then you look at his face, and you think, 'It was probably that eagle's mum that did that.' And he comes up to me and says in whatever, Pashtun, Farsi maybe, I don't know, 'You come with me.' And I didn't. He wanted me to go out to whatever hill, whatever cave he lived in, probably wanted to bugger me and slit my throat. Well, that was the opinion of the guy in the hotel, whose apricots I was selling, he knew the geezer, he said for sure that's what he would have done, fucked you senseless then killed you. But it would have been an adventure.

Anyway, so I didn't go with him. In fact, the excuse I gave myself for not checking it out was that this young English geezer called Boris had turned up, he was staying in the same hotel, and I was looking after him because he was really sick. Then I had learned from someone in London that David Lindahl who was meant to be turning up with my van was in London with all this stuff. And I'd been there several months by this time, just making enough to live on as I went. So I thought, 'Right, I've got two bob, and nothing in the pipeline,' even the apricot season had finished, and it's time to start heading home.

And I was with this Boris. We get on the steam train to Zahedan in Iran from Quetta. And this train was so slow, which was very fortunate because I had very bad shits, and I had to keep getting off the train, having a shit and getting back on the train again. I walked to the front of the train, and by the time I got there I'd need another shit, get off and repeat that, all through whatever mountains those are. I tell you where I got the shits from, I remember it well. The train, it stopped to take on water. And they're bringing tea round, and water. And you can see the water – it's water out of the fucking engine, rusty water, really rusty water. And it's one of the most dumb things I've ever done in my life, but I said to the geezer, 'Isn't there any better water than this?' And he looked a bit shifty, but went off and came back with this clear water. I swigged at it, and then I saw these mosquito larvae swimming about in it, and I thought, 'What have I done?' – I've just drunk some highly contaminated fucking water. They were giving you water from the engine, the second-hand boiler water. Because it had been boiled, and was therefore safe to drink, if a bit rusty. I got the really bad shits after that.

Anyway, going into Iran, the train stops and you get a bus into Zahedan, the nearby city. The customs at the railhead are very suspicious of me, don't like the cut of my jib, haul me off. They are convinced I'm some sort of smuggler or up to no good, and they want to give me a miserable time, they're convinced I'm a hash smuggler, diligently looking through all my stuff and blah di blah di blah. I tell Boris to go on and maybe I'll meet him on the other side. I've still got a couple of bags of stuff, which they're going through very closely. I did have about an ounce, just a personal smoke, but they didn't find it because I'd been very meticulous in hiding it. But I'm still fucking ill. I get a lift into the city the next day and am dropped off by a thing called a serai. Before you get into any town or village, there's an area which is just like a sort of parking lot, traditionally for the camel trains, but now used by camel trains and lorries. Called a serai. Caravanserai. The same in Afghanistan. They're called that same thing in Turkish as well, because there's popular Turkish football teams called Aksarai and Galatasarai. There's an area in Istanbul called the Galata and there's the Galata Bridge, and the Galata Sarai. Anyway, I've just got to this serai, and I'm walking the last bit into the town, and there's Boris walking out, coming to find me, as it turned out. So we reunite, but we've got to get out of the town because we've got no money for hotel beds or that sort of thing. It must have been quite early in the day, because we decide just to head out, roughly in the direction of Tehran but that's a long way away, several hundred miles. And the first place we've got to go through is called the Kerman Desert – you can imagine what that's like. A fucking desert, is what. So we're hitchhiking beside the road, we've got nothing, no water, no food, there's no shade there. I can't remember why we stopped at that particular place, we'd probably got a lift there, somebody going along this invisible track to some village in the mountains, so he dropped us there. So very little traffic, no cars, just lorries, the occasional bus, but we weren't going to flag down a bus because we had no fare. But all the lorries were probably going to Kerman – that's the next town – they'd say 'How much?'

and we'd say, 'We have no money' – 'Fuck you', sort of thing, and they'd
drive off. But one of those guys didn't say fuck you and drive off, he
said, 'Climb in the back.' The lorries out there have enormously high
sides, the sides are 8, 10 foot built up above the bed. So to climb in the
back you've got to climb up the side of a fucking lorry, with big bags,
which wasn't easy when you're ill and all that. We get to the top of the
side of the lorry and look down, it's a long way down but it's all covered
with straw. So we just drop our bags and roll off, no hanging on to the
side and lowering yourself down. Underneath this straw there's these
fucking hot overripe melons, the sundew-type melons, the yellow ones.
So we've got all this shit all over us, this melon pulp. But we're both
hungry and thirsty, so rather ill-advisedly we just grabbed a handful of
this stuff and necked it. Well, when you've got the shits, that's about the
worst thing you can fucking do.

So we get our lift to the first town, Kerman, and then to Yazd. Yazd
I already knew was the centre of Zoroastrianism. And right in the middle
of Yazd there was this wonderful place. There's a town square sort of
thing, with this impressive building picked out with pastel neon lights.
It is really tasteful, beautiful. And when you've just come in from several
days in the desert and you're feeling ill – 'Oh, look at that.' We head
towards it and as you get near you can see it's an ice-cream parlour.
Walked into the place because we just wanted to look at it. I look at the
price list on the wall and I knew we had just exactly enough money in
our pockets for an ice cream. So I say to the guy, 'One ice cream please.'
By this time my Farsi was fluent enough to ask for that. Anyway, he
starts doling out two ice creams and I say 'no', and he just hands us these
two ice creams. Oh, I could have hugged him, except I was just a filthy
unbeliever, and I don't know how the Zoroastrians square it with the
surrounding rabid Muslim types, but he was obviously a top man in the
town, and I suspect he knew the money we were buying the ice cream
with was all we had. I thought, 'I'd rather spend the money on an ice
cream' – it was sort of *Ice Cold in Alex*, if you've seen that. So me and
Boris ate our ice creams in Yazd. And I've had a great deal of love for
the Zoroastrian religion ever since.

I did have stuff to sell along the way, which is how I subsisted in
Tehran, because by the time I got to Tehran it was late at night, and I
didn't want to go stumbling into the first hotel I came across, because I
didn't have the strength for it. So I found a park in the middle of town
and lay down, head on my bag, coat over me, and had a pretty disturbed
night's sleep as the local toerags were trying to nick my bags from under

my head and I was able to fight them off without actually waking up, because you want to hang on to sleep. A pretty shitty night, really.

Boris had immediately fucked off, because as soon as we got to Tehran he went to the British embassy to be repatriated, and that was the last I saw of him. In the morning I found myself a cheap hotel, and bought myself some yogurt and local bread, which I figured would probably be the best sort of diet I could have – I was shitting snot and blood, nothing brown coming out, just transparent mucus with lumps of blood in it, not good. And it wasn't fucking helped by this English couple, I think they might have been staying at the same hotel. One of them was some sort of journalist and she had got an invite to the opening of a posh Iranian restaurant, and they had enough clout to get me in on their ticket. It's a pretty smart place and I'm dressed in rags sort of thing ... Anyway, we're in this smart Irani restaurant and I'm looking up at the ceiling thinking. 'That's the most amazing star-effect ceiling I've ever seen in my life' – and then a plane flew over, there was no roof to this really, really lavish restaurant, really good carpets on the floor, fancy tables, the only restaurant I'd ever been in Iran with linen tablecloths, a really fancy posh place. And on the table in every restaurant in Iran is this carafe with a Duralex glass inverted on the top of it. I think, 'I could do with a drink of water,' pour myself a glass – oh, it's vodka. Which is really what your already fucked-up stomach needs, a big mouthful of pretty raw vodka. You wouldn't be able to buy vodka in Tehran now.

I can tell you exactly when I was in Tehran – or I can tell you exactly when I left it, because I'd sold a rug or two and got just about well enough to travel, and I got a bus from Tehran to Istanbul, and while I was still in Iran, just before I left Tehran, men landed on the moon. So it's a very easy time to date, that. I wasn't too impressed by men getting to the moon anyway, it seemed to me if you throw enough fucking money at it you can do it. Try getting to Quetta and back on nothing, mate.

So I'm coming back to Istanbul, still really unwell, but I'm glad because at least Istanbul is familiar. But I was unwell. I was fucking unwell for ages; when I came back to England, I couldn't drink anything, I couldn't even drink half a pint of bitter for over a year. So yeah, I get to Istanbul. I'm in Istanbul but I'm skint. So I've got to acquire enough money to get me back to Blighty. I have to do some fucking dodgy things to get it. I could still be in prison, literally, for some of the things.

I met some Yanks, part of the Laguna Brotherhood they claimed, from Laguna Beach, middle-classy mafiosi sort of thing, and they wanted to buy some hash, and I said, 'I don't think Istanbul's a good place to buy bulk,' because they wanted bulk. But there was a little crew I knew, and I took them down there, they were just lining up to buy a small amount at first to see how it went. We were up in this ancient, local-type charming building. Suddenly there's a fucking crashing noise downstairs, and, 'POLICE! POLICE!' By this time the money and the hash is on the table, and the couple of guys we're dealing with, Turks, shout, 'Police, quick,' and leg it out through a window. And somehow I just thought, 'No, that happened too slick.' The window was already open, it was just too synchronised. And I couldn't hear boots thumping up the stairs either. So I thought, 'I'm going to stand my ground here.' And I did. No police came up the stairs, and after a while the geezers that had fled out the window came back looking sheepish. Which was slightly amusing. They're trying to get you to run and leave the money and the hash there, so when you get there half an hour later: 'Oh, all that money and hash has gone, the police must have taken it.'

So I'm with these same two Yanks, who had a virtually brand-new VW camper van. These guys I quickly came to loathe, because they earned it. The sort of Yanks who drive at the locals as if they're not there, as if they're less than cattle – 'They've got to get out of my way because I'm a Yank' – and driving at ridiculously fast speeds through the bazaar. I just wanted to fucking hit them. I suggested to them that if they wanted bulk amounts of hash they'd better go to the horse's mouth, which was an area beyond Gaziantep, which is the roughest part of Turkey. It's beyond the Mediterranean, east of the Mediterranean in Turkey, that's where all the hash comes from – some of it's grown in the Beqaa Valley on the other side of the border, the Syrian side – anyway, that's the place where all the Turkish hash comes from. So I said best to go down there and get it from the guys who are growing it, or their agents, rather than trying to find it in Istanbul. There is a lot of demand in Istanbul but you need to get to the source. Anyway, so we get to Gaziantep, to be met by soldiers sitting behind machine guns all over the place, all over the streets, heavily armed, in full battle gear. I go to a teahouse I'd been to before, and ask what's happening. 'Oh, some soldier shot some local kid who was the son of a local tribal leader, a high-ranking family, and there was a bit of trouble on the streets yesterday, and now it's total lock-down.' Right; not a good time to go and buy hash, because no one can fucking move or anything. So I ask, 'What hash have you got?' And he brings out some pretty good pollen, unpressed. So I tell the Yanks, 'Look, you see the situation out there, no one can move, and this geezer's got this bag of pollen, that's what there is.' And the Yanks say, 'No, we want ten keys.' I tell them, 'They ain't got it – and unless you're prepared to stay here till all this military have fucked off, which probably won't be for several weeks, we're fucked.' They were ignorant fucking bastards – 'No, we want ten keys.' So I tell the guy they want ten kilos, and they wanted it pressed. So he goes away for a few hours, comes back with this pressed hash. And it was obvious to me they'd just used whatever hash they had, and mixed it with flour, and pressed it. 'Right, you've got ten kilos' – that was it really, and I wanted to batter these people by this time, but I was basically living off them.

I'd got together just about enough money to get out of town, and I meet up with some American-born, Arab-descent geezer called Oran who was in a similar boat, and we start making our way north. Somehow get as far as Bulgaria, get all through Bulgaria OK somehow, I don't know how, then we get to over in Yugoslavia somewhere, and we're stuck at this motorway service station. It's not like an English motorway service station, it's much more casual and scruffy and it's smaller too. We're there for several days and no one will give us a lift – there's any amount of foreigners, Westerners, hippie types stop by, because anywhere you can get petrol you stop and fill up. So there's loads of traffic and we're going around saying, 'Hey, man, can you give us a lift to the town, blah di blah?' and, 'Oh no, man, my clutch is going' – there was always some reason they couldn't give us a lift, we were obviously skint and scruffy and all that. And how we got out of there, that was good. We'd been living for several days off unripe sweetcorn and unripe damsons. Then this guy pulls up in an old Volkswagen. And it splattered to extinction just a couple of hundred yards up the road. So Oran, the guy I was with, the Yank, he legs it up there, I fix his motor, and then the cunt tries to drive off. So I grab the driver's hair, cos he's a filthy long-haired hippie, and I ain't going to let go of it, and he knows that, so he gives us a lift up to the town.

Then we get to Vienna, and somehow we get into Germany from Austria, I don't know how we managed to do that but we did. And then into Holland.

We get to Amsterdam and I sell one of the Afghan nomad dresses I've got with me for a decent amount of dosh, so I've got a bit of money in my pocket. But it's the year when Amsterdam is the place where every pot smoker in the world wants to fucking be. And even if you was prepared to pay a thousand pounds you couldn't find a bed. Every bed in the town was fucking full. There were hundreds of people sleeping in the parks, hundreds more sleeping in shop doorways, which I was one of. We'd had a good night out, been to a club where we had good music and I bought some hash in a club with a whole ring of geezers with scales. Shouting out what they'd got. It's Amsterdam, isn't it, spice capital of the world.

So an ounce, a half-ounce or whatever, I had in my pocket, and I'm bedded down in some shop doorway, and I'm woken up by the police. They'd decided to have a swoop on the town and pull in every fucker who's sleeping on the streets and in the parks, and there are fucking hundreds of us. And the geezer next to me in the processing line, he's got 3,000 dollars in travellers' cheques on him, he's got a return ticket from wherever in the States to Brussels and back again to the States, and he's saying to me, 'I can't believe this, I'm being fucking busted for vagrancy.' Because he couldn't find a bed and had to sleep rough.

So they come to process me and it didn't take them long before they said, 'Right, you're being deported for vagrancy. Now you live in England, so we must prepay your ferry fare, how are you going to pay for this?' And I just happened to have a chequebook with me, a David Rowberry & Company chequebook. So, just having a laugh, I said, 'Oh, all right if I pay by cheque, then?' – thinking how absurd, taking a cheque from someone you're doing for vagrancy – 'Oh yes, that will be fine' – fucking hell, OK. And the only bad cheques I've ever written in my life were to Dutch police and to British Rail when I got to Harwich, to get to London.

And if you recall I started that trip with Vicki and Carol. So Carol lives in Battersea at the time, the last time I saw her she was starting this term at art school in Istanbul, but time had elapsed, I knew she'd be back in London, or probably. So I think, 'I'll swing round to Carol's place, get at least a bed for the night and try to have a wash-up and regroup.' Walked into Carol's place, and there she is in bed with fucking Vicki.

And I could not handle it, I could not handle it, man; I just turned around and walked away. I could not handle it.

I stir myself, and poke the stove.

The light of dawn is coming over Bredon Hill, and soon I will be able to see how high the water is.

Storm Imogen seems to have blown over, but the river is still rising. The bottom step of five up to the cabin is now skimmed with river water, and I have to splash to get out to my car, to check that it is mercifully still above the flood.

I come back into the cabin, and put the kettle on, which hurts. It hurts, because a few days back, I went over to West Wales to see old Perry Venus, and tripped over a kerb whilst looking for a chemist in Aberaeron. I seem to have cracked a few ribs, and it is uncomfortable, to say the least. In short, I have 'had a fall', my first. Late middle age is starting to morph into late late middle age. In Shakespearian terms, I am leaving Justice and entering Pantaloon, or Daft Old Cunt, as Younger Readers might have it. I am already wearing a pair of tartan leisure trousers from Boden. And tonight, I'm struck by the fact that these stories are from long long ago, like the stories my grandfather told me about being a boy sailor at the Battle of Jutland.

After all, the book is dedicated to my granddaughters. Sit up on Grandpop's knee, little ones, while I tell you about the time Uncle Bob crossed Iran off his tits on morphine.

I bloody wish I had some here, or at least a cup of Bob's lovely soothing opium tea.

All I have is medicalised health remedies, viz. ibuprofen and paracetamol, a lot of Yorkshire Tea and a little Pembrokeshire Smoking Mixture, which I have been getting through since my tumble. It doesn't help the pain, as such, but it does help me see the funny side.

I take a handful of painkillers with my tea, hoping I can sleep.

Because tomorrow is going to be a busy day.

Because Bob is back from Afghanistan, back to a changed world. Adventurers miss out on history. I'm reminded of my reaction to the *Star Wars* movie; there's been too much action, and not enough cod philosophy. I feel welcome in my own narrative again. It's back to the van in the woods for me.

Cos it's 1969, OK?

Oh Yeah, Let's have Some

By the end of February, there are stirrings of life in the wood, and as I arrive, Bob is up by the log pile, and insists on showing me something, and we step into the trees. There are snowdrops, and daffodils, but there are also shoots which Bob tells me are the beginnings of the bluebells.

'Fucking early, they are,' he says, pointing with his home-made walking stick, and, as ever, I see no reason to doubt him.

Inside, there is a bit more light than on my last visit, and as Bob makes the coffee, I notice again how sorted the old bus is. There's an aluminium Whitbread beer barrel raised from the floor on wooden blocks for water. Under its tap, a stainless-steel bowl for slops. There are two handmade shelves on the kitchen side, the driver's side, which run from the door to the wood-burner. On the bottom shelf, I can see sugar, Go-Cat, Cheerios, fruit and veg, and a couple of bottles of vodka. The top shelf is a work surface with the gas ring and the food preparation area, with tins for tea, coffee and sugar, and a pierced can of evaporated milk.

'Food preparation area' sounds a little like something from *Elle Interiors*, but, trust me, it wouldn't pass muster. Bob lives alone, and has done for twenty-five years. He has no running water, so he rations out what's in the Whitbread barrel. As our old friend Chas used to insist, 'You've got to eat a bit of dirt to build up your immune system.' Food for thought, if he hadn't predeceased both me and Bob.

Hanging from the ceiling are pots and pans, obscuring the light from one of the high narrow windows which run along both sides of the bus. And below the window, a narrow shelf with some curtain wire strung along it to hold safe a few plates and mugs should by some absurd miracle the bus ever move again.

The wood-burner is ill-served by being called a wood-burner. It's the size of a medium-sized wood-burner, and it burns wood, so it's easy to see why it gets called that. What it is really, though, is a miniature wood-burning range, a thing of beauty, built especially for Bob's van. It has a little oven, and it fits into the gap next to Bob's bed as it was designed to do. Life without it would be impossible.

Bob's bed, big enough for two, runs horizontally across the bus, just behind the driver's seat. It is covered in Afghan rugs and cushions. Bob's devices, his mini CD player and DVD viewer, his generic tablet with its concomitant dongle, his old-skool Nokia, twinkle as they recharge on the bed. The weather is cold, but the skies are clear, and that means electricity.

Turning to the passenger side, opposite the range (as we must now call it), there's a wooden chest, also from Afghanistan, covered in the empty bags that Bob brought back from the second trip, which serves as a guest seat. You must be careful not to knock your head when you get up, because the shelf on this side is waist height, and you're right at the end. It's Bob's workbench. An arc welding gun connects to gas canisters outside by tubing which coils through two holes drilled for the purpose in the side of the bus. Bits of newly made wind-powered mobiles hang from the ceiling. There are a couple of vices and a bench anvil. The bench is an explosion of creativity in metal, a jeweller's bench, an artist's bench, a right fucking mess. I like to sit on the stool which Bob uses when he's working, while he lounges on the bed. I like picking though the stuff on the bench; what's this? What does this do?

Then the moka starts to bubble, and while Bob puts the coffee together, I get back to picking through his head; why was it like this, how did that happen, or, 'Where did you go, that night you walked out of Carol's place?'

'I have no idea. Somewhere. No idea at all.'

'Because you were ill. Really quite ill. And penniless. And as you emphasised before, money means a welcome, but having no money, not so much. You went from being a Beat, to being a thief, to coming back to London as a Face, essentially – you know, you're out with the Montagus on boats, swanning about in your Jaguar XK20 with Guy, just living the high life – and then you weren't.'

'When I got back from the first trip I wanted to make it out and back on my own. Which I did. Afghanistan taught me a lot, you know, about life, and myself and that.'

'Yeah, but: Vicki, the house, the Jag, the high life – all gone. You gave all that up. For a Boy's Own Adventure. It was your Saturn Return, man.'

'Don't fucking start that,' Bob growls.

'No, but it was. You were the right sort of age, twenty-seven, twenty-eight. It's the moment in your life when Saturn returns to where it was on your chart when you were born. It's a time for pressing your self-destruct button. As it goes, I'm having my second Saturn Return right about now.'

'Bollocks.'

'But Bob, while you've been off swanning around selling apricots in Quetta, stuff has been happening. Those coats you brought back had lots of invisible cosmic fairy dust in the pockets, and now the acidy fairy types are indulging themselves in various arcane philosophies. I'm sorry. Astrology is the least of it.'

'I've stayed pretty clear of all the cosmic stuff, because quite honestly any people I've known who were part of that "cosmic" sort of crew, they're so fucking dishonest. Because that whole existential beat thing, it does have an inherent honesty, being straight. Whereas all that cosmic stuff, it ain't straight, and it buys into all that religion stuff, pretty well made up by blokes to control other blokes.'

'But you read Gurdjieff, for example.'

'Yeah, but there wasn't a sentence going on about cosmic shit, it was all about what he was doing. Whether it was lies or truth, it doesn't matter, they were basically adventure stories.'

'*Meetings with Remarkable Men*?'

'Yeah. He was travelling around, setting up wherever he was, and mending stuff for the locals. I modelled my trip to the Americas on that. It worked, it was great, I had a good time ... until that cunt at Montreal Airport.'

'We'll come back to that cunt in due course. In the meanwhile, open your heart chakra and let me tell you about the hidden springs of wisdom.'

Guy Stevens' protégés, Mott the Hoople, in their valedictory single 'Saturday Gigs', from 1974, sum up the atmosphere of the time: 'Sixty-nine was cheapo wine, have a good time, what's your sign? Float up to The Roundhouse on a Sunday afternoon ...'

They used 'What's your sign?' as a signifier for 1969, because by the time Bob got back from Afghanistan, the Age of Aquarius was kicking off. Ideas around 'spirituality' mattered a lot to the Freaks' culture. I wish I had more time to discuss these ideas, but Lord only knows this has been a long story already, and we still have a way to go. So I'm only going to examine a few: the influence of theosophy on Freak culture, ecstatic dance without Ecstasy, what happens to Satanists when they go soft, and why I know what my rising sign is. In the Appendix you can learn how to throw and read the *I Ching*. After that, O Younger Readers, the pathless path is yours to follow or not.

Theodor Adorno, whom Bob banned me from discussing right at the beginning of this book said, 'Occultism is the metaphysic of the dopes,' and he may have had a point. But also at the beginning of this book, I highlighted the great philosophical and spiritual problem of our age, which is that God is Dead; and, therefore, how do we live? Until about the 1860s, spiritual hunger in the West was fed by Christianity. There may have been innumerable sects, but they could all agree on a few things: that the Earth was created by God for a purpose, and that Jesus Christ was his Son, who died on the cross for the sins of Humankind, was resurrected three days later, and ascended into Heaven to be with his Father. Biblical criticism, theological revisionism, mass industrialisation and scientific innovation meant that it was not so easy for people to agree on these principles by the end of the nineteenth century. Then came Nietzsche's discovery of the corpse of God. And so, since spiritual hunger seems not to have gone away, myriad belief systems have come into being, many of them with their roots in India. And in the West, these belief systems found their way here largely thanks to the agency of Madame Helena Blavatsky.

As discussed briefly already, Blavatsky was a Russian mystic who claimed to have travelled in Tibet, where she was taught the 'Ancient Wisdom' by the 'Hidden Masters', a clan of 'ascended' teachers, who told Blavatsky that her job was to return to the West to propagate their teachings. Her fame first came about in the USA, where she gave an interview about her travels in Tibet to the *New York Times*, which attracted followers. She and several supporters established the Theosophical Society in 1875, and she wrote *Isis Unveiled* to explain her philosophy.

Theosophy, according to Blavatsky, is the rebirth of an ancient wisdom-religion, an occult guide to the cosmos, nature and to human life. The many faiths of Humankind derive from a universal religion known to Plato and ancient Hinduism. The Hidden Masters conversed with Blavatsky in Ancient Sanskrit to reveal their 'secret doctrine', which Blavatsky discussed further in her book of the same title, published in 1888. Broadly speaking, *The Secret Doctrine* argues that humans are co-evolving with the cosmos, and the aim of the Hidden Masters is to help Humankind reach a state of being where we are consciously participating in evolution. Blavatsky's ideas had traction in a world which was becoming sceptical of the claims of Christianity, but was not ready to let go of faith.

Blavatsky's greatest disciple was an avowed atheist, one of Britain's best known, one who helped reform the way the law treats atheists. But she illustrates the old argument that if someone doesn't believe in God, it leaves them free to believe anything. She allowed theosophy into the space where her Christianity and then her atheism had once been. She was a Socialist, an advocate of women's rights and birth control, first woman President of the Indian National Congress, and her name was Annie Besant.

She was born in 1847, and married the Rev. Frank Besant in 1867. By 1870, they had two children. But she began to doubt Christianity, and refused to attend Communion, and so her husband threw her out and obtained a formal separation. In 1874, she renounced Christianity, and joined the Secular Society, where she formed a close relationship with Charles Bradlaugh, at that time the de facto leader of secularism in England, and started to write for his magazine, the *National Reformer*. In 1877, Bradlaugh and Besant decided to publish a book called *The Fruits of Philosophy*, which advocated birth control for women, for which they were prosecuted, and found guilty. They were sentenced to six months' imprisonment each, but their conviction was overturned in the Court of Appeal. In 1880, Bradlaugh was elected MP for Northampton, but he asked to affirm on taking his seat, rather than take the Oath of Allegiance on the Bible. He was refused, and he said he would therefore take the Oath, and feel his conscience bound by it, even though he didn't believe in God. He was not allowed to take the Oath either, and was therefore barred from taking his seat. After an eight-year battle, Bradlaugh was finally allowed to affirm. One of his first speeches was in support of the famous matchgirls' strike, which was started due to an article by Annie Besant about the horrors of working in a match factory. Annie helped form the Match Girls Union, which, after a three-week strike, won considerable concessions from their employers, Bryant & May. Annie was the best known and most articulate woman atheist socialist campaigner of the late nineteenth century. An atheist's atheist. Atheisty McAtheistface.

In 1889, Annie read and subsequently reviewed Madame Blavatsky's *The Secret Doctrine*. So struck was she by the book that she arranged to meet Blavatsky, and quickly became involved in theosophy. In her autobiography, Annie wrote of Blavatsky, 'We bear witness to the unselfish beauty of her life, the nobility of her character, and we lay at her feet our most reverent gratitude for knowledge gained, lives purified, strength developed.' Annie was the first British woman to go on a 'journey' (dread word) from Christianity to atheism to 'New Age Spirituality', and she has had thousands of followers. I know, because I've sat smoking with them in the Healing Field at Glastonbury Festival, discussing chi energy.

In 1893, Annie moved to India, and abandoned atheism and socialism, although she did travel back to Britain to speak in favour of women's suffrage. In 1907, she became the second President of the Theosophical

Society, but she did not abandon politics; she was a supporter of Indian Home Rule, and was elected President of the Indian National Congress, the political movement that Gandhi would lead to independence. But her views of India were seen through the lens of theosophy; for Annie, India was 'the Mother of Spirituality'.

It was an important part of theosophical belief that the world was waiting for the coming of the Bodhisattva Maitreya, the World Teacher. In 1909, Annie's friend Charles Leadbeater found him, aged fourteen, swimming off the Theosophical Society's beach in Adyar, a few miles south of Madras (now Chennai). His name was Jiddu Krishnamurti, and Annie became his legal guardian as the Theosophists prepared him for his new role. Krishnamurti was groomed to be the Messiah, and the Theosophical Society set up an organisation for his benefit, the Order of the Star. They arranged for him to give talks all over the world explaining theosophy, including tours of the States. In 1922, on his way between talks, he stayed in a cottage near the town of Ojai, California, a cottage which his followers later bought for him, and where he was based for the rest of his long life. Thirty miles inland from Santa Barbara where the first vegetarian restaurant and shop was opened, Ojai has been a hippie town ever since. In 1929, Krishnamurti forswore theosophy, dissolved the Order of the Star and started to talk about 'the teachings':

I maintain that truth is a pathless land, and you cannot approach it by any path whatsoever, by any religion, by any sect. That is my point of view, and I adhere to that absolutely and unconditionally. Truth, being limitless, unconditioned, unapproachable by any path whatsoever, cannot be organized; nor should any organization be formed to lead or coerce people along a particular path. I do not want followers, and I mean this. The moment you follow someone you cease to follow Truth. I am not concerned whether you pay attention to what I say or not. I want to do a certain thing in the world and I am going to do it with unwavering concentration. I am concerning myself with only one essential thing: to set man free. I desire to free him from all cages, from all fears, and not to found religions, new sects, nor to establish new theories and new philosophies.

He insisted that he didn't want followers, and so he has lots, of a particular kind. They included Bruce Lee, Aldous Huxley and Deepak Chopra, I'm afraid. It's possible your mum has a Deepak Chopra book somewhere on her shelves, if she's the kind of mum who rubbed arnica on your bruises and had you called Sky in a naming ceremony. Krishnamurti's most important follower, though, was known as Osho, who very much belongs in the last chapter, in the colours of the twilight. Krishnamurti died in 1986, aged ninety. He may have forsworn theosophy, but he never denied being the World Teacher.

Krishnamurti was not the first Indian guru to appear in the West; that honour belongs to Swami Vivekananda, who was the first to popularise yoga in the West in the late nineteenth century. Nor was he the best known; that honour will always rest with the Maharishi, whom the Beatles visited in his ashram in India in 1967. But Krishnamurti was the first to become widely known, and discussed, and taken seriously. His words echo through the writings of Alan Watts, whose book *The Way of Zen*, together with a very large amount of powerful cannabis, turned me into the Buddha for a week, a hilarious episode which you can find recounted in my book *Something of the Night*. Whether he would like it or not (I would guess not), Krishnamurti's work is alive today in the soft cult of 'Mindfulness'.

I will admit to a fondness for the Indian god Krishna, mostly because of the Beatles. George Harrison embraced 'Krishna Consciousness', and he used the Hare Krishna mantra in his 1971 hit *My Sweet Lord*. The Hare Krishna Temple had a hit record themselves with the 'Hare Krishna Mantra' in 1969, and I liked that too, when I was eleven. It made me a bit pro Krishna at an impressionable age. The bald-headed orange-clad monks still parade and chant up Oxford Street most days; and you may be stopped by one of their mendicant monks in a street anywhere, with a clipboard and a copy of the *Bhagavad Gita* for you to buy. Tell them 'Gouranga' if you get stopped by them. Younger Readers who would like to know more of Krishna should try Peter Brooks' epic film of *The Mahabharata*.

Nor was I the only member of top light-entertainment duo Your Dad to have an interest in the mysteries of the Orient. I tell Bob, 'Chas was a Premmie – a follower of Prem Rawat, the Guru Maharaj Ji. Gumragi. The Divine Light Mission, and all that.'

'That really shocks me, actually; not many things shock me but that does. You know how I feel about religions – they were all invented by men. And I know that they work, some of these things, the same as Sufi dancing does ...'

'Yes; in fairness to Chas, who never tried to recruit me to the Divine Light Mission, why he did it is because it worked, from his point of view. He didn't have any belief system about it. Chas was an atheist, and a man of faith. There's a series of practices and they make you feel kind of high. When he was dying he was pretty much meditating all the time, in the way he learned from Gumragi.'

'And taking intravenous smack.'

'Yes. It was a beautiful end.'

From Quietist Gurus, therefore, to advocates of 'practice'. Yoga is one such discipline; by controlling the body, one controls the mind and frees the spirit. Another is dance. When I was a student at Lancaster University, one of my tutors liked to quote Nietzsche, thus: 'We should consider every day lost on which we have not danced,' and I agree. Ecstatic dancing has a long and glorious history. The most recent example of this on a large scale was the rave scene, one of the last moments of the counter-culture, a moment that Younger Readers themselves might have had some experience of. Like Osho, it belongs at the end of this story. In 1969, very few people danced. There were nightclubs, discos if you will, that played chart music, where straights went to meet. There was Northern Soul, if you were up north, but it was more concerned with dancing and fun than anything else. No bad thing; great music, but not Freak culture. And that was about it. Disco proper didn't happen till the seventies. People didn't really dance at gigs; they sat there, or lay there, as we shall discover on the Isle of Wight. The odd hippie chick or stoned loon stood up and freaked out, but if you look at films of gigs or festivals from the late sixties or early seventies, you'll see they were very much outliers, whose dancing bore scant relation to the music.

There were some who took dancing very seriously, though, especially the followers of Georges Ivanovich Gurdjieff, a Russian/Greek/Turkish/Armenian, who was born sometime between 1866 and 1877, and who died in 1949. Bob read Gurdjieff's 'account' of his travels in the Middle East, Afghanistan and India, *Meetings With Remarkable Men*, and was impressed enough to use his ideas when he was living in Mexico.

Gurdjieff's charismatic personality attracted attention to his views, and brought him lots of disciples, including old Tim Leary. Wrapped up in a lot of unreadable guff (that much of his writing is unreadable is part of the point, according to his followers) is a fairly simple idea, one with which it sometimes feels hard to argue. This is that, although humans think they are awake, they are actually asleep, and that it is only possible to change this with great effort. We all know that this is true, I think. We know we have wasted our lives in dreams which we never tried to make real. We know this is true: the less we do for ourselves, the more lifeless we are, and we fall into deepest sleep, lullabied by the Spectacle into docile alienation. Gurdjieff, and his slightly more readable disciple P.D. Ouspensky, wanted to wake us all up.

The best known part of Gurdjieff's method to bring about this awakening is a series of dance moves known as 'The Gurdjieff Movements'. You can see them online. They look very difficult but rather beautiful when performed in groups. Gurdjieff, when supervising 'the Work', as it was known to Gurdjieff's contemporary followers, would on occasion shout 'Stop', at which point the participants would have to hold themselves in whatever position they happened to be at that point in the dance. Gurdjieff once described himself as a dance teacher, seeing his movements as a method to achieve states of concentration and awareness that can only be reached by the wakeful. And when you are awake, you remember yourself and what it is that you're supposed to be doing, which is rarely working in a call centre in Kettering and living with your parents whilst saving for a deposit on a house. You know that is not what you're supposed to be doing, don't you? Not why you're here?

'Man is asleep,' said Gurdjieff, 'he has no real consciousness or will. He is not free; to him, everything "happens". He can become conscious and find his true place as a human being in the creation, but this requires a profound transformation. Man's possibilities are very great; you cannot conceive even a shadow of what man is capable of attaining. But modern man lives in sleep, in sleep he is born, and in sleep he dies. In the consciousness of the sleeping man his illusions, his dreams are mixed with reality. He lives in a subjective world and he can never escape from it. And this is the reason why he can never make use of all the powers he possesses and why he always lives in only a small part of himself.'

Gurdjieff's teachings, and those of Ouspensky, have had a profound influence on what is known as 'the Growth Movement'. The Growth Movement, whose natural home is at Esalen, Big Sur, California, takes many forms, most of them, so far as I can see, horrible. 'Personal Empowerment' is the thing, which might sound great. But I have been trapped at Islington dinner parties with members of Narcotics Anonymous who talk of Personal Growth and Empowerment all night, until I can barely digest my celeriac purée with spiced cauliflower and quail's eggs. I don't know what 'Personal Growth' is, except that which time throws at you. But I do know I need to wake my ideas up, as do we all. As my mum always says, 'What you need, boy, is a kick up the arse.' And you can't argue with that.

Gurdjieff based his movements on Sufi dancing. Sufis are the beleaguered mystical wing of Islam.

I say to Bob, 'I was looking at one of the things I saw you posted on Facebook the other day about how the highest you ever got was dancing with Sufis. You've never told me that story. What happened?'

'The first time I'd driven into Hay in my life, to do shopping, the same morning we woke up there, I opened the car door thinking I don't know anyone within a hundred miles, and a voice said, "Oi, Rowberry, what are you doing here?" And it was a bloke from the Kensal Rise end of the Portobello Road scene, an old mate called Simon, apparently living at Talgarth. Anyway, a few weeks later, it was coming up to Christmas and I see in a newspaper an advert for a flight to Istanbul and good hotel accommodation for thirty-eight quid or something, and I ask him if he fancies it, and he says, "Yeah." So I was with Simon in Istanbul, which I knew pretty well by this time, and I'd taken him to the whore streets and that, just to show him. And on this evening, this geezer comes up I'd met on many occasions before on previous visits, and I knew him to be a pisshead, who'd change money, buy hashish, a tourist hustler type. So he comes up and says, "You want to come Sufi dance?" And he's all slurry and seemed to be off his face. And we had nothing on, so I thought, "OK, let's go and check this out." I didn't ask him any questions about it.

'He led us to a nearby shared minibus, taxi sort of thing, which was really cheap. These dolmushes were basically transits with seats, that run a fixed route, go there, take you back, sort of thing, and they're cheap. So we got into one of them, which surprised me, because usually the tourist hustler type, the first thing they do is get you into a proper taxi. So we travelled to the edge of the town, out to the suburbs, and get to a big walled building, can't see what it is because it's getting a bit dark. Get to this gateway, into a yard, and get to a door and a building inside the outer wall, and this geezer becomes a different person – he says, "Take your shoes off here, be quiet and follow me." And he's changed, he's completely changed his whole persona, all of a sudden he's no longer slurring, he's crisp and together and sharp, and I think, "That's a bit odd."

'We go in, and fuck me it's a mosque. And there's a ring of geezers already dancing, and they're all – they look pretty well-to-do middle-class blokes, they're not bearded whirling dervish-y rag types by any means. And there's no word spoken; these geezers open their circle and allow us into it, and they continue with their circle dance. You have your arms linked, holding the other guy under the armpit or something, there's a lot of stooping and straightening as you're going round, and chanting, yeah?'

'No music? The music comes from the chanting?'

'Just the chanting, yeah. And I thought, "It's really forcing me into a very odd breathing pattern" – you couldn't do the stooping and the chanting without breathing in a certain way, it forced you into a breathing pattern which was not a usual one. And we came out of there, nobody laid anything on us, one of the guys said, "Are you going to the town centre?" – we said yes – "I'll give you a lift back." There was no hustle; they didn't want anything from us, but made me and Simon, who was a bit of a bad boy to say the least, feel really welcome. Simon was a part-time junkie, who would buy whatever he could get his hands on, and we both admitted we had never felt so high. Really, really high. And I've been trashed and wasted and off my tits, vomiting, crawling, all that, but this was something else, it really was, powerful – and you had to put a bit of effort into it.'

In summary, then, every day is lost on which we do not dance seriously.

I want to pick out one more group as emblematic of late-sixties spiritual thought, a group who called themselves the Process Church of The Final Judgment, and whose story I like very much. This time, rather than the New Age, or Personal Growth, they represent a renewal of interest in the Occult. In Magic, in their case what you might call Black Magic, because they worshipped Satan. Sort of.

They grew out of Scientology, the made-up religion that Tom Cruise belongs to. Mary Ann MacLean and Robert de Grimston met through a London Scientology centre, and borrowed some of its ideas to set up 'Compulsions Analysis', a personal growth psychotherapy group, which turned into a religious cult called 'The Process'. They produced a magazine, called *Process*, which stood out with its striking graphics and celebrity interviews with the likes of Mick Jagger and the boxer Henry Cooper, and with endorsements from singer Marianne Faithfull and the US actress Stefanie Powers. Bob remembers selling it in Karma Sigma. In 1966, de Grimston gave a talk at the Oxford Union, where he was roundly booed, and the group moved to the USA, where they incorporated as a church. Whilst in the US, de Grimston developed a theology (as befits a Messiah-like figure), which linked Jehovah, Christ, Satan and Lucifer in what he called 'The Game of the Gods'. At the end of time, these four deities would reunite. In the meantime, followers of The Process 'loved Satan', because Satan was Jesus' enemy, and Jesus told us to love our enemies. They set up a chain of meeting places and coffee shops, where interested parties would eat veggie burgers and listen to folk music and talks; none of them by de Grimston, who never spoke in public again after his humiliation in Oxford. Charles Manson, of whom more later, was reputed to have borrowed some of the group's theology. In 1974, de Grimston was removed as leader, and the reformed church, which now called itself the Foundation Church of the Millennium, repudiated much of his theology. They restarted the magazine, now called *Foundation*. Processians, as followers were known, were always fond of animals; in 1984, they moved to a ranch in Utah to make more room for their animals, and in 1991 changed their name again, to The Best Friends Animal Society. They now run one of the biggest and best known animal sanctuaries in the US: 2,000 homeless animals live on 36,000 acres of land. They run a chain of Community catch/neuter/return programmes for feral cats across America. The magazine changed its name again, to *Best Friends*, now published bi-monthly, and has over 200,000 subscribers. Their journey from a religious cult with a whiff of brimstone to a charity that looks after kittens fills me with glee.

I'm still not done, though. Mott the Hoople's question, 'What's your sign?' wants answering. Why do I know, not just what my sign is (Pisces), but also my rising sign (Leo)? How come I know that my Moon is in Capricorn (bad), and that it is unaspected (very bad)? Why can I tell Bob I'm due my second Saturn Return? Why do I know what it means? My mum doesn't know what her rising sign is. My daughters don't know. Why do I? It is estimated that eleven million people in the UK 'believe' in astrology in some sense, and I am not one of them, not exactly. So why do I know about it? Why did astrology come to have some credence for the counter-culture? Because – The New Age.

'The New Age' was an idea with its roots in eighteenth-century Transcendentalism, man. The first name to conjure with is that of Emmanuel Swedenborg. Metropolitan Young Readers on their way home to Hackney on top of the 38 bus may well have spotted 'Swedenborg House', round about Theobalds Road way. This was set up by the Swedenborg Society in 1810, thirty-eight years after his death, to propagate Swedenborg's ideas, which are, essentially, that the goal of humans is to transform themselves spiritually by subjecting themselves to 'rebirth'. The 'New Age' is the idea that the world itself trembles on the verge of spiritual transformation. Blavatsky was a Swedenborg fan; she called him 'the greatest of modern seers'. Blavatsky took this idea of humanity transforming itself in a spiritual regeneration, and made it central to her teachings. She was fascinated by astrology, and took its tenets as self-evident. 'The history of the World is written in the stars,' she wrote in *The Secret Doctrine*. The New Age, the so-called 'Age of Aquarius', would begin on the day the sun rises in Aquarius on 21 March. The snag with this is that no one knows for sure when it will happen, as it is not entirely predictable, since the twelve signs of the zodiac (Aries through Pisces) don't actually map onto the actual sky. This will not be a problem for astrology, as we shall see.

William Bloom, the Glastonbury-based New Age writer, author of such classics as *Working with Angels, Fairies, and Nature Spirits*, characterises New Age beliefs thus: that the Divine exists within each human; that the individual is the highest authority; that individual experience is the ultimate arbiter of truth; that belief systems are created to meet cultural needs; that the Universe is in a process of evolutionary development; that radical mystical transformation is a shared ideal, and that every individual must act to bring the New Age about by education and practice. Theosophical thinking is directed towards transformation and development. The New Age is largely interchangeable as an idea with 'The Age of Aquarius'.

Astrology is now the lingua franca of the New Age, its most public incarnation. You'll go a long long way to meet an adherent of New Age 'philosophy' who does not dabble in astrology to a greater or lesser extent. 'The Age of Aquarius', probably the best known astrological idea, is also the knockout song from the musical *Hair*. But in Blavatsky's time, astrology had been all but forgotten, other than by a handful of enthusiasts. As an idea, it had gone backwards since the late seventeenth century when, thanks to the ideas of Isaac Newton, astronomy had become a science. Astrological ideas were early victims of the efficacy of the scientific method. By 1880 it was largely discredited; eleven million people might 'believe' in astrology to some extent now, but at the turn of the twentieth century, its followers could be numbered in the hundreds. Astrology had always been concerned with predicting events. This was done by practitioners drawing up astrological charts which mapped planetary positions onto a future time and place, and drawing conclusions about what might occur.

This old-fashioned practice of astrology was transformed by William Frederick Allan, who worked under the name of Alan Leo. He was one of the few people still interested in 'event astrology'. In the 1880s he encountered Blavatsky's writings, and began a radical revision of the way astrology was organised. As a Theosophist, he took on board Blavatsky's cosmology (which has the sun as the conduit of spiritual force), and he reorganised astrology in order to fit the cosmology. Leo it was who emphasised the idea of the 'sun sign', and its developmental characteristics. He became Annie Besant's personal astrologer, but after a series of prosecutions for 'fortune telling' under the 1735 Witchcraft Act, he set out to establish that what he was doing was not fortune telling but mapping human character and charting developmental possibilities.

Leo published a dozen books, promoting the new astrology, and as such is regarded as the 'Father of Modern Astrology'. In particular, Leo took Blavatsky's idea that the zodiac represents development, from Aries (representing birth) through to Pisces (which represents death). If you look at an astrological column in a newspaper, you'll see that the sun signs which Leo promoted are listed in the order he devised, under Blavatsky's instruction. Astrology therefore accords with the theosophical cosmology, as opposed to the Newtonian one. Which is to say, an occult cosmology, rather than one based on the actual motion of the planets. This is why astrology doesn't worry too much about astronomy, and vice versa; their views of the universe are incommensurate.

Leo's work, together with the popularity of theosophical ideas, brought astrology back from the dead. By the 1930s, Leo's follower Dane Rudhyar had instigated the first twelve-paragraph horoscope column, based on Leo's system of sun signs, which appeared, appropriately enough, in *American Astrologer* magazine. (Incidentally, Rudhyar claimed that the Age of Aquarius would start in 2162, so no need to worry too much just yet.) It was a gimme for the popular press: the *New York Post* was publishing a daily column by 1936. In the UK, the first twelve-paragraph sun sign column was published in the *Sunday Express* in 1934, and it needed to educate the readership. Therefore, rather than 'Aries' or 'Pisces', each paragraph was headed 'for those born between March 21st and April the 20th', and so on. Paper rationing meant that the column wasn't produced during the Second World War, and it didn't reappear until 1955, in the *Daily Express*, at that time the best-selling newspaper in Britain. Which, you'll notice, is right at the beginning of the counter-culture in Britain (and three years after the repeal of the Witchcraft Act, which removed penalties from fortune tellers).

So; why do we know anything at all about astrology? It's because theosophical ideas of spiritual development had grown in popularity across the twentieth century. It's because Alan Leo's theosophical-inspired invention of sun sign astrology, regulated by his philosophy that 'the stars incline, they do not compel', fitted neatly into a twelve-paragraph newspaper column. It's because Leo's ideas were taken up by followers of Carl Gustav Jung, who gave Blavatsky's notion of personal spiritual development some traction. It's because hippie chicks (forgive me) learned how to draw up post-Leo developmental astrological charts, at first by means of 'ephemera', but now by computer programs. And everyone loves to read about themselves. Any time you read Mystic Meg or Russell Grant, you are buying into theosophical cosmology. Any time one of your mum's friends offers to 'do your chart' in order to find out something about your personality, you are following in the path of Madame Helena Blavatsky. From nothing to eleven million 'believers' in a little over a century takes some doing. I must leave it to your judgement as to whether or not it was worthwhile.

So what have we got from this brief look at some of the themes of late sixties spirituality? We've ended up with Deepak Chopra, mindfulness, fortune telling, empowering memes about how great you are, and kittens. We've ended up with the internet.

'Fuck,' says Bob. 'What else did I miss?'

'Politics, mate. Fucking loads of it. While you were poncing about being interrogated by Saddam Hussein, politics was all the rage. All the politics you'd grown up with and not noticed – the New Left, the Situationists – was all kicking off big time. Paris student uprisings! Vietnam! The Tet Offensive! The Democratic Party Convention in Chicago! The Prague Spring and the fucking Soviet tanks again! Nineteen sixty-eight, for fuck's sake! Bloody hell, even Mick Jagger was at it, demonstrating outside the US Embassy.'

'Not that interested.'

I sigh. I don't care.

Whole books have been written about 1968 – Mark Kurlansky's *1968* is an obvious example. In Peter Doggett's masterly *There's a Riot Going On*, which covers the links between radical politics and popular culture between 1966 and 1972, he says of 1968, that it had 'passed into mythology before it had ended'. 1968 is regarded as the high water mark of the counter-culture. After that, everything changed. 1969 was really the first year of the seventies. 1968 was the year when radical politics took to the streets, streets which, according to the Situationists, were covering up the beach. And Bob was off way-marking the hippie trail.

Let me take one event in Britain as symbolic of all that happened in 1968, to give some idea of the febrile political atmosphere that Bob had returned to. It's also an event that made a Freak of Essex County pole vaulter, R&B drummer and not terribly committed interior design student, Pete Mustill.

On 28 May 1968 students and some staff staged a one-day 'teach-in' at the Hornsey College of Art's Crouch End premises. Due mainly to the incompetence of the management, and to the bemusement of the students, it turned into a six-week occupation. The problems were educational, and had been five years in the making. The occupation may have seemed spontaneous, but the leap into action was preceded by a slowly growing awareness that change was needed, in the face of collapsing buildings and unpopular organisational reform.

For example, the occupiers didn't think you should have to have five O-Levels to get into art college, or that art schools should be merged with polytechnics, but should instead retain their separate identity. They also thought that Design should be kept as a discrete subject, distinct from Fine Art. Not quite the stuff to make people man the barricades, you'd imagine. But May 1968 was the time of student riots in France. Inevitably, given the moment, some of the Hornsey students took on many of the ideas of the Parisian *Enragés*. Students from other universities went over to Paris to join in the burning and looting fun over there, like Cambridge students John Barker and Jim Greenfield. But most stayed here, and made their own entertainment, and watched Paris almost fall from a distance.

The spark for the Paris student demonstrations had been struck in 1966 at the University of Strasbourg by five pro-Situationist students who got themselves elected onto the almost moribund Student Union Committee. They invited the Situationists to write something critical of the university, and Tunisian Situationist Mustapha/Omar Khayati stepped up with a pamphlet entitled 'On the Poverty of Student Life: A Consideration of Its Economic, Political, Sexual, Psychological and Notably Intellectual Aspects and of a Few Ways to Cure it'.

The students then essentially nicked all the Student Union funds, had 10,000 copies printed, and handed them out to new and returning students at the beginning of the autumn term. This caused something of a stir, and the students were excluded from the university. But what they had done was, for the first time, brought the ideas of the Situationists to a wider audience than a handful of radical art theorists. The ideas in the pamphlet spread quickly throughout the burgeoning student movements of Western Europe.

It was incendiary stuff; it still is – you'll find a link to the full text in the Appendix. It is against this book: 'The revolt is contained by overexposure: we are given it to contemplate so that we shall forget to participate.' It is against your phone: 'He devours the spectacle with his gaze, and enjoys it vicariously through the gaze of his friends. He is an other-directed voyeur.' It is against everything you've been taught to expect:

'The revolt of youth against an imposed and "given" way of life is the first sign of a total subversion. It is the prelude to a period of revolt – the revolt of those who can no longer live in our society.'

The cure that it promises is straightforward: 'Proletarian revolt is a festival or it is nothing; in revolution the road of excess leads once and for all to the palace of wisdom. A palace which knows only one rationality: the game. The rules are simple: to live instead of devising a lingering death, and to indulge untrammelled desire.' It was written as a call to action, and thousands of students in France, Germany and the UK read it as such.

The Hornsey occupation influenced other art students to occupy their colleges. Guildford Art College was the first, though it's difficult to imagine that anyone in Guildford has ever indulged untrammelled desires. You can hear the echo of the Situationists in *The Hornsey Affair*, a Penguin special on the occupation, put together by occupying students and staff, and published in 1969. This is from the end of a section entitled 'Evening's Entertainment' by 'A-R. And P.B-D', in which they talk about showing films every night. If they got bored, they showed them backwards, which made them '... roll around on the floor in helpless laughter at a film of vacuum-forming plastics technology in glorious Technicolor being shown backwards. This film summed up for us all the most bizarre aspects of the institutions and industrial concerns where people spend their lives obeying unexplained orders and doing things that were senseless.' (NB Younger Readers, drugs may have been used.)

It was fun. I know it was fun because Peter Mustill, who we must now introduce to our story, told me so.

'I did my foundation in Bournemouth. I'd wanted to be an architect, but I didn't get the grades, so I did Interior Design. There was a really funky interior design course there, and I was introduced to the work of a group of radical architects called Archigram. We rented these fuck-off big flats on the seafront all winter, and sat about smoking weed and talking and playing music. And partying. So I thought, "If I'm having a great time in Bournemouth, think how much of a great time I'd have in London," so I applied to transfer to the interior design course at Hornsey. I soon realised I'd made a huge mistake, because it was fucking shit. The department was housed in this tumbledown old primary school in Crouch End, and there was nothing happening, so I started hanging around the Royal College of Art. But as soon as the occupation was announced, I was right back in there. Stayed the whole six weeks. The best part was, every morning we'd have this big meeting, and people would come and talk to us, people like Buckminster Fuller and R.D. Laing. It was fucking great.'

The college was officially closed on the 4 July, when Haringey Council (who ran the place) sent in Securicor heavies with dogs. The students gave the guards tea and the dogs biscuits, and nobody moved. This was the so-called 'Day of the Dogs', which was seen as a triumph for the occupiers. But the building was besieged, and the authorities managed to negotiate an end to the sit-in on the 8 July. The college remained closed for the next six months. On the day after the Day of the Dogs, however, an exhibition documenting the work that had been done during the occupation opened at the ICA's new building on the Mall, only the second exhibition held in the new premises.

'I was there helping set that up,' Pete told me. 'It was brilliant, really exciting. It showed what could be done without administrators and bosses, if we could just run it ourselves.'

'So did you go back to college after the sit-in?'

'Nah. Much too boring. I'd met Bob and Sandy by then, and what they were doing seemed like much more fun. So I threw in my lot with them.'

'I never gave a fuck about politics,' says Bob.

'You sure missed a lot,' I say. 'A fucking shit-load. And a lot of music, too.'

'I caught up with the music. All right, it was Woodstock when I was out on my second trip. But I'd got back and I'd met up with a woman who had tickets for Crosby, Stills and Nash at the Albert Hall. And not only tickets, but there are twenty or thirty seats at the side of the stage, in the audience but virtually on the stage, and she had tickets for them. And it was the best concert I've ever, ever attended, particularly a sit-down concert. The band was so near, we were crying, the band was crying, everyone in sight had tears streaming down their faces. It was fucking wonderful. Really, really was. And I'd never heard them – heard of them, but not heard them.'

Since this is a book about the British counter-culture, so far as possible, I want to concentrate at this point, not on the US music scene, not on Laurel Canyon and the coming together of country and rock, of which Crosby, Stills and Nash (and sometimes Y, Neil Young) were standard-bearers, but on the new genre that was being invented in Britain, specifically England, in 1969; which was folk rock. Rob Young, in his remarkable book about British folk rock, *Electric Eden*, claims that you can hear Fairport Convention inventing it on 'A Sailor's Life', from their 1969 album *Unhalfbricking*, produced by snooty Joe Boyd.

But there was another highly successful and popular band operating in the UK at that time who could make claims to being the founding Fathers and Mothers of English Folk ... if not exactly rock ... then of jazzy inflected folk pop. They were called Pentangle. Which takes us all the way back to the first name that Bob dropped, his primary school playmate, John Renbourn. Renbourn and his friend Bert Jansch were regarded as two of the finest acoustic guitarists of the British folk scene, and by 1968 they had each released a couple of solo albums, and one album together. Singer Jacqui McShee had started joining them 'from the floor' at various folk clubs, and in 1968 they added bass player Danny Thompson and drummer Terry Cox; five members, hence 'Pentangle', though it also suited the quasi-mystical tone of the times. They were hugely successful very quickly, filling the Royal Festival Hall and playing at the Newport Folk Festival. One of the songs from their number-one album *Basket of Light*, 'Lite Flight', was used as the theme song for the BBC drama series *Take Three Girls*. Their sound has not aged well, but in 1968 and 1969, Pentangle were the acceptable face of the hippie culture. They were long-haired hippies, but clean and wholesome; my mum liked them.

My mum was not, however, generally a fan of long hair. I can remember, aged five, watching the Beatles doing 'She Loves You' on TV, and my mum saying, 'If ever you grow hair that long, I won't let you in the house.' In 1963, the Beatles' hair just about touched their collars; by 1973, mine was down on my shoulders, but my mum still let me in. Hair comes and goes; mostly goes, in my experience. Although waist-length hair was much more common in women than in men, men's hair in Victorian times was often grown long. Long hair was a status symbol; it showed that you had the time to look after it. It was the First World War that did for long hair, because it was a bit of a bother getting a decent shampoo in the trenches. Short hair was a sign of a soldier, and subsequently a veteran; admiration for veterans hadn't begun to fade before the start of the Second World War in 1939, when short hair became de rigueur again. Short hair was therefore associated with militarism; long hair was seen as a reaction against it. Hair was seen in a broader popular culture as the symbol of the hippies, one for which they were widely loathed and derided. Hair was therefore seen by the hippies as a badge of honour (including bodily hair: in 1969, men had beards, and hippie chicks had stopped shaving their legs). And that is why the legendary hippie musical, which contained obscenities, drug-taking, the burning of the American flag and onstage nudity, was called, naturally enough, *Hair*.

A Hero for High Times

It opened in London at the Shaftesbury Theatre on 27 September 1968 and ran for nearly 2,000 performances; it might have run for longer still had not the roof of the theatre fallen in five years later. The date is significant, because the day before, the Theatres Act of 1968 had come into force, which removed the power of the Lord Chamberlain to censor what could be performed in British theatres. The Lord Chamberlain's Office is that part of the Royal Household which is responsible for running the big set-piece events: royal weddings, state visits, garden parties, and so on. Until 1968, therefore, the censorship of theatre in the UK was a matter of Royal prerogative. Although in practice the Government exercises prerogative on behalf of the monarch, the control of what could and what couldn't appear on the British stage is a good example of how dyed-in-the-wool control over free expression is in the UK. No wonder the hippies grew their hair.

'So you were getting your head together?' I say.

'But slowly. I was fucking bad. I'm trying to remember how I regrouped. Motorbikes had a lot to do with it.'

'It must have been at about this time you met Pete Mustill.'

'That's right, that all happened through Sandy. Sandy had become mates with this Pete Mustill bloke. And I'd met Pete, and I'd bought myself a real weedy little motorbike and sold it to buy a better motorbike which we did up, and we spray-painted it over the course of several months, in Lady Locke's front room. Her real name was the Honourable Jean Kish – she was a very easy-going lady.'

'Was she a friend of yours?'

'Well, of course she was a friend, you wouldn't do spray-painting in someone's front room otherwise. Oh, you mean did I fuck her? Well yes, I did fuck her, but that was only somewhere along the line, because she wasn't a very particular lover. She was living with her husband, Sir Adam Kish – he was very laid back. I met her in fact because she was doing a bit of PR work for Forbidden Fruit – it's always good to have a nice-looking posh girl doing your PR. She was a close mate of Sue Miles.

'Anyway, so I've got a motorbike, I've got mates to knock around with – Pete Mustill, my brother, Dennis Rolfe who I knew from before, the photographer, and other people were around. And the Prince of Wales down Princedale Road was the pub of choice at the time.'

If you want a look at what a bunch of Prince of Wales regulars looked like, try to find a vinyl copy of Rod Stewart's 1974 album, *Smiler*. The picture in the middle of the gatefold sleeve shows what you might have been in for if you'd dropped by The Prince one Saturday lunchtime.

(Younger Readers should on no account listen to the album, as it is the first, but sadly by no means the last, of Rod's rubbish solo albums. The four solo albums before *Smiler*, though, are brilliant. No artist in the history of pop music went from genius to shite quicker than Rod, I'm afraid. Stevie Wonder, maybe. If ever I meet your dad, this is the kind of issue we'll discuss.)

'And where were you living?'

'Well, this was when I was squatting the vicarage at All Saints in Notting Hill. In the church hall of which, me and Duncan Laurie first projected an oil wheel light show on Pink Floyd.'

'Wasn't the squatters' community Frestonia round there?'

'This was a bit east of Frestonia. Yes, a good time for squatting in those days.'

Squatting has gone, really. In 2012, the Cameron/Clegg coalition government criminalised squatting in residential buildings. It was a good way to find somewhere cheap, or indeed free, to live; a way which, Younger Readers, is now as closed to you as the overland route to India. Its heyday was in the 1960s and '70s. Many of the groups who squatted empty properties organised themselves into Family Squatting Associations, which became legit over time, and morphed into Housing Associations. 'Frestonia', on Freston Road in Notting Hill, was a famous example of a squatting collective which became straight over time. In 1979, it's estimated that 50,000 people lived in squats. By 2001, it was down to about 15,000 people. Reader, I was one. Our squat, which called itself the Black Sheep Housing Collective, had three houses in Islington, all with the approval of Islington Council, which had given a long-term commitment to take over the houses, do them up into flats, and to bring the whole thing under council control; this has been carried out, and my old squat mates are now tenants of a housing association.

When Bob was squatting, it certainly was a good time. When he lived on the streets, Bob often slept in bomb craters; even by the late 1960s, large areas of North and West London had been effectively abandoned, and people moved into the houses which had often been left empty since the war. You pulled boards off the door, got in, and started to get the place together; connecting up water and electricity, mending windows and doors, and rescuing otherwise abandoned buildings. So popular a way of living was it that Bob's pal and counter-culture legend Heathcote Williams ran a squatters' housing bureau called Ruff Tuff Cream Puff. Freaks could rock up in London, and find themselves somewhere to live, either free or for a peppercorn rent. Criminalising squatting gives priority to the rights of wealthy absentee landlords over those of homeless people. Ownership always trumps need. That's the law.

'And what were you doing?'

'Bikes. Sandy and Pete Mustill and myself, we had a motorcycle business in a mews just behind Biba's in Kensington, just about fifty yards from Kensington High Street, in a basement, which ain't ideal for having a motorbike shop. It was a normal Georgian steps-down-to-the-basement house, so getting up and down was not the best fun in the world.'

Of course, Biba. What other shop would Bob have his bike shop behind? Founded by Polish immigrant Barbara Hulanicki and her husband Stephen Fitz-Simon in 1963 as a mail-order business, by 1969 Biba were in their third store, 120 Kensington High Street, selling not just their trademark clothes for women (cut beautifully in such a way as to make the wearers look skinny, but using material that kept their clothes affordable) but also branching out into menswear, make-up, jewellery and interiors. Inside, the shop was a thing of beauty and wonder, with dark velvet hangings and Art Nouveau mirrors. The make-up is the thing that is perhaps most recognisable today: for girls, neon lips and dark kohl around the eyes was *the* make-up look of the late 1960s and early 1970s. Biba was a place not just to shop, but to be seen; Jagger hung around to pick up dark-eyed girls, and Bowie and Marc Bolan were regulars. Biba was closed in May 1971, when the Angry Brigade set off a bomb inside the store; more of whom when we get to the seventies proper. This did not stop Hulanicki: in 1973, she took over the old Derry & Toms building, also on Kensington High Street, to set up Big Biba. It had seven floors and a roof garden (which you can still visit), and sold pretty much everything, including baked beans, in the trademark black and gold logo. It was so successful that it attracted as many as a million visitors a year. So successful that people got greedy and chucked out Hulanicki and Fitz-Simon – the store closed in 1975. But for a time, Biba dressed the nation's trendiest women, and stayed open just long enough for me to remember girls from my school going there.

'So what were you doing behind Biba?'

'We were doing up bikes for mates. Charging them, like. And we had to test the bikes. So me, Pete and Sandy were out on a motorbike ride out of London one day, to spend the weekend on army land where we were raised as kids. I had a good bit of hash in my pocket, and we were going to spend the night under the stars. We got to Virginia Water, and a motorbike cop pulls us. Two of us are riding customers' bikes – the customers are mates – and the copper says to me: "Is this your motorbike?" and I said, "Yes, it is", even though it was completely illegal in many other respects.

'Next he asks Pete, "Is this your motorbike?" and Pete says, "No." "Who does it belong to?" "The Marquess of Queensberry," which was an absolutely factual answer, true and honest. The copper took it to be some sort of sarcasm, so he said, "You're under arrest on suspicion of stealing a motorcycle." He came to Sandy: "Is this your motorcycle?" "It is not." "Who does it belong to?" "Dennis Rolfe." "Can I contact him?" "No, he is out sailing his yacht," which was, again, completely true and factual. "You're under arrest on suspicion of stealing a motorcycle." So he radios up a police car and all that, to take Pete and Sandy to the station, leaving their motorbikes on a grass verge somewhere near Virginia Water. I rode down to the station. Things weren't looking too wonderful, so I dumped the hash, somewhere I'd be able to find it again if I had to. Sandy tells them in answer to questions that he's a road manager for Led Zeppelin. They obviously don't know what a road manager is – they think it is some sort of big deal – and the copper says, "I'm going to phone my daughter." And then they get through to the Marquess of Queensberry, who is a hippie art teacher. And they manage to track him down when he's at a mate's place having supper. The cops say, "He's at a dinner party," even though he was just sitting around having a drink, they clearly pictured him with his ermine and a little coronet. And the cop eventually gets through to him: "I'm terribly sorry to disturb you, I know it sounds ridiculous, but we've arrested somebody riding a motorcycle they claim is yours, ha ha." "Is it Pete or Bob?" "Oh, his name *is* Peter, actually." You should have seen his face, he was touching his forelock, his face is draining – here are people who actually *know* the Marquess of Queensberry, the inventor of the rules of boxing on first-name terms; and a road manager for Led Zeppelin ... wow! We go out; the entire police station is fucking lined up to shake our fucking hands and ask for our autographs, can you believe? Of course we spurn all this sort of stuff ... but you should have heard the reverence in this copper's voice when he thought he was getting through to the Marquess of Queensberry.'

'I suppose his grandfather, his dad even, was Bosie, Lord Alfred Douglas, Oscar Wilde's downfall.'

'Yeah, he would have been; I hadn't thought of that.'

'And his great-grandfather did the rules of boxing. But he was having his bike done up at your place?'

'Yeah. And it's at that place where Taffy re-enters my life.'

Younger Readers, if they are close readers, will remember Taffy stabbing Kray heavy Joey King up the arse eight or so years ago. 'When Pete
and I had the motorcycle business, Taffy turned up there one day. Do
you know what an Auburn Cord is?'

'No.'

'One of the most astonishing cars ever built – one of the first cars to
have front-wheel drive, American, a totally Art Deco car, perhaps the
most beautiful car ever made. It came from the thirties; all aluminium,
handmade V8 engine, huge outside exhaust pipes, lots of them, painted
pink and black. He'd just blagged it off someone.

'Some mush we'd got to know lived along the block, he turned up
with Taffy in this car, who wanted to blag a motorbike off us or something, but we connected and I said, "You're the bloke who stabbed Joey
King." And he said, "Yeah," and so it went on from there.

'He's the nearest I've ever met to a true magician, without any bullshit,
hocus pocus or anything, he could just bend people to his will, people
couldn't deny him. That was his style. And he was by far and away the
most exciting thing around, and so I sort of threw in my lot with him,
basically. Doing up people's motorbikes was – well, me and Pete, we'd
just take their motorbikes, get an advance payment, spend it all on hash
and petrol and ride around on their motorbikes, and sometimes we'd
get the job done and sometimes not. Usually not! So that was easy to
abandon, I went on the road with Taffy.'

Just to be clear, Younger Readers, Pete Mustill is a good friend of
mine, who lives in Presteigne, where he writes cracking songs for his
band Little Rumba, promotes astounding music events, and edits our
local 'What's On' paper, which is called *Broad Sheep*. A most respectable
white-haired electric cycling enthusiast. His friend, and ex-girlfriend, Titi,
a Dutch lady, now in her mid-seventies and somewhat frail, also lives in
Presteigne, and both of them have been kind enough to tell me about
Taffy. Titi also told me about the shoot for the cover of the third Velvet
Underground album, as she was the photographer's assistant (and wife).
She also told me about actually watching the Velvet Underground, live,
in Warhol's Factory, on acid, whilst bouncing up and down on a tram-
poline. Frail white-haired ladies in their seventies are not always what
they may seem, and certainly not what they were in my day.

I tell Bob, 'The other day I was at Titi's flat talking to her and Pete
Mustill about Taffy. And Pete grabbed me by the arm and said, "Ian,
come with me. I've got to go and see a bloke in the Dukes now, who
owes me loads of money." And I said, "No, you're OK, Pete, I'm just

going to stay and talk to Titi." And Pete said, "Fuck ... I thought I'd see if I had the Taffy magic. There isn't a bloke in the Dukes who owes me lots of money, but that's the sort of thing that if Taffy said it you'd just go, "All right", whatever you were doing.

'When I hear people talk about him,' I say to Bob, 'the figure that I'm kind of reminded of is Charlie Manson. Manson seemed to have had that kind of charismatic pull.'

'Yeah ... or Hitler, or ... Taffy wasn't a big bloke, I never actually saw him get violent with anyone, I know that he got violent with quite a few people – after all, the first time I ever saw him, he stabbed a famous gangster up the arse. And I know for a fact that he had a shotgun under a bloke's chin, and all that. But his way was ... Well, he was a magician.'

The story of Charles Manson and his family is long and convoluted, and has been written about many times. There's a film, called *Helter Skelter*, and a wealth of stuff online. So this is the briefest possible precis, but one worth making, I think, because of how struck I am by the fact that every time I talk to someone about Taffy, Manson's name comes up.

Manson was born to a sixteen-year-old alcoholic prostitute in Cincinnati, Ohio, in 1934. His birth name was Maddox, but his mother was briefly married to a Mr Manson, and Charlie took his name. He was in and out of prisons and reformatories; so much so that when he was released in 1967, he had spent more than half his life behind bars.

During his last spell inside, Manson had met wannabe record producer and roadie Phil Kaufman, and on his release, Kaufman, some-what impressed by Manson's songwriting, said he'd introduce him to his showbiz friends, who included Doris Day's son Terry Melcher, a record producer who helped Manson record some demos, and Beach Boy drummer Dennis Wilson, who reworked Manson's song 'Cease to Exist' as 'Never Learn Not to Love' as a Beach Boys 'B' side.

Manson had been a cruel and manipulative boy, who learned that he could exert power over others. As well as pursuing his 'showbiz career' (using intimidation and fear, though the story runs that he didn't scare Dennis Wilson, who knocked Manson out in a fight). Manson began to acquire followers, who became known as the Family. At its height, the Family numbered over 100, but at its core were a group of young women who were attracted to Charlie by his charisma. One of this inner group was Linda Kasabian, after whom a meat-and-two-veg rock band were named. Kasabian said of Charlie, 'He would hold you for every second.' His first parole officer said that Charlie was what he needed to be at any given moment, and for the young unloved women who gathered around him, what he was, what he needed to be, was a cross between a father, a lover and the Messiah. One of his followers, Catherine Share, known as 'Gypsy' said, 'He never really had to say he was Jesus. I just thought he was the closest thing to Jesus that I would ever meet.'

And, like Jesus, Charlie demanded things of his followers. He believed that he had been warned by the Beatles song 'Helter Skelter' that his job was to prepare for a forthcoming apocalyptic race war. To this end, he moved his Family out to the Mojave Desert, to the Spahn Movie Ranch, a ranch that had been built as a movie set. From here, he sent the Family on a mission to kill, in order to bring 'Helter Skelter' about.

On 9 August 1969, four of the Family carried out a series of horrific murders at the home of film director Roman Polanski. Five people were killed, including Polanski's wife Sharon Tate, who was eight months' pregnant. She was horribly mutilated; one of the killers, Susan Atkins, testified that if she'd had more time, she'd have cut out Tate's unborn child. The following night, the Family murdered Leno and Rosemary LaBianca. At both crime scenes, investigators found words written in the victims' blood on the walls: Pigs. Death to Pigs. Helter Skelter.

No one suspected the Family; it was not until several members were arrested for vandalising the Mojave Desert National Park that they came under suspicion for the Tate/LaBianca murders. And it was not until 1971 that they were finally convicted. At the time of writing, Manson is still alive, in prison, and in denial.

Did Taffy have the kind of charisma that could lead people to kill? He got his pals to do some mad shit. Manson held an extraordinary hold over his followers, and the people that have talked to me about Taffy recognised that same mesmeric quality.

And the worst of it is this: if you watch film of Manson, and there is quite a bit to be found, you'll see that sometimes, just sometimes, from behind his madness, there emerges a beautiful, open smile, which is somehow more chilling than the swastika he carved on his forehead.

Manson's testimony at his trial is as good a summary as you'll find of core Freak existentialist philosophy: 'The truth is now; the truth is right here: the truth is this minute, and this minute we exist.'

I have made a would-be inspirational internet meme from this quote, superimposed on a serene background of lakes and forests and mountains. Lots of people like and share it. Very few notice where it comes from. #mindfulness.

The Manson Family killings were one of the two big events that signi-fied the failure of the sixties counter-culture to bring about a state of

Peace 'n' Love. The other was the Free Festival at the Altamont Speedway, in California, on 6 December 1969. The Stones were on tour in the US for the first time since 1966, doing a series of thirteen shows, but they had received complaints about the ticket prices ($8.50!). They decided to do a free concert in California, what they hoped would be seen as 'Woodstock West'. Negotiations began with the Grateful Dead, who agreed to be second on the bill to the Stones, and a venue was found: the Sears Point Raceway in Sonoma, California, right by the north end of one of the bays around San Francisco. The owners came up with a generous deal. The Stones would be responsible for the costs of the build and the take-down, for all the necessary licensing for health and safety, and for security. Otherwise there would be no charge, and any profits would be given to Vietnamese refugee children. Over the weeks of negotiation, a slight snag came to light: the owners of the Sonoma Raceway were a film production company, and all they wanted was the exclusive rights to any film that was made of the event, or $100,000. And another $100,000 upfront. So, a day before the festival was due to go ahead, the organisers moved the event to the Altamont Speedway, high in the Diablo Mountains above Oakland. The Diablo Mountains are called that because they are diabolical; scorching sun bakes them to a desert, and endless wind dries them out further. The well at the Speedway has so much sulphur in it that it smells of rotten eggs. As successive people who bought and tried to make a go of the Speedway discovered, it was a really stupid place for a race track, and until the festival, the largest crowd ever gathered there was 6,000. It was therefore also a fucking stupid place for a festival of any kind. With less than twenty-four hours' notice, an estimated crowd of 300,000 made their way up into the hills. The Dead had the good sense to pull out, especially when they saw that the notorious motorbike club the Hells Angels had been hired as the security. The Stones had used the Angels at their free concert in Hyde Park earlier that year, and it had, on the whole, worked well. What they overlooked was that the British Hells Angels were not really Hells Angels at all, but a bunch of relatively mild-mannered greebos. The California Hells Angels were very much nastier. They were offered $500 worth of beer to keep people off the stage, and, in fairness, they really did. As David Crosby of CSNY, who stepped up into second place on the bill when the Dead pulled out said, 'Remember, the Angels were asked to be there. They've always showed up at gatherings, but they were not asked to guard a stage. This time they were, and they did it. In their mind, guard a stage means guard it. That means, if anyone comes near it, you do them in, and in the Angels' style, if you do them in, you do them in.' Crosby was pointing the finger at the Grateful Dead's manager, Rock Scully, whose bright idea it was to hire them. It seems as though the Angels saw their remit as keeping off anyone who came vaguely near, and they prowled the front of the stage with loaded pool cues, attacking anyone within range. Jefferson Airplane singer Marty Balin was knocked unconscious for suggesting that they were being a wee bit overzealous. The violence reached its zenith with the murder of Meredith Hunter in front of the stage while the Rolling Stones played 'Sympathy for the Devil'. You can see the moment of his killing in the documentary made about that Stones tour, *Gimme Shelter*. Unsurprising, then, that this moment has come to symbolise the end of something.

'So there's Taffy, he turns up in the courtyard behind Biba's in the Cord. And he starts persuading you of things?'

'That was the first time he came by. The next time, he said, "Have you got a gun?" And I happened to have the gas gun I'd found that some Yardie types had hidden in our roof in the Portobello Road. And I had that, so he said, "Perfect", and we became quite matey after that. Adventuring with Taffy looked a lot more fun than anything else.'

'So how the fuck did Taffy have that truck, or bus – that extraordinary vehicle? Not the Auburn Cord, the Greville Wynne vehicle?'

'He got that about the same time that I met up with him.'

'And where did he get it?'

'There was someone – a very upmarket car dealer – Taffy had some relationship with him. I never queried the nature of the relationship, because Taffy never invited questions. But that was where he got the Cord from, and the GT40 that he fucking wrote off in the middle of London; this very valuable American Ford GT40, first polycarbon skin car, which Taffy hit a lamp-post with while doing a drag race along the road somewhere and the fucking thing exploded. But still he kept getting vehicles. You know the story of the bus, the previous history of it?'

'Tell me again.'

'It had been converted into a living and display space in the 1950s. Awnings pulled out on both sides. It was made for the British Government and it was on the secret list, we know that because when we went to get a head gasket for it, and the bloke said, "OK, what's the engine number?" and when we told him he said, "I'm really sorry, we can't sell you anything." I mean he was really sorry, he didn't come on all offi-cious, but this vehicle was on the Official Secrets list, so that's how we knew it was a government-built vehicle. It goes out behind the Iron Curtain, ostensibly doing a technical trade show, in the hands of a geezer called Greville Wynne.'

'Greville Wynne the spy, this is?'

'Yeah. Anyway, Greville Wynne got popped in Hungary when they found out that the whole fucking truck was all bugged up to fuck, yeah? And the Soviets busted him, bang to rights sort of thing, and you know the history.'

I do, and I'm not sure Bob is right, entirely. Greville Wynne was arrested because his Soviet contact, Oleg Penkovsky had been arrested, and named Wynne as his contact. Penkovsky was a colonel in Soviet military intelligence, who, worried that the world might find itself in a nuclear war, and disillusioned with the way that Soviet foreign policy seemed to be encouraging such a war, talked to Wynne, a businessman who sold electrical equipment, at a trade fair in Moscow early in 1961. Penkovsky told Wynne that he was willing to give information to British and US intelligence. Wynne had made a lot of trade trips behind the Iron Curtain, in his specially adapted mobile showroom, and was briefed in advance of the first meeting with Penkovsky by MI6. Penkovsky handed over information at that first meeting which was what in John Le Carré novels is known as 'gold'. And at a series of meetings with Wynne, Penkovsky continued to hand over information, particularly in the field of missile technology, in which Penkovsky was an expert; or, at least, had access to expert intelligence.

And here's a thing: it is at least arguable that you are alive today because of what Penkovsky did. He's known as 'The Spy Who Saved the World'. Because during the eighteen months or so that Penkovsky was operational and able to feed information to Greville Wynne, the world came as close to nuclear war as it had been before or has been since, due to an incident which is known as the Cuban Missile Crisis. The Cuban Missile Crisis was a diplomatic stand-off between the USA and the USSR, and between their respective leaders John F. Kennedy and Nikita Khrushchev. Cuba had undergone a revolution in 1959. Younger Readers will have seen Che Guevara T-shirts and posters, without perhaps knowing who he was. He was the most glamorous of the revolutionaries, but not the beardiest, a title which went to the Communist leader Fidel Castro, with a beard like a Hoxton hipster, one who smoked cigars rather than high-tech vaping devices.

If you were a Communist in 1959, chances were you were going to look for military support from the Soviet Union, and from 1960 onwards, the USSR obliged. By 1962, the USSR had grown so much in confidence that it started shipping the parts for nuclear missiles to Cuba. The problem with this from the US point of view is that Cuba lies ninety miles off the US coast. By having nukes in the Americans' backyard, the Russians would have a clear strategic advantage. Thanks to Penkovsky, Kennedy knew that this was happening; and knew that he had three days to stop it before the missiles became operational.

On 20 October, Kennedy decided to blockade Soviet naval access to Cuba. The president announced the presence of the missiles and the imposition of the blockade to the world in a television address on the evening of 22 October. For six nerve-shredding days, the world braced itself for nuclear war. During those six days, all the missile launchers that the USSR had sent to Cuba became operational. Because of Penkovsky's intelligence, Kennedy knew how many missiles were really there, and he called Khrushchev's bluff. Khrushchev backed down and agreed to withdraw all the missiles and launch equipment, and in exchange for the withdrawal, Washington agreed not to invade Cuba.

Sadly for Penkovsky, 20 October was also the date of his arrest. Opinions differ as to whether or not he was given away by double agents working at the CIA in Washington, or merely as a result of routine surveillance in Moscow. Within days, Penkovsky had given Wynne's name as his contact. Wynne, unfortunately for him, was with his converted bus/van/showroom at a trade fair in Budapest, where he was arrested and flown to Moscow. Penkovsky was executed for treason in 1963, and Greville Wynne, a portly English businessman in his mid forties, was sentenced to eight years hard labour, which, as he put it to his wife, was 'not exactly Butlins'. He was released in 1964 in a swap for the Soviet spy Gordon Lonsdale. Also thrown in were various ne'er-do-wells who were in prison in the USSR, one of whom was an early Freak called Mickey Green, who had been held by the Soviets after they caught him trying to smuggle dope out of Afghanistan via the air route through Tashkent. Bob will have cause to be grateful to him.

'It's *the* most important post-war case of spying' I tell Bob. 'The Master of Pembroke told me, and he should know. I asked him about it, because of knowing about Taffy's truck. He was fascinated to hear where Wynne's bus ended up. He told me Wynne was the wrong man in the right place at the right time. It's the case on which the entire fate of the earth turns. How did Taffy come by the bus that saved the world?'

'Through whatever circumstances, it came from behind the Iron Curtain, along with that Auburn Cord, in fact, that came out in the same deal. Rennick, Chris Rennick, that was the motor dealer's name.'

'So that came at the same time as Greville Wynne's bus? The Cord?'

'Well, apparently. They weren't things I ever questioned at the time. They came out of Eastern Europe in the same deal. And somehow Taffy got the bus, through his astonishingly persuasive ways, no threats, but people couldn't deny him. We were in the bus a few years later, middle of Amsterdam, when Taffy spots a van in the oncoming traffic. He says, "I've seen that van before, I want it." He gets out of the bus in the middle of the fucking traffic, says "I'll be back in a minute," leaves me in the bus in the middle of rush hour, great, goes up to the van and starts talking. Fuck me if I don't see the driver get out, Taffy get in and in about two minutes he comes back and says, "Let's go," and I followed him while he drove that van. Oh, and no money changed hands, Taffy didn't give him anything. Can you imagine, you're driving along in your home town, and some really wild-looking foreigner comes up to you and – what on earth could they say to you, how could they broach it, that you would get out of your fucking van and see him drive off in it? Without them putting more money than you'd hope to get for it in your hand?'

'No, I can't imagine it. What did Taffy look like?'

'Short, triangular-ish face, dark straightish brown hair, very slightly Mongolian cast of features, but only maybe 10 per cent, that sort of facial cast. Tattooed with Asian/Indian letters, words, signs or whatever, several of them on both hands, always wearing unusual clothes and usually pretty grubby, often very grubby – he might be wearing a Cacharel silk shirt but it would be thick with grease. I saw him in a suit once, but he just looked like a total wild-man tearaway, except in a suit.'

'So it wasn't through looks that he did it?'

'No – he looked like a fucking wild man. I mean, really. When he blagged that van in Amsterdam, he was wearing an Uzbeki horseman's coat, which are quilted velvet in several different colours, with a bit of fancy stitching here and there on it. No hint of convention there.'

'OK, you've got this truck, but why are you going to get Donovan's showman's wagon and how did you decide that you're going to be the backstage crew at the Isle of Wight Festival?'

'Well, I don't know. I didn't ask as it seemed it would be a futile exercise and we would fall out – I don't think there was any plan at all, cos that wasn't Taffy's way. He just said, "We're going to pick up Donovan's showman's wagon from his place in Skye, and we're taking it to the IOW Festival." So off we went in the famous bus, me and Taffy over the sea to Skye.'

'Let me tell you about Vashti Bunyan,' I say. 'To people who like folk rock, she's like a goddess. She's like Nick Drake, except a lady and alive. She made this album called *Just Another Diamond Day*, and it was a legendary album, and then she disappeared and gave up music. And then she got a letter from Devendra Banhart, who's an American folk artist, saying I fucking love your stuff, thirty years later, and I've devoted my life to finding you. At this time she didn't know, but copies of her album were selling for £5,000.'

'So she wasn't all computered up or anything?'

'No, she didn't have a clue. So they re-release *Just Another Diamond Day* on CD, and she becomes, if not a household name, very well known in folkie circles. And then she makes a new album and now she's making records with this folk elite.

'So she bowls up in London in about '66, and she wants to be a pop star. And she met, quite quickly, Andrew Loog Oldham, who signs her and gave her a Jagger/Richards song. And there are a few pictures of her on pop shows at the time, doing this single. But she didn't really like it, she's a vagabond girl in her heart, and out in Kent she met this bloke called Robert Kerr, and he's an artist, living in the middle of a wood, like you, with his artwork, in a place like here. They lived in this wood, and then they were chucked out and they walked out of their wood and met an old gypsy bloke, with a horse-drawn wagon, and he sold them his wagon and horse. Then they spent the next two years going from Kent to Donovan's place on Skye.'

'I doubt if those two people you're talking about had had anything to do with horses before, either.'

'No, they hadn't, they learned it all out on the way. They got there, but it took them two years.'

'What, the same horse?'

'Yeah, well, as Perry and I found out when we did *The Longest Crawl*, you spend most of your time if you've got a horse-drawn wagon walking alongside it.'

'Oh, yeah.'

'I imagined that you'd be riding on it.'

'Oh yeah, you walk, all sorts of reasons you walk. One reason, to take your weight off the wagon, you just lean alongside it. And safety, traffic safety, you make cars give you plenty of clearance, make sure they know you're there, sort of thing.'

'Have you done horse-drawn stuff?'

'I've never had any desire to have a wagon myself, but I've walked along with horse-drawn types.'

'So, this journey of Vashti Bunyan and her bloke, to Donovan's place on Skye, took two years. But while they were doing that, they'd stop places, and she'd nip down to London for a few weeks at a time, because she was recording this album with Joe Boyd for Island. The story is in this book called *Electric Eden*, by a bloke called Rob Young. The book opens with this story. It's become a mythical journey of English folk music. It took them two years to do the journey. And the best part of that to record the album, which sank without trace. At the time, people said she'd disappeared, but she hadn't; they kept going west from Donovan's place on Skye, and she ended up being a crofter in the Hebrides, and never gave the album much of a thought. Two years. And it took you what? Two days?'

'About that. I don't remember where we stopped, though we must have done. We bought some fish and chips in Glasgow, so we obviously went through Glasgow, then across Scotland to wherever it is you catch the ferry to Skye. We had just enough money to pay for the ferry and that was the last of our money so we had to blag the ferry back, the CalMac Ferry.'

'So why were you heading there?'

'Donovan was a dumb cunt, that sums it up. I mean, someone who got Taffy to drive that fucking bus to the Isle of Skye and back, towing a quite priceless piece of kit, just for half a day poncing around backstage? I can't remember much about it up there. Was Vashti Wotsit there when we went up and got the wagon, I wonder? They would have remembered it because I punched the lady of the house out, so people would remember that, I think.'

'You punched her?'

'Yeah.'

'Mrs Donovan, as it were?'

'Yeah. Someone happened to mention the date when we were up there, soon after we'd got the wagon hitched up and all that, and it was my birthday. So we were on a Scottish island, there's got to be someone making whisky there, so we got in the Land Rover, got a bottle, came back, drank it.'

'What Land Rover?'

'Donovan's Land Rover. We nicked that too. So we drank this bottle, and I said. "Right, I'll go and get another one," and I was quite drunk

because I drove the Land Rover over a little cliff, by mistake, not deliberately. But still, we got there and got the booze, and got back and we
drank it, and I'm not a practised drinker, and the woman of the house
said something behind me, she was talking to her mate, I just took
offence, I've no idea what it was. And I lamped her one.'

'And then, next morning, rather than arrive with a wagon, like lovely
Vashti, you steal their beautiful showman's wagon? After lamping
Donovan's old lady?'

'Yes. And now we're heading back to London. And we were about
halfway through what used to be the Caledonian forest, now bog, an
upland bog, and a very skinny road, almost straight, but where the edge
of the tarmac is it's just bog, there's nothing, zero, at the edge of the
tarmac and we're in a wagon on a double-decker bus chassis on a road
about a foot wider than a double-decker bus, and we're carrying a long
tow. The trouble is, because the road's so narrow, you couldn't
manoeuvre. It was left-hand drive: Taffy took a while to get used to that.
Taffy said the front left wheel of the wagon had gone off the road, and
he couldn't get it back on. About ten minutes later, he said, "Oh fuck,
the front of the showman's wagon has gone off." He didn't seem too
distressed by this news. And a few minutes after this, the whole fucking
thing, both the trailer and the bus, just start keeling over while we're
bowling along at forty miles an hour – and it's all dead slow, no panic
or anything, just going through this ninety degree rotation. So we slide
along a bit, no breaking glass or metal to be heard. But the whole thing
was on its side, in the middle of nowhere, with the big roots of trees
you see in the Caledonian forest. And a car stops and says, "There's an
artic full of aluminium ingots just done the same thing about half a mile
up the road." Anyway, Taffy sees there's nothing we can do ourselves,
thumbs a lift and goes off, and there's nothing for me to do, so I just
scout around the country, thinking I can get to this lorry and help myself
to a few aluminium ingots. And the lorry was on its side with thousands
of aluminium ingots strewn far into the heather, so I nicked a couple.
Within hours Taffy turns up with a fleet of heavy recovery vehicles.
We've got no money, no chequebook, cards or anything, all he's got is
a bit of paper with a letterhead of a totally non-existent company called
Atlantic Films, with an address in Chester Square, which various types
like Ronan O'Rahilly would use. But that's all he's got in the way of
currency, this totally phoney worthless bit of paper; except it wasn't
worthless, because it had us up and out of there. We had to make a new
bit for the turntable of the showman's wagon with an axe, we hadn't

got any spanners or anything but we had an axe, and we got a bit of wood from somewhere, made one on the spot and were away the same day. And the only damage: one of the windows of the showman's wagon had a crack that hadn't been there before. Astonishing you could turn on your side at forty miles an hour with such a rig and not do any damage.'

'Because it was a sort of peaty, soft landing?'

'Yeah, nothing of any substance there. But it unsettled Taffy. We're in Scotland still, driving south, and we pick up a couple of American student-type girl hitchhikers, not hippie types, just student types, over-awed by the whole experience. Anyway, Taffy gets into his head he wants to fuck one of them. He pulls over in the most unsuitable place, probably a motorway hard shoulder or something, and tells this girl he wants to fuck her, or whatever words he used. She was totally not having it, so they both done a runner. And without a word, Taffy gets out a fucking can of petrol and starts pouring it over the whole lot, his truck and Donovan's. I knew it was pointless asking him, so I just took the can off him. I chucked the can down, said, "I'm going to stop you," he said, "Why are you going to do that?" and I said "Because my passport's in there," so he said, "OK," and that was the end of it.'

'Back in the bus and continue?'

'Yeah. Continue back to London. Then our next park-up, with that whole rig, was a hundred yards from Kensington High Street, I kid you not, not far from where we were supposed to be mending bikes. Half a block away there was a short-term car park, grit, dirt floor, a guy with a hut, a National Car Park sort of thing, but there was an even greater space, a sort of old railway depot, long ago abandoned, and Taffy said, "We're going to pull in over there," and the car park guy folded and we never had any trouble from them, and we had quite a big fucking space, all buddleia and butterflies, quite pleasant. And we were there for quite a while, about a week, lots of people with binoculars up on the roof gardens, queues of people trying to clock us. Candy Carr, Donovan's drummer, turned up in the Land Rover, because he was playing with Donovan at the Isle of Wight Festival.

'A couple of spades turned up in very unusual gear for London, wearing the sort of gear that maybe a plantation owner would wear, camp sort of stuff, flared, skirted jackets, big hats. So there they were, with this jar of cocaine. We don't know them at all, but they had a nice jar of good quality coke and they said to us, "You might like a bit of coke, take the jar, see if you like it." Taffy takes a snort, passes it to me, I have a snort,

pass it to Candy, and so on. Then Taffy says. "Let's have another try."
I can see one of the geezers has just seen what's happening and is giving
up. Taffy keeps passing the jar round till it's about half gone, and then
says, "No thanks. Not for us."'

'Were the gentlemen pleased?'

'Not very. But what could they do?'

'What next?'

'From the car park on Kensington High Street we went down to the
Isle of Wight with no further adventures. Over to the island on the ferry,
no problem. And so we get to the gate of the festival.'

Let us pause with Bob at the gate, and look around us at the Isle of
Wight Festival, in the last week of August 1970. What have we come to?
We have come to Afton Down, overlooking Freshwater Bay. The festival
has been organised by the Foulk brothers, Ron and Ray, who have moved
the festival to this new site in the far west of the island from the farm
where it had been held for the previous two years.

If you have been to a festival, you have not been to one like this.
There is one stage, and an enclosure with burger vans and hot-dog stalls
around the perimeter. There are no artisanal dining opportunities, no
bars, no knick-knack stalls, no vintage clothing stalls, no fire-eating stilt
walkers, nothing to buy. In front of the stage, sit, lie and generally idle
about an estimated crowd of 600,000 stoned people. In 1970, the population of the Isle of Wight was about one-sixth the size of the crowd. It is
still the highest attendance of any festival in the UK; about three times
the size of Glastonbury at its most bloated. Around the 'arena' (the fences
were pretty much given up on when the Foulk brothers saw the size of
the crowd and reluctantly declared it a free festival), thousands of tents
cluster in the lee of the Downs.

A friend of mine, the naturalist Richard 'Bugman' Jones, wrote to me
recently about a trip to Afton Down with his father, not quite a year
after the festival:

On 23 June 1971 I was on holiday with our family, as was usual, in
the Isle of Wight. On that day, we went to Freshwater and whilst
the rest of the Joneses deported themselves on the beach, Dad and I
walked along the crest of Afton Down, above where the Freshwater
golf course now seems to be. It was a steep chalk hillside, reminis-
cent of the South Downs behind Newhaven, but I was surprised to
see lots of small earthworks. Hundreds of them amongst the short
sward. Each of these was about a metre and a half long, about 30 cm

high at the back, exposing the white chalk, with the spoil packed to the front to create a sort of ledge, also about 30–50 cm deep. These, according to my Dad's authoritative explanation, were where revellers at the festival had cut themselves seats into the hillside slope. A sort of hippie version of the amphitheatre.

Imagine what else future archaeologists might dig up (or naturalists; even at twelve, Richard's notebook was so meticulous that he could not just summon up the memory, but the date and the measurements). What the Bugman had found as a twelve-year-old boy was the evidence of the Foulk brothers' mistake in locating the festival in this beautiful place; it was, as Richard's dad pointed out, a natural amphitheatre. The sound system is great; you can sit up on the hill and hear perfectly well without buying a ticket.

The sun is shining in a cloudless sky. You are in for a treat, so far as music goes: The Who, Joni Mitchell, Sly and the Family Stone, The Doors, Miles Davis and, most famously Jimi Hendrix's last UK performance. You will, however, be going hungry, unless you thought to bring your own food. By Sunday, there will be no food to be had, other than some hot-dog buns. Six hundred thousand very stoned people with the munchies make for a weird trip, man. Back to Bob at the gate.

'We had no intention of stopping at all, but we saw that no way could we get through the gate, the vehicle was too wide, and probably too high as well. All the security was demanding papers and everything, of which we have none, we have no papers allowing us on site.'

'Your excuse was sort of to do with Donovan?'

'Yeah, Donovan had contracted Taffy to take his showman's wagon from the Isle of Skye to the Isle of Wight, purely so he could pose around in it.'

'And with Taffy to do it, which strikes me as a huge mistake.'

'Very much so. Anyway, there we are at the gate, we can't get in, and the security guys think we've stopped. And Taffy's certainly bolstering their assumption. I jump out, say to Candy who's in the Land Rover, "Pull through the gate," because I know there's a chain in the back of the Land Rover. I hooked the chain on to one side of the gate, and when it was hooked on I said, "OK, Candy, *go*" – and he went, he was into it. He went with enthusiasm, pulled out the gatepost and several metres of the fucking fencing, leaving astonished guards, astonished that we'd just ignored them. And we were in.

'There was virtually nothing in the backstage area at this time, we were there early, so we took the plum positions and set up. After a while the Foulk brothers came by and said, "Who are you, what are you doing here? We're not happy about it," and Taffy just waved his wand on them. I don't know what he said or did, but he was amazing. Anyway, so we were there. Then more people came and joined us: Pete Mustill, Dirty Al, my brother Sandy, and maybe Dennis Rolfe did too, because that was our little sort of motorcycle gang, and they'd come down on motorbikes. And they were mentioning they were having trouble getting about, because we were running about anywhere on the site, no wristband or that sort of stuff, and Taffy confronted the Foulk brothers saying "Some of our people are having difficulty getting through the various checkpoints, backstage area, offsite and onto site." We were next to this guy who was just lying on the ground, off his face. Taffy pulled all the buttons off this guy's greatcoat, biggish black naval type buttons, with an anchor on, a bit of rope round the edge, and said, "These are the go-anywhere pass, I'll give these to our crew, and you tell your security people that anyone with these buttons, no question." And that was sorted.'

'And the Foulk brothers were like, "Yeah, fine"?'

'I didn't witness that deal, but that's the bones of it. Anyway, Taffy comes back to the camp, gives me one of these buttons, and I immediately got on to a motorbike and went to the nearest haberdasher's shop I could find. And being on the Isle of Wight they all had almost identical buttons to the one I had, I bought fucking loads of them. The amount of beautiful groupie-type girls who got to hear about these buttons and would come up, literally offering a shag for these buttons . . .

'There was so much going on that it was just . . . it was like I had had an assertive behaviour pill, I just felt unstoppable.'

'And that was Taffy's thing, I suppose, assertiveness: "This is the case; get out of my van; why are you in my van?"'

'Yeah, maybe. One great incident there was in the second half of the long weekend, when I saw this girl who was a friend of Taffy's. I'd seen her round the Chelsea scene a bit, I didn't know her and hadn't spoken to her before that weekend, but she was round our camp. She had chartered a small aircraft to be like a taxi service between London and the Isle of Wight. And I saw this girl being dragged through the backstage area by one of the security guys, and she was protesting, fighting, she wasn't going quietly by any means, and I went over there, knight in shining armour and said, "Hey, man, let go of her, she's with us." And he said, "Who are you?" and what came out of my mouth was, "The family." And only later I realised that the Family, the band, were actually on the bill, and parked up quite near our camp.'

'Not the Family in the sense of Charlie Manson?'

'Well, there's that as well, I hadn't thought … Those were just the words that came out of my mouth without any connection to my brain, as far as I was aware. I knew I had to say something quick, and I wasn't thinking about the Charlie Manson thing …'

'Because Taffy was a bit …'

'Yeah, it could have gone that way … quite a common source of conversation was, "Shall we start up a cult?"'

'Because he could have pulled it off?'

'I think he could, yeah. So anyway, this had happened, so the girl sort of owes us one. Later on, the same day or the following day – are you aware of Tommy Weaver? Well, he was a sometime racing driver, extremely good-looking, beautiful, articulate, cultured, all that. He turns up in an old army lorry with a couple of his kids, Jake and Charlie. Tommy Weaver, you would have come across him in the book about the Stones down in the South of France. He was on that scene. He turns up with a bloke and introduces him to us as some ambassador's son. He was just some middle-class South American geezer. Sometime during the day, around the fire, someone says "Oh, Sly and the Family Stone. They are on later. If only we had some coke, they'd like that."'

'From a pop geek's point of view, at that moment, 1970, pretty much the best band in the world actually, that's worth pointing out.'

'Yeah, I liked them. Anyway, at this point this South American guy chirps up, "Oh, do you like cocaine?" And I think, "How come Tommy Weaver has come from London with some South American ambassador's son, without the subject of cocaine being brought up?" I mean, if someone introduced me to the ambassador's son, it wouldn't be many minutes before that would come up … Because diplomatic fucking luggage, come on … And the guy says, "Oh, I've got loads of cocaine back at home." And so I thought great, right, another brainwave – this girl, she owes us one. So I find Sue, or whatever her name was, I say this is the situation, and she was well into that, for obvious reasons, she'd get a good bit of Charlie, and square the books, sort of thing. So she'd take this guy to London in her plane, and I arranged for a motor-bike mate … In fact, Dennis Rolfe wasn't with us, now I come to think of it, that was Dennis Rolfe's involvement. He picked up this South American guy from the North London airfield, took him in to wherever it was and back out again. Plane comes back to the Isle of Wight, and the pilot is apparently telling the girl, "This is great, I'm getting lots of hours, and this is the very first job I've ever had flying an aircraft commercially." And my brother's by the airstrip in the Isle of Wight, on a motorbike, waiting to pick up the ambassador's son. I never knew why it happened, but the plane apparently crashed through a hedge by the road, through the hedge on the other side, into a caravan which was on the other side of that second hedge, trashed a load of caravans, took both wings off the plane ... My brother is watching this from whatever distance, and the cockpit opens and the guy just stands up and opens this briefcase he's got with him and smiles and closes it. We were fucking outrageous.'

'So you had coke, and did Sly and the Family Stone have some of that coke?'

'Well, I had no part of the transaction, all I saw was the bit that went up my nose, which was copious enough. I wasn't interested in money really, I knew I wasn't going to starve. The only girl I did take the time out to make love with was a girl called The Lovely Ro, for obvious reasons; we got together somewhere over that weekend. There was a huge underfloor toolbox under the wagon and that's where we ...'

'So romantic ... So the showman's wagon is sort of backstage hospitality?'

'Joni Mitchell saw it and obviously thought she wanted that to be part of her life, sort of thing, which is nice, and asked if she could use it as a warm-up room because it was close to the stage. The entrance to the steps up to the stage was nearer than where your car is today.'

'Twenty-five to thirty metres?'

'Twenty-five, yeah. Anyway, she's in there, and I'm just sitting on the steps outside making sure no one bothers her, hoping she'd come and ask for my services ... She didn't, I regret that. But when she went off to do her set I went in there, I did see a beautiful diamond and sapphire ring on the table there – it was the only thing on the table. It obviously couldn't have been accidentally taken off and not put back on again. It was a sort of thank-you – well, that's how I read it, maybe she took it off while she was playing the guitar and forgot to put it in her pocket.'

'What happened to the ring?'

'I flogged it. Well, it's only my word, isn't it, it hadn't got "this ring is the property of Joni Mitchell who left it in the showman's wagon backstage at the IOW" inscribed on the side, has it, so it's only my word. I was generally known, probably still am, as a pretty dodgy character.'

'Nonsense.'

'Well, some of it's deserved and some of it isn't. Anyway, I have been a thief, no bones about it. I know this ring was Joni Mitchell's; I'm not going to keep it in case I get engaged to a girl, and to say, "This ring was given to me by Joni Mitchell ..." So I just flogged it. I had a connection in an auction room. Someone Monica knew had a little North London antique-y auction room, and quite a lot of tom went through there.'

'Quite a lot of what went through there?'

'Tomfoolery, jewellery.'

'Oh! I've learned a new bit of rhyming slang.'

'It's a bit of a trap, because Tom is I reckon one of the most common prefixes, you've got tomfoolery, Tom Mix for fix, tomtit for shit. Tom More a prostitute. Tom Sawyer, lawyer. Anyway, I knew the ring was worth thirty quid, it wasn't a huge ring or anything particularly special about it, just a nice diamond and couple of sapphires ring.'

I say, 'And this was at a time when my old man was earning fifteen pounds a week – so a couple of weeks' wages.'

'What am I going to do, carry it around, give it to a pretty chick? No, I put it in the auction, got thirty quid for it, quite a lot of money for me.'

'So, back on the Isle of Wight, there was an attempt to rob all the money?'

'Yeah, we discovered where the house was that the Foulks brothers were using for their base, and figured that's where the dosh would be. Because it was in the days pre-debit cards, it was all cash, fucking big stacks of money. We had zero plan for how we were going to get away with it, zero. We just wanted to get it and then play it by ear from there. So a little team of us went up to the house – fuck knows how we got there, I think we walked. It was just over the other side of a little hill there, a sort of woody bit. We were going up the track and they've obviously fucking got word of it, because a big vehicle, might have been a Jag or whatever, came out of there really fast, tyres spinning, gravel going, all that. We went into the building and we knew that that was the money going out to meet a helicopter landing to get it. We went in the building, saw a pale-faced, terrified-looking girl behind the desk. How the fuck did we think we were going to get away with that? But it just seemed too good a thing not to try. It would mean losing all Taffy's fucking everything ... but we could get on bikes, we could get to the water, I knew a little bit about small boats, it was quite amusing. And the Jimi Hendrix thing ...'

'Oh yes, tell me about Jimi Hendrix. Oh, no, wait. Let me tell you about Jimi Hendrix.'

He was born a few months after Bob, 27 November 1942, in Seattle, Washington. He was christened Johnny Allen Hendrix; but in 1946 his parents changed his name to James Marshall Hendrix, which must have been a bit confusing. His home life was not great; his parents were chaotic alcoholics, who divorced when he was nine. When he was fifteen, in 1958, his mother died of cirrhosis of the liver, and his father bought him his first guitar by way of compensation. He was good from the off; forming his first band within three months of getting his guitar. And he was a left-hander; he had to learn the guitar upside down.

After stints in Seattle area R&B bands, Hendrix joined the US Army in 1961. He was a paratrooper, who undertook twenty-six jumps before an honourable discharge in 1962, mostly because it was clear that he hated being in the Army. He moved to Nashville, and started work as a session musician on what was known as the 'Chitlin' Circuit', i.e., gigs for black punters. Amongst many others, Hendrix played for Sam Cooke, Jackie Wilson, the Isley Brothers and Little Richard. By May 1966 he had made his way to New York, where he was fronting his own band, Jimmy James and the Blue Flames. He was scarily good. Mike Bloomfield, regarded at that time as the hottest white blues guitarist in the US, the man who had played electric guitar with Dylan at Newport '65, and played on Dylan's game-changing album *Highway 61 Revisited*, went to see Jimi play at the Cafe Wha? in Greenwich Village. Bloomfield said of the experience, 'I was the hot-shot guitarist on the block – I thought I was it. I went to see him … and in front of my eyes, he burned me to death … He just got right up in my face with that axe, and I didn't even want to pick up a guitar for the next year.' Ex-Animals bassist Chas Chandler saw him play; in particular, he played a song with which Chandler had been obsessed for a few months, called 'Hey Joe'. Chandler was sure that it would be a hit in the right hands; seeing Hendrix play the song convinced Chandler that he could be a star. On 24 September 1966, Hendrix flew into Britain, and that night played his first session at the Scotch of St James. Maybe Bob was there; certainly he saw Hendrix plenty of times, jamming around the clubs. Hendrix's reputation was such that everybody wanted to jam with him. He jammed onstage at the Regent Street Polytechnic with the newly formed supergroup Cream, whose lead guitarist was Bob's old chum, erstwhile banjo player Eric Clapton. Hendrix kicked into a Howlin' Wolf song, 'Killing Floor' and, unable to keep up, Clapton walked offstage halfway through the song. Chas Chandler found him in the wings, sucking hard on a fag. 'You never told me he was that fucking good,' Eric said to Chandler.

Within days of arriving, Hendrix had signed a deal with a new record company, Track, set up by Who manager Kit Lambert. 'Hey Joe' was Hendrix's first British hit in January 1967. He made four studio albums during his short but meteoric career: three great ones – *Are You Experienced?*, *Axis: Bold as Love* and *Electric Ladyland* – and one less great one, *Band of Gypsies*. Meteoric, I hear you complain. What else would you call it? In 1967, *Melody Maker* readers voted him 'Pop Musician of the Year'. *Rolling Stone* voted him 'Performer of the Year' in 1968. *Disc* magazine voted him World Top Musician of 1969 and 1970. By the time of the IOW Festival, he was the highest paid rock musician in the world. And for why? It was his guitar playing. It wasn't just playing it with his teeth, or behind his head, or when he'd set it on fire. He was just – the best. He was the first electric guitarist to fully realise the true differences between acoustic and electric guitars, the first to use wah-wah, the first to use the miracle of feedback to astounding effect, the first to make it really sing. He was the most gifted guitarist of his generation and, many have argued, the greatest of all time. He looked cool and sexy too; this helped.

'Now you tell me about Hendrix,' I say.

'One of our crew was an ex-Jesuit, Clancy, Irish, a very bad person with a gentle charm, shall we say. The backstage area was very small, just up to that tree there, not acres and acres of space. Hendrix was using just a 14 foot sort of tourer caravan. He hadn't brought it, it was provided by the management. Hendrix and his crew were in one of them and he's being carried out, literally, each arm over a girl's back, and they're helping him from the wagon to the stage. We can see all this because it's just there. Clancy turns to me and says, "There shouldn't be anyone else on the stage except the band," because there were cameras and all sorts of people ligging about on the stage. We couldn't see the stage but we knew there would be, because we'd seen it with the other acts. So we said OK, the band was on the stage and we just went up and told everyone else, including the security, to get off the stage. We had CBS complaining, "But we fronted the money for this festival," but we just said no, get off the stage, and then we got off it ourselves. So that's what happened.'

'Chas had a pal called Bill Lloyd. Top geezer. Played the bagpipes at Chas' funeral, and made me cry. His dad, Walter Lloyd, was on stage at IOW, because he was the bloke who threw water over Hendrix's guitar when he set it on fire. Walter was involved with setting up Festival Welfare Services because of what he saw there.'

'It was sad seeing Hendrix like that.'

'One of his last gigs, I think?'

'Yeah, it would have been.'

'And you'd seen him loads in clubs, at the beginning ...'

(It was actually the opening night of a short and catastrophic European tour, which ended a week later, on 6 September, at a German festival called 'Love and Peace' on the Baltic island of Fehmarn, which has become known as 'The German Altamont', due to excessive Hells Angel activity. Hendrix died in a Kensington hotel on 18 September.)

'What did you eat? Because that was a problem at the Isle of Wight Festival, wasn't it, they ran out of food?'

'Not us. We had effrontery on our side, and Donovan's Land Rover, which we would drive into the food marquee. For some reason, all the caterers were storing their food in one marquee, sort of an annexe to the backstage area. I'd drive in there with Candy or Sandy or whoever else was around, past security guards with their dogs, and help ourselves to whatever we wanted to chuck in the back. We were so blatantly obvious, we were just pushing it deliberately – we weren't just going to one caterer's stash, which everyone else would have been doing, taking what they needed and going out again. We were, "What's this? Oh yeah, let's have some." The day after the festival, we were talking to one of the security guards and his dog. Anyway, he was complaining to me how bad it was on the organisation's part that they hadn't supplied them with any food. They said they'd send food but they hadn't, and he'd been having to buy hot dogs and hamburgers to feed his dog. I went back to our wagon, where we had a whole box of big hams, you know those funny-shaped ones in tins. I went back and got one of these, carved a big chunk out and chucked it to the dog, and the man was almost weeping with gratitude for this thing we'd stolen right under his and his dog's nose.' Bob shakes his head.

'I mean, I play festivals,' I say, 'and I've played some titchy-tiny little nice festivals, one in Scotland last summer called Eden, on the little stage called the Melodrome that Chas set up, with acts on it all day. Backstage there, a loo, a couple of nice hippie done-up caravans, a big Green Room with sofas in, a kitchen which provided three meals a day for artists and crew. There was none of that at the Isle of Wight, and now even at a tiny little festival with a tiny little stage, everyone is sorted backstage.'

'Yeah. Well, we were well sorted. But I was astonished, to be quite honest, they were getting big acts from the States and England, world-class acts, and just these flimsy, shoddy little tourers, might only have been 12 foot, and with no attempt to jolly them up or anything.'

'I reckon that people weren't used to it, and as festivals have got more mature they've started to sort out backstage as well. But you were one of the tiny handful of people on the island who had any food. I interviewed this bloke at Abergavenny Food Festival called Smoky Joe, who was an old black hippie London chef bloke, and he'd bowled up at the Isle of Wight ...'

'I've met him, actually,' says Bob.

'He was doing catering at the Isle of Wight and he suddenly realised that there was nothing left, but that he had a large store of hot-dog buns. Just the buns. So for two days he was doling out hot-dog buns because that was pretty much all there was. And the Isle of Wight Festival, it's legendary, but there are very few photos – you couldn't possibly go to any festival now without there being a million photos posted online. But from IOW 1970, there are very few. So what was the atmosphere like? What sort of mood were the punters in? Because it had all gone tits-up, essentially. Too many people. They had to declare it a Free Festival, even though loads of people had paid.'

'To be quite honest, I didn't really have anything to do with the punters. We were never out in the audience area, all it was was a huge mass of people, all fanned out in front of one stage, like Red Indians surrounded by a circle of hot-dog and burger stalls, almost totally. And then I quite honestly can't even bring any memory of it, but there must have been loads of tents. But it was over there, we didn't have any business over there, there was no point going a quarter of a mile to get a hot dog when we had all the food.'

'Did you have any musical moments?'

'Errrr ...' Bob looks vague.

'You were up to no good, weren't you, none of this music nonsense?'

'To be quite honest, the music all seemed very secondary to what we were doing. I have absolutely no recollection at all of the music.'

'And when you say "what you were doing" – were you looking after the artists, or were you attempting to rob the artists, or what?'

'I mean, presumably Taffy was selling this coke we'd had flown in to people, but we just didn't have anything to do with the punters. We did have a fire there all the time, and there'd be a constant coming and going of artists around the fire. Firewood was a bit of a problem, because there fucking wasn't any – we had to ad-lib. In the backstage area they were keeping for some reason hundreds of folding wooden chairs, all wood with a couple of metal rods going through them, but nicely seasoned wood – well, that was the fire. Anyway, I think it was the last day, I was at the fire, breaking up these wooden chairs and putting them on the fire, when suddenly the gate, which was quite near, was full of these coppers including, and being led by, a really top-brass sort of copper, all the stuff on him. That guy and a sergeant came over to the fire, leaving the dozen or so coppers by the gate. Everyone round the fire's getting a bit nervous. The guy started to admonish me for breaking up the chairs which weren't my property, and I just asked him very politely if he wouldn't mind removing his people from the gate area, because they were upsetting these artists who are about to go on stage and perform before thousands of people. And he did! Fucked off, that was it – and he was the Chief Constable of Hampshire, which includes the Isle of Wight. No one could stop us.'

'Can you remember getting off the island, because again, this is one of the stories about Isle of Wight 1970, that the island started to run out of food, because the ferries weren't up to it. It was the largest festival ever in Britain, at least half a million people. They couldn't get all the people off the island.'

'That wouldn't have been a problem for us. Because we were in no hurry to leave. We had a nice park-up, lots of swagging and tatting to be done. It was quite a lot of days afterwards, because we were waiting to hear "yes, you can go any time you like". See, I was just looning around, I can't recall exactly what I was doing. Mind you, we were all acid-ed up, coked up, stoned ... not a lot of booze, it wasn't really a drinking culture.'

'You've done very well to remember as much as you have ...'

'I was just chatting to people, doing things, doing whatever it was. I did earn a very unexpected hundred dollars. We had got hold of an Elsan, a galvanised iron one, not a plastic one like you get now, no drainage tank or anything, which we'd kept pretty well hidden. Taffy comes in and said, "There are shitters that really need to be emptied," and no one's jumping up and down to do that. So I thought, "Fuck it, I'm not afraid to handle shit." I said I'd do it – dug a little hole and poured it in. Anyway, I get back and Taffy hands me a hundred-dollar bill, which is a lot of money.'

'Where did he get a hundred dollars from? On the Isle of Wight? Sly and the Family Stone?'

'I didn't ask, I just took it.'

'Again, it's amazing that there weren't shitters backstage, now you get showers and shitters no problem, only place to be at a festival, backstage.'

'I hadn't thought about that before, but you're right, the only shitter there was the one we had, and we weren't fucking advertising it.'

'Not even to Joni Mitchell?'

'Well, if she'd asked ... Presumably the stars were going to where there were some ... I don't remember ... it could only have been Elsans.'

'It's people like Andrew Kerr at Glastonbury that started to work out this sort of thing, the shitters, because no one had given it enough thought, had they? If you like, they discovered during the Isle of Wight Festival what it was they didn't know.'

'I was all right, because I'd learned out in Afghanistan about digging a small hole, shitting in it and putting the turf back on ... didn't worry me.'

Despite years of close friendship with Bob, this cheerful ability to shit in a hole in the woods is one in which I'm sadly lacking. On the odd occasion where I have been caught short whilst walking in the woods, Bob's sage words on the efficacy of sphagnum moss as an arse-wipe have stood me in good stead. But it would not be my first choice. It is the thing about the traveller life about which people are most curious, and which most people would find difficult. Years ago, Bob told me that he never used loo paper, but always washed his arse with water. I found this hard to believe. What, for example, if you're in a public loo? Do you hop over to the sink in front of all the other punters? Bob insisted that he did. A recently opened shopping centre in Hereford had an exhibition of photographs of 'Characters of Kington' in its loo. I've had a piss there, under an artfully taken black and white picture of Bob. If he used these lavatories, and had a 'Number Two', and hopped over to the sink to wash his shitty arse, he would certainly qualify as a character. I am not ambitious in this sense. The coffee has got things moving. I make my excuses, and head for home.

All Went Absolutely Sweet as a Nut

It's a beautiful evening in early June, and Bob is cooking fish pie. I love watching him do things, even simple things like cooking fish pie. It's the economy of movement, I reckon, that I like as much as anything. This is such a small space, and to work in it, you need grace, grace of movement, grace in the art of how to live in the moment. As Bob mashes his spuds for the topping, he adds a dash of evaporated milk, and I resolve to try it at home. Bob puts the lovingly assembled pie into the oven of his wood-burning range, and puts four or five logs on the fire, both to make sure it's cooked through and to brown the top.

Bob and I are sitting in the van, looking at my laptop. The evening sun is sinking behind the Whimble, Bob's trees are at their greenest, the flower candles of the horse chestnuts are in full bloom, de boids are singing, and we are emulating the behaviour of Millennials, viz, ignoring all this beauty, letting the moment pass, sitting together on his bed and gawping at technology.

On my laptop, I have a big bunch of photos, all but one from Bob's third trip to Afghanistan. His ex-girlfriend Monica had discovered them curling in a drawer in her house in Kington, and had popped them by a few weeks before. I took a bunch over to the West Coast, and old Perry Venus has digitised them for me. Now Bob and I, waiting for a fish pie, are sitting on his bed while I click through them.

'This is the one of you selling apricots in Quetta.'

The original is tiny, maybe nine centimetres square, so this is the first chance Bob's had to see it properly. There he is, look, in the middle, with scales to weigh the apricots.

'Fuck knows who took this,' says Bob. 'And, fuck, there's Boris!'

Bob points to the slight moustachioed figure to the right, leaning in the archway.

'Boris, the ill bloke you crossed Iran with?'

'That's him. Fuck. Who *took* this?'

I, of course, don't know. This is the only picture from the first two Afghan trips that we've found. The bulk of the pictures are from the third Afghan trip, and as Bob and I look at them, a story begins to emerge.

'I've got you going straight from the Isle of Wight to Afghanistan, but there was a bit of time between, wasn't there, you didn't just drive straight off the island to Afghanistan?'

'No, I already knew Monica, I think I had already teamed up with her, at least in a physical way, but I hadn't got the truck.'

'So you pretty much decided to go before you went to the Isle of Wight? You wanted to go back. I mean, you must have had some idea, because the third trip is so different from the other two. On the third trip you're living there. For a year.'

'Yeah, well, it turned out that Monica's life had taken this change. Monica was designing ranges of children's wear for Ladybird, and she had her own label, Ragdoll. Quite early on when I was seeing her, she got robbed of all her stock, and fabrics and that. And she had claimed insurance for it and I just happened to be there when the insurance company phoned up and started haggling, made her an offer, and I was right next to her so I could hear both ends of the conversation. And I could see she was just about to agree to it, so I said no, put some more on, which she did, and they went for it. So that was that; we had a bit of finance. Because she was already fed up, bored, with the world she was working in, and I told her how in Afghanistan you can buy beautiful fabrics very cheap, very little money at all, lovely fabrics, and people will work for fucking ten pence, twenty pence a day, and everyone out there would think you were overpaying them.

'So we bought this wonderful truck for seventy quid. And then Sandy got a truck, and then he got a caravan, and Pete Mustill went out with him. There was some talk about myself and Taffy in a truck, and Sandy in a truck, going out in convoy to Afghanistan, but that didn't happen, and Taffy left for Kabul before we were ready to get on the road.'

'And had he been before? Taffy?'

'Yeah, though to what degree I don't know. I'd never ask him questions. I think that's probably how we got on so well.'

'We had a few adventures on the trip out. In Iraq, there was like this internal border check, and I actually drove through a wooden pole across the road, with soldiers there. I'd been through customs a few miles back, but I'd been warned about this army customs point, a bit further on. Tom Harney had been through that same crossing some years before and he'd told me, "Cunts, they keep you there half the day for nothing, just amusing themselves basically, seeing what they can get off you." I thought, "Fuck it, I ain't going to stop," and I just smashed the pole, drove straight through it.'

'Yes, everyone wants to do that driving through a barrier thing, like in a car-park or something – but they're army, they've got guns ...'

'I could see they didn't have any motors, but I'd a biggish powerful truck, tough enough to smash through the barrier easily, so I thought by the time they get it together to start shooting I'm going to be more than a hundred yards away, so the chance of actually getting hit would be very small, because you're in a moving truck and they can't see you anyway because of the dust, so it would only be a lucky chance if they hit you, like. And they did fire off a few, but, I was right, they couldn't hit a moving truck, and on we went.

'Then, in Iran, we went along the top of the Caspian, as far as you can and be heading east, heading down to Meshed, and right on the eastern corner of the Caspian before it goes up north, there's a town. And when we went into a local shop, expecting to find the usual not very much of anything, we really lucked in. Not only did they have really superb goat's cheese, they had industrial amounts of fucking caviar, for cheap like you would not believe. Baked beans sort of price. And bottles of wine. All in this one little shop. And not only that, you could see it got suddenly very green, like being in Hampshire – beautiful streams full of trout, mossy banks. We learned later it was the Shah's private hunting ground, no one was allowed to live there or anything. There was a road through it, you could drive through it but that was it. But it was the only green, lovely place I saw in the whole country.

'It was always fucking great to cross into Afghanistan and get to Herat. We stopped in the café in the middle of the town to have something to eat, and because we had a three and a half ton lorry, and we knew it would be a possibility, I said to the boy, "Serve our meal out in the lorry," so we could just sit out there and have a smoke and be more relaxed than being in the cheap caff. So we were out there having our meal, when I heard a sound which surprised me – it sounded like a couple of Vespa scooters. I knew it wasn't the TukTuks, they don't make the same sound, the Vespas are much higher revs. So they pull up right beside me, but with the side of the truck between us so they don't know we're there; I peep out, and sure enough, it's a couple of South London skittles. Like mod-type boys. They just came out from South London on their Vespa GSs and they've got to this point in their lives. I so wished I'd recorded it. They were both very lucid and it had opened their eyes to who they were, where they were, and their relationship with each other. They were saying, "I know we've known each other all our lives, we went to school together, were best mates together and all that, but on this trip I've real-ised that although we like some of the same things, mostly you don't like what I like, and I don't like what you like," and went on to really laying it out on the line, all this. So they worked out they really had nothing in common ... and I kept schtum. Real South London boys.'

'So it was liberating, then, in a sense?'

'Yeah, they had grown up and they had realised, because they had seen all this other world outside South Wimbledon or wherever they came from, it made them realise who they were, and they weren't having to cling to the tribal thing of "we're friends because we live on the same street and went to the same school" sort of thing. They had suddenly realised it was time to shed all that and take it on a more existential level and move on.'

'And it shows that the Hippie Trail was in full swing,'

'It was. We arrived in Kabul with about two hundred quid and it went pretty good from there. Except Duncan Lawrie wasn't sending out the money from the clothes he was selling, which was a bit naughty of him. But then we met up with brother Sandy and Pete Mustill and Taffy.

'And Kabul was OK for a few weeks, but yeah, loads more travellers than before. But I'm a country boy, so I wanted to find a place outside town. The village Monica and Pete and I lived in was this place called Paghman, which is twenty miles outside Kabul. It was posh, in Afghan terms. The Queen of Afghanistan had a summer place there. I had this history of the Afghan wars with me. I'd gone off on a jaunt to Pakistan or somewhere, away for a couple of days, and when I get back, Pete's read this book. And he's looking a bit green about the gills. "I read your book, man. A whole regiment of the British Army got massacred right here, just outside our gates." "Yeah, Pete, that's why they like us here." He couldn't see it. That's why they prefer the English to all the other foreigners, because the English are the source of a lot of wealth for them, and a lot of tales of derring-do. "I remember when Grandad Mustapha went in, killed an Englishman and cut his dick off, my mum's still got it …" and all that – and as you're not posing any sort of threat at all, or calling them names, we're just guys in the bazaar, and we smoke together. Just be aware that you are completely at these people's mercy.

'I was in bed in this house in Paghman. They hadn't any putty there, the windows in this house were all just held in with a few tacks, two or three on each side. I heard this scratching noise which went on for a few minutes, realised someone was trying to take the fucking window out. I picked up the shotgun which was there, walked to the door, didn't have to open it as it was ajar anyway, and sure enough these two geezers with turbans on were trying to take the pane of glass out, because I'd got a little Honda generator and they were trying to get in and nick it. I thought, "I don't want any actual confrontation here" – but there again, I wanted them fucked off out of there. So I blew out the window beside them with the 12-bore. And I don't know if you've ever fired a shotgun inside a house …'

'Oddly, I never have …'.

'Well, it makes a noise like you wouldn't believe. So the window beside them just explodes, boom, and the whole room is lit up with the flash of the 12-bore. I really didn't want to hurt them, but I also wanted them to be very very sure that they wouldn't be doing that again. Of course they both ran like fuck; and that was the last I heard about it, there were no repercussions – if anything, our treatment was even better down in the village, because they'd be local boys and the story would have got about and they'd have had a laugh about it, because no one's been hurt, and I'm not going down the local police, so the only thing that's lost is my window which I've got to replace, so they probably had another laugh when they saw me carrying a pane of glass up the hill. In the morning, I found their sandals, because as I learned, when Afghans are scared and need to run, it's easier to leave your sandals behind and run barefoot. The next day, I took the sandals down the village and left them in the square, which everyone thought was dead funny, because they knew what had happened. So they thought we were all right.'

I click through the photos from Afghanistan.
'Who is this?' I ask Bob.

'The geezer was a New Zealander or a South African. Can't remember his name, but I didn't like him much. The girl is Sandy's girlfriend, Jayne Hodge, or Jayne Harries as she was before she got married. A poor little rich girl, a millionaire's daughter. Her dad owned Radio Rentals, the TV hire place. Sandy had got hold of this great little four-wheeler truck, ideal for two blokes, for him and Pete; you just stick a couple of mattresses in the back, and that's where you sleep on the journey. But Sandy had shacked up with this girl, and she insisted on coming with him. And she had loads and loads and loads of clothes. Like, she had twenty pairs of Chelsea Cobbler boots, a ridiculous amount of King's Road clothes, which are not what you need knocking about in the Hindu Kush. So Sandy had to get a caravan for all her stuff, and tow it behind this truck, which was not ideal, because it was fucked by the time he got to Kabul. She was married to the hairdresser, Gavin Hodge, before she buggered off to Afghanistan with Sandy. Ever heard of him?'

'I never have.' And I never had. So I Googled Gavin Hodge.

This is from his obituary in the Independent, 30/10/2009; he had died on the 22nd, aged sixty-five, from a brain haemorrhage.

[Hodge] ... made the front pages in 1968 when he eloped with a good-looking and rich debutante, Jayne Harries, in an incident which generated some shock even in swinging London: he was 23, she was 16. Harries often had her hair done by Hodge. He described her as 'the most stunning girl I had ever met'. As so often with him, one thing led to another and, to her family's horror, she became immersed in a world of sex, drink and drugs. Jayne, a talented showjumper, had a trial for the junior Olympic team, an event which, Hodge related to his journalist daughter Gavanndra, was a disaster.

'Someone brought out a hash cake,' according to Hodge. 'We all tried a bit, but Jayne, who had to do everything to excess, ate half the thing. The next day she fell off her horse at the first jump. She just lay on the grass giggling.'

With her parents trying desperately to extricate her from her relationship with Hodge, the pair eloped to Portugal. One version has it that she climbed out of her bedroom window at 2 a.m. clutching a mink coat; Hodge claimed with characteristic implausibility that she 'clambered out of an upstairs window with three mink coats and six huge Louis Vuitton trunks'.

They were married, apparently at her insistence, in Gibraltar, with the world's media following what was viewed as a sensational story. The pair careered around Europe and London, Hodge recalling that at one point they 'holed up' with the Rolling Stones guitarist Brian Jones in Tangiers.

Back in England they lived the high life. He said: 'There was a drawer full of money. One day she filled a shoebox with notes, went down the road and bought an Aston Martin; we crashed it that afternoon. The next day we went and bought a Jensen Interceptor.'

He said she became addicted to heroin when she travelled to Afghanistan with another man. According to Hodge she turned up one evening 'completely off her head'. He remembered: 'I walked out. It was selfish but I didn't know what to do with her. She was in a bad way. The girl I knew was gone – instead there was this rather bloated, confused person.'

Four days later she was dead, having taken an overdose of heroin in a public lavatory in Guildford. He was not present at her funeral service: 'I tried to contact her family because I wanted to go to the funeral,' he said, 'but I got no response.'

The 'other man', of course, was brother Sandy, a professional, practised junkie.

Bob says, 'The most decadent thing I ever saw was one time round at her and Sandy's place in Kabul, and her dressed like a slave girl, like a *houri*, sitting on silks and cushions, with lots of her flesh showing, with all these merchants kneeling in front of her, displaying their wares. And I thought, "Nah, I don't want any part of this." She went back after a few months, and the plane couldn't take all her stuff. She'd bought mountains of shit: silks, carpets, clothes. The poor fucking thing couldn't flap its wings, so she had to leave loads of stuff behind. One of the things she left was an aluminium flight case with these state-of-the-art cameras; and she said, "Bob, will you take this, and bring 'em back to London." I told her I'd take care of 'em. Which I did.'

'And so that's how come you had a camera?'

'Yep.'

We click through more of the photos Bob took in Afghanistan.

'This is Monica?'

'By the truck, yeah. We must have been out there for a few months by then, because you can see I've had it decorated up, Afghan style.'

'You weren't living in it at the time?'

'No, we were living in Paghman.'

'So this is Monica outside the house?'

'Yeah, with our dogs. Royal dogs, them. It's a Tazi dog. You can have one, on the understanding that it still belongs to the King.'

'Who is the other woman in this photo?'

'She was a Yank, called Carole. She was all right. She was living in one of the other empty houses in Paghman with her bloke. There were hundreds of Freaks up there. Well, half a dozen.'

'How come?

'All these houses had been built by Russians fleeing the Revolution, and they'd lived in 'em up to the fifties/early sixties, before they all buggered off somewhere else. And the locals wouldn't live in them, because they'd been built by unbeliever dogs. But they were quite happy for other unbelievers to live in them, because they bought a bit of money to the area. That's why the hippie invasion of Afghanistan was the only invasion that has ever worked. Because we went there to trade, and show 'em a bit of respect by living like them.'

'And it was a good life?'

'Yeah. I got to ride around on horses and motorbikes with a gun over my back. It was the Wild West. Best place in the world. I still think that.

'So I started just taking the camera out with me. You've got to be careful, like. People don't always like having a camera shoved in their face. It's stealing their souls, or something.'

'Or Islamic ambivalence about making images?'

'Yeah, probably.'

' These girls look a bit unsure.'

'Yeah. I didn't want to scare them. These were our gardener's kids. It was OK because they knew us a bit.'

'Where's this?'

'In a Kabul woodyard. It was next to the truck-yard where they were decorating my vehicle. Look at that poor bastard carrying that fucking thing. And Freaky Pete Mustill watching him.'

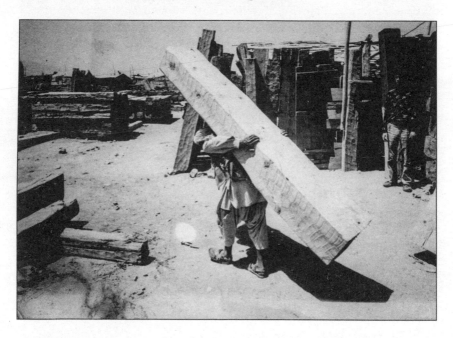

'That's Pete? Fuck me, he's changed.'

'Haven't we all.'

Pete travelled out to Afghanistan with Sandy and Jayne Hodge, about a fortnight behind Bob and Monica. He told me that Bob's estimate that Jane had twenty pairs of boots was way under; that in fact she had seventy-two pairs of boots and several mink coats in the little caravan that they dragged out behind them.

In Istanbul, Sandy, Jane and Pete encountered Wavy Gravy and the Hog Farm, travelling in a bus, like that of Ken Kesey and the Merry Pranksters, heading towards India.

'They had a hermit with them,' Pete told me. 'He lived in the luggage compartment.'

Wavy Gravy was a peace activist and performer (and still is – at the time of writing, he has just celebrated his eightieth birthday), who at one time was the official clown to the Grateful Dead. The Hog Farm (which also still exists) is regarded as America's oldest extant hippie commune. Wavy Gravy and the Hog Farm were recruited by the organisers of Woodstock; firstly to build fire-pits and a free kitchen, but eventually to run the security at the festival, which Wavy Gravy described as the 'Please Force' (their motto was, 'Please don't do that, please do this instead'). In 1970, Wavy Gravy and the Hog Farm arrived in Britain, and made a living setting up and decorating stages, and then used the money they made to finance their bus trip to India. Their progress matched that of Pete and Sandy and Jane, and they often parked up together on their way across Turkey, Iraq and Iran, and then hung out together in Kabul.

On arrival in Kabul, Pete palled up with the French ambassador's son, who had several electric guitars, an amp, and a rudimentary drum-kit. They formed a band, called the Blue Sharks. Pete felt there was a gap in the market in Kabul for 'western music', and so they found themselves a residency in Kabul's top restaurant, who clearly felt that a western rock band would add some cachet; though, as Pete told me, 'they probably weren't expecting a couple of herberts playing Hendrix covers at full volume'. Wavy Gravy and the Hog Farm didn't stay too long in Afghanistan, but moved on, intending to drive through the Khyber Pass and down into Pakistan. And Monica and Bob, together with Pete's band, drove with them as far as Jalalabad. And there, incredibly, Pete set up the 'Jalalabad Rock Festival'. There were only two acts: the Blue Sharks and some musicians from the Hog Farm. They played in an open-sided structure, much like a veranda, and Pete can only remember a couple of dozen bemused locals watching in puzzlement. But to set up such a thing, in a country where music was regarded with ambivalence, at best, takes a huge amount of chutzpah. Pete is still setting up festivals, and spaces at festivals (on the day he told me about the Jalalabad Rock Festival, he was getting ready to run a backstage area at Green Man Festival); but he started in Jalalabad.

Pete's exit from Afghanistan is worth mentioning. American Carole, pictured with Monica above, had a VW van. Her baby got sick; Pete thinks it had malnutrition. So she wanted to get back to the West as quickly as she could; specifically, to a clinic in Switzerland. And Pete, after a year in the mysterious East, was wanting to get back home. So he drove that VW van, with Carole and her sick baby in the back, from Kabul to Trieste in northern Italy, in ten days. In Trieste, the VW gave up, and Carole and her baby caught a train up into Switzerland, while Pete slept for a few nights on a park bench, waiting for his folks to spot him a train fare home.

'So was Taffy out there at the same time too?' I ask Bob.

'He set off before us, but arrived about six weeks after us. Up to all sorts of mischief. Political mischief, I think, some of it. When the sixties moved into the seventies, it suddenly got a lot tighter – the Americans particularly were basically buying up the country through the head of state.

'When Taffy arrived he was with this very lovely New York model girl, whom he had met in London. She was enthralled by the whole lifestyle and went along on the trip to Afghanistan. Taffy still had Donovan's show-man's wagon behind the Greville Wynne bus. Anyway, the girl decides she's had enough of Afghanistan and the increasing down-to-earthness of things, no toilet, that sort of thing – an American girl, you can imagine. She stuck it out for quite a few months, but somehow she met up with this American geezer who may or may not have been CIA, because there were starting to be a lot of them about. This guy, Taffy had a shotgun under his fucking chin, and Taffy gave him a bit of a knocking about and told him to fuck off, but he slipped back in the shadows, picked up this Paula and took her to the American embassy – a place of sanctuary, so she could get her ticket to go home. Taffy turns up at the American embassy, demands to see his missis, sort of thing. The vice-consul declined his request, and Taffy decks the vice-consul. He's promptly grabbed by the marines or whoever, and they lock him up. And the consul gets on to his Afghan oppo, says, "I've just slammed up this English guy – do me a favour and come and take him away." And then they ascertained who this guy was, a guy who was doing deals with several members of the government and was generally liked, when at that time the Yanks weren't. The *Kabul Times* had published a complete list of the CIA agents in Kabul, the entire front page, with their names and addresses, so the Yanks weren't in good odour and Taffy was, because he was doing deals with the Prime Minister. The land he was camped up on was the Prime Minister's fucking land. And the Afghans said, "Well, no – him smacking you in the gob happened on American soil, your embassy is American soil, he hasn't committed any crime in Afghanistan, we like him, we're happy with him." This put the Yanks in a bit of a spot. They didn't want to keep this extremely unruly Englishman in the cells, and so they upped a two-million-dollar aid deal, they upped it to six mill, if you take this guy off our hands.'

'So is that how he ended up inside? Is that what he was in prison in Afghanistan for?'

'Yeah. And he was put in the old fire station. It wasn't what you think of as a fire station, it was a compound, walled all the way round, accom-modation and sheds on the insides of the walls, but most of the thing was an open area in the middle. And the only security was a guy with a gun at the gate, which was generally just open. So it was pretty casual, you rocked up to see him any time you liked, carrying whatever, generally only food and that sort of thing, they'd have a look in your bag, but very laid back, to say the least.'

'No pictures of Taffy, I suppose?'

'No, man,' says Bob. 'Taffy wouldn't allow photos.'

(As this is Taffy's last appearance in this story, I should say that he went from Afghanistan to the South of France, via Amsterdam, in the Greville Wynne bus, towing the Donovan showman's wagon, to supply the Rolling Stones with dope for the recording of *Exile on Main Street*. After that, he was based full-time in Amsterdam. Although Bob and Pete stayed in touch with him there, both are uncertain what happened to him. I know that he died in Amsterdam sometime in the mid-1980s; according to one source, he drowned in a canal.)

'So what were you and Monica doing?'

'Making dresses for Forbidden Fruit. Monica was designing them out there, and then we were getting them made, and shipping them back to London.'

Also with the photos, Monica has found one of the sketchbooks she was using in Afghanistan.

'When Monica and I got back a year or so later, we went to the gig of the moment at the Roundhouse. The Roundhouse has got seats in it by this time – when we first started going there, it was basically just a railway turntable shed, with nothing at all, dirt swept out. But it had gone all middle-class with seats. I don't remember what the gig was, but I do remember the front row, and virtually everyone on the front row was wearing our clothes, because we were doing shirts as well.

'After a bit I had to fly back to London to straighten out the geezers we were sending the clothes to: they hadn't been very good about sending the money out for the clothes, and they sent me back with pictures of pages of *Vogue* magazine showing our clothes, but without any dosh. We were having to middleman dope just to pay the tailors and pay for the cloth we were buying. And that was quite exciting too, because we needed so much of this cloth, and it was made in Russia, it was Russian fabric, really nice, very much like Liberty prints, sort of schoolgirl-knicker colours – dark green, brown and maroon sort of colours – but with delicate little floral prints on them. And cheap, if you were buying them with black market change money, you got a 5 to 1 advantage on that, which ain't bad ...'

'And would that be dollars or pounds, or didn't they mind?'

'Don't matter, so long as it ain't roubles or Afghanis. We'd have to go out of Kabul when there was a big load coming in, because the cloth merchant we were dealing with was worried about it, because it was being smuggled over the border on camel trains. And we had to meet this bunch of nomad types with camels, quite a long way out of Kabul, many tens of miles out of Kabul, in this one place, and we just had to look out for a little sign, a little paraffin lamp on a stick by the road. After half an hour's drive, there it was – we wondered if this was a bit iffy. Everyone was a bit worried about getting this much cloth in without it being tumbled by somebody who'd want a big cut of it. So me, Monica and the cloth merchant bundled out there in a taxi to meet the cameleers, and do the deal. I felt a bit nervous; I'd got a big wodge of dosh by local standards, certainly, and we were stopped in the middle of nowhere, basically, doing a deal with people who are criminals. And people who are taking their lives in their hands smuggling stuff out of Russia.'

'And who have guns, presumably.'

'Oh, yeah. There was a quick burst of gunfire, but that was it; money changed hands, cloth changed hands, all went absolutely sweet as a nut.'

'I saw a thing on eBay recently which was a Forbidden Fruit dress. They're quite rare, you know, quite collectable.'

'Yeah, I've heard from quite a few people that our dresses are on the internet.'

We click on through the photos.

'One time, I was riding back up into Paghman, and I'm riding parallel to the road. And on the road there's this 4x4, labouring up the road, because it's nothing but stones and potholes, and it's chauffeur driven, and in the back seat there's this posh lady. And I think, "Fuck me, it's the Queen." Because her summer residence was in Paghman, not far from our place. Without thinking, I spurred the horse into a gallop to try to beat her. And she sees me, and starts berating her driver, urging him on. And really, this road is so bad it's three miles an hour, sort of thing. So you can hear the thing crashing, and chucking up clouds of dust, and I urge the horse on, and she's still berating her driver, almost beating him.'

'Who won?'

'We came to the turning before her house, and it crossed in front of our track, so I thought I'd better let her go in front of me. But it was close.'

'This is the road to Paghman, I guess?'

'Yeah. Close to us. He looks like a Tajik guy to me. But I don't know who he is.'

'So what's this?'

'This is our garden. Those are some more of the gardener's kids.'

'It looks like the trees have been banked up,' I say.

'No. That's an irrigation channel. There's probably still a bit of mois-ture in there, that's what the donkeys are after. We shared a water source with our neighbour, and once a day, the water was supposed to be

directed into our garden and round all the channels. But our gardener was always arguing with him about it, saying that he didn't let us have the water for long enough, or not enough of it. This is the neighbour, with the tools he used for diverting the water.'

'Mustill tells a story about you buying a gun in a little village with him. Do you remember that story? You turned up in this village that sells guns. Everyone there has guns, except you. And you have money for guns. In short, you have money, they have guns, and all is not well. You ask to try a gun, and put a couple of rounds into the breech. And to test it you shoot this pigeon up on a roof, at which point the locals applauded. And all was well.'

Bob laughs. 'Yeah, a place called Haddah, which is a little village heading towards no man's land, where the main industry is making handguns. But I have a big regret about guns out there.'

'What's that?'

'Well, me and Monica were heading off somewhere for a few weeks, can't remember for sure where. We went up north to look at Kunduz at one stage. Another time we went down to Goa. I don't know. But I asked the gardener to look after the house while we were gone. And I bought him a gun, to guard the house.'

'This is him with the gun, and his family, presumably?'

'Yeah, and Monica in one of our dresses.'

'To give us a send-off, and to say thank you for the gun, he killed a sheep and cooked us a feast in our garden. I watched him kill that sheep, and it was amazing. He got the sheep lying down, and then he lay down with it, stroking it, and kind of singing to it. He hypnotised it. And when it was completely relaxed, he cut its throat.'

'That was a really nice day. It really was. They were pleased about the gun, but they also just liked us. It was a real honour for us that they slaughtered a sheep.'

Bob shifts on his bed, and reaches for his tobacco tin.

'And then the next day Monica and I headed off for a few weeks for this trip in the truck.

'And as soon as we'd gone, our gardener took this gun that I'd got for him, and went round the neighbour's, and fucking killed him. Shot him dead.'

'Fucking hell, Bob. This guy? The water guy?'

'Yeah. And they arrested our gardener for it, and they hanged him. So, thanks to me, two guys lost their lives. And the family lost their father.'

And for the first time in all the years I've known him, Bob is crying.

The Hippie Trail might have been a trip, a Magic Bus ride. And the hippie invaders might have come to trade, and not to kill. But, you know what? It was still colonialism. The softest of soft colonialism, maybe, but colonialism nonetheless. Even Bob, with his profound love of and respect for the Afghan people, couldn't walk softly enough.

In particular, the hippies' views of the East smack of a particular strain of cultural colonialism called 'Orientalism', after the 1978 book of the same title by Edward Said.

According to Said, Orientalism is the approach taken by the West (and Western scholars in particular) towards the Mysterious Orient. In the Orientalist worldview, the West is active and structuring while the Orient is passive and disorganised. The West writes, and the Orient is written about; the West investigates, because the Orient needs investigation; the West has knowledge and produces knowledge, and the Orient is raw data waiting to be shaped into knowledge. The Oriental lacks knowledge of himself, and needs it, and can only obtain it from the structuring Western mind.

The American scholar Trent Cunningham has identified a variant of Orientalism which he calls, 'psychedelic orientalism'.

Bob was born when India was still part of the British empire, and was five at Indian independence in 1947. As well as Kipling, his boyhood reading was H. Rider Haggard and Boy's Own magazine with their tales of derring-do starring plucky British soldiers and agents pitting their wits against the 'wily Pathan'. Bob was, and is, motivated more by adventure than by mysticism. The Orient was a field for adventure; mysterious adventure with a bit of woo-woo thrown in sometimes, but mostly adventure. This would have been the prevailing view of the 'Orient' in Bob's youth, and it still has traction; see Indiana Jones and the Temple of Doom', which is Steven Spielberg's take on how the East was viewed in popular culture. Viewed, that is, until four lovable mop-haired lads from Liverpool who had shaken the world went to India and shook it up again. The musicologist Jonathan Bellman wrote: 'The main publicists for Indian culture (however imperfectly understood) were the Beatles.'

The Beatles first encountered India at Twickenham Film Studios during the making of their second film, Help!, in early 1965. It has belly dancers, a fakir lying on a bed of nails, the young Eleanor Bron as a dusky priestess in blackface, and hypnotic Indian music. So far, so Orientalist.

The set of the film was the first place that George Harrison became intrigued by the sitar, when he had seen one lying about. Later, during the filming of the bicycle scene in the Bahamas, a devotee of Krishna approached the Fabs, and gave them some Hindu devotional literature, which sparked George's life-long interest. George started to practise yoga, and to experiment with the sitar, which he first used on the track 'Norwegian Wood' on the Fabs' 1965 album, *Rubber Soul*. This is regarded as their spliff album, as they were stoned for the whole process of making the album, and as they also were for the filming of *Help!*

In July 1965, Harrison and Lennon took acid for the first time, which was slipped into their coffee by a society dentist. Which is another reason not to trust dentists. They found the experience terrifying, but they wanted to try it again. Six weeks later, Lennon had read Tim Leary's *Psychedelic Experience*, published the year before, whilst Harrison had tapes of Indian classical music. The two Beatles dropped their acid together and relaxed on lilos in Harrison's pool, with the music playing over loudspeakers. According to Bob Spitz's 2005 biography of the Beatles, 'John dropped acid according to Leary's instructions. "I did it just like he said in the book", he recalled.'

The Psychedelic Experience is a rewrite of the first English translation of *The Tibetan Book of the Dead* by Walter Evans-Wentz, published in 1927. Evans-Wentz was a life-long Theosophist, and he used Theosophical thinking to interpret the text. Madame Blavatsky's view of the world was therefore transmitted, through Leary's interpretation of how the Psychedelic Experience mapped onto her view of Tibetan Buddhism, pop!, into the acid-altered head of John Lennon. The gods in the Himalayas are now fully awake and starting to enjoy themselves.

What came out of that acid trip was 'Tomorrow Never Knows', the final track on their 1966 album, *Revolver*, although it was the first track the band recorded for the album. No one was/is better than this. All four of the Fabs were involved. Harrison brought the droning sitar-like tambura, and the brilliant guitar break; McCartney, the one who had jammed with Cornelius Cardew and was fascinated by experimental music brought the tape loops; Ringo brought the title – and those drums, that extraordinary repeating drum pattern. Lennon wrote the lyrics and the mantra-like melody. He wanted producer George Martin to make him sound like 'the Dalai Lama singing on a mountain top'.

'Tomorrow Never Knows' is one of a handful of game-changing pop songs, after which nothing would ever be the same. The fact that it was made by the world's biggest pop band (indeed, you might argue, at that time the world's biggest entertainment brand,) makes it all the more remarkable. Trent Cunningham has published a paper which demonstrates the similarities between the lyrics of 'Tomorrow Never Knows' and the 'First Bardo' from Leary's interpretation of *The Tibetan Book of the Dead*.

The song is an attempt to recreate an LSD trip, one which uses the language and music of the East to try to get close to the acid experience. Over the next couple of years, the Beatles were to continue to experiment with Indian music and culture in order to communicate the 'insights' which they felt came with dropping acid. After the recording of *Revolver*, George spent six weeks in the autumn of 1966 in India, with the great classical sitar player Ravi Shankar, learning the rudiments of the instrument, and, as a necessary part of the process (according to Shankar), immersing himself in Indian mysticism. George brought this sensibility to the recording of 1967's *Sgt Pepper's Lonely Hearts Club Band*, where the Indian influences (and the drug references) have become even more explicit.

Sgt Pepper was released on 1 June 1967, to all but universal acclaim. It launched the 'Second Wave of Beatlemania'; not to the sound of screaming this time, but rather to a hushed reverence. They had become as gods in the eyes of the fans. Tim Leary said of them that they were 'evolutionary agents sent by God endowed with mysterious powers to create a new human species'. Which is quite a big ask.

Lennon's way through was acid. He arranged to buy a lifetime's supply of Owsley acid, smuggled into Britain in film canisters, which arrived in time for the worldwide live broadcast of 'All You Need is Love' on 25 June. Owsley acid, the acid that Bob had been given by a chap who wandered in off the Portobello Road, and some of which he had sold to Ronnie Laing, was always going to be further out than anything Lennon had tried before. In the weeks following the release of *Pepper's*, he was tripped out 24/7.

Harrison was still Lennon's main tripping partner, but he was beginning to feel that he could 'get' whatever Lennon was getting through yoga and meditation. A 'spiritual goal' was what he was looking for; as Trent Cunningham argues, it was a spiritual goal which was framed in terms of the psychedelic experience it was supposed to supplant. George's wife, the model Patti Boyd shared his interest in Eastern mysticism. (Patti was the subject of two of the great love songs of her day, George's 'Something' and 'Layla', by Jo Bramley's ex-boyfriend, Eric Clapton). On 24 August 1967, she persuaded George, John and Paul to go with her to a lecture at the Hilton Hotel, overlooking Hyde Park, by the man who is still the best known of the Indian gurus who have appeared in the West since Vivekananda in the 1890s.

Say 'namaste' to the Maharishi.

No one is 100 per cent sure of his real name, or where he was from, or when he was born (though 1917 seems the best guess). In 1942 Mahesh Yogi (Maharishi is an honorific title) became the 'beloved pupil' of an Indian teacher known as 'Guru Dev'. If you, or your dad, or let's face it. (since this book is dedicated to my granddaughters), your grandad, are Beatles nuts, you might be familiar with 'Across the Universe', with its mantra-like refrain 'Jai Guru Deva, om', which means 'All Praise to Guru Dev', and was, according to Lennon, something of a refrain for the Maharishi.

According to his own account, from 1945 until 1955 the Maharishi meditated alone in the Himalayas, before launching himself on the West. He toured the world extensively from 1958 onwards, and his giggling face, framed by the longest hair anyone's mum had ever complained about, and with a white beard down to his navel, became a familiar sight on billboards and TV shows in the US and Britain. He was, therefore, a well-known figure when Patti Boyd persuaded the Beatles to go and hear him talk. And they were impressed; so impressed that they signed up for a weekend away with the Maharishi, at University College, Bangor, starting the next day, Friday, 25 August.

They went by train (which Lennon's wife Cynthia just missed, stranding her at Euston). Ringo came along too (and so did Mick Jagger, Marianne Faithfull and Donovan), and they spent a day learning to meditate. On Saturday, each of the participants was given a mantra by the Maharishi, which was supposed to be unique to them, though it later transpired they had all been given the same one, which was 'I-ing'. They enjoyed being on the university campus; they were not used, after all, to austerity. The other 200 or so participants on the course treated them just as fellow students, and by Sunday afternoon they were relaxed and intrigued by what the Maharishi had to tell them. At 3 p.m., on Sunday 27 August, the communal pay-phone in the hall of the dormitory block rang. It was a message for Paul, to share with the others. The Beatles' manager, Brian Epstein, had been found dead at his flat in London.

According to Bob Spitz, the Beatles 'traipsed off' to see the Maharishi to tell him the news. Ringo reported that the Maharishi told them, 'You have to grieve for him and love him, and now you send him on his way.' Lennon faced the press later that day, and reported what the Maharishi had said: 'Well, Brian is just passing into the next phase. His spirit is still around and always will be. It's a physical memory we have of him, and as men we will build on that memory.'

This is an extraordinary statement. Previously, entertainers faced with a similar situation would have invoked Christian beliefs, if they made any kind of religious statement at all. This is the first time 'New Age' beliefs were openly voiced by major international figures. It's hard to compute now; it sounds anodyne, just the sort of thing Gwyneth Paltrow would say if her dog died. In the summer of 1967, the Beatles were 'evolutionary agents,' and what they said had the force of gospel. It was a moment when the world took a step down the road to internet dating sites where people can write of themselves, 'I'm spiritual, but not religious.'

In February 1968, the Beatles went to Rishikesh, in the Indian state of Uttar Pradesh, to stay at the Maharishi's ashram. The visit was not a huge success, in terms of what they had hoped to achieve, which was to study the Maharishi's system of 'transcendental meditation' for three months. Ringo and his wife saw it as a holiday, and left after a fortnight. Paul and his girlfriend Jane Asher left a fortnight later, and John and George a few weeks after that. They had not achieved Enlightenment; in fact, what they mostly did was write what became *The White Album*, including Lennon's song 'Sexy Sadie', which rejected the Maharishi and his teachings. But they were the Beatles, and they were gods. The Hippie Trail, which had been pioneered by Bob and his friends became a Hippie Stampede. Tens of thousands of long-haired Freaks (and a couple of mods on Vespas) made the overland trek; bus companies sprang up to facilitate the trip.

They were in search of … what? A bit of Beatle magic? Some of that adventure that people like Bob had sought and found? Or 'themselves'? Usually, it was the latter. In India, the Freaks felt, they would be able to 'find themselves'. Which always implies that there is a self to be found other than that with which the individual is familiar. So there is an 'other' self, a more authentic self, located for ever over the Eastern horizon, in the land of Shangri-La. Orientalism had turned inwards; and young westerners' view of the East became something that could be 'found within'. Would Jayne Hodge have wanted to go East if the Beatles hadn't gone, if Indian attitudes and Afghan dresses had not become the height of fashion? Bob was equipped to make the trip, but lots of people weren't.

The British travel writer Bruce Chatwin was one of the first young white Westerners to travel overland to Afghanistan in 1962. In his essay 'A Lament for Afghanistan' he tried to blame the hippies for bringing in ideas which made young Afghan intellectuals susceptible to Marxism, and thus paved the way for the Soviet invasion of 1978, which closed the overland route. This seems a little harsh. However it came about,

Afghanistan is now a place of fear, a place where 'heroes' lose their lives and limbs in the name of … again, what? And the traffic is the other way, on foot, in the trucks of smugglers, in inflatable dinghies, across a hostile Europe to hope to find safety in a largely mythical 'West', driven by a catastrophic Occidentalist view of what safety and freedom might be.

Bob declares the fish pie ready, and he shares it out onto two tin plates. We both sit on Afghan rugs to eat our meals.

'There's no going back, is there?' I say.

Bob looks sad. He wishes there was. But there isn't.

I Loved it from the Word Go

Bob is sorting out his garden; spring is turning into summer, and there's lots to do in the woodland garden. I'm sitting in the van, still looking at the photos.

Bob has a friend over to help him with the gardening. Her name is Briar, and she lives in a yurt which is currently in Clyro, over towards Hay. She is in her late forties, I guess, as pretty as a berry. While Bob cuts corrugated iron sheets into strips to make a roof for a small garden structure, Briar comes into the van and makes some Rooibos tea for her and some tea tea for me, and then we share a smoke.

We talk about life, as hippies do on a spring afternoon..

The thing that puzzles Briar and me today is Why Do People Work To Keep the System Going? Briar earns a bit of money from gardening, enough to live on so she doesn't need to claim benefit. She's working today; Bob pays her for her services. Powys CC don't like her living in her yurt, even though you can't see it until you get up close, so they'd like to move her on. Briar doesn't make enough money from gardening to afford a flat. So, if Powys CC succeed in stopping her living in the yurt, she'll have to turn to the council for help, and will need to be in receipt of housing benefit in return for living in a place where she doesn't want to live. Our Masters might say, 'Well, we'll help you earn more money, so you *can* afford a flat. What's more, if you get a shitty forty-hour-a-week job on minimum wage, we'll subsidise your landlord *and* your employer, and make sure you've got enough to hover just above the poverty line.'

But here's the thing: Briar doesn't *want* to earn more money. She doesn't want your flat, or your benefits. She has a nice life, and only wants to continue living in her yurt, which she can afford to do, and enjoys. A yurt is what ... twelve feet across and six high? Hardly an eyesore.

When Briar goes, so will her yurt. She will have walked lightly on the earth, which she will have every right to feel proud about. There are lots and lots of people in the UK with more money than Bob and Briar and me. Lots more money. And stuff. Lord, the stuff .... Cars, phones, conservatories, extensions, an island kitchen, designer clothes ... stuff.

Fair dues; it's their money that they've worked hard for, on the whole, and their right to spend that money on stuff.

But we are not all that interested in stuff, and we are sitting in a wood, free to come and go, drinking tea, and smoking and talking about things which seem to matter, at least to us. And we can't for the life of us work out why people would rather have stuff than freedom.

Starting in the late 1960s, and for the next twenty or so years, tens of thousands of people uninterested in stuff and influenced by counter-cultural ideas migrated to the countryside. They (we) came to the deep countryside; into the Highlands of Scotland, into Cornwall, into Somerset, into Cumbria, and into the south-west of Ireland. But mostly, they (we) came to Wales; to West Wales, Pembrokeshire and Mid-Wales.

London was becoming harder to take. I've heard from a few ex-travellers the apocryphal tale of how, unable to take the smoke any more, they got in a van and headed west, until the van broke down, and then just stayed. It's a story I've heard in Lampeter, in Llanidloes and in Presteigne. (NB Younger Readers might need to spark up their map apps. So might anyone else not familiar with Mid-Wales.)

Large parts of Mid-Wales are taken up with the Great Green Desert. It is the most lightly populated part of the UK apart from the Scottish Highlands, only a four-hour drive from London. In the late sixties, there was nothing going on in vast tracts of what had once been hill-farming country. The farms couldn't support extended families, and people moved away. There weren't many houses, but of those that there were, many stood empty. The small market towns were increasingly isolated by the Beeching cuts to the railways and economically endangered by the falling price of meat and wool, and by imports of lamb from New Zealand and timber from Scandinavia. Populations all across rural Wales were falling. In ecological terms, a niche had been created for a new population. Rural Wales offered cheap housing, to rent or to buy, often with land attached. It was lightly policed, and with all the magic mushrooms you could eat. In its heyday, in the seventies and eighties, it was the Wild fucking West, it really was.

Younger Readers will notice that this is another way in which it has become much harder for them to get housed. The squats have gone, because squatting has been made illegal. Cheap housing in rural areas has gone, not so much because of the Freaks, but because of second-home owners. People like Briar are not allowed to erect temporary structures because of dumb planning laws. And as we shall learn towards the end of the book, since 1994, it has become all but impossible to find somewhere to park up a living vehicle. But fear not; in the last part of the book, you will learn how to build a bender, the simplest hippie structure imaginable, and all you will need is some branches, a tarpaulin, and a willingness to see that your need for housing outweighs corrupt planning laws.

Bob comes back into the van, Briar heads back to her gardening, and Bob and I start to talk.

'When me and Monica got back to London we were having trouble getting any money we were owed from Duncan at Forbidden Fruit. We took a really nice squat in the Chalk Farm area, really nice Victorian house, but we didn't want to live in London really.'

'Why not?'

'Because it had changed. The whole vibe had changed, the whole happy hippie pot-smoking thing had changed to smack, the whole Chinese heroin thing had completely changed the atmosphere. Because almost all the people that you knew previously, had partied with and clubbed with and this and that, they were all doing smack. I mean, I've had a little taste of that myself, but just as an occasional treat sort of thing, rather than a daily fucking tie. Which is why I never really got into it, because it's such a tie. So we didn't want to be in London any more. We'd done the clothes thing – it was in some ways a great success, the public response to it was fucking terrific, but we were still owed more than enough money ... I mean, only about twelve grand but then you could have bought a farm round here for that. And Monica and I had both really loved living out in the hills in Afghanistan.'

'I know the story of Monica and Titi, them coming up here to look around for a place, and how they found Bryn Ceinon,' I say. 'What was it like when you first rocked up?'

'Fucking great. I was raised in the country, remember, I am a country boy. So it was great. I hadn't ever seen Wales until we drove down here at night.'

'When you say "we", was Monica already here by then?'

'Yeah.'

'So "we" was you and Peter?'

'I don't remember whether Pete and Titi came down in the same van, or if they came in convoy – I don't think they came in convoy, I honestly don't remember the logistics of the move. I remember waking up in the morning and thinking, "Fuck me, you could grow so much dope up there." This is before I knew about sheep and all that. But that was my first thought when I got up in the morning and looked out. I loved it from the word go.

'I mean, I'd nip up to London, probably once a week, for purely frivolous reasons, sex drugs and rock 'n' roll basically, but I was always glad to get back. In those days you could have a last drink in the Prince of Wales on Princedale Road, have a last-orders drink there, and have a pint at the Baskerville Arms in Clyro just before you did the last couple of miles up the hill. Them were the days. Two o'clock in the morning, and generally the local copper would be in the pub. How it's changed, it's astonishing.'

'It was Downhome.'

'It was.'

Downhome was a dream shared by many of the migrating hippies. Downhome is a mythical place: a stone-built cottage on a hillside with roaring wood-burning stoves, half a dozen goats to milk, some weed in the greenhouse, some children in Clothkits dungarees gathering vegetables from the organic kitchen garden and, at its heart, a smiling Old Lady throwing coins to do an *I Ching* reading for the baby in her belly on the reclaimed scrubbed pine table in a warm loving kitchen smelling of fresh-baked wholemeal bread.

The greatest of the 1970s pub rock bands, Brinsley Schwarz, actually lived and played together in a series of houses they called 'Downhome', which was also the name of their management company. The first house they shared was in suburban Northwood, where they rehearsed in the front room, which was lined with mattresses to keep the noise down for their bowler-hatted neighbours. Their third album, *Silver Pistol*, was recorded in the house in Northwood on the old Pye mobile studio, which was parked in the driveway. In 1973, they moved to leafy Beaconsfield, where they had a barn as a rehearsal space – not exactly the middle of nowhere, but country nonetheless.

The Brinsleys, as fans like me call them, were one of the most cruelly under-rated bands of their day. Younger Readers will find them in the playlist at the back of the book. They were funky, eclectic, and light on their feet. Paul McCartney liked them so much he booked them as support for the first Wings tour. All the musicians travelled together on a coach, hired from Foxes of Hayes, which turned out to be the very same coach that the Beatles used for *The Magical Mystery Tour*. I imagine Macca had flashbacks.

The Brinsleys made six stonking albums between 1970 and 1975, but in the end they gave up the ghost due to lack of commercial success. This commercial failure was, to some extent, of their own making, as an over-reaction to a crass piece of record company nonsense. Their first album was the victim of a press stunt that went badly wrong. Their label, United Artists, excited by their new signings, set up a gig for the band at Fillmore East in New York supporting Van Morrison, and arranged to fly the British music press out to see the show. The band's flight was delayed, so they barely had a chance to soundcheck; the journos' plane was delayed by fog, so the journos got pished, and most of them missed the gig. The resulting press reports were all about the idiocies of record company 'hype', and none of them about the music.

The Brinsleys reacted by reinventing themselves and going underground. They recruited a new member, guitarist singer and songwriter Ian Gomm, and hid themselves away in 'Downhome', writing great songs, and taking a low-key approach to performance. They played lots of free festivals (including Glastonbury Fayre in 1971), and they started to play in pubs in London. Up until this time, bands with recording contracts didn't play in pubs. The Brinsleys were part of a scene which included Ducks Deluxe, Kokomo, Ian Dury's band Kilburn and the High Roads and even, towards the bottom of the bill, old Chas Ambler's band, The Louts. The pub rock bands helped to establish a circuit of small venues, such as The Tally Ho in Kentish Town, the Hope and Anchor in Islington and the Half Moon in Putney, which would prove invaluable to the punk bands a few years later. I loved these bands. They were about the only UK corrective to prog.

Living and working together for five years had its highs and lows for the Brinsleys. There were eleven people in both the houses. In the evenings, if they weren't gigging or rehearsing, they would sit about listening to albums. It's hard to find an album that eleven people would all agree on, but there was one band that everyone loved, and would listen to over and again. The band that they loved the most, the band whose music haunts the early Brinsleys albums, the band that they most wanted to be a UK version of were, er, The Band. The Band, you might remember, had played with Dylan at the legendary Manchester Free Trade Hall gig in 1966.

One day in 1974, the Brinsleys' manager called to say that The Band were playing at Wembley in support of CSNY on the morrow, and needed somewhere to rehearse, and could they use the barn at Downhome? The Brinsleys said yes, as you would. Ian Gomm told me, 'The next day, this stretch limo pulls up outside our house, and we all go, "Fuck me, it's them." And they're here in our barn, using our backline. Brinsley had spent a fortune buying guitars and amps so that he could sound like Robbie Robertson, and here's Robbie using Brinsley's Orange amp, and he's sounding like Robbie, which annoyed Brinsley, who never could. But they were dead quiet, so the five of us stood with our ears pressed to the barn door to hear them. Levon Helm had a problem with his vocal mic, and I'd built the Brinsley's PA, so I went in to sort it. Levon says, "My voice sounds like it's in a hollow zone, man", and I'm thinking I don't know where the hollow zone fader is ... so I fiddled about a bit, and he said, "Yeah, that's great, man." Richard Manuel came into the house, drinking from a bottle of Tia Maria, the sort of thing you get a thimbleful of at Christmas, and he's just glugging it down. Twenty minutes later we got the word that they had finished, and I went in the barn, and Richard Manuel had collapsed on his keyboard. So they said they'd done enough, and they half supported, half carried him back to the car. Garth Hudson was the last to pack up, and he showed me and Bob Andrews his custom Lowry organ. Bob loses his cool, and says, "You're the greatest keyboard player in the world," and Garth Hudson stands up and says, "No I'm not,", and fucks off.' (NB Younger Readers – Garth Hudson certainly was the greatest keyboard player in the world at this time.)

So why did The Band want to borrow a barn in the country to rehearse, rather than use a sprauncy West End rehearsal studio? Because that was their world. Downhome was where they were from.

In 1967, The Band had moved together into a house they called 'Big Pink' in West Saugerties in upstate New York, six miles from where

Bob Dylan was living in the town of Woodstock. (The Festival, incidentally, was only named after Woodstock, where it had originally been
planned to take place, but was actually held in Bethel, some sixty miles
away.) In this house The Band recorded the *Basement Tapes* with Dylan,
who was getting his head together after a motorbike crash in 1966. Here
too they wrote the material for their own first album, *Music from Big
Pink*. There had long been a lively music scene in Woodstock, but
Dylan's presence attracted more musicians to the area: Tim Hardin, Jimi
Hendrix, Van Morrison, Todd Rundgren. It was close enough to New
York (about two hours' drive) so that you didn't feel cut off, but hidden
deep enough in the Catskill Mountains that it felt like a different world.
Getting your head together in the country meant Woodstock, at least
for a while; you took a house, and played all day. In 1970, The Band
recorded their third album, *Stage Fright* in the Woodstock Playhouse,
engineered by Todd Rundgren. In 1972, Dylan's by then ex-manager
Alfred Grossman built a studio in Bearsville, a suburb of Woodstock,
so as to take advantage of the increasing number of rock bands who
wanted to hang out and record in the countryside. Getting it together
in the country was clearly the way to go.

For many musicians at the time, not just the Brinsleys, The Band were
the Band, the guys that everyone wanted to emulate. And Dylan was
regarded as little less than a god. If Dylan did it, and if The Band did it,
it had to be the right thing to do. British bands had taken to the countryside before, including the Incredible String Band, who lived for a time
in a house in Llandegley, just over the hill from Bob. Guy Stevens had
visited Bob and Vicki when they lived in Wiltshire to score some dope
for Traffic, who were recording nearby. But the desire to recreate the
spirit of Old Old Woodstock (the town, not the festival) meant that more
and more British bands were looking to move to the countryside.
According to Barney Hoskyns, author of *Small Town Talk*, a book about
Woodstock's place in musical history, pretty much all musical migration
was as a consequence of players wanting to do like Dylan and The Band
did. McCartney had taken himself off to Scotland, to a farm on the Mull
of Kintyre, I'm afraid, and Led Zep's guitarist Jimmy Page had moved
up to Scotland too, to Boleskine House, which had once been owned by
the magician Aleister Crowley. Donovan, as we have seen, was attempting
to set up an artist's community on Skye, hampered by Taffy and Bob.
Eric Clapton moved to a house in Ewhurst, Surrey, where my grandmother and aunt had once been in service. Bands headed for Mid-Wales
too, to live a Downhome dream for a few weeks or even months. In the

mid sixties, brothers Charles and Kingsley Ward had opened a residential studio in the village of Rockfield, in Monmouthshire. It was slow to take off, and it was not until after The Band and Dylan made it fashionable to record in the country that it located its mojo. But then, from about 1970, take off it did. In the 1970s, amongst many others, Black Sabbath, Motörhead, Hawkwind, Graham Parker and the Rumour and Dr Feelgood all recorded there. Even the Brinsleys left their own Downhome, and went out to Rockfield to record their last album. In 1975, rock band Queen recorded 'Bohemian Rhapsody' there, as I suppose it had to be recorded somewhere. It's still going; in the early nineties the Stone Roses pretty much moved in for a year, and spent 347 ten-hour days working on their second album. Oasis decamped to Rockfield to record their second album *(What's the story) Morning Glory*. Staying and playing in the countryside still has great appeal.

But there was no place like Woodstock, and it is fair to say that Downhome in all its incarnations was an American phenomenon. It combines an idea of freedom (to play music, or make art, or just to 'be') with the long American tradition of 'homesteading', of becoming self-sufficient – which takes us back to the first of the hippies, Henry David Thoreau.

The idea of homesteading was to become autonomous: to grow your own food, to make your own entertainment and to live with as little money as possible. By the 1930s, a new breed of homesteaders were mixing Thoreau's ideals with the German immigrant Nature Boys' taste for 'wholefood', together with a healthy dash of Blavatsky's cosmology. Taken together, these influences morphed into a new set of ideas, whose most vigorous proponent was a Hungarian-born naturalised American academic, Edmund Bordeaux Szekely, who died in 1979, aged seventy-four.

Szekely wrote over eighty books, usually translated into English by his follower, L. Purcell Weaver. One of these was *Medicine Tomorrow: An Introduction to Cosmotherapy with Guide to Treatment*, published in 1938. According to Weaver, Szekely led the 'International Cosmotherapeutic Expedition 1939–1940', which 'studied the therapeutic application of the cosmic, solar terrestrial and human radiations in different parts of the world'.

What, you ask, is Cosmotherapy? According to Szekely, Cosmotherapy works by 'helping us to progress towards an understanding of and an alignment with the Universal or Cosmo-logical Self, allowing us to centre ourselves within all Universal Forms'. With which there is no arguing.

Szekely saw himself as a healer, and is regarded as a key figure in the rise of 'Naturopathy', a bundle of various healing therapies which include colour therapy, hair analysis and colonic irrigation. If your name is Willow, the chances are that you have been subject to some of Szekely's ideas, such as when you had a cold, your mum waved crystals over your head or made you look at something red. His most influential book was the 841 pages of *Cosmos, Man and Society: A Paneubiotic Synthesis*, published in 1948; and if you can find out what Paneubiotic means, you are a better non-gender-specific person than I.

In 1940 (presumably on his return from the International Cosmotherapeutic Expedition), Szekely and his wife Deborah opened a camp in Tecate, Baja California, Mexico, hard up against the US border. It was (still is) called 'Rancho la Puerta'. The camp had one adobe hut (visitors had to bring their own tents) and the Szekelys grew organic produce, kept goats and made cheese, and invited like-minded people to visit, for $17.50 a week. In return for this bargain price, guests worked in the garden, chopped wood, milked goats and listened to Szekely's lectures on achieving good health and long life by means of becoming aware of the interdependence of mind, body and spirit. Szekely spoke against herbicides, pesticides, artificial fertilisers, cigarettes and fats in the American diet. He recommended a way of life familiar to the habitués of Sexauer's Health Food Store in Santa Barbara – pure air and pure water, lots of exercise, and a grow-your-own wholefood vegetarian diet (though he seems not to have shared the Nature Boys' enthusiasm for nudity).

The camp became a spa in the early 1950s when visitor numbers grew. Szekely and his wife began hiring specialists in yoga and Gurdjieffian mind/body exercises, to develop the spiritual side of their guests. You can still visit now (the price has gone up a bit); Szekely's wife Deborah was described as 'the godmother of wellness', which gives you an idea of what you'll be in for: no fags, no booze, lots of lovely crunchy raw sprouting mung bean salads and a large dose of occult nature therapy, 'Wellness' being one of those things of which everyone is very much in favour, without being quite sure what it means.

One of Szekely's readers was a classical violinist called Helen Knothe, who had studied with and been a lover of Krishnamurti in the 1920s. She visited Rancho la Puerta with her husband, Scott Nearing, in 1948, and was inspired by the visit. She continued to cite *Cosmos, Man and Society* as one of her great influences, and to describe Szekely as a great teacher and philosopher. Scott Nearing was twenty years older than Helen. He was what would now be called a radical economist. From 1905 to 1915, he taught at the University of Pennsylvania Business School, where he advocated a tax system based on land value rather than income, an economic idea that is known as Georgism—

'Not fucking economics,' groans Bob from the bed.

'Yes. Shut up ...'

'It's my van.'

'It's my book. Now, listen ...'

You will have encountered Georgist economic thinking most Christmases, because Nearing is credited with spreading the popularity among students of the Landlord Game, the forerunner of Monopoly, which he used as a tool to teach his students. Whether Georgism states that you should buy the orange ones is unclear. Nearing was sacked from his position in 1915 for denouncing the use of child labour by American corporations, and went to work for the Socialist Party of America. In 1919 his avowed pacifism got him prosecuted for trying to dissuade young men from joining the Army.

Scott and Helen decided to try to remove themselves from capitalist alienation, and they moved to Vermont to homestead in 1932. They built their own house, grew their own food, and bought some extra land covered in sugarbushes from a neighbour. They earned any money they needed by producing syrup. They moved in 1952 to avoid a new ski resort which was being built in the Green Mountains of Vermont, and started again on a beautiful but bleak site on the coast of Maine, where you can still visit their homestead, now known as The Good Life Center.

Scott Nearing insisted that the secret of their success was that they kept meticulous records which helped them remember what they had learned. These records fed into the homesteading guides they had started to write. In 1954, they published *Living the Good Life: How to Live Simply and Sanely in a Troubled World*, which is a 'How To ...' guide to self-sufficient living. Many people read the book, and had dreams, but got no further. It found its real readership in the 1970s after a reprint, as young people took up the ideas. The population of Maine grew by 4.4 per cent in the mid 1970s, the fastest growing population of any state in the USA; in 1974, there were 6,000 farms in Maine; by 1978, there were 8,500. New homesteaders were learning from *Living the Good Life*. It's a practical book; it talks a lot about composting, crop rotation and how to build an underground root storage cellar.

Shortly before his death, aged 100, in 1983, Scott Nearing said, 'Do one thing you believe in. Do it with all your might. Keep at it no matter what. The life we have been living is so far away from the really worthwhile goals of life that we've got to stop fooling around and move toward a new way of living.' He died consciously; a few weeks after his last birthday, he decided to fast until death. Helen died in 1994, aged ninety-two. Hard to say they weren't onto something. Fittingly for these disciples of the First Hippie, their archives and papers are lodged at the Thoreau Institute in Walden Woods.

The hands-on, how-to ethic of *Living the Good Life* was continued in the US by the *Whole Earth Catalog*, put together and published between 1968 and 1980 by Californian Stewart Brand, a one-time acid evangelist and ex-US Army parachutist turned Futurist. The *Whole Earth Catalog* was just that: a catalogue. It told readers where to buy tools, with the widest possible definition of what a tool might be: spades and rakes, yes, but also solar panels, goat feed, books, plans; where to obtain them, and what was best for a particular job. These days, it's known as 'The Hippies' Internet' because that was how it functioned. You wanted a micro hydro-electric plant, or plans for building a yurt, or a thing for sharpening your scythe – you looked it up in the index, and you found who did the best one, or the most reasonably priced, and contacted them. Brand was one of the first people to understand the possibilities of the computer, and set up an early digital networking project, called The WELL, in 1985, seven years before the arrival of the internet. Brand stopped producing the WEC in 1994, because he understood that it had been superseded by the internet. I've carried my 1980 edition, *The Next Whole Earth Catalog*, around for years, and it's in pretty poor shape, but I still thrill to turn the pages. My daughters argue about who is going to get it when I die; not bad for a thirty-five-year-old out-of-date catalogue of stuff. Now, of course, the Hippies' Internet is available on the internet, and you'll find a link in the Appendix, but nothing will take the place of my tatty print copy. It's hard to get for much less than fifty quid these days.

There was a short-lived British version, called the *Index of Possibilities*, but British Freaks who dreamed of a self-sufficient life could, and did, get hold of the original, even if they seldom wrote off to the States to buy galvanised zinc or long-handled hay rakes. But British self-sufficiency had a low profile, until a few inciting events of the mid-1970s sparked the exodus to the country in earnest. Some of these events were lovely carrots drawing people to the countryside by opening up new possibilities – and some were horrid scary sticks that put the fear of societal collapse into the wannabe homesteaders' hearts.

Two lovely crunchy organic carrots were a book by John Seymour called *The Complete Book of Self-Sufficiency* – and a sitcom. *The Nearings* is the first use of 'The Good Life' in the sense of self-sufficient living, but it was BBC TV's *The Good Life* which fed the British fashion for dropping out and moving to the country to grow your own and raise a few goats. Scott and Helen, it could be argued, are the originals of Tom and Barbara Good, played in the series by Richard Briers and Felicity Kendal. It started in 1975, and ran for four seasons, until 1978. Tom leaves his well-paid job as a designer, with Barbara's support, to turn his Surbiton house and garden into a smallholding. His next-door neighbours, Margo and Jerry Leadbetter, are not happy at the situation. It was voted ninth in a poll of Britain's best ever sitcoms, and it is still funny. Odd as it may seem, the hard-working but happy Tom and Barbara were seen as role models, and thousands of people are reputed to have tried their hands at smallholding as a consequence.

Those brave souls who did sell up and head for the British hills had a bible to guide them, which was John Seymour's *The Complete Book of Self-Sufficiency*, published in 1976. It should really also credit his wife Sally, who did many of the wonderful illustrations. It should also perhaps credit Christopher Dorling and Peter Kindersley, who edited and designed the book for Faber and took over publication of subsequent editions for their own highly successful publishing house. The book promised a lot; this is the back cover:

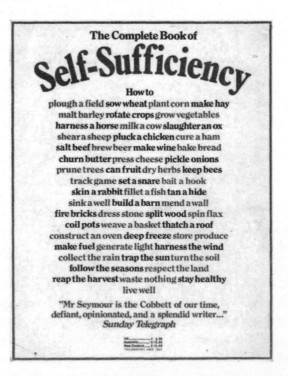

Seymour was nobody's hippie; as you can tell from the cover, he didn't go along with the Nearings' ideas about vegetarianism, and I suspect he would have popped you on the chin if you'd gone near him with a healing crystal. An ex-military man who had attended agricultural college before the war, he was a writer and broadcaster who turned his hand to self-sufficiency. His two wonderful books on the English canals and rivers, *Sailing Through England* (1956) and *Voyage into England* (1966), are second only to L.T.C. Rolt's *Narrow Boat* in the canon of British canal books. Somewhat blunt in his style, I've long suspected he might not have been terribly good company. His books are rather didactic, and can make the reader feel inadequate as much as empowered. But he lived what he preached, and clearly knew of what he wrote – his book is beautifully illustrated and designed, and every tyro smallholder had a copy on their shelf. Lots of people used it as a dream book; like the *Whole Earth Catalog*, I've had a copy for years, even though I could no more skin a rabbit or weave a basket than I could fly an airship. It is an easy find in charity shops, and the revised edition is still in print; have a look.

'Did you ever have a copy, Bob?' I ask.

'I must have seen it. But no.'

'Do you see yourself as a Good-Lifer? You grow lots of your own veg, you shoot the odd rabbit, make your own booze, you chop your own wood, you built a shack, you generate your own electricity ...'

'I've lived a good life. I dunno. It just seemed right for me. I just like it.'

'Come the collapse of capitalism, you could manage. I'd be first to the fucking wall.'

'You'd cope.'

It's nice to have your friend's goodwill. But I'm not sure he's right. I watched *The Good Life* and read the *Whole Earth Catalog* and *Self-Sufficiency*, but I was always only a homesteader in my dreams, rather than in any kind of reality.

To complement these Good Life carrots there were also the scary sticks of doom. Two books in particular fed into seventies uncertainty about the future, an uncertainty which made people across Europe and the USA feel that homesteading was an essential rather than a merely desirable lifestyle. One was *Limits to Growth*, published in 1972. It was authored by a think tank called the Club of Rome who used computer modelling (then in its infancy) to map the uses of global resources against population growth. Their prediction was that 'If the present growth trends in world population, industrialisation, pollution, food production, and resource depletion continue unchanged, the limits to growth on this planet will be reached sometime within the next one hundred years. The most probable result will be a rather sudden and uncontrollable decline in both population and industrial capacity.' *Limits to Growth* is the best-selling environmental book ever, with an estimated global sale of seventeen million in its three editions. It unnerved people, as I hope it will unnerve you if you read it.

If you Google the Club of Rome, incidentally, you will find lots of great stuff about how they are an Illuminati front, the Illuminati being a shadowy group of conspirators who wish to establish 'A New World Order'. *The Illuminatus! Trilogy* was a huge book for the Freaks. Published in 1975 by Leary collaborator Robert Anton Wilson and his colleague as *Playboy*'s letters editor, Robert Shea, it's a funny, sexy and mad SF novel, which was supposed to be a satire, but which, sadly, has ended up being part of the reason that conspiracy theory has bloomed like cancer in a post-truth world. If ever your dad points out instances of the number 23 to you, ask him if he's read it.

The other game-changing book of the period was Paul and Annie Ehrlich's *Population Bomb* of 1968, which was even more apocalyptic in tone. It predicted mass starvation by the 1980s, unless population growth was brought under control, by forced sterilisation if necessary. It was very very unnerving, though largely discredited now. But it scared readers; sometimes, scared them into action. An interview with Ehrlich in *Playboy* in 1972 led two solicitors from Daventry in Northamptonshire, Tony and Lesley Whittaker, to set up a political party called PEOPLE. At its 1973 conference it adopted the *Manifesto for a Sustainable Society*. This remarkable document is one of the cornerstones of Green political thought. In its opening section, 'Philosophies', the authors sum up their thinking thus:

> The overriding principle is that Man should take care not to upset or do irreparable damage to the ecological equilibrium of Nature. When applied in conjunction with ideals of conservation, self-sufficiency and economic steady state, this principle acts as a restraint on the type and scope of any development. Dramatic changes are necessary in agricultural techniques, waste disposal, town and community planning, quarrying and mining methods, transport facilities, when they are subjected to ecological constraints, and it is this principle which unifies all the others and gives them a corporate identity.

There would have been, at most, fifty members present at the 1973 conference. The party stood six candidates in the February 1974 election, and received 4,500 votes; and five candidates at the October election of the same year, when it got less than 2,000. At its 1975 conference, PEOPLE changed its name to the Ecology Party. At the 1983 election, they put up 100 candidates, and got over 50,000 votes (one of them mine – I've been a member since 1982, I should perhaps admit). At the 1985 conference, they changed their name again, to the Green Party. At the 2015 election, they had a candidate in every seat, and received 1.1 million votes. And one MP, Caroline Lucas, the first Green politician anywhere on earth to win a seat under the first past the post system. PEOPLE is regarded as the earliest Green political party anywhere in the world, and the ideas in *Manifesto for a Sustainable Society*, including self-sufficiency, are still at the heart of Green Party policy-making.

Bob Dylan and The Band, books both encouraging and frightening, and even good-natured sitcoms are perhaps not quite enough to fully account for the drift to the country in the 1970s and '80s. So how about some geopolitics? In particular, the October 1973 Yom Kippur War between Israel and Egypt and her ally Syria caused a great shift in thinking about energy. America supported Israel, and the Arab-controlled oil-producing nations (OPEC) embargoed oil sales to the USA, and dropped their production by 5 per cent. Oil prices rose from $3 a barrel to $11 a barrel in two years, and the UK government prepared for petrol rationing.

Or how about some good old-fashioned industrial action? Due to a strike by coal miners, between 1 January and 7 March 1974, the Tory government ordered the 'Three-Day Week', in an attempt to save power. Workplaces (and homes) only got electricity for three days a week. TV companies shut down at 10.30 every night. It looked like the good times of the late 1950s and early 1960s were over. Government seemed to be breaking down as the lights went off. People were scared. *Manifesto for a Sustainable Society* might have been forward looking, but it was also a tad alarmist, even a wee bit survivalist in tone.

There was even a darkside equivalent to *The Good Life*, called *Doomwatch*, in which a team of plucky investigators and scientists attempted against the odds to protect Britain from inevitable ecological disaster. Many of the people who were interested in self-sufficiency were concerned for their families' immediate future; none more so than groups we might describe as 'hippie survivalists'.

If you put the postcode SA19 7EE into Google maps, you will find yourself hovering over a valley in the Great Green Desert of Mid-Wales, about eight miles north of Llandeilo, and fifteen south of Lampeter. If you start to zoom in, you'll see some fuzzy dots. Zoom in further, and you'll see the dots resolve into a remarkable series of tipis, yurts and roundhouses, with polytunnels and neat gardens. This is Tipi Valley, the still-beating secret heart of British hippiedom. It is, in essence, a small village, whose population fluctuates as new residents come and old hands are forced by infirmity into houses, but which is usually somewhere about 100. Since 1975, people have been moving here as an escape from the alienated world, in hope of being able to discover a way of life that is authentic.

Long-term resident Chris Waite is credited as the first man in the UK to build a tipi, at the 1974 Windsor Free Festival. He learned how to do it from drawings and plans in the *Whole Earth Catalog*. He did it, he says, to be closer to the earth, because Lord knows if you want to be close to the Earth, you can't do much better than a tipi. There is a fire in the middle, and a hole in the top; you might think of it as a sort of leaky cape surrounding a fire. If you're lucky, the smoke goes out through the fire flaps; if not, the whole structure fills with smoke. If you're lucky, the weather stays dry; if not, or if you have not put your tipi up properly, then rainwater drips down the poles and onto your pointy little head while you are crashed out, man. They look great, but have been superseded in traveller life by the much cosier and more efficient yurt, which has a small portable wood-burner at its heart. Some residents of Tipi Valley have built roundhouses: semi-permanent structures which look a bit like they'd be at home in Hobbiton. The villagers insist that semi-permanent structures like this cannot be sold, because 'the land belongs to itself'.

The village has no leader, or any formal organisational structure. Over the years, as they've acquired bits of money, they have bought small parcels of land from the neighbouring farmers, but Tipi Valley is not a commune. Such mutual decisions that have to be made are made by consensus, through conversations between neighbours. Although there are no leaders, there are very much elders, chief of whom would have to be Rik the Vic, who is, in fact, a Church of England priest who has lived in the village for thirty-five years. He lives in a geodesic dome tucked inside a tipi, amongst gardens and polytunnels where he grows most of his own vegetables. He says that the residents, whatever their religion, share a basic paganism, which expresses itself as a love for nature. Living in a tipi or a yurt pretty much amounts to living outdoors, after all. Like any survivalist, staying warm is a major preoccupation, and gathering firewood takes up a lot of the residents' time. Like Bob's van, most of the structures have solar panels to make their own electricity for things like a bit of lighting and running a music system (or a laptop these days, though there is no way to get online, as there's no mobile reception in Tipi Valley). As Rik says of the village residents, they wouldn't be regarded as normal, but they are all sane; especially so in a world where the lights are going out.

There is a shared structure, a tipi called The Big Lodge; and sometimes meals are cooked communally on special occasions; but for most of the time, it is a village, where all the residents are free to live as they wish, so long as they live in temporary structures, and take their shoes off when they enter a dwelling, which is pretty much the only rule in Tipi Valley. But in the 1970s, communal life seemed attractive to many people who wanted to find new ways of living. For thousands of young people, wanting to escape from an alienated society into a Brave New World of their own making, but unable to afford a bit of land, living in a commune seemed like it was a way forward.

There were an estimated 500 UK communes at the movement's height in 1981. Although there were (and still are) urban communes, in the rural versions, people would grow food together, cook together, and often raise children together. Over time, only a handful of people could hack it. Bob wouldn't fancy it; too much of a loner. I wouldn't fancy it; too much of a pig. If you think about what it's like to live with your own fucking family, and then multiply that by five, then you'd have some idea of the possible tensions. But the model has evolved, rather than having been abandoned altogether. There are housing co-ops and co-housing schemes, and self-build communities where a group of people acquire some land for development, and then take it in turns to help one another build their own houses. Finding somewhere to live away from your parents has never been harder, but there are alternatives to saving up for a mortgage. They are few and far between, but if Younger Readers decide to become politicised in the broadest sense, these alternatives could represent a realistic way forward; ways of sharing resources without having to argue about whose turn it is to clean the bogs. (Probably mine, he said, shame-facedly.)

'I haven't got one,' says Bob.

'I know.'

'So I never have to clean it.'

'No, I know.'

'Because I shit in the woods.'

Sigh.

One more thought about why people moved to the country in the 1970s and 1980s before I move on; which is, why here? Why is Bob shitting in these woods in particular? Much as it pains me as a Presteigne man to admit it, it's probably something to do with our neighbour, Hay-on-Wye, twenty miles south-south-west. It's probably due to one remarkable man, Richard Booth, the King of Hay.

Booth is a well-to-do Hay native, who came back to the town after he graduated from Oxford, worried that young people had no opportunities in Hay, and no choice but to move away. The answer, it seemed to Booth, was books. Second-hand books.

Richard Booth opened his first bookshop in Hay-on-Wye in 1961, in the disused fire station. Everything in Hay at that time was pretty much disused. It was a small market town on the verge of collapse. It is very beautiful, rising above the banks of the river and framed by Hay Bluff and the Black Mountain plateau, and it had been something of a tourist destination in the early twentieth century. But after the Second World War, it was through. The last passenger train to Hay ran on 31 December 1962, even before the Beeching Report. British Rail didn't need to be told there was no future in the line. (Younger Readers, wondering what the Beeching Report might have been, are urged to buy my excellent book on railways, *Parallel Lines*, where they can read all about it. If you are in Hay, and find a second-hand copy, check to see if it's one of the rare unsigned ones.)

Booth didn't just open a bookshop; he taught his home town a trade. Booth bought books on an industrial scale. He went to the USA, and bought up whole libraries, and always took a few likely lads with him. Local people learned how to buy and price second-hand books, how to sell them, how to put a catalogue together. People started to visit Hay again, so more bookshops opened in vacant, cheap-to-rent shops. By the time Bob and Monica bowled up in 1971, there were a dozen or more. Monica was one of the first people to realise that non-bookshops might do well, too; her clothes shop, Monica of Hay only closed in 2014. (Her London shop, Monica of Hampstead, is still open, though, and still selling Monica's designs.) At its height in the early twenty-first century, Hay had over forty bookshops; now there are only two dozen or so, but the chance that Booth had offered entrepreneurial hippies is still there. For example, if you are in Hay for the festival, you will certainly want to try Shepherd's ice cream, set up by two old Freak pals of Bob and Pete Mustill, Martin Orbach and Juliet Noble.

'Is this book about me?' says Bob. 'Or are you just promoting Hay?'

'You, my darlin'. Your life and times. Your geopolitical background. The socio-economic conditions that prevailed at such and such a moment. Etc. It's all about you. And the kids.'

'What kids?'

'The kids. Hippie kids.'

Up until 1969, the counter-culture had been an urban experience. If it can be revived and reinvented, then I guess it will be an urban experience again, that will happen in places like Bristol and Brighton. One of the reasons for this is second- and third- generation hippie migration out of the countryside, and back into cities. What is there for young people to do in the countryside any more? If the dream didn't come off entirely, it came close enough that a lot of hippies set up home, raised families, and colonised large parts of mid and west Wales. It is their children, my children, who are moving away.

Younger Readers will have met these hippie children if they have ever visited festivals such as Glastonbury, Secret Garden Party, Latitude, etc., because it is they who run the festivals. They are the fire-eaters, stilt-walkers, burlesque dancers, musicians. They run the stalls; it is they who sell you sheep's milk ice cream and crepes and vintage clothing. A young couple of my acquaintance, Bill and Bex, themselves the children of New Age Travellers, run a coconut shy round innumerable festivals from April to September, and drive their living vehicle to Portugal for the rest of the year.

I have seen figures claiming that fourteen million people in the UK visit at least one 'music festival' per annum, and spend an estimated £2.3 billion annually. Festivals are huge business. While we are doing dubious statistics, and if you doubt my thesis that things have changed, in 2015, *Time Out* claimed that 22 per cent of festivalgoers that year had taken drugs – 22 per cent! It makes me want to sit down. What are the other 78 per cent doing? Also according to *Time Out*, 97 per cent have drunk alcohol, but take it from me, booze is not going to get you through Glastonbury. It will make you carefree, when what you need to be is paranoid, in order to stand a chance of coming out alive. I'd wager that at the Glastonbury Fayre in 1971, the figures would have been the other way round.

There are dozens and dozens of music festivals every year. July is the peak month (according to *Time Out* again, there were sixty-five in July 2015), but every year from April till October you can spend pretty much all your weekends in a field of mud, camped next to some cunts from Swindon (Reading), Islington (Latitude) or Chipping Norton (Wilderness);

eating burgers (Reading), artisanal fava bean falafels (Latitude) or a three-course meal curated by Yotam Ottolenghi (Wilderness); and listening to AC/DC (Reading), A.C. Grayling (Latitude) or Pop Up Opera's production of Emmanuel Chabrier's rarely performed *Une Education Manquée* (Wilderness).

Many of these festivals, your Downloads and your Vs and your T-in-the-Parks, are direct heirs of the Reading Festival, and need not concern us here; they are as counter-cultural as a toe-tapping monarch or a BBC One sitcom. Another group of festivals (Creamfields, for example, or Lovebox) grew out of nightclubs, looking for a legal way to promote raves, and I've kicked the rave scene into the last chapter. There is, however, a third group, which do have their roots firmly in the counter-culture. Glastonbury is the mother and father of these.

It's easy to imagine if you are there that you are at a rock festival, much like any other, just a bit bigger. The BBC's woeful annual coverage gives this impression too. But if you head out of Babylon, up the Main Drag towards the Sacred Space (not sacred, full of fucknuts doing Nox, good loos if you don't mind queuing), then once you cross the old railway line, you will be in the Green Fields, which are the remnants of Glastonbury Fayre. Linger at Croissant Neuf, and hope to catch Biggles War Time Band. Do one in the Peace Garden. Chat to anarcho-syndicalists in Green Futures. Go through Green Crafts, and ask the exhibitors to tell you their favourite Bob Rowberry story (he was a resident metal-worker for many years). Do another one in the Tepee Circle, and then bimble across to the Healing Field to get your chakras balanced in a gong workshop. It's still, just about, the real deal. You can watch the rock festival on catch-up when you get home.

Then you have the smaller boutique festivals. I have fallen out of love with them a bit. I got busted by a narc in the shape of a darling spaniel going into Secret Garden Party with nothing more than a couple of blims; have been chucked out of Wilderness for telling a child called Atticus to fuck off, on mic, at a kids' event, while dressed as a vicar, because his name was Atticus; and have endured the indignity of being last on in the literature tent at Latitude while Elbow played 'One Day Like This', accompanied by a massive fireworks display, on the Main Stage, just a couple of hundred metres away from where I was trying to read some of my deathless prose to a handful of too-whacked-to-move stoners. I'm too old for BoomTown, and too cynical for Shambala. These days, my favourites are the oop-north ones: Solfest, Eden, and the legendary Beat-Herder. I like these because I go as part of the Melodrome crew. The

Melodrome is a mobile stage, painted by Panit Dave (who will be showing you how to build a bender right at the end of this book), and set up by old Chas Ambler.

Chas was a festival geek. He loved nothing better than to sit round an all-night fire by an internal gate, shitting on about the difficulties of organising vehicle movements across the site at Glastonbury. Playing hundreds of festival gigs with him over the twenty years or so we worked together as Your Dad, I got to hear his festival theories a lot. Some were managerial. Some were socio-economic. Some were political. And some were historical. These, I feel, are the ones which stand up to scrutiny. And his central historical theory was that contemporary festivals have their roots in a) the big free festivals of the 1970s and early 1980s (Glastonbury Fayre, Windsor and Stonehenge) and b) the almost forgotten Albion Fairs, held in East Anglia between 1972 and 1986.

'But I never went to the Albion Fairs,' says Bob.

'Nor did I. But Chas did and the dead can do no wrong. People usually only acknowledge the free festivals. But Albion mattered, quite a bit. So we'll look at both points of his theory.'

'Really?'

'Really. At great length.'

Bob groans.

'Our story starts at the Bath Festival of Blues and Progressive Music, which was held at the Royal Bath and West Showground in Shepton Mallet, Somerset, on the weekend of 28 and 29 June 1970 ...'

'I was at that,' says Bob.

'Were you?'

'Yeah. I played at it, too ...'

'Did you? I didn't know you could play anything.'

'I can't. But brother Sandy was Led Zep's roadie, remember? So me and Mustill were backstage, and Jimmy Page was looking at my bike, and offered me money for it, like, but I said no. Then he said, "Oh, we're on, man. And we need people to come onstage with us and bang tambourines and shake maracas and shit. Do you fancy it?" Fucking dead right we did. So up we went. Sadly, Mustill was so pissed he fell off the back of the stage.'

'Chas was there too. It was his first festival; he always reckoned he'd only gone to see Hot Tuna. He sat through the Floyd doing "Atom Heart Mother" for the first time; said they went on so late and went on so long, that by the time they were finishing, the sun was coming up.'

See, this is why non-fiction is so much more fun to do than fiction. In fiction, it would seem contrived to have the two main characters (one active, one passive, one talking, one talked about, one alive, one dead) in the same place at the same time without meeting till years later. No one would buy it. Especially at the point where a local farmer and his partner bunked in through the hedge, and liked what they saw.

Athelstan Joseph Michael Eavis and his then girlfriend and soon to be second wife Jean lived on his family's land, called Worthy Farm, just outside the pretty village of Pilton, about four miles from the showground, and about six from Glastonbury. Eavis had taken over his family farm in 1954 when he was nineteen, though he had never wanted to, and had trained for a career in the Merchant Navy. Life wasn't easy; there was an overdraft of £5,000 on the farm, and Eavis had to work for a few years as a coalminer to make ends meet. So long ago and far away is this story, that not only where there such things as coalminers, but there were such things as coalminers in Somerset.

Eavis was so impressed by the festival that he'd bunked into without paying, that he decided he'd start his own at Worthy Farm. He thought it might pay off part of the overdraft. He says that he 'thought there might be a way of combining the traditions of the country fair with the ideals of the pop festival culture'. He got on the phone, called a few agents, and booked some bands. It wasn't called 'The Glastonbury Festival'; it was called 'Pilton Pop Folk and Blues'. The Kinks were supposed to be top of the bill, but by the time the festival came around, on 19 and 20 September, they had hit single 'Lola' to promote, so at the last minute, they pulled out. Eavis replaced them with Marc Bolan and T. Rex. Other acts included Stackridge, Amazing Blondel and Keith Christmas – names to conjure with, no? It was supposed to cost a pound to get in (though few people seemed to have paid) and festivalgoers were entitled to free milk from the Worthy Farm herd. It was held on the weekend that Hendrix died, which reputedly cast 'a bit of a downer' over proceedings. Estimates of how many people attended range between one and two thousand, and Eavis reckons he lost £1,500 on the event. And that would have been that, had not Eavis received a call a few weeks after the festival from well-to-do hippie Andrew Kerr.

Kerr had been appalled by IOW 1970, both by the dreadful organisation and by its commercialism. Driving back to London from the island, he said to his carload of hippies, 'We've got to have a proper festival, and it's got to have some cosmic significance.' He thought of Stonehenge, but decided that it wasn't viable because it was surrounded by arable fields – the beauty of Worthy Farm is that it is a dairy farm, so no crops are being grown to get trampled underfoot by the punters. The word having got about amongst the beautiful people that Andrew was looking to set up a festival, he got a few calls from friends telling him about the little event at Eavis' place. Andrew went to Pilton to meet Eavis to tell him his plan for a free festival, and Eavis said yes. In October 1970, Kerr moved into the farmhouse to begin preparations for the Fayre, which took place over the Solstice Weekend, 22–26 June 1971.

Kerr had previously been assistant to Randolph Churchill, son and official biographer of Sir Winston. Randolph Churchill died in 1968, and Kerr was heartbroken, describing him as being like a surrogate father. He had known Randolph's daughter Arabella since she was eight; Kerr invited her to visit him at Worthy Farm – and she moved in too. As she said, 'Basically, that was the end of my straight life.' Kerr's first job was, of course, to site the main stage in relation to the ley line from Glastonbury Tor to Stonehenge by means of dowsing earth energy. More of which soon, man.

Having put a stake in the ground for the most energetically positive site for the main stage, all Kerr and Arabella had to do was raise loads of money, book acts and get the stage actually built. The idea was that it was to be a free festival. Woodstock and IOW 1970 had both ended up free by dint of poor organisation rather than by intent. Kerr and Arabella wanted it to be free from the start. Michael Eavis had little actual involvement; all he wanted to do was recoup his losses from the 1970 event, and said that if the organisers paid him a bit of rent, they could get on and do what they liked. Kerr put what money he had into the event; Arabella had just received four grand from a family trust, so she put that in too. But, as it was a free festival, Eavis didn't get paid, and he just ended up losing more money.

A guy called Bill Harkin turned up with a design for a stage which had come to him during meditation. It was to be a pyramid, with translucent plastic sheets as siding. They found an innovative sound engineer, Tony Andrews, who had built the prototype for the Turbosound system that was to change for ever the way outdoor music was heard. As the stage was being built, Andrew and Bella booked their acts, amongst them Traffic, Melanie and Fairport Convention. David Bowie, best known at that time as a one-hit wonder after his 1969 hit 'Space Oddity', was fitted in towards the bottom of the bill. (At the 2000 Glastonbury Festival, he was top of the bill, and we in Your Dad were bottom, from which I've taken hope over the years.)

Brinsley Schwarz were there. They were on the Pyramid Stage, and all was going well. They were using their own PA, and sounding good. Then, a Rolls-Royce came through the crowd, and, as Ian Gomm tells it, 'Loads of people in robes got out. And everyone's going, "Ooh, he's here."' And these people come up and say, "You've got to stop playing." And this woman comes up behind me, and actually pulls my hand off my guitar, and says, "You've got to stop." In the end, they had to pull the plug on us. And they brought up this throne, and threw white rose petals all over the place. And this kid sits on the throne and starts speaking. But what they've overlooked is that it's our PA, and our manager Dave Robinson says, "We're fuckin' taking it down." So this kid is speaking, but no one can hear him, so they have to find him another PA. When they got it going, he starts all over again, and says the same thing all over again: "I'm a Perfect Master, I'm here to show you the way", and all that. And at the end, he says, "And to do my work, I need your money." And he's the one who's turned up at a free festival in a Roller.'

This was the thirteen-year-old Guru Mahara Ji, Gumragi to his followers, the founder of the favourite hippie cult of the 1970s, the Divine Light Mission. He spoke for twenty minutes; amongst his topics was 'the dangers of drugs', which was a bit like standing in front of the crowd at Wembley on Cup Final Day and arguing that contemporary dance is more fun than Association Football. Andrew Kerr, like Chas, was a Premmie, a follower of the Guru Mahara Ji (Kerr had invited him), and, like Chas, he didn't seem to take much notice of the No Drugs bit.

British filmmakers Nic Roeg and David Puttnam made a film of the event, called *Glastonbury Fayre*, and there was a triple album too, which includes a long track from the Grateful Dead, who didn't actually play, a version of 'Silver Machine' by Hawkwind which was really recorded at the Roundhouse, and several studio recordings, including ones from Marc Bolan, David Bowie and Brinsley Schwarz. Despite these spin-offs, the thing was a financial disaster, and Eavis decided that he was done with festivals. He never quite managed it. From 1972 until 1977, a bunch of hippies always used to turn up for solstice, and Eavis, tolerant man that he is, let them stay. In 1978, the police forced Eavis to have a festival. A group of hippie travellers had attempted to hold a festival in nearby Buttleigh Wood, and the police had tried to move them on. Faced with lanes full of hippie living vehicles, the police asked Eavis to host them, which he did, for three weeks. Hawkwind legend Nik Turner bought his own portable pyramid stage, and Kerr told him the event was 'better than 1971'. The pressure was mounting; so in 1979, Arabella persuaded

Eavis to have another go, to hold a second, but paying, Glastonbury Fayre, to raise money for the UNICEF Year of the Child. Peter Gabriel was top of the bill, performing for free. Eavis was much more involved in the planning and execution than he had been in 1971, and seems finally to have admitted to himself that he enjoyed it, so in 1981, the Glastonbury Festival of Contemporary Performing Arts as we know it today was held for the first time. A permanent Pyramid Stage was built on the site Andrew Kerr had dowsed. The real legacy of the 1971 Festival was that Eavis had found his core team: Bill Harkin, Tony Andrews, Arabella Churchill and Andrew Kerr.

Yeah, man. Andrew Kerr. Namaste.

I never saw Andrew when he wasn't smiling. The first time I met him was in 1997. Your Dad had been booked by Arabella to run a variety show in the Theatre and Circus Camping backstage restaurant. (Theatre and Circus remained Bella's domain until her death in 2007; the field where the Cabaret Tent is situated is now called 'Bella's Field' in her memory.) If you had paid £75 to get into the festival, you wouldn't have been able to see us; there is a whole festival behind the festival for performers and workers that ye olde punters never get to see; eateries and bars, each with a stage for bands to play. We were booked to 'curate' (dread word) various entertainments from five in the evening till two in the morning; a sort of 'best of' some of the Outer Reaches of the festival for other performers to see. But Glasto 1997 was a terribly wet and cold year, so wet and cold that I abandoned the big tent I was supposed to be sharing with Chas, and begged Bob, who was working in Green Crafts, to let me stay in his van, which he was kind enough to do. When Chas and I turned up at the venue, there was no stage as such, just a muddy corner in a wet marquee, with a pile of old pallets and a bit of tarp to put over them. Neither Chas nor I were terribly competent stage builders, so when a beautiful smiling man turned up and offered to help, it seemed like a small miracle. Twenty minutes later, the pallets had been turned into a sturdy stage, the grubby tarp spread over them took on the aspect of an expensive Persian carpet, and Chas and I were setting up our sound system.

'That was amazing,' I said to the smiling man. 'How did you learn to do that?' His smile widened, and he showed me his laminate. (At a big festival like Glastonbury, it's all about how good your laminate is.)

It read: *Andrew Kerr. Co-founder, Glastonbury Festival. Access all areas at all times.*

He said, 'I was the site manager from 1971 until 1987, darling.'

So that was how he learned. He was kind enough to stay and watch our sometimes patchy shows. After that, on all the eight or nine occasions we played Pilton, Andrew would turn up and cheer us on; every year, he'd come and sit round our fire in Green Performers Camping, and give us all the festival gossip; his day-job at the festival was to ride round the site in a Land Rover with Michael Eavis every morning, trouble shooting. Then at some point, he'd wander off with Chas to find Jonathan Cainer, the astrologer, and they'd do satsang together. It's a Premmie thing.

Andrew's memoirs, *Intolerably Hip*, give something of the flavour of a great man. He never could get away; he lived in Pilton till his death in 2011.

That Glastonbury Fayre provided a blueprint for the Glastonbury Festival is unsurprising. It also proved to be a blueprint for the wider free festival movement of the 1970s. Free festivals were not a sixties thing; they were very much a child of the 1970s. It takes a while for the British to unbutton.

In 1972, it looked like there wouldn't be a big free festival. This seemed like a bad idea to a couple of hippies living in a squatted commune in North London, Sid Rawle and William Ubique Dwyer. Ubi was an anarchist acid evangelist who had started taking the drug in Sydney, where he was buying it at first from the cops, who controlled Sydney's acid market. He ran a club for acidheads called The Cellar; when he swapped suppliers, he was busted, imprisoned for two years, and then deported to Ireland, where he had been born.

Ubi made his way across to London, where he became well known for standing at Speakers' Corner ranting about acid. The idea for the Windsor Free Festival came to him while tripping in Windsor Great Park, where he received a vision of 'a giant festival in the grandest park in the kingdom'. Well and good, were it not for the fact that Windsor Great Park belongs to the Queen; it is what you might call her back garden. Ubi became obsessed with the idea, and although Sid Rawle helped, it was always Ubi's vision. Ubi wrote to invite the Queen; and one of her officials wrote back to say, thanks, but no thanks, as she'd be in Balmoral. Ubi saw the fact that she replied at all as an endorsement for his plans. By his own account, he had 200,000 flyers printed advertising the event – he was, oddly, a civil servant by day, working at HM Stationery Office, and could get access to free copying.

There were three Windsor Free festivals in all, in 1972, '73 and '74. Estimates vary widely as to the attendance. According to some accounts, there were 700 people at the first one; according to others, as few as 150. The second one was bigger at around 1500. Or 8,000. Or 20,000, even. And at the third and final Windsor Free in 1974, there were ten or twelve or fifteen or twenty thousand people. The reason that figures vary so widely are perhaps explained by Andy Roberts' summation of the philosophy underlying the festival in his indispensable book *Albion's Dreaming*: 'LSD underpinned the creation of environments in which people could live unhindered by what they saw as petty laws and restrictions.' Everyone there was off their nut; it's not surprising that no one can come up with accurate figures.

No one has managed to come up with a definitive list of who played there either, but certainly the usual suspects, Gong, Hawkwind, the Pink Fairies, etc., put in an appearance at one stage or another over the three years the festival ran. So did some of the pub rock bands; not the Brinsleys for once, but Ace, Bees Make Honey and Ducks Deluxe all seem to have done a turn in one or other of the years. Also present were the excellent Global Village Trucking Company, who, like the Brinsleys, lived and played together, and who, like the Brinsleys, had real doubts about the music business, so much so, that they turned down several recording deals, in the spirit of the times. They would not have been paid: Ubi's slogan for the festivals was, 'Pay no rent.' Free food was provided for the first two years; in '74, to the horror of the purists, Ubi let food vendors onto the site. He also let God in. He always claimed that his permission to hold the festival at all came direct from the Big Guy. As Ubi said in one of his flyers, 'We want to bring God down out of the sky and put him where he belongs – in the human heart.'

And what better way to let God into your heart than through the ingestion of massive amounts of acid? And, in the spirit of the thing, acid could be had for nothing. In 1974, a gentleman in a suit turned up at the side of the stage with a briefcase containing thousands of microdots, each kept separate from the other by being stuck on strips of Sellotape. An announcement was made from the stage that this gentleman was giving acid away, and the crowd rushed the stage.

One of the few accurate accounts of the 1974 festival comes from drug charity Release. Their report makes for a delightful read. They said that 'the first wave of trippers inundated us fairly early. An inordinate number of them seemed to be "wankers", i.e. sexually repressed individuals liberated in a bizarre kind of way by the acid.' And anyone who has been around people tripping cannot help but sympathise with, 'worst of all were the juvenile philosophers who bellowed tedious cosmic observations about the state of the universe'. Someone had made a notice board with 'dropping times' to show what was the optimum time between dropping acid and your favourite band coming on, which would account nicely for no one being 100 per cent sure who was playing. The Divine Light Mission were also running a bad trip tent, where unfortunates who had overdone it were calmed down, or not, by premmies chanting satsang at them.

As Andy Roberts writes, 'Windsor 1974 seems to have had more acid casualties than any other free festival.' The problem seems to have been the strength of the free acid. It wasn't impure; it was very good. The brown acid which the organisers cautioned festival goers about was tested as being at 200μg, which was very high strength. Where it came from, we shall discover.

On 29 August the festival was broken up by 800 policemen invading the campsite, and they used brutal tactics to throw the festival attendees out of the Queen's garden. It never happened again; in 1975 Sid Rawle and Ubi Dwyer were imprisoned for attempting to promote that year's event; on their release, Ubi went back to Ireland, and Sid ... Sid did Watchfield.

There were a raft of newsletters and publications during and after the event, one of which was called *Maya*. On the masthead, it said, 'We shall celebrate with such fierce dancing the death of your institutions.' Which might neatly precis the seventies hippie philosophy, were it not for one of the strangest episodes in the counter-culture – the institutionalised free festival that was Watchfield.

Ubi and Sid worked hard to make Windsor '75 happen (that's why they were both imprisoned, after all) and the UK government worked hard to make sure it didn't. Lest Younger Readers doubt that the free festival movement was a strictly underground phenomenon, be in no doubt that it excited the British press very much. Whilst admittedly, August is the traditional silly season, when politics doesn't really happen, the Windsor Free Festival generated a lot of column inches. Hillsborough deniers the *Sun* even covered the police breaking up of Windsor with the front-page headline, 'Were The Police Too Tough?' *The Times* wrote that 'festivals ... are basically amiable gatherings which with a degree of tolerance it should be possible to accommodate'. The Home Secretary Roy Jenkins took a similar line, and over the winter of 1974/5, he initiated negotiations with the organisers of the People's Free Festival to find a mutually agreed site. He set up a committee, under the chairmanship of Rev. Steven Verney, Canon of the Chapel Royal in Windsor

Castle. Ubi wanted nothing to do with it, and so it was Sid Rawle, the self-styled 'King of the Hippies', who entered into discussions with Jenkins's department.

Sid told historian Andy Beckett that he thought Ubi was wrong not to talk with the government. The free festival movement was young, and Sid thought it would be lost if there was no follow-on from Windsor. He told Beckett, 'I've always seen these things as trade fairs for alternative lifestyles.' The committee offered Sid a few sites, but they eventually latched onto Watchfield, a disused Second World War aerodrome. It was bleak, and windswept, but Sid went for it because it was possible to see the White Horse of Uffington from the site, which he saw as a good omen. Although the Government didn't provide any funding, as such, it facilitated alcohol licensing and laid on telephones (pay phones in those days, of course), water and chemical toilets (which the festivalgoers boycotted in favour of digging their own latrines, feeling they were more environmentally friendly). A mere 350 police surrounded the site, them and much of the British press, between 23 and 31 of August 1975. I was at my first festival at that time, just up the road in Reading, and a few of the acts appeared at both; bands like Gong and Hawkwind, stalwarts and in some ways instigators of the free festival movement. Steve Winwood and Jim Capaldi from Traffic turned up and played a drunken set with Vivian Stanshall from the Bonzo Dog Doo-Dah Band. There was a taste, too, of things to come: pub rock R&B band The 101ers did a fiery set, fronted by Joe Strummer, who was about to be poached by the nascent Clash.

Andy Beckett's account of the festival in *When the Lights Went Out*, his history of *What Really Happened to Britain in the Seventies* is hard to better. It was a fairly heavy scene, man, as the Hells Angels turned up and took over the one remaining empty hanger as their headquarters. There wasn't much acid about, which perhaps contributed to the heavy atmosphere. But Ubi Dwyer would argue that the real reason that it was heavy was because it was, to a great extent, government sponsored, or, at least, government approved. In the end, the Government didn't see that they got much out of it, and Verney's committee never met again. Although there were a few more 'People's Free Festivals', it seemed as though the steam had gone out of them. Sid Rawle went off to be one of the founders of Tipi Valley and, subsequently, the Peace Convoy. The free festival movement kept going, however, and the heart and focus of the movement shifted to Stonehenge, both for the festivalgoers, and for the authorities determined to stop them.

According to old Chas Ambler's theory, contemporary boutique festivals have their roots not just in the free festival movement, but in the
so-called Albion Fairs, which ran across East Anglia in the years from
1972 until 1986. And because they were a very different beast, organised
along radically different lines, to different ends from the free festivals,
I'm going to finish festivalgoing for now with a quick look at them,
before heading back to the 'Henge for some stone hugging.

After spending a bit of time at the Glastonbury Fayre or the Windsor
Free, it would be easy to imagine that, in the rural 1970s, everyone who
moved to the countryside or even just went for the weekend was off their
tits on acid and dope all the time. Of course, this was not the case. Most
middle-class incomers to the countryside were more like Tom and Barbara
Good. They drank red wine, perhaps shared a joint at louche dinner
parties, and may have dropped a tab while they were at university, but
they weren't acid evangelists out to change humankind. What they wanted
– what all incomers want, then as now – was to be accepted as a local.

This is never going to happen. The desire of the counter-culture to
alter the consciousness of all humankind and thus to instigate a whole
new way of living based on authenticity and love and peace and coexist-
ence with Nature is much more likely to come to fruition than that
anyone born and bred in your new village is going to regard you with
anything other than deep suspicion. When I first moved to the deep
countryside in the late 1980s, I asked a builder who was doing some work
on the house what it took to be regarded as a local. 'Three generations
in the grave,' he said, but over time I've come to regard that as over-
optimistic. My neighbour Jan has been married to her husband John for
forty years. He was born in the house where they still live. But Jan is
from 'off', and old Presteigne residents have not forgotten. 'I'll never be
a local,' Jan said to me recently. She is from Llandrindod Wells, twenty
miles off.

From our front door to the border with England is a thirty-second
walk, but, make no mistake, Presteigne people see themselves as every
bit as Welsh as a rugby-playing leek-eating coalmining daffodil-breeding
male-voice chorister from the Rhondda, even though they sound like the
inhabitants of Ambridge. And quite right, too. If we have to have borders,
they have to be drawn somewhere. It just happens to be here. Borders
are two-dimensional; you are either one side or the other; it's a binary
thing. From here – or from off.

It must be remembered that the natives saw the incomers as essentially
mad. They had grown up in draughty old shit holes with no running

water and no electricity; until, after a lifetime of hard work, they managed to get enough money together to build a smart new bungalow nearer to the road with central heating, double glazing and wipe-clean surfaces. Then a bunch of loons from That London rock up, clap their hands in delight at the fact that the old house has no electricity and that water comes from a well in the garden, and offer you thirty grand for it. This hardly seems rational.

What incomers bring is energy and a romantic commitment to this place they have chosen to make their home. One of the things they (we) like very much are 'traditions'. We feel they connect us to a deep past (even though most rural traditions that have survived are often late-Victorian revivals). We want to join in. We want to be part of it. Over a few years, we realise that whatever it is, it would be much better if we just got our sleeves rolled up, formed a committee, and organised the thing ourselves. However innovative and joyous the East Anglian Fairs were, it must be faced that they sprang from incomers' romantic attachment to a place that they had staked their future on and a past that never was, and their passionate desire to demonstrate this attachment by getting things done.

A group of Suffolk incomers from London started meeting in local pubs in 1971. They set up The East Anglian Arts Trust, and decided to hold a 'medieval craft fair' as a fund-raiser for various artistic endeavours in the region, although over the years, the Fairs became their main focus. The first of the Faires was held at Barsham, south of Beccles, in 1972. It wasn't free – it cost 25p to get in. It was a legal event, as were all the Faires. What this meant in practice was that they ended up being lightly policed – there were two constables and an inspector at the first Barsham Faire. People did drop acid, and they did wander about smoking spliff, but they were primarily community events, which local people and their children came to take to their hearts. The medieval theme meant that there was no electricity supply (and therefore no amplified music), and that no vehicles were allowed on site. All products had to be made by stallholders (including food), and all stalls and structures hand built. Fair-goers were encouraged to attend in medieval costume, although this was loosely interpreted, as the focus was on participation rather than historical re-enactment. Medieval costume was seen as easy to do; you could turn up in rags, and count as a beggar.

It was so successful that it was held for four years, and introduced to the festival scene walk-about participatory theatre, kids events, jugglers, fire-eaters, and artisanal food stalls before there was such a thing as artisanal food. Barsham Faire became a victim of its own success; by the time of the Last Barsham Faire in 1976, thousands of people were turning up (including Chas, who first attended in 1974), and the loose structure of the organisation made it too much to keep getting together. There is a film which was made of the Last Faire, and I've included a link to it in the Appendix; have a look. Despite my Old Punk Rocker's aversion to all things folk, it does look great. No one is visibly tripped out, yet it still looks wild and anarchic. And if I've played down the druggy side, I apologise; the very very posh organisers are filmed smoking spliff and sharing a bong while chatting to camera; it was, after all, the seventies. Looking at the film, you can see Chas's point, I think: small stalls, small stages, actors wandering about making mischief, loads of kids and dogs, punters wandering around enjoying themselves dressed as medieval peasants.

The energy of Barsham did not die with the Faire; it turned into an organisation called 'Albion Fairs', which supported Barsham's successor events for the next ten years; often these fairs are known collectively as Albion Fairs, though this is perhaps to exaggerate the influence of the organisation. Bungay Horse Fair in particular is still spoken of with great affection; it combined a 'traditional' country fair with the hippie-ish energy of Barsham. A friend of mine who was there as a child with her hippie parents remembers it as a joyful time, joyful and quite scary.

One of the Faire's legacies was a book, called *Build Another Barsham* by Sandra Bell, published in 1976. It was written right at the end of the Barsham Faires, and is a 'How to' guide for putting together what we must now call 'boutique festivals'. It was used as a blueprint for many of the small to medium festivals of the 1980s, such as the late-lamented Elephant Fayre in Cornwall, now transmuted into the Port Eliot Literary Festival. This is from Sandra Bell's introduction:

> I suppose that if Barsham Faire stands for anything it is a belief in the creative energy of every individual, which is a good enough reason to hold a celebration. Anyone can do it on whatever scale they choose and with whatever modifications suit best. Barsham with its thousands is getting rather large for a small organisation to handle every year, but our hope is that other groups, villages, parishes, even streets will want to launch their own Faires. That is why we have written this small book to offer some practical information as to how we sorted out the problems.
>
> May the Greens of England echo to your rejoicing.

'I wish I'd gone now,' says Bob.

'Me too. But instead, we need to make our way to Stonehenge. Not for the festival, not yet. I'm festivalled out. I want a great big shit, a long long bath, and fourteen hours' sleep. I need time to recover. No, my friend, we're going to Stonehenge for the energy.'

'What energy?'

'Earth energy, man.'

Stonehenge Free Festival, although it started in 1974, seems to me an eighties phenomenon, and I will discuss it, and the reaction to it, in the final chapter. Stonehenge's spiritual dimension, however, is very much a thing of the late 1960s and 1970s. Astute Younger Readers will still be wondering 'Why *did* Andrew Kerr think it was important to site the Pyramid Stage on a ley line?' And what is a ley line anyway? What indeed?

Do not be fooled by those who tell you why Stonehenge was built, because nobody knows. Archaeologists have done wonders investigating the thing; they can date the stages of construction and use of the site between about 3100 BCE and 1600 BCE, which is the latest established prehistoric date of activity. As to how or why it was built, or by whom, or for what purpose, that is subject to archaeological theory; highly intelligent informed conjecture, but conjecture nonetheless. What is beyond dispute is that at sunset on the day of the Winter Solstice, and at sunrise on the day of the Summer Solstice, the sun is aligned with the Heel Stone, the embanked avenue and the five great 'Trilithons' that make up the central horseshoe. It would be a brave person who asserted that it had no astronomical significance. More than that, we cannot say. The presence of so many bones, and of bluestones from the Preseli Mountains in Pembrokeshire, which were probably held in regard by pre-historic healers, suggest that it might have been a Neolithic Lourdes, a place where people were taken in the hope of a cure. It's big, and would have taken a lot of building, so it's possibly also a site of communal significance and therefore religious ceremonies; possibly celebrating a coming together of culture after a time of strife. As I say, these are informed conjectures by archaeologists based on the evidence.

And then you have the other kind of conjectures, which are by Keith in the pub, and are based on the Interweb. Aliens, right, built it, like they built the Pyramids, because how else could you move the stones, and it was a star portal, etc., etc. But Keith, as I'm sure you're aware, isn't always right (#brexit), and I think we may discount him for now.

As a historian, though, there are things I can tell you; in particular how Stonehenge has been understood in the late twentieth century. Also,

I have hugged the stones at Stonehenge. I spent Winter Solstice there a few years back, in company of Panit Dave. I met official druids, neo-pagan hippie ladies *d'un certain âge*, King Arthur, and amused though sceptical security guards. It was one of the hippie ladies who insisted that I hug the stones, and that the point was to feel their energy.

I must say, try as I might, I was unable to feel any energy. Those who live life as Bob does, through action, might well be able to feel this energy. But as a pipe-sucking man of theory, while I was hugging the stones all I could think was, 'Energy? What energy? Kinetic? Thermal? Radiant? What? What sort of energy sits about in stones waiting to be hugged?'

Upon reflection, there are two possible answers. The first, and most tempting to me, is: no sort. There is no huggy energy in stones, however mysterious they may be. The second, and most tempting to neo-pagans, is potential energy. Potential energy is energy that is stored in a force field. There are three kinds of force fields: gravitational, electric, and magnetic. Magnetic and gravitational forces have both been invoked to explain the energy that is consequently stored in standing stones. The planet is subject to both gravitational and electromagnetic forces, after all. So why shouldn't it be stored in stones? And how is this energy transmitted to the stones? By ley lines. Ley lines carry energy, by virtue of being the lines of the planet's magnetic (or gravitational) fields. Stonehenge is located at the hub of several networks of ley lines, and is thus regarded as a vortex of energy, which sits in the stones until someone comes along and hugs them.

'This valley is thick with ley lines,' I say.

'Is it?'

'Blimey, yes. The Radnor Valley is where ley lines were discovered.'

Which is, up to a point at least, true. The ley lines of the Radnor Valley were the first to be analysed in detail. The discovery, or invention, of ley lines was made by a man called Alfred Watkins, who was very much not a hippie, and not even a late nineteenth-century dabbler in theosophical ideas. He was born in Hereford in 1855 to an on-the-up family, who came to own a large brewing concern, with thirty-five pubs, and a mill and commercial bakery that sold bread up into Birmingham. He started his career as an 'outrider'; travelling around Herefordshire on horseback, taking orders from pubs for the family beer, and then changed to working for the milling side, also travelling around the Hereford and Radnorshire countryside. During his travels, he became intimate with his native landscape. He was a pioneer of landscape photography, and he also wrote extensively on features of the countryside. He was what is known as a 'topographer', which is to say, someone who takes great notice of their locality, and records it. In 1921, he delivered a paper to the Woolshope Naturalists Club on ancient British trackways, because he thought he had noticed something in the landscape that no one had noticed before. This was that standing stones, stone crosses, the sites of old churches, burial mounds, barrows, etc., could all be shown to be aligned with one another. Watkins argued that Neolithic travellers had deliberately built their structures in a straight line in order to aid cross-country navigation. Retired from the family business, he set out to prove his thesis, and in 1925 he published the book for which he is best known (and which is still in print), *The Old Straight Track*.

It will help Younger Readers immensely at this point if they avail themselves of a copy of *The Old Straight Track*, which they should be able to find in most reputable charity bookshops. Turn to the second inserted section of photographs. The photo across the Radnor Valley to Old Radnor church is taken from outside The Rack, the house where I lived with my family from 1987 to 1990, and where I first met Bob. According to Watkins' calculations, the Radnor Valley (or the Walton Basin to archaeologists), is criss-crossed by ley lines, so that it comes to resemble a spider's web.

The Walton Basin (or the Radnor Valley to non-archaeologists) is an astounding place from an archaeological point of view, behind only Great Orme Head and the Preseli mountains as Neolithic sites of importance in Wales. Sadly, there is almost nothing to see, except four stones known wittily as 'The Four Stones' by the side of a back road in a farmer's field, and they're Bronze Age anyway. I once had to undergo a pagan divorce ceremony there.

The largest Neolithic wooden enclosure ever discovered in Europe was found by aerial photography in 1979, which first detected crop marks showing that something huge was going on in the Walton Basin. It is so vast that you could fit five Olympic stadiums into it; archaeologists estimate that it would have taken 3,300 tonnes of wood to build. That is far from all. There are a total of eight palisades and cursuses in the valley, often built on top of one another. No one has a clue what they were for. The largest was built round about the same time Stonehenge was started. No wonder the Radnor Valley is thick with ley lines. Presumably, the Radnor Valley is full of huggy energy.

Watkins didn't know these structures were there when he visited 'Radnor Vale' for his book. He did know (as anyone who has visited will know) that it is a very beautiful and haunted place. He describes the air as being like wine. Perhaps we are lucky that our remarkable Neolithic monuments have been lost from sight, other than by pilots, at certain times of the year, or the A44 would be like the A303, and Bob, far from being able to hide quietly in his wood, would be host to a permanent festival.

The wisdom of the ancients, and the British ancients in particular, have fascinated the Freaks since the late sixties, with the rediscovery of *The Old Straight Track* by writer and 'sacred geometer' John Michell. Trained as a surveyor, but with a vocation as a sage, Michell's best known and most influential book was his re-imagining of Watkins' work, *The View over Atlantis*, published in 1969. He was prolific, to say the least. He believed in, and wrote about, UFOs, the Divine Right of Kings (let the Queen run everything), Imperial Measurement (the thing your gran goes on about in her 'Why can't we have pounds and ounces like we used to' rants at Christmas), and the British-Israelite Movement (mad). He was a Platonist, a *Telegraph* reader and a screaming pot-head.

It was Michell who made Glastonbury sacred. *The View over Atlantis* argues that we live in the ruins of a global Neolithic civilisation. Watkins had found something much more remarkable than straight tracks. He had found the pathways by which the earth energy is transmitted, marked and mapped against the zodiac by our distant ancestors. According to Michell, 'From the rocks mountains and headlands a mysterious current once flowed down avenues of standing stones over mounds and earthworks towards some central hill dedicated to Mercury. Below the hill an instrument of solar generation produced the spark by which the current became animated and recoiled in a wave of fertility through the hidden veins of the land, urged on by the music and clamour of the rejoicing people.' These hidden veins, of course, are ley lines, and they can still be mapped by means of sacred geometry.

Many of them meet around Glastonbury; for Michell, Glastonbury was the 'New Jerusalem', the deliberately chosen successor site to Stonehenge, and he sets out to establish that it was laid out according to the principles of this lost geometry. The great ley line from Glastonbury Abbey to Stonehenge passes through Worthy Farm. Michell was a practitioner of dowsing for these lines of power, and some accounts have him doing the dowsing for the ideal spot for the Pyramid Stage, rather than Andrew Kerr. I like to imagine them doing it together, stoned as stoned can be, searching for the optimum energetics with bent bits of wire, staking out the place in triumph. There have been three Pyramid Stages so far; all on the same propitious site. Michell also calculated the dimensions for Bill Harkins' 1971 Pyramid Stage, using the principles of sacred geometry.

There have been a few scientists the Freaks took to heart, like James Lovelock (author of the Gaia hypothesis, which treats the Earth as a living organism), Nikola Tesla (pioneer of AC electrical transmission, now with an electric car builder named after him), Wilhelm Reich (subject of the Kate Bush song 'Cloudbusting'), Lyall Watson (subject of Cerrone's 1977 euro-disco hit 'Supernature'), Fritjof Capra (*The Tao of Physics*, worth a read) and Rupert Sheldrake (morphic resonance, don't ask) et al. Some are less credible than others, but all are interesting.

Michell was the Freaks' Newton, the one who did the sums. Unlike those of Sir Isaac, however, Michell's ideas cannot be argued with. This is not to do him down. He explicitly invoked traditions of 'knowledge' other than scientific. In the preface to *View over Atlantis* he writes: 'The important discoveries about the past have been made not so much through the present refined techniques of treasure hunting and grave robbing (i.e. archaeology) but through the intuition of those whose faith in poetry led them to a scientific truth.' Michell was a teaching fellow at the Temenos Academy, whose patron is HRH Charles, the Prince of Wales. Temenos runs courses in what it calls 'the Perennial Philosophy', and encourages students not just to learn philosophy, but to try to live it. The role of Temenos, as it sees itself, as indeed its patron sees it, is to balance these two kinds of knowledge: that of science and poetic, intuitive revelation. That is the part of Michell's ideas, the Blakean poetic vision of a great beneficent pattern laid over a sacred landscape, which you can't argue with. You should be able to find *The View over Atlantis* in the same charity bookshop where you got *The Old Straight Track*, and shelved next to it. I think the beauty of Michell's vision has much going for it, even if the bit you can argue with, the science bit, suggests it is probably nonsense.

My own hero in this place where science meets spirit was a trained scientist, turned theologian, turned historian, turned Catholic priest called Ivan Illich. He spoke at least ten languages, and set up a language school-cum-radical theological college in Cuernavaca in Mexico. His most famous book was called *De-Schooling Society*, from 1970, and it will change your head, man, if you let it. As you might imagine, it was highly influential in the radical 'De-schooling' movement of the 1970s. All his books are fascinating, if somewhat dense, and they'll all change your head. Like

Michell, he was a fierce critic of modernity, but unlike Michell, he put forward proposals for the elimination of alienation. Read Michell for fun, and Illich for real.

Briar pushes a wheelbarrow past the van door, and Bob throws a few logs onto the wood-burner.

'So were there already other hippie types here when you arrived, a sort of community?'

'Oh yes, we were by no means the first hippies. Like I say, first morning in Hay, I met Simon, for example, who I went to Istanbul with. He was living in a house with about half a dozen other hippie types. And on the other side of the hill, we quickly learned, were the Count and Countess de la Falaise, well-established in society. She was a model and one of her best mates Jean Shrimpton often used to come down, and Mick Jagger used to visit occasionally. There was quite a lot of what I used to call aristo heads, who had already moved down to this area, the Ormsby-Gores and so on – some of them I did know from London, in fact, but I met more of them down here than I did up in London.'

I say, 'When I arrived in Mid-Wales in 1976, there were lots of hippies. There was a place called Llangybi Common, which was a big park-up for the travellers' vans. Sid Rawle parked up there for a bit. And in Lampeter there was Smudge's health food shop, and because he had scales, you would go in and weigh out your drugs there. "All right, Smudge?" "Yeah, all right." "Can I borrow the scales?" Yeah, no problem."'

'I've done that more than once, obviously with some sort of, in an envelope or something, just walk into the shop, no conversation, just walk out leaving them a bit surprised and shocked. Well, when you want to weigh something, Post Offices are good for that now, because they've got very good little scales on the customer side of the counter.'

'You very quickly became part of the hippie scene down here, people were pleased to see you?'

'Oh yes, we were already part of it, weren't we, wherever we went we would be part of that scene.'

'But at this point, it seems to me really interesting in view of what we were talking about earlier about the importance of money. Because when you were with Vicki, you were well-to-do, well-heeled, Scotch of St James, all of that, a high-functioning hippie. And then you're in Afghanistan and all right, you got ripped off for the money but still, you're all right for a bob or two.'

'Oh yes, we certainly weren't starving, and we were having a good time, which seemed far more important than sitting in some fucking office trying to find some other way to fiddle the books, sort of thing.'

'But still – you might disagree – when you came here that was sort of an end to material prosperity, in a way. You've spoken to me about being here in the eighties and having no money and living off rabbits and stuff. You could have set up a jeweller's bench somewhere, started to employ people ... set up a hippie easterny jewellery empire ...'

'No, I couldn't; I didn't know how to make jewellery. That's when I learned to make jewellery, after my motorbike crash.'

'My point being that lots of hippies turned into Richard Branson. You know, they became quite well-to-do, and although they've kept some of the idealism lots of them ended up doing all right. And I'm not saying, "You're a cunt, you could have been rich, what's fucking wrong with you?" But it's like that wasn't the path you chose to take ...'

'Yeah, but there was a time when I was rich, or had all the advantages of being rich, when I was with Vicki, but I walked away from that. And I gave away half of 25 Belsize Square, which is quite a big house in Hampstead. I was half owner of it.'

'Signed it over when you split?'

'Signed it over. And I volunteered that, it wasn't Vicki making a fuss, it wasn't any of that. When I decided to leave I said to Vicki, "Have someone draw up a paper that I can sign, making over the house entirely to you." I didn't have to do that, I could have said, "I'm the fucking half-owner," but I'm just on my way.'

'But it's one of the things that interests me; you know, you didn't go, "I've got to have all that money, or life won't be worth living."'

'No, because I had had a taste of where I could buy anything I wanted. And I saw what having lots of money bought. It bought fucking toadies, basically. No day passed when there wasn't someone coming round because you'd got good drugs, nice place, wine, food, sound system, that sort of thing – no, money ain't the great panacea, is that the word?'

'I think it's a very good word.'

'And subsequently I have noticed, rather oddly, that nearly all the people I know who have topped themselves have been very rich. And that's got to tell you something, hasn't it?'

'So when you first came down here, how were you making a living?'

'When I was down here the first time, before I was doing the metal-work and everything? Well, we had stock from Afghanistan, lots of tasty stuff. We didn't really have space to store it in the tiny house we were living in, and we saw this really nice little shop by the clock tower in Hay. On the road as you're passing through Hay, you come over the bridge, turn right and go straight along, and just opposite the clock tower on that road, there are a couple of shops. One of them was empty, fifteen quid a week rent, nice little shop and so we opened it as a shop with our clothes and soft furnishings. And in the back of the shop, because we found it difficult to find hippie-type food, we had lentils, chickpeas, that sort of stuff. When we had the squat in Chalk Farm, we were a hundred yards away from one of the first wholefood wholesalers, so we knew them. So we'd go up to London every week, buy a few sacks of whatever, put the sacks in dustbins, and take them back to Hay. We had a pair of scales and scoops and bags there. And we bought a big range of herbs and spices in sweet jars as well. It was a loss-leader, because every hippie in the area would hear about it, and they might have been a bit snotty about going into the clothes shop, but when they were there buying their food they might think, "Oh, there's rather a nice dress there." So it worked like that.'

Wholefood, vegetarian food, natural food, were essential elements of the Nature Boys' philosophy. Sexauer's Health Food store in Santa Barbara and the Eutropheon Live Food Cafeteria in Los Angeles were central in importance to the birth of the Freaks. The Eutropheon was described as the place where 'the torch of the counter-culture was lit.'

Involuntary vegetarianism has persisted for most of the existence of the human race. When we were hunter-gatherers, the fruits of the gathering formed the bulk of our diet, as it was done by women, whilst successful hunting was something of a bonus, as the male hunters spent a lot of time doing their make-up and in ecstatic dance. With the advent of agriculture and animal husbandry, meat became more available, although not universally. In Britain in the nineteenth century, a labouring family might keep a pig, but the meat from that pig would have to last a year. Meat, for most of human history, was expensive and rare. The Vegetarian Society was formed in 1847 from various Christian groups who condemned the eating of meat for biblical reasons. This is the first recorded use of the word. Abstinence from meat, they argued, was a Christian duty, as it has always been in Hinduism and Buddhism. The Vegetarian Society had some success, and London had several popular vegetarian restaurants by the 1890s. The early twentieth century saw a shift as people like George Bernard Shaw, Aldous Huxley and Adolf Hitler choose vegetarianism because of their compassion for animals, rather than because of a religious impulse.

Now, although high moral considerations still apply for many vegetarians, it has become a lifestyle choice. A large preponderance of Death Metal Bands are vegetarian, for example. As many as 20 per cent of Younger Readers are currently vegetarian. (I made that up, but I bet it's true.) A lot of people are 'meat avoiders' – they will eat fish or chicken but not red meat, for example. A survey for the BBC in 2009 claimed that 10 per cent of Britons are 'meat reducers', people who are trying to eat less meat for health or (in my case) political reasons. I eat vegetarian once a week; in a sane society, I realise that I would eat meat once a week. But I come from a different world, a world of post-war home cooking, and vegetarian dishes other than Alphabetti Spaghetti on toast were not on offer. Something of a bible to contemporary English chefs, Dorothy Hartley's *Food in England*, published in 1954, has no mention at all of vegetarianism. *The Good Housekeeping Cookbook*, published in 1976, has a short paragraph at the end, which expresses concern about where proteins will be found in the diet. According to the Vegetarian Society's own figures, in 1945, at the end of the Second World War, there were 100,000 vegetarians in the UK; now there are somewhere in the order of three million – it is a very modern thing. I'm sure all vegetarians have their favourite story about elderly relatives getting it wrong. I once had lunch, in company with eight or nine other Arvon employees, with Helen Osborne, widow of the playwright John Osborne. She had cooked shepherd's pie.

'I know two of you are vegetarian,' she said. 'Do help yourselves to bread and cheese.'

The spread of vegetarianism is due, at least in part, to the Freaks. But the Freaks being the Freaks, many of them were not just vegetarians, but freaky vegetarians. Their diet was not merely vegetarian – but macrobiotic.

Macrobiotics insists that you should eat mostly wholemeal grain and pulses (and yes, we're talking brown rice and lentils here), together with fresh organic vegetables, all of which should be properly chewed before swallowing. It's an early twentieth-century idea from Japan, where Zen Macrobiotics was used as a healing practice. The man who came up with the idea was called Sagen Ishizuka, known to his patients as 'the vegetable doctor'. The aim of the macrobiotic diet was to bring harmony to the body, by balancing yin and yang energy in the body. What energy, you ask? Chi energy, I answer.

Macrobiotics is not so much moral or political or even ethical, as personal. It is for your health, for your own good. It was the ideal diet for a world which was moving away from ideas of salvation in the next world, to notions of therapeutic self-improvement in this.

In 1966, there was pretty much only one person in Britain who followed the macrobiotic diet, a Japanese experimental artist named Yoko Ono. Yoko belonged to a performance art group called Fluxus, and if you want to annoy your dad, tell him, 'Lennon broke up Fluxus, man.' Yoko turned John macrobiotic, a diet he stuck to up until his assassination in 1980.

All well and good. But what were John and Yoko actually to eat? Step up young American entrepreneur and macrobiotic evangelist, Craig Sams, who arrived in London in 1966, keen to spread the good wholesome news.

Like Scott Nearing, Craig Sams had attended the Wharton School of Business at the University of Philadelphia, which is beginning to look to me like a fairly funky place to go if you want to study business. Sams was a Freak, and his first gig in London was selling home-prepared macrobiotic food through the snack bar at the UFO club in Tottenham Court Road. The Freaks chewed long and hard while Pink Floyd, the Soft Machine and the Crazy World of Arthur Brown all played. He opened Seed in 1968, in the basement of the Gloucester Hotel on Westbourne Terrace, which was hailed as Europe's first macrobiotic restaurant. Regular customers included not just John Lennon and Yoko Ono, but Marc Bolan, who met his collaborator in T. Rex, Micky Finn, in the restaurant. John and Yoko's presence was enough to ensure that Seed became achingly trendy. As the actor Terence Stamp said, 'It was a cool place to hang out for those who were health conscious.' It was a little bit of Hollywood come to West London.

Seed took up two rooms. One had cushions on the floor set around tables made out of the reels that mains electrical cable was wound around, whilst in the second room, there was a tent thing hanging from the ceiling and normal square wooden tables with bentwood chairs. If I'd been forced to go, I'd want to sit in one of the chairs while eating beans, rather than the cushions, wouldn't you? There was always taped music, mostly psychedelic rock, which would have added to the farty ambiance.

The basic dish (called 'Tomorrow's You') was rice and vegetables for 4 shillings, but there were specials too, which you could tell apart by the size of the earthenware bowl they were served in. Top of the range was the 'Heavy Special' for 10 bob, which was brown rice and vegetables and a choice from two other portions which might include vegetable tempura, a bean dish, falafel, tabbouleh or hummus. In the spirit of the age, for a while Seed provided a free meal of brown rice and vegetables plus a cup of kukicha, and I don't even want to know what that is.

Sams and his brother Greg were just getting going. In 1969 they opened Ceres Grain Shop in All Saints Road, Notting Hill, from where they decided to set up a wholefood wholesale business as well, called Harmony. The Harmony trademark showed a yin-yang symbol with two stylised leaves on the upward side and two roots on the downward side. Their big seller was Harmony Whole Rice in 2 pound paper bags. So successful were they that they moved Ceres Grain Shop and Harmony to much larger premises on the Portobello Road, where Bob and Monica bought their rice and lentils wholesale to sell on in Hay.

The Sams brothers worked with Andrew Kerr and Bella Churchill, and were the only food suppliers at Glastonbury Fayre in 1971. If you hadn't bought your own grub, all the food you could get was macrobiotic – muesli, brown rice, red bean stew, porridge and unleavened bread with tahini or miso spread, unless you could somehow blag your way into the farmhouse and eat bacon and eggs with Farmer Eavis. The lavatories at Glastonbury Fayre were no more than planks over holes dug in the ground, separated into cubicles by sacking, and they must have seen a lot of trade.

Also in 1971 the Sams founded *Seed: The Journal of Organic Living*, edited by their father. It ran until 1977, and it's great. In the Appendix, there's a link to a website where you can read all the issues, and having read this far, in this book, you should now be equipped to have a look. They interviewed rock stars and writers and actors who were following the macrobiotic lifestyle. Terence Stamp was on the cover of issue No. 2 in 1971; in his interview he says: 'My mother's not much into grains. She's very Leo and into meat and potatoes,' which explains a lot to me, as I have Leo rising, yeah? As well as articles extolling the benefits of the macrobiotic diet (such as how macrobiotics might develop your sixth sense) and natural healing (such as how to do acupuncture on a baby's thumb) they were also keen on Freak Science, carrying long reviews of Lyall Watson's *Supernature* (which attempted to offer biological explanations for supernatural phenomena) and a series of articles by John Michell attacking Darwinism.

Despite the magazine folding in 1977, Harmony Foods is still with us; its 'Whole Earth' peanut butter is the second top selling brand in the UK. In 1991 Craig Sams and his wife Josephine Fairley were travelling in Africa looking for organic peanuts for the peanut butter. They didn't find any that passed their stringent tests, but they did find organic growers producing cocoa beans. So they founded Green & Black's chocolate. Sams says, 'People ask how we managed to create a new confectionery brand in a sector where there have been no new brands in decades and I often think it's because of being macrobiotic.' In 2005, the couple sold Green & Black's to Cadbury for twenty million pounds; Sams is still president of the company, and tries to ensure it stays true to its macrobiotic roots. Not bad going for a Freak from Nebraska – Sams is the great unsung hippie entrepreneur, and the man who taught the Freaks to eat well, if sometimes unappetisingly.

As I mentioned in passing earlier, macrobiotic diets aim to bring into harmony the yin and yang forces in your chi energy. This is the 'life energy', an idea which bears a family resemblance to the earth energy carried in ley lines. Is there therefore a bodily equivalent of ley lines? Most certainly there is. They are called body meridians.

They are energy channels 'transporting' the chi throughout your body. If there are blockages in your body meridians, you are fucked, basically. Your chakras are in danger of becoming seriously unbalanced, and it'll be off to a gong chakra rebalancing workshop for you before you can say, *Om Namah Shivaya*. According to the many and various strands of energy therapy, of which acupuncture is the best known, all health problems, whether physical, mental or spiritual, can be traced to energy blockages in the body meridians. Energy blockages can be the result of stress, an injury or trauma, or bad living habits such as poor diet, addictions and lack of exercise, all of which I have in spades. The chi energy trying to crawl through my body meridians must feel like motorists waiting to get through the Dartford Tunnel on a Bank Holiday Friday night. Luckily for me, there is no actual medical evidence for body meridians.

But the Freaks wanted no part of industrialised medicine. The Nature Boys, Edmund Bordeaux Szekely, and Craig Sams all emphasised what is now taken as axiomatic: a vegetable-based diet, no smoking, not too much booze, clean water and lots of fresh air and mild exercise are going to do you no end of good. All this, science confirms.

But the therapies, the homeopathy, the crystal healing, the reiki, the acupuncture, etc., are good things precisely *because* they are un-scientific, because they are poetic and intuitive. The industrialisation of the pharmaceutical industry coincides with the medicalisation of health. Medicine started working, sometime in the nineteenth century, because it had discovered science. It had become evidence based. And medical evidence is uptight, phallocentric and controlled by Big Pharma. Fuck 'em. Our bodies are not all that we are.

Sometimes this demand for non-medicalised health is good; other times less so. Chas Ambler was a big believer in alternative therapies and post-Sams diets, and he felt that by following these regimes, he had managed to mask the pain from his cancer, thus delaying his diagnosis until it was too late. In the end, he became sceptical of non-morphine-based medicine. He did like a bit of cannabis oil rubbed on his temples, though, right up to the end. The person who had gifted him the oil is an evangelist for the stuff. In every sense an evangelist.

This person told me, 'It's what was in myrrh, Ian. That's why the Wise Men gave it as a gift. It's the anointing oil.'

The most serious case of how Freak Science manages to ignore evidence is vaccination. Vaccination works, and is a good thing, but this has not prevented many Freaks of whatever stripe from stopping their children getting vaccinated. In 2016, there was an outbreak of measles at the Glastonbury Festival amongst the children of gullible hippies. You can have hours of fun Googling the reasons why hippie parents didn't want their kids vaccinated, but as you trawl through millions of pages of [dis]information, don't forget that they are *all* bollocks. If *you* have hippie parents, please check that your vaccinations are up to date.

I will get letters for this.

The death of God, as we have seen, did not mean the end of faith. New Age therapies are faith-based in many ways (as well as, I admit, commonsensical in their approach to nutrition and exercise.) Freak Science's faith in 'energy' might be in many ways anti-scientific, but it is explicable.

Models of consciousness have often followed scientific and techno-logical development. In the early seventeenth century, craftsmen learned how to make beautiful automata, and philosophers thought the universe was clockwork in its workings. Alexander Graham Bell invented the first practical telephone in 1876, and early-twentieth-century psychologists modelled the working of the brain on telephone switchboards. Now, according to many neuro-physiologists, the brain is like a computer. But consciousness and gravity are the two great mysteries of science, and if scientists are honest, they will tell you they don't have a clue (or, rather, a few clues, none of which add up to a solution). This does not stop people from modelling what they don't know onto the things they do know. In the century that came up with radio, and radioactivity, and where $E=MC^2$ is seen as *the* popular icon of scientific thought, perhaps it is unsurprising that Freak Science latched onto the idea of occult vibrating energetic frequencies as its big idea, even if they are undetectable by actual sciencey science.

After all, old Tim Leary's mantra, 'Turn on, Tune in, Drop out', implies that humans are living radios, that we can flick the on switch with LSD, and tune into frequencies where we will detect subtle vibrations. If you did this, you would be able to detect bad vibes or good vibes. The greatest pop single ever, 'Good Vibrations', by Brian Wilson and the Beach Boys, runs with this image. And if Brian was picking up good vibrations, who am I to say he was wrong?

'What else, Bob?' I ask. 'What else were you up to when you got down here?'

He seems to have given up on gardening for the day. I think he likes watching Briar do it, though. He reaches for his tin.

'As well as the shop, I also had this job as warden of a camp on a farm owned by the people we were renting Bryn Ceinon from, our next-door neighbours. Monica's dad was the chief youth officer north of the river in London, and he wanted to bring a load of kids down for a bit of adventure. So I'd hired a lorry in London to take all the camping equipment down to the farm. Now I'd heard, and Pete Mustill had heard, that there was an American in London paying really top dollar for any upright piano. So myself and Pete Mustill, we whipped round everyone we knew in the Hay area, and got four upright pianos. Loaded them on to this lorry, because I'd got to get the lorry back to London and I thought if we could make a few bob on this, great. Get to London, go to David Black's antique shop on Princedale Road, and he says, "He's gone" – the geezer who's buying these pianos. So we've got this lorry which we've got to take back to wherever it came from, and now we've got to lose these pianos. And we only had a couple of hours to do it in, so it's a problem. So we went down Charles Road, by St Giles's Hospital, down Hampton Road area, a long, straight, slightly uphill road, running more or less parallel to Ladbroke Grove, but a couple of streets west. So I said to Pete, "Get in the back, open up the doors and I'll accelerate really fast, and when I do, you shove a piano out." And we did that, we emptied them all out while driving along the road, which was a bit cheeky, I know. If there had been YouTube, we'd have gone viral.

'Anyway, here we are, down in Bryn Ceinon. There was myself and Monica, Pete and Titi, and my brother Sandy. And it's a nice sunny day, when unexpectedly down the track comes these three Volvo cars with Dutch plates on, identical model Volvos, each with a driver in it and no one else. So alarm bells start ringing, and I think, "This is odd." I know the driver of the first car, Titi's brother Pieter. I know him to be a bit of a bad boy, into this and that, especially dodgy motors. So I said, "Hello, Piet, what's happening, mate?" and he said, "Oh, it's me and my friends, we're just on a tour." I said something to the effect of, "Don't give me that shit, because if three mates are on a tour they go in one car, they don't take a car each. I think you're up to something quite heavy, and either I'm part of it or I'm not part of it. And as I think you're lying to me, I don't want to be involved in something I'm not part of, so have a cup of tea and fuck off." That's more or less how the conversation went verbatim. So they had a cup of tea and fucked off.

'That evening Monica and I went over to a friend's place by Talgarth for a meal, and we were on our way home when we meet one of these Volvos on the hill. It's a very narrow road so we slowed up the motor, wound down the window for a chat like they do round here. It's Dutch Pieter, Pete Mustill and my brother in this motor. I ask them what they're doing. So Pieter owns up. "We were delivering a huge amount of hash, the boots of all the motors were full of hash; we delivered it to a place in Wiltshire. The hash came in from Pakistan through Shannon Airport, and then from Cork to Swansea with the IRA's say-so, and now we're going to go back and rip a load of it off."

'I looked at Pete Mustill and say, "I'm surprised you're going along with this, Peter; you were always a bit goody-goody" – Sandy I knew wasn't above such things, as he and I had done similar things in the past. And I said to the Dutch guy, "What's the name of the village?" And he told me, and I knew a geezer who lived there who I knew was one of Howard Marks's crew. I knew this was David Talbot. Anyway, so Pete Mustill bows out.'

'Pete was telling me the other day he's still grateful you talked him out of it.'

'So he fucking should be. So he gets out, and Sandy and Dutch Pieter are off, but I said to Sandy very distinctly, "Right, you're doing this, don't bring it back to my place, because since I can figure it out, the people at the other end can figure out the same thing in reverse." Sandy, being the sort of person he was, did in fact bring it back to our place the next day. I said, "I don't want it here, man. There are going to be repercussions, and I certainly don't want to be involved."'

'So they went to Wiltshire and nicked back the dope they'd just delivered?'

'Yeah, a hundredweight of dope or whatever, lots of dope. So I knew there would be repercussions, and the next night, Dutch Piet and Sandy are still there. Pete Mustill and Titi had found somewhere else to be. To get to our place you had to go round a big field, more than half a mile on a very bad track, so you could hear motors that were coming for several minutes before they got to you. People used to go up there for a shag. Eleven thirty, twelve at night it's shaggers, that's no problem, but one o'clock, that's not shaggers. About one o'clock in the night, I heard motors coming down the track. So I said, "This is trouble." So I gave an old rifle and a shotgun to Sandy and Pieter, sent them upstairs. I said to them, "You go up there, and cover me." Anyway, one o'clock there's a knock on the door …'

'Presumably Sandy and Piet hadn't knocked on their door when they took the stuff …'

'They took it from a lock-up garage, and they weren't seen doing it. But who else knew it was there to be nicked? So I opened the door, and there were two Irish geezers standing there, both with their hands in their pockets. There's a small porch, so my boys couldn't see them. I walked between them across the yard to a pile of logs, picked up a log, split it and walked back with axe in hand, and one of the Irish geezers flashed his coat open and showed me an automatic machine pistol, he didn't point it at me but just let me know he'd got it. The other one is standing with his hands in his pockets, suggestively, making out like he might have a gun in his pocket too. I said, "Why are you here, what are you after?" and he said, "We're looking for this Dutch Pieter," and I says "There's no one else here." A tense moment, and then we heard the double click of a pair of fucking shotgun hammers being pulled back and the very definite snick as the rifle bolt is pushed forward. Anyone who knows anything about guns would recognise what those sounds were, because we were only from about here to that tree away. The Irish guy had a real sense of humour. After a tense pause, he said, "Oh well, if there's no one else here, we'll be off," and that was it.

'Later the same day or a day or two later, they found out where my mother lived down in Margate and had her against the wall with a gun at her head, demanding to know where Sandy was. She said she didn't know, although the hash was, in fact, stashed in her deep freeze. Dutch Pieter had a small coaster ship he had just purchased, and when he got back to Amsterdam and went to his boat, these Irish guys are waiting for him. They have got a mounted machine gun on the deck, not the sort you hold, one of the ones you sit behind, and they pointed it at anyone who came up, and these Irish guys take Pieter for a tour of this boat, and show him the explosive charges they've rigged up all over it, and put a proposition to him that he signs over every fucking thing that he owns, which was quite a lot. He had substantial holdings about the place, motors and property as well as the boat. Sign it over, they said, or we send you out for a ride on your boat and you'll make a dramatic exit from this world. So he did exactly as they suggested.

'I went to visit the place I knew in the Maida Vale area which Graham Plinston and Howard Marks were using as a bit of a base. This was a bit iffy, because you were going into the camp of people who think that you had robbed them considerably. I told them the whole story. Of course they knew that Sandy was involved, or the IRA wouldn't have gone down to see my mum. And I straightened it with Graham and Mr Marks, and said I'd get whatever Sandy hadn't sold back from him, which I did, and I told them I don't want anyone else going down there bothering my mum, as you would.'

'So was it the Marks guys who'd been and troubled your mum or was it the IRA?'

'It was the IRA – the geezer was at the time the most or second-most wanted man in the British Isles, geezer called James McCann. I think he was number two on the Most Wanted.'

The Irish Republican Army were a real and present danger when I was growing up. It wasn't just that we saw the battles being fought on the streets of Belfast and Londonderry on TV every night, although we did. It was the fact that they brought their campaign so successfully to Great Britain. For example; on 5 October 1974, in Guildford, where my parents had met, where I was born, and where my grandparents and uncles and aunties and cousins still lived, the IRA exploded bombs in the Seven Stars and the Horse and Groom pubs. Five people were killed, and sixty-five wounded; none of them my family, but neighbours and workmates and friends of friends. On 21 November 1974, the IRA planted bombs in the Mulberry Bush and Tavern in the Town pubs in Birmingham, killing twenty-one and wounding 182. Years later, I helped a young man write his father's story of being wounded that night, as part of his attempt to understand the trauma that had scarred his father's life. In the middle of the night of 12 October 1984, I was at home in Brighton looking after my daughter while my wife was away on a business trip, when I heard a 'whump'. I got out of bed and went outside, and looked towards the seafront, where I could see a glow and smoke rising in the sky. The IRA had exploded a bomb at the main Tory Party Conference hotel, the

Grand. Five people were killed, and thirty-one were injured. The IRA weren't bogeys – they were all too real. Bob was right to be alarmed at their appearance at his door. Nor were they any kind of Freaks. The 'counter-culture' didn't have much traction in Northern Ireland until the advent of punk. Both sides, Republican and Nationalist, wanted to show themselves as being worthy of political power; both sides kept their hair short (for the seventies!), and wore suits and ties. The conflict in Northern Ireland was taken much too seriously for anyone to be dropping acid and throwing the *I Ching*.

Nor were the Palestinian Liberation Organisation pissing about. The world watched terrified as PLO allies Black September kidnapped, held to ransom and subsequently killed eleven Israeli athletes at the Olympic Games in Munich, in 1972. The seventies felt like dangerous times. But there *were* Freak terrorists, though usually with less well-defined political purpose than the IRA or the PLO. In Germany, there was the Red Army Faction, the so-called Baader-Meinhof gang; in the States there was the Weather Underground, amongst others: and in good old Blighty, there was the Angry Brigade.

Between May 1970 and August 1971, the Angries carried out a series of twenty-five bombings, in which no one was killed and only one person was slightly injured. Amongst others, they bombed banks, Conservative Party offices, the Italian Trade Centre, and the 1970 Miss World competition (a small bomb under a BBC van outside the Albert Hall the day before transmission; the event itself was disrupted by sisters from the Women's Movement who threw bags of flour at presenter Bob Hope). They often delivered 'communiqués' after their activities, printed using an old John Bull printing kit. This is Communiqué 1, outlining a list of potential targets:

FASCISM & OPPRESSION

WILL BE SMASHED

EMBASSIES (SPANISH EMBASSY MACHINE GUNNED THURSDAY)

HIGH PIGS

SPECTACLES

JUDGES

PROPERTY

'Spectacles' doesn't mean goggles, but spectacles in a Situationist sense. Miss World 1970 was certainly one of these. Communiqué 6 gives an idea of their aims and ideology:

OUR attack is violent . . .

Our violence is organised.

The question is not whether the revolution will be violent. Organised militant struggle and organised terrorism go side by side. These are the tactics of the revolutionary class movement. Where two or three revolutionaries use organised violence to attack the class system . . . there is the Angry Brigade.

Revolutionaries all over England are already using the name to publicise their attacks on the system.

No revolution was ever won without violence.

Just as the structures and programmes of a new revolutionary society must be incorporated into every organised base at every point in the struggle, so must organised violence accompany every point of the struggle until the armed revolutionary working class overthrows the capitalist system.

Communiqué 6

The Angry Brigade

Communiqué 9 demonstrates their widening target list:

WE are getting closer.

We are slowly destroying the long tentacles of the oppressive State machine . . .

secret files in the universities

work study in the factories

the census at home

social security files

computers

TV

Giro passports

work permits

insurance cards.

Bureaucracy and technology used against the people . . .

to speed up our work

to slow down our minds and actions

to obliterate the truth.

Police computers cannot tell the truth. They just record our 'crimes'. The pig murders go unrecorded. Stephen McCarthy, Peter Savva, David Owale – The murder of these brothers is not written on any secret card.

We will avenge our brothers.

If they murder another brother or sister, pig blood will flow in the streets.

168 explosions last year. Hundreds of threatening telephone calls to government, bosses, leaders.

The AB is the man or woman sitting next to you. They have guns in their pockets and anger in their minds.

We are getting closer.

Off the system and its property.

Power to the people.

And Communiqué 13 still stands, in my view, as one of the pithiest condemnations of the capitalist system:

Capitalism is a vicious circle.

People's sweat and blood is used and exploited. They make us produce shit ... they give us next to nothing while their class pockets huge profits ... the ruling class ...

Then, when we put the overalls aside, we clean up the muck from our faces and we take the boring bus or train home and they suddenly transform us into consumers.

In other words, when we are not working they make us buy the same shit we produced. The miserable wage packet they gave us they make us spend on useless food, on machines specially designed to break down, and on houses we know look and feel like prisons.

Prisons we helped build. And paid (more specifically promised to pay) over the next twenty years for we never have enough dough to pay for a house or a car or anything for that matter – they have to exploit us even more by making us pay interest for them. We build the prisons and then we live in them. We produce shit and then we eat it.

Producers of shit. Consumers of shit.

The Angry Brigade's most spectacular activity was the bombing of Robert Carr's house, in January 1971. (As Angry Brigade member John Barker said in 2007, 'The AB was, ironically, spectacular, given that I and others were much influenced by Guy Debord's *The Society of the Spectacle*.') Robert Carr was the Secretary of State for Employment, and was negotiating at that time with the trade unions over the controversial Industrial Relations Act. This made him a legitimate target in the view of the Angry Brigade. He was at home in Hertfordshire with his wife and thirteen-year-old daughter when the two bombs exploded, blowing in windows and the front door. The Government started to take the Angries seriously. The Bomb Squad (now known as the Anti-Terrorist Unit) was set up in January 1971 in order to catch them; the IRA didn't start their GB bombing campaign till 1973.

Who were the Angry Brigade? No one is entirely sure. Five people were eventually convicted of Angry Brigade activities, and it's a fair bet that all five were guilty to a greater or a lesser extent. But there were others, and bombings continued after the convictions. As the Angries themselves stated in Communiqué 7, THEY COULD NOT JAIL US FOR WE DID NOT EXIST. There was no central organisation, no committee, no leader. Anyone who acted in the name of revolutionary libertarian socialism could and did claim to be part of the Angry Brigade; groups were claiming the Angry Brigade mantle as late as 1984.

In June 1971, when the home of William Batty, a director of the Ford plant at Dagenham, was damaged by an Angry Brigade bomb, the *Daily Telegraph* reported that the Metropolitan Police Commissioner Sir John Waldron had been instructed to 'smash the Angry Brigade'. The raids on squats, communes and bookshops that followed were a direct attack on the counter-culture. They culminated in a raid on 359 Amhurst Road, in what people who live there today call Stoke Newington, but in those days was simply Hackney.

The police found more than sixty rounds of ammunition, a Browning revolver, a Sten gun, and a polythene bag stuffed with thirty-three sticks of gelignite, together with detonators. They also found the John Bull children's printing set used to print the Communiqués. Eight people were arrested over the course of a few days including Anna Mendelson, Hilary Creek, Jim Greenfield and John Barker. Barker and Greenfield, you might remember, had gone to Paris to join in with the student uprisings of 1968. Mendelson and Creek had been students together at Essex University, rightly regarded as a hot bed of left-wing student activism. They were known collectively as 'The Stoke Newington Eight'. The Old Bailey trial, where Mendelson, Creek and Barker defended themselves, and which lasted from May to December in 1972, demonstrated that the arsenal at Amhurst Road had been planted by the police. John Barker said in a book review he wrote in 2007 that 'It is not so disrespectful to see the trial as one of the few achievements of the AB and that this was so because it was no longer clandestine.'

Their defence was highly effective, managing to cast serious doubt on most police evidence against them. Government forensics and fingerprinting experts found their professional credibility brought seriously into doubt. Barker, Greenfield, Creek and Mendelson all received ten-year sentences, reduced from fifteen after pleas of clemency from the jury, for 'conspiring to cause explosions likely to endanger life or cause serious injury to property'. The other four defendants were acquitted.

Why were they jailed in spite of being fitted up? Because they were certainly responsible for some of the bombings, and for the production of the communiqués. As Barker says, 'In my case, the police framed a guilty man.' And less you doubt that they were proper Freaks (who, after all, are all about Peace 'n' Love, yeah?), Barker also said, 'We never took it seriously anyway: what I mean is that like many people then and now we smoked a lot of dope and spent a lot of time having a good time.'

But wait, I hear you cry. Four people were convicted at the Stoke Newington Eight Trial? But you said that five people were convicted for involvement with the Angry Brigade! Yes indeed. The fifth was Jake Prescott, a burglar and heroin addict from Fife, who had got mixed up in the politics of the Angry Brigade, and who had already been sentenced to fifteen years in November 1971 for his part in the Carr bombing, although this was later reduced to ten at the Old Bailey trial to keep his sentence in line with the other defendants. He too had been convicted of conspiracy, because the only charge that could be made to stick was that he had addressed three of the envelopes that the communiqués were sent in. Jake said that he had no idea that the contents of the envelopes were claims of responsibility for the attack on Robert Carr's house.

Put into an orphanage at seven, convicted of stealing a box of paints aged eleven, and a drug addict and burglar by the time he was in his teens, Jake saw himself as a professional criminal. In the mid sixties, when he was sent to Albany Prison on the Isle of Wight for possession of a firearm, he discovered the revolutionary politics of the black civil rights movement. He told the *Observer* in 2002: 'I took it all to heart. I had no objectivity. So when I got out of jail I thought, "London here I come." I wanted to live it.'

In Albany, he'd met Ian Purdie, an avowed anarchist who was serving nine months for throwing a petrol bomb at an army recruitment office. Through Purdie he was introduced to a commune in Grosvenor Avenue, Islington, where Barker, Mendelson, Creek and Greenfield were living before moving to Amhurst Road.

As it happens, I lived in a squat on Grosvenor Avenue in the early 2000s. I also met, and liked very much, Jake Prescott. I spent New Year's Eve 2001 at the house Jake shared with his wife and children in Hackney.

He was happy to talk to me about what had happened. While all around us whooped and sang 'Auld Lang Syne', Jake and I, the only two teetotallers in the place, sat and shared a spliff.

'Make noo mistake, Ian. I was a fucking criminal. I'd always been a criminal. I'd planted bombs at a man's hoose while he was inside with his family. If that's not criminal, I don't know what is.'

When he got out of prison, Jake wrote to Robert Carr apologising for his involvement. By that time Lord Carr of Hadley, he invited Jake to meet him at the House of Lords, where he accepted the apology over tea. Jake said that was the moment he started to turn it around. He found a job at a citizens' advice bureau in Sheffield and trained in employment law. When I met him, he was a stay-at- home dad, while his wife worked as a high-ranking official for Hackney Council. He told me in so many words what he'd go on to tell the *Observer* in the 2002 interview: 'As the only working-class member, I was not surprised to be the first in and last out of prison. When I look back on it, I was the one who was angry and the people I met were more like the Slightly Cross Brigade.'

Bob doesn't like thinking about politics, so I guide him back onto safer territory.

'Didn't you come across that very same stash of dope in Afghanistan?'

'Yeah. Graham Plinston rented the Swedish legation building in Kabul, because the Swedish legation had fucked off. It was a nice bungalow type place, with a big three-car garage, because the diplomats would have needed cars. There was room to have three big motors in there, and plenty of room to get round them all, and workshop space and benches. Graham Plinston said in a comment I'll never forget, "I wouldn't show this to everyone, but have a look at this." He opened the door of this garage and the whole floor was four inches deep in round "flying saucers" of hash. It was a lot of fucking hash. It was because of that moment of trust – you're really putting yourself on the line showing someone something like that in your own house – that when Dutch Pieter and Sandy did this scam, I thought, "No, I'm not going to be part of robbing this." I mean, I had been robbing people years before, but there was a certain level of trust and honour that comes into it. Sounds like bullshit, but it's true. It's something that used to be far more prevalent in the old days.'

'So did you like Howard Marks? Was he, in fact, Mr Nice?'

'The only time I recall meeting him was at that Maida Vale, St John's Wood place. I never had any dealings with him. Graham I knew pretty well, he was in Kabul for quite a long time. The first time I saw him, me and Monica were just outside Kandahar, in the lorry heading towards Kabul, and this geezer who turned out to be Graham was in a taxi with this really dodgy-looking Afghan geezer. Me and Monica knew exactly what the situation was, so we cracked up laughing as we tried to pass the taxi. That was the first time we saw him, but we subsequently met him in Kabul.

'Graham had rented a house up by Monaughty [a house local to Presteigne where, it is reputed, the sixteenth-century magician and spy Dr John Dee was born] and a geezer who was also out in Afghanistan, Skip Ehrlich, over from Los Angeles, he wasn't actually a Hell's Angel but that sort of thing, he looked after Graham's wife Mandy while Graham was off running around the world being Howard Marks's lieutenant. Skip and Mandy were living at Monaughty. So I have this long-running link with Graham.'

'I was talking to Mustill the other day, and he told me the story about the Diamond Roadster, the bike he designed.'

'I remember the Diamond Roadster – that was something he did with Mark Williams, though.'

'He claims that you ended up with the one remaining prototype.'

'Possibly, yeah.'

'Wonder if it's here?'

'No. I know where it is, where it's gone. It was an all right little bike.'

'I remember you telling me about the first time you met Mark Williams, as well.'

'Oh yeah, it was in Sue Miles's bed.'

'Where I think he was quite disappointed to find you?'

'Yeah, he did like a double, twofold thing, both barrels.'

So; here we are. About 1972. In bed with Sue Miles. And this is really the first time it makes sense to talk about women and the counter-culture.

I feel ashamed about this. I always thought it was going to be a problem, but not such a big problem as it turned out to be. I might have woven the story of the Women's Movement into the rest of the book, somehow, but that felt falsely optimistic. It would have meant ignoring the narrative that says 'Old Ladies and Hippie Chicks are there to fuck, to look after kids, to type and to cook up some brown rice', which I feel runs through the book up to this point. It is about one old freaky geezer, and written by another, middle-aged freaky geezer, and this makes for an inevitable bias, I guess. I hope, however, that I was aware of this bias, and kept my eyes on it. It's just that there really wasn't much to say, up until now, the early 1970s, not if I was going to be somehow true to the lives of women. 'The lives of women in the British counter-culture, after the publication of Betty Friedan's *The Feminine Mystique* in 1963, but before the publication of Germaine Greer's *The Female Eunuch* in 1970' might make a good PhD for a women's historian. One theme that might emerge, I suspect, is that the Pill was more fun for men than for women in the 1960s.

I feel uncomfortable about writing a potted history of the Women's Movement. For one thing, there isn't room to do it justice. As with the politics of 1968, or the US counter-culture, or John 'Hoppy' Hopkins, I have kicked the problem into the Appendix, and have listed some recommended reading. Rosalind Miles's *Women's History of the World* graced every sister's bookshelf in the 1990s and is still a good place to start. If you fancy a go at one of the founding texts of second-wave feminist, Shulamith Firestone's *Dialectic of Sex: The Case for Feminist Revolution*, although very much of its time (1970), is bold and brave.

I feel uncomfortable because I must get it wrong. I do much more housework than my dad did. I've spent much more time looking after children than he did. I've worked under women bosses more than I have boss men, and I've always liked it. (I don't think they did, not because they were women, but because they were my boss.) I've worked with extraordinary women writers, musicians and performers. I know to put the lavatory seat down. I've learned, broadly, the location of the clitoris. None of this was my doing, and none of it was by choice. I'm not a great bloke. Anything the Women's Movement has achieved at work or in the home has been achieved by women. As much as I celebrate those achievements (my life has been much nicer than my dad's, and I am the father of daughters and the grandfather of granddaughters, after all), it's just not a story I'm in a position to judge.

For example, Nicola Lane, who drew the Dennis the Dope and Wanker cartoon reproduced in this chapter, says she didn't start to think about feminism until she read Germaine Greer. The playwright Michelene Wandor, on the other hand, has said that '[Germaine] ... made no difference one way or another. She was a useful populariser, but had no political function as a figure.' So, I don't know. I have joked for years that I first achieved orgasm on the day of publication of *The Female Eunuch*, and like so many of my jokes, it's funny cos it's truthy. I've never had a girlfriend who wasn't to a lesser or a greater degree part of, or at least interested in, the Women's Movement. That's why I cook and look after kids and try to hit the pan when I'm pissing: because I was told to, by women. This does not qualify me as a women's historian. I'm especially not qualified to write about the Women's Movement as a social reform movement. Hippie chicks burning their bras made for better photographs than the work that women like Sheila Rowbotham were doing.

One of the issues that made me start thinking about this book was when a student, a talented and bright student with a hint of goth about her, in 2012 FFS, came into my office, looked over her shoulder, closed the office door behind her, and said, in a whisper, 'Ian, please don't tell anyone, but I think I might be a feminist.' I told her I was honoured that she had chosen to come out to me, and that it was a good thing. But I took her point. It does not seem to be fashionable any more to be a feminist. All too often, I've heard young women express a distaste for feminism which is couched in terms not far from those of the Lad culture of the mid nineties. All too often, I've heard young women take what seems to be the Beyoncé line: *because* they are feminists, they can therefore wear what they like (i.e. not much), and, what's more, shake their booties on camera. This version of 'empowerment' is by a long shot my favourite outcome of feminism, if feminism it be. Which I doubt.

Charles Shaar Murray gets it mostly right, I think, talking to Jonathon Green in *Days in the Life*:

> The way women were treated on *OZ* was very influential on *Spare Rib* and had a lot to do with the founding of post-hippie feminism. The treatment they got was so offhand and casual, verging on the contemptuous. I'm not surprised that they eventually thought 'fuck this shit'. It was all 'Yay, freedom, let everyone do what they want', but the little woman is still over in the corner. She may be wearing a flowered dress and a headband, but she's still the one who rolls the joints, cooks up the vegetable messes that everybody used to pretend they liked, and generally does what Jann Wenner refers to with his normal exquisite tact as 'the chick work'. A lot of the girls were trying to be good hippies, doing whatever good hippies did, which meant that a lot of them would literally fuck anybody, do all the washing-up, and so on. Then they suddenly realised that no matter how important it was to be a good hippie, it was more important not to take this shit. So feminism was not so much an outgrowth of the hippie movement as a reaction against it.

To confirm his point, *OZ* 11, the April 1968 issue, carried this advertisement in the classified section:

> *OZ needs a talented, beautiful, energetic secretary who can TYPE, RE-SEARCH, INTERVIEW, WRITE and who is capable of enduring mundane clerical work (e.g. handling subscriptions). She should be able to sell advertising. SHORTHAND is not essential, but would help. Salary by negotiation. Do not apply if such things as SECURITY and SUPERANNUATION are important. OZ Girl, 38a Palace Gardens Terrace, London W8.*

This kind of advertisement was outlawed in the 1975 Sex Discrimination Act. *OZ*, at the cutting edge of what was and was not permissible in the permissive society, was clearly not at the forefront of moves to end sexual discrimination. Traditionally punk is seen as the first reaction to 'the hippie movement', but if CSM is right, then the Women's Movement was too, at least in part. Perhaps that's why punk and the Women's Movement fitted together so well, for a time.

I think there's one thing I can put right, though. Deciding not to write too much about things that have been written about extensively elsewhere (such as John 'Hoppy' Hopkins), and trying to stick to places that Bob went, or was involved with, even if somewhat marginally, I've skated over several key moments in the history of Freak culture. For example, I've only mentioned in passing the setting up in 1966 of the Indica Gallery and Bookshop, which was funded by Paul McCartney, and was where Yoko Ono met John Lennon. I've not said a lot about the setting up of *International Times*. I've not touched at all on the 'International Poetry Incarnation' in 1965, where between six and seven thousand young people, on the cusp of changing from Beats into hippies, went to the Royal Albert Hall to listen to writers like Adrian Henri, Gregory Corso, Lawrence Ferlinghetti, Alexander Trocchi, William Burroughs, and top of the bill, Allen Ginsberg (though there wasn't actually anything as hierarchical as a bill). All the accounts of these events credit 'Miles', aka Barry Miles, or Mr Sue as I call him, as co-founder of Indica and the *International Times*, and as co-organiser of the 'International Poetry Incarnation'. Nigel Fountain, in *Underground*, his history of the underground press in the UK, refers to 'Sue Miles, wife of *IT* co-founder Barry Miles'. Grrrr, quite frankly.

Let it be shouted from the rooftops – Sue Miles was *also* a co-founder of *IT, also* a co-proprietor of the Indica Gallery, and *also* a co-organiser of the Albert Hall event. She was not just someone's wife, so much as a collaborator, who has been written out of most narratives of the time. She was chosen by Richard Neville to run 'The Friends of OZ' pressure group, which supported the defendants in the obscenity trial. She was one of the first women in the underground press to refuse to make the tea and roll the joints, and insist on actually writing something. She became the restaurant critic for *Time Out* in the early 1970s, and stepped across from there into becoming 'the doyenne of the new wave of chefs who transformed London restaurants during the 1980s'. She died of lung cancer in 2010. Jonathon Green in his obituary of Sue says that she was 'impressed by nothing'; but those of my friends who loved her say that she was herself impressive, and warm and talented and clever. I wish I'd met her.

Bob says, 'Yeah, she was all right, was Sue.'

'When you were seeing her, was that when you were based down this way?'

'I had been based down here. I had left Monica after an ill-judged liaison with a bit of posh totty living in London. So I left Monica in the lurch, and even though she was keen to patch it up afterwards I just knew I'd do it again, I just couldn't ... I felt really shit about it but knowing me I knew I'd do it again. It's odd, the complexities of the human mind.'

'So you split up with Monica, and then did you go back to London?'

'Yeah, I'd got a van, a lorry, an ex-GPO work van, made into a living van, so I went to live in London or wherever.'

'Was that the first time you'd lived in a living vehicle, outside of Afghanistan?'

'Yeah. Even without any windows apart from the ones in the cab, I thought, "This is great." And it was, fucking great – seventy quid and you had a beautiful home, and you could take it wherever you liked. There were so many boxes it ticked in my life.'

'When I first came here,' I say, 'there wasn't just you, there were loads of people in vans. I bought records off lots of them, because they couldn't run turntables off twelve-volt batteries. Gone, isn't it? There's just you left really, round here? There's people round Glastonbury way, but here, it's just you.'

'Yeah. There was a passing fashion where a lot of people came to the same conclusion – fuck me, for a hundred quid you can buy your home. I know there's fuel, but the legal aspects of it, it's the same as running a car, same tax, and insurance is often cheaper. The first truck I put together when I was living down here cost thirteen quid to insure and that was in the late seventies.'

'So what was it like to park up in London?'

'Because I knew Hampstead well, there was a row of Victorian houses, if you're coming down to Hampstead Heath, there's a little section of land which is tarmacked, the upper side of that triangle, there's one road of Victorian houses, on the other side there's a mini-heath, a dead-end road only used by the people who live in those houses. That's where I used to park, on that road. I'd pull up there at night, and fuck off in the morning after I'd had a cup of tea – I wouldn't actually live there. I don't know if it was the days before yellow lines, but there weren't any yellow lines there. Sometimes I'd just park up wherever I was, it wasn't a problem at that time. The only time it was a problem, I was parked on some sort of line where I shouldn't have been, it was in the morning, I was just going into this girl's place I was parked outside to have a dump because I needed one. It was Arabella Churchill, in fact. But I could see a parking warden heading my way, and I knew I hadn't time to go in the house and have a shit and I really needed to. There was a wooden trap door in the back to get to the axle to fill it with oil and stuff. So I rather shamefully just had a crap into that, straight on to the road, and drove off, leaving a presumably steaming turd where I'd been. I don't feel proud of that.'

'Chas once spent a torrid night with Arabella in her tent, as it goes.'

'Did he now? I never knew that.'

'Had you stayed connected with that hip London, with Guy Stevens, for example?'

'Well, he died ...'

'Yes, but not until the early eighties.'

'No, once we left London, I lost touch with Guy. He used to come and visit us in Wiltshire while I was still with Vicki. I'd been to Afghanistan on the first trip and I'd still meet up with him, must have been after the first two trips to Afghanistan that I lost touch with him.'

'The next band he did after Procol Harum were Mott the Hoople, from Hereford and Shrewsbury. The nearest thing we've ever had to a local superstar band.'

'I was still in touch with Guy when Mott the Hoople were happening, I remember talking to him about it, about the Escher picture of lizards on the cover of the first album.'

'Tell me about the bike crash.'

'Right. Well, I was living in London, mostly, but still up and down here. I had a girlfriend, the lovely Sara, and she was friends with the Lambton girls, Lucy and Linda ...'

I hold my breath and hold my heart.

'Lucy? Lucinda Lambton?'

'Yeah.'

'I love her. One of *the* great TV presenters.'

'Yeah. Her and her sister were good friends with Sara. Graham Plinston had bought this place called the Palace of Ben Abu, which is a proper old Moroccan palace in the middle of Tangier. It was in a shit state when he found it, unkempt, and he asked Skip Ehrlich to go and tidy it up in preparation for sale. So Skip and I went over. And he also said he'd left this state-of-the-art Sherpa motorbike at his place in Ibiza, if we wanted to go over afterwards; and coincidentally Sara was on Ibiza, and I knew the bike was at the same place, so that was a double reason to go to Ibiza. So we did a preliminary tidy-up of the Palace of Ben Abu, which was amazing, doors at least twelve foot high that you could drive a coach through, proper four-inch thick. No water in the place, pretty much derelict, so you had to go out of the door in the morning to get water. And there would be dozens of tourists, mostly Japanese, all photographing the place, a bit of an odd situation. After a week or so, I got a bus up to where you get the boat to Ibiza, spent a day there waiting for the boat. I went down to the scrapyard while I was waiting, more my sort of place than the beach with people who'd rent a deckchair to sit in the sun. Caught a boat to Ibiza and then on to this house, Casa Canrubio, where the Lambton girls and Sara were, and the motorbike, this fantastic dirt bike.

'The motorbike crash itself was stupid. A few days before, I was razzing around in the dirt on the bike, forgetting I had bloody Indian flip-flop sandals on, and I did a foot-down slide, and broke my big toe. It was the side the gear change was on, so I couldn't change gear with my foot. A day or so later, I was out on the road, the girls had gone up to a bar and I thought I'd join them there and have a drink. So I was changing gear with my hand, also looking backwards because the mudguard had got a bit bent when I fell off the bike, so I was looking to see how bad that was, and riding on the wrong side of the road at this point, forgetting I was in a foreign land. The first thing I knew about the car was when I was flying over it, wondering what it was doing there, and being able to work out it was a taxi because a bit of paint over the driver's door near the roof was worn down to the grey primer, and you've probably noticed in sunny places when a taxi is waiting for a fare, the driver often stands there with a rag in hand ostensibly cleaning the car but really just rubbing the bit that's just above the door. So a taxi was the only sort of car that would be worn to the undercoat primer just above the door – that thought was running through my head as I'm flying over it. The next thought was to see where I'm going. When I saw where I was going, which happened to be a rock face, I had the wonderful thought, "I'd better shut my eyes," and I did. For quite a long time.

'First time I opened them there was a nun standing next to me. I don't know where I am. I could see she's definitely holding a veterinary-size hypodermic in one hand. And in the other hand, held quite high, is what I initially think is a Russian flag. I'm trying to work this out, and then I notice little bits of white on the edge of this flag, and I realise it's the edge of a bloodstained sheet. I gradually realise it's *my* bloodstained sheet; the nun is looking directly ahead, but I'm down there. I can't move, can't move anything. While still looking fixedly at the horizon, she brings this hypodermic down whump into my leg – because I'm naked she can't look at me – and I flake out. Next time I opened my eyes, there's a friendlier figure and one known to me, a geezer called Mickey Green – a dope smuggler of the day, the one who was released by the Russians the same time as Greville Wynne – he's leaning over me with a custom-grown little fingernail full of brown powder. He'd grown his nail to snort various powders. He said, "Do you want a snort?" – "Yes" – so I passed out again. Next thing I knew I'd been loaded on to a plane. I was flown out by Sara and the Lambton girls, with Sara as company, back to England. They'd turned up at the hospital in Ibiza literally as they were wheeling me to the operating theatre to cut my leg off.'

'So they saved your leg?'

'Fucking right they did. When I came out of hospital, I was all smashed up, with several limbs in plaster, and I was basically living in the broom cupboard under the stairs, with a mattress in there, in a sort of a junkie household in the Kensal end of Portobello Road, just off the Harrow Road. I tell you what it was like. My pal Sir Adam Kish comes running in, because he lived literally round the corner. Adam comes in, saying, "I've just found a great new gig!" "What's that, Adam?" "Going to the supermarket in Aldgate, pick a tin of beans, jam it in the till so they can't close it, grab all the money and run." And that was his view of a good gig! And he had a big fistful of money. That was how people in that place were living. It was no good.'

'I saw that picture you posted on Facebook, of you on crutches, I've never seen you look so frail, in all the years I've known you.'

'Well, my head had been smashed open, I had loads of broken bones, I wasn't in very good shape. But I knew this bloke called Tony Bruegger, whose mum was one of the Rees-Mogg family.'

Bruegger's uncle was William Rees-Mogg, editor of *The Times*, who had written a famous leader column in 1967 titled 'Who breaks a butterfly on a wheel?', condemning Mick Jagger's imprisonment for drugs offences. Bruegger's cousin is loathsome Tory MP Jacob Rees-Mogg. One of the themes of Bob's life has been his contact with, and love of, the aristocracy. Aristos were vital to the counter-culture, providing money and support to the wilder elements. When fashion moved away from the Freaks, in the late seventies, the aristos moved with it.

'Tony Bruegger said to me, "I've got this house you can stay in, in Temple Cloud, south of Bristol. Why don't you get yourself down there? Fresh air, good food, all that, give you time to heal. There are a few friends staying there already, but I'm sure they won't mind you moving in." So that's what I did.

'What Tony had neglected to say was that his friends were paying rent. They were a bit miffed at first when this cripple turned up, saying Tony says I can move in. It's a bit off, when you're paying rent and your landlord just says to a mate, you can live there free. But those girls – Ween, Jill Vickers and Kate Hooper – were lovely. And their friend Maureen Leopard, who lived down the road. They looked after a complete stranger they'd never met before. That's big.'

'How long were you there?'

'Three months or so. I was in much better shape after that, but not right for ages.'

To emphasise the aristo connection: 'Ween', aka Margaret Messenger, married David Lascelles, aka Viscount Lascelles, now the Earl of Harewood, in 1979. Bob's girlfriend Sara was a regular visitor to the house in Temple Cloud too, and a few years back, I met Ween and Sara when they spun by Bob's van for an afternoon of jewellery buying. Bob is right – they were lovely. Bob has an extraordinary knack of being on good terms with his ex-girlfriends. Ween (no longer the Viscountess Lascelles) had brought him a birthday present; Sara had made him a cake.

Maureen Leopard, also an occasional visitor to Presteigne, married aristocracy too, though of a different order. She's married to Robert Hunter, lyricist and 'non-performing' member of the Grateful Dead. Amongst the hundreds of songs that Hunter wrote with Dead frontman Jerry Garcia was 'Truckin'', with its killer line, 'Lately it occurs to me, what a long strange trip it's been,' an epitaph for the counter-culture if ever there was one.

Any account of the Freak scene in Britain is always going to include John 'Hoppy' Hopkins and Heathcote Williams. Since this book is both an account of Bob's life and an introduction to his times, and some of the ideas that formed those times, I can just about get away with my promise to old Perry Venus to sideline 'Hoppy', since he only had a walk-on part in Bob's story, and his wider role in counter-cultural London is overdone elsewhere. But Heathcote Williams really was a bona fide Bob pal. Williams is a poet, an activist, a playwright, an actor, a rascal. He was a one-time organiser of squats: he ran a housing agency for squatters in the 1970s called Ruff Tuff Cream Puff, and he was integral to the setting up of the Free State of Frestonia, the squatters' community in Notting Hill which declared itself independent of the UK in 1977. Heathcote was Frestonia's Ambassador to the Court of St James. Google him; you'll thank me. On his Wikipedia page it says 'Williams has had a somewhat turbulent personal life', which is something of an understatement. Two of Bob's favourite Heathcote stories might illustrate why.

Bob and Heathcote met in Brilley, in the hills around Hay, introduced by Bob's old pal Sir Adam Kish, in whose wife's flat Bob and Pete Mustill had spray-painted motorbikes.

'You'll like this guy, Adam says to me, and he was right. One day, me and Adam were going up Hay Bluff in Heathcote's wife's Austin A35 van. In front of us there was this French-registered car, with a family in it, obviously enjoying a day out in the Black Mountains. They were going very very slowly, and Heathcote says, "Shall I give 'em a nudge?" Me and Adam, being up for stuff, go, "Yeah," thinking he's going to give them a little nudge. But, fuck me, he drops it a cog, accelerates like fuck, and rams them up the back. And then he does it again, and the poor bastards drive off the road. You know what that road's like? Single track all the way, and they drive off down a gully, where they are not going to get out without a tow from a tractor. And Heathcote grins and drives on.

'And then there was a time a few years later in London, where me and Heathcote were skint, and fancied a drink. And there was a sign up on a telegraph pole saying "Cat Missing, Reward £5". And fuck me, there was this cat, sitting under the poster ...'

At this point, I hand over to cartoonist Nicola Lane, who turned this anecdote into a cartoon for *International Times* in May 1977, starring Heathcote Williams as Dennis the Dope and Bob Rowberry as Wanker. Ms Lane says that she used a few of her friends' true stories for cartoons in *IT* at that time.

Bob swears this is a true story.

International Times was still being published regularly up until 1973. Although homosexuality had been legalised in 1967, it was still illegal for men to actually find ways of meeting openly, and in October 1973, the magazine was prosecuted for publishing gay contact ads. At which point, it ceased publication. Although it was revived by various publishers intermittently until the mid eighties, its great days were gone.

If *IT* was the main newspaper of Freak culture, *OZ* was its *Vogue*, its glossy coffee-table must-read status symbol. Somewhere towards the very end of making this book, Richard Neville died, aged seventy-four. Neville was the founder and the guiding genius of *OZ* magazine, which between 1967 and 1973 was seen as the most authentic voice of the counter-culture. It looked beautiful (it still does; you can access and download all forty-eight issues via the University of Wollongong website, link in the Appendix), but it is very much of its time.

By the early 1970s, sex has moved on since Larkin's 'Annus Mirabilis' in 1963. The Pill has been put into widespread use. Homosexuality and abortion have been legalised. The Lady Chatterley trial and the 1968 Theatres Act have opened up culture to a new frank discussion of sex and sexuality. And the Gay Liberation Front, post legalisation, were setting up situations and demonstrations to demand not just a furtive legalisation, but full equality.

The moment of *OZ* came at a time when open pleasure in sex was on the up, as it were. Today, much of it reads as though a bunch of schoolboys were finally allowed to pass round all the smutty notes they liked. It assumes that sex and drugs and rock 'n' roll are available to all, on equal terms, but especially men; the attitude towards women noted by Charles Shaar Murray comes across in many of the pieces. This attitude to sex is neatly summed up by Richard Neville in his book, *Playpower*, also published in 1970, when it seemed that he could do no wrong:

> When boy meets girl, within minutes of drifting off to a comfortable location, boy can be happily splashing about in girl's cunt, both of them up each other's arses, sucking and fucking with compassionate enthusiasm. No more tedious 'will she or won't she by Saturday?' but a total tactile information exchange, and an unambiguous foundation on which to build a temporary or permanent relationship. The pot of gold at the end of the rainbow comes first; later one decides whether the rainbow is worth having for its own sake. If the attraction is only biological, nothing is lost except a few million sper-

matozoa and both patients continue their separate ways. If there is a deeper involvement, the relationship becomes richer, and so does the sexual experience. The way to a girl's mind is through her cunt.

In our own very different (and post-Women's Movement) world, there's lots here we might find difficult. The few million spermatozoa have the ability, last time I checked, to make babies. Neville takes for granted that the chick is on the Pill, yeah? This takes away, if not quite her right to say no, then certainly several lines of defence. *No more tedious will she or won't she*? And I know a great number of Sisters who might have something to say about the last line. Lest it be forgotten, however, the Sexual Revolution of the 1960s follows hard on the heels of the hypocrisy and prudery of the 1950s. Neville's language, and the somewhat grubby boyish glee of the writers of OZ that they have been let out to play, if not excusable, is at least explicable in the light of what had gone before.

Nor did the uptight world go away. Also in 1970, Evangelical missionaries Peter and Janet Hill came back from a four-year stint in India, and found themselves shocked by how far the 'Permissive Society' had advanced in their absence. They set up an organisation called 'The Nationwide Festival of Light', and quickly attracted approval from the moral guardians of the day; the Earl of Longford, Malcolm Muggeridge and Mrs Mary Whitehouse. They attracted some celebrity support too, such as actors Dora Bryan and David Kossoff, and the legendary announcer Bob Danvers-Walker, who did the voice-overs for Pathé News during the Second World War. He said: 'This is the age when men with dirty minds and tongues flourish because up till now there has been no militancy against those degenerates who befoul every form of art.' The Festival of Light hoped to offer militant opposition to the sexual revolutionaries. On 25 September 1971, 40,000 people gathered in Trafalgar Square for speeches by Whitehouse, Longford and Muggeridge, who said in his speech, 'I felt an abiding sense of being so in need of salvation myself, that for me the Festival has been an immense clarification ... Man's true problem is his attempt to live without God, to live with fantasies that he's a God himself ... Without God, we are irretrievably lost in the darkness of mortality. Praise the Lord!' The Festival of Light-goers then marched behind a Sally Army band to Hyde Park, where they joined another 50,000 or so people to listen to an evening of Christian music, headlined by Cliff Richard. The Gay Liberation Front, sisters from The Women's Movement and the staff of OZ had organised 'Operation

Rupert': lots of Freaks heckled the poor marchers, but they were kettled by the police into a corner of the park, and did little to upset the staid goings on.

But Richard Neville, his co-editor Jim Anderson and business manager Felix Dennis had more to worry about than The Festival of Light. Because they were just out of prison, pending appeal, having been found guilty of publishing an obscene magazine in the longest running obscenity trial in British history, which ended up seeing them sentenced to fifteen, twelve and nine months, respectively.

Their troubles had started quietly enough, as troubles often do. In the February 1970 edition *OZ* 26, Neville had published a shout-out:

> Some of us at *OZ* are feeling old and boring, so we invite any of our readers who are under eighteen to come and edit the April issue. Apply at the *OZ* office in Princedale Road, W11, any time from 10 a.m. to 7 p.m. on Friday, March 13. We will choose one person, several, or accept collective applications from a group of friends. You will receive no money, except expenses. You will enjoy almost complete editorial freedom. *OZ* staff will assist in purely an administrative capacity. If you like, write before March 13 and tell us who you are and would like to do with a 48-page two-colour magazine. *OZ* belongs to you.

A few dozen kids wrote in, and spent a few weekends in Jim Anderson's flat putting it together. One of these was Charles Shaar Murray, who told the *Guardian* in 2001 about his fellow editors:

> The company of schoolkid editors included Peter Popham, subsequently a respected foreign correspondent for the *Independent*; Deyan Sudjic – the posse's sole skinhead – founder of Blueprint, editor of *Architectural Digest* and a front-rank commentator on architectural issues; Colin Thomas, a successful photographer; Trudi Braun, who became a senior editor at *Harper's*; Steve Havers, cultural commentator turned web designer; and Vivian Berger, whose juxtaposition of the head of Rupert Bear with a Rabelaisian cartoon by Robert Crumb helped generate some of the most surreal exchanges ever heard in a British court.

This cartoon, of kiddies' favourite Rupert Bear with a great big hard-on, tupping a very large lady, was made by Berger as a collage; he had juxtaposed Rupert's head on a Robert Crumb cartoon. It's a classic of the Situationist technique of *détournement*, and it got everyone into a great deal of trouble. *OZ* 28, The Schoolkids Issue, was published in April 1970. It wasn't explicitly *for* Schoolkids; the point is, it was *by* them. The Rupert Bear cartoon is smutty and childish, as you'd expect from a fifteen-year-old boy. Perhaps the thing that our modern sensibilities would have most trouble coming to terms with was the picture on page three: a clearly under-age schoolgirl in her uniform, captioned, *Jailbait of the Month*.

On 8 June, the offices at Princedale Road (just up the road from Bob's old local, The Prince of Wales) were busted by the Metropolitan Police's notoriously corrupt Obscene Publication Squad. Neville, Anderson and Dennis were charged with conspiracy to debauch and corrupt children. At their committal hearing in October, all three wore schoolboy uniforms. Meanwhile, *OZ* continued publication, unreconstructed; in *OZ* 32, published in January 1971, Neville wrote, 'It's about time straight society got things in perspective and realised that many of their kids are smoking dope, dropping acid and fucking freely, quite unconcernedly.'

The trial proper started on 23 June 1971. It lasted six weeks, with twenty-seven days in court. Neville defended himself; Anderson and Dennis were represented by John Mortimer, the author of the *Rumpole of the Bailey* TV series, with, as his junior, Geoffrey Robertson, who wrote an account of the trial for TV in 1991, starring Hugh Grant in a wig as Richard Neville.

The trial hinged on what was meant by obscene. The judge was agin 'em from the start, as in so many episodes of *Rumpole*. He pointed to the classified advertisements for penis enlargers and vibrators. He dwelled over the small ads, which, like those in *IT*, were often for male models. The defence called up expert witnesses like the psychologist Hans Eysenck and DJ John Peel. Everyone agreed that the star witness was jazz singer George Melly, who was asked by Neville to define 'cunnilingus', hitherto unknown to the judge (and presumably, his poor wife). 'Gobbling,' said George, 'going down. Sucking off. As we used to call it in the Navy, "yodelling in the canyon".' The judge was not amused; he had already banned laughing in the courtroom.

The three Freaks were found 'not guilty' of the conspiracy charge, but the judge directed the jury to find them guilty of publishing an obscene magazine. Given his lack of sympathy, it was expected that he would send the *OZ* editorial team to jail, but even so, the sentences he passed were seen as draconian. The three were released after twelve days, and were finally exonerated on appeal in November 1971, on the grounds of the judge's misdirection of the jury.

Richard Neville went back to Australia, Jim Anderson went to Ghana and *OZ* limped on under Felix Dennis's editorship until 1973, when, like *IT*, the levels of prosecution proved too much to bear. The underground press retired hurt. Many of the writers decamped to the *New Musical Express*, of which more in the next chapter.

Not all magazines that were published in this era were straightfor-wardly 'underground'; independent would be better. *Time Out*, still very much with us, comes out of this tradition; so does *Bike*, now the UK's top selling motorcycle magazine, which was founded by Bob's old ally, Mark Williams, as *the* hippie bike magazine. Most important was feminist magazine *Spare Rib*, founded in 1972 by Rosie Boycott and Marsha Rowe, in reaction to *OZ* as much as to the straight women's magazines like *Woman's Realm*. *Spare Rib* had a distribution deal with W.H. Smith, and was much too professionally produced to count as 'underground'. It closed in 1993, right at the end of my period, when the counter-cultural project had finally run out of steam. It too is available online, through the British Library, link in the Appendix. Read it, Younger Sisters, and wish for something like it again.

I like looking at *OZ*, but for me, it leaves a bad taste in the mouth. It reminds me of what I didn't like at the time: not so much the sex, as the noodling music. If the Women's Movement was the first and greatest reaction against the hippies, punk was the loudest. And Bob don't dig punk.

'Before I write about punk, and you bugger off to the States, tell me why you were on an island in Sweden.'

'It must have been the winter before I went to the States. I can't honestly remember why I was there. There must have been some reason. I'd gone to visit some people I knew, David Lindahl – the guy who'd let me down in Afghanistan – and his Swedish wife, and they're living several hours north of Stockholm, and I was there for some reason. I don't know why I was there; I do know I was there with a Morris Minor van. His place was near Tierp, in a village called Mehedeby, and David had taken me out to an island that the family owned an equipped shack on, with all the fishing tackle you'd ever need and a boat with a little motor. So I thought I'd really like to spend time on a little island near the Baltic coast, fishing. The place is more water than land, it's like a whole series of islands, granite rocks, beautifully wooded islands, pine and birch, and then at the more rocky end of it loads of juniper, which made it smell really nice. The mosquitoes are a bit of a fucker.'

'So how long were you on that island for? And were you making jewellery?'

'Yeah, making jewellery. I was there a few weeks, I guess, I don't remember. And while I was there I had a very pleasant time. A bit of a thrill was when I was going along a narrow bit of water that the boat could just fit along, and there was a crashing noise like a bulldozer coming through the brush on one side, and a fucking moose came crashing through. It did not break its stride for the fucking stream; just leapt over it in front of me. That was a bit of a treat.

'Anyway, suddenly it turned winter, and I woke up in the morning and what had been sparkling running water with my nets across to catch the fish and all that, it's fucking ice. I thought, "Fuck," because I knew winter was coming, but I thought there would be a bit of ice around the edge and I would know it was time to go, but no, it was just ice. And the home base, the place where you could land a boat, was a couple of miles away by water. So I looked at the ice, and poked it a bit. All I had was a rowing boat with an outboard motor, but obviously it ain't going to go through two inches of ice.'

'And let's just emphasise for Younger Readers, there's no mobile phones . . .'

'No, of course not, nothing. But the ice looked thick enough to walk on. I thought fuck me, it wasn't there yesterday, and the water underneath it wasn't a placid pond, it was fast-flowing water, so if you fall through the ice you're fucked. You're dead, there's no way out, you'd be whipped along by the current, and you ain't going to swim your way back to the hole where you fell in, because the water's running faster than I could swim. So I thought, "I want to get across to the other side." I cut a long thin pole, and got a bit of line and tied it round my waist, and made a train of my possessions, because I didn't want to be carrying stuff. I had the pole under my armpits, the thinking being, "If I go through the ice, I won't go all the way through, I'll have something to pull myself out on that ain't crumbling away." I had my box of scrap silver with me on the island, but in a fortunate decision which really paid off, I left that box on the island because I had quite a few pounds of scrap silver in there. Silver was really cheap at the time, and I'd never parted with my offcuts. And I thought, "It's silly to carry an extra few pounds, I'll leave it there and catch up with it some other time." I looked all round the island, which was only small, about here to the woodshed sort of thing, at its longest, and a third of that in its width – I went all round it, looking at the ice – and I saw a fucking moose footprint on it, I kid you not – just in one place, it had made a crossing from one bit of land to another, so I thought, "It knows what it's doing, it's a sight bigger than me." And obviously, it worked. I tied my stuff to the fishing line, and got me across the ice, which hadn't been there the day before.'

'So you just walked off the island, across the ice, leaving your silver behind?'

'Yeah, leaving the silver behind, which played so well in my favour …'

'Because it comes back, just at the right moment?'

'Yeah.'

It's been a long afternoon. Bob yawns and stretches on his bed, kicking some of the photos of Afghanistan to the floor. I pick them up, and stand to go. Briar is tidying up outside before she gets into her ex-Post office Commer Van and heads back to her yurt.

As we walk up to my car, Bob says to Briar, 'Did you know Ian was Chas's comedy partner?' – And Briar hugs me, saying that she didn't know, and tells me how she's spent many happy hours sitting with Chas on various internal gates at festivals, talking of this and that, sharing a drink and a smoke and a laugh around an all-night fire.

The small surviving remnant of the Freaks that are left all know one another, one way and another. A couple of degrees of separation, no more. Each year, more fall away; and who then will man the internal gates?

I pull out onto the empty A44. Within minutes, an Audi comes screaming up in my rear-view mirror, and sits on my fucking arse. The driver is much more important than me, as he's driving an Audi, but there's a bit coming up where the road winds for a mile or so, so I slow down, and let him stew. I doubt that he will appreciate my grandmotherly kindness. At the next possible straight bit of road, he comes skittling past, on his way to somewhere important. I wish him well. I wind down my window, and bimble back towards Presteigne.

I hear a bird sing in the hedgerow.

'Poo-tee-weet.'

I Use the NME

This part of the book isn't set in Bob's van. Bob isn't in this bit. This part is just me, alone with Peggy the dog, in the cabin on stilts, by the western bank of the Severn, a little north of Tewkesbury.

The storms have subsided, and, at last, after a week, the water has too. The river is only a few feet above its summer average. Boats from Upton Rowing Club are back, fighting against the stream. A narrowboat puttered up-river this morning. My ribs are agonising from my fall. I have to prop myself up in bed to try to sleep, and I'm tired. I sit out on the decking, taking my breakfast in full-spectrum sunshine. It's cold, though; there is a silvering of frost on the part of the decking that has yet to come into the sun. Dog walkers bimble up the footpath on the opposite side of the Severn, and Peggy, emboldened by thirty metres of fast-flowing river water between her and their dogs, barks and barks and barks at them.

Bob isn't in this part of the book because it is about punk, and Bob just didn't get it, wasn't at all interested. Pete Mustill summed up the views of his generation, talking to me about punk a few years back.

'We worshipped Little Feat. We'd spent years practising to get good. And then you fuckers came along with your three shit chords and your shit guitars ...'

The fact of the matter is, by the time punk happened, Bob was the enemy.

He liked trad jazz, he projected psychedelic oil-wheel patterns onto Pink Floyd, Procol Harum were named after his cat, he was the first person to introduce Afghan coats to the UK, and he had played tambourine live on stage with Led Zep. Who was the enemy, if not Bob? The oldest of the old hippies? The dinosaur's dinosaur?

Bob always sensed this, I think. As he told me, he 'just didn't dig what was happening'. That's why, for much of 1978 and 1979 he packed up and went off to Canada, California and Mexico, and the story of that trip, and Bob's story in general, picks up in the next chapter. Not to worry too much, though, because by 1980, Bob will be back from the States, and the punks and the hippies will become allies and then friends and then just fellow Freaks, so much so that they will become increasingly indistinguishable from one another through the eighties and early nineties.

But in the beginning, in 1976 and 1977, the hippies were the baddies. Hippie bands. Hippie record label bosses. Hippie DJs. Hippie haircuts. Hippie clothes. Hippie values, and their failure. Fuck Peace and Love. The punks wanted authenticity back on the agenda. We meant it, maaan.

Without punk stories, no attempt to talk about 'the counter-culture' in the UK would make sense. So this is my punk story. I was never a terribly convincing punk, but punk changed everything for me, and for the counter-culture too. It was a chance for reinvention on a massive scale.

I was born, as I've said, a week before Elvis joined the Army. Elvis joined the Army on 21 March 1958, whilst Bob was shagging Jo Bramley in a pile of coats in the corner of Ken Colyer's club. The counter-culture, as I have defined it, was off the blocks and down the first straight. This world I have been trying to describe, the World of Bob, is the world in which I grew up. The counter-culture, so far as I was concerned as a kid and as a teenager, was just our culture. Bob and his friends were trying to discover something new, but we were bobbing along in their wake. What they were trying to find out, we believed. What was scary and new for the hippie pioneers was just the way of things for us.

In 1968, Bob was in Afghanistan, Pete Mustill was taking part in the Hornsey Art School Strike and Chas Ambler was playing drums in a ballroom dance band in an end-of-the-pier show in Blackpool after smoking his first jay backstage with Englebert Humperdinck's backing band. Many of my teachers at secondary school were leaving teacher training college, several of them determined to help us discover the beach beneath the street. I was ten, and I was in a band called the Marmites. I've been in bands, without a break, ever since.

The first group I can remember seeing on TV was the Beatles, then the Stones. The first record I hated was 'Stranger on the Shore' by Mr Acker Bilk. The first record I bought with my own money, aged nine, was *The Magical Mystery Tour* EP; acid by Owsley Stanley, you'll recall. Before 1967 and the Broadcasting Act, my mum usually listened to Radio London while she was cooking, a pirate radio station. 'Something in the Air' by Thunderclap Newman was number one in 1969; can you imagine that now? 'We've got to get together sooner or later, because the Revolution's Here?' Of course we believed the Revolution was just around the corner. It was number one in the hit parade when I was eleven. Why wouldn't we believe it? When I saw John Lennon going to bed with Yoko for world peace on TV, I thought that was a good thing to do, because I loved the Beatles. I loved pop music. Pop music good, war bad, that's what I learned as a kid.

I had two road to Damascus moments that twisted this love into fanatical devotion. The first must have been in February 1972. I was a member of the Air Training Corps, because I hoped one day to be in the RAF. I liked aeroplanes. I had friends who liked aeroplanes, and I went to the ATC with them. We used to go on gliding trips with the ATC, often to West Malling in Kent, an old Battle of Britain airfield. Coming back from a gliding trip on a coach one evening, sitting next to my pal Jeff, King of Aeroplane Enthusiasts, I heard a piece of music that sent a shock through me. The guy in the seat behind us had a radio, and he was listening to the Sunday-night chart show on Radio One.

'What's that?' I asked.

'"Meet Me on the Corner", by Lindisfarne.'

I think I bought the single the next day; my first since *Magical Mystery Tour*. That week, I watched *Top of the Pops*, hoping to see Lindisfarne. I was not disappointed. My mum screeched in horror at the sight of Alan Hull's hair. In fairness, your mum would probably screech too; it is quite a do. I was a fan at once. The follicles of my own hair, upon seeing Alan Hull's, started laying down the foundations for several years' unfettered growth, growth that would see wavy hair down to my shoulders by early 1976.

All my paper-round money started to go on records. The following weekend, I bought the Lindisfarne album, *Nicely Out of Tune*. A week later, I bought Paul and Linda McCartney's album *Ram*.

The second decisive moment, the moment I became a punk, was a week or so after that. I was ill from school (I wasn't ill, obvs, but faking a sore throat, as it was probably PE). My mum and old feller were out at work, and after a bit of a doze, I came downstairs in my dressing gown, made myself a lovely cup of tea, and lay down on the sofa to watch schools TV. In those days, Younger Readers, not only were there only three channels – which you had to get up to change, yeah? – but there was no daytime TV, other than schools. So I watched schools TV. That day, there was a music programme on, a twenty-five-minute kiddies' music programme, with children biffing xylophones and glockenspiels and wood blocks. The presenters sang songs on the acoustic guitar about quavers and crotchets, accompanied by some of the teeny percussionists. And then they played an animation, a crude cartoon, which depicted hot air balloons moving diagonally against an immobile sky. And they played a recording over it. I had never heard anything approaching it. It had a xylophone, yes. But it also had a girl's voice like no other, which gave the song a beauty beyond all compare. I sat up on the sofa. The presenters said something along the lines of, 'Wasn't that a pretty song? It was called "I'll Be Your Mirror" by the Velvet Underground and Nico.'

The Velvet Underground and Nico! I'd seen that album at the weekend, in Noise, Newhaven's record shop, when I'd been buying *Ram*. The one with the banana! The next day, miraculously recovered from my illness, I bought it. I was just fourteen.

The Velvet Underground and Nico! Imagine how depraved the producers of that kiddies' schools TV show must have been. What were they thinking? I remain eternally in their debt. A fortnight later, after a few listenings to 'Heroin' and 'I'm Waiting for My Man', I left the Air Training Corps, as you would. I took the radio up to my room, and found John Peel. I monopolised the record player in the front room, to my parents' horror, and they bought themselves a new stereo to play their stuff on (very good stuff, too: Nat King Cole, Ella, Sarah Vaughan) – and gave me the old record player. Which I took to my room, to play my rapidly expanding collection as loud as I could get away with. My parents didn't seem to miss 'Femme Fatale'.

When Bob was growing up a rebel, there were few obvious avenues open to him. He tried crime and didn't like it, so he and his friends had to find a way to live that enabled them to live with authenticity. For us wannabe rebel kids of the early seventies, this other way, the path that Bob and his friends had carved through the jungle of normality, was wide open and increasingly well-trodden, and the path was mapped out for us by the *NME*.

Up until I was fourteen, my mum had bought me the *Beano* every week, and had it delivered with the *Mirror*. I asked her if I could change to the *New Musical Express*, and she agreed. After that, fashion, attitude, politics, ambition were all copied from the inky pages of my new comic. It was my education, that and O-Level History. History lessons were the only lessons I liked. I liked them because I was being taught by a *soixante-huitard* who gave lessons on the inherent evils of the capitalist mode of production, disguised as a course on the Industrial Revolution. That's right, Younger Readers; comprehensive schools in the seventies were full of Marxists. Governments were getting worried, and really for the first time started taking an interest in what happened in schools. As a measure of how hands-off the British Government had been, the first ever speech by a prime minister on the subject of education was by Jim Callaghan in 1976.

I read the *NME*, and did what it told me to do. I had the *Little Red Schoolbook*, with its killer line, 'All Grown-Ups are Paper Tigers,' because the *NME* alerted me to its existence. It couldn't be bought in Dee's Newsagents, High Street, Newhaven, but it could be had in the Public House bookshop in Brighton, our nearest radical bookshop. Younger Readers have no idea where their nearest radical bookshop is, because there are none left. One afternoon, after hearing about the National Union of School Students, our year refused to go back to lessons, because we wanted an end to uniforms, and we stood out on the playground until the headmaster came and shouted at us through a megaphone.

Who was writing for the *NME* at that time? Who was shaping my world view as an impressionable teenager? Charles Shaar Murray, who, in 1970, had been one of the editors of the *OZ* Schoolkids issue; Mick Farren, erstwhile doorman at the UFO club, friend of the MC5 and lead singer in the Social Deviants; Nick Kent, junkie friend of the Stones, whose series in the *NME* on the Beach Boys in 1975 was probably the most important piece of 'rock' criticism ever published in Britain up to that point; Miles, Barry Miles, Mr Sue Miles, reviewed records; Chrissie 'Pretenders' Hynde was interviewing, and clearly shagging, Brian Eno; and, in 1977, the *NME* unearthed the great contrarian Julie Burchill, sixteen and gun-slinging for trouble.

Wayne Kramer was the guitarist in the MC5. The MC5 were the most obscure of the Detroit bands my handful of equally obsessed pals worshipped; Alice Cooper (the band, not the man), Iggy and the Stooges, the Motor City 5. Mick Farren was visiting Wayne Kramer when he was busted (framed, as Farren thought), for cocaine possession, and Kramer was subsequently imprisoned for a mad length of time. Farren wrote about the case in the *NME*. And what did we do as fifteen-year-olds? We carved 'Free Wayne Kramer' on our school desks. Our parents never thought to look in the *NME*. The contemporary equivalent would be worrying about your fifteen-year-old listening to gangsta rap, I guess. I'm sure my parents worried about what I was listening to, but really what they should have been worrying about was what I was reading.

The *NME* is still about, the last of the music weeklies, the 'inkies' as they were known, because the ink came off on your hands. In a last-ditch attempt to save the paper, it has reinvented itself as a free-sheet, which means it is more than ever in hock to its advertisers. I picked up a copy at a tube station last time I was in That London, and I thought I might weep. To compare it with the old *NME* would be like comparing Marx's

German Ideology with *The Very Hungry Caterpillar*. The new *NME* thing seems to be a lifestyle mag (i.e., things to buy) with a bit of music thrown in. I threw it away. And then I picked it out of the bin, and reread it with great enthusiasm, remembering just in time that they might have a book review section, and I could just have alienated them. Doubt it. Probably not. Fuck it. Threw it away again.

Before the shift to the new model in 2015, the *NME* sold just over 18,000 copies a week; some of them, I'm sure, to people who've never stopped reading it. But back in the day, when I sucked it up like gospel, it sold 300,000 copies a week. *Melody Maker* sold 205,000, *Sounds* 100,000, and *Record Mirror* about 75,000. Some people bought them all, but I didn't. I was an *NME* man to the core of my impressionable being.

Here's a thing: when you went to see bands, you sat down. If you went to see a 'big band' in Brighton (for example, Wishbone Ash or Focus), you went to the Dome – and sat down. If you went to see an up-and-coming band – Be Bop Deluxe, for example, or Renaissance – you went to the Sussex University Student Union Hall – and sat down on cushions. Very few people had the nerve to actually dance. It could not have been duller. After the gigs, my pals and I would discuss what gear the bands had been using. That was as interesting as it got. The first band I saw standing up was pub-rock pioneers Ducks Deluxe in the Hungry Years in Brighton, in about 1975. That was better, but only slightly. Even the audience for Kool and the Gang, *circa* '75/'76, in Brighton's Top Rank, where movement was at least possible, hardly budged.

I'd never got off on the Big Beast Bands of the seventies. Couldn't be doing with Zep, as I had no interest in being screeched at about witches and dragons. 'Piper at the Gates of Dawn' aside, Floyd left me cold, until *Dark Side*, when I started to get hot with anger. Never could stand those first-wave metal bands, like Deep Purple and Uriah Heep, or the noodling of the likes of Genesis or ELP. Strange to relate, I could stand the noodling of Yes, in small doses, but by the mid seventies Yes weren't trading in small doses.

I liked Mott, Bowie, Roxy, the Faces, the Beatles, the Beach Boys, the Stones, Alice Cooper, the Velvet Underground, the Stooges, the MC5. I liked singer-songwriters: Van Morrison, Jackson Browne, Tim Buckley (Jeff's dad to Younger Readers), Joni Mitchell, Stevie Wonder. Despite my early Lindisfarne flirtations, I didn't like folk rock (though I did have *Fairport Nine*), but I did like country rock. Although the *NME* was gospel, there was apocrypha too. For years, I subscribed to a music nuts' mag called *ZigZag*, and I also bought what they liked: the Byrds, the Flying Burrito Brothers, Gram Parsons, Emmylou Harris, Big Star. As a subscriber, you got a free album every year, and in January 1976 it was the Joe Boyd produced eponymous album by Kate and Anna McGarrigle, which I loved. Through the good offices of *ZigZag*, I'd found Tom Waits, and had his first three albums on import. Import was the only way to go. These records needed finding. There were very few record shops that sold anything outside the charts. The Newhaven record shop, run by Mrs Gloria Noise, as we called her, would order you stuff, but imported records were only to be found in Virgin Records in Brighton (lots of unattainable pre-Raphaelite girls, shop smelt of dope, signs up saying 'No dealing on the premises', cushions on the floor with dangling head-phones), or on a precious day in London picking up stuff. Seeing Springsteen doing 'Rosalita' on the *Old Grey Whistle Test* was a revelatory moment, as was, of course, Bob Marley and the Wailers *Live at the Rainbow* (I wasn't there, but the album rocked). And I liked a lot of blue-eyed soul, especially Todd Rundgren and Hall & Oates, and I liked a bit of disco, of course I did. Still do. Disco means dancing, dancing means girls, and I like girls. Above all, I liked pub rock; I liked Brinsley Schwarz and Ducks Deluxe and Kokomo.

I was Punk/New Wave's core audience. I'd been looking forward to something new for years.

In January 1976, Mick Farren wrote an article in the *NME* calling for the overthrow of the rock dinosaurs, a point he remade later in the year with a piece calling for a new generation of bands to sink the luxurious complacent *Titanic* of the rock behemoths. I agreed; it was in the *NME*, after all.

The 21 February 1976 issue of the *NME* is a good way to see some of the then current obsessions of the paper's staff. Patti Smith is on the cover – the tagline promises an interview with Patti on the subject of French poet Arthur Rimbaud. There was an article about the difference between U-Roy and I-Roy, two Jamaican reggae stars. The article was illustrated by the two men wreathed in impenetrable clouds of ganja smoke, the joke being that when they got their bongs going, it was impossible to tell them apart. And tucked away in the corner of the reviews page, 'Don't look over your shoulder, but the Sex Pistols are coming', by *NME* staffer (now professional astrologer) Neil Spencer. This was the first published review of the Pistols. It ended with a mini inter-view between Spencer and guitarist Steve Jones. 'Actually, we're not into music.' 'Wot then?' 'We're into chaos.'

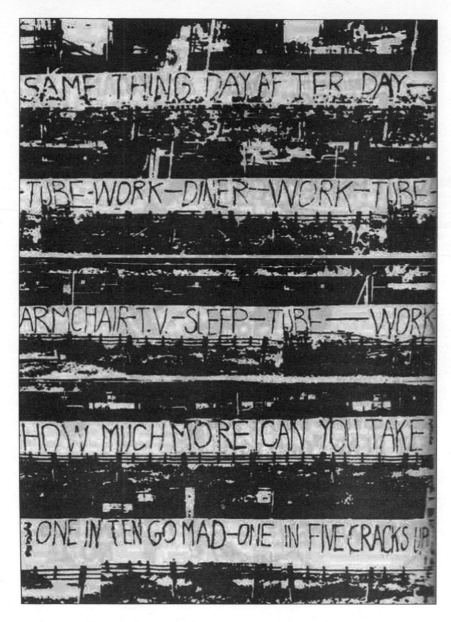

This excellent graffito depressed commuters on the Hammersmith & City Line between Westbourne Park and Ladbroke Grove for many years. They could hardly miss it, since it took up half a mile of trackside wall. It would do as a neat description of the lived reality of the alienated life. It was the work of a British group of Situationist wannabes called King Mob. Apart from graffiti, their only 'Situation' was when, in December

1968, a group of King Mob supporters invaded the toy department at
Selfridges. One of their number was dressed as Santa, and they handed
out the store's stock of toys to passing kids. They also handed out a flyer
entitled 'It was meant to be great but it's horrible', which purported to
be 'The Confessions of S Claus'. One of these art terrorists was called
Malcolm McLaren, who, with his friend Jamie Reed, had also been part
of an art-school sit-in in 1968; at Croydon, rather than Hornsey.

By the early 1970s, McLaren had met his partner Vivienne Westwood,
and opened a series of clothes shops selling Westwood's designs. The
shops were always in the same premises at World's End on the King's
Road in Chelsea, but Westwood and McLaren couldn't settle on an
identity; it turned from Let it Rock into Too Fast to Live Too Young to
Die, until in 1974, it became SEX. In December 1975, I saw my first punk,
waiting for the Seaford train on Lewes station. Her name was Jordan,
and she was the shop assistant in SEX. She wore a rubber tutu, torn
fishnet tights, ankle-length boots, had her hair in an impossible white-as-
bone bleached bouffant beehive, and instead of the big mascara eyes of
the hippie girls, she wore a stripe of black across her eyes, like a super-
hero mask. She commuted everyday between SEX and Seaford, the next
town to Newhaven. She rocked my world.

Westwood's designs in SEX became the blueprint for the look of punk.
Malcolm's brief and unsuccessful management of the New York Dolls
became the blueprint for his management of a band formed by SEX
habitués Paul Cook and Steve Jones. McLaren introduced them to his
Saturday assistant, Glenn Matlock, who became their bassist. As their
singer, he chose another customer, John Lydon, who impressed McLaren
with his green hair, green teeth (hence Rotten) and home-made 'I Hate
Pink Floyd' T-shirt. McLaren got Lydon to sing along with Alice Cooper's
'I'm Eighteen' on the shop jukebox, and he was in. They played their
first gig on 6 November 1975. The gig which Spencer had so tantalisingly
reviewed was at the Marquee, supporting Eddie and the Hot Rods, on
12 February 1976. It was their ninth gig.

Reading that review, a few weeks before my eighteenth birthday, I
rubbed my hands in gleeful anticipation. My great friend Perry Venus,
whom I was to meet later that year, rubbed his, up in Wiltshire. All over
the country, boys and girls were rubbing their hands in gleeful anticipation. Two hip Manchester lads, Howard Devoto and Peter Shelley, trem-
bling on the verge of trying out something similar, booked the Pistols
into the Lesser Free Trade Hall Manchester, and opened for them with
the first gig of their new band, the Buzzcocks, on 4 June 1976. I really

don't know anyone who was there. Estimates of the crowd vary between forty and twenty-one. If anyone tells you they *were* there, they are lying, unless they are Tony Wilson and Martin Hannett, the founders of Factory Records (who are both dead, so if someone tells you they're them, they're lying), or Morrissey, or Mark E. Smith from the Fall, or Peter Hook from New Order, or, God forbid, Mick Hucknall, all of whom were certifiably there. The Pistols just made people want to start a band. I was already in one, our sixth-form band Ruby Crystal and the Diamonds, but all we could play was a blues jam for hours on end. I wanted to be in a punk band. By now I had connected that fabulous figure on Lewes station with the Pistols. I hadn't heard a note, and I almost didn't care.

On 14 August, just as I was thinking about the Reading Festival in a few weeks' time, and university in six weeks' time, Stiff Records came into being, with the release of their first single, 'So It Goes / Heart of the City', by one of my heroes, the bass player from Brinsley Schwarz, Nick Lowe. It could only be got by mail order, so I ordered one by mail. Stiff was the first truly independent UK record company to start up in years. It had a home-made feel. It seemed reachable, human-scale. After that, I bought everything on Stiff for the next eighteen months. It felt like my record label.

It was the hottest summer in living memory. 1975 had been very dry; and so forty days without rain in 1976 meant that the Government introduced water rationing. Mains water to many houses was cut off, and people queued at standpipes on street corners. This is one reason, maybe, that the Reading Festival that year was so bad-tempered – it was too hot. There were only a handful of bands that I actually wanted to see: 801 with Phil Manzanera and Eno from Roxy Music; Eddie and the Hot Rods, who were, if not exactly proto-punks, at least a speeded up R&B outfit; and U-Roy and the Mighty Diamonds, two reggae bands, both with Sly and Robbie from the Wailers playing bass and drums. When the reggae bands were announced, a couple of hundred of us made our way to the front through the supine hippies. Perry was one of these, though we didn't meet till a few months later. We were going to dance, against the wishes of the majority. The remaining 29,800 people at the festival, or so it felt, stood behind us, and screamed at the stage in anger, and pelted us and the bands in a rain of beer cans. It was described afterwards by the local press as a mini-riot, but it didn't feel that mini at the time. Was it racist? Or just an outpouring of anger at the idea of change among the generally highly conservative rock audience, there to see AC/DC? It felt like both. I came away from it with a deep loathing of rock's old guard, no longer just aesthetic, but now also personal. The rain broke for the first time in six weeks as we drove away from the site.

In October 1976, with characteristic bad timing, given that punk was kicking off up the road in London, I left Newhaven to live in Mid-Wales, to attend St David's University College, Lampeter, to study philosophy. It would have been harder to get further away from the epicentre of punk.

Just before I left sixth form, a girl I knew from the year below asked me why I was going to university, as it was a thing people from our school did but very rarely. I did not hesitate. 'To lose my virginity. To take drugs. And to form a rock 'n' roll band.' Three fine ideals. I chose Lampeter because it was a long way from Newhaven and it didn't ask for a foreign language O-Level (I only had three altogether), because when I went up for an open day, I met a beautiful hippie chick on a little bridge over the stream that bifurcated the campus; because there was sun in the sky and snow on the hills, and because the head of the students' union who showed us round made it clear that he would be able to sort out a bit of hash. I only asked one question: 'What bands do you get?', and he said, 'In 1972, we had the Velvet Underground.' To this day that's the Lampeter Student Union Entertainment Committee's finest moment, and even then it was only the Mark Three Version, with none of the original members. But at the time, I was impressed.

I found my ambitions harder to realise than I had at first hoped, until after six weeks or so, I met Perry Venus at a Union Hall disco, and discovered that his list of what he hoped to achieve at university was the same as mine. He already knew cooler people than I did, including an actual drummer, who had some actual cannabis. Things started looking up. In November 1976, Stiff released what is regarded as the first punk single, 'New Rose' by The Damned, and we played it till it became see-through. By then, Perry and I and about half a dozen like-minded pals were sitting about all day in his student bedsit, listening to Alice Cooper and the Ramones (who were a band before they were a T-shirt), Patti Smith, the Stooges, the MC5, the Blue Öyster Cult and the New York Dolls, learning how to roll joints, and plotting our own earth-shattering entry into the world of punk. Inevitably, we formed a band.

More accurately, Perry formed a band with two like-minded souls, the drummer, who was called Phazer, and Wee Boab, a cool-as-fuck guitarist, both of whom had leather jackets and attitude. Perry played bass, and looked like a blond Ramone. I sulked for a few weeks, till they deigned to give me an audition. They took me to Conti's Café on Lampeter High Street, and I sang along to 'Carwash' on the jukebox. Just like Johnny

Rotten did! And I was in. I was the singer in a punk rock band called the Repeaters. I had ticked off drugs and being in a band. I shall draw a veil over my achievement of my third ambition, though it is worth noting, perhaps, that it became a great deal easier after I became the singer in a punk band. My new compadres were *NME* readers to a man. Wee Boab and Perry had both learned to play from *The NME Book of the Guitar*, a series of pull-out sections which were the Bert Weedon of the punk generation. (Bert Weedon was a first-generation rock 'n' roll guitarist, who wrote a bestselling how-to-play guitar book in the late fifties.) Wee Boab described *The NME Book of the Guitar* to me recently as being 'like a big brother, helping you to learn'. The *NME* told us what to listen to; it nagged at us to form bands; and then it taught us how to play.

On 26 November, the Pistols released their first single, 'Anarchy in the UK', on the EMI label. My pals and I all had it on order, so six copies were sold on the first day in Lampeter alone. Probably did us all right, too; I sold mine in 1984 for fifty quid.

On 1 December, the loathsome Queen pulled out of an interview on the London ITV news programme, *Today*, presented by Bill Grundy. Queen, not so much an actual band as a brand, were fellow EMI artists, and so it was suggested by their mutual label that they were replaced by latest signings, the Sex Pistols. The interview went out live, at 6.35 p.m. As well as the Pistols, there were four fans, two of whom, Siouxsie Sioux and Steve Severin, would go on to form Siouxsie and the Banshees. Grundy was, by all accounts, terribly terribly drunk. There's a link to the interview in the Appendix; it's probably the most famous interview ever given by a band, and you should watch it if your dad hasn't shown it to you already. Grundy is clearly hating the experience as much as he hates the band. John says shit, and Grundy makes him repeat it. Grundy flirts with Siouxsie, and Steve Jones calls him a 'dirty sod'. Grundy tells him he has ten seconds to say something outrageous. Jones calls him a 'dirty bastard'. Grundy urges him on. Jones says, 'You dirty fucker. You fucking rotter.' And the interview ends. The next morning, the Pistols were front page news in the *Sun*, the *Express* and the *Mail*. The *Daily Mirror*'s headline was: 'The Filth and the Fury.' A man kicked his TV in. From being an obscure cult for music-mad kids wanting a bit of grit back in their lives, punk had become, overnight, the most notorious youth movement ever, topping skinheads and the mod/rocker battles of the mid sixties by a mile. It was a moral panic, and we few mild lads in a student bedsit in Mid-Wales felt more connected than ever. We were punks, and we were the avowed enemies of all that was decent.

Bliss it was in that dawn to be alive, but to be young was very heaven.

I got my hair cut when I went home for Christmas, and so, according to me, I just got under the wire to count as a '76 vintage punk, even though the band didn't actually get to do a gig until Spring '77.

So there we were: the first punk band in Mid-Wales. As firsts go, it's not a patch on any of Bob's, but it's the best I can do. It was hard to see punk bands in Mid-Wales. We had nothing to judge ourselves against. We didn't really have a peer group, other than ourselves; all we had was the *NME*. You could get the records, but the bands were far away. Perry had seen Patti Smith and the Ramones. Wee Boab was from High Wycombe, so hung out at legendary venue the Nags Head, and got to see some of the early bands. Our lyricist and later rhythm guitarist, Yammerman, actually saw the Sex Pistols/Clash/Damned tour in December 1976, which had been banned from just about everywhere except his home town of Plymouth. But I never did see many punk bands, and can't even remember for sure which was the first I actually saw; Iggy in Aylesbury, maybe, in the spring of 1977, or perhaps New York second-leaguers Richard Hell and the Voidoids. I didn't see an actual British punk band until I saw the Jam at the Top Rank in Brighton in the summer of 1977, and the Jam barely counted. Our geographical isolation from the scene did not stop us feeling part of it, however. For young people in Mid-Wales at that time, the Repeaters were the first punk band that anybody saw. For punters in Newcastle Emlyn, Llanybydder, Aberystwyth and Lampeter, our version of the Clash song '1977' was *the* version, since no one else but us for miles in any direction was listening to Clash B-sides. To be honest, we never would have cut it in London. We were too soft, too safe, more outer outer suburbs than inner outer, more Sevenoaks than Bromley. Also, we took acid.

In 1977, I lived in the only village in Mid-Wales that Younger Readers who are not from Mid -Wales have ever heard of, which is Llanddewi-Brefi, home of Gareth, 'The Only Gay in the Village', from the sketch show *Little Britain*. The most famous gay who had ever lived in the village was called David Litvinoff, an old Soho habitué who had run away from Town to Llanddewi, where he was visited by Hendrix, Marc Bolan, and John Lennon and Yoko Ono. An old Lampeter hand told me recently about hitching from London to Llanddewi to deliver Litvinoff a note from the Angry Brigade and to take back a packet of cash. He was surprised to find Mick Jagger and Keith Richards pissed and stoned in Litvinoff's front room, as you would be. But by early 1977, Litvinoff was dead, and there were only three industries in Llanddewi-Brefi: sheep farming, forestry and the manufacture and distribution of vast quantities of LSD.

Students at Lampeter had suspected as much for a few years, given the extraordinary ease with which acid could be got in the area. Our drummer, Phazer, had a girlfriend, called Bee, who very much enjoyed her acid, and who was happy to supply it to her fellow students. She wrote to friends in Birmingham, telling them how easy it was to get acid. It came via a local man, Alston Hughes, known to everyone in the area as 'Smiles', and he was getting it from a hippie couple who had recently moved to a secluded cottage a few miles away, just outside Tregaron. They were Richard Kemp and Christine Bott. Christine was a goat enthusiast and sometime locum GP; I was treated by her at the doctor's in Lampeter in the early spring of 1977. Kemp was an acid evangelist who believed that the world could be changed for the better by the universal ingestion of LSD. He had devised methods of making pure LSD more cheaply and easily than anyone had done before. He was a member of and a supporter of 'The Brotherhood of Eternal Love', an underground organisation that believed humankind could only be saved by 'turning on'. By 1973, the main lab was in Carno, near Newtown; Bott would drive Kemp over there once a week so that he could pick up another batch, and oversee that week's production.

Kemp was scrupulous in his production methods. He insisted that all the tablets should have 200µg of acid, and tested random samples to make sure his product was up to scratch. In Andy Roberts' book about UK acid use, *Albion Dreaming*, he speculates that the famous 'brown acid' which was distributed free to such devastating effect at the 1974 Windsor Free Festival was provided by the Kemp set-up; Smiles has confirmed to me that this was in fact the case. There was another lab in London that was part of the same organisation, using Kemp's method, and it is estimated that by 1976 they were making 90 per cent of all the LSD in Europe. Samples of their work were found all over Europe, in the US, and in South Africa. They made millions of tabs, which Smiles was helping to distribute across the globe. They made so much acid, that after they were busted, the price in London went up from £1 to £5 a tab. And the days of easy acid in Lampeter were over.

The police operation to track the Welsh acid ring was called Operation Julie, and was the biggest undercover drugs bust in Britain up to that point. It was named after one of the investigating officers, Sgt Julie Taylor, and Bob suspects that she came to Bryn Ceinon on a scouting expedition during the early part of the investigation. The investigation started properly in February 1976, and came to fruition at 5 a.m. on 26 March 1977 when over 800 police, drawn from all over the country, simultaneously raided eighty-nine premises in England and Wales.

Unfortunately, one of these houses was the one where Bee lived with Phazer, just outside Lampeter. One of her letters, boasting of the ease with which she could get acid, had been intercepted by the Julie squad. And so she had her door kicked in first thing, which is never fun. Bee and Phazer were in bed, and old Perry Venus, who had been staying over for a few days during the Easter vacation, was sleeping on cushions on the floor. Perry it was who invented what we used to call 'The Lampeter Rule', which was that if you only had a small amount of dope left, there was no point in hanging on to it, and you'd be better off doing the lot in. This excellent rule saved a lot of hassle, because there was almost nothing to be found. There was a bowl in which they had crumbled some hash into some melted chocolate, which Perry had the foresight to push under a chair with his foot. But nothing else. So the house was clean – except for two tabs of acid in Bee's purse. She was arrested, and six months later was fined £200 for possession at Tregaron magistrates' court. Me, Perry Venus and Yammerman went with her in solidarity. At the main trial, in 1978, Kemp got thirteen years. Smiles, Alston Hughes, got eight.

Smiles was kind enough to write to me during the writing of this book, and I reproduce what he said to me here:

I did and do feel that LSD is a major force for good. The whole hippie thing and the ideals that were being espoused are as important today as they were then, if not more so. I do think acid should not be illegal, nor any other drug of intoxication – it seems crazy to me that the state should attempt to stop individuals changing their consciousness so long as they do no harm to others. They are going to do it anyway and as we have seen criminalisation serves only to line the pockets of corrupt persons in positions of power and is grist to the mill of the prison system.

I think it has to be considered that there was a recession on and money was tight for most people. We spread a lot of money about the community, from buying the drinks, or doing small favours (and some big ones) or putting envelopes full of money through postboxes at night anonymously (though I think most people sussed that one). We were wild but kind, I guess you could say. You may say I am a dreamer, as our John said, but I am not the only one and I do

believe that if there is a future for our species, we had better wise up
a bit sharpish. It is later than we think. Psychedelics were pointing
us to a better way of living by sharing and caring; and we now live
in the alternative and it is fucking awful.

Smiles was released in January 1982. Lyn Ebenezer, a local reporter who
wrote a book about the case, says that if ever Smiles went back to
Llanddewi, he would be greeted as a long-lost friend. Smiles told me that
he'd been back three times, and that he'd always had a really warm
welcome. It's almost as if the locals, in a conservative Welsh farming
community, didn't really see what they were doing as a crime.

Christine Bott got nine years, even though she was not found in
possession, nor could she be linked to the production. She got nine years
for 'knowledge and support', although she might have got much less if
she had not courageously stood in the dock at Bristol Crown Court and
defended LSD use. She said that, as a doctor, she felt that LSD was 'an
agent which if used in the right controlled conditions could have a
beneficial effect on the lives of those who took it'. This did not go down
well with the judge.

I feel a bibliographical note coming on, one which illustrates the
ubiquity of the counter-culture. In order to fully understand Llanddewi-
Brefi's place in the counter-culture, you would need to read *Jumpin' Jack
Flash*, a recently published biography of David Litvinoff by Keiron Pim;
Leaf Fielding's excellent *To Live Outside the Law* (Fielding was part of the
distribution team, and was at one time the man who made the LSD
Kemp was churning out into tablets. Some of his stories are in fact things
that happened to Smiles, and were used with his permission); Lyn
Ebenezer's local's eye view, *Operation Julie*, and Andy Roberts' indispensable overview of acid use in Britain, *Albion Dreaming*. And that's just
one Mid-Wales village. Population 500. This book is largely set in the
Mid-Wales town of Presteigne, population 2,000, and look at the size of
it. Imagine what went on in your town. Imagine what you could find
out if you asked around.

From a consciousness-altering point of view, the end of cheap acid
didn't really make much difference to us, as the Brefi valley is one of the
best places in the UK to collect psilocybin mushrooms. To this day, it's
still the only wild mushroom I can confidently identify.

So, we ended up an acid punk band, influenced by psychedelia as
much as rama lama 180 bpm heads-down stripped-back rock 'n' roll. In
1979, we all moved down to Brighton, where we were just another

struggling Brighton New Wave act. We changed our name to the Airtight Garage, and we had half a dozen fans, mostly because of our opening number, 'Don't Look Back', originally by sixties US garage punk band the Remains. Our half-dozen fans, like us, were devotees of the compilation album *Nuggets*, a beautiful celebration of the highlights of sixties US garage punk. We should've done more of that stuff, but we would insist on turning gloomy; Manchester might have suited us, but Brighton's light-hearted scene didn't. We split up in 1980, having released no records.

After the band split, man, I kept playing in bands, all based in Newhaven. I was still in thrall to the *NME*. In the eighties, I liked Paul Morley and Ian Penman, who were writing about music in theoretical terms that interested me. Morley in particular seemed like a dude. Where previous rock journalists, like CSM, Mick Farren or Nick Kent had wanted to be rock stars, Morley seemed to want to be a cross between Malcolm McLaren and Roland Barthes, the French philosopher. He seemed to want to be a writer. In 1983, Morley left the *NME* to form Zang Tuum Tumb records with composer Jill Sinclair and her husband, producer Trevor Horn. Their first great success was with Frankie Goes to Hollywood, and Morley is credited with the brilliant promotional and marketing campaign that helped their first three singles reach number one. The slogans on the T-shirts are reputed to have been written by Paul Morley: 'Frankie Says Relax', 'Frankie Says Arm the Unemployed'. A band was more than a bunch of musicians. It could be ideas. I tried to bring some of this thinking about the nature of what pop music might mean to my two subsequent bands. I wanted to be Newhaven's answer to Scritti Pollitti. My bandmates thought I was a wanker. Writing prose started to seem more attractive to me than trying to explain why I'd just written a song about Heidegger to a bunch of junkies. Practice never suited me so much as theory. Thinking about it now, the *NME* in its early/mid eighties incarnation as a champion of the Frankfurt School lit my way out of playing music, as the golden years of the seventies showed me the way into it.

In 2011, the Airtight Garage got back together for a one-off gig at a festival called 'Punk Brighton', a celebration of the great days of the Brighton scene. We were, of course, bottom of the bill. Phazer couldn't make it, because he was writing up his PhD in Musicology. We now live in a world where even drummers have doctorates. So we used a drum machine: turns up on time, keeps the beat, doesn't fuck about at rehearsals, and doesn't feel the need to explain the use of the Dorian and Mixolydian modes in Krautrock, 1969–74.

Top of the bill on the Sunday night were the most successful Brighton punk band ever, Peter and the Test Tube Babies, who ended up being the punk band I saw more than any other, because my brother Trapper was the bass player. That boy has never bothered about theory, or history, or what things mean. He just had a right fucking laugh making records and touring the world for ten years, before he switched to being a tour manager and guitar tech for the likes of Skunk Anansie, the Waterboys, and, SQUEEEE Younger Readers, Sam Smith. Punk as fuck, my brother still is.

If I was asked to list the UK's ten greatest punk singles, the first three would be by the Sex Pistols, the next three by the Clash, the next three by the Buzzcocks, and at number ten, 'New Rose' by the Damned. Looked at from a pop-music point of view, it was 'The New Wave' that produced the most enduring music, rather than the straightforward punk bands. As an attitude, however, punk changed everything. That attitude had its roots in Situationism. Carrot-topped Malcolm McClaren and his friend Jamie Reed were always conscious of what they had learned in King Mob. Jamie Reed's famous artwork for the Pistols – the Queen with a safety pin through her nose, the ripped-up and glued-down lettering – are among the best known example of what the Situationists called 'détournement'. McLaren found a bunch of louts hanging about in his shop who wanted to form a band, and saw his chance for some playful subversion of pop music. He said he'd find them a singer, and he found them the only true genius of UK punk, Johnny Rotten. Peace and love seemed out of time in the political turmoil of 1970s Britain, and it was the moment for hate and war. It's a great story, but one that doesn't interest Bob, so it's nearly time to find out what he was up to while young people were pogo-ing and gobbing on one another.

The real motto of punk was: it was easy, it was cheap, go and do it, which features in a song by the Desperate Bicycles. Dinosaurs can be killed. Authenticity is the thing. Do It Yourself, whatever it is; new music, new publications, new art, new politics, new ways of living, all could be taken control of.

After punk, the world was full of new possibilities. If you are interested, here's some more further reading. The two best books on punk are *Clothes, Music, Boys* by Viv Albertine, and *England's Dreaming* by Jon Savage. If you are interested in the link between Situationism and punk, *Lipstick Traces* by Greil Marcus is unbeatable.

Yet this was the moment the world of fashion and the counter-culture parted company, after fifteen or so fruitful years. Punk was fast and dirty and exciting, but it was also earnest. In order to get gigs, you had to do benefits, for punk causes: to raise money for Rape Crisis lines, or women's shelters, or community centres. We did them as a matter of course, because we needed gigs. We were good people, too, but that's not why we did them. We did them because they were there, and they were there because of a do-it-yourself political mentality that grew up very quickly. This was fund raising for radical causes, for causes which felt close to home. These days, bands do gigs to raise money for Help for Heroes or Cancer Research, for causes which are beyond their control. It became a scene where great music could be heard; but it didn't always make for a fun night out.

Disco was much more fun. The clothes were fun, the dancing was fun, and the drugs were fun. In the world just before AIDS, sex was both fun and plentiful. People had even started to enjoy it. Disco wasn't earnest, wasn't violent, wasn't challenging. And so fashion headed off to the Blitz Club in Covent Garden to become the New Romantic Movement. The New Romantics were not Freaks, though they looked freaky. In the 1980s, shiny pop was due to have its day in the sun. Hedonism had come out into the open, as Thatcherism celebrated materialist success. Club Tropicana, drinks are free. It was a youth movement with no ideological baggage at all, its aim was to have fun. Which, after all, is no bad thing when you are young.

Punk marked the end of something as much as it did a new beginning. There was still a discernible counter-culture, one which assimilated many punks over the course of a few years. Lots of people still dipped their toes in the freaky waters. But punk marked the true birth of tribalism in youth movements. Before punk, if you weren't a hippie, what were you? By the early 1980s, you could be all sorts of things: a punk, a New Romantic, a soul-boy, a ska-girl. The Freaks changed direction, and high fashion lost interest in what the Freaks were doing and learned how to dance; the pop music of the early 1980s was depoliticised, defanged and fun.

The counter-culture, the world of the Freaks, whose rise to glory Bob has been part of, has reached its apogee and is entering its twilight years. After 1976, it savagely divided into punks and hippies. Bob was the enemy for a while. In 1978, my band the Repeaters played a gig in Tipi Village. Jim, our new drummer (Phazer having thrown over student life and headed off to London), was horrified when we got out of our van to be greeted by a naked four-year-old child with a bicycle pump, who went round each member of the band, pretending to inject us with speed. Her

huge and hairy father looked on with evident approval. They had a barn
with electricity; we set up, and played through our twenty-five-minute
set in fine order. By this time, we were used to people actually dancing,
or throwing themselves about at least. This audience remained sitting
on cushions, nodding, and saying 'Yeah' at the end of each number. After
we finished, we started to pack up our stuff. One of the organisers came
up to us and asked what we were doing. 'Packing up,' we said. 'Is that
it?' he said. 'Bands usually play all night.' I said, 'Well, we're a punk band,
and we play for twenty-five minutes.' We thought they were ludicrous,
out of touch, a bunch of outdated hippies who just didn't get it. I suspect
they thought we were a bunch of upstart cunts who just made noise.

These differences reached their peak at the Stonehenge Free Festival
in 1980. The festival scene had lived on through punk. Buses and tipis
were parked up and put up around the Sacred Stones. Fey girls in long
skirts still floated about. Long-haired weirdos still drifted around after
them. Flabby self-indulgent hippie bands still noodled about on mini
pyramid stages. But there was a difference from previous free festivals:
this one had punks. Several hundred had turned up to hear anarchist
punk band Crass. In his book *The Last of the Hippies*, Crass drummer
Penny Rimbaud told the story of what happened next. He said that Crass's
presence on the bill attracted several hundred punks who were not used
to going to festivals; they, in turn, attracted interest from various people
to whom punk was equally new. As people were listening to the music,
suddenly, for no apparent reason, a group of bikers stormed the stage
saying that they were not going to tolerate punks at 'Their festival'.
Bikers armed with bottles, chains and clubs stalked around the site
viciously attacking any punk that they set eyes on. The members of Crass
attempted to protect themselves and other terrified punks from being
beaten up. 'There were screams of terror as people were dragged off into
the darkness to be given lessons on peace and love; it was hopeless trying
to save anyone because, in the blackness of the night, they were impossible to find. Meanwhile, the predominantly hippie gathering, lost in the
soft blur of their stoned reality, remained oblivious of our fate.'

But by 1981, these differences seem to have started to heal. More and
more punk and new-wave bands started to play the festivals, and the
audience changed, as large numbers of punky new-wavey types attended
and the hippies' taste in music shifted. Punks moved into buses. Hippies
learned to dance.

All seemed to be well again, and Bob was no longer the enemy. It
looked like the counter-culture was stronger than ever. But all was not

well. Punk was the equivalent of the German spring offensive of 1918. It looked to be highly successful, but the supply lines broke down, and what seemed to be a renewed, reactivated counter-culture was, paradoxically, entering its last stages.

Every other day, I've needed to get out of the cabin to get supplies. At first, in the flood, Peggy and I would clamber over the Road Closed barrier, and wade up into Upton, or, to get coal, drive eight miles to the Countrywide store which is about a quarter of a mile away in non-flooded times and easily visible from the cabin's road gate, but inaccessible when the river is as high as it's been. After my fall, though, with my broken ribs, it's too painful to walk into Upton for groceries, even though the river is back to navigable levels and the road is open. I've taken to doing a shop at supermarkets with car parks in nearby towns; Tewkesbury mainly, but also Pershore and, today, Great Malvern. Not much walking for me, or for Peggy, I'm afraid. She stayed in the car while I hobbled around Morrisons.

Driving back to the cabin, I saw a fingerpost to the left for Madresfield. I had noticed the name while looking at the OS map of the area a few days back.

So I followed the sign.

Ah, Madresfield! Country headquarters of Evelyn Waugh and his friends the Lygons. Their house, Madresfield Court, was the model for Brideshead. There is little to see from the road: a mock-Tudor gatehouse, a sign saying 'Madresfield Court, Private' in gold letters on a British racing-green background, and a drive disappearing over the brow of a low rise, which obscures the house from view from the road. I parked the car by the end of the drive, and waited while Peggy had a shit on the verge.

Waugh wrote *Brideshead Revisited* in a fit of nostalgia for the world of country houses that the Second World War had brought to an end. So effective is *Brideshead* as a vehicle for nostalgic sentiment that standing at the end of the drive to the hidden house, I too felt nostalgic for a world that was never real, and never mine. Here Charles Ryder and Sebastian Flyte had spent languorous summers, here Charles and Julia had lived as man and wife, here Lord Marchmain had found his way back to God, dying in the Chinese drawing room. Was Nanny still tucked away somewhere upstairs?

Nostalgia is a thing, I find, to which I am increasingly subject. Everyone is nostalgic for their late teens and early twenties, I guess, as they approach their sixties. It's just that mine were spent in a welter of creativity at a time of renewal and hope, in a momentary bubble of freedom. Or that is how it seems to me now. I hope that Younger Readers can still feel the world is like that. But I'm not at all sure they can.

I pick up Peggy's shit, and climb painfully back into the car.

There's an east wind blowing tonight, and it's cold in the cabin. I stoke up the stove, poke it with an old long-throw screwdriver, and listen to the midnight news on the wireless, sitting as close as I can to the fire in a straight-backed chair, hoping for some relief from my discomfort, thinking about the past, like an old man.

Libre El Gringo!

'You've had a makeover!' I say as I climb into the van.

And he has, or rather the van has. Bob has faced facts, accepted that this old bus is going nowhere, cut out the steering column, removed the driver and passenger seats, and replaced them with bookshelves and a chest of drawers. The bus, whilst not quite up to the cabin porn standards of my retreat by the River Severn, is looking rather glam.

And he's replaced his mattress, Bob tells me.

'I felt it was infested with living things,' which is as good a reason to change your mattress as I know.

'And you've grown a beard,' I say. And he has. It's knocked years off him, actually, because the moustache bit and the side bits are still black. The moustache bit is ... Zapata-esque, and it makes me smile, because of the time it saved his bacon, in Mexico, where Zapata moustaches are regarded as a good thing.

The wood-burner is blazing, the coffee pot is on, the evaporated milk tin is open, the fags are going, and Bob is talking.

In narrative terms, we have arrived at the moment where, while the young me awaited the arrival of 'Anarchy in the UK' and the concomitant Sten guns in Knightsbridge, Bob went west.

There are countless books, films, TV shows and records about hippie culture in the States. There are so many that you could, if you wished, now pause here for ten, twenty years or so, and bring yourself up to speed before we go to California, meet Mary Freewind, and drive south in a VW Bug to the land of Carlos Castaneda. I'd rather you came back to it, clearly. When you do, try *The Electric Kool-Aid Acid Test* by Tom Wolfe, *There's a Riot Going On* by Pete Doggett, and *The Illuminatus! Trilogy* by Robert Shea and Robert Anton Wilson, all of which would be good places to start.

'So, the States. Why the States? You met this lady?'

'Yeah, I told you about the meeting on Hay Bluff, didn't I?'

'The one which culminated in a lovemaking session, as the *Sun* would call it?'

'Yes, not twenty minutes had passed from initial encounter, me on a motorbike, her towing a home-made caravan, to us shagging on the bonnet of her car. She was looking for a place about a mile from where we were. I thought I knew where it was so I guided her down a narrow road off Hay Bluff. She was over here visiting a friend called Norma Levine that Monica sold our shop to, the wholefood and clothes shop ...'

'You sold the business?'

'We sold the goodwill, that's all. I headed back to London. I was getting it together pretty well with jewellery, and I was living on an island on the Thames, called Tagg's Island, in a beautiful Edwardian showman's wagon. Like Eel Pie Island, there had been an Edwardian dance hall, gin palace sort of thing, but I didn't ever see that. And there were lots of trees there, lots of trees felled to make way for demolition work, which I logged up and sold in London for firewood. Anyway, I made jewellery, sold it, got together five hundred quid in cash, and got a multiple entry visa to the States.

'I only thought about getting the visa because I met this bad boy who I used to know, called Vaughan Ingham, and I said, "Hello, Vaughan, haven't seen you for a while," and he said, "No, I'm just back from the States." So I said, "How did you get in, did you have a false passport or something?", because he'd done time for drugs, and he said, "No, they gave me a visa – they don't ask, they've changed their visa application form, all they want to know is your name and address and your age." So I thought, "I've got a name and address and an age."'

'A name and an age, anyway.'

'Well, there are loads of addresses in the world, aren't there? And Freddie Laker tickets were going for sixty quid for a flight to New York. So I took a Freddie Laker across the Atlantic, and landed in New York.'

'When was this – '77, '78?'

'Seventy-eight. I'm in New York, I had a ticket from the airport to the bus station, so I went there and checked on the next bus to Montreal, and it was quite soon, and I was a bit disappointed because I thought at least I'd have a couple of hours looking around New York. I went out of the bus station into the first place I could buy a beer, and I soaked up the atmosphere, then boom, on the bus to Montreal. I really liked the vibe in New York, and determined to come back. I had no problem getting into Canada, where I met up with the lovely Linda Gaboriau.'

'The lady on the bonnet of the car? She was a married lady?'

'Yes, her. Married but divorced. She'd been married to a bloke who was this radical new-wave councillor in Montreal, called Nick Auf der Maur. I mean, this geezer was radical enough to get pulled in with a score of other known radical types when the French President, probably de Gaulle, was coming on a visit to Montreal. The police pulled in a load of known radicals and just fucking locked them up. And this bloke was one of them.

'Anyway, Linda Gaboriau was tasty ... You might have heard of her daughter? Mark Williams has just come back from New York and had seen this girl singer, Melissa Auf der Maur?'

A nerdy bell rang, and from somewhere deep in my memory, a Heath Robinson engine made up of useless facts about pop music and the inland waterways of Great Britain, a metaphorical index card came down a metaphorical zip wire and made itself known.

'Melissa Auf der Maur? Wasn't she the bass player in Hole?'

'Was she?'

(Google says yes.)

'Anyway, Mark Williams was greatly enthused by this girl, and was raving about her. I asked if she was Canadian, and he said, yes, so I said, "I nearly put her head through the window of a car," which I did. We'd borrowed a car, and I said to Linda and her daughter, "Hold on, I'll try the brakes on this to see what they're like," because a car you've never driven before, especially an old American car, you want to know that sort of stuff before you actually need to. And I don't know, they just didn't hold on, and the brakes were much stronger than I expected, and Melissa flew from the passenger seat and hit her head on the windscreen and cracked it – the windscreen, not her head.'

'In short, you nearly killed the bass player in Hole when she was a child.'

'I don't know who Hole are.'

'All-girl grunge band. Early nineties. Courtney Love's band.'

'I don't know who Courtney Love is.'

'Kurt Cobain's wife?'

'I don't know who Kurt Cobain is.'

I sigh, and move on.

'So were you living with Linda and her daughter?'

'I stayed with her for a while, and I think it was a mutual sort of thing, we both liked fucking each other but living with each other maybe not. I'd met people in Montreal and I met this one girl called Joy Nolan who was also lovely and a lefty, radical, Jewish. She was living about twenty, thirty miles out of Montreal, in a place called Shawbridge. Her family had the use of a lot of woodland with a shack, similar to the Swedish shack, and they let me stay there. Her dad came up to see how I was keeping his cabin. He asked, "How do you go to the toilet?" and I said,

"Well, same place as the bears," and he laughed, and we were mates after that.

'There was a lake next to the shack, and it was quite warm. I'd noticed a gas bottle about the place, and wondered about it. Anyway, her dad gets one of these gas bottles, goes to a deflated air bed and fills it up. He says, "Nitrous oxide." The crack is, you go out on the water on the air bed, take in a breath, there you go. You can imagine it. I follow his advice, the bed gets floppier and floppier, you get floppier and floppier … Not the sort of thing you want to be doing every day, but for a one-off experience it was a treat. Anyway, so I was there, making jewellery and doing other stuff, a bit of decorating work, among the intellectual elite of Montreal, and enjoying the Montreal nightlife, which was very accessible and all that.

'I did meet Baldry there for the last time. On the local radio, they announced that Long John Baldry will be playing at such and such a place, a couple of nights hence. So obviously I headed into town, and just happened to get to the place as Long John arrived, which was serendipitous. He was with some very lovely squeaky gay creatures, and we go into this quite small venue and John goes to get ready to sing, and we have a chat and that.'

'He didn't know you were coming?'

'No. I mean, how would he? It was still in the days before mobile phones.'

'So was he surprised to see you?'

'Surprised and delighted. In fact, he did his opening song, and said how nice it is to see Bob blah di blah. In fact, he's the only bloke I've deliberately handled his willy. So we were pretty matey, shall we say, pretty relaxed with each other. That was only a brief encounter, but a very pleasant one.'

'So you're in the shack, in the woods, shitting with the bears …'

'Shitting with the bears, and having a pleasant time. Sometimes staying in the city, while doing work for a couple called Quinn and Joanne. Joanne was working for an agency defending the rights of the indigenous population, the Indian, Eskimo types, and she was currently working on how to prevent a valley from being flooded to provide water for New York City. And I said, "Joanne, there's so much fucking space here, what does it matter if one valley gets flooded?" And after I'd done my devil's advocate bit, she said, "Hmmm, sounds like what you don't realise is that this valley is bigger than Italy." I said, "You're joking." And she took down the atlas and looked at the square miles and she was right, it was bigger than fucking Italy. There were thousands and thousands of people lived there. That was a shocker. I don't think I'd really cottoned on how big it is out there.'

'When you say you were working for them, you were making jewellery?'

'No, no, I was making jewellery some of the time, and some of the time I was making slight alterations to people's homes to make them look nicer. The amazing thing is, I'd never done any of that sort of work at all, but it was the sort of thing that you could see escalate, I could stay the rest of my life and do interior design. It wasn't what I wanted to be doing, it was just a few nice little jobs, just to get some money. Because the jewellery, I wasn't trying to sell. I was just amassing a bunch of it so I could send it to London.

'And then something happened. It got cold. I mean, I met up with other beautiful women, and I was having a nice time. It's the only place I've ever gone into a bar, there was a jazz bar there, where a waitress came up to me and said, "I'm knocking in half an hour, I want you to come home with me ..." It left no doubt whatsoever, not "If I play my cards right I could have her ..." Anyway. I met some nice girls there, it was a pleasant time, easy accessible nightlife, and good music as well, like I met the McGarrigle sisters there. I was already a fan. I'd got a couple of their tapes in England and I knew they were Canadian but then the girl I'd gone over to see, Linda, said, "The McGarrigle sisters are playing at a local venue, would you like to come?" Fucking right I would. And it turned out she was a mate of theirs, so I met them just briefly at the gig, but then a couple of weeks later I was in a local fruit and veg street market, and there they were, so I steams in like a fucking battleship.'

'Were they nice girls?'

'Oh yes, absolutely.'

'One of them was married to Loudon Wainwright. And is the mother of Rufus Wainwright and Martha Wainwright.'

'I still play McGarrigle sisters tapes, they're wonderful. Straight-from-the-heart girls, no doubt about it.'

'That's very interesting to me,' I say, 'because you've left London pretty much at the high water mark of punk, and the New Wave starting to happen. And the McGarrigle sisters were – I mean, they were very trendy, actually, over here.'

I start singing 'Heart like a Wheel'.

'See, I had that as a seventeen-year-old, eighteen-year-old boy,' I say. 'They were one of the acts who, although we liked punk and New Wave, we still liked country music, soul, jazz, and they were one of the acts that carried through punk and out the other side.'

'Folk, they would be sold under, I'd imagine.'

'Oh yes ... but in 1977, 1978 we'd play a bit of Sex Pistols and we'd play a bit of Elvis Costello and we'd play a bit of Kate and Anna McGarrigle. For music nuts, they were it. They were absolutely the bomb. I've gone all shuddery. So you met the McGarrigles, you're in that Montreal scene?'

'Yeah – not going to a lot of parties or anything, just good clubs, there was one that had films on, then a band, good bands, and the drinks weren't rip-off prices. But winter came and that was it. It started to fucking snow. And it's proper winter, and I'm not equipped for an Arctic winter, and I don't want to be. It was all right living in the shack, but it was a summer shack, it certainly wasn't a winter shack.

'And I had a good contact in California, and that sounded like a sensible direction to go. And I thought, "could I get a drive-away car to do it in"? I had a fucking arm in plaster, in a sling, because I'd been doing something to a tree and a branch had flicked back on my arm and broken a small bone in it. So when I went into the drive-away car office my arm was in plaster, and a bit cheekily I said, "Have you got anything that needs going to California in the next week?" – He looked through his books, "No" – "Have you got anything in the south-west area?" – "Yeah, Tucson, Arizona. A one-year-old Oldsmobile Cutlass." So I said to the guy in the office, "Yes, fine." He signs me up for it, arranges a date and time, and I'm leaving his office, I'm actually at the door, and I say, "You've asked me for no identification whatever, you must know I'm neither American nor Canadian, and I've got an arm in plaster," and he laughed. I said, "What's to stop me going all along the Pan-American highway in this car?" And he said, "Yeah, but you're not going to, are you?" And he didn't even ask about the arm in plaster, I was all ready to tell him it was nothing to worry about, but he wasn't worried about it. And so I picked up this pretty much brand-new American car to have adventures cruising along the highways. It was about the time the Americans had gone for economy engines, and in fact it did about 32 to the gallon. There was a double nickel, 55 mph speed limit all over the States, which is pretty slow when you think how far it is between places. So I kept to the speed limit because I wanted to get as much mileage as possible and also not get an on-the-spot fine or flung into a redneck jail.'

'Because with those car delivery gigs, you have to pay for the petrol yourself?'

'Yeah. I had a friend in one of the halfway-down towns – Louisville, Kentucky – so I contacted him one night, and stayed with him while I examined maps. The way I chose to go down, I headed straight south, which took me past Nashville. You could see it about five or six miles away across a flat landscape, you can see the skyscrapers, which look fucking bizarre. I stopped by a roadside caff, bypassing Nashville. There were only a few punters in the place, it was really early morning, before-work early morning, four, five o'clock sort of thing. And there was this really cracking what you might call an octoroon girl, Negro clearly there but skin no darker than mine, perhaps a bit of Spanish blood there too, and fucking handsome. And she was shouting out something wicked at me, she was obviously kitchen staff and wouldn't be allowed out, so I went out the other side of the counter and asked, "Are you married? What time do you knock off?" And she said, "Two hours' time. Yeah, I am married, but you've got a car, haven't you?'

I thought about waiting there in this horrible neon-lit scene, antici-pating a shag. The car from the back seat backwards was rammed full of the guy's fucking stuff. The owner of the car was a snowbird, like a lot of Northern US and Canadians, they move south for the winter, and he wanted all his tat with him, so the front seat was fine but all the back was completely rammed with stuff. So I thought, it's about two hours' waiting, and I was already a bit jangled from driving through the night, you get white line fever, so the thought of waiting in this horrible place with these redneck types, none of them looking remotely friendly or interesting, and I thought, "I don't want it," just for an uncomfortable shag in a car. That's why I asked about the husband, because I thought it would be good to go to her place, go to bed, have a great shag, crash out, wake up a few hours later, have another nice shag and something to eat, then fuck off – but the thought of having a quick shag in the front of a car ... I mean, I sort of regret it because she was fucking gorgeous. Of course, there's also the added thing that you might have a husband blowing your head off, because it was the sort of place you could buy handguns, pistols, anything. They had them in petrol stations like you might get specs here.'

'So you arrive in Tucson, Arizona?'

'Yeah, with the car; I'd got there a couple of days before I had to deliver it, so I had it to tour around a bit. It's a sort of cowboy film town. I stayed there a few days, in this really cheap old flop-house, a place where the local winos lived, smelt of urine and so on, but a room, like. I even did a bit of jewellery work there. And checking out the Tucson nightlife as well, which was very accessible and low rent, not expensive. The places I went in the States and Canada, as long as you've got the dosh and you're not totally obnoxious and rude to the door staff – I mean, they've got bouncers there, but you could get in, there was good music everywhere. I had a drink under a bridge with Red Indian types, in the middle of Tucson, not feathers and buckskins and that, but they were in an underpass passing a bottle about, and they were the first Indians I'd seen. I stopped, and they must have realised I was friendly and not after scalps or anything, so we connected and they passed me their bottle, and I drank out of it.'

'But you're still trying to get to California?'

'Yeah, so after a week I caught a bus up to San Luis Obispo, a town on Central Coast Highway 101, about halfway between LA and San Francisco. And I had a mate, a bloke I'm still in touch with, Sir Adam Kish, who was currently living outside the town and who offered me a place to stay, because there was a local geezer called Al Kinkel and his lovely missis who had a house there who would let you stay on their land.

'So, here we are in California, in Al Kinkel's place, where I had the use of a barn to make a bed for myself, any part I wanted. I'd made myself a little stove out of house bricks and had a Coleman gasoline stove, but it wasn't as warm as I was expecting – I spent Christmas there – and there was thin ice on the puddles in the morning. So that was a bit of a surprise. I thought California would be blazing sunshine, though the weather in the day was all right. But I was there for a while and got a local girlfriend, called Mary Freewind.'

'That's beautiful. Made up, but beautiful. Couldn't get more California, really.'

'We were at a party, and my mate, the English guy from London, the one I'd gone to visit, Sir Adam Kish, he was there, and this girl comes up to me and says, "I want to fuck an Englishman tonight, I'm not sure whether it's you or Adam."'

'Al Kinkel's place was a plot of land with a number of interesting old vehicles on it. It was up in the hills near Creston Grade. I never knew exactly what was their land and what wasn't, there were no fences, just a bunch of caravans and a wooden barn and various types living there. There was me and my mate, Sir Adam, and a girl living in a single horsebox-size U-Haul trailer, several people. I got on with all of them, and I was fucking both of the good-looking women there, because it was California in the 1970s ...'

'And it was possible? Pre-AIDS?'

'It was expected. Yeah, I had a good time there. But Mary Freewind lived on Star Route, Creston, with a parrot.'

'Star Route Creston, if you Google it, is the address where L. Ron Hubbard died.'

'There you go – I used to live there for a while, I certainly don't recall L. Ron Hubbard's name, but then I don't recall anyone's name, except the parrot's. Sam Weller his name was.

'Then it was time to head south, because I wanted sunshine. I was looking for a vehicle to take me down to Mexico. I was looking for an old American pick-up, but all the ones I could see that were in my range were past it, worn-out V8 engine, about eight miles to the gallon, sort of thing. I had met a guy who was living in a Ford saloon car, a relatively compact saloon car as Americans go, and he'd got it sorted, he'd taken out the partition behind the back seat and the boot, but kept the front seats as it was, and I'd never thought of that. He lived in the back of it, and he could get in and put his feet in the boot, and I thought that was fine, that would do. So I was just looking for a car basically, and I met this geezer and he said, "I've got a VW Bug, but the suspension and steering's all shot, man, all shot." And I'd had some Beetles, so I knew a little bit about them, so I went to have a look at it and got underneath it, nothing wrong with it at all from what I could see, so I said give us the keys, so I turned the wheel to see what it felt like. And the steering lock don't come off when you turn the key. And I got back under the motor again, had another look, and I realised what was wrong with it was that the steering lock don't come off, and this dumb twat hasn't worked this out.

'So I asked, "How much do you want for this?" – twenty bucks – gave him twenty dollars, and said, "Have you got a big hammer?" He went and got me this hammer, so I just beat the steering lock off. It had been standing so long so I needed to jump start it, and it was facing downhill so I just took the handbrake off, started into life as I was getting to the bottom of the hill. Just then a copper was walking out just across the road and I nearly had to run him over not to lose the engine catching, and the copper quite rightly came over because not only had I just run him over but the engine was making this fucking revving sound. He said, "What's your game, sunshine?" or whatever the local equivalent was, so I told him the truth and he was absolutely cool about it.'

'So you got a Bug?'

'I got a Bug, and I says to Mary Freewind, "Fancy going to Mexico for a while?" because I thought it would be fun to take a nice-looking willing shag with you on such a jaunt, and she spoke some Spanish as well because she'd hung out with a lot of Mexicans, so I thought that wouldn't be a bad thing. I did a quick conversion job on the Bug to make it comfortable, and then she said, "Ah. I've got a daughter down in LA, I'd like to take her with us." So I said, "OK."

'We stopped in this south LA suburb to pick up the girl. Can't remember her name. The father of this child—'

'How old was the kid?'

'Ten? The father is pissed off with Mary Freewind, but there's no point me stepping in, until he starts to hold her between the car and the door and starts hitting her with the door, and I tell him he's got to stop that. He says, "It's none of your business," and I say, "It is my business, because you're fucking hitting my girlfriend with my car."'

'It's the definition of your business, I'd have thought.'

'And he shouts out – obviously there's someone else in the house at the end of the drive – "Bring my rifle!" So I say to Mary, "Get in the car, we're going ..." There I was in a suburban American street, and I knew there would be no good result even if I won the brawl, I was going to get cops on my trail ... The girl was already in the motor, she was all right.'

'So she went all the way to Mexico with you?'

'Oh yeah, we had a nice time.'

Bob and Mary Freewind and her nameless daughter made it as far south as the tiny town of Tetipac, very roughly halfway between Mexico City and Acapulco. Here, they stopped. Thanks to the wonders of the internet, you can go on Google Maps and zoom into Street View and wander around the little town, which looks to be unchanged since Bob's day. The last time I checked, there was even a time-worn VW Bug, parked on a slope, waiting for a bump start.

'I thought, "I'm going to Mexico – I don't know anything about Mexico." Nothing except what a Yank had told me, which was the further south you go the better, and everywhere you go the first thing you say is, "I'm not American." The only place I knew anything at all about was this place called Taxco, and the only thing I knew about it was that they produce all the silver jewellery that comes out of Mexico. So I looked where it was on the map and it was perfect, between Mexico City and Acapulco, quite a long way down south. So I thought I'd head for there. Then I met this geezer who was the owner of a house in Tetipac, an hour or so away from Taxco. He lived in Mexico City most of the time, and there was this separate building in the corner of the garden. So

I rented this little place in Tetipac. It had been built as a granny flat or servants' quarters in the grounds of this nice house, in a garden in this little town. The garden was bananas, citrus trees, coffee bushes, it wasn't like an English garden, it was a mini-jungle.

'The gardener was getting funny with us. I'd got matey with a couple of lads in the village, my own age, and we were definitely the bad boys of the village, the smokers, and the gardener got funny. There was an erratic water supply, as there often is in these places, but it was more erratic than made sense and I found out the gardener was playing silly fucking tricks and cutting off our water supply. Anyway, I met these local lads one day and they said, "We came round to see you the other day but there was a big chain on the gate, we couldn't get in." So I went and saw the gardener and said, "Are you locking the gate so I can't get in or out and my friends can't come to see me?" And I gave him a hard slap, because I didn't want that sort of behaviour. He whips out a fucking shiv and I think, "Right, I don't want to die for this, so I leg it back into my house to pick up a weapon, but Emiliano had split, left the premises.'

'That was the gardener?'

'Yeah. So half an hour later, in our little house, I look out of the window and see a bunch of guys coming up the track, armed with clubs and machetes. So I bolt the front door. It was a flat-roofed, two rooms and bathroom building, built up against the wall of a neighbour's garden. I get out of the back window of the place, where you couldn't be seen by the people coming towards us, up on to the flat roof where I could observe. And I see that a branch has fallen off the walnut tree that was overhanging the roof, so I've got a three-, four-foot-long handy bit of branch. And I wait, quite a few minutes pass, these guys haven't come straight up to the door, they've hidden in the undergrowth like they weren't there.

'Anyway, I didn't know what their plan was, and obviously they didn't either – they must have thought I'd just walk out of the door. So they come out of their hiding places and pick up a ladder and put it against the wall of the place, and two of them start climbing up. So I wait till the head of the leading one is coming up, and I start shouting out these newly learned abusive terms in Spanish, and swing this branch like I'm going to hit them on the head. They don't wait to see if I'm really going to hit them on the head. The top guy falls backwards off this ladder, and knocks down the guy who's coming up behind him, so they're both sitting on their arses on the ground. The one who was coming up first has a big hat, and he pulls out a fucking enormous revolver and starts aiming at me. I'm not going to wait to see how good his aim is, or how serious he is, so I leg it over the wall into the neighbour's place. I'd been working on the neighbour's truck earlier in the day, and he'd showed me this .32 automatic pistol, like blokes do. So I said, "Lend us your pistol, because I've got a load of drunks up at my place and they've got a gun." He said, "Yeah, OK, but I'll come with my pistol." Back-up, fine! So we walked up the roadway up to my place and he saw the one with the big hat who'd pulled the gun and my neighbour said, "Oh fuck, that's the Commandante." The local chief of police! It was turning bad because there were a couple of guys there, I don't know who they were but they weren't from the village. And they really started to hit me with things, and it looked like it might be contagious as well, they weren't hitting me in the face, they were prodding me and trying to get it going. And fortunately I'd learned a word that day, it was "*castillo*", which means "prison". And I knew they had a simple jail in the village. So I turned to the Commandante whom I'd met often in the bar. I just thought he was the local drunk – well, he was, as well as the chief of police. I said, "You, me, now jail," as grammatically correctly as I could, because I could see he was floundering and didn't know what to do and could see it was going to get bad very quick. After all, I had threatened to knock him off my roof with a fucking great big stick. So I made him arrest me.

'So I'm off to jail, so I knew the guys doing the prodding would stop, because I was in the custody of the local police, even if he was a halfwit. So we get to the jail and I'm put in this ludicrously designed cell, you could not believe it – anyone in the street could get anything into that cell, be it a bottle of beer, sandwich, packet of fags or a fucking hand grenade. So all night there's, if not the hand grenade, all the aforementioned sort of thing arriving. People are coming and passing me stuff. And in the morning I hear this chant outside, "*Libre el gringo! Libre el gringo!*" And all the fucking villagers had got together, and were standing outside the place, shouting, "*Libre el gringo*" – which they did.'

'Because that's where you were doing your Gurdjieffian mending of things? So you'd been helping them all?'

'Yeah.'

'What did Mary Freewind think?'

'She didn't last much longer after that. It was time for her to go when she got the hots for some local Mexican geezer and was sneaking off to shag him ... Bit of a shame that she was a slag, basically, but it was all right, she was a good fuck and nice to be around most of the time ... Just this one slight problem ...'

'She got on well with the locals too.'

'Yeah. The real big disappointment in Mexico, though, was music. I was expecting flamenco, mariachi trumpets, but when I was out there, it was the worst trash pop music you could possibly imagine, trying to be comical as well sometimes – urgghh, fuck off. Anyway, so I was a bit starved of music more than anything else, and a geezer turned up with a record player, and he had a completely scratched-up Jimi Hendrix album. And there was only one track playable, which was "All Along the Watchtower". And I fixed his record player but kept lying to him that I was having difficulty getting it right, so that I could hear "All Along the Watchtower". That was the first thing I mended.'

'So I was mending things, and making nice jewellery, which some of them had seen and admired. After I'd been in this place for quite a while, about four months, and put it about that I repair things, this old lady brought along a pair of spectacles, and they had a metal frame, which was broken in several areas. It's quite an easy job, about half, three-quarters of an hour's work, and I sorted them out. But I was surprised that some local silversmiths, which there were fucking hundreds of, hadn't fixed the glasses. So anyway, I fixed the glasses and she put them on; and it was, "This is the first time I've been able to see for years." She really was bowled over, and I thought, "Yeah!" – it was so good.'

'This is where they ended up calling you El Maestro?'

'That was one of the proudest accolades I've ever gained, I think.'

'How did that come about?'

'Progressively; it started out I was addressed as "gringo", then I became "El Gringo", then I became "Señor Gringo", then, much to my embarrassment, I started to be addressed as "Maestro".'

'Did you mend vehicles?'

'I mended several, though there was one I wished I hadn't. There was a family lived outside the village, a mile or two off, a sweet family, and one of the family's sons I really got on well with, he was a nice bloke. And he said, "Can you come because there's an old pick-up, we can't use it because there's something broken, can you come up and have a look at it and find out what's wrong with it?" So it needs an axle rod or something, and I ask, "Where's the nearest scrapyard?" 150 miles away, it turned out. I had to chug off in my VW to get the part. It taught me one thing, if ever I wanted to be a smuggler in that area, forget about taking dope from Mexico, take fucking car parts from the US. Fuck me, you wouldn't have believed how much they were. For a second-hand VW crankshaft, not re-machined, just taken out of the car, two hundred dollars. Which is a lot of money down there. The sort of thing you could get here for next to fuck all. So I get their truck running, have a little test drive and come back and say, "Look, it's got hardly any brakes, it really needs the brakes looking at." I'm happy to do it but they say they can do that themselves and I didn't insist. And the next day the whole fucking family went off the road in it, the entire family.'

'Oh ... that's horrible, Bob ...'

'Yeah, you can imagine I didn't feel good about it. I'd done something, and that whole family would still be alive if I hadn't've done. An act I had done had led to the death of half a dozen people ... And I thought there might be repercussions, people saying, "This is all your fault, you gringo bastard, fuck off where you came from," which would not be all that unreasonable. But far from it, quite the reverse ...'

Bob wipes away a tear.

I say, 'That's not great, Bob.'

'No, not great. But all the other mending was great.'

'How long were you there? I'd have been tempted to leave after the prison break.'

'No, no, come on – I mean, the place where the whole village says "*Libre el gringo*" – they supply me with food and drink all night, saying, "Free the man." I was only in prison because I told the fucking sheriff to put me there, remember? No, it was cool.

'The bloke I really got on with in the village was a similar type to myself. And he had a lovely daughter. He was a person who made the local fireworks. He had to start from scratch, made his own gunpowder, for the very fizzy bangy sort of fiestas they often have – God, I couldn't believe them. They called him maestro too.

'I think it was the fifth of May festival, don't know what it was about, but anyway, the Cinco de Mayo was their main fiesta of the year and they said to me, "We would like you to be the bull." So I asked, "What's involved here, then?" So they say this guy, the other Maestro, he makes a bull from wickerwork ...'

'You weren't thinking "Wicker Man" at this point?'

'Well, yeah. He makes a bull, it has fireworks in it, someone must put the bull on their head and then chase all the pretty girls with the bull while the fireworks are going off. So I thought, "Yes, I'll go for it." It was a what-you-see-in-the-films sort of village, nice handsome warm buildings round a central square with a fountain in it, a church at one end of the square and then the rest of it's filled with various commercial places. Anyway, the church is lovely and ancient, with twelve-foot-high wooden doors, and they're piling up all this wood around them, not just little twigs but quite substantial bits of wood. So I ask, "What are you doing that for?" – "We're going to burn it." – "But won't the doors catch fire?" – "Oh yeah" – "Oh, OK . . ." So there's a lot of stuff going on, drink flowing and that, and then the bull turns up, the one I'm going to be wearing, and sure enough it's wickerwork, it's not huge – but it's completely interwoven with fireworks, not little fizzy things, no, they're bangers – all home-made and twisted into one continuous fucking thing. I think, "I'm going to keep my hat on for this" – fucking good thing I did; I barely had anything left of the shoulders of my shirt. They lit this thing and it was fucking insane – ksh, ksh, ksh – you've seen a Chinese fireworks festival, with many, many, multiple fireworks – imagine wearing that as a fucking hat, yeah? And you've still got to keep it together to spot the pretty girls and chase them, which fortunately wasn't so hard, it was fun . . . And then when I'd done that, with many minor burns, they're lighting the fucking bonfire they've built up against the church door . . . They light it, and they let it burn, until you could see the church doors starting to roar up, I think, "What are you fucking doing?" Then at some point someone must have given a signal and they pull all the burning wood away and they had water buckets stashed about, and they put water on the fire that's on the church door and put it out.'

'And they do that every year?'

'Yeah. Wild. Another fiesta day, and the two guys forming the local bad boys, they said, "Can we borrow your knife?" "Well, what for? You've all got knives, you're fucking Mexicans." "No, no, there's a special cere-mony tomorrow, and we need the best knife we can get for it, and we know you've got a good one." (I had a Buck folding knife.) So I say, "OK, but I'm going to get it back? I don't want you running off with my knife," and they say, "No, no, you'll get it back for sure, and you'll see it in use, because we want you to come down and sit in the chair of honour." As far as I knew it was just some Catholic procession through the village, picturesque and all that but . . . Anyway, I find I'm sitting between the priest and the fucking mayor, and we're on the basketball pitch, on the edge of town. The procession comes in, usual sort of Catholic tat, you've seen the films, the entire village is here in the procession, but leading the procession is the two bad boys who had borrowed my knife. And they've got between them a tasty young local girl. And there's a table in the middle of the basketball pitch . . . and I'm thinking, "It can't be what I'm thinking it's going to be," and so I keep shtum, and they get to the middle, the crowd all gets to the other side of the action and leaves us with a ringside seat of what's happening. And my two bad boys, they're between us and the girl who, as you've guessed, is laid out on the table, and there is my knife, being held up in a fucking stabbing position, and appears to stab down into this gorgeous girl. A moment later, what appears to be a human heart is held aloft ...'

'Fucking hell.'

'They obviously haven't murdered this girl and taken out her heart; but I look at the priest, and he looks at me and shrugs, goes, "You've got to do what you've got to do," sort of thing.'

A quick note here about Mexican mysticism and Carlos Castaneda, perhaps the most read author of the counter-culture, who published twelve books which sold a total of twenty-eight million copies. His first book, *The Teachings of Don Juan*, was published in 1968, and was pretty much a set text for any self-respecting Freak. This, and two subsequent volumes, purport to be the research notes for his degree in Anthropology, from the University of California in Los Angeles (UCLA), which he gained in 1960. Therefore, the books are presented as ethnography. They deal with Castaneda's training as a shaman in Mexico with a 'master' called Don Juan Matus, who, by means of the ingestion of a great deal of magic mushrooms and jimson weed, learned to fly, and to turn himself into various animals. For the hippies, the idea that drugs could lift you onto a higher spiritual plane was very heaven, of course. Lots of my pals had at least the first book on their shelves. But there was a problem.

Wallace Sampson, in 'Science-based Medicine', writing about Richard de Mille's 1980 publication, *The Don Juan Papers*, says that the book:

traces Castaneda's academic works in cultural anthropology at UCLA, through comments from his advisers, others who had input into the granting of the degree, and outside observers. The conclusion of most: the thesis was a work of fiction, perhaps based in some personal experiences, but mostly in works of others, knowledge of other cultural rituals and myths, synthesized into a nearly plausible epic analysis of the occult mysteries of native American tribes.

So I think it fair to say that if you read Castaneda's books, you should take them with a pinch of salt, like with tequila, and read them as novels.

I never got on with them myself. If you want a nearly plausible epic of occult mysteries, I much preferred *The Third Eye*, by a Tibetan Lama called T. Lobsang Rampa, published in 1956. The book told of Rampa's upbringing in a Tibetan monastery, and was, for some unknown reason, in my school library, where I devoured it in a couple of sittings. It was a huge bestseller, one which, once again, found its way onto a lot of Freaks' bookshelves. I thought it was great; as one of the reviewers said, it was 'something close to a work of art'. The problem here was that T. Lobsang Rampa was in fact a plumber from Devon called Cyril Hoskin, who had never been closer to Tibet than Okehampton. He was outed in 1958, but was happy to admit that, yes, he was born Cyril Hoskin, and had never been to Tibet; but after an accident where he fell from a tree, was inhabited by the spirit of Lobsang Rampa, who 'wrote' the book. He went on to write seventeen more books, one of which, *Living with the Lama*, was supposedly dictated to him by his cat. Although *The Third Eye* is nonsense, it really is quite a good book, which sparked a counter-cultural interest in Tibet, just as much as Tim Leary's espousal of *The Tibetan Book of the Dead*.

'Another adventure there, this group of people came from another village about forty miles away because they had heard about me, and they came in a Volkswagen Beetle, and said, "There's some motor in our village needs sorting out, will you come and have a look at it?" And so I say, "Yeah, sure," and there were already four of them in this motor, and they say, "Will you do us the honour of driving?" We come over the brow of a hill and I look and in front of us there's like a rope-and-plank bridge over a canyon. It seemed like a quarter of a mile down, at least twice as far as here to that woodshed. No sides to the bridge, nothing, and I think, "This is a bit of an unexpected test," and I know one thing, the less time I'm on that fucking bridge the better, so I just floored it and hit it as fast as I could. I look around at everyone else and they're all fucking green ... "*Señor*, we should have told you, everyone gets out except the driver usually ..." They were more frightened than I was. Anyway, we get to this other village and it's also the day they're having this bull festival, and there's a corral like you see in cowboy films, wooden rails, and it's a bull-riding thing, local lads are trying their hand at riding these long-horned cattle. One of the guys takes a tumble and the bulls all start to move in on him and have a go at him, and I'm nearest, I'm lying down so I've only got to roll under the rail and I'm there, so I think I'd better do something. So I go and grab hold of the bull and wrestle with it, to stop it gouging this poor bugger. As soon as he was out of the way I'm off over the fence, quickest bolt I've ever done. But that put me in well with the local people there.'

'How long where you in Tetipac?'

'More than six months. So long my visa had run out.'

'To get back into the States?'

'Yeah, and I had dumped the motor in Tetipac, because it had broken its crankshaft. I knew that because I took the engine out and took it apart and all that, very easy to do on the VW. So I was there without a motor, the two girls had gone a couple of months or so prior to that. And I was missing England; I was missing being somewhere I could understand every word that's being said, and just my own culture, really. So it was time to go. But Mexico was really good to me, I had a nice time there, learned a bit of Spanish, smoked some marijuana ... and they protected me, you know?

'There were only about three shops in the village that sold food, and they were all bars as well. I was in one of these, there were one or two local customers in there, and the patron and his wife. I got on really well with the patron and his wife. I was sitting on a roll of wire in the corner, because there was agricultural stuff and things about, having a beer. I'd been there at least four or five months so I was the right colour, I had a Zapata moustache, same hat as everyone else was wearing, same sandals as everyone else, so as long as I kept my mouth shut I'd pass. And I kept my mouth shut when three geezers walked in, dressed the same as everyone else but carrying automatic weapons, which wasn't usual. And they were obviously "Federale" police, because of the way they didn't pay for their beer. What the Federale do, they find people like myself, find they've got dope on them and then take everything they've fucking got, they're just licensed robbers, basically. And my language skills had got good enough to know that they were asking for me at the bar – "We hear that there's a gringo living here." So I think, I've got, not a vast amount of weed, but certainly a bag of it, at the place where I lived, and once they got hold of me it wouldn't take long to find out where I lived. I did not want them to get hold of me, so I kept my head down, shtum. They had a couple of beers, and they directly asked the couple who owned the place if they knew me, and they said, "No." So you can imagine how I felt towards them, you're putting yourself at serious risk here by denying that, so I was very touched by that. Anyway, the guys have another beer and fuck off. Phew ... About a minute later a little boy comes in, a local boy; his face really ashen, very upset, saying "I'm so sorry ... but their truck won't start, and they asked if there was a mechanic here, and I said yes, because we are so proud of you ..." And then he clicked in his little head, because everyone knew they were looking for me, by this time the whole village knew that, and the whole village was keeping shtum, and this little guy had said, "Yes, we have a mechanic – oh fuck, it's the guy they are looking for that we've said ain't here, and now I've told them you're here, not you as in the guy they're looking for but as in the mechanic."

So I've got to go out, and deal with them. I think, "How the fuck am I going to handle this?", because although I've got enough Mexican Spanish to get about on, and to understand at least half of most conversations, I've certainly not nearly enough to pass myself off as a fucking local. I go out to the door, and do a big show of Hercules, circus strongman type movements. And then, with an arrogant swagger, looking as though I'm about twice as big as I am, I move towards the back of the truck and make a real show, and hoping they've got the wit to – because although I knew what the word for "handbrake" was it was too much for me to say without giving away the accent – so I hope they'd got the sense to take it off. So I go out there and say *"Arriba"* – get up – I can get away with that – and I start to push. And fortunately for me there's a very slight decline in the road – it's dirt, but there's a very slight slope, and it started to roll, and I'm giving it everything I've got, because I want them gone. It just happens that that day I'd learned the word for "clutch", which happens to be "clutch". Anyway, the truck started, and I never had to buy a drink in that village from that moment onwards, the whole place fell apart ... So it was a good moment.'

'How did you leave?'

'I just felt it was time to go. Oh yeah, there was this fifteen-year-old schoolgirl who was the daughter of my fireworks mate. She was fucking gorgeous. I mean, people get married at fifteen there. She was showing out to me, and at that time, I'd moved out of the rich guy's place and was just renting a small room in another property, with a window overlooking the road where every morning and evening this lovely girl walked by. So, you know, we had a good definite eye contact, she was pleased to see me looking at her and I was pleased to see her looking at me. Anyway, I forget who it was came up to me, it might have been the Commandante, anyway he came up to me and said Raimondo (the fireworks guy) asked me to tell you he is loading his pistol for you ... basically saying, "Keep your eyes off my daughter, you gringo scum bag, even though we're friends I'm going to shoot you if you try to shag my fifteen-year-old daughter." It made me think. There were a few tasty women about, but the Catholic thing is almost as bad as the Muslim thing in those deep rural Catholic places. Once the American girl had gone home, I was not getting any nookie.

'I wanted to have another look at Montreal, because there were a few girls I knew up there. And I still hadn't done New York – the little twenty-minute beer break I'd had on a doorstep in New York had whetted my appetite, and my plan was to regroup a bit, and then get something sorted out in New York, so I wasn't going there totally cold with no contact at all.'

'How did you get from Tetipac to Montreal?'

'By bus. I went by local bus to Mexico City, and then a bus from there back to the States.

'When I got to the border, I had my fingers well crossed, because I was leaving without the car that I'd gone in with. If they had spotted that I would have been in quite deep shit. I'd given the car to a Mexican family who'd done me favours. I said, "You can have this car, free of charge, only one proviso, if I don't get through the border because they notice I don't have this car with me, I'm going to have to come back and get that car to the nearest customs post, and get it written off my passport. I knew that was the deal because I'd had to do that sort of thing in Iran. I wanted to avoid that expense and hassle and take a chance I'd get out of Mexico without them noticing, and without them noticing my visa was fucking well out of date. Anyway, that was fine, got out of Mexico, got to the States. The Yank redneck type border guard was a bit sharper than his Mexican compadres over the border, and said, "Hey, you went into Mexico with a car and came out without it," and I said, "Yeah, it broke its crankshaft." He really didn't fucking like it, man, and he was going to send me back to Mexican Customs, but I said, "I'm out of Mexico; it's their business, not yours." He was taking it as a kind of personal insult, until a couple of his fellow officers came over and they were more reasonable and said, "He's right, it's none of our business, you're just being nasty to the guy for no reason." It was a squeaky moment – and no one noticed my visa was out of date.

'So anyway, I got a bus to New Orleans, walked out of the bus station, and a local motor pulls over, a guy leans out and he's got a big fucking automatic pistol just stuck in his waistband, with a guy in the back seat obviously OD-ing from smack, and asks, "Do you know where the nearest hospital is?" I almost said, "Can I come with you? You look like my sort of people." But I didn't. Now I was in New Orleans, young, cheap and single. And you're already in the French Quarter, where the bus station is, you're smack in the middle of it.'

'Where I've actually been.'

'I'm sure you have. If you've been to New Orleans you'd be dumb not to go to the French Quarter. I walked into the first bar that looked jolly and lively and absolutely rammed and I hadn't been in there more than a few seconds, and a guy comes along and says, "What do you want?" So I say, "A drink." And he thought I was being funny, I didn't say "a Bud" or "a Coors" or whatever, I wasn't really focused on what I wanted to drink, I was just looking at the people and what sort of types they were. And he legs it to the far end of the bar, picked up a billy club, had a whispery word with some hard-looking cats who were there too, and starts pushing his way through the crowd to get to me to batter me. So I think, "Fuck this," and I was out the door and down the street. Heard some nice dancing music coming out of another bar, walked in, and there's some really fucking horny-looking chicks dancing together on a little stage. I think, "This looks all right." I order a drink and, "Hang on, they're not chicks, they're fucking geezers." It's a gay bar, which is usually a good laugh, so I decide to have another drink, then I need a pee so I go to the bog and some geezer comes along and cups my balls, so I say, "I'm not really gay and I've only been in town half an hour ..."

'I bought some emeralds in New Orleans. I thought it would be a good place to buy emeralds and it was. I knew there'd be a trade coming up from South America with whatever people could carry in their pockets. But I thought I'm going to get into trouble here if people are so fucking volatile that you can go into a bar and ask for a drink and they're ready to bash your skull in, so I got out of there pretty quick.

'I thought I'd spend a bit of time in Montreal and then get something organised in New York, maybe find just one person I can stay a night with and learn a bit. The next day I got a bus up to New York, and then back to Montreal. I stayed with my friends Quinn and Joanne.

'And in Montreal Joanne the Indian affairs girl who I'd done work for was talking to her friend in New York on the phone. "Yes, this English guy's here, did some nice original work on the place ... yeah, he's a jeweller as well ... yeah, hang on, I'll ask him ... My friend in New York here wants someone to do some work in her East Village pad, are you up for it?" She knew I wanted to go there, and I said, "Yeah." And it turned out to be the wife of Tuli Kupferberg. So it was lined up that I go there, stay there in the East Village pad, with the missis who is probably a tasty hippie chick, and her mates would be the same, and paid work, doing up the place, and I had a pocket full of jewellery.

'Tuli Kupferberg out of the Fugs?'

'Yeah.'

'The Fugs were great. He appears in *Howl,* you know. He's the guy "who jumped off the Brooklyn Bridge and walked away unknown and forgotten into the ghostly daze of Chinatown".'

'Was he? I'm even more pissed off that I didn't get to meet him, then. And I'd heard the Clash were playing in New York. There was an American hippie magazine which used to publish the key to the Bell telephone code, so you could just look up any number, apply the code to it, and call anywhere in the world for the price of a local call. So I got through to Johnny Green, who was the then tour manager of the Clash, and said, "Hello, Johnny, I'm thinking of coming to New York tomorrow," and he said, "Yeah, be great to see you, we'll put your name on the door so you can come straight backstage." So I think, "Great, this is fucking set up." I'd get into New York, straight round Tuli Kupferberg's place, drop my bags off, say, "I've just got to go and get in to one of the Clash gigs, in whatever big hall it was in New York, I'll be back later this evening." And I thought, "Sorted, or what! New York here I come!"'

'So what happened?'

'So the girl I was seeing at the time drove me to Montreal airport, and I came across this situation where US immigration is inside the Canadian airport. The American immigration guy didn't like the look of me, saw I'd overstayed my visa in Mexico, and not only that but I'd taken a car into Mexico and hadn't taken it out, and he really didn't like that. Basically, he didn't like my face. He said, "I suspect you are working over here?" and I said, "Yes, I am working." I'd kept all the documentary evidence to show that I'd been sending stuff to London and the bank things for when it arrived. And he wouldn't wear it. And of course I'd been half a year in Mexico, and he noticed the whole car thing, and he said I couldn't go back into the States. I said, "That's a nuisance." He had his hand on his gun so he grabbed it and said, "What's that you say?" I said, "I said that's a nuisance." And he's coming across the counter, nearly climbed across the fucking counter to get at me, till he realised he couldn't get away with hitting me. Fucking American immigration wouldn't let me get on the plane, even.

'Thinking there might be a problem, I'd asked Frances, the girl I'd been seeing, to wait until I got through immigration, which she had done. She took me back into town, and I was fuming. Got to a posh suburb of Montreal, and I asked Frances to let me out and walk. Walking along this suburban street, a taxi pulls up in front of me, a woman gets out, and in the road where the taxi was is a fucking enormous roll of money. So I pick it up, and it's fucking huge, thousands of dollars. And

I saw her going up the steps into this house, and I thought, "Fuck." So I called out to her, and she wept when I gave her the money. And I fucking felt like weeping myself.

'I just wanted to leave that continent then, it was just one thing after another. I just wanted to get the next plane out of town after all that.'

'So did you?'

'Yeah. Cost me all the money I had left, which was a fucker really, because Frances said, "I'll drive you to New York," which she would have done, and maybe it would have been fine crossing the US border by road, but I was just pissed off, angry that it should be in the hands of these fucking twats where I went and what I did. I was doing honest work, good creative work, and not being allowed to enter the land of the brave and free.

'So I landed at Heathrow, absolutely skint and pissed off, frankly. Not even enough to buy duty-free baccy or anything, nothing. But some fucker meanwhile had been playing around with the world commodity price of silver, and manipulated the price hugely, four times, five times more than it had ever been. And I'd landed in Heathrow and thought, "My box of silver." My box of silver I left in Sweden. So I phoned up my mate in Sweden, and said, "David, have you still got that box of silver I left on the island?" – "Yes, I've got it here." – "Could you post it to me in London, please, it would be handy to have it." – "Better than that, I'm coming to London tomorrow, I can bring it." And I met him at the airport, took it to a silversmiths, weighed it in, and got five hundred quid, which would have been the equivalent of a couple of grand now.'

'And so the adventure could start again.'

'Yeah.'

'And you moved back round here?'

'Yeah'

'And then seven or eight years later, you met me.'

'Did I?'

'Yes. You remember everything else, you cunt, but you don't remember meeting me.'

Bob reaches for his tin.

'Remind me,' he says.

Now Here I am, Wheels Flattened

I first met Bob Rowberry in 1987, when I moved with my then girlfriend Lily and my seven-year-old daughter Charlie to an isolated cottage on the side of the Radnor Valley. We had come to get our heads together in the country. All the way from Brighton.

We had enough money to buy a house, and we wanted to get away from the south-east; we looked at the Marches of Wales, mostly because Charlie's aunts lived nearby, in the Forest of Dean. Charlie's mum had just died, and it seemed wise to be within an hour's drive of them. We looked at a few places. When we saw the information for The Rack in Kinnerton, a few miles outside New Radnor, we liked the look of it at once. As we drove west along the A44, past Kington, to where the road rises up a hill before descending into the wide isolated basin, we gasped at the beauty of the Radnor Valley, surrounded by high hills, dominated by the Whimble; and when we drove up a steep winding lane with hedges decked with honeysuckle and roses to see the cottage in front of us, with its stunning view over the valley, we were sold. It had a large garden, and we saw ourselves cultivating veg and maybe the odd chicken. We were in the last wave of rural migrants, looking for Downhome.

After us, the dream was coming to an end. We didn't know that then, but it is obvious now. We made friends with a few young families who lived in the valley, and Charlie became friends with their children. Those no-longer-young families are still in the valley, some of them in the same houses, and are still my friends, but their, our, children have moved way, almost without exception. Very few new families have arrived since the late 1980s.

Like all good stoners, my first priority on arriving in a new place was to find somewhere I could score, and the people I met by the bus stop in the morning to send our kids off to school all looked like they wouldn't mind being asked. In this part of the world, at that time, you could ask people you'd only just met that sort of thing without embarrassment, standing in a shelter waiting for the school bus.

So I asked one of them; and I was right, she didn't mind being asked at all. She told me she'd mention me to 'Black Bob'. A few days later, he pulled up outside our cottage on a motorbike, and that was that. I have no memory of social awkwardness of any kind. We just hit it off. It got to be the case that he'd drop by once or twice a week, and we'd sit at our dining-room table, and we'd chat, and smoke, and he started telling me these stories. The first time my parents visited our little bit of Downhome, Bob called by, and I can remember my mum melting into what I can only call girlish giggles in the face of his charm and beauty. The very same mum who had told me, when I was five, that if I came home with long hair, she wouldn't let me in the house. I was buying logs from Bob as well, and he was also 'helping me do up my car', i.e., he was doing up my car while I made tea and revised for exams. This was the time when we devised 'Theory & Practice, General Builders'. And here we are thirty years later, still smoking and chatting.

One Bob story has entered family legend. He popped by one morning with a piece of draw as big as a baby's fist, and we sat as usual, chatting and smoking. I bought a bit off him. At this time, Lily's younger sister Kerry was visiting. Always easy on the eye, Kerry was, on this particular day, wearing a pink miniskirt. Bob didn't actually speak to her, but followed her comings and goings, shall we say, and it was clear that he was reluctant to leave. He stayed for three or four hours, chatting, smoking, and eyeing up Kerry.

The next morning, I was outside chopping logs when Bob pulled up again on his motorbike. From inside his leather jacket, he pulled out a gun, which he pointed at me.

'Oi, Marchant! If you don't skin up, I'll fucking shoot you.'

Having chopped enough logs to get us through a day, this seemed like an offer it would be churlish to refuse, so he came in, and I made tea and rolled a spliff. Kerry was still our house guest, no longer wearing the pink miniskirt, but rather a pair of jeans. This time, Bob did speak to her.

'Do you want to come up the forestry for a ride round on my bike?'

Kerry giggled. 'Oh, I don't know. Should I?'

'I'll look after you,' he said. 'Come for a ride up the forestry.'

Kerry blushed and giggled some more. 'Ooh, I don't know if I should ...'

I could tell that she was sorely tempted.

'Lily,' said Kerry, 'do you think I should go for a ride with Bob on his bike up the forestry?'

Lily shrugged. 'It's up to you.'

Bob said, 'Yeah, come on. Come for a ride.'

Kerry giggled, blushed and giggled. And blushed and giggled and blushed.

'Well ...' she said, clearly having decided that she would.

'The only thing is,' said Bob, 'could you pop on that pink miniskirt you was wearing yesterday?'

Kerry screamed, and ran from the room. Even Bob overplays his hand sometimes.

We are sitting outside today. It's a beautiful day, the day of the autumn equinox. Bob's been cutting up logs with his chainsaw before I arrive, getting ready for what's to come, though the winter seems far off in the warmth of the sunshine. We sit in the wheelchairs that Bob uses as outdoor seating, and I remind him of the Kerry story. He smiles at the memory.

It's interesting to me that Bob's remarkable memory gets less sharp as we come closer to the present day. Not, I think, because he's losing it, but because he has settled into his own version of domesticity, and the crazy stuff is still bright, whilst domesticity doesn't always create memorable moments. This doesn't mean he's bored – far from it. He takes huge, unbounded pleasure in the here and now; each day is a gift, a jewel.

'So what happened when you got back from America?'

'After I got back from the States, early 1980 maybe, Monica lent me this Edwardian showman's wagon she had, which was on Tagg's Island in the Thames, where I'd been before I headed off. There were also these three wrecked Morris Minors. None of them worked, so I put together a drivable car out of them; and I drove down here, because I was going to a party at Richard Booth's place in Cusop. I met this bloke called Dan and his girlfriend Vanessa there. And I said, "I'm maybe wanting to live down this way again." And they said, "We've got this place you can have, rent free, like." So I went and saw it and thought, "Yeah, this'll do me." It's called the Old Lodge, in Dorstone. I lived there with my dog for a couple of years.' (Dorstone is a little to the south-east of Hay, in an area known as the Golden Valley.)

'What were you doing?'

'Jewellery. Welding up people's cars. Shooting rabbits. Doing the festivals. And then I met Patsy, and I'd been seeing her for a bit, she said do you want to move in with me, like?'

'In New Radnor?'

'Yeah, up Harley Dingle.'

'So you moved from the Old Lodge?'

'Yeah. And we got on all right at first.'

'And you had Roo? Your daughter?'

'Yeah. But Patsy couldn't stand my snoring, so I took the back off a van I had, and put it on this rickety old caravan chassis in Patsy's garden; I didn't even fasten it on, it was held on by Isaac Newton and the wheel arches . . .'

'Good name for a band . . .'

'. . . so I lived in there. In her garden.'

'That's where you were living when I met you. You brought me up here, to this wood, because it was where you were getting the logs you were selling. We bimbled about on your old dumper truck, too fast for me. I was shitting it.'

'Yeah. I had the thinnings from the Forestry Commission. I paid sixty quid a year, for all the trees they hadn't marked that they wanted to keep. Yeah, that was a major part of my income at that time.'

'So when you split up with Patsy, then you went in the van?'

'Well, no, I squatted that house up the road from you in Presteigne.'

Hard as it may seem to believe, this squat still exists, a tiny one-bedroomed place, one of a handful of squats left in existence. Welsh Heritage should preserve it. It should be on the Presteigne Tourist Trail. The current incumbent, a high-brow hippie gentleman in his late sixties, likes to catch me on the street so he can discuss Freud's *Interpretation of Dreams*. He should be paid to do this for tourists who come to see the last unreconstructed hippie squat in Mid-Wales.

'Because you knew Presteigne really well. And Pete Mustill's here, Mark Williams is here . . .'

'Of course. Been coming here for years. But after that squat, I was going to so many festivals, I just ended up in my van. Mercedes, the first two were, before I got this.'

'And you were parking up pretty much where ever you wanted?'

'Yeah, but always no more than ten miles or so from here, so that I could help bring up Roo.'

'And you didn't get hassle?'

'Not till after fucking Castlemorton, no.'

'That whole festival world didn't really happen until you came back in the eighties.'

'It had changed hugely. It was all coincidental with the New Age Traveller thing. It became so that the crew at Glastonbury, virtually all of them, were what you would call New Age Travellers. All of them had live-in vans, most of them were living on the road, sort of thing, and that was the best time, when people were coming over the Glastonbury fences like on the Somme. And there was a lot of stuff that was nothing to do with the organisers, entrepreneurial in a small way. It was a happening scene, and it's not now. It's rich cunts and crooks who have got their hands on it now.'

'Did you know Sid Rawle at all?'

'Yeah, I knew him from the Portobello Road days. He used to come to the shop after school.'

'Was he a mild-mannered schoolboy? You imagine people coming along in their school uniform, and then thinking, "No, I'll grow my hair and drop out. I met him when we did a gig at Tipi Valley, a hundred years ago.'

'I can't even remember what he looked like back then, but I know he used to come to the Portobello Road shop to score a bit of puff, basically.'

'But you never did that convoy thing that Sid was into?'

'No. I've never been one for groups. Whenever I found myself walking through London as it was in the early days, there'd be a little clique of you, leaving the pub and going up to the next pub or whatever. I always felt very uncomfortable being part of a group, so I'd just slip off. That's just the way I am. It seems like in life you have more opportunities if you're on your own, I think. And you have more ability to seize those opportunities.'

'I used to say to my students, if you want to write, you've got to be very happy in your own company. It's one of the first things I say; and you can see that half of the class, at that point, have already dropped out. Applies to any sort of artist, really, except perhaps an actor or a muso; you've got to be self-sufficient, in spiritual terms.'

'You have.'

Just because Windsor/Watchfield and the 'People's Free Festival' had come to an end, this did not spell the end of the free festival movement. By the late 1970s, it was pretty much possible to spend each weekend from May to September at either a free festival or a cheap community event, like the Albion Fairs. In 1970, at the Isle of Wight Festival, Taffy was one of the few people to have 'a living vehicle'. In 1974 Chris Waite had found guidance from the *Whole Earth Catalog* and built the first tipi. By the late 1970s, the idea of living in a movable space was catching on. You'd move from Stonehenge and up to Worthy Farm, on to the Albion Fairs, and back to Wales for the Psilocybin Festival in September. Until

1990, the Glastonbury Festival had a field set aside inside the festival for the travellers, and they subsequently got in free; because, given the size of some of those vehicles, how were you going to keep them out anyway? There was trouble in the early nineties, and the travellers were moved to a site outside the fence, which led to the fence being pulled down both in 1994 and in 1995 by those who had been excluded.

Chas, at this time, was running an on-site pop-up Pilton festival news-paper, called *The Glastonbury Global*. Arabella had fixed it so that Chas and his team of reporters and newspaper sellers had a Portakabin and a couple of photocopiers to knock out the paper. No computers, so they were all typed and photocopied. They sold papers in the morning, wrote and edited them in the afternoon and evening, and printed 'em out over night. Watching the fence come down by the Sacred Circle in 1994 was one of Chas's best loved stories, which he told me for the one hundredth time a few weeks before died. I'd tell it to you, but I never really listened.

One of Chas's reporters for this enterprise was Pete Mustill. By the early 1980s, they had both washed up in Bath. Chas was drumming and acting with the Natural Theatre Company, and learning how to play piano by sitting in piano showrooms till they chucked him out. He lived in a van, the squalor of which defies all description, as did all his subse-quent homes. Think *Heart of Darkness*. The squalor ... the squalor ... One of the places he parked up outside so that he could barge in and use their facilities without asking or knocking was the squat where Pete was living; they palled up, and played in bands together for many fruitful years. Chas found his way up to Lancaster, and Pete back to Hay and Radnorshire. Pete now runs a What's On magazine like no other, the splendid *Broad Sheep*, which covers gigs, films, theatre events and chakra rebalancing workshops over a vast area of the Marches, Shropshire, Herefordshire and the Great Green Desert. Pete has made a culture out of the hip communities that still exist in this area. And he first learned how to write copy and edit a magazine while working with old Chas Ambler on *The Glastonbury Global*, one of the very last of the handmade underground magazines.

One of the reasons Glastonbury has managed to survive, not as the rock festival you see on the BBC, but as a hippie free festival, is because many of the travellers are back on the Glastonbury site, working. Bob, Chas, Pete Mustill, m'self, and thousands like us, get to decide if we want to go to Glastonbury or not. If yes, we see who needs a bit of metal-working/space-fixing/piano-playing/walk-about, and we're in. Chas would never miss it, and could always get a job manning internal gates, far and away the best gig going. Now the travellers are not unlike the travelling showmen who bring fairs to the towns; they still follow the festivals, but the festivals are licensed, they cost a great deal to get into, and the travellers are being paid to be there.

As the festival circuit played its merry round, those people who were spending their summers on the road travelling between festivities started travelling together. Travelling in convoy was convivial; it meant there would be parties en route between festival sites. Also, it must be faced, many of the vehicles were on their last legs, a few degrees better than Bob's van, but still pretty cronky. If you broke down, which you did, a lot, your mates should be able to sort you out and get you going.

Living vehicles were often associated with squats, and in winter many streets around squatted houses would be full of parked-up living vehicles. In the 1980s, in particular in London, squat parties became commonplace, where sound systems would play early techno house to squatters and travellers alike. It was, on one level, a culture of the dispossessed, of people who lived in squats and vans on very little money, hassled by the authorities, moved on, and ideally stamped out. It was a hard life. You'd make sure you picked up water at every garage you passed, as much as you could carry, because you never knew for sure when the police might stop you moving on, and water might be hard to find. (NB How the world has changed, Number ∞. In those days, you didn't buy water at garages. You filled your barrel at the tap. In those days, you couldn't buy water anywhere, as it was free.)

There are lots of ways to be dispossessed, and being a traveller isn't always the easiest. But although it might be hard, it's a way to try living an unalienated life. You have no boss, no bills other than fuel and bottled gas, you are free to at least try to park up where you like. You spend a lot of time outdoors, often in beautiful places. You will most probably home-school your kids; sometimes this works out fine, other times, less so.

It's not easy to fight alienation off.

At the height of the 'movement' in the early 90s, there were an esti-mated 2,000 living vehicles in the UK, and around 8,000 'New Age Travellers'.

The problem for local people was not that they moved, but that they might stay.

Stonehenge Free Festival was the great annual meet-up for the travel-lers. It was set up in 1974 by a man known as Wally Hope, who was banged up and medicalised in a psychiatric hospital by way of thanks from the authorities. Lots of people headed there after Windsor Free Festival. At least one of the stages was taken from Windsor down to Stonehenge. Everyone who went to the festival called themselves 'Wally', and for years afterwards, you would hear old festival hands shouting 'Wally' in hope of an answering call from someone else who was there.

From 1975 until 1979, Stonehenge Free Festival continued to grow: 2,000 people in 1975, and 5,000 or so for the years up until 1980. According to people I've met who were there, it was an extraordinary experience. Panit Dave put it to me thus: 'You had witches, warlocks, schizos, mystics, psychiatrics, every type of brain state you could imagine. They were all there at the same time, all raising their consciousness. The energy that was raised there was fucking mad. There was an openness, everyone had their eyes up, was looking one another in the eye. It was like meeting your fellow humans for the first time.'

In 1980, Stonehenge started to get big. This was the first festival that the punks came to in numbers, and some of them never went away. You can see festival fashion changing from old photographs; from floaty skirts and long hair in 1974 to leather jackets and mohicans by 1985. By 1980, The New Age Travellers were starting to be a phenomenon that interested the press. In 1982, an estimated 30,000 people attended Stonehenge. Punk had not destroyed the counter-culture. What, after all, did anarchy amount to?

Various anarchists have called themselves Albion Free State, and 'Albion' is an idea that runs through much of the New Age political thought. What is Albion, apart from an excellent football club representing the fine city of Brighton and Hove? Heathcote Williams was one of the architects of Albion Free State, and in his 1974 manifesto he writes, 'Albion is the other England of peace and love which William Blake foresaw in a vision – a country freed of dark satanic mills and similar Big-Brother machinations.' Albion is what the twelfth-century writer Geoffrey of Monmouth called the island of Great Britain, claiming that before Brutus came from Troy and named it after himself, Albion was the original name. It was a land once inhabited by giants, now long dead. Twelfth-century writers could see no explanation for the stone circles dotted over the landscape, other than they had been built by giants. Albion means the White Isle; shining and pure. No wonder the Freaks played with the idea of Albion; it allowed them to lay claim to a lost lineage of pure shining wisdom, going back to the builders of Stonehenge. It is the Britain of John Michell and Andrew Kerr, true in the sense that it is poetic.

In practice, Stonehenge Free Festival was anarchist in its organisation. That is to say, it depended on mutual aid. Where stages were set up, where people camped and parked, these kinds of decisions were made by consensus, if they could be called decisions at all. The festival, for some of the further-out thinkers, represented a model of non-organisation for society. Or rather for a forthcoming society, for Albion.

After the 1982 festival, large numbers of the Travellers felt that they wanted to continue the party. A hundred and fifty vehicles left the site in convoy, heading for the RAF base at Greenham Common, where a Women's Peace Camp had been set up in protest against the presence of US short-range missiles, known as cruise missiles. Because the convoy was heading for the Women's Peace Camp, somebody stencilled 'Peace Convoy' on one of the lead vehicles. Two moral-panic-causing situations were about to meet.

The Cold War had fallen quiet after the end of the Vietnam War in 1972. The coming to power of Margaret Thatcher in the UK and Ronald Reagan in the US ended this period of relative quiet. They were alarmed by the Soviet invasion of Afghanistan in 1979, and by improvements in Soviet missile technology, and they resolved to up the ante. In June 1980, the UK government announced that it would play host to 160 Pershing cruise missiles, armed with nuclear warheads, to be based at RAF Greenham Common in Berkshire and RAF Molesworth in Cambridgeshire. The point about cruise missiles is that they are mounted on the back of movable launchers, rather than being fired from bombers, silos or submarines. They were therefore able to move to different sites, and were less susceptible to attack. As a footnote, some historians claim that Reagan was a peacenik, who would never have 'pressed the button', and that his Chiefs of Staff knew this. But he talked loud and shook a big stick.

In September 1981, a group of women marchers from Cardiff called 'Women for Life on Earth' arrived at Greenham and set a 'Peace Camp' outside the main gate. On 28 December 1981, members of the Fellowship of Reconciliation, on a pilgrimage from Iona Abbey to Canterbury Cathedral, established a similar peace camp at the south-east gate of Molesworth, though this included both sexes.

In May 1982, 250 women attempted to blockade Greenham, to stop preparations for the deployment of the missiles. It was righteous, it made the front pages; and so, on 30 June 1982, the Peace Convoy rocked up at Greenham, to run what they called the Cosmic Counter Culture Carnival; by every account, a good time was had by all. Most usefully, the travellers taught the women how to make benders. Not everyone was comfortable, as the Greenham camp had been declared a 'women-only space', and after a week, the travellers started to drift off; they came together as a convoy in the summers of 1983, '84 and '85.

This was not a fringe affair; my first wife Rowan was an occasional weekend visitor to the camp, including the day of 'Reflect the Base' in December 1983, when 50,000 women surrounded Greenham, holding up mirrors so that the soldiers guarding the base could see what they had become.

My Presteigne friend (and Bob acquaintance) Nicola Jones, Nix, spent a year camped at Greenham. She talked to me about life in the Greenham Women's Peace Camp.

'I had a beautiful job. I was modelling all over the world, earning lots of money. I had a lovely house in Bristol. And I jacked it all in to go to Greenham. My main reason was to support women. I thought they'd all be hippies, but they weren't, not all of them. There were doctors and lawyers and teachers, all kinds of women.

'For me, it was escapism; I wanted to get rid of my coke habit and be around women. It was a chance to be really naughty. You could cut down fences, fight soldiers and live like a bohemian in the woods. I bloody loved sleeping in the woods. And getting chucked out of local shops; I loved all that. But I was very CND.

'I lived in a bender. I built it myself from tarp and twigs. I had fur coats underneath me, duvets on top, but I mostly slept in my clothes. And there was a fire going all the time, and we had like a field kitchen. We'd eat what we were given, veggie stews mostly, but there was always a pot of soup on, bubbling like a witches' cauldron. The main gate was where the heavy women were, the Green Gate. There were at least seven different camps, all with colours; I was in Indigo. In our camp, we'd all eat together at 7 p.m., and we had rotas to take it in turns with the kitchen, or digging shit pits. There was a pub, can't remember what it was called, where they were really kind, and they let us wash in there.

'We spent a lot of time singing. Chant Down Greenham, you know?

'We scored dope off the soldiers; some of them wanted out. We'd chat with 'em, but they were a long way away, because of all the razor wire. Mind you, some of the soldiers used to handcuff us against the fences and wank on us.

'I lost count of how many times I got arrested. Dragged off in the back of a police van for a night in the cells; at least we got a wash.

'I was there a year, and then just got up and left. But I could do anything after Greenham; it was a beautiful place and a terrible place.'

I have shared a link in the Appendix to scenes of the blockade at Greenham. Thousands of women were prepared to lie down in front of Army vehicles. Hundreds of police, some of them mounted, were used to push and frighten and drag the women out of the road. Looking at footage of Greenham, you can see what Nix means when she says that not all the women were hippies, but hopefully you can see the courage of the sisters. Greenham Common airbase is now an industrial park, and you have to drive past it if you're boycotting the Newbury bypass. There's a memorial to those remarkable women by the old main gate; stop one day, and say namaste.

Meanwhile, the Molesworth Peace Camp ticked along, attracting less attention from the press. Having been founded by pilgrims from Iona, it retained its Christian character. The original People's Peace Camp was set up at 'Peace Corner', on Old Weston Road, by the wartime entrance to the base. A simple wooden multi-faith peace chapel, known as Eirene (Greek for 'peace') was built in spring 1982. On 26 July 1983, the camp was evicted and the chapel destroyed. The camp moved a short way to Warren Lane on the west side of the base. Here it was decided to build a more permanent peace chapel, using rubble from the old runway. An organisation called Architects for Peace helped draw up the plans. The cornerstone was laid on 14 April 1984, and on 2 September, still roof-less, the chapel was dedicated for all faiths, with the blessing of the Bishop of Huntingdon. Wheat was planted on the base, ostensibly to grow food for the starving in Eritrea.

In 1984 it was the site for the Green Gathering, half festival, half Ecology Party rally. The Peace Convoy, or some of it, attended, and some of them decided to stay, including Sid Rawle, who was living in a bender.

This grew into the Green Village, and then into Rainbow Fields Village, where about 100 people lived on the base in vans and benders and tents, some of them from the original Christian camp, but most of them now Freaks.

On 6 February 1985, 1,500 Royal Engineers, 100 Military Police, and 600 civilian police were deployed to secure the seven-mile station perimeter for the Ministry of Defence. According to the *Daily Telegraph* defence correspondent, it was the largest single Royal Engineers operation since the crossing of the Rhine in 1944. They evicted the Rainbow Village and erected a razor-wire fence around Molesworth. The Peace Chapel and the wheatfields were also enclosed by razor wire.

Famously, Secretary of State for Defence Michael Heseltine arrived by RAF helicopter, wearing pancake make-up and a camouflage jacket over his suit, and strutted for the TV cameras and the world's press. The cost of the operation to clear 100 Freaks and fence in RAF Molesworth was somewhere in the region of £6.5 million.

In 1986, Reagan and his Soviet counterpart Mikhail Gorbachev agreed in talks in Iceland to remove cruise missile systems in Europe; the last weapons of mass destruction left Greenham and Molesworth in 1991.

The clearing of Molesworth was relatively peaceful compared to the steps Wiltshire police took to stop Stonehenge 1985. First they surrounded the stones with razor wire. They flung road blocks up to stop a convoy of 150 vehicles getting onto the site for that year's Free Festival. The Convoy, still trying to assert what they felt was their right to get up to the stones for their celebration, turned off the road and into an adjacent field, on the edge of Savernake Forest, where they were surrounded by over 1,000 police and put under siege.

Then the police came into the field, and smashed the Travellers' vans to bits. This is known as 'The Battle of the Beanfield'. The *Observer*'s home affairs correspondent Nick Davies was there. He wrote:

> There was glass breaking, people screaming, black smoke towering out of burning caravans and everywhere there seemed to be people being bashed and flattened and pulled by the hair ... Men, women and children were led away, shivering, swearing, crying, bleeding, leaving their homes in pieces ... over the years I have seen all kinds of horrible and frightening things and always managed to grin and write it. But as I left the beanfield, for the first time, I felt sick enough to cry.

There was an ITN news crew present. The reporter, Kim Sabido, speaking to the camera said, 'What we – the ITN crew and myself as a reporter – have seen in the last thirty minutes here in this field has been some of the most brutal police treatment of people that I've witnessed in my entire career as a journalist. The number of people who have been hit by policemen, who have been clubbed whilst holding babies in their arms in coaches around this field is yet to be counted ... There must surely be an inquiry.' No such inquiry was ever held.

Step up the unlikely hero of the day, David Brudenell-Bruce, the Earl of Cardigan. He witnessed and had been horrified by Beanfield, and allowed the shocked and now homeless Freaks (the ones who hadn't been arrested, at least) onto his land in the Savernake Forest.

Nix was in Bristol, and got a phone call from a couple of friends whose homes had been first trashed, and then impounded, and were now being blocked in the woods by the same police force who had brutalised them earlier. Nix made her way there, to do what she could to help; the skills of living in the woods at Greenham would come in useful.

She told me women and kids who'd been taken to the police station were being thrown out at 2 a.m., with no warm clothes, and nowhere to go.

'People were just living in the woods, there was nothing, it was scary. People came down with stuff, tipis, shelters, and local people brought clothes, but they were there for weeks waiting to get their trashed vehicles back. The police shat in their vehicles, man. People's homes.'

Panit Dave had seen which way the wind was blowing, and had avoided Stonehenge that year. A few weeks after Beanfield, he packed his family into his living vehicle and caught the ferry from Fishguard to Rosslare.

'In Ireland, they knew the score. I had a goat and half a dozen chickens in my van, and they just waved us through.' Many travellers reacted in the same way, and headed for the area around Dunmanway in south-west Cork. Many of them are still there; Panit judged it safe to come back after three years.

Characteristically, he told me that he'd been told by someone in the know, that the police for Beanfield had been chosen because 'they all had Mars rising in their signs'.

George McKay in his 1996 book *Senseless Acts of Beauty*, quotes Shannon, a late-period post-Beanfield traveller: 'In the early eighties it was mostly alternative-y type people who picked up an alternative life-style, now it's basically people who are fucked off with the city. It's not the rosy rainbow hippie scene it was in the seventies and eighties, people trying to live in love and peace. That isn't going to exist in the nineties.'

She was quite right. The forces that had smashed the Peace Convoy at the Battle of the Beanfield would see to it.

'So, that whole festival scene, Goffee got you into that, you say?' I ask Bob.

'No, Goffee got me into Glastonbury for the first time, but I had already started going to festivals, because I had a van, a live-in van, and I had a skill that could get me in to festivals for free. The Goffee thing came up because he came to me and asked me to make gadgets, flame-throwers and that. I was actually being paid to stand, with thousands of people around, and operate these home-made, totally illegal flame-throwers.'

'It's Bob heaven, really, isn't it?'

'It was. My favourite was at one of the small Welsh festivals. There was going to be a torch procession through the site. I used to take flame-throwers to festivals; I'd just take them in my kit-bag. Anyway, this geezer knew about this and he said, "How about we have a bit of drama?" There's a gap you go through, where tractors would go through into the next field, and there's a bridge there. So we arranged I'd bar him from crossing the bridge with the flame-thrower and get the bridge burning, and he'd do whatever would defeat me, the villain, and all that. So I'm sitting up the hill, 150, 200 yards from the meet place. I can see the procession but don't want to go down there too early and be standing there like a twat, so I wait, and then work out, "All right, time to leave now." With a flame-thrower you've got to keep the pilot alight, and you've got to give it an occasional squirt to keep it rejuvenated. So I'm walking down this hill, across this field, giving this thing an occasional little burst. And somebody said to me later on, "Did you see those coppers? While you was going along giving the flame-thrower a little burst, there were these two coppers following you, one of them clearly wanted to wrestle you to the ground, and his mate was trying to stop him from doing it." Because I was obviously legitimate, and it was a legit part of the show, so I wouldn't have been kind to them, sort of thing, if they'd jumped on me and started interfering, which would have been an extremely dangerous thing to do, attack a bloke with a flame-thrower.'

'How do they work? If we wanted to build a flame-thrower?'

'The simplest way: get a fire extinguisher that's already got a car-type valve in it. Some of them even have a little pressure gauge. You empty whatever is in there out, you unscrew the top, half-fill them with fuel, which in my case was petrol, paraffin and diesel, mixed, but more petrol than anything else. You take off the rubber hose and replace it with a metal one, a car brake pipe sort of thing, and arrange a pilot light on the end, just wick-type soaked in fuel, and then pressurise it, put it up to about 150PSI and there you go.'

'Nothing could be simpler,' I say, not really understanding anything he said, but hoping, nonetheless, that an enterprising Younger Reader might have a go.

The last great free festival was held at Castlemorton Common, near Malvern, between 22 and 29 May 1992. Somewhere between 20 and 50,000 people attended. Attendance was fuelled by the fact that Castlemorton was the lead story on the BBC Six O'Clock News on the Friday and Saturday nights, and the coverage drew people from across the country.

The festival had been prompted, to a large extent, by Somerset and Avon police, who banned the Avon Free Festival, a regular May Bank Holiday gathering near Bristol. But rather than provoke a confrontation, the police encouraged the sound systems to head north towards Castlemorton Common, a few square miles of public land, about six miles from my borrowed cabin outside Upton upon Severn.

At least ten sound systems were funnelled onto Castlemorton Common, including Club Dog and Bedlam; but the most notorious were Spiral Tribe, who mixed John Michell's ideas of ley lines and cosmic geometry with a determination to 'make some fucking noise', and who had by far the biggest and loudest sound system.

Convoys were guided to the Common, setting up something between a festival, an outdoor rave and a tented city. The sound systems ran all day and night. And the more the media reported what was happening, the more people turned up.

The by-now-old-school New Age Travellers knew from the start that there was a problem. Some of the clubbers embraced rave as a major counter-cultural force, and had taken on ideas like eco-activism, anti-capitalism and New Age paganism. But many of them didn't give a toss; they were there to party. Worryingly from the Travellers' point of view, they hadn't learned to shit outside by burying their turds. The travellers who had acquired this basic life skill, and who relied on the kindness of landowners and the relative discretion of the police, were almost as outraged by this behaviour as *Daily Mail* readers sitting at home in Haslemere and frothing at the mouth. The endless techno music drove locals and some of the travellers who had been forced onto the site to the point of insanity. The media didn't trouble to point out the difference between weekend ravers and long-term travellers, and drew a picture of reckless travellers spending their benefit cheques on drugs before shitting on the common.

I talked to Tina Beans, who had been on the door at both Club Dog and Bedlam in London. She got the door gig because 'I was unblaggable'. She was amongst the travellers who were directed away from the Avon Free Festival and onto Castlemorton Common.

'Was it fun?'

'Fun in a very trippy way. The E at the time were those big brown things that had a lot of speed in, hence they were called disco biscuits. Kept you up for three days. My thing was the candy flip (acid and E) so I didn't like these quite manic people (mainly blokes) on biscuits. It was the first time I realised that there were loads of us trying out different lifestyles. I came at it from the more "let's relax dude angle," as opposed to the "let's do drugs and partay" thing. There were too many people. I went to sleep and it was OK; the next morning it was like being in Oxford Street. I think that was Sunday. It felt really busy in the main areas where Spiral were but we were well away from that with the hippies. It felt lawless, to be honest.'

'It was amazing,' Lol Hammond of techno duo the Drum Club told Tim Guest for the *Observer*, 'but you knew it couldn't go on.'

When the fun finally ground to a halt, West Mercia police swooped on Spiral Tribe, impounding their equipment and arresting thirteen members, charging them with 'Conspiracy to Cause a Public Nuisance'. They were all found not guilty; between them, the policing operation and the court case cost the long-suffering British taxpayer somewhere in the order of five million pounds.

These not guilty verdicts did not stop demands for action from the Government. At the Tory Party conference in October 1992, Prime Minister John Major said: 'New Age Travellers? Not in this age. Not in any age.' Castlemorton was the climax of the moral panic which led to the 1994 Criminal Justice and Public Order Act.

Criminal justice bills usually run together a lot of issues. This particular iteration bundled together a lot of things that applied to court procedure on things like bail and the treatment of young offenders, with some admirable ideas, such as tightening laws on child pornography, and allowing children to testify via video in court cases. It was part five of the Act, pertaining to pubic order, that did for the travellers. It introduced the offence of aggravated trespass. It gave powers to confiscate sound equipment. It gave the police powers to stop people who they 'reasonably believed' were on their way to attend an unlicensed rave. It gave the police powers to remove persons and vehicles that were unlawfully on land which had previously been open, and it changed for ever the law concerning common land.

Most shamefully, it repealed The Caravan Sites Act of 1968, a fairly benign piece of legislation which obliged local authorities to provide permanent 'halt sites' for 'gipsies'. It defined 'gipsies' as 'persons of nomadic habit of life'. Not all travellers are 'New Age'. This vindictive clause was just another attack on one of the most despised communities of all, not one of whom would have been anywhere near Castlemorton.

'It became really difficult,' says Bob. 'That's when I started my business, Vanguard House.'

'What did you do?'

'I guarded people's houses in my van.'

'It did what it said on the tin?'

'It did. When posh people were away, I'd park my van up in their gardens, and look after them, water their plants and that. I was up by Castle Ring a lot of the time, too. They were building a house up there, so I sort of guarded the site.'

At the same time Bob was becoming more grounded in the Radnor Valley, I was starting to move away, to study, but also, unknowingly, to bear witness to the last days of the counter-culture.

In 1989, aged thirty-one, I went to Lancaster University to study the history and philosophy of science (with a creative writing minor), a qualification which has largely debarred me from paid employment ever since. For my first year, I commuted weekly from Radnorshire. In a new place, starting a new course, it should have proved the ideal opportunity for a radical reinvention, but old habits die hard, and so it was that I found myself on the first night of Freshers' Week in the kitchen of a student flat, at least twelve years older than anyone else who was there, trying to make a connection.

I had been here before, in 1976, when I started at Lampeter. In Lampeter, in 1976, cannabis was as easy to obtain as a bacon sandwich at a roadside catering van. Lancaster in 1989 seemed tougher going at first, but I made connections that night which stood me in good stead for the next ten years. My first eighteen-year-old pal (all mature students like making pals with students of a more appropriate age) was a pug-ugly thug from Sketty, just outside Swansea, who was called Ziggy. His real first name is unpronounceable even to Welsh people. Like me, he's one of those people who get chatty after a few spliffs, and we sat there talking about girls and fighting, of which Ziggy was something of an aficionado, his main tip being that to be a good fighter, you had to first be a good runner.

We discovered that we were both doing philosophy. Over the next three years I discovered that I would always have to work at it, but that some people are just gifted. Philosophy is a practice, but practice seldom makes perfect. If I practised football all day, and Lionel Messi didn't, Messi would still be a much better footballer than me. So it was with Zig. He was a natural philosopher, whose uproarious lifestyle merely fuelled him to greater heights of philosophical success. After being awarded the inevitable First, he turned into a spliff dealer to fund his MA and PhD, and was shifting a couple of eight bars a week at his height in the mid nineties. (I wish I could tell you his name, but since he is now

Head of First Year Studies in the highly ranked Philosophy Department of a major Russell Group university, I'd better not.)

Friday night was scoring night, and the house he shared with fellow postgrads was a cheery meeting place for academically and artistically inclined stoners for years after. We fell into two camps: the older, more sober members of the party, who were going home or to the pub after scoring, and the younger, giddier portion of the crowd, who were off out to Preston or Manchester. Ziggy used the profits from retailing spliff to go clubbing and to take industrial volumes of E, and he liked his chums to go with him.

The younger students I met through Ziggy at Lancaster were stoner music fans with radical politics. They might have been twelve or thirteen years younger, but we clearly belonged to a similar culture, or at least, cultures which bore strong family resemblances to one another. The difference between us was they were going to raves, and I was going home to be a single dad. M' young chums, led by Ziggy, used to go clubbing most weekends; Lancaster is an hour's train ride away from Manchester, and the Manc thing was big in Lancaster. I didn't fancy the rave culture, because I didn't fancy E.

Confession time: I have never taken E, and neither has Bob.

With E, came Love. It was Huxley's soma, in a way. The so-called 'Second Summer of Love' happened in 1987 as MDMA took off in warehouse parties; and in the charts. D-Mob's innocuous 'We Call it Acieeeeed!' was banned from the BBC after one play of the video on *Top of the Pops*. The same BBC that showed *The Magical Mystery Tour* on Boxing Day 1967, which was fuelled by Owsley acid.

Ecstasy, MDMA, as I mentioned at the beginning of the book, was discovered by a German chemist called Anton Köllisch, and patented by Merck, the drug company he was employed by, on Christmas Eve 1912. Legend has it that it was developed as an appetite suppressant, but legend is wrong: Merck were researching blood-clotting agents, and MDMA was a by-product of this work.

Köllisch was killed on the Somme in 1916, and no one at Merck showed much interest in his discovery. They would try it out occasionally; it was tested on animals in 1927, and on flies in 1952, which showed only that it is toxic to flies. If those flies had started going 'big fish, little fish, cardboard box' with their wings, the experimenters might have been more interested. The US Airforce is also said to have tested it on animals, in their search for a truth serum, though what questions the animals might have answered it is impossible to imagine.

It is unclear when exactly MDMA was first tested on humans. There are 'insinuations' in the Merck archives that one of their scientists may have tested it on humans in a search for stimulants for pilots in 1959. The recipe for ecstasy was first published in 1960 in a Polish scientific journal, which hardly makes for accessibility, though it perhaps implies that it was being tested behind the Iron Curtain. It first turned up in street pills in Chicago in 1970, though no one is quite sure of the journey between Polish scientific journals and the South Side.

In 1976 it was introduced to Alexander Shulgin by one of his students. Shulgin was an independent drug developer, who was especially interested in the use of psychedelic drugs in psychiatric work. Shulgin developed over 200 different psychedelic drugs over the course of his career, all of which he tested on himself. He also developed the Shulgin Rating Scale for reporting the subjective effect of psychoactive drugs. If, for example, you're going, 'Is this doing anything? Is this working? Did I just buy an aspirin again?' then you are having a +/- experience on the Shulgin Rating Scale. If, however, you are chatting with Krishna whilst you ride unicorns together over luxuriant fields of purple grass, then you are at ++++.

Shulgin had his own licensed laboratory, outside San Francisco, known as the Farm. He found new methods of synthesising the drug, and used it on himself, and this is actually the first documented test on a human. He thought it was mildly interesting, and he liked it. He used it to unwind, describing it as a bit like an after-work martini, but given that he took an estimated 4,000 trips over the course of his long life, on many and various outré psychedelics, who can say now what he found a mildly relaxing intoxicant, and what took him all the way to ++++?

Shulgin introduced the drug to researchers who he thought might be interested, one of whom was psychotherapist Leo Zeff, who had been using LSD in his work with patients since the early sixties. Zeff thought it had great potential in therapy. He called it 'Adam', feeling that it took patients back to a pre-lapsarian state of innocence. Zeff trained an estimated 4,000 therapists in its use, both in the US and in Europe. They liked it because it decreased fear, increased communication, but, above all, increased empathy in patients. Therapees needed less input from the therapist after taking MDMA, because they finally got to see things from their mum's point of view.

It's estimated that 10,000 recreational doses of MDMA were taken in 1976. The researchers and therapists wanted to keep it quiet, in case the Drug Enforcement Agency called for its criminalisation. It was finding its way into clubs like the very upmarket Studio 54 in New York, but supply was intermittent. It is further estimated that 500,000 doses of MDMA were sold in the USA between the mid seventies and criminalisation in the mid eighties. As is pretty much always the case, criminalisation caused sales to rocket. The US congress had passed a law which allowed the DEA to ban any drug it thought dangerous to human health. In 1985, the DEA exercised their new prerogative for the first time, and made Ecstasy illegal.

They were sued in a high-profile case by a group of therapists, who wanted to continue to use it with patients. In court, the judge decided that it should be put on 'Schedule Three', which meant that it could be manufactured, tested on humans and made available on prescription. The DEA ignored this, and placed it on Schedule One, and thus put it into the hands of criminals, who have an interest in expanding their market. According to an article in *Mixmag* from March 2015, 25,000 kilograms of E is consumed in the UK each year.

The point is the empathy. After taking Ecstasy, you love everybody. People who took it were looking to be 'loved up'. And so, a last note on sex.

E is not necessarily sexy. It is huggy. Younger Readers are quite huggy too, I find. Same-sex hugging leaves me a bit cold, I'm afraid. The first time I was hugged by a loved-up man, I stiffened, and not in a good way. The poet Matt Harvey says, 'If you don't like being hugged by another man, you probably shouldn't even *be* in a vegetarian restaurant in Totnes,' which is just one of the reasons I never *have* been in a vegetarian restaurant in Totnes, as he put me off. A handshake is quite enough, thank you. But huggy was just the job for a world where sex had turned very quickly from something fun and joyous to something dangerous and life-threatening. AIDS changed everything. Many young people who grew up in the sixties and seventies had a sexually transmitted disease at one stage, of one kind or another, but they were almost a badge of pride. Waiting in the fluorescent light of a 'clap clinic' could even be a fairly social occasion, because there was a fair chance one or two of your mates would be in. Treatment wasn't pleasant, but if treated right, STDs were no longer life-threatening, or rather, were no longer seen to be life-threatening. AIDS killed: an estimated twenty-five million world wide, so far.

This led in the mid to late 1980s to the promotion of 'safe sex', which sounds a bit like a contradiction in terms. The invention of the Pill saw the demise of the condom, or 'rubber johnnies' as they were known. The arrival of AIDS saw an unprecedented revival in their use. As I've tried to argue, the arrival of the Pill was not a universally good thing for women. It took away a line of defence, a powerful line, the threat of pregnancy, from women who didn't want sex. Even now, we have to run campaigns that say 'No Means No'. Saying 'No' in the 1970s just meant you were an uptight bitch. Perhaps a drug that increased empathy at the same time as reducing libido was not altogether a bad thing.

As to what sex is like now – I'm the one remaining living member of top light-entertainment duo Your Dad, and I'm sure Younger Readers would appreciate it if I backed off, which I will.

Ecstasy's growing popularity post-criminalisation fitted perfectly with a new kind of electronic dance music, called, I'm never quite sure what.

Dance music, house music, acid house music, techno, techno house, jungle, drum and bass, breaks, glitch hop, trip-hop, etc., etc., was the music that I had been waiting for since punk. I always knew it would come, and always thought it would be a good healthy thing when it did. I would know it when it came because I wouldn't like it, most of it. It would leave me cold, like Pete Mustill and Bob go 'meh' at punk. I would, in my turn, become the enemy, with my guitars and drums and my 'Anti-Nazi League' T-shirt and my, look at me, I'm the Anti-Christ, and oooh, I'm having a White Riot. And Lo! It has come to pass; I don't like it, most of it, and I still think that's a good and healthy thing. As my daughter Minnie says, 'Grandma likes Nat King Cole. You like Nat King Cole and the Stone Roses. I like Nat King Cole, the Stone Roses, and things you've never heard of.' This is right and proper.

Central to my problem, I think, is the fact that I've never taken Ecstasy. Toby Weymouth, boss of Lancaster sound system and rave organisers Acme Bass Company, pointed out to me that Ecstasy draws people to repetitive beats: 'It makes you feel part of a thing. Everyone is dancing together, almost like they've been choreographed. You can feel vibration, like you're part of something. E lets people dance who can't dance.'

This is another problem from my point of view; I can dance. I like the less regimented feel of funk. The repetitive thing inhibits me. To my ears, the problem with techno old school house acid grime drum and bass is that it doesn't swing, and so I can't dance. Old Chas Ambler couldn't dance, but he liked nothing more than getting out on the floor and showing people the quite extraordinary extent to which he couldn't dance, and he loved a drop of MDMA to remove what tiny shreds he ever had of inhibition. I was the designated driver after most of our gigs, so that he could partake.

Bob puts it beautifully, I think: 'That music's shit. I don't want to take one of those Es, in case I start liking it.'

But, it doesn't matter what I think of the music. It's not my culture. If I'd done E at the time, I might hear it differently, but my serotonin levels were so fucked for so long, I didn't fancy it. And so the music has passed me by. But the sound of techno is the sound of the last days of the counter-culture, and Ecstasy its last drug. On Friday nights at Ziggy's, I would say goodnight as the young people got ready to party, and go home, or toddle down to the pub to spend the rest of the evening in company with other mature students, to talk about Elvis Costello, our divorces and what we did during the miners' strike.

My own contemporaries as undergraduates at Lancaster were the usual suspects, if you were filming *The Usual Suspects* using mature students from 1989. Feminist green activists, feminist SWP activists, feminist queer activists, jazz trumpeters, longhairs, Buddhist gurus back from India, comic-book cartoonists, ex-working girls, ex-prisoners, ex-biker drug casualties, a guy who'd spent five years living at Molesworth Peace Camp, and a bloke who'd been in the SAS who, on being dumped by a feminist girlfriend because of his unreconstructed ways, had come to Lancaster to do women's studies. I liked him, because almost everyone else was a vegetarian. We sat together most days, all of us, talking and smoking and drinking coffee in the Nelson Mandela Coffee Bar, which acted as an unofficial mature students' common room.

Younger Readers who are currently at British universities have no chance of meeting people like this, as mature students have all but gone. And if anyone knows of a still-existing coffee bar anywhere on a UK campus named after Nelson Mandela, and can produce a receipt, please write in to claim a small prize (ian@moodindex.co.uk).

The campus was smothered in political posters, calling for meetings on this and action on that. I belonged to the Anarchist Society (insert own jokes). The Women's Society went into the Student Union shop and pulled the *Sun*, lads' mags, etc., from the shelves and littered them around campus. There were two student occupations in my three years at Lancaster, and I'm happy to say I was able to support them both, though what they were about, I have no clue. Campus buzzed with engaged activism of a type familiar to me for fifteen-odd years. It was fun.

In Lancaster itself, there was a wholefood Co-Op and café which doubled as a radical bookshop, an independent record shop, several 'alternative pubs' and lots of great venues both to hear bands and to play in. This local music scene was supported by a monthly alternative 'What's

On' magazine, and the excellent Lancaster Musicians' Co-Operative. There were open your heart chakra workshops in the Gregson community centre.

And then there was Mystic City.

It was part wholefood café, part nightclub. I only went in a couple of times, because I found the atmosphere a bit odd. Odd, because it was staffed by 'Orange People.' Lancaster had more than its fair share of 'Orange People' in the late '80s and early 1990s. You would see them wandering about the city streets, a few of them in orange robes, but more often in orange T-shirts and baggy trousers. Orange was supposed to be one of the colours of the sunrise. At some point, they started to change colour, and the orange turned to purple, the 'colours of the sunset'. These were 'sannyasin', followers of Bhagwan Shree Rajneesh, who preferred to be known as 'Osho'. The sannyasin were one of the last visible evidences of hippie orientalism.

Osho was born into Jainism, rather than Hinduism, which sets him slightly apart from his contemporaries like Guru Mahara Ji and the Maharishi, who were from a Hindu tradition. He had trained and lectured in philosophy, and toured India giving talks throughout the 1960s. In 1974, he set up an ashram in Pune, a couple of hours' drive south-east of Mumbai. Westerners soon found their way there, because Osho had devised what he called 'dynamic meditation' for Western spiritual appetites. It was the perfect union of post-Krishnamurti quietism and Gurdjieffian action. He didn't ask his disciples to be ascetic. He loved money, and thought it a jolly good thing. At one time, he had ninety-three Rolls-Royces – it was his followers' aim to get him up to 365, one for each day of the year.

His theology was simple: there is no God other than life itself, life is now and here, and we should all live wakefully. The dynamic meditations were designed to wake practitioners up, much as had been Gurdjieff's aim. He also taught that love is prayer, and that making love – if, and only if, between a man and a lady – was the most sacred of human acts. Osho's ashrams saw some serious action over the years.

Along with his frankly anodyne pronouncements, very similar after all to what Charles Manson said, he had a dark side to his teachings. Homosexuals were perverts. Crippled or blind children should be killed at birth. Yet by 1981, his ashram was attracting 30,000 visitors a year, and Osho felt the need to move to bigger premises. His followers paid $5.7 million for 67,000 acres of land in Oregon; and they started to build, not so much an ashram, as a city. At its height in 1985, it had 7,000 inhabitants, and was growing. They called the city Rajneeshpuram.

Difficulties with the local authorities forced the hand of Osho's principal sidekick, Ma Sheela. In order to keep growing, the city needed to be incorporated, and locals objected. So Ma Sheela poisoned the salad bars of ten local restaurants, causing 750 people to fall ill, which Ma Sheela thought would stop them from voting against the incorporation of Rajneeshpuram. Osho reputedly didn't know, and when he found out, he dobbed Ma Sheela in; she was sentenced to twenty years in prison, whilst Osho was deported from the US. He attempted to set up residence elsewhere, but was refused entry into twenty-seven countries. He ended up back at his meditation centre in Pune, where he died in 1990.

Yet he still continued to attract followers, and he still does. You can visit his thriving centre in Pune. A pal of mine called Tim Guest wrote a memoir about being raised by a sannyasin mother in Osho's various ashrams. The book is called My Life in Orange, and I highly recommend it. Sadly, I couldn't talk to Tim whilst I was writing this book, because he died of a morphine overdose in 2010.

So I spoke to a Lancaster sannyasin, a good friend of mine, who was given the name Divyam Aranya. A dropped-out druggy student from Wolverhampton, in the early eighties he lived on Blade Street in Lancaster, where he encountered, and became part of, a community of Orange People. He was initiated at a workshop led by Ma Prem Vismaya (aka Tim Guest's mum,) who was running the UK Rajneesh centre near Newmarket in Suffolk. Even after Osho's deportation from Rajneeshpuram, Divyam stayed true, travelling to Crete to see Osho while he was trying to obtain permission to stay there. Divyam was the guy who booked music into Mystic City, where he regularly hired Chas to play a bit of jazz piano. Divyam never renounced it, whatever it is, although he'll give you a look if you call him anything other than Mark these days. And I've never seen him wear orange.

The Osho thing is hard to understand, harder than either Guru Mahara Ji, or the Maharishi. He's quite funny if you watch a clip of him on YouTube, but not much else. He liked sex, Rollers and nitrous oxide; but thousands, perhaps hundred of thousands of people dedicated their lives to him. Old Tim Guest gets the last word; he says of Osho in My Life in Orange, that he was 'a lovable rogue who got away with doing his own thing'.

In 1989, at a British university, therefore, it was not just possible, but inevitable, that one would be surrounded by people who had been marked in some way by Freak culture.

If you Google Lancaster University, 1989, this is not what you will find.

What you will find is the speech by Kenneth Baker, the then Education Secretary, which altered for ever the course of British universities, by means of the slow introduction of a system which has no place either for radical politics or for ragamuffins looking to learn. The counter-culture may not have come out of the universities, but it thrived there, and its influence was felt strongest, and lasted longest, in university towns.

Baker's speech concerned the announcement of the restructuring of universities and polytechnics, and the introduction of student loans, and therefore, eventually, tuition fees.

Younger Readers have too much at stake to fuck about. If they are students, they work too hard at actual jobs to support themselves to be the least bit interested in educating, organising and agitating. If you go to 'uni', and stick at the student thing, you get a bit of paper which, you hope, will be a magic amulet which opens the door to a career, a mortgage, a nice car and a new phone every year. The loans and tuition fees have turned students into consumers, who demand what they have paid for.

Something else was happening in 1989 at Lancaster, I think, which shifted British universities away from a counter-cultural recent-ish past. The public and the Tory government had a particular view of plate-glass universities as incubators of counter-cultural vice. Malcolm Bradbury's History Man was filmed on the Lancaster campus. Bradbury's anti-hero, Howard Kirk, played in the TV series by Anthony Sher, was the ultimate countercultural figure, a pot-smoking Marxist sociologist who exercised power over his students in flared crushed-velvet trousers. There are many candidates for who Bradbury based Kirk on, but my money is on David Craig, who was head of the Creative Writing Department at Lancaster, and who therefore taught me.

Back when Lancaster University was two or three years old, i.e. 1966, when Craig was teaching English, he was censured (so the story runs), for marking up the papers of those students who adhered most closely to Marxist orthodoxy. The university wanted to dismiss him, so we were assured by those who were there, but they couldn't, because he had tenure. (Ask your older tutors, and hear them sigh.) According to legend, there were demonstrations, library occupations, pamphlets and counter pamphlets, one of which, The Case Against David Craig, is rumoured to be kept in the Closed Collection in the library, though no one ever seems to have seen it. Bradbury's novel, a top read, incidentally, is a liberal conservative critique of the plate-glass universities (in which he himself taught) and of the inherent hypocrisies of the counter-culture, of free love and cheap drugs and go with the flow and don't work for The Man.

Successive governments made deliberate policy against counter-cultural elements in the UK, and Baker's speech is one. *The History Man* was pretty much how the Tory government saw the universities, and something had to be done.

The thing I didn't really take notice of in 1989 was the rise of management as an academic subject. I would wish to argue that Baker's speech, together with the ascendancy of management and business studies as university subjects marked a profound moment in the history of British universities.

In the Middle Ages, and up to the beginning of the nineteenth century, theology was the 'Queen of Sciences', and at the centre of a university's concerns. They were run by ordained priests. In the early nineteenth century, new kinds of universities appeared, which had philosophy, including natural philosophy (science as it is now known) at their heart; and so universities came to be run by philosophers and scientists. From 1989 onwards, the central subject increasingly became management studies. So now, the universities are run by managers. The universities keep the humanities only out of nostalgia or guilt.

The last heroes of the counter-culture were the road protesters, and its last pin-up boy was called Daniel Hooper, aka 'Swampy'. In 1989, the Thatcher government published *Roads for Prosperity*, a White Paper which proposed a massive investment in the UK's road network. There were 500 proposed schemes, at a cost of twenty-three billion pounds. This was needed, the Government argued, because there would be a 142 per cent increase in road use by 2025. A sane government would have been working to reduce that figure by spending on public transport. A sane society would be getting rid of roads. Thatcher's government, certainly in its last days, was not sane, but deranged. So sane people tried to stop them building these new roads. And try very hard they did.

At the site of the M3 extension at Twyford Down in 1992, at the M11 extension into East London in 1994, and at the site of the proposed Newbury bypass in 1996, protesters did everything possible to stop the roads being built. They built treehouses. They tied themselves to trees. Most famously, they built tunnels. Swampy was the expert digger, who built networks of tunnels under the Newbury site.

Even old Bob spun by for a night.

'So I'd been down south for some reason, and I was coming by where the Newbury road protest camp was, so I thought I'd stop and have a look, because I knew this girl I was courting at the time, Anna, was there. When I turned up and saw the situation, it became obvious that there were several small camps, and I wasn't going to go wandering off to try to find Anna, in case she was entertaining gentleman callers, like. So I had a bit of a wander round. I found this group trying to take down this wooden bridge, to try and stop the diggers getting through and ripping up the trees. They were making a right fucking pig's ear of it, so I went and got my chainsaw from the van, and cut the bridge up for 'em. So that was all right, and I sat about the fire, talking to the eco-warriors and that. But the next morning, at about eight, I was woken by 'Good Morning Campers!', and I looked out my window, and there was this long line of coppers, coming through the adjacent cornfield in single file. Which was one of the most surreal things I've ever seen. And all these coppers were really calm, and they stood on one side of the stream, while all the road protesters stood on the other, screaming abuse at 'em. And I thought, "Nah, I don't fancy this," so I headed off.'

The nine miles of road cost 10,000 trees and 100 million pounds to build, a fifth of that on policing and security. The protesters built twenty-seven camps. In January 1996 750 people were arrested under the terms of the 1994 Criminal Justice Act. Swampy was the last person to be evicted from the site, tucked away in the furthest reaches of one of his tunnels. He had to be excavated from his underground lair by a specialist in the rescue of people who were trapped in confined spaces. Swampy played the same trick at Fairmile in Devon the following year, and was unearthed by the same guy. Swampy became so famous, he appeared as a guest on *Have I Got News For You* in 1997. He had been tamed, to an extent, made safe by light entertainment, but he wasn't a fair-weather Freak. He works as a tree surgeon these days, and lives with his family in a yurt in Tipi Valley.

In the late 1980s and early 1990s Lancaster was full of crusties. Some of them played the didgeridoo, unfortunately, but many of them just asked for money. They were against washing, because they wanted people to think they were road protesters, had dreadlocks (they were exclusively white), and their drug of choice was a four-pack of Special Brew. They would get to the odd rave, if they were lucky, but mostly they were too pissed. Their equivalent at festivals was 'the Brew Crew', who could be violent and deeply unpleasant; strong drink, and lots of it, had never been the festivalgoers' drug of choice, and the Brew Crew came as a shock. Both Bob and Nix are still annoyed by the fact that they didn't know how to brew their own beer. There was a scene, of sorts, and a handful of bands: the Levellers, The Wonder Stuff, Back to the Planet, Ozric Tentacles, who dressed like their fans, and espoused simple political ideas. Many of the crusties had dogs on ropes. Often, for a homeless person, a dog is pretty much all you can rely on. He's loyal, and he'll watch over you. And some crusties were homeless, but for many, it was a weekend thing. They'd pull on homeless chic and get pissed, and sit about on the streets, so they had to have dogs on ropes too. The crusties, it always seemed to me, were taking on a few of the attitudes they had seen at festivals, and turning them into not much really.

It could be argued that the crusties came from a different place. They were Thatcher's babies, disaffected yoof without jobs, or education, or a future. Some of their attitudes might remind you of Bob as a young man living on the streets of London as a Beat. But none of them could quote *Howl*. They were not hip. Nobody could aspire to be a crustie. By 1994, what was hip was something else again.

On the cover of the book, and in the first chapter, I said I'd end in 1994, because I thought that you could say that by then 'The' counter-culture, the unified high counter-culture, the one that engaged musicians, writers, poets, artists, dreamers, radical politicos and Freak scientists for nearly forty years had run out of steam and left the popular consciousness. No Elvis, Beatles, Rolling Stones or The Clash. No fashion spreads in *Vogue*. No front pages in the papers, no shock horror from the press. The Criminal Justice Act had done for the raves, and for the travellers. Tony Blair had become leader of the opposition, and pretty much everyone was hoping for nothing much more than that he could defeat the Tories.

James Brown (not *the* James Brown) was a music journalist, who, during an unsuccessful job interview for the editorship of the *NME* sometime in 1993, had ended up pitching an idea for a new magazine for men; in fact, 'For men who should know better.' This was *Loaded*, named after a song by Primal Scream.

According to the PR blurb, '*Loaded* is a new magazine dedicated to life, liberty and the pursuit of sex, drink, football and less serious matters. *Loaded* is music, film, relationships, humour, travel, sport, hard news and popular culture. *Loaded* is clubbing, drinking, eating, playing and eating. *Loaded* is for the man who believes he can do anything, if only he wasn't hungover.' The first issue came out in May 1994, featuring an interview bigged up on the cover between 'super-lads' Gary Oldman, Paul Weller and Eric Cantona.

Sport was one of those things the counter-culture just didn't do. Those of us who were football nuts kept quiet about it. My old friend and colleague Yammerman and I would occasionally slope off to games together, but we were hardly out about it. Nick Hornby's *Fever Pitch*, published in 1992, made it OK to like football openly. It is also accused of bringing a middle class crowd to games, but I'm down with that these days. By the early 1990s, hooliganism was on the decrease; the football terraces started to quiet down round about the time of the appearance of E, oddly enough. And the game had remade itself; the Premiership was first contested in the season 1992–1993. The game became glamorous for the first time since George Best hung up his boots. (If you are a Freak looking for a team to support, incidentally, you should go for Forest Green Rovers, the world's first vegan football club, whose pitch at their ground, The New Lawn, is the world's only organically grown playing surface. Their chairman is Dale Vince, boss of Ecotricity, a former New Age Traveller who learned to run windmills and solar panels at the Glastonbury Festival. (There are links in the Appendix to both Ecotricity and the Phone Co-Op, incidentally, if you're wanting to Freak up your utility providers.)

New Laddism arrived at just the moment that Blur, Pulp and in particular Oasis were in their pomp. Oasis were the perfect soundtrack for New Laddism: loud, brash, hedonistic, working-class, football-loving Beatles impersonators. This was the time of 'Britpop', and it swept all before it, largely because it was very good. Blur in particular have stood the test of time, but if you look at pictures of them from their early days, you'll see that they are wearing Fred Perry shirts and Farah slacks, while the Levellers are dressed like crusties. Girls are much more likely to go for Damon Albarn than Jeremy out of the Levellers.

If New Laddism was good for football, Britpop and for the drinks industry, it was bad for the Women's Movement. *Loaded*, and its competitors like *FHM*, *Maxim*, *GQ*, *Nuts* and *Zoo* featured soft-core photos of glamour models, but this was not enough to put off a new generation of women determined to be (forgive me) New Laddettes, whose aim seemed to be to keep up with the lads, pint by pint. A new generation of women who felt that feminism was a foregone conclusion. Whose job was done. Which didn't matter any more; that it was OK for their mums or their big sisters, but for them, it was outdated, outmoded, through. They wanted to shag and get pissed and get their tits out for the lads.

Three last things, two of which involve fire. On 13 June 1994, the Pyramid Stage at Glastonbury burned down in the middle of the night, with ten days to go before the start of the festival. Am I not supposed to find this symbolic? And on 23 August 1994, came what was arguably the last 'happening' of the counter-culture: the burning of a million quid by the KLF in a boathouse on the Inner Hebridean island of Jura.

The KLF were Jimmy Cauty and Bill Drummond, and they started as a band, who used a series of different names, such as the Justified Ancients of Mu Mu and the Timelords. As the Timelords, they had a Number One hit single in 1988 with 'Doctoring the Tardis', a mash-up of the *Doctor Who* theme and Gary Glitters 'Rock 'n' roll'. Rather than making a straightforward follow-up record, they wrote a book, called *The Manual: How to have a number one hit the easy way*, long out of print, and heart-stoppingly expensive on the second-hand market. The Justified Ancients of Mu Mu, or the JAMS, took their name from the classic Freak novel *Illuminatus*, with which both men were obsessed. This obsession went so far that they persuaded country legend Tammy Wynette to sing the lyrics 'They're justified and they're ancient and they drive an ice-cream van' on their hit record 'Justified and Ancient'.

In 1991, the KLF were the biggest selling singles artists in the world. In 1992, they won 'Best British Group' at the Brit awards. They appeared onstage at the award ceremony with speed-punk band Extreme Noise Terror, playing a version of their hit single '3 a.m. Eternal'. At the conclusion of the performance, Bill Drummond sprayed the audience of the music industry's great and good with blanks from a machine gun, and dumped a dead sheep in the hospitality room, signifying what they thought of the UK music bosses. They then announced their retirement from music, and deleted their entire back catalogue. The KLF meant it; their back catalogue remains deleted. They buried their statuette from the ceremony in a field near Stonehenge.

They then changed their name again, to the K Foundation, and turned themselves into artists. Their medium was money. They announced the K Foundation award for the 'worst artist of the year'. The prize money was £40,000, twice the amount of the annual Turner Prize for contemporary art. The winner was Rachel Whiteread, who, coincidentally, also won the Turner on the same evening. Showing enormous ill-humour, Whiteread refused the K Foundation's money, until they threatened to burn it, at which point she grumpily accepted the cash, saying that she would use it for grants for young artists. The K Foundation also exhibited a series of artworks, which featured large amounts of cash stuck to boards. They were on sale at less than the face value of the cash; one work, which reputedly featured a million pounds nailed to a bit of wood, was on sale for £500,000.

Drummond and Cauty estimated that what they had left from the music business at this stage was a million quid. It was this million quid they burned in the boathouse on Jura. There's a film of the event, called *Watch the K Foundation Burn A Million Quid*. Shot on Super 8 film, it shows Drummond and Cauty doing just that on an open fireplace. It's not easy to burn a million quid. In 2004 I was on Jura, and met a couple of locals who recall walking along the beach the next morning and finding slightly singed fifty-pound notes, which had simply been sucked up the chimney.

Drummond seems unsure now why they did it, and friends of friends have told me that his children are particularly put out. But I think it was magnificent, the greatest Situationist stunt of all. If any major pop groups have Situationist inclinations any more, they keep them well hidden; Situationism, the art movement that radical students and radical pop groups loved, is now the sole preserve of academics. The ashes of the KLF's money, which they have hung on to, symbolise the end of a time when bands who were disgusted with the business side, the spectacular side of the industry, were prepared to do something about it.

My last last thing is a sad thing. This is the disappearance of Richey Edwards, on 1 February 1995. Richey was the rhythm guitarist and lyric writer for the Manic Street Preachers. I would wish to argue that if the Sex Pistols were the first real British punk band, then the Manics were the last. In an interview with journalist and now 6 Music DJ Steve Lamacq in 1991, Edwards cut the words '4 Real' on his forearm with a razorblade, in order to demonstrate his authenticity, his belief in the 'ideals' of punk. After his disappearance, there were several sightings of Richey in South Wales; but on the 14th, his car was found at Aust services on the M48 next to the River Severn. His body has never been found, but it is widely presumed that he committed suicide by jumping off the Severn Bridge. Inevitably, there are those who think he is still alive; Goa is a favourite candidate for where he ended up. Richey Edwards seems to me to be a proper counter-cultural figure, one of the youngest in this book. He believed in something that no one believes in any more: the power of rock music, pop music, whatever, to change the world. He sought, not peace and love, but authenticity, the existential ideal of being true to oneself, in a world which had decided that authenticity was not worth having.

So why did the counter-culture fail? Why has it gone?

Several reasons, I think.

Firstly, fashion.

Being a hippie was once, a long time ago, a fashionable thing to be. Young aristocrats saw something there they could take and use for their own purpose. The easiest way to live a superficially non-alienated life is just to have lots of money. The Upper Classes of Old England abhor 'trade.' Not working, after all, is one of the best things about being both rich and a Freak. Above all things, the upper classes are in search of fun. The prospect of a glamorous and sexy way of life was just as attractive to rich young people as it was to Bob, and much easier for them to sustain. What, after all, did a deb of 1958 have to look forward to? It was the last year that debutantes were presented to the Queen, and they could expect a dreary round of balls and dances, visits to race meetings and horse shows, in return for the chance of meeting a man from the same class background, getting engaged, and marrying into money, big houses, grand estates, Liberty headscarves, waxed jackets, dogs, horses and the obligation to produce 'an heir and a spare'. A young lady 'coming out' in 1964 (not what Younger Readers mean by 'coming out', but coming out into 'Society'), had different prospects, including marrying a 'rock star'. It didn't take long for rock stars to be assimilated into Society; the Stones in particular were prone to what Bob calls 'upper-class totty'.

By 1979, High Society and High Fashion had found its way to different clubs, different drugs, and different political ideas. Being a hippie was no longer hip. Being a Freak was freaky. By the early 1990s, although it was possible to unearth a few 'trustafarians', no one interested in fashion was going to be attracted by crusties. A few days at Glasto in Cath Kidston wellies is one thing; Turning On, Tuning In and Dropping Out another thing altogether. And fashion was led by pop music. The Rolling Stones and most especially the Beatles came from the beatnik culture, and there was nothing more fashionable than the Beatles and the Stones. With the 'genre-isation' of pop music, there is no band that has the same reach. I'm not even sure that pop music is fashionable any more.

Then you have recuperation.

This is a Situationist idea, and it's a good one. Straight society takes anything threatening, and turns it into spectacle. It takes anything radical, and debollocks it. The free festivals turn into five days coverage of rock bands at Glastonbury on the BBC. Johnny Rotten advertises butter. Iggy Pop advertises car insurance. Vegetarianism becomes a mainstream lifestyle choice; but one which demands Yotam Ottolenghi cookbooks and easy access to zather, manouri and membrillo. HRH The Prince of Wales and His Holiness Jeremy Corbyn advocate homeopathy. Young men wear CND T-shirts without knowing what CND is. Young women think the

Ramones is a T-shirt brand. Macca and Jagger are Knights of the Realm. Religion is something mad people do, a long way away, whilst in the West, no one thinks twice about describing themselves as 'spiritual but not religious' as though it means something. The Women's Movement became so successful that it produced a powerful backlash – which ends in one of my students not wanting anyone to know that she regards herself as a Feminist. Gay Liberation (and boy, will I get letters for this) is now being normalised to such an extent that the Church of England is debating whether or not it should support gay marriage. Does this mean young gay men are feeling pressure to marry and settle down? I fear it does. They are no longer 'other'. Being 'other' is bad. Everyone must be just like 'us'.

That which can't be normalised is legislated against. There are so few 'New Age Travellers' any more that none of my students knew what I meant by the term. Underground magazines were busted for obscenity. Unlicensed free festivals and parties were replaced by boutique festivals which cost £200 to get in to. Heroin is not generally a good thing (though Chas was grateful that he was being given it in large quantities at the end of his life); but The War on Drugs has turned against cannabis, Ecstasy and LSD, whilst governments cheerfully allow powerful multinational companies to peddle booze and fags.

Then we have exhaustion.

As Robert Hunter wrote for the Grateful Dead, it's been a long strange trip. Very long. The acid evangelists of the 1960s and 1970s thought that theirs would be a fairly easy job; once everyone had done acid, everything would change. They discussed putting acid in the water supply, to turn on as many people as possible in one go. Sex and drugs and rock 'n' roll were so obviously good things, so much better than what was on offer, that it could only be a matter of a few years before the New Age dawned. But the Millennium didn't come, people got fed up with waiting, cut their hair and got jobs. The anarchy foretold by the Pistols never materialised either, except in the dreamworld of Albion Free State. Instead, Margaret Thatcher's Tories won the general elections of 1979, 1983, 1987 and, under her successor John Major, 1992. The historian Dominic Sandbrook argues that rather than seeing say, John Lennon as the archetypical sixties figure, actually John Major would be a much better candidate. While the Freaks made headlines, most people in Britain worked hard to buy their own homes, a car, a foreign holiday. To get on.

Geo-politics played a part, too. Two things in particular, both from 1989: the Tiananmen Square Massacre in Beijing, and the fall of the Berlin Wall. These events took away both illusion and fear. Mao was something of a hero to the counter-culture, because it was felt that he was doing the thing properly. He wasn't just trying to do State Capitalism, or so it seemed from half a world away. Most old heads of my generation have a copy of Mao's *Little Red Book* tucked away on their shelves, somewhat shamefacedly. I was a wee bit pro-Mao myself, until Tiananmen Square, when the People's Liberation Army of China killed between 200 and 2,500 students on the night of 4 June 1989. (The lowest figure being the official Party line, the highest coming from the Red Cross.) The famous picture of the lone man standing in front of a column of tanks leaving Tiananmen Square was taken the next day, and conveys the feeling of betrayal: that the PLA would turn on the people. No one could cling to the illusion that Maoism was somehow different any more.

The fall of the Berlin Wall, which started on 9 November 1989 and ended less than a year later with the reunification of Germany, signified the end of the Cold War. It was clear, from early on, that this was the case. The Russian leader Mikhail Gorbachev did not send in the tanks, and the world breathed a huge sigh of relief. With the end of the Warsaw Pact, nuclear war was no longer a danger. Membership of CND at its highest in 1985 reached 110,000. Twenty years later, it had fallen to 32,000. It was felt to be an irrelevance in an age where the threat of nuclear war was seen to be a thing of the past. Nuclear disarmament, the unifying political cause of the counter-culture, had been achieved. The fear lifted. The counter-culture wasn't needed any more. Universal unconditional love could be had in pill form, and peace had come. Job done.

Then you have what we might think of as existentialism triumphant. Charles Shaar Murray has written that the hedonistic excesses of the counter-culture, and a view of existentialism which equates it with self-interest, led directly to the culture of the yuppies, and embraced that view of capitalism which is known as neo-liberalism. From this perspective, the Freaks did more harm than good.

Bob blames the widespread use of heroin; once heroin got into the system, hippiedom was through. Cannabis and LSD are creative drugs; smack isn't. You might say the same of cocaine, the Yuppies drug of choice. They both involve a particular kind of turning inward which inflates the ego, rather than dissolving it.

But Bob has another thought, which is key, I reckon.

'I was thinking about your question "What happened to the hippies?"'

'What do you think?'

'Well, there weren't really a lot of us. There were a lot of people who looked like the public perception hippies, dressing up like hippies, with their long hair and smoking dope and taking acid, yeah, sure. And going to the festies and whatever. But they weren't really there, sort of thing.'

'Weekenders?'

'Yeah.'

There never were that many 'real' Freaks. Lots less than you might think.

It's like the Shakers. The Shakers were an eighteenth-century offshoot of Quakerism, who made a few converts in the States in the mid nineteenth century. To become a Shaker, you had to sign a covenant, committing yourself to lifelong celibacy. This meant they had very few children. There never were many Shakers, and their abhorrence of sexual contact meant that they all but died out; in 2009, there were three, living in the Sabbathday Lake community in Maine. But, by gum, they could make kitchen furniture. It's the kitchen furniture that has kept the Shakers in our collective memories, rather than the innumerable other apocalyptic Christian sects of the nineteenth century. Googling 'Shaker style' brings up almost three million hits.

The counter-culture is remembered in a certain way because its equivalent of Shaker kitchen furniture was pop music in its Golden Age. The music remains, but the ideas and sentiments have long gone.

The Freaks made a lot of noise. Good noise. But much of it, in the end, signified nothing.

It's night in the old bus, and Bob and I are still talking. He's been up to see his friend Dave the Bronze today, and he's telling me about going into Dave's workshop, and how it's like an alchemist's laboratory. In the solar-generated light, you could say that about Bob's place, no doubt. Coffee is bubbling on the gas ring. The eternal fire that is Bob's wood-burner keeps us warm; too warm, even on a late-September night. The workbench is a brilliant clutter of creativity. Mobiles hanging from the roof cast shadows of strange birds on the floor of the bus. I am coming to the end of my questions.

'So how did you end up in this wood?'

'Ah well, I was parked up in a lay-by on the way back from a festival in the Cotswolds next to some chainsaw carvers, who'd put their statues out so that people would stop and look at their wares, like. They're mates of mine, so I'm parked up next to them, with my wares on show too. And this couple stop, and they're looking at my hooks, and they say, "These are amazing. Where do you get the wire from?" And I say, "Well, I get it from alongside the old abandoned railway line that goes through a wood outside New Radnor."

'And she says, "Not Far Lost Wood?"'

'And I say, "Yeah, how have you heard of Far Lost Wood?"'

'She says, "We've just bought it off the Forestry." So I saw my opportunity, and I said, "Would you mind if I parked up there sometimes?"'

And I swear Bob blushes and looks coy as he says, 'And I just kept coming back here more and more.'

'Until ...'

'Until, I ended up staying. Fifteen years now. They've been all right.'

'They're homeopathic vets, aren't they?'

'Yeah, but they're sussed. They helped me get my gypsy status off Powys County Council. So I can stay as long as I want, without altering the residential status of the wood, so long as I pay a peppercorn rent (currently 5p a year), and don't put up any permanent structures.'

And so here he is.

'Do you remember right at the beginning of this, I asked you how you felt about me doing it?'

'Of course.'

'And you said that you didn't mind, because the past is a pleasant void, the future is a less pleasant void, waiting to be filled, but the present is lovely.'

'Did I?'

'Yes. Do you still think that? I mean, I've sort of filled the void of the past.'

'You'll fuck it up. You'll cut and paste and miss loads out. I'm still going to write my autobiography.'

'I look forward to reading it. What about the future?'

'What about it? It's only a probability, a possibility even. Who can say?'

'The present?'

Bob leans forward.

'It's a miracle, isn't it? When you think of all the elements that had to come together, all the accidents that had to happen for life to occur. That this planet is in this sweet spot, where it's not too hot and not too cold so that we get liquid water. What are the chances? All of the stuff that we're made of comes from stars, man. And here we are, to witness it, to be part of it. What's that, if it's not a miracle? And now, here I am, wheels flattened, going nowhere, but in this moment. In this miraculous present.'

That'll do, I think.

Namaste.

May you be blessed with happiness, health and prosperity.

Epilogue

in which the author describes how to get your head together in the country

I drove in bright winter sunshine from Lancaster out to Andy Yurt's Ground, high in the Tatham Fells, to visit the grave of old Chas Ambler. I parked by the side of a one track moorland road and walked down through a soon-to-be wood. Andy has planted thousands of saplings which, year by year, are turning into trees.

Chas was buried in a cardboard coffin, painted by genius dyslexic signwriter, Panit Dave.

It makes me happy to be back here, remembering the night we held the wake on Chas's mobile stage, the Melodrome, right on this spot, and how Chas's coffin was on stage the whole time, raised on trestles. I remember my opening line: 'Well, Chas has often died on stage before, but up until now he's never actually been dead.' I remember all the musicians who played that night. I remember the next day, when a brass band came and played 'When The Saints' in proper New Orleans fashion, as we walked with his coffin to the grave, followed by seventy or so mourners, who had come from all over Britain to be in this isolated place. I remember as they lowered him in, as I said a few words, and how all the mourners lent a hand to fill in the grave, Bill Lloyd playing the pipes. I remember crying, and I'm crying now.

At the head of the grave, there's a large homemade dreamcatcher, which will fall apart with time and weather. Chas's girlfriend Viv has bought a yew tree, which has been planted somewhere about where his chest would be. Andy's put a marker at the foot of the grave; a stone he found at a garden centre, marked with the four cardinal points of the compass.

It is one of the most beautiful places I know, and the most ironic. Beautiful, as I turn to face the four points of the compass in this brilliant sunlight. North to the Lake District mountains; west to the sea; east to the bulk of Ingleborough, and behind it Pen-y-Ghent and Whernside, covered in snow like icing sugar on a cake; and to the south, rising away to block the view, the dark mass of Tatham Fells.

It's ironic, because Old Chas couldn't give a fuck about scenery or nature, he really couldn't. Nothing would interest him less than that he was buried in a beautiful place. He came from Ealing, and his taste in landscape, such as it was, extended no further than the suburban. As Andy Yurt said to me, 'Chas was much more interested in the people *in* the field rather than where the field was', referring to Chas's love of festivals, Glastonbury Festival in particular. Chas got our almost semi-legendary act Your Dad on the bill at Pilton for twelve years or so, and it was there that I first met Panit, through Chas's agency.

I remember sitting with Chas and Panit outside the Mocha Berry Cafe in Glastonbury during Frost Fair a few years ago. Frost Fair is the weekend at the beginning of December, when the streets of Glastonbury are closed to traffic, and stalls pop up selling crystals and dreamcatchers, which is pretty much what the shops sell anyway. The Melodrome is here, owned and run by Chas, but decorated by Panit, playing host to a series of bands, one of them (bottom of the bill) Your Dad. It is, in short, a mini festival, seven miles and six months away from Pilton. If you wanted to be perverse, you could call it the Glastonbury Festival. There's a link to Pilton Festival, though; the Glastonbury Town Band, traditionally the first act on the Pyramid Stage on Sunday, are outside the George and Pilgrim, playing 'Hark the Herald Angels Sing'.

At least one in three people on the streets is a straightforward hippie. It's cold, so they are wrapped up warm; warm but ethnic. There are a lot of unfortunate hats. A few people are wearing what look very like Afghan coats. Many of the young people have dreadlocks, and knitted bags slung over their shoulders. Some of the younger children are wearing skirts that might have been designed by Monica. It's hard to believe that the Freak culture has gone away at all, here on the Isle of Avalon.

Panit tells me a Bob story:

'I was parked up at a festival next to him once. And I know I talk loud, and there were a few people gathered around my fire, laughing and that. And we may well have been playing music. All of a sudden, Bob comes steaming out of his van, going, "Will you fucking shut up, Dave? I'm trying to sleep." And I say, "In fairness, Bob, it is three o'clock in the afternoon."'

'That's very good.'

'I soothed him by offering him a bottle and a spliff. Not that he needed soothing once I'd told him what time it was.'

There's a reason why I've got Dave talking, and it's not just for Bob stories.

'Dave: how do you build a bender? I want people to know how to get their heads together in the country.'

Panit lived in benders for a long time; so long that there are those who call him Bender Dave.

'I haven't seen a proper bender for years. Most people live in hovels, where they get poles, bend 'em into semicircles, and put tarpaulins over. That's no good. You've got to bend it like an egg shape, like a bow-top wagon, and then the rain don't go anywhere near where you're sitting, especially if you've put like a small trench round it.'

'Where do I start?'

'You get some poles, like thin branches, about seven or eight feet long, about two inches in diameter at the base. Ten or twelve should do, but it depends on the size of your tarp. You put a couple of holes in the ground, and you get your two strongest poles, stick 'em in the holes, and bend them over so that they meet, for most of their length, into an arch. Then you weave and twist the ends of the poles together, and tie 'em up with baler twine, if you've got it. But, remember, what you're after is like a horseshoe, not a semicircle. Then you get another couple of good poles, and do it again in the opposite corners, and do the same so that they cross the first two. Then you tie them together to the first lot, so you've got a cross. Then you get some more of your poles, and some of them you do the same, so that they all meet in a star shape in the middle, and the rest you weave them horizontally in and out of your arches.

'Then you get your tarps and throw them over. We used stolen lorry tarps. There was a hierarchy of coverings. Some tipis would have these custom-made covers, like Sid Rawle's crew did. But other people were more renegade, and did ramshackle tipis, with tarps of all different colours, that had lorry firms' names on them and that. Ideally, you have a couple, one for the walls and one for the ceiling. You weigh the wall ones down with logs, or stones, or something, and tie the roof one on. Then, in the day, you take the roof off, otherwise a bender can fucking stink. It's organic. If you can, you should put fresh reeds on the floor every day.'

'How did you stay warm?'

'I used tin-can stoves. Laziness is the only way to get cold. You make a stove from a can, but you've got to keep it going, got to make sure you've got all your wood together. If it snows, you bank it up against your walls. It gets lovely in there. But don't get too messy with 'em; don't fuss too much, once you've got the shape right you'll be fine. Often, if I was going somewhere I knew I could find poles, I'd just take my tarps with me, and not bother lugging the poles about. See, tipis, the Native Americans might use buffalo-skin coverings, and these bloody great big poles as a frame. They were big and heavy, so you might leave them up most of the time. But a bender, that's what they called a wigwam, and they were light, and made for travelling.'

'How long did you live in benders?'

'Years. Years and years.'

'But you're not travelling now?'

'Very few people actually travel now, not for fifteen years or more. All the park-ups and pull-ins have been sussed. All you get is hassle.'

'But you don't live in a house?'

'I couldn't bear a house. You can feel the electricity running round the walls. Everything hums. You can't feel the wind. No, I live in a beautiful showman's wagon built in the sixties. My wagon rocks in the wind, I know what's happening. I can hear the rain over my head. I like being in the weather. If it's raining, I open the windows. I've woken up in the morning with a bit of frost in me beard; I love that. No, buildings, central heating, air conditioning, all that. That's not right.'

'Because you don't believe anyone should own land?'

'Of course not. It's *our* land, we're just looking after it. No, the only three bits of land you own are the bit you're standing on, the bit you're having a crap on, and the bit you're buried in.'

So I guess old Chas owns this bit of the Fells, three feet wide and six foot long. I smoke a fag, say a prayer, and head back to my car.

As I drive away, I turn the radio on to listen to the news. War is coming. We will have no say in it. We don't own this place, and the people who do own it don't give a toss what happens to us. War is here, and there's nothing we can do.

There was a time, say from about 1989 to about 1992, when I didn't live my life in the shadow of war. Other than that, though, war has been one of the defining themes of my life. I grew up in a world where all the grown-ups had been in, or at least lived through, the war. My dad liked to talk about his time doing National Service, my stepdad about his in the Home Guard. I played with soldiers, read war comics, played war at school, watched war movies and talked a lot about war to my pals.

By 1967, my parents were reaching the end of their marriage in oper-atic style, and every night they would scream at one another for hours at a stretch. I remember being in the next room during one particularly appalling fight, watching black-and-white TV footage of the Six-Day War with tanks and marching armies racing across the Sinai Desert. I was nine; and I thought that the soldiers boots were going to smash through the television. Every night on the TV was Vietnam, and Biafra, and then, from 1969 on, Northern Ireland. The IRA blew up Guildford, where I was born; later, Brighton, where I lived.

When I was twelve, I joined the Air Training Corps, and learned how to shoot a First World War Lee Enfield .303 rifle, and how to identify Soviet Aircraft. I left a year later, after discovering The Velvet Underground. 'Heroin' was my gateway drug to the counter-culture; a week after buying the first Velvet Underground album, I was out of the ATC, but not out of war. Even civil war seemed not unlikely. Britain was locked in conflict with itself for much of the seventies. Night after night, the lights went out, and we lived by candlelight while angry strikers and complacent plutocrats shouted at one another across picket lines, and in smoke-filled rooms.

All these conflicts were nested in the one big conflict that was the Cold War. We grew up under the shadow of all-out thermonuclear war. In the eighties, with Thatcher and Reagan increasingly stepping up pres-sure on the Soviets, the threat of that world-ending conflict seemed particularly acute.

We were scared. Cruise missiles upped the stakes, it seemed. My wife went to Greenham. The profits from Glastonbury all went to CND. It was real. The clock was ticking towards midnight. In 1980, the Government published a pamphlet called *Protect and Survive*, which advised citizens what to do in case of nuclear attack, which amounted to not much more than stay at home and die there. In 1989, when the Berlin Wall came down, we stopped worrying about nukes, somehow. Hardly anyone worries any more. The UK has 215 nuclear weapons, France 300, Israel 80, Pakistan and India more than 100 each. China has about 250, and now North Korea have them too. Each of these weapons are many times more powerful than the bombs dropped on Hiroshima and Nagasaki at the end of the Second World War.

The US and Russia have about 7,000 nuclear weapons each. Thanks to treaties limiting their use, they each have a mere 1,800 at any one time armed and ready to fire at a few minutes notice. We should still be scared. You should be scared. You should know what that symbol on your T-shirt means.

It was not just me who was affected by war, of course, but entire generations. My whole generation, Bob's generation, all of us. Millions of us. Even though most of us have never fought in one. It haunts this planet.

This book is out of date. If you go on adventures, like Bob, you might miss history, but if you write history, you are always behind the moment. But I started by saying that the concerns of the counter-culture have been lost, or forgotten, or recuperated at best. So I feel I have to come as close to the present as I dare, to test my thesis.

We live in a time of war, and a time of great upheaval and change.

Change is coming because of worsening economic circumstances in the West, and the unfettered rise of AI to replace human productivity. The banking crisis of 2008 was followed by years of stagnant economic growth. Incomes have shrunk in what the real world calls real terms. People are homeless, and queuing for food. Governments slash budgets. There is record high youth unemployment all over Europe. No jobs, no food, nowhere to live. Just a phone. Britain leaving the European Union gives the opportunity for lovely low-paid, low-regulation work, enough for all!

Meanwhile, the wars go on. The Arab Spring? Funny fucking kind of spring. Our masters delight in destabilising the least stable part of the world. Thousands of tonnes of bombs are dropped on people's homes, so they pack up, pick up and walk away, and try to get to somewhere safe, like here. What would you do?

Imagine a man from sub-Saharan Africa with no food, no clean water, no prospect of economically productive work, who is getting bombed by his own government, but who happens to speak English. He decides to head north in search of a better life. He crosses the Sahara Desert, somehow gets across the hellhole that is Libya, and manages to find a boat on the coast. There are 354 people on a tiny fishing boat which flounders in choppy waters; they get picked up, thankfully, by the Italian coastguard, and taken to Sicily. Your man gets put in a holding camp, before being processed, and then starts to head across a hostile Europe to Calais, where he somehow survives for a few months before bunking into the back of a wagon on a ferry to Dover, at which point he applies for asylum. He gets bunged into an Immigration Detention Centre for at least six months, but maybe three, four, five years. He is given £37 a week to live on.

He should be welcomed with open arms, shouldn't he? Not out of altruism, but because someone as smart and resourceful as him is going to come in handy. Companies send their management on three-day team-building exercises where they have to do shit like build rafts. This guy has just been on the most exhausting management course imaginable. We should give him the keys to the place, not lock him up.

But these brave resourceful people are now seen as scum, as the enemies of Western Europe. This is because people moving causes wages to drop. In his book *23 Things They Don't Tell You About Capitalism*, the economist Ha-Joon Chang makes it clear that high European and US wages are only maintained by immigration controls. Free movement of people, at best, is redistributative. Capital, which does not suffer restrictions on its free movement, goes where it will.

These economic pressures cause anger because a hungry man is an angry man. People need food and shelter before they can begin to think about overcoming alienation.

Politics is making a slight return amongst young people, there is no doubt. It really needs to. The UK is leaving the EU partly because too many Millennials didn't look up from the black mirror in time to vote. But, perhaps, because of the victory of Leave in the Euro referendum, in the General Election of June 2017 it looks like they did. Younger voters decided they liked Jeremy Corbyn, a sixty-eight-year-old allotment holder and vegetarian who doesn't drink and has never smoked a spliff, but a guy at least who knows what the CND symbol looks like. Because younger voters have never seen a 'left-winger', mainstream North European Social Democratic Corbyn seems like one to them. Seems like one to lots of folk. At the Glastonbury Festival in 2017, thousand of people gathered in front of the Pyramid to chant Corbyn's name. At Glastonbury Fayre in 1971, it was Gumraji, sitting on his white throne, trying to address the Freaks through the Brinsley's PA. Who offers the greater vision, the Social Democrat or the Freak?

Social Democrats want a world where there is well-paid work for all, good socialised heath care, good educational provision from ages four to twenty-one, good security against both terrorist activities and environmental degradation, and where hard work can still lead to moderate prosperity. The Freaks wanted a world where free, authentic individuals live in abundant playful communities, peacefully co-existing and educating their curiosity in a world of equal plenty.

I reckon, if you're going to be an idealist, you might as well go large, but the Freak alternative is no longer on offer. As you've probably noticed, it remains more of an outline for an idealistic planet visited by the crew of the *Starship Enterprise* in one of those episodes where Spock falls in love with an alien with big hair and short skirt, rather than the actual Real World, a place I've always found over-rated.

It hasn't come off yet, I admit that. I've tried in this book to think about why these ideas have disappeared so far from view, when for a time they seemed to be coming into focus. I'm trying to argue that young people should look at them again. If you've got nowhere to live, build a bender. The countryside needs you back. If you've got no job, do something else instead, at least for a time. Pay for it by living cheap. Be consciously economically inactive.

What worries me is that Younger Readers will welcome new road developments, feeling that borrowing to invest in infrastructure will benefit the economy in the long term, because that is the sort of thing Social Democrats do, and that they will not consider chaining themselves to trees in order to stop the developers, which is what Freaks do.

To go back to the beginning: the Freaks thought that in order to change society, you first had to change the individual. This was the point of the acid, according to Tim Leary, to John Lennon, to the League of Spiritual Discovery, to Christine Bott and to Smiles. Once, religion had the same aim. To redeem the individual from the world. Alchemy, too; turning base metal into gold is a metaphor for individual transformation. The counter-culture was responding to Nietzsche. How are we to exist in a world without God? Without God, what's the fucking point of all this fucking shit? But, really? What is the point? To be schooled, worked, bred from, pensioned off and cremated? The answer, according to the Freaks, was to play; to play God even, in a world where creativity and wonder and good old-fashioned fun were prized above stuff and status and stress. And this, above all else: to thine own self be true.

We live in conservative times. Social media gives voice to a herd mentality, herded together in algorithmic bubbles. Humans are being reconstructed in the norms of social media. Digital natives see the world differently from those of us who are not. A quarter of people under thirty in London are teetotallers. Income for young people has dropped by 30 per cent in the ten years since 2006. Illegal drug use is dropping, as are teenage pregnancies. Truancy is at an all-time low. The universities are hotbeds of managerialism led by bureaucrats fearful of their paying customers. Fear is big. The fear of lack of money, the fear that it's hard to get into the job market, the fear of homelessness.

It seems to me that the Unthinkable has become unthinkable. No one could think of driving to Afghanistan and buying a few coats. Imagination in the young, I worry, has been caused to run in deep yet narrow channels, never to break free of the levee and wash the old world away.

Still, mine is not to worry, I guess. But old men must be allowed their memories. I grew up in the shadow of the war. You grew up in the shadow of the Freaks. The Freaks have gone. It's your world now. Yours, my Younger Readers, my granddaughters. Good luck with it. Fuck it up less than we did.

The phone rings on the seat beside me. It's Bob. I pull into a lay-by and call him back. He wants to tell me about his visit to London yesterday.

'I was staying last night with Dennis Rolfe and his missis. And they've got this quite posh house, like, so there's no smoking indoors. They'd gone to bed an hour, and I fancied a fag. I'm just in my dressing gown, but it's a warm night. I was leaning against the door to keep it open, but I underestimated the springiness of it, and it slammed shut behind me. And I know the doorbell's not working, so I start knocking really loud. But Dennis's bedroom is at the back of the house, and I think, "Fuck me. All I've got is some tobacco, my walking staff, and my dressing gown. I haven't even got the keys to my van." So I keep knocking and knocking. Nothing. I think, "I'm going to have to flag down the Old Bill and get them to lock me up for the night." So I do one last really loud knocking. And the upstairs window of the house next door opens, and this lady pokes her head out and says, "Are you in trouble?" And I say, "I am really," and explained the situation. So she comes down in her dressing gown, and she says come in. I'm in my dressing gown, and I'm leaning on a staff like fucking Gandalf, and she's got Dennis's number on her phone, so she lends me her phone, and Dennis comes down. And that lady was Helena Bonham Carter.'

'You and Helena Bonham Carter were standing about in your dressing gowns together last night at one in the morning? In her house?'

'Yep.'

And I laugh. And Bob Rowberry, Big Blinking Black Bob the Hook, the Beat, the Face, the Travelling Freak, El Maestro, the greatest unhailed foot soldier of the counter-culture, who lives deep in a wood in a valley on the Welsh border, alongside a long ago abandoned railway line, in a superannuated school bus, now painted battleship grey, whose engine has died and whose wheels have fallen off, he laughs too.

An Appendix and an Afterword

Books

The main bibliography seemed not to fit with my over-arching intention for this book, that it serve as an introduction, and not be too dauntingly academic. So my full referenced reading list can be found online at http://www.moodindex.co.uk/wordpress2010/wordpress/a-hero-for-high-times/bibliography-and-references/

I have acknowledged a few of my sources in the text, because I want you to read them, and didn't want to tuck them away at the back of the book. The books I have mentioned in the text are (most of them) readable and easy to find, and I hope you have a look.

This is a list of books that might constitute a well-read Freak's library. The counter-culture was a literary culture. Everyone read, or pretended to read, but of course, not everybody read everything.

John Allegro, *The Sacred Mushroom and the Cross*
Richard Bach, *Jonathan Livingston Seagull*
Richard Ballantine, *Richard's Bicycle Book*
Richard Brautigan, *Trout Fishing in America*
Dee Brown, *Bury My Heart at Wounded Knee*
Mikhail Bulgakov, *The Master and Margarita*
William Burroughs, *Junkie*
Rachel Carson, *Silent Spring*
Carlos Castaneda, *The Teachings of Don Juan*
Quentin Crisp, *The Naked Civil Servant*
Ram Dass, *Be Here Now*
Guy Debord, *Society of the Spectacle*
Allen Ginsberg, *Howl*
G.I. Gurdjieff, *Meetings with Remarkable Men*
Robert Heinlein, *Stranger in a Strange Land*
Joseph Heller, *Catch-22*
Frank Herbert, *Dune*
Herman Hesse, *Steppenwolf, Siddhartha, The Glass Bead Game*
Abbie Hoffman, *Steal This Book*

Christmas Humphreys, *Buddhism*
Aldous Huxley, *The Doors of Perception*
Erica Jong, *Fear of Flying*
Jack Kerouac, *On the Road*
Sheldon Kopp, *If you meet the Buddha on the Road, Kill Him!*
R.D. Laing, *Knots*
Lao Tzu, *Tao Te Ching*
Tim Leary, *Politics of Ecstasy*
Ursula K. Le Guin, *The EarthseaTrilogy, The Dispossessed, The Left Hand*
    of Darkness, Always Coming Home
T. Lobsang Rampa, *The Third Eye*
H.P. Lovecraft, *The Call of Cthulhu*
Richard Mabey, *Food For Free*
Herbert Marcuse, *One-Dimensional Man*
John Michell, *The View Over Atlantis*
Michael Moorcock, *Hawkmoon: The History of the Runestaff, The Final*
    Programme, Elric of Melniboné
Richard Neville, *Play Power*
Friedrich Nietzsche, *Ecce Homo*
Jeff Nuttall, *Bomb Culture*
Mervyn Peake, *The Gormenghast Trilogy*
Robert M. Pirsig, *Zen and the Art of Motorcycle Maintenance*
Thomas Pynchon, *Gravity's Rainbow*
Luke Rhinehart, *The Dice Man*
Tom Robbins, *Even Cowgirls Get the Blues, Another Roadside Attraction,*
    Jitterbug Perfume
J.D. Salinger, *The Catcher in the Rye*
John Seymour, *The Complete Book of Self-Sufficiency*
Robert Shea and Robert Anton Wilson, *The Illuminatus! Trilogy*
Idries Shah, *The Way of the Sufi*
Gilbert Shelton, *The Fabulous Furry Freak Brothers Omnibus*
George R. Stewart, *Earth Abides*
Henry David Thoreau, *Walden*
Hunter S. Thompson, *Fear and Loathing in Las Vegas*
J.R.R. Tolkien, *The Hobbit, The Lord of the Rings, The Silmarillion*
The Harvard Lampoon, *Bored of the Rings*
Kurt Vonnegut, *Slaughterhouse–Five, Cat's Cradle, Breakfast of Champions*
Lyall Watson, *The Romeo Error, Supernature*
Alan Watts, *The Way of Zen*
Whole Earth Catalog

Richard Wilhelm (translator), *I Ching*
Tom Wolfe, *The Electric Kool-Aid Acid Test*

Cannabis

You may have noticed, as I have, that although I've discussed both LSD and heroin at some length, and MDMA in passing, I've not so much written about cannabis as sat about smoking it.

Smoking is bad, and it kills you. I wish I didn't smoke. I wish I had never smoked. I'm desperate to stop. If you don't smoke, please don't be encouraged to try by old farts like me and Bob.

I wish I had just stuck to hash cakes.

In the culture I have been writing about, cannabis is a bit like tea. It's a polite thing to offer your guests.

It's called weed because it's a weed. It pretty much grows anywhere. If it gets too much sunlight while it is budding, it produces an oil to protect itself from the UV rays. That oil is what makes hemp fun, as well as medicinally useful. That's why the good shit comes from sunny places. But it will grow quite happily in your garden or in a window box.

According to Professor David Nutt's classification of dangerous drugs, cannabis is at number 11. Heroin is top, cocaine second, downers third, methadone fourth, alcohol fifth, and you take that with your gran at Christmas. Tobacco trails in at nine, LSD is at 14, and Ecstasy at 18. Professor Nutt was sacked from his job as the UK Government's advisor on drug use for saying that more people are killed riding ponies in gymkhanas than from taking E. It was true, but they still sacked him.

There are a few dangers associated with using dope, but death is not one of them. No one has ever died of a cannabis overdose. Scientists can't really inject humans with cannabis to see how much would kill them, but when they tried it with rats, by giving them vast amounts of cannabis, all the rats did was sleep for three days. But it may affect concentration, at work and at school. Most certainly, you shouldn't use spliff and drive. Weight gain is a worry, as you might find yourself fancying cake and lovely pork pies at inappropriate times. But the big danger with cannabis is psychosis.

I've known four guys who have had cannabis psychosis, and it's not pretty. It can be temporary, but it can last a lifetime. I've lost count of how many people I've had a smoke with over the years, certainly into the thousands, but I remember those four guys.

There is growing evidence that teenagers who smoke large amounts of weed are more likely to display symptoms of schizophrenia than those who don't. In those who have a predilection, such as a family history of severe mental illness, it can accelerate the onset of schizophrenia by two and a half years. These effects seem to drop off after users pass the age of eighteen.

For me, I'm glad it came into my life. Millions of other people are too.

I am a member of the Green Party, and party policy calls for immediate decriminalisation, followed by a Royal Commission on ways and means to establish a legal and regulated trade. I think that is a good idea.

Uruguay has fully legalised cannabis use since 2012, and it will be interesting to see how that goes for them. It's currently legal for recreational use in the US States of Alaska, California, Colorado, Maine, Massachusetts, Nevada, Oregon and Washington. It's legal to use but not to buy in DC. Canada is trying it next. In Spain, it is legal to grow cannabis plants for personal use, so long as no one can see them. That makes perfect sense to me. You wouldn't want some fucknut to nick them, after all.

What is not sensible, in my view, is putting the distribution of largely benign substances into the control of criminals, and so as well as legalising cannabis, I think LSD and Ecstasy should be available in pharmacies, and heroin on prescription. I think that alcohol should not be on sale in supermarkets, but only in pubs and off-licences, and that it should be taxed in a way that takes into account the individual and social harms it causes, as tobacco is.

Films: A list by Tony Lawson

A few years ago, I was at Pembroke College in Cambridge giving a talk, and they sat me next to the Master at dinner. Funny business, dining at High Table at an Oxbridge college. You sit up on a dais overlooking a hall full of poshed-up students. Ye Olde Master reads aloud a prayer in Latin, and then you tuck in to this extraordinary grub. Over dinner we made conversation, the Master of Pembroke and I. He asked what I was working on, and I told him it was a biography of a friend of mine, but also a study of the high times, the counterculture, and how it came about, and why it ended.

He said, 'Oh, I was a student at Cambridge from 1963-66, and it was a wonderful, free, liberating time, sex, drugs, freedom, marvellous. I remember the quad here at Pembroke decked with political banners; you wouldn't get that now. And because of that, wherever I went in my work, and I travelled a lot, all over the world, I always remembered the freedom of those times, and felt as though I carried that sense of freedom and liberation with me. I suppose you'll be writing about New Wave Cinema?'

'.... er ....'

'It's important not to forget the importance of New Wave Cinema in the growth of the counterculture, Ian,' he said.

I asked him what his work was, that had taken him all over the world. He said, 'I ran British Intelligence. I was the head of MI6.'

I've thought about it since. How did someone who thought of themselves as a hip counter-cultural guy end up as the UK's spymaster, as 'M'? I reckon it's to do with freedom; maybe at the time, the Soviets seemed like the enemies of freedom, and fighting them seemed like a way of fighting for freedom. I don't know.

But I do know I've got to find a way to say something about cinema, in case MI6 come in after me.

I recruited my pal, Presteigne resident Tony Lawson. I don't know a great deal about film. But Tony does, not in the sense of being a bloke who's seen a few films and is a bit interested, but in the sense that he edited *Straw Dogs*, *Don't Look Back*, *Barry Lyndon*, etc. Tony has been Nicolas Roeg's editor of choice since the seventies.

I reckon this list will keep you going for a bit. It's a list by a man who is both a cinéaste and a top professional, compiled with love. He says in his note to me 'I'm sure there are more, I just can't think of them.'

The Wages of Fear (1953)
Seven Samurai (1954)
La Strada (1954)
A Generation (1955)
Kanal (1957)
Ashes and Diamonds (1958)
The Four Hundred Blows (1959)
Hiroshima Mon Amour (1959)
Zazie in the Metro (1960)
Breathless (1960)
Shoot the Pianist (1960)
La Dolce Vita (1960)
Peeping Tom (1960)

L'Avventura (1960)

WR – Mysteries of the Organism (1961)

Jules et Jim (1962)

Knife in the Water (1962)

The Loneliness of the Long Distance Runner (1962)

The Exterminating Angel (1962)

Cleo of 5 to 7 (1962)

8 1/2 (1963)

The Servant (1963)

Tom Jones (1963)

This Sporting Life (1963)

Dr Strangelove (1964)

A Hard Day's Night (1964)

Alphaville (1965)

Darling (1965)

The Ipcress File (1965)

Repulsion (1965)

The War Game (1965)

The Spy Who Came in from the Cold (1965)

Le Bonheur (1965)

The Shop on Main Street (1965)

Loves of a Blonde (1965)

Morgan, A Suitable Case for Treatment (1966)

Closely Watched Trains (1966)

Alfie (1966)

The Battle of Algiers (1966)

Blow-Up (1966)

Georgy Girl (1966)

Balthazar (1966)

Accident (1967)

Bonnie and Clyde (1967)

The Graduate (1967)

Point Blank (1967)

Week End (1967)

The Firemen's Ball (1967)

Faces (1968)

If ... (1968)

Midnight Cowboy (1969)

Easy Rider (1969)

The Wild Bunch (1969)

Z (1969)
My Night at Maud's (1969)
MASH (1970)
The Butcher (1970)
Performance (1970)
Zabriskie Point (1970)
Aguirre, The Wrath of God (1972)
The Bitter Tears of Petra von Kant (1972)
Mean Streets (1973)
Celine and Julie Go Boating (1974)

Hitching

The Lancaster University campus is about three miles south of the city. For many years, students wanting a lift from the city onto campus stood by a lamp-post beside the A6, known as the hitching post. Sometimes there would be as many as twenty people queuing there. My friend Mickey Lips met his wife in that queue. Students and staff members would expect to pick up a few hitchers on the way in. On campus there's a shelter where students hitch for a lift back into town.

No one uses it any more. But why? Is the world that much less safe? Are students so much richer now that they all have cars? So much less willing to spend ten minutes in the company of strangers? When did you last see a hitchhiker anywhere? They are becoming scarce.

Hitching could be safer than ever, if people would be willing to rethink it a little. It should be the convention that the person hitching takes a photo of the registration number of the car they are getting into, and sends it to a friend. Drivers would see the sense of it, I think, and if it became a convention, I'm sure they wouldn't mind. It was never that unsafe, anyway.

I Ching

If Younger Readers want to try dipping their metaphorical toes into the watery spiritual zeitgeist of the counter-culture, I recommend trying the *I Ching*. Bob snorts with contempt, but I still do it from time to time. It translates from Chinese as 'The Book of Changes', and it makes no claims for itself. Tradition has it that one of its authors was Lao Tzu, 'Old Man', the Father of Chinese philosophy and in particular of Taoism. Way back towards the beginning of the book, I spoke about how Taoism is, in some ways, the controlling philosophy of the counter-culture, from which it derived the idea that you should 'Go With the Flow'. This is a wildly simplistic view of Taoism, but if you want more, you will have to find out for yourself, by the very nature of the thing, because 'those who know do not say, and those who say do not know'.

The *I Ching* that we have today is largely the work of Confucius, the greatest of China's philosophers. If you are worried that you might get sucked into a religious cult, please don't be. Confucius was concerned with how to live well in this life, not with theology or the hereafter. You should not read the *I Ching* as a way of telling the future, so much as a way to take the temperature of the fleeting moment by reading a short series of texts, written by a very wise gentleman. The best translation is by a German called Richard Wilhelm. It was translated into English by Cary Baynes, and the book with its black and red cover was a must on many Freaks' bookshelves. It does have a fair old bit in it about fifth century BCE Chinese politics, but you can skip that by buying the excellent *Pocket I Ching* by W.S. Boardman, based on the work of Wilhelm and Baynes, which gives readings for each of the sixty-four hexagrams, and shows how to generate those hexagrams using three coins.

As the name implies, a hexagram is made of six lines. These days, I use the interweb to generate mine. It's not really worth asking questions, I'd say; just try it and see what it says. I used a website to generate a hexagram to share with you here.

The hexagram it gave me was this,

which is Hexagram 14, 'Possession in Great Measure.' But the top lines are what is known as 'changing lines'. So as well as reading the text for Hexagram 14, you read the text for the lines that are changing, in this case lines 1 and 2. These are on the page opposite the main reading. If a line changes, it changes into its opposite, which gives a second Hexagram, in this case Hexagram 43, Breakthrough.

You then read the text for the second Hexagram. If you have no 'changing lines', then you just read the text for the first Hexagram. What does this reading tell me? It tells me I'm glad I've introduced you to the *I Ching*. I could have faked a reading, of course, but I didn't.

Links

These links can also be found via my website, where you can also find the full bibliography:
http://www.ianmarchant.com/

This is a very good link to the history and archaeology of the Radnor Valley:
http://www.rgreen.org.uk/Radnor.html

These three links will take you to the story of how Marcus Gray proved beyond all reasonable doubt that Procol Harum were named after Bob's cat (Vicki's cat really).
http://www.procolharum.com/young_cat-claude1.htm
http://www.procolharum.com/young_cat-claude++2+.htm
http://www.procolharum.com/young_cat-claude+33-s.htm

Here are some excellent magazine archives:
OZ: http://ro.uow.edu.au/ozlondon/
International Times: http://www.internationaltimes.it/archive/
Spare Rib: https://journalarchives.jisc.ac.uk/britishlibrary/sparerib
Seed: https://craigsams.com/writings/seed-magazine/
The Whole Earth Catalog: http://www.wholeearth.com/index.php

This is the link to the Royal College of Psychiatrists' entry on the dangers of cannabis:
http://www.rcpsych.ac.uk/healthadvice/problemsdisorders/cannabis.aspx
and this is the link to the Cannabis Law Reform Group, which argues for legalisation:
http://www.clear-uk.org/

Here's some useful information about squatting:
https://www.squatter.org.uk/about-ass/
and some about why you should: 'on the poverty of student life'
http://library.nothingness.org/articles/SI/en/display/4

You can still listen to Radio Caroline,
http://www.radiocaroline.co.uk/#home.html
learn ecstatic dance
http://gurdjieff-movements.net/
throw the *I Ching*
www.ichingonline.net
and visit Scott and Helen Nearing's Good Life Center in Maine
http://goodlife.org/
(although it might be easier to get to the Centre for Alternative
Technology, near Machynlleth)
http://www.cat.org.uk/index.html

This is a joyous film of the Last Barsham Faire from 1976, which shows,
I think, both why Freak culture was wonderful and why it needed
updating:
http://www.eafa.org.uk/catalogue/703
Six months or so later, the makeover started, as Bill Grundy interviewed
the *Sex Pistols*:
https://www.youtube.com/watch?v=0knFHyDD150

Here are a couple of clips showing some of the violence that the Freaks
were subjected to under Tory rule in the 1980s; first Greenham,
https://www.youtube.com/watch?v=vMdrXW72jaw
and then the Battle of the Beanfield
https://www.youtube.com/watch?v=6LHizyCtakw

If you'd like to Freak up your utilities, have a look at Ecotricity, for all
your energy needs,
https://www.ecotricity.co.uk/for-your-home/
and for broadband and mobile, you can't do better than the Phone Co-op.
You can become a member, as well as a customer, and share in any
profits.
https://www.thephone.coop/

I realise that not everybody is fortunate enough to live in Wales, but
I'm also sharing a link to Dwr Cymru, aka Welsh Water. This is worth
looking at because Welsh Water is not part of a huge multinational, but
is owned by a not-for-profit company controlled by the Welsh Government.
It is, in short, a nationalised industry in all but name. It is morally wrong,
isn't it, to profit from water? You may not be able to get your water from

Dwr Cymru, but have a look at how they are structured, and wonder why something like this doesn't operate anywhere else in the UK. http://www.dwrcymru.com/en.aspx

If you are a vegan who believes in sustainable energy and organic cultivation methods, and who also enjoys Association Football, then follow follow follow the Green Devils, Forest Green Rovers. https://www.forestgreenroversfc.com/

And finally, who can resist these two lovable scamps? Yes, it's no-longer-extant festival cabaret troupers Your Dad at the Glastonbury Frost Fair on the Melodrome Stage in 2012. The stage was painted by Panit, who seems to be talking over me, as per. https://www.youtube.com/watch?feature=player_embedded&v=5qqOuDHKoGo

Money

Before decimal currency arrived in 1971, just after my thirteenth birthday, and just before Bob's thirtieth, money was different. It was based, not on the number ten, but on the number sixty, which was the basis of Babylonian mathematics. It was therefore probably ripe for re-inventing, as the Babylonians were so through by 1971.

There were twenty shillings to the pound, and twelve pennies to a shilling. An old shilling was therefore worth five pence; or 'New Pence' as I still call them. A shilling was known as a 'bob'. A 'tanner' was sixpence; two and a half new pence. There was a little silver sixpence coin. Two shillings and six pence (Twelve and a half New Pence) was my pocket money. It was called a half crown, and there was a coin for that too. For my paper round as a lad, I got seven shillings and sixpence a week, though this doubled after decimalisation to 75p. A guinea was a pound and one shilling, and although there were no longer guinea coins, some posh shops still priced things in guineas into the 1980s.

Music

If I was to think too much about this, I really would go mad. My life has been dedicated to listening to pop music, thinking about pop music, playing pop music. I've even delivered an academic paper on why 'Bohemian Rhapsody' is objectively shit. No; if I give this anything but the most cursory thought, I'd go insane. When I am an old man, I will get this volume down, and shake my head in shame.

After much soul-searching, I've decided to boil this down to fifty songs. I tried to make the list as British as possible, but as its roots are in America, the first few songs really had to be there. The other exceptions are Hendrix, who first found success in Britain, and Kate and Anna McGarrigle, who are Canadian, and whom Bob met, but who have earned their place by representing music that came through punk largely unscathed, because it was good. Only the Beatles get three songs, which is still to underplay their significance.

The playlist also tells a story, I hope.

You can listen to it via Spotify – https://open.spotify.com/user/bartle-booth23/playlist/7c6JgQQlDIjMb54VFfclYK

Nat King Cole, *Nature Boy*

Charlie Parker and Dizzy Gillespie, *A Night in Tunisia*

Ken Colyer's Jazzmen, *Sheik of Araby*

Elvis Presley, *Heartbreak Hotel*

Carl Perkins, *Blue Suede Shoes*

Gene Vincent, *Be Bop A Lula*

Little Richard, *Tutti Frutti*

Lonnie Donegan, *Rock Island Line*

Beatles, *Sheik of Araby*

Long John Baldry with Blues Incorporated, *Rain is Such a Lonesome Sound*

Rolling Stones, *Little Red Rooster*

Davy Graham, *Angi*

Wizz Jones, *Ballad of Hollis Brown*

Animals, *The House of the Rising Sun*

Beatles, *Tomorrow Never Knows*

Incredible String Band, *Painting Box*

Pink Floyd, *Chapter 24*

Donovan, *Sunny South Kensington*

Procol Harum, *Conquistador*

Beatles, *Helter Skelter*

Pentangle, *Light Flight*

Fairport Convention, *A Sailor's Life*

Jimi Hendrix, *All Along the Watchtower*

Thunderclap Newman, *Something in the Air*

Rolling Stones, *All Down the Line*

Vashti Bunyan, *Diamond Day*
Trees, *The Garden of Jane Delawny*
Quintessence, *Notting Hill Gate*
Mighty Baby, *A Blanket in my Muesli*
Mott the Hoople, *Saturday Gigs*
The Deviants, *Let's Loot the Supermarket*
The Pink Fairies, *Portobello Shuffle*
Hawkwind, *Orgone Accumulator*
Kate and Anna McGarrigle, *Heart Like a Wheel*
Nick Lowe, *Heart of the City*
The Damned, *New Rose*
The Sex Pistols, *Anarchy in the UK*
The Clash, *White Man in Hammersmith Palais*
Aswad, *Natural Progression*
Steel Pulse, *Handsworth Revolution*
Crass, *Punk is Dead*
Robert Wyatt, *Shipbuilding*
The Waterboys, *Fisherman's Blues*
D-Mob, *We Call It Acieeed*
Julian Cope, *Hanging Out and Hung Up on the Line*
The KLF, *3 a.m. Eternal*
Manic Street Preachers, *Motorcycle Emptiness*
Flowered Up, *Weekender*
Two Bad Mice, *Bombscare*
Alison Krauss and Yo Yo Ma, *Simple Gifts*

Women's Movement

In the text, I've recommended Rosalind Miles' *Women's History of the World*, Shulamith Firestone's *The Dialectic of Sex* and, of course, Germaine Greer's *The Female Eunuch*. Valerie Solanas' *The Scum Manifesto* will give you pause for thought, too.

But this freaky version of what the Women's Movement was/is/will be again ignores a major strand of the movement; arguably, in fact, a much larger part of the story, which grew out of the Women's Suffrage movement and twentieth-century social reform. To find out about this, you can't do better than to read the work of Sheila Rowbotham. Try *Women's Consciousness*, *Women, Resistance and Revolution* and *Dutiful Daughters* (written with Jean McCrindle).

In 1970, there was a two-day conference at Ruskin College, Oxford, which is sometimes cited as the start of the Women's Movement in the UK. This conference came up with what were known as 'The Four Demands':

1. Equal pay.
2. Equal education and job opportunities.
3. Free contraception and abortion on demand.
4. Free 24-hour nurseries.

At a further series of conferences in the 1970s, another three were added:

5. Legal and financial independence for women.
6. The right to a self-defined sexuality.
7. Freedom from intimidation by the threat or use of male violence.

If you think these demands have been achieved – well, you are wrong. If you think they are still worth fighting for, then fight.

Afterword

9 June 2017

It is always a mistake to declare the End of History, but maybe I'm just in time to hop back on as it kicks back into partial life. Watching the opposition to Trump has made me hopeful again. When I started writing this book, I saw no signs amongst the students I was teaching or amongst the great majority of the young people that I was meeting while performing at festivals, of any real knowledge of, or interest in, what I have called 'Freak Culture'. I've defined this culture as an existential movement, which was convinced that only by living in a fully realised momentary now can the individual, and thus society, be freed from alienation; and that these moments, being unalienated, would be lived joyfully, playfully.

Bob would say that's bollocks. Bob might say, turn on, tune in, drop out. Go with the flow. The moment is all. Make art, make love, live in peace. You are part of the Universe. Good advice, I reckon.

The punk in me says get pissed, destroy, also good advice under the right circumstances, but he also says, it was cheap, it was easy, go and do it, and maybe that's the best advice the counter-culture can offer a new generation of young engaged political activists.

Brexit and Trump and Mrs Theresa May in 2017 could be the equivalent to my Younger Readers of what the invasions of Hungary and Suez were for the Freaks in 1956.

Now you need a Ginsberg and a Ken Colyer and an Elvis of your own. Maybe they will come, not in the form of poets and pop musicians, but as something else. I don't know what though.

Or maybe you don't. Maybe you have enough to go on already.

Good luck; the Freaks are on your side.

Acknowledgements

Thanks

To David Robert Rowberry, collaborator, co-conspirator, for putting up with years of questioning, for going along with all this, for the photos and for everything. Well played, Maestro.

To Colin Midson, for encouraging me, to my agents Annette Green and David Smith for holding me, to my editor Dan Franklin, without whose work over thirty years or so, there would be no history of the counterculture.

To Paul Williams, aka Perry Venus, for his invaluable knowledge of the period, his work on Bob's photos, the photo at the end, and for always being up for coming on a trip. To Yammerman, Phazer, Jet, Wee Boab and Big Jimmy Mac, the first punks in the Great Green Desert.

To Christopher Charles 'Chas' Ambler and Nicola 'Nix' Jones, my dear and irreplaceable friends. To John Moat and Andrew Kerr. To Tim Guest and Jonathan Cainer.

To the nomadic people: Peter Mustill, Panit Dave (aka Dave Panit), Alston Hughes, Francis Stonor, David Goff Everleigh, Alison Parry, Hugh Pope, Briar Miller, Dennis Rolfe, Monica Meyer, Rachel Francis, Andy Yurt and Vicki, Titi Poelsma, Annette Vanstokkem, Palfi Rinehart.

To Lois Pryce and Austin Vince, for the loan of the cabin on stilts. Thank you squared.

To Nicola Lane for 'Dennis the Dope and Wanker'.

To people who answered my questions: Ian Gomm, George Szirtes, Kevin Jackson, Charles Shaar Murray, Nicola Lane, Andrew Hussey, Stewart Home, Barney Hoskyns, Andy Roberts, Keith Christmas, Peter Everett, Tony Lawson, Mark Williams, Simon Norfolk, Toby Weymouth, Joe McNally, Christine Lawson, Rick Mayes, Mark Wildman, Noel Flay Cass, Richard Jones, Ian Quance, Sue Sanders,

Clare Stuteley, Jillian Stuteley, Christopher Doyle, John and Janet Graham, John Rogers, Matt Harvey and Tina Griffiths.

To people who questioned my answers: Dr Ursula Howard, Samantha Heywood, Dr Peter Jackson, Dr Gregory Leadbetter, Dr Lucy Fraser, Dr David Littlewood, Dr Saleel Nurbhai, Dr Seiriol Morgan

To my ex-students, especially Hayley Harman, Sophie Clarke and Ross Horton. To Kerry Morgan at the Spar, High Street, Presteigne, for trying to stop me buying tobacco – and for selling me tobacco in return for a mention. To ECWM, EJMM, VCM and SKS. To Peggy the dog.

To the Melodrome crew, esp Mick and Chel and Martin and Kath and Lucy. To Chrissie Gladwin and Viv Carradice. To dear Tony Green. To the Village Hall crew. To my co-habitees in the Black Sheep Co-Op, esp Uncle Richard Salmon. To all the people round the fire who've ever talked to me. To all the people who've explained to me that this whole universe could be like an atom? In a whole other Universe? And, like, there's no way of telling?

And thank you to Hilary Marchant. It's traditional, in listing narrative non-fiction acknowledgements, to thank your long-suffering spouse last, even if really they should come first. Hilary transcribed 100-odd hours of taped conversations between me and Bob. About one third of the keystrokes that went into the making of this book are hers. She did a first proof-read of my dyslexic prose, though any remaining mistakes are all mine. Her critical intelligence and unwavering indifference to the doings of a bunch of stoned old Freaks were the lights that lit the path as we made our way together through the valley of the shadow of Bob. Without you HJ, my love, nothing.

Index

Page references in *italics* indicate photographs or illustrations.
BR indicates Bob Rowberry.

Old Grey Whistle Test 369
Oldham, Andrew Loog 244
Olympic Games (1972), Munich 338
101ers 317
Ono, Yoko 6, 141, 163, 330, 347, 364, 375
OPEC 303
Operation Julie (1976–7) 5, 376–7, 378
Operation Rupert (1971) 357–8
opium 122–6, 133, 171, 179, 198–9, 203, 211
O'Rahilly, Ronan 102–3, 104, 156, 246
Oram, Neil 77; *The Warp* 77
Orbach, Martin 306
Orbison, Roy 56
Order of the Star 218
orientalism 25, 151, 282, 286, 431
Ormsby-Gores 159, 161, 326
Orwell, George 42, 48
Osborne, Helen 329
Osborne, John 329; *Look Back in Anger* 54
Osho 219, 220, 431, 432
Ouspensky, P.D. 221
Oxford Union 223, 224
OZ 165, 166, 346–7, 348, 355, 356–60, 367; trial
   (1971) 5, 358–60

Paddick, Hugh 95
Page, Jimmy 295, 309
Paghman, Afghanistan 264–5, 269, 270, 270, 277,
   278
Pakistan 174, 183, 199, 204, 264–5, 273, 335, 449
Palace of Ben Abu, Tangier 350
Palestinian Liberation Organisation (PLO) 338
Panit Dave 121, 309, 322, 416, 421, 445, 446–7,
   465
Panorama 81
Paperback Bookstore 163
Parallel Lines (Marchant) 70, 306
Paramounts, The 158
Paris student unrest (1968) 149, 227, 228
Parker, Colonel Tom 56
Parker, Edie 71
Partisan, the, Soho, London 78–82, 80, 92
Pashtun Match Company 184
Pathé News 357
Patsy (BR's girlfriend) 411–12
Paul Butterfield Blue Band 153
peace and love 21, 68, 149, 150, 364, 380, 382,
   416, 439
Peace Convoy, The 5, 13, 317, 417–18, 419, 421
Pearson, Gabriel 79
Peel, John 11, 64, 104, 161, 359, 366
Peggy the Dog 173, 174, 363, 383, 384
Penguin 170, 229
Penkovsky, Oleg 113, 241, 242
Penman, Ian 379
Pentangle 35, 231; 'Light flight' 231, 466
PEOPLE party 302; *Manifesto for a Sustainable
   Society* 302, 303
Perkins, Carl 54, 127, 466
permissive society 347, 357
Pester, Bill 26–7, 28
Peter and the Test Tube Babies 380
Phazer 373, 376, 377, 379, 381

phenomenology 68, 136
Philadelphia Association 136
Phillips, Dewey 56
Phillips, Sam 55–6
Pill, arrival of (1961) 112, 127, 345, 356, 357,
   428–9
Pilton Festival 446
Pink Floyd 132, 133, 158, 161, 162, 164, 165, 233,
   309, 330, 363, 368, 371, 466
pirate radio 102–5, 364, 464
plate-glass universities 141, 433–4 *see also*
   universities
Plato 216
Playboy 302
playlist, music 466–7
Plinston, Graham 337, 343, 344, 350
Plinston, Mandy 344
Poelsma, Titi 236, 237, 291, 334, 335, 336
Polanski, Roman 238
Polari 95
Polari 95
Pop, Iggy 367, 375, 440
Popham, Peter 358
pop music 28; Britpop/1990s and 11–12, 437;
   Elvis as first modern pop star 55; folk pop
   see folk pop; game-changing pop songs
   283; genre and 152, 153, 154, 155, 440;
   greatest pop single ever 'Good Vibrations'
   334; Guy Stevens and 156–7; Ian Marchant
   love of/devotion to 365, 465–6; invention
   of modern 57; Mexican 397; New
   Romantics and 381; 1950s 42–3; pirate
   radio and 104; playlist 466–7; punk and
   379, 380; rock 'n' roll and 57, 152, 153, 154,
   155; situationist ideas and 439, 440 *see also
   under individual artist and song name*
Port Eliot Literary Festival, Cornwall 320
Portobello Road, London 151, 188, 222, 232,
   240, 275, 276, 284, 291, 331, 351, 413
Posthuma, Simon 166, 167
Pound, Ezra 163
Powers, Stefanie 223
Powys County Council, Wales 1, 444
Prague Spring (1968) 227
Prescott, Jake 342, 343
Preseli Mountains, Wales 321, 323
Presley, Elvis 6, 11, 43, 46, 51, 54–5, 56–7, 59, 60,
   82, 102, 127, 128, 168, 364, 436, 466, 469
Presteigne, Wales 78, 118, 121, 125, 163, 236, 290,
   306, 318–19, 344, 352, 362, 378, 412, 418, 459
Price, Alan 107
Priestley, J.B. 84
Prima, Diane di 74
Prince 95–6
Prince of Wales, Princedale Road, London
   232–3, 292
Private Eye 79, 112, 114
Process 223
Process, The/Processians 223–4
Procol Harum (band) 3, 4, 132, 156, 158, 159,
   160, 167, 349, 363, 463, 466
Procol Harum (cat) 3, 4, 132, 156, 158, 363, 463
Profumo Affair (1961) 13, 111–18, 129
Profumo, John 'Jack' 112, 113, 114–15